THE LONGMAN STANDARD HISTORY OF MEDIEVAL PHILOSOPHY

THE LONGMAN STANDARD HISTORY OF MEDIEVAL PHILOSOPHY

DANIEL KOLAK

William Paterson University of New Jersey

GARRETT THOMSON

College of Wooster

PEARSON

Longman

New York San Francisco Boston
London Toronto Sydney Tokyo Singapore Madrid
Mexico City Munich Paris Cape Town Hong Kong Montreal

Editor-in-Chief: Eric Stano
Executive Marketing Manager: Ann Stypuloski
Production Manager: Denise Phillip
Project Coordination, Text Design, and Electronic Page Makeup: WestWords, Inc.
Senior Cover Design Manager/Cover Designer: Nancy Danahy
Cover image: Wooden bridge across moat, Bodiam Castle, Sussex, England. © Stone/Getty Images, Inc.
Senior Manufacturing Buyer: Dennis J. Para
Printer and Binder: Courier Corporation
Cover Printer: Courier Corporation

Library of Congress Cataloging-in-Publication Data
Kolak, Daniel.
  The Longman standard history of philosophy / Daniel Kolak, Garrett Thomson.
      p. cm.
  Includes bibliographical references and index.
   ISBN 0-321-23511-8 (volume 6 (comprehensive) : alk. paper)—ISBN 0-321-23513-4
(volume 1 (ancient) : alk. paper)—ISBN 0-321-23512-6 (volume 3 (modern) : alk. paper)—
ISBN 0-321-23510-X (volume 5 (20th century) : alk. paper)
   1. Philosophy—History. I. Title: Standard history of philosophy. II. Thomson, Garrett. III. Title.
   B72.K635 2006
   190—dc22
                                                          2002010370

Please visit us at http://www.ablongman.com

ISBN-13:   978-0-321-23514-5
ISBN-10:   0-321-23514-2

1 2 3 4 5 6 7 8 9 10—CRS—10 09 08 07

◆ CONTENTS ◆

◆ PREFACE ◆

Philosophy may not be the oldest profession, but it is the oldest discipline and the source of our views about reality, knowledge, and morality. To understand the revolutionary nature of the evolutionary history of philosophy is to understand ourselves and our world anew. Without the blinders of naive answers to questions about reality, knowledge, and morality, inspired by the intellectual intimacy that philosophy affords, the mind is broadened and refreshed. In that sense philosophy is always anything but old—awash with new possibilities of inquiry and understanding, the illuminating questions of philosophy instead liberate us from the obviousness of present answers, the blinders of our individual and collective biases.

Philosophy progresses, evolves, and rarely stands still. Though philosophers build upon the work of their predecessors, they continually revise and often overthrow the views of those predecessors—sometimes, even those of their own teachers. One of the most famous examples is the sequence from Socrates to Plato to Aristotle. And yet throughout the evolution of thought that philosophy heralds much remains the same: the call to wonder, dispute, question, liberate, ponder, inquire, understand everything one can about the whole of our being—reality, knowledge, and morality—without becoming closed off ourselves. To behold the whole without being conquered by the wholeness of the vision is the sum and substance of the western intellectual tradition made possible by philosophy—a delicate balance that is anything but delicate when it is attained.

To see new wisdom in the old and old wisdom in the new is to be not just learned, but wise. And to not just tolerate such expansive openness but to *love* it now and then is what it means to *be* a philosopher, both in the past and present.

This book provides you with everything you need to unlock the secrets of medieval philosophy. With over 30 of the greatest works by 17 of the most important western philosophers of the Middle Ages, this volume assembles into one book some of the most profound and edifying ideas from this astounding era of human thought. Suitable for a one-semester introduction to medieval thought, history of medieval philosophy, medieval history of ideas, or medieval intellectual history, this book is an assembly with a purpose, to bring the profound philosophy of the Middle Ages to you, but even more importantly: to bring you to a profound level of understanding of the true philosophical light of the so-called Dark Ages.

We have structured the book to make this possible. The volume as a whole is divided into six standard divisions: Section I, Plotinus, Section II, Augustine, Section III, The Early Medieval Philosophers, Section IV, Islamic and Jewish Philosophers, Section V, Aquinas, and Section Six, Thirteenth Century and Late Medieval Philosophers. Each section opens with a General Introduction that provides an overview of the standard major themes and historical developments. A Prologue opens each chapter, offering context for specific philosophers or to key schools of thought. These are designed to let you in on what has come before, so that you don't enter the conversation in the middle. Individual Biographical Histories give pertinent details about the life and times of each philosopher. The purpose is to show you that philosophers are neither divine demigods nor depersonalized thinking machines, but individual human beings with a penchant for grappling with the perennial "Big Questions," come what may. The purpose of the Philosophical Overviews to each philosopher is twofold: first, to show how that philosopher's thinking about reality, knowledge, and morality integrate into a coherent view; second, to integrate each particular philosopher into a broader philosophical context. Each reading selection comes with its own concise introduction designed to quicken your entry into the issues and prepare you for what is to come. The selections themselves have been chosen for their profundity and edited to highlight the central importance, while leaving in the all-important methods, processes, and development of the views expressed therein. Where translations are involved, we have in each case selected the most lucid. The Study Questions at the end of each reading provide comprehension questions as well as wider discussion questions; these are for you to test yourself and to see how well you have understood what you have read. The Philosophical Bridges, such as "Augustine's Influence," show how what has come before makes possible what comes after, namely that philosophy's perennial questions lead to ever more evolving views.

Special thanks to each of the following reviewers, whose comments about one or more of the volumes in the "Longman Standard History of Philosophy" series helped to enhance each book.

Michael L. Anderson, University of Maryland
Marina P. Banchetti-Robino, Florida Atlantic University
David Boersema, Pacific University
Stephen Braude, University of Maryland Baltimore County
Cynthia K. Brown, Catholic University of America
Richard J. Burke, Oakland University
Marina Bykova, North Carolina State University
Jeffrey Carr, Christopher Newport University
James P. Cooney, Montgomery County Community College
Elmer H. Duncan, Baylor University
Christian Early, Eastern Mennonite University
Emma L. Easteppe, Boise State University
James E. Falcouner, Brigham Young University
Chris L. Firestone, Trinity International University
Merigala Gabriel, Georgia Southern University
Bruce Hauptli, Florida International University
Larry Hauser, Alma College
David J. Hilditch, Webster University
Mary Beth Ingham, Loyola Marymount University
Betty Kiehl, Palomar College
John H. Kulten, Jr., University of Missouri
Nelson P. Lande, University of Massachusetts
Dorothea Lotter, Wake Forest University

Charles S. MacKenzie, Reformed Theological Seminary
Thomas J. Martin, University of North Carolina Charlotte
D. A. Masolo, University of Louisville
Leemon B. McHenry, California State University, Northridge
John T. Meadors, Mississippi College
Glenn Melancon, Southeastern Oklahoma State University
Mark Michael, Austin Peay State University
Thomas Osborne, University of Nevada, Las Vegas
Walter Ott, East Tennessee State University
Anna Christina Ribeiro, University of Maryland
Stefanie Rocknak, Hartwick College
George Rudebusch, Northern Arizona University
Ari Santas, Valdosta State University
Candice Shelby, University of Colorado-Denver
Daniel Silber, Florida Southern College
Allan Silverman, Ohio State University
James K. Swindler, Illinois State University
David B. Twetten, Marquette University
Thomas Upton, Gannon University
Barry F. Vaughan, Mesa Community College
Daniel R. White, Florida Atlantic University
David M. Wisdo, Columbus State University
Evelyn Wortsman Deluty, Nassau Community College

We would like to thank the following people for their help. Brandon West of the College of Wooster for his sterling work as a student research assistant. Amy Erickson and Patrice Reeder of the College of Wooster for their unfailing secretarial help. Professors Martin Gunderson, Ron Hustwit, Henry Kreuzman, Adrian Moore, Elizabeth Schiltz, and Philip Turetzsky for their useful comments. Everyone at Longman Publishers for their very professional work, especially Priscilla McGeehon and Eric Stano, who have supported the project with tireless energy and enthusiasm. Our wives, Wendy and Helena, for their help and understanding. Finally, we would like to dedicate this volume to our children: Julia, Sophia, Dylan, and Andre Kolak; and to Andrew, Frances, Verena, Susana, and Robert Thomson.

In general terms the so-called medieval era spans roughly a thousand years in European history between the fall of the Roman Empire around 450 C.E.[1] to the so-called Italian Renaissance in the latter half of the fifteenth century. It almost goes without saying that what happened in philosophy during these thousand years between Rome and the Renaissance is pivotal to understanding modern and contemporary thought. But it is equally important to try and understand medieval ideas in their own right, not just as stepping stones to the modern world view. Just as in art and music, sometimes appreciating the intrinsic value of a work illuminates it in ways that may make it shine more, not less, than what came after. In this book we shall thus try to learn and appreciate not only the evolutionary, but also the *revolutionary*, aspects of medieval philosophy.

The severe blow dealt to the political, intellectual, artistic, and knowledge-seeking enterprises during the third and fourth centuries came as a great shock to many: books were burned, schools closed, and the Roman Empire—which had inherited the legacy of the Greeks—fell, destroyed from within. The Hellenic philosophical genius and the distinctly anti-authoritarian sentiments of the Epicurean and Stoic philosophers, developed during the rise of the Roman Empire, was confronted by the sudden rise of a slew of cults and emerging religions vying for people's beliefs. With the fall of the Roman Empire, numerous Christian cults began to draw large numbers of followers and superstition was rampant. Even the Roman aristocracy began to worship its emperors as gods, while the common people divided themselves among various cults vying for power. Isis combined the worship of Greek and Egyptian gods, the Mithraic cult worshiped the sun, the Phrygian cult worshiped the Mother of the Gods. Christian sects, no longer persecuted as they had been under Marcus Aurelius, began to win converts, and eventually, to draw more than all the other cults combined. Before long it came to pass that within philosophy itself the question of the nature and role of authority, especially in relation to revelation, divine or otherwise, always hovering in the background since ancient times, was thrust into the forefront.

The Question of Authority

The emphasis in ancient (classical) Greek philosophy on the self-mastery and self-certainty available to the individual through reflection, exemplified and perfected in the systems of Plato and Aristotle, continued into the so-called Hellenistic era, spanning

---

[1] "Common Era," which corresponds to A.D.; B.C.E. will be used to note "Before the Common Era," which coincides with "B.C."

roughly 323 B.C.E. (the death of Alexander the Great) to 30 B.C.E (when Augustus established the Roman Empire) and the Roman era (from 30 B.C.E. to the fall of Rome in 450 C.E.) With time, the great sages of the past came themselves to be revered as oracular-like authorities whose wisdom superceded any that ordinary learners were capable of acquiring on their own. In this way philosophy itself came to play a more authoritarian-like role in the search for knowledge and wisdom. This is perhaps deeply ironic, given its distinctly anti-authoritarian Socratic origins. Socrates, more so than any other ancient figure, made the art of questioning authority one of philosophy's central, perhaps even fundamental, activities. Now the schools founded by his pupils, Plato and Aristotle, each of which lasted nearly a thousand years until the fall of Rome, had become the new authority.

This new development was itself, however, a natural development in the progess of civilization. So much knowledge, so many systems, had come to pass, that individuals, especially in the western traditions, began to feel that they could no longer achieve the enlightenment or salvation they sought on their own. The ideas promulgated by religious groups of the time, no less so than today, emphasized the authority of special learned masters whose works could be studied as vehicles to not only inward illumination, but also *divine* revelation. This, of course, was hardly a new idea. Even Socrates himself talked of the gods and of listening to them, and we must not forget the important role played by the ancient Oracles at the Greek temples, who it was believed spoke directly with divine authority as the voices of the Gods. That being said, virtually all subsequent philosophical traditions, even as practiced under the umbrella of orthodox religious systems (inclusive of the Christian, Jewish, and Muslim traditions, as we shall see), relied on a series of commentaries and criticisms of the great past masters, less as sources of infallible views but, rather, as a means of confirming or enhancing the commentators' own views.

In this way, throughout the medieval era, the intellectual tension between these two sources of authority—the sage wisdom of past masters versus that of divine revelation—evolved into a series of more or less *collaborative* systems of thought. The rift widened with an even deeper tension, unresolved throughout the Middle Ages, between the *mediated* authority of *historically* accredited revelation verses the *immediate* authority of "divine illumination." Indeed, even before Plotinus the neo-Pythagoreans had begun to elevate the works of Aristotle, Plato, and Pythagoras to the level of religious doctrines. Among the key figures that began this trend was the Greek philosopher Numenius (second century C.E.), who had a doctrine of three gods. The first, identical with Plato's Form of the Good, exists as a self-contained transcendence. The second is identical to Plato's demiurge, as described in Plato's *Timaeus*, the intermediary conveyor between the ideal forms and the matter in which he creates the universe. The third is the universe itself, what the ancient Greeks called the *Kosmos*. But Numenius went even further, arguing in his works, which were key sources studied by Plotinus and his students, that Pythagoras and Plato had merely reformed and reshaped the ancient wisdom of the Brahmans, Jews, and Egyptians, and that Aristotle's Intellect was identical to the Good, which became the Plotinian "One," to which we shall turn in our first section. This, of course, provided the foundation for the integration of philosophy into the newly developing Christian theology, as we shall see, starting with Augustine.

Out of these complex hierarchical systems of dynamic authority, philosophy began to develop and flourish for the next thousand years, albeit in a very different manner from the classical Greek, Hellenistic, and Roman eras as it evolved under the strict super-vision and authority—one might even say, protection—of the ruling religious orthodoxy.

Plotinus, Augustine, and the Early Medievals

There are any number of ways to categorize the vast collaborative philosophical systems produced during the early part of the medieval era. We follow a roughly chronological order, and begin with Plotinus, arguably the last of the great ancient philosophers, and certainly a pivotal figure at the crossroads between the Greek tradition spanning the seven centuries from Thales to Sextus Empiricus and the beginning of Christendom. The Catholic philosophy that followed arose from the views of Plato, the Stoics and neo-Platonists, and developed by four leading Latin church founders: St. Ambrose, St. Jerome, St. Augustine, and Pope Gregory the Great. But clearly the most influential philosopher among them was Augustine, whose ideas lay the foundation for western philosophy for the next thousand years, up to the Renaissance and beyond. These two figures—Plotinus and Augustine—comprise the first two sections of this book.

The Rise of Scholasticism

The shift in our third section from a figure to a period, what generally is called Early Medieval Philosophy, signals the shift from individuals to schools, or systems, of orthodoxy within which philosophy, though still infused and inspired by the work of brilliant individuals, was by and large driven by collective decision-making regarding inquiry into the fundamental questions of reality, knowledge, and ethics. Lest anyone think that this in and of itself is too primitive, backward, or intellectually suppressive to be considered worthy of the attention of philosophers, it is well worth pointing out that contemporary science has on this point more in common with medieval philosophy then it does with contemporary philosophy, insofar as science today is still (as it was in the Middle Ages) by and large a collective enterprise. During this Early Medieval Period we focus on the contributions of Boethius, John Scotus Erigena, St. Anselm, Abelard, Hildegard of Bingen, and John of Salisbury.

Islamic and Jewish Thought

Our fourth section contains the pivotal work of the Islamic and Jewish Philosophers: Avicenna (Ibn Sina), al-Ghazali, Averroës (Ibn-Rushd), and Maimonides. What is especially fascinating about the Islamic influence is that after the fall of the Roman Empire, when Justinian closed the schools of Athens in 529 C.E., and the great works of the ancients philosophers were burned or denounced by the papal authorities as pagan heresies, philosophers escaped to Persia. They took their Greek books with them, which were translated first into Syriac and then Arabic, where Plato and Aristotle began to influence a whole generation of Islamic and Jewish thinkers. Had it not been for the schools in Alexandria, Syria, and Persia, the great works of western philosophy in ancient Greece would have been lost forever. What is also becoming clearer is the great influence of these Islamic and Jewish writers on the subsequent development of philosophy through their own writings, both as commentaries on Plato and Aristotle and original works, which we shall study in this section.

Aquinas and the Revival of Aristotelianism

The fifth section is devoted, once again, to an individual: Aquinas. Whereas Plato was the dominant influence on Augustine, Aquinas—following in the footsteps of the Islamic and Jewish commentators—finds his main inspiration in Aristotle. Aquinas' system was the dominant force behind subsequent philosophical innovation within Christendom.

Prelude to the Renaissance

Our sixth and final section puts together the deepest thinkers of the thirteenth and so-called "Late Medieval" period out of which the Renaissance and modern philosophy developed. Indeed, the contributions of Bacon, John Duns Scotus, William of Ockham, and Nicolas of Cusa help us to understand philosophy's complex and often turbulent historical development. Not only do these works form a bridge between the ancient and modern world, many of the concepts and categories forged therein have become the standard tools and techniques of philosophy up to the present day.

SECTION I

◆ PLOTINUS ◆

PROLOGUE

The abrupt ending of Greek and Roman philosophy as it had evolved from the golden age of Greece heralded the inward turn of the Early Medieval Period. Starting in the third century, against the backdrop of the rapidly disintegrating Roman Empire, Early Medieval philosophy emerged as a unique blend of religious mysticism and esoteric logic. As Roman military campaigns took their economic toll on both citizens and cities, the great cultural centers of the empire began to unravel. The aristocracy fled to escape the huge taxes and worsening health conditions; nearly a third of the population was wiped out either from war or the plague. The Roman military gained power over the citizens, even over the emperors. People turned away from culture and education, seeking solace in otherworldly religions.

PLOTINUS (205–270)

Biographical History

It is against this tumultuous sociopolitical backdrop that Plotinus, the last of the great ancient philosophers, tried to rekindle the flame of Greek thought. Born and raised in Egypt, he studied philosophy in Alexandria. In 243 he went east, joining the expedition of Gordian III with the idea that he could thereby study Indian and Persian philosophy more authentically, not just by reading, but by traveling to the places where it originated. After Gordian III was assassinated Plotinus returned to Rome, where he continued his studies in the libraries and with books he had acquired. He devoted himself for the rest of his life to teaching and writing philosophy that, because of his emphasis on the primacy of Plato, is known as "neo-Platonism."

Plotinus' vast metaphysical system inspired many devoted followers. He convinced Emperor Gallienus to build a second city near Rome, based on Plato's *Republic*, that was to be called Platonopolis, but the project was never completed. Plotinus' greatest work, posthumously edited by his student Porphyry into six books of nine sections (*Enneads*) each, is a vast metaphysical vision inspired by Parmenides, Pythagoras, and most of all Plato. Plotinus argues against the materialistic atomism of the Stoics, Epicureans, and Skeptics, whose materialistic philosophy he regarded as impotent for dealing with the growing superstitions of the time.

Philosophical Overview

As already mentioned in the General Introduction, one of the main inspirational sources for Plotinus came from the second century Greek philosopher Numenius, whose works were an attempt to integrate the ancient wisdom into a systematic theological vision in which the world itself was divine, a "third level" or "visible" God, itself a product of and yet in some mystical way identical to the "first God," the One, the supreme form of the Good. This raises many deep metaphysical and logical problems of identity, especially of how the One can give rise to and also be the many, a problem that plagued both Plato and Aristotle and which became the chief preoccupation of Plotinus.

Plotinus distinguishes three levels of reality that are but one ultimate reality, much in the way that Christian theologians viewed the Holy Trinity. A key difference, of course, is that the Plotinian hypostases consists of three metaphysical *principles*, whereas the Christian Trinity consists of three *persons*. But the logical foundations paved the way for much subsequent Christian theology.

The Parmenidean One, which Plotinus calls "God," transcends Being. In that sense the One, in Plotinus' view, is equivalent to Plato's fundamental concept of the supreme, ideal form of the *Good*. Because the One, which precedes the Good, is essentially indefinable, no predicates can be attributed to it. Technically speaking, this means that you can't say it is large or small, one or many, and so on, and attach any precise or logical meaning to your statement. All we can say about the One is that "It is." Everything that is, was and will be exists as an emanation of the One, which is the ultimate and eternal source of all being.

The next, second level, below the One, is its first *emanation*, meaning that it is a product of, or the result of, the One in the sense that it consists in the *image* of the One, which Plotinus identifies with *nous*. This ancient Greek notion has variously been translated as "mind," "spirit," and "intellectual principle." *Nous* exists as a result of the One trying to understand itself; *nous* gives to the One *vision*, the power of seeing—it is the "light" by which the One sees itself.

The next emanation is the third, lowest level of reality, which Plotinus calls *psyche*, or *soul*, which in turn is the creator not only of all living things but also of the sun, moon and stars. The soul makes possible the visible world because it has two parts, the inner soul that faces the *nous* and the outer soul that faces the external world. These three metaphysical "levels"—the One, the *nous*, and the soul—correspond, respectively, to three distinct levels of consciousness: mystical awareness, intuitive thought, and discursive thought.

ENNEADS: FIRST ENNEAD, SIXTH TRACTATE: BEAUTY

In this selection Plotinus distinguishes, first, the perception of a thing from the thing itself and, second, the perception of beauty or ugliness from the perception of the thing. While all that the soul sees are ideas that themselves emanate from the soul, the soul does not have to be like what it sees in order to see it—in fact, it has to separate and distinguish itself as subject from object. Putting it most simply: to see a chair (just like in a dream) the perceiving intellect must separate itself as perceiving subject from the object, to differentiate itself; the mind (just like in a dream) cannot see *itself* as a chair, it must see the chair as non-mind, as emanating from something other than the mind that perceives it. But this is *not* the case with beauty; here the soul, the conscious, seeing, perceiving intellect, must in some sense itself *be* or *become* beautiful to see the true ideal form of beauty. This is how in approaching the true aesthetic the soul approaches its own ultimate cosmic nature, the ideal form of the Good.

1.

Beauty addresses itself chiefly to sight; but there is a beauty for the hearing too, as in certain combinations of words and in all kinds of music, for melodies and cadences are beautiful; and minds that lift themselves above the realm of sense to a higher order are aware of beauty in the conduct of life, in actions, in character, in the pursuits of the intellect; and there is the beauty of the virtues. What loftier beauty there may be, yet, our argument will bring to light. What, then, is it that gives comeliness to material forms and draws the ear to the sweetness perceived in sounds, and what is the secret of the beauty there is in all that derives from soul? Is there some one principle from which all take their grace, or is there a beauty peculiar to the embodied and another for the bodiless? Finally, one or many, what would such a principle be? Consider that some things, material shapes for instance, are gracious not by anything inherent but by something communicated, while others are lovely of themselves, as, for example, virtue. The same bodies appear sometimes beautiful, sometimes not: so that there is a good deal between being body and being beautiful. What, then, is this something that shows itself in certain material forms? This is the natural beginning of our inquiry. What is it that attracts the eyes of those to whom a beautiful object is presented, and calls them, lures them, toward it, and fills them with joy at the sight? If we possess ourselves of this, we have at once a standpoint for the wider survey. Almost everyone declares that the symmetry of parts toward each other and toward a whole, with, besides, a certain charm of color, constitutes the beauty recognized by the eye, that in visible things, as indeed in all else, universally, the beautiful thing is essentially symmetrical, patterned.

But think what this means. Only a compound can be beautiful, never anything devoid of parts: and only a whole; the several parts will have beauty, not in themselves, but only as working together to give a comely total. Yet beauty in an aggregate demands beauty in details; it cannot be constructed out of ugliness; its law must run throughout. All the loveliness of color and even the light of the sun, being devoid of parts and so not beautiful by symmetry, must be ruled out of the realm of beauty. And how comes gold to be a beautiful thing? And lightning by night, and the stars, why are these so fair? In sounds also the simple must be proscribed, though often in a whole noble composition each several tone is delicious in itself. Again since the one face, constant in symmetry, appears sometimes fair and sometimes not, can we doubt that beauty is something more than symmetry, that symmetry itself owes its beauty to a remoter principle? Turn to what is attractive in methods of life or in the expression of thought; are we to call in symmetry here? What symmetry is to be found in noble conduct, or excellent laws, in any form of mental pursuit? What symmetry can there be in points of abstract thought? The symmetry of being accordant with each other? But there may be accordance or entire identity where there is nothing but ugliness: the proposition that honesty is merely a generous artlessness chimes in the most perfect harmony with the proposition that morality means weakness of will: the accordance is complete. Then again, all the virtues are a beauty of the soul, a beauty authentic beyond any of these others: but how does symmetry enter here? The soul, it is true, is not a simple unity, but still its virtue cannot have the symmetry of size or of number: what standard of measurement could preside over the compromise or the coalescence of the soul's faculties or purposes? Finally,

Plotinus, from *The Six Enneads*, translated by Stephen MacKenna, (London: Medici Society, 1917) emendations by Daniel Kolak.

how by this theory would there be beauty in the intellectual principle, essentially the solitary?

2.

Let us, then, go back to the source, and indicate at once the principle that bestows beauty on material things. Undoubtedly this principle exists; it is something that is perceived at the first glance, something which the soul names as from an ancient knowledge and, recognizing, welcomes it, enters into unison with it. But let the soul fall in with the ugly and at once it shrinks within itself, denies the thing, turns away from it, not accordant, resenting it. Our interpretation is that the soul—by the very truth of its nature, by its affiliation to the noblest existents in the hierarchy of Being—when it sees anything of that kin, or any trace of that kinship, thrills with an immediate delight, takes its own to itself, and thus stirs anew to the sense of its nature and of all its affinity. But, is there any such likeness between the loveliness of this world and the splendors in the supreme? Such a likeness in the particulars would make the two orders alike: but what is there in common between beauty here and beauty there? We hold that all the loveliness of this world comes by communion in ideal form. All shapelessness whose kind admits of pattern and form, as long as it remains outside of reason and idea, is ugly by that very isolation from the divine thought. And this is the absolute ugly: an ugly thing is something that has not been entirely mastered by pattern, that is by reason, the matter not yielding at all points and in all respects to ideal form. But where the ideal form has entered, it has grouped and coordinated what from a diversity of parts was to become a unity: it has rallied confusion into co-operation: it has made the sum one harmonious coherence: for the idea is a unity and what it molds must come to unity as far as multiplicity may. And on what has thus been compacted to unity, beauty enthrones itself, giving itself to the parts as to the sum: when it lights on some natural unity, a thing of like parts, then it gives itself to that whole. Thus, for an illustration, there is the beauty, conferred by craftsmanship, of all a house with all its parts, and the beauty which some natural quality may give to a single stone. This, then, is how the material thing becomes beautiful, by communicating in the thought that flows from the divine.

3.

And the soul includes a faculty peculiarly addressed to beauty, one incomparably sure in the appreciation of its own, never in doubt whenever any lovely thing presents itself for judgment. Or perhaps the soul itself acts immediately, affirming the beautiful where it finds something accordant with the ideal form within itself, using this idea as a canon of accuracy in its decision. But what accordance is there between the material and that which antedates all matter? On what principle does the architect, when he finds the house standing before him correspondent with his inner ideal of a house, pronounce it beautiful? Is it not that the house before him, the stones apart, is the inner idea stamped upon the mass of exterior matter, the indivisible exhibited in diversity? So with the perceptive faculty: discerning in certain objects the ideal form which has bound and controlled shapeless matter, opposed in nature to idea, seeing further stamped upon the common shapes some shape excellent above the common, it gathers into unity what still remains fragmentary, catches it up and carries it within, no longer a thing of parts, and presents it to the ideal principle as something concordant and congenial, a natural friend: the joy here is like that of a good man who discerns in a youth the early signs of a virtue consonant with the achieved perfection within his own soul. The beauty of color is also the outcome of a unification: it derives from shape, from the conquest of the darkness inherent in matter by the pouring-in of light, the unembodied, which is a rational principle and an ideal form. Hence it is that fire itself is splendid beyond all material bodies, holding the rank of ideal principle to the other elements, making ever upwards, the subtlest and sprightliest of all bodies, as very near to the unembodied; itself alone admitting no other, all the others penetrated by it: for they take warmth but this is never cold; it has color primally; they receive the form of color from it: hence the splendor of its light, the splendor that belongs to the idea. And all that has resisted and is but uncertainly held by its light remains outside of beauty, as not having absorbed the plenitude of the form of color. And harmonies unheard in sound create the harmonies we hear, and wake the soul to the consciousness of beauty, showing it the one essence in another kind: for the measures of our sensible music are not arbitrary but are determined by the principle whose labor is to dominate matter and bring pattern into being. Thus far of the beauties of the realm of sense, images and shadow pictures, fugitives that have entered into matter to adorn, and to ravish, where they are seen.

4.

But there are earlier and loftier beauties than these. In the sense-bound life we are no longer granted to know them, but the soul, taking no help from the organs, sees and proclaims them. To the vision of these we must mount, leaving sense to its own low place. As it is not for those to speak of the graceful forms of the material world who have never seen them or known their grace—men born blind, let us suppose—in the same way those must be silent upon the beauty of noble conduct and of learning and all that order who have never cared for such things, nor may those tell of the splendour of virtue who have never known the face of justice and of moral wisdom beautiful beyond the beauty of evening and of dawn. Such vision is for those only who see with the soul's sight, and at the vision, they will rejoice; awe will fall upon them and a trouble deeper than all the rest could ever stir, for now they are moving in the realm of truth. This is the spirit that beauty must ever induce, wonderment and a delicious trouble, longing and love and a trembling that is all delight. For the unseen all this may be felt as for the seen; and this the souls feel for it, every soul in some degree, but those the more deeply that are the more truly apt to this higher love—just as all take delight in the beauty of the body but all are not stung as sharply, and those only that feel the keener wound are known as lovers.

5.

These lovers, then, lovers of the beauty outside of sense, must be made to declare themselves. What do you feel in presence of the grace you discern in actions, in manners, in sound morality, in all the works and fruits of virtue, in the beauty of souls? When you see that you yourselves are beautiful within, what do you feel? What is this Dionysian exultation that thrills through your being, this straining upwards of all your soul, this longing to break away from the body and live sunken within the veritable self? These are no other than the emotions of souls under the spell of love. But

what is it that awakens all this passion? No shape, no color, no grandeur of mass: all is for a soul, something whose beauty rests upon no color, for the moral wisdom the soul enshrines and all the other hueless splendour of the virtues. It is that you find in yourself, or admire in another, loftiness of spirit; righteousness of life: disciplined purity: courage of the majestic face; gravity; modesty that goes fearless and tranquil and passionless; and, shining down upon all, the light of Godlike intellection. All these noble qualities are to be reverenced and loved, no doubt, but what entitles them to be called beautiful? They exist: they manifest themselves to us: anyone that sees them must admit that they have reality of being; and is not real being, really beautiful? But we have not yet shown by what property in them they have wrought the soul to loveliness: what is this grace, this splendor as of light, resting upon all the virtues? Let us take the contrary, the ugliness of the soul, and set that against its beauty: to understand, at once, what this ugliness is and how it comes to appear in the soul will certainly open our way before us. Let us then suppose an ugly soul, dissolute, unrighteous: teeming with all the lusts; torn by internal discord; beset by the fears of its cowardice and the envies of its pettiness; thinking, in the little thought it has, only of the perishable and the base; perverse in all, its the friend of unclean pleasures; living the life of abandonment to bodily sensation and delighting in its deformity. What must we think but that all this shame is something that has gathered about the soul, some foreign bane outraging it, soiling it, so that, encumbered with all manner of turpitude, it has no longer a clean activity or a clean sensation, but commands only a life smouldering dully under the crust of evil: that, sunk in manifold death, it no longer sees what a soul should see, may no longer rest in its own being, dragged ever as it is towards the outer, the lower, the dark? An unclean thing, I dare to say; flickering hither and thither at the call of objects of sense, deeply infected with the taint of body, occupied always in matter, and absorbing matter into itself; in its commerce with the Ignoble it has trafficked away for an alien nature its own essential Idea. If a man has been immersed in filth or daubed with mud his native comeliness disappears and all that is seen is the foul stuff besmearing him: his ugly condition is due to alien matter that has encrusted him, and if he is to win back his grace it must be his business to scour and purify himself and make himself what he was. So, we may justly say, a soul becomes ugly by something foisted upon it, by sinking itself into the alien, by a fall, a descent into body, into matter. The dishonor of the soul is in its ceasing to be clean and apart. Gold is degraded when it is mixed with earthy particles; if these be worked out, the gold is left and is beautiful, isolated from all that is foreign, gold with gold alone. And so the soul; let it be but cleared of the desires that come by its too intimate converse with the body, emancipated from all the passions, purged of all that embodiment has thrust upon it, withdrawn, a solitary, to itself again—in that moment the ugliness that came only from the alien is stripped away.

6.

For, as the ancient teaching was, moral discipline and courage and every virtue, not even excepting wisdom itself, all is purification. Hence the mysteries with good reason adumbrate the immersion of the unpurified in filth, even in the nether world, since the unclean loves filth for its very filthiness, and swine foul of body find their joy in foulness. What else is Sophrosyne, rightly so-called, but to take no part in the pleasures of the body, to break away from them as unclean and unworthy of the clean? So too, courage is but being fearless of the death which is but the parting of the soul from the body, an event which no one can dread whose delight is to be his unmingled self. And magnanimity is but disregard for the lure of things here. And wisdom is but the act of the intellectual principle withdrawn from the lower places and leading the soul to the above. The soul thus cleansed is all idea and reason, wholly free of body, intellective, entirely of that divine order from which the wellspring of beauty rises and all the race of beauty. Hence the soul heightened to the intellectual principle is beautiful to all its power. For intellection and all that proceeds from intellection are the soul's beauty, a graciousness native to it and not foreign, for only with these is it truly soul. And it is just to say that in the soul's becoming a good and beautiful thing is its becoming like to God. for from the divine comes all the beauty and all the good in beings. We may even say that beauty is the authentic existents and ugliness is the principle contrary to existence: and the ugly is also the primal evil; therefore its contrary is at once

good and beautiful, or is good and beauty: and hence the one method will discover to us the beauty-good and the ugliness-evil. And beauty, this beauty which is also the good, must be posed as the first: directly deriving from this first is the intellectual principle which is pre-eminently the manifestation of beauty; through the intellectual principle soul is beautiful. The beauty in things of a lower order—actions and pursuits for instance—comes by operation of the shaping soul which is also the author of the beauty found in the world of sense. For the soul, a divine thing, a fragment as it were of the primal beauty, makes beautiful to the fullness of their capacity all things whatsoever that it grasps and molds.

7.

Therefore we must ascend again toward the good, every soul. Anyone that has seen this, knows what I intend when I say that it is beautiful. Even the desire of it is to be desired as a good. To attain it is for those that will take the upward path, who will set all their forces towards it, who will divest themselves of all that we have put on in our descent—so, to those that approach the holy celebrations of the mysteries, there are appointed purifications and the laying aside of the garments worn before, and the entry in nakedness until, passing, on the upward way, all that is other than the God, each in the solitude of himself shall behold that solitary-dwelling existence, the apart, the unmingled, the pure, that from which all things depend, for which all look and live and act and know, the source of life and of intellection and of being. And one that shall know this vision—with what passion of love shall he not be seized, with what pang of desire, what longing to be molten into one with this, what wondering delight! If he that has never seen this being must hunger for it as for all his welfare, he that has known must love and reverence it as the very beauty; he will be flooded with awe and gladness, stricken by a salutary terror; he loves with a veritable love, with sharp desire; all other loves than this he must despise, and disdain all that once seemed fair. This, indeed, is the mood even of those who, having witnessed the manifestation of Gods, can never again feel the old delight in the comeliness of material forms: what then are we to think of one that contemplates absolute beauty in its essential integrity, no accumulation of flesh and matter, no dweller on earth or in the heavens, so perfect its purity, far above all such things in that they are non-essential, composite, not primal but descending from this? Beholding this being, the choragos of all existence, the self-intent that ever gives forth and never takes resting, rapt, in the vision and possession of so lofty a loveliness, growing to its likeness, what beauty can the soul yet lack? For this, the beauty supreme, the absolute, and the primal, fashions its lovers to beauty and makes them also worthy of love. And for this, the sternest and the uttermost combat is set before the souls; all our labor is for this, lest we be left without part in this noblest vision, which to attain is to be blessed in the blissful sight, which to fail of is to fail utterly. For not he that has failed of the joy that is in color or in visible forms, not he that has failed of power or of honors or of kingdom has failed, but only he that has failed of only this, for whose winning he should renounce kingdoms and command over earth and ocean and sky, if only, spurning the world of sense from beneath his feet, and straining to this, he may see.

8.

But what must we do? How lies the path? How come to vision of the inaccessible beauty, dwelling as if in consecrated precincts, apart from the common ways where all may see, even the profane? He that has the strength, let him arise and withdraw into himself, foregoing all that is known by the eyes, turning away for ever from the material beauty that once made his joy. When he perceives those shapes of grace that show in body, let him not pursue: he must know them for copies, vestiges, shadows, and hasten away towards that they tell of. For if anyone follow what is like a beautiful shape playing over water—is there not a myth telling in symbol of such a dupe, how he sank into the depths of the current and was swept away to nothingness? So too, one that is held by material beauty and will not break free shall be precipitated, not in body but in soul, down to the dark depths loathed of the intellective being, where, blind even in the lower world, he shall have commerce only with shadows, there as here. "Let us flee then to the beloved Fatherland," this is the soundest counsel. But what is this flight? How are we to gain the open sea? For Odysseus is surely a parable to us when he commands the flight from the sorceries of Circe or Calypso, not content to linger for all the pleasure offered to his eyes

and all the delight of sense filling his days. The Fatherland to us is there whence we have come, and there is the Father. What then is our course, what the manner of our flight? This is not a journey for the feet; the feet bring us only from land to land: nor need you think of coach or ship to carry you away; all this order of things you must set aside and refuse to see: you must close the eyes and call instead upon another vision which is to be waked within you, a vision, the birthright of all, which few turn to use.

9.

And this inner vision, what is its operation? Newly awakened it is all too feeble to bear the ultimate splendor. Therefore the soul must be trained to the habit of remarking, first, all noble pursuits, then the works of beauty produced not by the labor of the arts but by the virtue of men known for their goodness: lastly, you must search the souls of those that have shaped these beautiful forms. But how are you to see into a virtuous soul and know its loveliness? Withdraw into yourself and look. And if you do not find yourself beautiful yet, act as does the creator of a statue that is to be made beautiful: he cuts away here, he smoothes there, he makes this line lighter, this other purer, until a lovely face has grown upon his work. So do you also: cut away all that is excessive, straighten all that is crooked, bring light to all that is overcast, labour to make all one glow of beauty and never cease chiselling your statue, until there shall shine out on you from it the godlike splendor of virtue, until you shall see the perfect goodness surely established in the stainless shrine. When you know that you have become this perfect work, when you are self-gathered in the purity of your being, nothing now remaining that can shatter that inner unity, nothing from without clinging to the authentic man, when you find yourself wholly true to your essential nature, wholly that only veritable light which is not measured by space, not narrowed to any circumscribed form nor again diffused as a thing void of term, but ever unmeasurable as something greater than all measure and more than all quantity—when you perceive that you have grown to this, you are now become very vision: now call up all your confidence, strike forward yet a step—you need a guide no longer—strain, and see. This is the only eye that sees the mighty beauty. If the eye that adventures the vision be dimmed by vice, impure, or weak, and unable in its cowardly blanching to see the uttermost brightness, then it sees nothing even though another point to what lies plain to sight before it. To any vision must be brought an eye adapted to what is to be seen, and having some likeness to it. Never did eye see the sun unless it had first become sunlike, and never can the soul have vision of the first beauty unless itself be beautiful. Therefore, first let each become godlike and each beautiful who cares to see God and beauty. So, mounting, the soul will come first to the intellectual principle and survey all the beautiful ideas in the supreme and will avow that this is beauty, that the ideas are beauty. For by their efficacy comes all beauty else, but the offspring and essence of the intellectual being. What is beyond the intellectual principle we affirm to be the nature of good radiating beauty before it. So that, treating the intellectual cosmos as one, the first is the beautiful: if we make distinction there, the realm of ideas constitutes the beauty of the intellectual sphere; and the good, which lies beyond, is the fountain at once and principle of beauty: the primal good and the primal beauty have the one dwelling place and, thus, always, beauty's seat is there.

STUDY QUESTIONS: PLOTINUS, *FIRST ENNEAD, SIXTH TRACTATE: BEAUTY*

1. What does Plotinus mean by "beauty," and how does it apply to the intellectual realm?
2. What is the "intellectual principle?"
3. In what ways is his view of the ideal forms similar to Plato's? In what ways different?
4. What is the nature of love between two souls? How does it occur? What makes it possible? How do you know when you are in love in this way, and how does it differ from love that is merely physical?
5. What does he mean by saying that the good is the soul's own natural act?
6. Why must we each become beautiful and godlike before we can see and know God?

ENNEADS: FOURTH ENNEAD, NINTH TRACTATE: ARE ALL SOULS ONE?

In this selection Plotinus, like Plato before him, argues that the soul by descending into the world of appearances forgets that it is but an emanation of "the One," the cosmic all-soul. This is necessary: there is no existence for us without forgetting. However, drawing on Aristotle's notion that thought, or contemplation, receives the form of the object contemplated, Plotinus explains how it is nevertheless possible for the soul, through self-contemplation, to transcend its own limitations. It is possible for us to thus glimpse not only that of which we are each a reflective emanation—*nous*—but also that of which the *nous* itself is a reflective emanation—the One. Because the soul, unlike the *nous* and the One, can only contemplate its objects in succession, it also thereby in virtue of this necessary limitation gives rise to time, space, and matter. In this quasi-real state the soul is thus further able to then contemplate, in a dreamlike state, the existence of nonconscious matter. Going still further in the "inward" direction, the soul becomes "divinely possessed and inspired" to see beyond itself to the next higher level. The fragmented image within us of the One is therefore but "thought thinking itself," the *nous*, a "unity-in-diversity." In this mystical state the soul is in direct contact with itself as the One. In this way we are each one and the same numerically identical soul in many different bodies, each one of us is the same being, an emanation of the one "all-soul." Plotinus admits that this may seem like a preposterous idea. How can you and I be one? I feel happy, you feel pain—does that not make us different? I am a philosophy professor, you a student; how then can we, who know different things, be one and the same numerically identical being? Remarkably, Plotinus considers carefully each and every obvious objection to his thesis, explaining how what may at first glance seem like an idea too strange to contemplate is the best possible explanation of our experience, better, even, that the ordinary commonsense view which has its own problems.

1.

That the soul of every individual is one thing we deduce from the fact that it is present entire at every point of the body—the sign of veritable unity—not some part of it here and another part there. In all sensitive beings the sensitive soul is an omnipresent unity, and so in the forms of plant life the plant soul is entire at each several point throughout the organism. Now are we to hold similarly that your soul and mine and all are one, and that the same thing is true of the universe, the soul in all the several forms of life being one soul, not parcelled out in separate items, but an omnipresent identity? If the soul in me is a unity, why need that in the universe be otherwise seeing that there is no longer any question of bulk or body? And if that, too, is one soul and yours, and mine, belongs to it, then yours and mine must also be one: and if, again, the soul of the universe and mine depend from one soul, once more all must be one. What then in itself is this one soul? First we must assure ourselves of the possibility of all souls being one as that of any given individual is: It must, no doubt, seem strange that my soul and that of any and everybody else should be one thing only: it might mean my feelings being felt by someone else, my goodness another's too, my desire, his desire, all our experience shared with each other and with the (one-souled) universe, so that the very universe itself would feel whatever I felt. Besides how are we to reconcile this unity with the distinction of reasoning soul and unreasoning, animal soul and plant? Yet if we reject that unity, the universe itself ceases to be one thing and souls can no longer be included under any one principle.

2.

Now to begin with, the unity of soul, mine and another's, is not enough to make the two totals of soul and body identical. An identical thing in different recipients will have different experiences; the identity man, in me as I move and you at rest, moves in me and is stationary in you: there is nothing stranger, nothing impossible, in any other form of identity between you and me: nor would it entail the transference of my emotion to any outside point: when in any one body a hand is in pain, the distress is felt not in the other but in the hand as represented in the centralizing unity. In order that my feelings should of necessity be yours, the unity would have to be corporeal: only if the two recipient bodies made one, would the souls feel as one. We must keep in mind, moreover, that many things that happen even in one same body escape the notice of the entire being, especially when the bulk is large: thus in huge sea-beasts, it is said, the animal as a whole will be quite unaffected by some membral accident too slight to traverse the organism. Thus unity in the subject of any experience does not imply that the resultant sensation will be necessarily felt with any force upon the entire being and at every point of it: some transmission of the experience may be expected, and is indeed undeniable, but a full impression on the sense there need not be. That one identical soul should be virtuous in me and vicious in someone else is not strange: it is only saying that an identical thing may be active here and inactive there. We are not asserting the unity of soul in the sense of a complete negation of multiplicity—only of the supreme can that be affirmed—we are thinking of soul as simultaneously one and many, participant in the nature divided in body, but at the same time a unity by virtue of belonging to that order which suffers no division. In myself some experience occurring in a part of the body may take no effect upon the entire man but anything occurring in the higher reaches would tell upon the partial: in the same way any influx from the all upon the individual will have manifest effect since the points of sympathetic contact are numerous—but as to any operation from ourselves upon the all there can be no certainty.

3.

Yet, looking at another set of facts, reflection tells us that we are in sympathetic relation to each other, suffering, overcome, at the sight of pain, naturally drawn to forming attachments; and all this can be due only to some unity among us. Again, if spells and other forms of magic are efficient even at a distance to attract us into sympathetic relations, the agency can be no other than the one soul. A quiet word induces changes in a remote object, and makes itself heard at vast distances—proof of the oneness of all things within the one soul. But how to reconcile this unity with the existence of a reasoning soul, an unreasoning, even a plant soul? The indivisible phase is classed as reasoning because it is not in division among bodies, but there is the later phase, divided among bodies, but still one thing and distinct only so as to secure sense-perception throughout; this is to be classed as yet another power; and there is the forming and making phase which again is a power. But a variety of powers does not conflict with unity: seed contains many powers and yet it is one thing, and from that unity rises, again, a variety which is also a unity. But why are not all the powers of this unity present everywhere? The answer is that even in the case of the individual soul described, similarly, as permeating its body, sensation is not equally present in all the parts, reason does not operate at every point, the principle of growth is at work where there is no sensation, and yet all these powers join in the one soul when the body is laid aside. The nourishing faculty as dependent from the all belongs also to the all-soul: why then does it not come equally from ours? Because what is nourished by the action of this power is a member of the all, which itself has sensation passively: but the perception, which is an intellectual judgement, is individual and has no need to create what already exists, though it would have done so had the power not been previously included, of necessity, in the nature of the all.

4.

These reflections should show that there is nothing strange in that reduction of all souls to one. But it is still necessary to enquire into the mode and conditions of the unity. Is it the unity of origin in a unity? And if so, is the one divided or does it remain entire and yet produce variety? And how can an essential being, while remaining its one self, bring forth others? Invoking God to become our helper, let us assert, that the very existence of many souls makes certain that there is first one from which the many rise. Let us suppose, even, the first soul to be corporeal. Then the many souls could result only from the splitting up of that entity, each an entirely different substance: if this body-soul be uniform in kind, each of the resultant souls must be of the one kind; they will all carry the one form undividedly and will differ only in their volumes. Now, if their being souls depended upon their volumes they would be distinct; but if it is ideal form that makes them souls, then all are, in virtue of this idea, one. But this is simply saying that there is one identical soul dispersed among many bodies, and that, preceding this, there is yet another not thus dispersed, the source of the soul in dispersion which may be thought of as a widely repeated image of the soul in unity—much as a multitude of seals bear the impression of one ring. By that first mode the soul is a unit broken up into a variety of points: in the second mode it is incorporeal. Similarly, if the soul were a condition or modification of body, we could not wonder that this quality, this one thing from one source, should be present in many objects. The same reasoning would apply if soul were an effect of the conjoint. We, of course, hold it to be bodiless, an essential existence.

5.

How then can a multitude of essential beings be really one? Obviously either the one essence will be entire in all, or the many will rise from a one which remains unaltered and yet includes the one—many in virtue of giving itself, without self-abandonment, to its own multiplication. It is competent thus to give and remain, because while it penetrates all things it can never itself be sundered: this is an identity in variety. There is no reason for dismissing this explanation: we may think of a science with its constituents standing as one total, the source of all those various elements: again, there is the seed, a whole, producing those new parts in which it comes to its division; each of the new growths is a whole while the whole remains undiminished: only the material element is under the mode of part, and all the multiplicity remains an entire identity still. It may be objected that in the case of science the constituents are not each the whole. But even in the science, while the constituent selected for handling to meet a particular need is present actually and takes the lead, still all the other constituents accompany it in a potential presence, so that the whole is in every part: only in this sense is the whole science distinguished from the part: all, we may say, is here simultaneously effected: each part is at your disposal as you choose to take it; the part invites the immediate interest, but its value consists in its approach to the whole. The detail cannot be considered as something separate from the entire body of speculation: so treated it would have no technical or scientific value; it would be childish divagation. The one detail, when it is a matter of science, potentially includes all. Grasping one such constituent of his science, the expert deduces the rest by force of sequence. The geometrician, in his analysis, shows that the single proposition includes all the items that go to constitute it and all the propositions which can be developed from it. It is our feebleness that leads to doubt in these matters: the body obscures the truth, but there all stands out clear and separate.

STUDY QUESTIONS: PLOTINUS, *FOURTH ENNEAD*: *NINTH TRICTATE, ARE ALL SOULS ONE?*

1. How does Plotinus deduce that "the soul of every individual is one thing?" What is the argument? Is it persuasive? Why?
2. Does Soul A in Body A = Soul B in Body B also mean that Body A and Body B are the same body? In other words, given that in Plotinus' view you and I are the same soul, are we therefore also the same body? Why?
3. What does Plotinus mean by "essential existence?" Is bodily existence essential?
4. What is the relationship between "unity" and "identity?"
5. Plotinus claims that there is "nothing strange" in his reduction of all souls to one soul. Do you agree? Why? If not, what are your objections and how do you suppose Plotinus would reply to you?

Philosophical Bridges: The Influence of Plotinus

Plotinism lasted as a school of Greek and Latin philosophers throughout the fifth century, inspiring philosophers such as Porphyry, Apuleius, Jamblichus, Julian the Apostate, Tehmistius, Simplicius, Macrobius and Proclus. Plotinus' revival of Plato's metaphysical idealism also inspired philosophers such as Augustine, Dionysius the Pseudo-Areopagite, and John Scotus Eriugena, to incorporate Plato's thought into Church doctrine.

Islamic philosophers such as Avicenna, Al Gazali, and Averröes were all deeply influenced by Plotinus. His emanation theory found its way even into the Jewish tradition through Avicebron's *Fons Vitae*. Meister Eckhart and Nicholas of Cusa were also inspired by him. Modern vestiges of his thought can be found in the British idealism of George Berkeley and more recent British idealists, such as F. H. Bradley and T. H. Greene. Among the Germans, Hegel, Fichte, Schelling, and Schopenhauer developed equally vast metaphysical systems of absolute idealism. Among American philosophers, the view that we the many are each the emanation of the one world soul culminated in the late nineteenth and early twentieth century philosophy of Josiah Royce. More recently, a number of prominent twentieth-century physicists held this view, among them Erwin Schrödinger, Fred Hoyle, and Freeman Dyson. Schrödinger, one of the originators of quantum mechanics, puts it like this:

It is not possible that this unity of knowledge, feeling and choice which you call your own should have sprung into being from nothingness at a given moment not so long ago; rather this knowledge, feeling and choice are essentially eternal and unchangeable and numerically one in all men, nay in all sensitive beings. But not in this sense—that you are a part, a piece, of an eternal, infinite being, an aspect or modification of it, as in Spinoza's pantheism. For we should have the same baffling question: which part, which aspect are you? What, objectively, differentiates it from the others? No, but inconceivable as it seems to ordinary reason, you—and all other conscious beings as such—are all in all. Hence this life of yours which you are living is not merely a piece of the entire existence, but is in a certain sense the whole; only this whole is not so constituted that it can be surveyed in one single glance. [Schrodinger, *What is Life*, Cambridge University Press 1967]

In his *I Am You: The Metaphysical Foundations for Global Ethics* (Springer 2004), Daniel Kolak argues that we are all the same person is the *best* possible view of personal identity. He writes:

The central thesis of *I Am You*—that we are all the same person—is apt to strike many readers as obviously false or even absurd. How could you be me and Hitler and Gandhi and Jesus and Buddha and Greta Garbo and everybody else in the past, present and future? This is the best explanation of who we are for a variety of reasons, not the least of which is that it provides the metaphysical foundations for global ethics. (p. xii)

BIBLIOGRAPHY

GENERAL
Primary
Plotinus, from *The Enneads*, translated by Stephen MacKenna, Pantheon, 1957; abridged and reissued, with introduction and commentary by John M. Dillion, Penguin Classics, 1991

The Essential Plotinus, translated by Elmer O'Brien, American Library, 1964; reissued by Hackett Publishing Co, 1975

Secondary
Armstrong, A.H. *The Architecture of the Intelligible Universe in the Philosophy of Plotinus*, A.M. Hakkert, 1967

Brehier, E., *The Philosophy of Plotinus*, University of Chicago, 1958

Mayhall, C. W., *On Plotinus*, Wadsworth, 2004

Gerson, L., *Plotinus*, Routledge, 1998

Gerson, L., *The Cambridge Companion to Plotinus*, Cambridge University Press, 1996

Graeser, A., *Plotinus and the Stoics*, Brill, 1972

Gregory, J., *The Neoplatonists*, Routledge, 1991

Inge, W. R., *The Philosophy of Plotinus*, Greenwood Press, 1968

O'Meara, D., *Plotinus: An Introduction to the Enneads*, Oxford University Press, 1993

Rist, J., *Plotinus: The Road to Reality*, Cambridge University Press, 1967

SECTION II

◆ AUGUSTINE ◆→

PROLOGUE

With more than a little help, either directly or indirectly, from the works of Plato, Aristotle, the Stoics, and the neo-Platonists, Christian philosophy dominated western thought for a thousand years, from the fall of Rome until the Renaissance. Four of its main Latin Church founders—St. Ambrose, St. Jerome, St. Augustine, and Pope Gregory the Great— were all well versed in philosophical methods and techniques, especially Augustine (Aurelius Augustinus of Hippo), whose influence upon the church and subsequent developments was deepest and most lasting.

Many have speculated as to why, after nearly a thousand years of robust development from Thales and the other pre-Socratic philosophers, through Plato and Aristotle, culminating with the distinctly anti-religious turn of the Epicureans, Stoics and Skeptics, western civilization seemed suddenly to revert into rampant superstition, chaos, and religious fundamentalism. Plotinus, as we already pointed out, blamed the latter philosophers themselves. He was not alone. His solution—build an even better philosophy, founded on a logically grounded epistemology with an even more vast and all-encompassing, thoroughly cosmic metaphysics—inspired the next generation of philosophers who, regardless of how repressed they may have been by the orthodox church doctrines within which they had to live and work, were at the same time extraordinarily empowered by the sheer magnitude of protection and authority afforded to them by the emerging power of the church. Among these newly hierarchical thinkers, Augustine was arguably the greatest.

AUGUSTINE (354–430)

Biographical History

Like Plotinus, who inspired and influenced him most deeply, Augustine was himself a bridge between ancient and medieval thought. He was born at Tagaste in North Africa (near present day Tripoli) during the final years of the decline and fall of the Roman

Empire. He studied and taught rhetoric—"the art of persuasion"—in Carthage, Rome, and Milan, until he became a devout believer in Manicheism. This powerful Persian religion, the product of a strange mix of Christianity and Zoroastrianism by its Magian founder, Mani (Greek *Manes*, Latinized *Manichaeus*), teaches that the human struggle between good and evil is itself a comic manifestation of an eternal duel between angelic forces of light and demonic forces of darkness. Mani's unique marriage of Zoroastrian ideas caught young Augustine's fancy, especially the claim that Christ himself was an incarnation of the same immortal spirit as Buddha and Zarathustra. He believed that Christ was the original first soul of humanity created by the "mother of light" as a guide in our cosmic ballet between light and darkness. No sooner did Augustine accept this teaching than he discovered the Skeptics and altogether dropped Manicheism in favor of a new guiding light: doubt everything that can be doubted. But then he discovered Plotinus and became a devout neo-platonist. To Plotinus's religious interpretation of Plato he added Zoroastrian and Manichaean themes: the struggle between good and evil, sin and salvation, a philosophical tension which remained the focal point of his thought even after his final conversion to Christianity.

You may think that with so many "conversions" Augustine was wishy-washy or a pushover. He wasn't. The fact is that the most highly esteemed Roman lawyers noted him as an intellectual wizard for his abilities to train young lawyers in rhetoric—"the art of persuasion"—which he delighted in using to plead the most unimaginably unpopular cases. He became the leading professor of rhetoric at the University of Milan, until the year 387, when he suddenly converted to Christianity, returned to his birthplace in Africa, and devoted himself to building monasteries and writing philosophy. He was ordained as a priest in 391 and five years later appointed bishop of Hippo, a city near Carthage, where he remained for the rest of his life.

Philosophical Overview

Plato did metaphysics and epistemology for their own sake. Not Augustine. He saw philosophy in a more Socratic light: the purpose is not knowledge or wisdom for their own sake but, rather, the moral development of individual souls. The goal is salvation, by which he means the ending of suffering and the attainment of happiness, both in this world and in the next. Augustine cleverly augments this ancient Socratic ideal with all the best arguments and tools developed by the Epicureans, Stoics, and Skeptics.

In the works of the neo-Platonists such as Plotinus, Augustine found "all things but one—the *Logos* made flesh." This problem he than himself solved by laying a firm philosophical foundation for Christianity using their views, especially Plotinus. Augustine's unorthodox Christian reinterpretation of neo-Platonism culminates in his view that only a select few individuals can obtain ultimate knowledge of reality via a mystical intuition, "the supreme Form of the Good," "Being," "God." His unique form of introspective empiricism begins with a study of the sensations of the external world and proceeds inward with a rigorous psychology of the self. His *City of God*, written shortly after the fall of the Roman Empire in 410, provides the philosophical foundations for a new religious state modeled after and inspired by Plato's *Republic*. Augustine sees a major flaw in Plato's thought: to *know* the truth does not guarantee that you will *do* the truth. He finds a similar error in Aristotle: the essence of humanity is not rationality, as Aristotle thought, but *will*. Furthermore, it therefore follows, according to Augustine, that you cannot believe in God unless first you *will* yourself to believe. Logic, rationality and argument are impotent against the will. Augustine's understanding of free will further complicates his astounding vision. The idea, basically, is that we are not free to believe in God or not. Only through "divine grace" can you or I come to believe that God exists. But it is not as simple as that, either. There are several crucially important things that we can and must do to prepare ourselves to receive God's grace. Interestingly enough, this religious preparation is, thoroughly and deeply, philosophical.

This point about the role of philosophy in Augustine's thought is easily, and often has been, missed by many religious as well as secular philosophers (but *not*, most notably, among subsequent philosophers, by Descartes or Kant). Philosophy in Augustine's conception is not opposed to but in fact *essential* to religion. This is because true reality can only be understood when we first understand the world of appearances to be false. And although through philosophy we can come to understand that the appearances are deceiving, that for instance we do not directly perceive external reality, and so on, but we cannot no matter what we do come in actuality to *believe* that this is so. This profound point—that, essentially, we cannot "believe" what philosophy teaches us for instance about perception and reality—would be either a bone of contention or the foundation for deep insight for philosophy throughout the ages up to the present day; on the one hand, it provided the fodder for transcendental arguments (see the sections on Descartes and Kant) and, on the other, the pragmatic turn in nineteenth and twentieth century thought. But as far as Augustine was concerned, this inner, transcendental revelation of the truth—whether it be about perception, psychological introspection, metaphysics, or God himself, Augustine calls *faith*. On *no* account can reason provide such faith. One must start, "God willing," with philosophically inspired insights and only then reason to the truth, a method that would be further developed into a very potent philosophy by Descartes. In other words: one cannot reason *to* faith, one must reason *from* faith. Hence Augustine's famous dictum, "I believe in order to understand."

Here, then, are the truths that Augustine found by his revolutionary method of inquiry:

1. *the mind cannot grasp the true reality on its own*
2. *without special training into a state of illumination, we cannot ever know God*
3. *God must illuminate the mind through inner revelation so that the true reality can be grasped*
4. *Knowledge of God is predestined by God and there is nothing any of us can do to attain such knowledge; no amount of study will help, no amount of learning, not even prayer makes any difference.*

Few, if any, professing Christians believe these doctrines today. According to most versions of contemporary Christianity, what you do can and does affect whether or not you attain knowledge of God, salvation, and so on. According to Augustine, however, such "illumination" either will or will not happen, independently of what you do. Even your salvation, or damnation, is preordained, in advance of anything you do, by God. God's grace cannot be earned but must be bequeathed to you directly by God, apparently for no rationally discoverable reason. Again, however, this vision is complicated by Augustine's insistence that although we cannot reach God by rational means we are nevertheless obliged to seek the impossible, knowing fully well in advance that we cannot know whether we will ever succeed! We must seek truth and enlightenment even though we cannot ever know whether we are on the correct path. There *is* no "correct path." This sounds contradictory but it is the seed of a very powerful idea that gripped and inspired minds of both religious and antireligious persuasions for generations to come.

Augustine provides an equally provocative answer to Plotinus' question as to why the mind is not fully aware of itself: because, to function properly, the mind must be seduced by its own images, to see its own mental representations of things not as images or representations but as things in themselves. Thus it is only by *properly deceiving* itself that the mind can operate in and among the appearances, under a veiled, false or hidden, view of its own operations. To become fully illuminated to itself, to its own existence as such, the mind must detach itself, in the manner of the Buddhist, Stoic, and Skeptic, from its own perceptions and the things to which it is attracted by desire. In other words, the mind must remove itself from the seduction of its own images. This view is no doubt reminiscent of the path of the philosopher who leaves the darkness of Plato's cave for the light of the sun. This the mind can attain when it becomes aware of its three distinct faculties as separately functioning aspects of one entity of the mind. These three faculties—memory, understanding, and will—are, Augustine claims, the direct image within us of the Holy Trinity.

AGAINST THE MANICHAEANS

In this work Augustine criticizes the Manichaean version of Zoroastrianism, the religious order from which he converted to Christianity. Here he argues that we must accept the reality of a perfect and omnipotent force beyond the grasp of human consciousness and intellect, what he calls *God*. The existence of God, he thinks, is not difficult to establish. The problem is how to rectify an imperfect and limited world created by a perfect and unlimited being. Some medieval theologians argued that because there is evil in the world God must be evil, that the purpose of our existence is to suffer. Others argued that really there was no evil, that pain and suffering are but illusions. Augustine takes a different approach. Evil is neither an illusion, nor is God in any way corrupt. Rather, evil is itself a necessary tool for carrying out God's plan for ourselves and the world.

HAPPINESS IS IN THE ENJOYMENT OF MAN'S CHIEF GOOD. TWO CONDITIONS OF THE CHIEF GOOD: 1ST, NOTHING IS BETTER THAN IT; 2ND, IT CANNOT BE LOST AGAINST THE WILL.

How then, according to reason, ought man to live? We all certainly desire to live happily; and there is no human being but assents to this statement almost before it is made. But the title happy cannot, in my opinion, belong either to him who has not what he loves, whatever it may be, or to him who has what he loves if it is hurtful, or to him who does not love what he has, although it is good in perfection. For one who seeks what he cannot obtain suffers torture, and one

who has got what is not desirable is cheated, and one who does not seek for what is worth seeking for is diseased. Now in all these cases the mind cannot but be unhappy, and happiness and unhappiness cannot reside at the same time in one man: so in none of these cases can the man be happy. I find, then, a fourth case, where the happy life exists—when that which is man's chief good is both loved and possessed. For what do we call enjoyment but having at hand the objects of love? And no one can be happy who does not enjoy what is man's chief good, nor is there any one who enjoys this who is not happy. We must then have at hand our chief good, if we think of living happily.

Augustine, from *The Writings against the Manichaeans and against the Donatists* (a Select Library of the Nicene and post-Nicene Fathers), First Series, ed. Philip Schaff, vol. 4 (New York: Christian Literature Publishing Co., 1886–1890).

We must now inquire what is man's chief good, which of course cannot be anything inferior to man himself. For whoever follows after what is inferior to himself, becomes himself inferior. But every man is bound to follow what is best. Wherefore, man's chief good is not inferior to man. Is it then something similar to man himself? It must be so, if there is nothing above man which he is capable of enjoying. But if we find something which is both superior to man, and can be possessed by the man who loves it, who can doubt that in seeking for happiness man should endeavor to reach that which is more excellent than the being who makes the endeavor? For if happiness consists in the enjoyment of a good than which there is nothing better, which we call the chief good, how can a man be properly called happy who has not yet attained to his chief good? or how can that be the chief good beyond which something better remains for us to arrive at? Such, then, being the chief good, it must be something which cannot be lost against the will. For no one can feel confident regarding a good which he knows can be taken from him, although he wishes to keep and cherish it. But if a man feels no confidence regarding the good which he enjoys, how can he be happy while in such fear of losing it?

MAN—WHAT?

Let us then see what is better than man. This must necessarily be hard to find, unless we first ask and examine what man is. I am not now called upon to give a definition of man. The question here seems to me to be—since almost all agree, or at least, which is enough, those I have now to do with are of the same opinion with me, that we are made up of soul and body—what is man? Is he both of these? or is he the body only, or the soul only? For although the things are two, soul and body, and although neither without the other could be called man (for the body would not be man without the soul, nor again would the soul be man if there were not a body animated by it), still it is possible that one of these may be held to be man, and may be called so. What then do we call man? Is he soul and body, as in a double harness, or like a centaur? Or do we mean the body only, as being in the service of the soul which rules it, as the word lamp denotes not the light and the case together, but only the case, yet it is on account of the light that it is so called? Or do we mean only the mind, and that on account of the body which it rules, as horseman means not the man and the horse, but the man only, and that as employed in ruling the horse? This dispute is not easy to settle; or, if the proof is plain, the statement requires time. This is an expenditure of time and strength which we need not incur. For whether the name man belongs to both, or only to the soul, the chief good of man is not the chief good of the body: but what is the chief good either of both soul and body, or of the soul only, that is man's chief good.

MAN'S CHIEF GOOD IS NOT THE CHIEF GOOD OF THE BODY ONLY, BUT THE CHIEF GOOD OF THE SOUL.

Now if we ask what is the chief good of the body, reason obliges us to admit that it is that by means of which the body comes to be in its best state. But of all the things which invigorate the body, there is nothing better or greater than the soul. The chief good of the body, then, is not bodily pleasure, not absence of pain, not strength, not beauty, not swiftness, or whatever else is usually reckoned among the goods of the body, but simply the soul. For all the things mentioned the soul supplies to the body by its presence, and, what is above them all, life. Hence, I conclude that the soul is not the chief good of man, whether we give the name of man to soul and body together, or to the soul alone. For as, according to reason, the chief good of the body is that which is better than the body and from which the body receives vigor and life, so whether the soul itself is man, or soul and body both, we must discover whether there is anything which goes before the soul itself, in following which the soul comes to the perfection of good of which it is capable in its own kind. If such a thing can be found, all uncertainty must be at an end, and we must pronounce this to be really and truly the chief good of man.

If, again, the body is man, it must be admitted that the soul is the chief good of man. But clearly, when we treat of morals—when we inquire what manner of life must be held in order to obtain happiness—it is not the body to which the precepts are addressed, it is not bodily discipline which we discuss. In short, the observance of good *customs* belongs to that part of us which inquires and learns, which are the prerogatives of the soul; so, when we speak of attaining to virtue, the question does not regard the body. But if it follows, as it does, that the body which is ruled over by a soul possessed of virtue is ruled both better and more honorably, and is in its greatest perfection in consequence of the perfection of the soul which rightfully governs it, that which gives perfection to the soul will be man's chief good, though we call the body man. For if my coachman, in obedience to me, feeds and drives the horses he has charge of in the most satisfactory manner, himself enjoying the more of my bounty in proportion to his good conduct, can any one deny that the good condition of the horses, as well as that of the coachman, is due to me? So the question seems to me to be not, whether soul and body is man, or the soul only, or the body only, but what gives perfection to the soul; for when this is obtained, a man cannot but be either perfect, or at least much better than in the absence of this one thing. . . .

GOD IS THE CHIEF GOOD, WHOM WE ARE TO SEEK AFTER WITH SUPREME AFFECTION.

Let us see how the Lord Himself in the gospel has taught us to live; how, too, Paul the apostle—for the Manichaeans dare not reject these Scriptures. Let us hear, O Christ, what chief end Thou dost prescribe to us: and that is evidently the chief end after which we are told to strive with supreme affection. "Thou shalt love." He says, "the Lord thy God." Tell me also, I pray Thee, what must be the measure of love; for I fear lest the desire enkindled in my heart should exceed or come short in fervor. "With all thy heart," He says. Nor is that enough. "With all thy soul." Nor is it enough yet. "With all thy mind." What do you wish more? I might, perhaps, wish more if I could see the possibility of more. What does Paul say on this? "We know," he says, "that all things issue in good to them that love God." Let him, too, say what is the measure of love. "Who then," he says, "shall separate us from the love of Christ? Shall tribulation, or distress, or persecution, or famine, or nakedness, or peril, or the sword?" We have heard, then, what and how much we must love; this we must strive after, and to this we must refer all our plans. The perfection of all our good things and our perfect good is God. We must neither come short of this nor go beyond it: the one is dangerous, the other impossible. . . .

THAT IN ALL NATURES, OF EVERY KIND AND RANK, GOD IS GLORIFIED.

All natures, then, inasmuch as they are, and have, therefore, a rank and species of their own, and a kind of internal harmony, are certainly good. And when they are in the places assigned to them by the order of their nature, they preserve such being as they have received. And those things which have received everlasting being, are altered for better or for worse, so as to suit the wants and notions of those things to which the Creator's law has made them subservient; and thus they tend in the divine providence to that end which is embraced in the general scheme of the government of the universe. So that, though the corruption of transitory and perishable things brings them to utter destruction, it does not prevent their producing that which was designed to be their result. And this being so, God, who supremely is, and who therefore created every being which has not supreme existence (for that which was made of nothing could not be equal to Him, and indeed could not be at all had He not made it), is not to be found fault with on account of the creature's faults, but is to be praised in view of the natures He has made. . . .

THAT WE OUGHT NOT TO EXPECT TO FIND ANY EFFICIENT CAUSE OF THE EVIL WILL.

Let no one, therefore, look for an efficient cause of the evil will; for it is not efficient, but deficient, as the will itself is not an effecting of something, but a defect. For defection from that which supremely is, to that which has less of being—this is to begin to have an evil will. Now, to seek to discover the causes of these defections—causes, as I have said, not efficient, but deficient—is as if someone sought to see darkness, or hear silence. Yet both of these are known by us, and the former by means only of the eye, the latter only by the ear; but not by their positive actuality, but by their want of it. Let no one, then seek to know from me what I know that I do not know; unless he perhaps wishes to learn to be ignorant of that of which all we know is, that it cannot be known. For those things which are known not by their actuality, but by their want of it, are known, if our expression may be allowed and understood, by not knowing them, that by knowing them they may be not known. For when the eyesight surveys objects that strike the sense, it nowhere sees darkness but where it begins not to see. And so no other sense but the ear can perceive silence, and yet it is only perceived by not hearing. Thus, too, our mind perceives intelligible forms by understanding them; but when they are deficient, it knows them by not knowing them; for who can understand defects?

OF THE MISDIRECTED LOVE WHEREBY THE WILL FELL AWAY FROM THE IMMUTABLE TO THE MUTABLE GOOD.

This I do know, that the nature of God can never, nowhere, nowise be defective, and that natures made of nothing can. These latter, however, the more being they have, and the more good they do (for then they do something positive), the more they have efficient causes; but in so far as they are defective in being, and consequently do evil (for then what is their work but vanity?) they have deficient causes. And I know likewise, that the will could not become evil, were it unwilling to become so; and therefore its failings are justly punished, being not necessary, but voluntary. For its defections are not to evil things, but are themselves evil; that is to say, are not toward things that are naturally and in themselves evil, but the defection of the will is evil, because it is contrary to the order of nature, and an abandonment of that which has supreme being for that which has less. For avarice is not a fault inherent in gold, but in the man who inordinately loves gold, to the detriment of justice, which ought to be held in incomparably higher regard than gold. Neither is luxury the fault of lovely and charming objects, but of the heart that inordinately loves sensual pleasures, to the neglect of temperance, which attaches us to objects more lovely in their spirituality, and more delectable by their incorruptibility. Nor yet is boasting the fault of human praise but of the soul that is inordinately fond of the applause of men, and that makes light of the voice of conscience. Pride, too, is not the fault of him who delegates power, nor of power itself, but of the soul that is inordinately enamored of its own power, and despises the more just dominion of a higher authority. Consequently he who inordinately loves the good which any nature possesses, even though he obtain it, him-

self becomes evil in the good, and wretched because deprived of a greater good. . . .

THAT EVEN THE FIERCENESS OF WAR AND ALL THE DISQUIETUDE OF MEN MAKE TOWARDS THIS ONE END OF PEACE, WHICH EVERY NATURE DESIRES.

Whoever gives even moderate attention to human affairs and to our common nature, will recognize that if there is no man who does not wish to be joyful, neither is there any one who does not wish to have peace. For even they who make war desire nothing but victory—desire, that is to say, to attain to peace with glory. For what else is victory than the conquest of those who resist us? And when this is done there is peace. It is therefore with the desire for peace that wars are waged, even by those who take pleasure in exercising their warlike nature in command and battle. And hence it is obvious that peace is the end sought for by war. For every man seeks peace by waging war, but no man seeks war by making peace. For even they who intentionally interrupt the peace in which they are living have no hatred of peace, but only wish it changed into a peace that suits them better. They do not, therefore, wish to have no peace, but only one more to their mind. And in the case of sedition, when men have separated themselves from the community, they yet do not effect what they wish, unless they maintain some kind of peace with their fellow-conspirators. And therefore even robbers take care to maintain peace with their comrades, that they may with greater effect and greater safety invade the peace of other men. And if an individual happens to be of such unrivalled strength, and to be so jealous of partnership, that he trusts himself with no comrades, but makes his own plots, and commits depredations and murders on his own account, yet he maintains some shadow of peace with such persons as he is unable to kill, and from whom he wishes to conceal his deeds. In his own home, too, he makes it his aim to be at peace with his wife and children, and any other members of his household; for unquestionably their prompt obedience to his every look is a source of pleasure to him. And if this be not rendered, he is angry, he chides and punishes; and even by this storm he secures the calm peace of his own home, as occasion demands. For he sees that peace cannot be maintained unless all the members of the same domestic circle be subject to one head, such as he himself is in his own house. And therefore if a city or nation offered to submit itself to him, to serve him in the same style as he had made his household serve him, he would no longer lurk in a brigand's hiding-places, but lift his head in open day as a king, though the same coveteousness and wickedness should remain in him. And thus all men desire to have peace with their own circle whom they wish to govern as suits themselves. For even those whom they make war against they wish to make their own, and impose on them the laws of their own peace.

But let us suppose a man such as poetry and mythology speak of—a man so insociable and savage as to be called rather a semi-man than a man. Although, then, his kingdom was the solitude of a dreary cave, and he himself was so singularly bad-hearted that he was named Kaxos, which is the Greek word for *bad*; though he had no wife to soothe him with endearing talk, no children to play with, no sons to do his bidding, no friend to enliven him with intercourse, not even his father Vulcan (though in one respect he was happier than his father, not having begotten a monster like himself); although he gave to no man, but took as he wished whatever he could, from whomsoever he could, when he could; yet in that solitary den, the floor of which, as Virgil says, was always reeking with recent slaughter, there was nothing else than peace sought, a peace in which no one should molest him, or disquiet him with any assault or alarm. With his own body he desired to be at peace, and he was satisfied only in proportion as he had this peace. For he ruled his members, and they obeyed him; and for the sake of pacifying his mortal nature, which rebelled when it needed anything, and of allaying the sedition of hunger which threatened to banish the soul from the body, he made forays, slew, and devoured, but used the ferocity and savageness he displayed in these actions only for the preservation of his own life's peace. So that, had he been willing to make with other men the same peace which he made with himself in his own cave, he would neither have been called bad, nor a monster, nor a semi-man. Or if the appearance of his body and his vomiting smoky fires frightened men from having any dealings with him, perhaps his fierce ways arose not from a desire to do mischief, but from the necessity of finding a living.

But he may have had no existence, or, at least, he was not such as the poets fancifully describe him, for they had to exalt Hercules, and did so at the expense of Cacus. It is better, then, to believe that such a man or semi-man never existed, and that this, in common with many other fancies of the poets, is mere fiction. For the most savage animals (and he is said to have been almost a wild beast) encompass their own species with a ring of protecting peace. They cohabit, beget, produce, suckle, and bring up their young, though very many of them are not gregarious, but solitary—not like sheep, deer, pigeons, starlings, bees, but such as lions, foxes, eagles, bats. For what tigress does not gently purr over her cubs, and lay aside her ferocity to fondle them? What kite, solitary as he is when circling over his prey, does not seek a mate, build a nest, hatch the eggs, bring up the young birds, and maintain with the mother of his family as peaceful a domestic alliance as he can? How much more powerfully do the laws of man's nature move him to hold fellowship and maintain peace with all men so far as in him lies, since even wicked men wage war to maintain the peace of their own circle, and wish that, if possible, all men belonged to them, that all men and things might serve but one head, and might, either through love or fear, yield themselves to peace with him! It is thus that pride in its perversity apes God. It abhors equality with other men under Him; but, instead of His rule, it seeks to impose a rule of its own upon its equals. It abhors, that is to say, the just peace of God, and loves its own unjust peace; but it cannot help loving peace of one kind or other. For there is no vice so clean contrary to nature that it obliterates even the faintest traces of nature.

He, then, who prefers what is right to what is wrong, and what is well-ordered to what is perverted, sees that the peace of unjust men is not worthy to be called peace in comparison with the peace of the just. And yet even what is perverted must of necessity be in harmony with, and in dependence on, and in some part of the order of things, for otherwise it would have no existence at all. Suppose a man hangs with his head downwards, this is certainly a perverted attitude of body and arrangement of its members; for that which nature requires to be above is beneath, and *vice versa*. This perversity disturbs the peace of the body, and is therefore painful. Nevertheless the spirit is at peace with its body, and labors for its preservation, and hence the suffering; but if it is banished from the body by its pains, then, so long as the bodily framework holds together, there is in the remains a kind of peace among the members, and hence the body remains suspended. And inasmuch as the earthly body tends towards the earth, and rests on the bond by which it is suspended, it tends thus to its natural peace, and the voice of its own weight demands a place for it to rest; and though now lifeless and without feeling, it does not fall from the peace that is natural to its place in creation, whether it already has it, or is tending towards it. For if you apply embalming preparations to prevent the bodily frame from mouldering and dissolving, a kind of peace still unites part to part, and keeps the whole body in a suitable place on the earth—in other words, in a place that is at peace with the body. If, on the other hand, the body receive no such care, but be left to the natural course, it is disturbed by exhalations that do not harmonize with one another, and that offend our senses; for it is this which is perceived in putrefaction until it is assimilated to the elements of the world, and particle by particle enters into peace with them. Yet throughout this process the laws of the most high Creator and Governor are strictly observed, for it is by Him the peace of the universe is administered. For although minute animals are produced from the carcass of a larger animal, all these little atoms, by the law of the same Creator, serve the animals they belong to in peace. And although the flesh of dead animals be eaten by others, no matter where it be carried, nor what it be brought into contact with, nor what it be converted and changed into, it still is ruled by the same laws which pervade all things for the conservation of every mortal race, and which bring things that fit one another into harmony.

OF THE UNIVERSAL PLACE WHICH THE LAW OF NATURE PRESERVES THROUGH ALL DISTURBANCES, AND BY WHICH EVERY ONE REACHES HIS DESERT IN A WAY REGULATED BY THE JUST JUDGE.

The peace of the body then consists in the duly proportioned arrangement of its parts. The peace of the irrational soul is the harmonious repose of the appetites, and that of the rational soul the harmony of knowledge and action. The peace of body and soul is the well-ordered and harmonious life and health of the living creature. Peace between man and God is the well-ordered obedience of faith to eternal law. Peace between man and man is well-ordered concord. Domestic peace is the well-ordered concord between those of the family who rule and those who obey. Civil peace is a similar concord among the citizens. The peace of the celestial city is the perfectly ordered and harmonious enjoyment of God, and of one another in God. The peace of all things is the tranquility of order. Order is the distribution which allots things equal and unequal, each to its own place. And hence, though the miserable, in so far as they are such, do certainly not enjoy peace, but are severed from that tranquillity of order in which there is no disturbance, nevertheless, inasmuch as they are deservedly and justly miserable, they are by their very misery connected with order. They are not, indeed, conjoined with the blessed, but they are disjoined from them by the law of order. And though they are disquieted, their circumstances are notwithstanding adjusted to them, and consequently they have some tranquillity of order, and therefore some peace. But they are wretched because, although not wholly miserable, they are not in that place where any mixture of misery is impossible. They would, however, be more wretched if they had not that peace which arises from being in harmony with the natural order of things. When they suffer, their peace is in so far disturbed; but their peace continues in so far as they do not suffer, and in so far as their nature continues to exist. As, then, there may be life without pain, while there cannot be pain without some kind of life, so there may be peace without war, but there cannot be war without some kind of peace, because war supposes the existence of some natures to wage it, and these natures cannot exist without peace of one kind or other.

And, therefore, there is a nature in which evil does not or even cannot exist: but there cannot be a nature in which there is no good. Hence not even the nature of the devil himself is evil, in so far as it is nature, but it was made evil by being perverted. . . .

STUDY QUESTIONS: AUGUSTINE, *AGAINST THE MANICHAEANS*

1. What is happiness?
2. How should we leave our lives? Why?
3. What is the chief good of our existence?
4. How do mind and body differ?
5. Does evil will have an efficient cause? Why?
6. How does the mind perceive intelligible forms?
7. What is the point of the Hercules example? What does it show?
8. What makes social harmony possible? By what means is this best attained?

ENCHIRIDION

Here Augustine argues that although God is perfectly good and all powerful, God's creations need not be perfect, nor good. God knew, when God created the world, that people would sometimes choose evil. But God foresaw exactly how through our evil acts God's perfectly good will would be fulfilled. The problem is not with God but with the human mind's inability to understand God's infinite wisdom. Subtly, Augustine implies that God needs us. The reason God needs human beings is that we can do what God cannot, namely, evil things, act in ignorance, and so on. We are thus a necessary force in God's vision, we help create reality which without our intervention would not be possible in all its complex glory.

What is called evil in the universe is but the absence of good . . . In the bodies of animals, disease and wounds mean nothing but the absence of health; for when a cure is effected, that does not mean that the evils which were present—namely, the diseases and wounds—go away from the body and dwell elsewhere: they altogether cease to exist; for the wound or disease is not a substance, but a defect in the fleshly substance—the flesh itself being a substance, and therefore something good, of which those evils—that is, privations of the good which we call health—are accidents. Just in the same way, what are called vices in the soul are nothing but privations of natural good. And when they are cured, they are not transferred elsewhere: when they cease to exist in the healthy soul, they cannot exist anywhere else.

All beings were made good, but not being made perfectly good, are liable to corruption: all things that exist, therefore, seeing that the Creator of them all is supremely good, are themselves good. But because they are not, like their Creator, supremely and unchangeably good, their good may be diminished and increased. But for good to be diminished is an evil, although, however much it may be diminished, it is necessary, if the being is to continue, that some good should remain to constitute the being. For however small or of whatever kind the being may be, the good which makes it a being cannot be destroyed without destroying the being itself. An uncorrupted nature is justly held in esteem. But if, still further, it be incorruptible, it is undoubtedly considered of still higher value. When it is corrupted, however, its corruption is an evil, because it is deprived of some sort of good. For if it be deprived of no good, it receives no injury; but it does receive injury, therefore it is deprived of good. Therefore, so long as a being is in process of corruption, there is in it some good of which it is being deprived; and if a part of the being

Saint Augustine, from *Enchiridion*, translated by J. F. Shaw, in *The Works of Aurelius Augustine*, ed. M. Dods (Edinburgh: T. & T. Clark, 1892).

should remain which cannot be corrupted, this will certainly be an incorruptible being, and accordingly the process of corruption will result in the manifestation of this great good. But if it does not cease to be corrupted, neither can it cease to possess good of which corruption may deprive it. But if it should be thoroughly and completely consumed by corruption, there will then be no good left, because there will be no being. Wherefore corruption can consume the good only by consuming the being. Every being, therefore, is a good; a great good, if it cannot be corrupted; a little good, if it can; but in any case, only the foolish or ignorant will deny that it is a good. And if it be wholly consumed by corruption, then the corruption itself must cease to exist, as there is no being left in which it can dwell. . . .

The omnipotent God does well even in the permission of evil: nor can we doubt that God does well even in the permission of what is evil. For He permits it only in the justice of His judgment. And surely all that is just is good. Although, therefore, evil, insofar as it is evil, is not a good; yet the fact that evil as well as good exists, is a good. For if it were not a good that evil should exist, its existence would not be permitted by the omnipotent God, who without doubt can as easily refuse to permit what He does not wish, as bring about what He does wish. And if we do not believe this, the very first sentence of our creed is endangered, wherein we profess to believe in God the Father Almighty. For He is not truly called Almighty if He cannot do whatsoever He pleases, or if the power of His almighty will is hindered by the will of any creature whatsoever. . . .

The will of God is never defeated, though much is done that is contrary to His will: these are the great works of the Lord, sought out according to all His pleasure, and so wisely sought out, that when the intelligent creation, both angelic and human, sinned, doing not His will but their own, He used the very will of the creature which was working in opposition to the Creator's will as an instrument for carrying out His will, the supremely Good thus turning to good

account even what is evil, to the condemnation of those whom in His justice He has predestined to punishment, and to the salvation of those whom in His mercy He has predestined to grace. For, as far as relates to their own consciousness, these creatures did what God wished not to be done: but in view of God's omnipotence, they could in no wise effect their purpose. For in the very fact that they acted in opposition to His will, His will concerning them was fulfilled. And hence it is that "the works of the Lord are great, sought out according to all His pleasure," because in a way unspeakably strange and wonderful, even what is done in opposition to His will does not defeat His will. For it would not be done did He not permit it (and of course His permission is not unwilling, but willing); nor would a Good Being permit evil to be done that in His omnipotence He can turn evil into good.

The will of God, which is always good, is sometimes fulfilled through the evil will of man: Sometimes, however, a man in the goodness of his will desires something that God does not desire, even though God's will is also good, nay, much more fully and more surely good (for His will never can be evil): for example, if a good son is anxious that his father should live, when it is God's goodwill that he should die. Again, it is possible for a man with evil will to desire what God wills in His goodness: for example, if a bad son wishes his father to die, when this is also the will of God. It is plain that the former wishes what God does not wish, and that the latter wishes what God does wish; and yet the filial love of the former is more in harmony with the goodwill of God, though its desire is different from God's, than the want of filial affection of the latter, though its desire is the same as God's. So necessary is it, in determining whether a man's desire is one to be approved or disapproved, to consider what it is proper for man, and what it is proper for God, to desire, and what is in each case the real motive of the will. For God accomplishes some of His purposes, which of course are all good, through the evil desires of wicked men.

STUDY QUESTIONS: AUGUSTINE, *ENCHIRIDION*

1. What is evil? How is it related to good?
2. What makes us corruptible? Is there any way to avoid this? Why?
3. Is corruption always an evil?

4. Does God permit evil? Why?
5. Can anything defeat God's will?
6. How can an act of human evil fulfill God's will, which is always good?
7. Are all of God's purposes good?

SELF-KNOWLEDGE AND
THE THREE-FOLD NATURE OF MIND

In this selection Augustine methodically explains what makes self-knowledge possible, arguing at the same time that this is something very difficult for us to attain. His answer has to do with the nature of the mind. First of all, the mind must come to recognize that most of its beliefs about itself are false. This is something that the skeptics, too, agreed with. It is precisely for this reason that the skeptics claimed that self-knowledge is, therefore, impossible. Augustine agrees with their premise but not their conclusion. He argues, to the contrary, that in spite of the falseness of most of our opinions, especially about ourselves, there is nevertheless something that we can know about ourselves with absolute, perfect certainty. For even if we come, through the recognition of the falseness of so many of our opinions, to doubt everything that we think we know, there is one thing we cannot doubt: our own existence. For in the act of doubting nothing can be more certain than that the doubter exists: since doubting requires thought, and without a thinker there can be no thoughts, the doubting itself affirms the existence of the doubting self. In this way Augustine anticipates, and lays the logical groundwork, for Descartes' argument that would shake up the philosophy world more than a thousand years later and herald the age of modern philosophy. When Descartes says, "I think, therefore I am," he is to a certain extent echoing Augustine's argument in these passages, which are taken from his *City of God* and *The Trinity*.

Now, whereas Plotinus had merely asked, without clearly answering, the question of why the soul, or mind, is not fully aware of itself, Augustine provides a full-blown theory. The answer, and it is as profound as it is logical, with ramifications for subsequent science of the mind and brain, is that the mind *cannot* know itself for the simple reason that to function properly it must have images of things that it takes to be not images but things in themselves. Thus here Augustine is also anticipating the groundbreaking work of Immanuel Kant. In other words, it is through deceiving itself into (mis)understanding its own representations as being not aspects of the mind but as things in themselves existing independently of the mind, that enables the mind to have experience. Without a false view of its own operations, the mind cannot have any experience of the external world, for it would then take its own conjurations, thoughts, perceptions, and images for what they are: mental events. Once the mind understands properly the seductive power of its own images to deceive itself, and why this deception is necessary, the mind begins the path towards philosophical enlightenment. If it persists, it will attain, ultimately, an understanding of the three-fold aspect of itself functioning as three different faculties which even though they are different do not destroy identity. The three minds (mental faculties) are one being. This three-fold aspect of the mind, according to Augustine, mirrors the Holy Trinity; indeed, these three faculties—memory, understanding, and will—are themselves each a direct representation of the threefold aspect of God, namely, the Holy Trinity.

CHAPTER 26. OF THE IMAGE OF THE SUPREME TRINITY, WHICH WE FIND IN SOLVE SORT IN HUMAN NATURE EVEN IN ITS PRESENT STATE.

And we indeed recognize in ourselves the image of God, that is, of the supreme Trinity, an image which, though it be not equal to God, or rather, though it be very far removed from Him, being neither co-eternal, nor, to say all in a word, consubstantial with Him, is yet nearer to Him in nature than any other of His works, and is destined to be yet restored, that it may bear a still closer resemblance. For we both are, and know that we are, and delight in our being, and our knowledge of it. Moreover, in these three things no true-seeming illusion disturbs us: for we do not come into contact with these by some bodily sense, as we perceive the things outside of us, colors, for example, by seeing, sounds by hearing, smells by smelling, tastes by tasting, hard and soft objects by touching, of all which sensible objects it is the images resembling them, but not themselves which we perceive in the mind and hold in the memory, and which excite us to desire the objects. But, without any delusive representation of images or phantasms, I am most certain that I am, and that I know and delight in this. In respect of these truths, I am not at all afraid of the arguments of the academicians, who say, What if you are deceived? For if I am deceived, I am. For he who is not, cannot be deceived; and if I am deceived, by this same token I am. And since I am if I am deceived, how am I deceived in believing that I am? For it is certain that I am if I am deceived. Since, therefore, I, the person deceived, should be, even if I were deceived, certainly I am not deceived in this knowledge that I am. And, consequently, neither am I deceived in knowing that I know. For, as I know that I am, so I know this also, that I know. And when I love these two things, I add to them a certain third thing, namely, my love, which is of equal moment. For neither am I deceived in this, that I love, since in those things which I love I am not deceived; though even if these were false, it would still be true that I *loved* false things. For how could I justly be blamed and prohibited from loving false things, if it were false that I loved them? But, since they are true and real, who doubts that when they are loved, the love of them is itself true and real? Further, as there is no one who does not wish to be happy, so there is no one who does not wish to be. For how can he be happy, if he is nothing?

CHAPTER 6: THE OPINION WHICH THE MIND HAS OF ITSELF IS DECEITFUL.

But the mind errs, when it so lovingly and intimately connects itself with these images, as even to consider itself to be something of the same kind. For so it is conformed to them to some extent, not by being this, but by thinking it is so: not that it thinks itself to be an image, but outright that very thing itself of which it entertains the image. For there still lives in it the power of distinguishing the corporeal thing which it leaves without, from the image of that corporeal thing which it contains therefrom within itself; except when these images are so projected as if felt without and not thought within, as in the case of people who are asleep, or mad, or in a trance.

CHAPTER 7: THE OPINIONS OF PHILOSOPHERS RESPECTING THE SUBSTANCE OF THE SOUL. THE ERROR OF THOSE WHO ARE OF THE OPINION THAT THE SOUL IS CORPOREAL, DOES NOT ARISE FROM DEFECTIVE KNOWLEDGE OF THE SOUL, BUT FROM THEIR ADDING THERETO SOMETHING FOREIGN TO IT. WHAT IS MEANT BY FINDING.

When, therefore, it thinks itself to be something of this kind, it thinks itself to be a corporeal thing; and since it is perfectly conscious of its own superiority, by which it rules the body, it has hence come to pass that the question has been raised what part of the body has the greater power in the body; and the opinion has been held that this is the mind, nay, that it is even the whole soul altogether. And some accordingly think it to be the blood, others the brain, others the heart; not as the Scripture says, "I will praise

Augustine, from *The City of God*, translated by Marcus Dods (Modern Library, 1950).

Augustine, from *History of the Christian Church*, Vol. III: *Nicene and Post-Nicene Fathers*, ed. Philip Schaff (New York: Charles Scribner's Sons, 1884).

Thee, O Lord, with my whole heart"; and, "Thou shalt love the Lord thy God with all thine heart"; for this word by misapplication or metaphor is transferred from the body to the soul; but they have simply thought it to be that small part itself of the body, which we see when the inward parts are rent asunder. Others, again, have believed the soul to be made up of very minute and individual corpuscles, which they call atoms, meeting in themselves and cohering. Others have said that its substance is air, others fire. Others have been of opinion that it is no substance at all, since they could not think any substance unless it is body, and they did not find that the soul was body; but it was in their opinion the tempering together itself of our body, or the combining together of the elements, by which that flesh is as it were conjoined. And, hence, all of these have held the soul to be mortal; since, whether it were body, or some combination of body, certainly it could not in either case continue always without death. But they who have held its substance to be some kind of life the reverse of corporeal, since they have found it to be a life that animates and quickens every living body, have by consequence striven also, according as each was able, to prove it immortal, since life cannot be without life.

For as to that fifth kind of body, I know not what, which some have added to the four well-known elements of the world, and have said that the soul was made of this, I do not think we need spend time in discussing it in this place. For either they mean by body what we mean by it, namely that of which a part is less than the whole in extension of place, and they are to be reckoned among those who have believed the mind to be corporeal: or if they call either all substance, or all changeable substance, body, whereas they know that not all substance is contained in extension of place by any length and breadth and height, we need not contend with them about a question of words.

Now, in the case of all these opinions, any one who sees that the nature of the mind is at once substance, and yet not corporeal—that is, that it does not occupy a less extension of place with a less part of itself, and a greater with a greater—must needs see at the same time that they who are of opinion that it is corporeal, do not err from defect of knowledge concerning mind, but because they associate with it qualities without which they are not able to conceive any nature at all. For if you bid them conceive of exis-

tence that is without corporeal phantasms, they hold it merely nothing. And so the mind would not seek itself, as though wanting to itself. For what is so present to knowledge as that which is present to the mind? Or what is so present to the mind as the mind itself? And hence what is called "invention," if we consider the origin of the word, what else does it mean, unless that to find out (*invenire*) is to "come into" that which is sought? Those things accordingly which come into the mind as it were of themselves, are not usually said to be found out (*inventa*), although they may be said to be known; since we did not endeavor by seeking to come into them, that is, to invent or find them out. And, therefore, as the mind itself really seeks those things which are sought by the eyes or by any other sense of the body (for the mind directs even the carnal sense, and then finds out or invents, when that sense comes to the things which are sought); so, too, it finds out or invents other things which it ought to know, not with the medium of corporeal sense, but through itself, when it "comes into" them; and this, whether in the case of the higher substance that is in God, or of the other parts of the soul; just as it does when it judges of bodily images themselves; for it finds these within, in the soul, impressed through the body.

CHAPTER 8: HOW THE SOUL INQUIRES INTO ITSELF. WHENCE COMES THE ERROR OF THE SOUL CONCERNING ITSELF.

It is then a wonderful question, in what manner the soul seeks and finds itself; at what it aims in order to seek, or whither it comes, that it may come into or find out. For what is so much in the mind as the mind itself? But because it is *in* those things which it thinks of with love, and is wont to be in sensible, that is, in corporeal things with love, it is unable to be in itself without the images of those corporeal things. And hence shameful error arises to block its way, whilst it cannot separate from itself the images of sensible things, so as to see itself alone. For they have marvelously cohered with it by the close adhesion of love. And herein consists its uncleanness; since, while it strives to think of itself alone, it fancies itself to be that, without which it cannot think of itself. When, therefore, it is bidden to become acquainted with itself, let it not seek itself as though it were withdrawn from itself; but let it withdraw that which it has added to itself. For itself lies more deeply within not only than those sensible things, which are clearly without, but also than the images of them; which are indeed in some part of the soul, namely that which beasts also have, although these want understanding, which is proper to the mind. As, therefore, the mind is within, it goes forth in some sort from itself, when it exerts the affection of love towards these, as it were, footprints of many acts of attention. And these footprints are, as it were, imprinted on the memory, at the time when the corporeal things which are without are perceived in such way, that even when those corporeal things are absent, yet the images of them are at hand to those who think of them. Therefore, let the mind become acquainted with itself, and not seek itself as if it were absent; but fix upon itself the act of [voluntary] attention, by which it was wandering among other things, and let it think of itself. So it will see that at no time did it ever not love itself, at no time did it ever not know itself; but by loving another thing together with itself it has confounded itself with it, and in some sense has grown one with it. And so, while it embraces diverse things, as though they were one, it has come to think those things to be one which are diverse.

CHAPTER 9: THE MIND KNOWS ITSELF, BY THE VERY ACT OF UNDERSTANDING THE PRECEPT TO KNOW ITSELF.

Let it not, therefore, seek to discern itself as though absent, but take pains to discern itself as present. Nor let it take knowledge of itself as if it did not know itself, but let it distinguish itself from that which it knows to be another. For how will it take pains to obey that very precept which is given it, "Know thyself," if it knows not either what "know" means or what "thyself" means? But if it knows both, then it knows also itself. Since "know thyself" is not so said to the mind as is "Know the cherubim and the seraphim"; for they are absent, and we believe concerning them, and according to that belief they are declared to be certain celestial powers. Nor yet again as it is said, Know the will of that man: for this it is not within our reach to perceive at all, either by sense or understanding, unless by corporeal signs actually set forth; and this in such a way that we rather

believe than understand. Nor yet again as it is said to a man, Behold thy own face; which he can only do in a looking glass. For even our own face itself is out of the reach of our own seeing it; because it is not there where our look can be directed. But when it is said to the mind, know thyself; then it knows itself by that very act by which it understands the word "thyself"; and this for no other reason than that it is present to itself. But if it does not understand what is said, then certainly it does not do as it is bid to do. And, therefore, it is bidden to do that thing which it does do, when it understands the very precept that bids it.

CHAPTER 10: EVERY MIND KNOWS CERTAINLY THREE THINGS CONCERNING ITSELF—THAT IT UNDERSTANDS, THAT IT IS, AND THAT IT LIVES.

Let it not then add anything to that which it knows itself to be, when it is bidden to know itself. For it knows, at any rate, that this is said to itself; namely, to the self that is, and that lives, and that understands. But a dead body also is, and cattle live; but neither a dead body nor cattle understand. Therefore, it so knows that it so is, and that it so lives, as an understanding is and lives. When, therefore, for example's sake, the mind thinks itself air, it thinks that air understands; it knows, however, that itself understands, but it does not know itself to be air, but only thinks so. Let it separate that which it thinks itself; let it discern that which it knows; let this remain to it, about which not even have they doubted who have thought the mind to be this corporeal thing or that. For certainly every mind does not consider itself to be air; but some think themselves fire, others the brain, and some one kind of corporeal thing, others another, as I have mentioned before; yet all know that they themselves understand, and are, and live; but they refer understanding to that which they understand, but to be, and to live, to themselves. And no one doubts, either that no one understands who does not live, or that no one lives of whom it is not true that he is; and that therefore by consequence that which understands both is and lives; not as a dead body is which does not live, nor as a soul lives which does not understand, but in some proper and more excellent manner. Further, they know that they will, and they equally know that no one can will who is not and who does not live; and they also refer that will itself to something which they will with that will. They know also that they remember; and they know at the same time that nobody could remember, unless he both was and lived; but we refer memory itself also to something, in that we remember those things. Therefore the knowledge and science of many things are contained in two of these three, memory and understanding; but will must be present, that we may enjoy or use them. For we enjoy things known, in which things themselves the will finds delight for their own sake, and so reposes; but we use those things, which we refer to some other thing which we are to enjoy. Neither is the life of man vicious and culpable in any other way, than as wrongly using and wrongly enjoying. But it is no place here to discuss this.

But since we treat of the nature of the mind, let us remove from our consideration all knowledge which is received from without, through the senses of the body, and attend more carefully to the position which we have laid down, that all minds know and are certain concerning themselves. For men certainly have doubted whether the power of living, of remembering, of understanding, of willing, of thinking, of knowing, of judging, be of air, or of fire, or of the brain, or of the blood, or of atoms, or besides the usual four elements of a fifth kind of body, I know not what; or whether the combining or tempering together of this our flesh itself has power to accomplish these things. And one has attempted to establish this, and another to establish that. Yet who ever doubts that he himself lives, and remembers, and understands, and wills, and thinks, and knows, and judges? Seeing that even if he doubts, he lives; if he doubts, he remembers why he doubts; if he doubts, he understands that he doubts; if he doubts, he wishes to be certain; if he doubts, he thinks; if he doubts, he knows that he does not know; if he doubts, he judges that he ought not to assent rashly. Whosoever therefore doubts about anything else, ought not to doubt of all these things; which if they were not, he would not be able to doubt of anything.

They who think the mind to be either a body or the combination or tempering of the body, will have all these things to seem to be in a subject, so that the substance is air, or fire, or some other corporeal thing, which they think to be the mind; but that the understanding (*intelligentia*) is *in* this corporeal thing as its

quality, so that this corporeal thing is the subject, but the understanding is in the subject: namely that the mind is the subject, which they judge to be a corporeal thing, but the understanding [intelligence], or any other of those things which we have mentioned as certain to us, is in that subject. They also hold nearly the same opinion who deny the mind itself to be body, but think it to be the combination or tempering together of the body; for there is this difference, that the former say that the mind itself is the substance, in which the understanding [intelligence] is, as in a subject; but the latter say that the mind itself is in a subject, namely in the body, of which it is the combination or tempering together. And, hence, by consequence, what else can they think, except that the understanding also is in the same body as in a subject?

And all these do not perceive that the mind knows itself, even when it seeks for itself, as we have already shown. But nothing is at all rightly said to be known while its substance is not known. And therefore, when the mind knows itself, it knows its own substance. But it is certain about itself, as those things which are said above prove convincingly; although it is not at all certain whether itself is air, or fire, or some body, or some function of body. Therefore, it is not any of these. And to the whole which is bidden to know itself, belongs this, that it is certain that it is not any of those things of which it is uncertain, and is certain that it is that only, which only it is certain that it is. For it thinks in this way of fire, or air, and whatever else of the body it thinks of. Neither can it in any way be brought to pass that it should so think that which itself is, as it thinks that which itself is not. Since it thinks all these things through an imaginary phantasy, whether fire, or air, or this or that body or that part or combination and tempering together of the body: nor assuredly is it said to be all those things, but some one of them. But if it were any one of them, it would think this one in a different manner from the rest, namely not through an imaginary phantasy, as absent things are thought, which either themselves or some of like kind have been touched by the bodily sense; but by some inward, not feigned, but true presence (for nothing is more present to it than itself); just as it thinks that itself lives, and remembers, and understands, and wills. For it knows these things in itself, and does not imagine them as though it had touched them by the sense outside itself, as corporeal things are touched. And if it attaches nothing to itself from the thought of these things, so as to think itself to be something of the kind, then whatsoever remains to it from itself, that alone is itself.

CHAPTER 11: IN MEMORY, UNDERSTANDING [OR INTELLIGENCE], AND WILL, WE HAVE TO NOTE ABILITY, LEARNING AND USE. MEMORY, UNDERSTANDING, AND WILL ARE ONE ESSENTIALLY, AND THREE RELATIVELY.

Putting aside, then, for a little while all other things, of which the mind is certain concerning itself, let us especially consider and discuss these three—memory, understanding, and will. For we may commonly discern in these three the character of the abilities of the young also; since the more tenaciously and easily a boy remembers, and the more acutely he understands, and the more ardently he studies, the more praiseworthy is he in point of ability. But when the question is about any one's learning, then we ask not how solidly and easily he remembers, or how shrewdly he understands; but what it is that he remembers, and what it is that he understands. And because the mind is regarded as praiseworthy, not only as being learned, but also as being good, one gives heed not only to what he remembers and what he understands, but also to what he wills (*velit*); not how ardently he wills, but first, what it is he wills, and then how greatly he wills it. For the mind that loves eagerly is then to be praised, when it loves that which ought to be loved eagerly. Since then, we speak of these three—ability, knowledge, and use—the first of these is to be considered under the three heads, of what a man can do in memory, and understanding, and will. The second of them is to be considered in regard to that which any one has in his memory and in his understanding, which he has attained by a studious will. But the third, namely use, lies in the will, which handles those things that are contained in the memory and understanding, whether it refer them to anything further, or rest satisfied with them as an end. For to use, is to take up something into the power of the will; and to enjoy, is to use with joy, not any longer of hope, but of the actual thing. Accordingly, everyone who enjoys, uses; for he takes up something into the power of the will, wherein he also is satisfied as with an end. But not every one who uses, enjoys, if he has sought after that, which he takes up into the power of the will, not on account of the thing itself, but on account of something else.

Since, then, these three, memory, understanding, will, are not three lives, but one life, not three minds, but one mind; it follows certainly that neither are they three substances, but one substance. Since memory, which is called life, and mind, and substance, is so called in respect to itself; but it is called memory, relatively to something. And I should say the same also of understanding and of will, since they are called understanding and will, relatively to something; but each in respect to itself is life, and mind, and essence. And hence these three are one, in that they are one life, one mind, one essence; and whatever else they are severally called in respect to themselves, they are called also together, not plurally, but in the singular number. But they are three, in that wherein they are mutually referred to each other; and if they were not equal, and this not only each to each, but also each to all, they certainly could not mutually contain each other; for not only is each contained by each, but also all by each. For I remember that I have memory and understanding, and will; and I understand that I understand, and will, and remember; and I will that I will, and remember, and understand; and I remember together my whole memory, and understanding, and will. For that of my memory which I do not remember, is not in my memory; and nothing is so much in the memory as memory itself. Therefore I remember the whole memory. Also, whatever I understand I know that I understand, and I know that I will whatever I will; but whatever I know I remember. Therefore I remember the whole of my understanding, and the whole of my will. Likewise, when I understand these three things, I understand them together as a whole. For there is none of things intelligible which I do not understand, except what I do not know; but what I do not know, I neither remember, nor will. Therefore, whatever of things intelligible I do not understand, it follows also that I neither remember nor will. And whatever of things intelligible I remember and will, it follows that I understand. My will also embraces my whole understanding and my whole memory, whilst I use the whole that I understand and remember. And, therefore, while all are mutually comprehended by each, and as wholes, each as a whole is equal to each as a whole, and each as a whole at the same time to all as wholes; and these three are one, one life, one mind, and one essence.

CHAPTER 12. THE MIND IS AN IMAGE OF THE TRINITY IN ITS OWN MEMORY, AND UNDERSTANDING, AND WILL.

Are we, then, now to go upward, with whatever strength of purpose we may, to that chiefest and highest essence, of which the human mind is an inadequate image, yet an image? Or are these same three things to be yet more distinctly made plain in the soul, by means of those things which we receive from without, through the bodily sense, wherein the knowledge of corporeal things is impressed upon us in time? Since we found the mind itself to be such in its own memory, and understanding, and will, that since it was understood always to know and always to will itself, it was understood also at the same time always to remember itself, always to understand and love itself, although nor always to think of itself as *separate* from those things which are not itself; and hence its memory of itself, and understanding of itself, are with difficulty discerned in it. For in this case, where these two things are very closely conjoined, and one is not preceded by the other by any time at all, it looks as if they were not two things, but one called by two names; and love itself is not so plainly felt to exist when the sense of need does not disclose it, since what is loved is always at hand. And, hence, these things may be more lucidly set forth, even to men of duller minds, if such topics are treated of as are brought within reach of the mind in time, and happen to it in time; while it remembers what it did not remember before, and sees what it did not see before, and loves what it did not love before. But this discussion demands now another beginning, by reason of the measure of the present book.

STUDY QUESTIONS: AUGUSTINE, *SELF-KNOWLEDGE AND THE THREE-FOLD NATURE OF MIND*

1. How do we recognize the image of God in ourselves?
2. Why is Augustine not afraid of the arguments of the Academicians?
3. What makes Augustine so certain that he exists, that about this he cannot possibly be deceived?
4. Does Augustine apply his method of doubt to the love of God? Why?
5. What is the role of memory with regard to questions of faith and God?
6. What is the source of the soul's (mind's) false opinions about itself? Why does the mind (soul) not see itself exactly as it really is?
7. What are the three things that each mind knows with absolute certainty?
8. What is the significance of the ancient percept, "Know Thyself?"
9. How does Augustine argue that memory, understanding, and will are not three but one?

ON FREE WILL

Here Augustine gives his famous argument that God gave us free will even though it is free will that makes it possible to sin against God. Notice that in his debate with Evodius, Augustine begins by distinguishing *clear* ideas, as Descartes would later do, known directly by one's own judgment, from those that are known (if at all) only by or through authority. Augustine then argues that although it is, indeed, free will that makes it possible for us to sin it is free will too that makes it possible for us to act *rightly*. Without free will there would be no question of right or wrong. In other words, just as Kant would later do, Augustine sees in the concept of free will a necessary condition for the having of something that is a given presupposition of the argument, namely, that the distinction between right and wrong is itself real. Notice, also, in the beginning of Chapter III how Augustine gets Evodius to acknowledge the certainty of his own existence: "since it is clear to you that you are, and since it would not be otherwise be clear to you unless you lived." This argument we will see taken up again, with even greater force, by Descartes.

In Chapter IV Augustine distinguishes the "inner" from the "outer" sense by which the mind knows itself and its perceptions. In naming this "the understanding," he is referring to that faculty by which ideas (perceptions) are intuited by the mind. Many centuries later Locke, Berkeley and Hume will talk of "the faculty of the understanding" in this same way. Thus, if you asked them or Augustine the question, "how does the mind see (or know) the objects of its contemplation, be they perceptions or ideas?" the answer would be the same: with the faculty of the understanding. Except Augustine is fundamentally not an empiricist but a rationalist in the Platonic tradition; it is the inner light of reason that is the highest faculty of the mind, of which there is none higher but one: God (Chapter VI).

In Chapter VII he takes up the difficult question that any representational theory of mind and perception must address, namely: how can two different minds perceive one and the same object? And here he boldly puts forth a theory of public vs. private experience that anticipates subsequent developments in philosophy well into the twentieth century. As if this weren't enough to make him one of the truly great and original thinkers, he goes on to make the case, as William James would do, that beyond reason is a will to believe which Augustine boldly identifies with wisdom itself.

BOOK II

In which, a difficulty having arisen from the circumstance that freedom, by which sin is committed, was given by God, the following three questions are inquired into: by what reason it is manifest that God is; whether all goods are from God; whether the free will is to be considered among the number of goods.

CHAPTER I

Why Freedom, by Which Sin Is Committed, Was Given by God.

1.

Evodius. Now explain to me, if you can, why God gave man free judgment of will, for obviously, if man had not received free will, he would not be able to sin.

Augustine. Is it certain and known to you then that God gave man this which you do not think should have been given?

E. So far as the preceding book is concerned I seem to have understood both that we have free judgment of will and that we sin only by it.

A. I too recall that that has already been made clear to us. But I have just asked whether you know that God gave us this which we clearly have and by which clearly we sin.

E. I think no other than God. For we are from him; and whether we sin or act rightly, we merit punishment or reward from him.

A. I want to know also whether you know this clearly or whether you are moved, not unwillingly, to believe it by authority even though you do not know it.

E. I answer that in what concerns this thing I first believed by authority. But what is more true than that every good is from God and that every just act is good, and that the punishment of sinners and the reward of those who act rightly are just? From this it comes about both that sinners are afflicted by God

---

Sancti Aubelii Augustini, Hipponensis Episcopi, *De Libero Arbitrio, Lib. II*, in *Opera Omnia*, J. P. Migne, *Patrologia Latina*, vol. 32, col. 1239–1266.

Augustine, from *On Free Will*, Book II, 1–46, translated by Richard McKeon in Richard McKeon, ed., *Selections from Medieval Philosophers*, vol. 1, Charles Scribner's Sons, 1929, pp. 11–64.

with misery and that those who act rightly are visited with felicity.

2.

A. To that I have no objection, but I raise this other question: how do you know that we are from him? For this you have not yet explained, but you have explained that we merit from him either punishment or reward.

E. That, too, I see is clear no otherwise than because we know already that God judges sins. Certainly, all justice is from him. For as it is not characteristic of any goodness to show its benefits in what is alien to it, so it is not of justice to judge in what is alien to it. Wherefore, it is clear that we pertain to him, not only because he is most benign in showing his benefits in us but also most just in judging. Finally, from what I have stated and from what you have conceded, every good, including man, can be understood to be from God. For man himself in so far as he is man is something good, because he can, when he so wishes, live rightly.

3.

A. Clearly if these things are so, the question which you proposed has been solved. For if man is something good and can not act rightly except when he wishes, he ought to have a free will without which he could not act rightly. For it is not to be believed that, because sin is committed by it too, God gave free will for sin. Therefore, since without it man can not live rightly, there is cause enough why it should have been given. It can, moreover, be understood to have been given for this and on this account, because if anyone shall have used it for sinning, it is condemned in him by God. But this would be done unjustly if free will had been given, not only that one might live rightly, but also that one might sin. For how could he be punished justly who had used his will for that purpose for which it has been given? But then, when God punishes the sinner, what else does he seem to you to say except, Why have you not used your free will for the purpose for which I gave it to you, that is, for doing rightly? Further, if man lacked free judgment of will, how would that be good, for which justice itself is commended when it condemns sins and honors deeds rightly done? For that which was not done by the will would be neither sinfully nor rightly

done. And according to this if man did not have free will, both punishment and reward would be unjust. However, there must have been justice in both punishment and reward, since it is one of the goods which are from God. *Therefore*, God must have given man free will.

CHAPTER II

Objection: How Is the Free Will Pliant to Evil If It Has Been Given for Good?

4.

E. I concede now that God gave it. But I ask you, does it not seem to you that, if it has been given for acting rightly, it should not be susceptible of being turned to sinning? As in the case of justice itself, which was given to man that he might live well: for can anyone live evilly by his justice? So too, no one would be able by will to sin, if the will had been given for acting rightly.

A. God will grant, I hope, that I shall be able to answer you, or rather that you reply to yourself by the same truth, teaching within, which is the supreme mistress of all. But I want you to tell me briefly, if you hold as certain and known that of which I have asked you, that God has given us free will, whether or not it be necessary to say that that should not have been given which we acknowledge God to have given. For if it is uncertain whether or not he gave it, we inquire rightly whether it was well given, that it may be discovered also, when we shall have found it was well given, that he gave it by whom all goods have been given to man; if however we should find that it was not well given, we may understand that he did not give it, whom to blame is sinful. But if it is certain that he himself gave it we must acknowledge that, in whatsoever manner it has been given, it should neither not be given nor be given otherwise than it was given. For he gave it whose deed can not rightly be reprehended in any stipulation.

5.

E. Although I hold these things with unshaken faith, still, since I do not yet hold them in knowledge; let us inquire as if all things were uncertain. For I see, since it is uncertain whether free will was given for doing rightly (since we can also sin by it) that it becomes uncertain too whether it should have been given. For if it is uncertain that it was given for doing rightly, it is also uncertain that it should have been given, and by that it will also be uncertain whether God gave it; because if it is uncertain that it should have been given, it is uncertain that it has been given by him, of whom it is sinful to believe that he has given anything which should not have been given.

A. At all events you are certain that God is.

E. That too I hold unshakable, not by contemplation, but by belief.

A. If, then, any of those fools of whom it is written, "the fool hath said in his heart, there is no God,"[1] should say that to you, and should not wish to believe with you what you believe, but wished to know whether you believed the truth; would you leave the man, or would you judge that he was to be persuaded in some way of what you hold unshakable, particularly if he wished, not to oppose it obstinately, but seriously to learn it?

E. That which you stated last warns me sufficiently what I should answer him. For, of course, even if he were extremely stupid, he would grant me that one must not argue deceitfully and obstinately about anything whatever, and particularly not about so great a thing. After he had conceded that, it would first be important to me that I should believe he inquired this in good faith and did not conceal within himself any obstinacy and deceit in what pertains to this question. Then I should demonstrate (which I think would be extremely easy for any one), how much more reasonable it would be (since he was willing to believe another who was not acquainted with them in respect to hidden matters of his own mind, which he himself knew) to believe also from the Books of so many men who left testimony in letters that they lived with the Son of God, that God is; for they have written that they saw deeds which could never have been done if there were no God; and he would be very stupid, if he, who for himself wanted

me to believe these things, should reprove me for believing them. Moreover, since he would not be able to reprove me rightly, he would in no ways find a reason why he too should not imitate me.

A. If, then, you think it sufficient in the question of the existence of God for us to have judged that so many men could not have believed thoughtlessly, why, I ask you, do you not think similarly that the authority of those same men is to be credited in those matters too, which, uncertain and obviously unknown, we have undertaken to examine, and so spare us the labor of further investigation of them?

E. But we wish to know and to understand that which we believe.

6.

A. You remember correctly what we undeniably asserted at the beginning of our previous discussion.[2] For if to believe were not one thing and to understand another and if we did not have to believe first whatever great and divine truths we wished to understand, the prophet would have said in vain, "if ye will not believe, ye shall not understand."[3] Our Lord himself also urged by both his words and his deeds that they whom he called to salvation should first believe. But later when he spoke of the very gift which was to be given those who believe he did not say, and this is life eternal, that they should believe; but he said, "and this is life eternal that they should know thee the only true God and him whom thou didst send, Jesus Christ."[4] Then again he says to believers, "seek and ye shall find;"[5] for neither can that be said to have been found which is believed while unknown, nor is any one made suitable to find God unless he shall first believe what later he is to know. Wherefore, obedient to the precepts of God, let us seek earnestly. For what we seek when he urges us, we shall find by his pointing the way, so far as these things can be found in this life and by such as we: for it is to be

---

[1] *Psalm* 53:1; or in the Vulgate, *Psalm* 52:1.

[2] Book I, chapter 2.

[3] *Isaiah* 7:9, sec. LXX. In the Vulgate version *intelligetis* becomes *permanebitis*; the passage, consequently is now rendered, *If ye will not believe, surely ye shall not be established.* The early writings of Augustine antecede, of course, the Vulgate translation, and for a time Augustine seems to have opposed the project of translation, although in his later works the version of St. Jerome not infrequently appears in his biblical citations.

[4] *John* 17:2.

[5] *Matthew* 7:7.

believed that they can be distinguished and known very evidently and very perfectly by better men even while they inhabit this earth, and certainly by all good and pious men after this life; and it is to be hoped that it will be so with us. Once earthly and human things have been despised, these things are in every manner to be desired and loved.

CHAPTER III

That It May Become Manifest that God Is, It Is Inquired What Is Most Excellent in Man.

7.

Let us, however, if that pleases you, take up the question in this order: first, how it is manifest that God is; then, whether all things whatsoever, in so far as they are good, are from him; finally, whether free will is to be numbered among the goods. When these have been resolved it will appear sufficiently, I think, whether free will was rightly given to man. So, to begin with what is most manifest, I ask you first whether you yourself are. Or perhaps you have fears lest you be led astray in that question, although surely if you were not, you could not in the least be led astray?

E. Go on instead to the other questions.

A. Then, since it is clear to you that you are, and since it would not otherwise be clear to you unless you lived, this also is clear, that you live; do you understand these two to be extremely true?

E. I understand that immediately.

A. Therefore this third proposition too is clear, namely, that you understand.

E. Clearly.

A. Which of the three seems to you to excel?

E. Understanding.

A. Why does that seem so to you?

E. Because since there are these three, to be, to live, and to understand; and a stone is, and an animal lives, but nevertheless I do not think a stone lives nor an animal understands; but on the other hand it is most certain that he who understands both is and lives; so, I do not hesitate to judge that more excellent to which all three are present than that from which two or one are absent. For that which lives, surely also is, but it does not follow that it also understands: such I judge is the life of an animal. But, on the other hand it surely does not follow from the fact

that something is, that it also lives and understands: for I may say that a corpse is, but no one would say that it lives. Moreover, that which does not live, much less understands.

A. We hold, then, that of these three two are absent from the corpse, one from the animal, and none from man.

E. That is true.

A. We hold further that that is most excellent in the three which man has together with the other two, namely, to understand; and having that it follows also that he is and lives.

E. Surely.

8.

A. Tell me now, whether you know that you have those ordinary senses of the body, seeing, and hearing, and smelling, and tasting, and touching.

E. I do.

A. What do you think pertains to the sense of seeing? That is, what do you think we perceive in seeing?

E. All corporeal things.

A. Do we also perceive the hard and the soft by sight?

E. No.

A. Therefore, what pertains properly to the eyes, which we perceive through them?

E. Color.

A. What to the ears?

E. Sound.

A. What to smell?

E. Odor.

A. What to taste?

E. Flavor.

A. What to touch?

E. Soft or hard, smooth or rough, and many such qualities.

A. Then, do we not perceive the forms of bodies, large, small, square, round, and whatever other qualities there are of this sort, by both touching and seeing, therefore can they not be attributed to neither sight nor touch properly, but to both?

E. I understand.

A. Do you understand then also, that single senses have certain properties concerning which they report, and that some of the senses have certain properties in common?

E. I understand this too.

A. Are we able then to distinguish by any one of the senses what pertains to each, and what all or certain of the senses have in common among them?

E. That can be distinguished in no way except by a certain interior sense.

A. Is that perhaps reason itself, which the beasts lack? For I believe, by reason we understand these things and know that they are so related.

E. Rather I think we understand by reason that there is a certain interior sense, to which all things are referred from those very well known five. For the beast sees by one process, by another he avoids or desires that which he perceives in seeing: for the one sense is in his eyes, but the other is within him, in the soul itself, by which animals either desire and seize if pleased, or turn from and reject if displeased, not only those things which are seen, but also those which are heard, and those which are grasped by other senses of the body. This sense, however, can not be called sight, nor hearing, nor smell, nor taste, nor touch, but something else which presides over all of them in common. This, as I have said, we may comprehend with reason, but we can not call it itself reason, since it is clear that it is present in beasts.

9.

A. I recognize this, whatever it is, and I do not hesitate to call it the interior sense. But that which is referred to us by the senses of the body, unless it also pass beyond this interior sense, can not come to knowledge. For whatever we know, we comprehend by reason. We know, however, to say nothing of many other facts, that colors can not be perceived by hearing nor voices by sight. And although we know this, we know it neither by eyes, nor ears, nor again by that interior sense which beasts do not lack. For it is not to be believed that they know that light is not perceived by the ears, nor the voice by the eyes, since we distinguish such things only by rational reflection and thought.

E. I can not say that I have observed that. In fact, what follows if they judge too by the interior sense, which you concede they do not lack, that colors can not be perceived by hearing, nor voices by sight?

A. Do you think also that they can distinguish these four one from the other—the color which is perceived, and the sense which is in the eye, and that interior sense in the soul, and the reason by which these are defined and enumerated one after the other?

E. Not at all.

A. Then, would reason be able to distinguish these four, one from the other, and determine them in definitions, if there were not referred to it, color through the sense of the eyes, and also that sense itself through the interior sense which presides over it, and the same interior sense through itself, if there is not still another intermediary interposed?

E. I do not see how it could be otherwise.

A. Do you see then that color is perceived by the sense of the eyes, but that the sense itself is not perceived by the same sense? For you do not see the seeing itself with the same sense by which you see color.

E. Not at all.

A. Try also to make this distinction: for I think that you do not deny that it is one thing to be color and another to see color, and that again it is still another thing to have the sense, when color is not present, by which it could be seen if it were present.

E. I see that too, and I concede that they differ from each other.

A. Do you see any of these three, besides color, with the eyes?

E. None.

A. Tell me then whence it is that you see the other two, for you would not be able to distinguish them if you had not seen them.

E. I know nothing further; I know that they are, nothing more.

A. You do not know then whether it is reason, or that life, which we call the interior sense, excelling the senses of the body, or something else?

E. I do not know.

A. This however you know: that it can not be defined except by reason, nor can reason define it except with reference to those things which are offered to it for examination.

E. That is certain.

A. Whatever else there is, then, by which all that we know can be perceived, it is in the service of reason, to which it brings and reports whatever it touches, so that the things which are perceived can be distinguished by their ends and can be comprehended not only by being perceived but also by being known.

E. That is so.

A. Reason itself distinguishes its servant-senses and that which they bring to it from each other, and further recognizes what separates them from itself, and proves itself to be more powerful than they. Does it then comprehend itself by some other thing than itself, that is, by reason? Or would you know that you have reason otherwise than by perceiving it by reason?

E. Very true.

A. Since, therefore, when we perceive color, we do not in like manner perceive, by the sense itself, ourselves perceiving; nor when we hear a sound, do we also hear our own hearing; nor when we smell a rose, does our very smelling also emit some odor to us; nor when we taste something, does taste itself savor in our mouth; nor when we touch something, are we able also to touch the sense of touch itself; it is clear that these five senses can be perceived by no one of the senses, although all corporeal things are perceived by them.

E. That is clear.

CHAPTER IV

The Interior Sense Perceives Itself Perceiving: Whether It also Distinguishes Itself Apart.

10.

A. I think it is clear also that not only does that interior sense perceive those things which it has received from the five senses of the body, but also that the senses themselves are perceived by it. For no otherwise would a beast move itself either in desiring something or in fleeing it, except by perceiving itself perceive, not in order to know, for this is the property of reason, but only in order to move, which surely it perceives by no one of those five senses. But if this point is still obscure it will be clarified if you consider, for example, what is clear enough in any one of the senses, as in sight. For, to open the eye and to move it that it may look at that which it wishes to see, would in no way be possible, if, when the eye was closed or not so moved, the interior sense did not perceive that it did not see the thing. If, however, it perceives that it does not see when it does not see, it is necessary too that it perceive that it sees when it does see; because it indicates that it perceives both, since it does not move the eye when it sees by that appetite by which it moves the eye

when it does not see. But it is not so clear whether this life, which perceives itself perceiving corporeal things, also perceives itself, except that any one who inquires within himself finds that every living thing flees death; since death is the contrary of life, it is necessary that life, which flees its contrary, perceive itself too. But if it is still not clear, let it be passed over, that we may go on only by certain and clear instances to that which we wish. For the following points are clear, that corporeal things are perceived by the bodily sense; but sense itself can not be perceived by this same sense; yet both are perceived by the interior sense—corporeal things (by way of a sense of the body) and the sense of the body itself; finally, that by reason all these and reason itself are made known, and are held together in knowledge: does it not seem so to you?

E. It seems clearly so.

A. Proceed then; tell me now how the question arises which has kept us so long on this path in our efforts to solve it.

CHAPTER V

The Interior Sense Excels the External Senses of Which It Is the Moderator and Judge.

11.

E. As I remember, the first of those three questions which we posed a little while ago to establish an order for this discussion is now being considered, that is, how, even though it is to be believed most tenaciously and most firmly, it can be made clear that God is.

A. You recall that correctly, but I want you to bear this diligently in mind too, that when I asked you whether you knew that you were, not only this but two other facts which you knew appeared to us.

E. I remember that too.

A. Now then consider to which of those three you would say pertains all that the bodily sense perceives; that is, in which class of things does it seem to you must be placed whatever our sense touches whether by means of the eyes or by any other instrument of the body; is it to be placed in the class which only is, or in that which also lives, or in that which also understands?

E. In that which only is.

A. Then, in which class of these three do you judge the sense itself to fall?

E. In that which lives.

A. Which of these two then do you judge to be the better? The sense itself or that which the sense perceives?

E. The sense surely.

A. Why?

E. Because that which also lives is better than that which only is.

12.

A. Will you hesitate, then, to place above this sense by which we perceive body (and which you have just said is to be placed above the body itself) that interior sense which in what precedes we have looked for beneath reason and even as common in us with the beasts?

E. I should certainly not hesitate.

A. I want you to tell me too why you do not hesitate. For you can not say that this interior sense must now be put in that one of those three classes which also understands, but only in that which both is and lives, although it lacks understanding: for this sense is also present in beasts in which there is no understanding. Since these things are so, I ask you why you place the interior sense above the sense by which we perceive corporeal things, since they are both in the class which lives. Moreover, you have placed sense, which perceives bodies, above bodies, because they are in that class which only is, whereas sense is in the class which also lives: and since the interior sense is found in that class too, tell me why you think it is better. For if you should say, because it perceives this sense, I do not believe that you will find a rule by which we can establish that all perceiving is better than that which is perceived by it, lest perchance we be compelled by that to say also that all understanding is better than that which is understood by it. That in fact is false, because man understands wisdom and is not better than wisdom itself. Wherefore, consider by what cause it appeared to you that the interior sense is to be preferred to this sense by which we perceive bodies.

E. Because I know it to be a kind of moderator and judge of the other. For if something should be lacking to it in the exercise of its function, it

demands it as due from its servant, as was brought out a little while ago in the discussion. For the sense of the eye does not see itself see or not see, and because it does not see, it can not judge what is lacking to it or what is sufficient; but the interior sense does this, and by it the soul of the beast is admonished to open the closed eye and to supply that which it perceives to be lacking. But no one doubts that that which judges is better than that which is judged.

A. Do you see then that in a certain way this sense of the body also judges of bodies? For pleasure and pain pertain to sense when it comes in contact smoothly or roughly with a body. For just as the interior sense judges what is missing or what is sufficient to the sense of the eyes, so the sense of the eyes itself judges what is missing or what is sufficient in colors. Likewise, just as the interior sense judges whether our hearing is too little or sufficiently intent, so hearing itself judges in voices, which of them flows smoothly or which resounds harshly. We need not proceed further with the other senses of the body, for I believe you are now aware of what I mean, that obviously the interior sense judges of these senses of the body when it examines their integrity and when it demands what is needed, just as the senses of the body judge of bodies, accepting a smooth touch in them and rejecting the contrary.

E. I see clearly, and I grant that it is very true.

CHAPTER VI

Reason Excels Other Functions in Man; If There Is Anything Which Excels It, It Is God.

13.

A. Consider now whether reason judges also of this interior sense. For now I do not ask whether you think that reason is better than it, because I have no doubt that you do; although again I do not think that it need even be asked whether reason judges of this sense. For how would one thing be better than another among the things which are below reason, that is, in bodies and in the senses of the body and in that interior sense, and how would reason itself be more excellent than the others, which indeed it is, unless it proclaimed this itself? Which certainly it could in no way do unless it judged of them.

E. That is clear.

A. Then, since the nature which not only is, but also lives, but does not understand (such as the soul of beasts) stands above the nature which only is and does not live nor understand (such as an inanimate body); and again since above that there stands the nature which at the same time is and lives and understands (such as the rational mind in man) would you not think that in us, more particularly in those things by which our nature is fulfilled that we may be men, something could be found more excellent than what we placed in the third place in these three? For it is clear that we have a body, and a certain life by which the body itself is animated and quickened, which two we also recognize in beasts, and a third something which the nature of beasts does not have, the head or eye of our soul, as it were, or any other name by which reason and understanding may be designated more appropriately. Wherefore consider, I pray you, whether you can find in the nature of man something more sublime than reason.

E. I see absolutely nothing better.

14.

A. Well, then, if we could find something which you not only do not doubt to be, but also to be more excellent than our reason itself, will you hesitate to call that, whatever it is, God?

E. I should not necessarily say, if I could find something better than that which is best in my nature, that it is God. For it does not please me to name God that to which my reason is inferior, but rather that to which nothing is superior.

A. Plainly so: for he has himself given to this reason of yours the power to feel so piously and truly of him. But I ask you again, if you did not find that there was anything above our reason except what is eternal and immutable, would you hesitate to call that God? For you know that bodies are mutable, and it is clear that the very life by which the body is animated does not lack mutability in various states; and reason itself is surely shown to be mutable, since it sometimes attempts to arrive at truth and sometimes does not attempt to, and sometimes arrives and sometimes does not. It may be granted that if reason with the aid of no instrument of the body, not by touch, nor by taste, nor by smell, nor by ears, nor by eyes, nor by any other sense inferior to it, but by itself, discerns something eternal and immutable and at the same time discerns itself inferior to it, that must be its God.

E. I will readily grant that that is God than which nothing is known to be superior.

A. You hold a good doctrine: for it will be enough for me to show that there is something of that sort, which either you will grant to be God, or if there is something above, you will concede that that itself is God. Wherefore whether there be something above or not, it will be manifest that God is, since I shall have shown, with his aid, that which I promised, that there is something above reason.

E. Then demonstrate what you promised.

CHAPTER VII

In What Manner the Same Thing May Be Perceived by Many, as a Whole, or Not as a Whole, and at the Same Time by Different Persons.

15.

A. I shall do that, but first I ask whether my bodily sense is the same as yours, or whether definitely mine is only mine, and yours is only yours; because if it were not so, I would not be able to see anything with my eyes which you did not see.

E. I concede readily that although they are of the same genus, nevertheless, we have each of us senses of seeing, or hearing, or any one of the others. For a man can not only see but can also hear what another man does not hear, and one man can perceive by any of the other senses what another does not perceive. Wherefore it is clear both that your sense is only yours, and mine is only mine.

A. Will you make this same answer concerning that interior sense too? Or will you say something else?

E. Absolutely nothing else. For surely that sense of mine perceives my sense and yours perceives yours: for that very reason I am asked very frequently by a person who sees something, whether I too see it, because I perceive myself seeing or not seeing but he who asks does not.

A. And then, does not each one of us have his own reason? Inasmuch as it can happen that I understand something when you do not understand it; and you can not know whether I understand it; but I know.

E. It is clear, too, that we have, each of us, individual rational minds.

16.

A. Will you be able to say too that we have the individual suns, which we see, or moons, or morningstars, or other things of that sort, even though each one sees them with his own and proper sense?

E. I should certainly not say that.

A. Many of us, then, are able to see a single thing at the same time, although we have, each single one of us, our individual senses, by all of which we perceive that one thing which we see at the same time, so that although my sense is one and yours another, it may nevertheless happen that what we see is not one mine and another yours; but one only may be present for both of us, and may be seen by both at the same time.

E. That is very clear.

A. We can also hear some single voice at the same time, so that although my hearing is one and yours another, there is not, for all that, one voice mine and another voice yours which we hear at the same time, nor is one part of it caught by my hearing and another by yours, but whatsoever has sounded will be there to be heard at one time, one and whole, by both of us.

E. That too is clear.

17.

A. Now you may also consider what we say in relation to the other senses of the body, that, with respect to what pertains to this thing, they are not constituted wholly as the two senses of eyes and ears, nor are they constituted wholly differently. For because you and I can fill our lungs from the same air and perceive the state of the air by odor; and again because we can both taste of the same honey or of any other food or drink, and perceive its state by flavor, even though it is one and our senses are individual, yours to you and mine to me, so that although we both perceive one odor and one flavor, nevertheless you do not perceive it with my sense, nor I with yours, nor with any one sense which could be common to both of us, but truly my sense is mine and yours is yours, even though a single odor or flavor is perceived by both: in this respect, therefore, these senses are found to have something like the above two in sight and hearing; but they are unlike in this (in so far as it pertains to what we are now treating) that although we both draw one air into our nostrils or both take one food to taste it, nevertheless I do not draw in that part of the air which you do, nor do I take the same part of the

food as you, but I take one and you another: and therefore of all the air I take a part, when I breathe, such as is sufficient for me, and you too take, of all of it, another part such as is sufficient for you: and although the food be consumed one and all by both of us, still it can not be consumed all by me and all by you, in the manner in which I hear a whole word and you the whole word at the same time, and as I see a certain species as much as you too see it at the same time; but it is necessary that one part of the food or drink pass into me and another part into you; do you understand these things clearly enough?

E. By all means; I grant them to be very apparent and most certain.

18.

A. Do you think the sense of touch is to be compared with the senses of the eyes and ears in this matter which is now being discussed; because not only can we both perceive one body by touching it, but also you will be able to touch the same part as I have touched, so that we can both perceive by touch not only the same body but also the same part of the body? For in touching it is not as in eating of a given food, when we can not both of us, I and you, take all of it; but that which I have touched you will be able to touch, one and all, so that both of us touch it, not in single parts, but each of us the whole.

E. I confess that this sense of touch is in this respect very much like the two higher senses; but I see that they are unlike in this respect, that we can both see and hear at the same time, that is, at one time some single whole, but we can not both touch any whole at one time. but only single parts, and we can touch the same part only at separate times, for I can not touch any part which you are inspecting by touch unless you remove your touch.

19.

A. You have replied very carefully, but you must see this too, that since of all the things which we perceive there are some which both of us perceive and others which we may perceive individually, we perceive surely our senses themselves, as individuals, each his own, so that I do not perceive your sense nor you mine, because we can not both perceive, but only singly, anything of those things which are perceived by us through the senses of the body, that is, of corporeal things, except what is so made ours that we are able to transform and change it into ourselves, as is the case with food and drink, of which you will be able to perceive no part that I have perceived; for even in the case of nurses who give children masticated food, nevertheless that which the taste has taken therefrom and has changed to the viscera of the chewer, can in no way be recalled that it may be made again into food of the child. For when the throat tastes something with pleasure, it claims for itself an irrevocable part, however small, and this must be done because such is the nature of the body: for if it were not so, no savor would remain in the mouth after those masticated bits had been passed on or spit out. This can rightly be said also of the parts of the air which we draw into the nostrils; for although you may draw in some of the air which I have expelled, nevertheless you can not draw in that which has gone from the air into my nutriment, because that can not be returned. Physicians say that we take nutriment through the nostrils too; which nutriment I alone can perceive by breathing, and I can not return it by breathing it out again for you to draw into your nostrils and perceive too. For there are other sensibles which although we perceive them, still we do not in perceiving change them into our body and corrupt them; we both can perceive them, whether at one time or successively at different times, inasmuch as either the whole or the part which I perceive, may be perceived by you too; of such sort are light or sound or bodies which we touch but nevertheless do not alter.

E. I understand.

A. It is clear then that those things which we do not alter and which we nevertheless perceive with the senses of the body, do not pertain to the nature of our senses and rather on that account are common to us, because they are not changed and altered into something proper, and as it were, private to us.

E. I agree readily.

A. Therefore, that must be understood to be proper and as it were, private, which belongs to each one of us alone and which each alone perceives in himself, because it pertains properly to his nature; but that must be understood to be common, and as it were, public, which is perceived by all who are sentient, with no corruption or alteration of itself.

E. It is so.

CHAPTER VIII

The Reason or Nature of Numbers Is Perceived by No Sense of the Body; by Whomsoever It Is Perceived in Understanding, It Is One and Immutable.

20.

A. Attend now, and tell me whether something may be found which all who reason see in common, each with his own reason and mind, since that which is seen is present to all and is not altered for the use of those to whom it is present, as food or drink, but remains uncorrupted and whole whether they see it or do not see it: or would you perhaps think that there is nothing of this sort?

E. On the contrary, I see that there are many such things, of which it suffices to mention one: that the reason and truth of number is present to all who reason, so that every computer individually tries to apprehend it with his reason and understanding; and one can do it rather easily, another with more difficulty, still another can not do it at all: although notwithstanding it offers itself equally to all who can grasp it; nor when perceived by any one is it changed and altered for the nutriment, as it were, of its perceiver; nor does it cease when some one is deceived in it, but he is so much the more in error the less he sees it, while it remains true and whole.

21.

A. Clearly true; but I notice that you found what you said quickly as if you were not unused to these things; nevertheless, if some one were to say to you that these numbers are not impressed on our mind by some nature of theirs, but by those things which we come upon by the bodily sense, as it were, certain images of visible things; what would you reply? Or do you also think thus?

E. I should certainly not have thought thus: for if I have perceived numbers by the sense of the body, I have not thereby been able by the sense of the body to perceive also the nature of the separation and combination of numbers. For by this light of the mind I refute him who would report a false sum when he computes whether in adding or subtracting. And I do not know how long anything I touch by a bodily sense will persist, as for instance, this sky and this land, and whatever other bodies I perceive in them;

but seven and three are ten, and not only now, but always; nor have seven and three in any way at any time not been ten, nor will seven and three at any time not be ten. I have said, therefore, that this incorruptible truth of number is common to me and any one at all who reasons.

22.

A. I do not oppose you when you reply so very truly and with such certainty. But you will see also that numbers themselves are not easily drawn out by the sense of the body, if you will have considered that any number whatsoever is given its value according to the number of times it contains one; for example, if it contains one twice it is called two; if three times, three, and if it contains one ten times, then it is called ten: and the number of times that any number whatsoever contains one, that is its name, and it is called that much. Certainly whoever ponders one very truly, finds forthwith that it can not be perceived by the senses of the body. For whatever is touched upon by such a sense, is proved immediately to be not one but many: for it is body, and therefore has innumerable parts. But not to trace out any extremely minute and still more finely divided particles, however small that tiny body be, it surely has a right part and a left part; one higher and another lower; or one further and another nearer: or some at the ends and another in the middle; for it is necessary that these be present in the tiny mode of body however tiny we may say it is; and because of this we do not concede that any body is truly and purely one in which, notwithstanding, so many could be enumerated except for the discrete consideration of that one. For when I seek one in body, and when I have no doubt that I shall not find it, I know certainly what I seek there, and what I shall and what I shall not find there, and what can not be found there or rather can not be there at all. When therefore I know that body is not one, I know what one is: for if I did not know one I should not be able to enumerate the many in body. But wherever it may have been that I know one, I surely do not know it through the sense of the body, because through the sense of the body I know only body, which we are persuaded is not truly and purely one. Moreover, if we have not perceived one by the sense of the body, we have perceived no number by that sense, at least so far as those numbers are concerned which we distinguish by the understanding. For there is none of them which is not given its value according to the number of times it contains one, and the perception of one is not encompassed by the sense of the body. For the half of any small body whatsoever makes up a whole of two halves, and it itself contains its half. Therefore, these two parts are in the body in such fashion that they are not simply two themselves. But since the number which is called two is called two because it contains twice that which is simply one, the half of it, that is, that which is itself simply one, can not further have a half or a third part or any part whatsoever, since it is simple and truly one.

23.

A. Furthermore, whereas when we follow the order of numbers we see two after one, which, number, compared to one, is found to be double; the double of two is not joined next in series, but four which is the double of two follows after the interposition of three. And this relation is carried out through all the other numbers by a most certain and immutable law, that the first number after one, that is, after the first of all numbers, itself excepted, is double one, and in fact two follows one. The second number after the second moreover, that is, after two, itself excepted, is double two: indeed, after two there is first three, second four, which is double the second. The third number after the third, that is, three, itself excepted, is the double of three: indeed, after the third, that is, after three, there is first four, second fire, third six, which is twice the third. And so, too, after the fourth, the fourth number, itself exempted, is double four: for after the fourth, that is after four, there is first five, second six, third seven, fourth eight, which is double the fourth. And so you will find through all the others what has been found in the sequence of the first numbers, that is, in one and two, that the double of any number is as many units after it as the original number is after one. Whence do we perceive this, then, which we perceive to be immobile, firm and uncorrupted through all numbers? For no one has perceived all the numbers by any sense of the body for they are innumerable: whence then do we know that this is so through all; or by what phantasy or by what apparition is to certain a truth of number to be contemplated so faithfully through countless numbers except by an Interior light which the corporeal senses do not know?

24.

A. From these and many similar instances it must be granted by all inquirers to whom God has given natural perception and whom obstinacy has not overcast in obscurity, that the reason and truth of numbers is not perceived by the senses of the body, and that it persists unalterable and pure, and that it is common to be seen by all who use reason. Wherefore, although many other things can be found, which are present in common and as it were publicly to those who reason, and are seen by them by way of the mind and by way of the reason of each and every one who perceives, and these things remain inviolate and immutable, nevertheless I have taken it not unwillingly, that this reason and truth of numbers should occur most insistently to you when you wanted to answer what I asked: for not for nothing is number joined to wisdom in the Sacred Books where it was said: "*I turned about and I inclined my heart that I might know and consider and inquire the wisdom and the number.*"[1]

CHAPTER IX

What Wisdom Is, Without Which No One Is Happy; Whether It Is One in All Wise Men.

25.

A. Nevertheless, I ask you, what do you think must be judged of wisdom itself? Do you think that each individual man has his own individual wisdom? Or do you think that one wisdom is present in common for all, of which the more one is made participant the wiser he is?

E. I do not yet know what you call wisdom, inasmuch as I see that what is done and said wisely appears variously to men: for those who fight seem, to themselves to act wisely, and those who, despising military matters, supervise the care and labor of cultivating the field, praise rather this and attribute it to wisdom; and those who are astute in thinking out ways of acquiring money, seem to themselves to be wise; and those who neglect or cast off all these and all things that are temporal of this sort, and turn their whole care to the investigation of truth that they

may know themselves and God, they judge this to be the great reward of wisdom; and they who do not wish to give themselves to this leisure of seeking and contemplating the truth, but instead exercise extremely laborious cares and offices such as counseling men and busying themselves in the activity of moderating and governing human affairs, they judge themselves to be wise; and those who do both of these, and live partly in the contemplation of truth and partly in official labors, which they think they owe to human society, they seem to themselves to hold the palm of wisdom. I omit innumerable sects of which there is none that does not place its own spectators above all others and hold them alone to be wise. Wherefore since it is a question with us now, not of what we may believe the answer should be, but of what we are convinced by clear understanding, I shall in no ways be able to answer what you ask unless I also know by contemplating and by discerning with reason what I hold by believing, and this is wisdom itself.

26.

A. Do you think there is any wisdom other than truth, in which the supreme good is discerned and known? For all those different spectators whom you mentioned seek good and avoid evil; but with that in view they pursue different things because different things seem good to different people. Therefore, he who desires what should not have been desired, even though he would not have desired it if it had not seemed good to him, nevertheless errs. However, neither he who desires nothing nor he who desires what he should desire can err. In so far therefore as all men desire a happy life they do not err. But in so far as any one does not hold to that way of life which leads to happiness, although he avows and professes himself to wish nothing except to arrive at happiness, he errs to that extent. For error is to follow something which does not lead to that at which we wish to arrive. And the more one errs in the way of life, the less is one wise. For one is that much the further removed from the truth in which the supreme good is discerned and known. When the

---

[1] *Eccles.* 7:26. The Vulgate has *sapientiam et rationem* instead of *sapientiam et numerum*. *Ratio* is usually rendered the *reason of things* in the translation of this text; *Eccles.* 7:25, in english translation.

supreme good, however, is pursued and achieved, every one is made happy because we all without controversy wish the supreme good. As therefore it is certain that we wish to be happy, so it is certain that we wish to be wise, because no one is happy without wisdom. For no one is happy except by the supreme good, which is discerned and known in that truth which we call wisdom. Just as, therefore, before we are happy, a notion of happiness is notwithstanding impressed upon our minds, for through it we know and we say confidently and without uncertainty that we wish to be happy; so too before we are wise, we have a notion of wisdom impressed in our mind, by which each of us, if he were asked whether he wished to be wise, would reply without any obscurity of doubt that he did.

27.

A. Wherefore, if it is now clear to us what wisdom is, which perhaps you were not able to explain in words (for if you did not at all discern it by the mind, you would by no means know both that you wish to be wise and that you ought to wish it; which I do not think you will deny), I want you now to tell me whether you think that wisdom too, like the reason and truth of number, exhibits itself in common to all who use reason; or whether you think that, since there are as many minds of men as there are men, whence it is that I do not discern anything of your mind nor you of mine, there are also as many wisdoms as there could be wise men.

E. If the supreme good is one to all, the truth in which it is discerned and known, that is, wisdom, must likewise be one and common to all.

A. But do you doubt that the supreme good, whatever it is, one for all men?

E. I doubt it very much, because I see different people enjoying different things as their own supreme goods.

A. I should have wished that no one have doubts of this sort about the supreme good, just as no one doubts that man can be made happy only by securing it, whatever it is. But since this is a great question, and since it calls urgently for a long discourse, let us consider that there are just as many supreme goods as there are different things which are desired by different people as supreme goods: does it not follow there-

fore that wisdom itself likewise is not one and common to all, because those goods which men distinguish and choose in it are many and diverse? For if you think that, you can doubt too with regard to the light of the sun, whether it is one, since there are many and diverse things which we see in it. From these many, each one chooses by will what he enjoys through the sense of the eyes: and one man willingly looks upon the height of a mountain and enjoys this sight; another the even surface of a field; another the convexity of valleys; another the greenness of woods; another the moving smoothness of the sea; another all of these or whichever of them are beautiful together and contribute to the joy of seeing. Therefore, just as these things are many and diverse which men see and choose for enjoyment in the light of the sun, and still the light itself is one in which the glance of each one who looks sees and knows that which he enjoys: so too, although the goods are many and diverse from which each one chooses that which he wishes and sets it up rightly and truly to be seen and known for his own enjoyment of the supreme good, nevertheless it can happen that the very light of wisdom in which these can be seen and known may be one and common to all wise men.

E. I grant that that can happen, nor is there anything to prevent that there be one wisdom common to all, even though there are many and diverse supreme goods; but I should want to know whether it is so. For if we concede that it can happen that that be so, we do not necessarily concede that it is so.

A. We know, meanwhile, that there is wisdom: but whether there is one wisdom common to all or whether each wise man has his own as he has his own soul or mind, that we do not yet know.

E. That is so.

CHAPTER X

There Is One Light of Wisdom Common to All Wise Men.

28.

A. Where, then do we see this which we know, whether it be the fact that wisdom is or that all men desire to be wise and happy? For I should by no means have doubted that you see it and that it is true. But do you see this truth as your own thought in such a way that if you do not communicate it to me I ignore it utterly? Or do you understand it in such ways that this truth can be seen by me, even if it is not told to me by you?

E. Certainly in such ways that I do not doubt, it can be seen by you too, even though I were unwilling.

A. Consequently since we both see one truth with separate minds, is it not common to both of us?

E. Most clearly.

A. Again I believe that you do not deny that one must apply oneself diligently to wisdom and that you concede this is true.

E. I do not doubt that in the least.

A. Shall we, further, be able to deny that this truth is one and is common to be seen by all who know it, although each one contemplates it, not in my mind, nor in yours, nor in the mind of any one else; but in his own mind, since that which is contemplated is present in common to all who contemplate?

E. Not at all.

A. Again, will you not grant that this is very true and present in common to me as well as to you and to all who see it, that one must see justly, that the worse must be subordinated to the better, and that equals must be compared with equals, and that to each one must be rendered his due?

E. I agree.

A. Can you deny that any uncorrupted thing is better than a corrupted thing, an eternal thing than a temporal one, an inviolable than a violable?

E. Who can?

A. Can anyone therefore call this truth his own, since it is present immutably to be contemplated by all who are able to contemplate it?

E. No one would say that this truly is his own, since, as it is true, so it is one and common to all.

A. Again, who denies that the mind must be turned away from corruption and turned to incorruption, that is, not corruption but incorruption must be sought out? Or who, when he grants that truth is, does not understand it also as immutable and does not see it to be present in common to all minds able to contemplate it?

E. That is very true.

A. Then, will any one doubt that that life which is not turned by adversities from a sure and honorable way of thinking, is better than that which is broken and upturned easily by temporal inconveniences?

E. Who would doubt that?

29.

A. I shall ask no more questions of this sort now for it is enough that you see as I do and that you concede that it is very certain that these, as it were, rules and certain lights of virtue are true and immutable and are present in common each or all to be contemplated by those who are able to conceive them, each by his own reason and mind. But I ask, of course, whether these seem to you to pertain to wisdom? For I believe that he seems to you to be wise who has acquired wisdom.

E. Most certainly he does.

A. Well, would he who lives justly be able to live so, if he did not see the inferior things he subordinates to the preferable ones, and the equal things he joins to each other and things due to each which he distributes?

E. He could not.

A. Will you deny then that he who sees these things, sees wisely?

E. I do not deny it.

A. Then, does not he who lives prudently choose incorruption and does he not perceive that incorruption is to be placed before corruption?

E. Clearly.

A. Therefore, when he chooses that to which he turns his mind, which no one doubts should he chosen, could it be denied that he chooses wisely?

E. I should certainly not deny it.

A. Therefore, when he turns his mind to that which he chooses wisely, he assuredly turns wisely.

E. That is certain.

A. And he who can not be thrust away by terrors and pains from that which he chose wisely and from that to which he turned himself wisely no doubt acts wisely.

E. Beyond any doubt.

A. It is very clear, then, that all these things which we called rules and lights of virtues, pertain to wisdom: seeing that the more any one uses them for the conduct of life and lives his life according to them, the more he lives and acts wisely; anything however which is done wisely can not rightly be said to be separated from wisdom.

E. That is absolutely so.

A. Just as, therefore, there are true and immutable rules of numbers, the reason and the truth of which you said are present immutably and in common to all who see them, so there are true and immutable rules of wisdom, which, you replied a moment ago when you were questioned concerning a few of them one by one, are true and manifest, and you concede that they are present in common to be contemplated by all who are able to consider them.

CHAPTER XI

Wisdom and Number Are the Same, or Else Exist One from the Other or One in the Other.

30.

E. I can not doubt that. But I should want particularly to know whether these two, namely wisdom and number, are contained in some single genus, because you have pointed out that they have been joined together even in the Holy Scriptures; or whether the one exists dependent on the other or consists in the other, as if number existed derived from wisdom or in wisdom. For I should not dare to say that wisdom exists from number or consists in number: in fact it strikes me somehow, since I have known many arithmeticians or numberers or whatever else they may be called, who compute extremely well and admirably, but only very few wise men or perhaps none, that wisdom is much more venerable than number.

A. You say something at which I too always wonder. For when I consider to myself the immutable truth of numbers, and the lair, as it were, and innermost part of it, or the sort of region, or whatever other word can be found appropriate to name the manner, as it were, of dwelling place and seat of numbers, I am removed far from the body: and finding perhaps something which I can think, but not finding anything which I can set in words, I return as if wearied to these things of ours that I may speak, and I talk of things which are located before the eyes, as they are wont to be talked of. This occurs to me too when, so far as I am able, I reflect very watchfully and very intently on wisdom. And because of this I wonder a great deal, since these two are in the most secret and the most certain truth: and the testimony of the Scriptures is added too, in which they are mentioned conjointly, as I have pointed out; I wonder most of all

as I have said, why number is of trifling value to the multitude of men and wisdom dear. But doubtless it is this, that wisdom and number are a certain single and same thing; but yet, since it is none the less said of wisdom in the divine Books "that it reaches from end even to the end vigorously and it disposes all things agreeably,"[1] that power by which "it reaches from end even to the end vigorously" is perchance called number: and surely that by which "*it disposes all things agreeably*," is then properly called wisdom; since both are of one and the same wisdom.

31.

But because he gave numbers to all things even the lowest and to those placed in the end of things and indeed all bodies have their numbers even though they are most remote in things; yet he did not grant to bodies to be wise nor even to all souls, but only to rational souls, as if he placed in them a seat for himself from which he may dispose all these things, even the lowest, to which he gave numbers: so since we judge easily of bodies, as of things which are ordered beneath us, on which we distinguish numbers impressed beneath us; and because of that we hold them to be of lesser value. But when we began to turn about as if upwards, we found that numbers also transcend our minds, and that they remain immutable in truth itself. And because few can be wise, notwithstanding that it is granted even to the stupid to count, men admire wisdom and despise numbers. The learned, however, and the scholarly, the more remote they are from earthly blemish, the more they look upon both number and wisdom in truth itself and hold both dear: and in comparison with its truth, gold and silver and other things for which men fight, are not for them, but for them grow worthless.

32.

Nor should you wonder that numbers have been so little valued by men and that wisdom is so dear, because men can more easily count than be wise, since you see that they hold gold more dear than the light of a lamp, and they would laugh to have gold compared with it. But a thing far inferior is honored more, because even a beggar kindles a lamp for himself, but few have gold: although wisdom may be absent so that in comparison

---

[1]*Book of Wisdom* 8:1.

with number it is found inferior, despite that they are the same, still it seeks the eye by which it can be seen. But just as, to express it thus, brightness and heat are perceived consubstantial in one fire, nor can they be separated from each other, and yet heat passes only to such things as are moved close, whereas brightness is diffused also further and more broadly: so too by the power of understanding which is present in wisdom, things which are nearer, such as the rational souls, grow warm; but those which are more remote, such as bodies, do not attain to the heat of being wise, but are steeped in the light of numbers: this perhaps is obscure to you. For no likeness of visible thing can be fitted to an invisible thing in complete accord. Consider only this, which is sufficient for the question which we have taken up and which manifests itself even to humbler minds, such as we are, that although it can not be clear to us whether number is in wisdom or from wisdom or whether wisdom itself is from number or in number, or whether both can be shown to be the names of one thing; this certainly is clear, that both are true and immutably true.

CHAPTER XII

There Is a Single and Immutable Truth in All Understandings and It Is Superior to Our Mind.

33.

Wherefore, you would certainly not deny that there is an immutable truth, containing all these things which are immutable true, which you can not say is yours or mine or any one man's, but is present and proffers itself in common to all who discern immutable truths, as a secret and public light in wondrous ways: but who would say that all that which is present in common to every one who reasons and understands, pertains properly to the nature of any of them? For you remember, I suppose, what was gone over a little while ago in relation to the senses of the body; namely that those things which we touch in common by the sense of the eyes or the ears, such as colors and sounds, which I and you see at the same time, or hear at the same time, do not pertain to the nature of our eyes or ears, but are common to us to be perceived. So too, therefore, you would never say that those things which I and you each with his own mind perceive in common, pertain to the nature of the mind of either one of us. For you can not say that what the eyes of two people see at the same time, is the eyes of this one or the other one, but a third something to which the glance of both is turned.

E. That is very apparent and very true.

34.

A. Do you think then that this truth of which we have been speaking for a long time now and in which, though it is single, we see so many things, do you think it is more excellent than our mind is, or equal to our mind, or else inferior? But if it were inferior we should judge, not according to it, but of it, just as we judge of bodies because they are lower, and we say commonly not only that they are so and not so, but that they ought to be so and not so: so too in regard to our minds, we know not only that the mind is so, but frequently too that it ought to be so. And we judge thus of bodies when we say, It is less white than it should have been, or less square, and many others similarly; moreover, we say of minds, It is less apt than it should be, or less smooth, or less vehement, according as the nature of our customs may have disclosed. And we judge these things according to those interior rules or truth which we discern in common: of them on the other hand no one in any manner judges. For although one would say that eternal are greater than temporal things, or that seven and three are ten, no one says that they should have been thus, but knowing them only to be so, one does not correct as an examiner but only rejoices as a discoverer. It, however, this truth of equals were in our minds, it too would be mutable. For our minds sometimes see it more, sometimes less, and by this they show themselves to be mutable: whereas it, continuing in itself, neither advances when it is seen by us more, nor grows less when it is seen less, but whole and uncorrupted it rejoices those who are turned to the light and punishes those who are turned away in blindness. Why is it that we judge of our minds themselves according to it, when we can in no way judge of it? For we say of the mind, It understands less than it should, or it understands as much as it should. The amount, however, that a mind ought to understand is according as it has been able to be moved more near to, and to inhere in, the immutable truth. Wherefore if the truth is neither inferior nor equal, it remains that it be superior and more excellent.

CHAPTER XIII

Exhortation to Embracing Truth which Alone Makes Men Happy.

35.

However, I had promised, if you remember, that I should demonstrate to you that there is something which is more sublime than our mind and reason. Behold it is truth itself: embrace it if you can, and enjoy it, and delight in the Lord, and he will give you the desires of your heart.[1] What more, indeed, do you seek than that you be happy? And who is more happy than he who enjoys the unshaken and immutable and most excellent truth? But do men cry forth that they are happy when they embrace the beautiful bodies, of wives or even of prostitutes, for which they have lusted with great desire: and do we doubt that we are happy in the embrace of truth? Do men cry that they are happy when, their jaws arid with heat, they come upon an abundant and healthgiving fountain, or when, hungry, they find a meal or dinner splendidly furnished and plentiful: and will we deny that we are happy when we slacken our thirst and feed on truth? We are used to hear voices of those crying out that they are happy if they lie down in roses or other flowers or even if they enjoy very sweet smelling unguents: what is more fragrant and what more pleasing than the inspiration of truth? And do we hesitate to call ourselves happy when we are inspired by it? Many make for themselves a happy life in the song of voices and of strings and of flutes, and when these are taken from them, they judge themselves miserable; but when they are present they are carried away with joy: and shall we seek some other happy life when, with no crashing, so to speak, of songs, a kind of eloquent silence of truth flows into our minds, and shall we not enjoy the happiness so certain and so present? Men who are delighted in the light of gold and silver, in the lustre of gems and of other colors, or in the clearness and the joy of the very light which is proper to the eyes, whether in terrestrial fires or in stars or the moon or the sun, seem to themselves happy when they are not recalled from this pleasure by any vexation or by any need, and they wish to live always for these: and have we feared to place the happy life in the light of truth?

36.

By all means, since the supreme good is known and secured in truth, and since that truth is wisdom, let us see the supreme good in truth, and let us secure and enjoy it. He is surely happy who enjoys the supreme good. For this truth reveals all goods which are true, which men of understanding, each according to his capacity, choose singly or together to enjoy. But just as they who choose in the light of the sun that which they look at willingly and are rejoiced by that sight; whereas if perchance there were any among them endowed with very vigorous and healthy and very strong eyes, they would look upon nothing more willingly than the sun itself, which likewise lights up other things by which weaker eyes are pleased: so the keen and vigorous perception of the mind when it has gazed with sure reason on many true and immutable things, directs itself to that truth itself by which all things are shown forth, and inhering in it, as it were, forgets other things, and at once in it enjoys them all. For whatsoever is pleasant in other truths, is pleasant assuredly in the truth itself.

37.

This is our freedom when we are subjected to this truth: and it itself is our God, who frees us from death, that is, from the condition of sin. For truth itself speaking as man with men, says to those who believe in him: "if you have abided by my word, then truly you are my disciples and you will know the truth and the truth will make you free."[2] For the soul enjoys no thing with freedom except that which it enjoys with security.

CHAPTER XIV

Truth Is Possessed with Security.

But no one is secure in those goods which he can lose while he is unwilling. No one, however, loses truth and wisdom against his will: for no one can be separated from them in space, but what is called a separation from truth and wisdom is a perverse will, by which inferior things are chosen. No one, however, wants any thing when he does not want it. We have,

---

[1] *Psalms* 36 (or 37): 4.

[2] *John* 8:31, 32.

therefore, what all may enjoy equally and in common: there are no straitnesses, there is no defect in it. All its lovers it receives with none in the least envious of it, and it is common to all and chaste to each. No one says to another: go back that I too may come near; take away your hand that I too way embrace. All cling to it and all touch it. The food of it is destroyed in no part; you drink nothing of it which I can not. For you do not change anything from its common participation into your private property; but what you take from it remains whole for me. I do not wait that what it inspired you be returned from you, and that thus I may be inspired by it: for there is not anything of it which is ever made the property of one or of several persons, but it is all common at one time to all.

38.

Therefore, those things which we touch, or which we taste, or which we smell, are less like this truth, but those which we hear and see are more like it: because every word by whomsoever it is heard, is heard whole by all, and at the same time whole by each; and every species which is contiguous to the eyes, is seen at the same time as much by one as by another. But even these are similar at a very long interval: for no voice sounds wholly at once, because it is stretched out and produced in time, and some of it sounds first, some later; and every visible species spreads out, as it were, through space and is not all everywhere. And certainly all of these are borne away while we are unwilling, and we are hindered by certain difficulties from enjoying them. For even if some one's sweet singing could be eternal, and even if those devoted to him should come earnestly to hear him, they would be crowded together, and they would fight for places according as their number was large that each might be nearer to him who sings, and they would try to remain shut within themselves, hearing nothing else, but they would be touched by all the fleeting voices. Moreover, if I should want to gaze upon this sun, and if I could do that persistently, it could disappear from me by setting, and it could be veiled over by a cloud, and I could lose the pleasure of seeing it by many other obstacles, although against my will. Finally, even if the sweetness, both of seeing light and of hearing a voice, were always there, what great thing would come to me, since it is common to me and to

beasts? But that beauty of truth and wisdom, so long as there is a persevering will to enjoy it, does not shut off those who come in a crowded multitude of hearers, nor does it move along in time, nor does it migrate in space, nor is it interrupted by night, nor is it blocked off by shadows, nor does it fall under the senses of the body. Of all the world it is nearest to all those turned toward it who enjoy it, it is eternal to all; it is in no place, it is never away; it admonishes abroad, it teaches within; it changes all who see it to the better, it is changed by none to worse; no one judges of it, no one judges well without it. And it is thereby clear that truth is without doubt more excellent than our minds, which are each made wise by it alone; and of it you may not judge but by it you may judge others.

CHAPTER XV

That God Is, Is Known Certainly Now from a Complete Application of Reason.

39.

Moreover, you had conceded that if I should show you that there is something above our minds, you would confess that it is God, provided there were nothing still loftier. I had said, acceding to this concession of yours, that it would be sufficient to demonstrate this. For if there is something still more excellent, that rather is God: if however there is nothing, then truth itself is God. Whether, therefore, that more excellent something is or is not, you nevertheless can not deny that God is: Which was the question set to be discussed and treated by us. For if this affects you, that in the sacrosanct discipline of Christ we accept in faith the doctrine that God is the Father of Wisdom, remember that we also accept this in faith, that equal to the eternal Father is the Wisdom which is begotten of him. Whence nothing further need be inquired, but only held with unshaken faith. For God is, and he is truly and supremely. This we not only hold now undoubted in faith, as I believe, but we also touch it in a sure, although still very tenuous, form of knowledge; but it suffices for the question which we took up, that we are able to explain some aspects which pertain to the thing: unless you have something which you oppose to this.

E. On the contrary, I accept these things and I am overcome utterly by an incredible joy which I can not explain to you in words, and I cry out that they are most certain. I cry out, moreover, with an interior voice with which I wish to be heard by that very truth and to cling to it: because I concede it to be not only good but the supreme good and the maker of blessedness.

40.

A. Rightly so, and I too rejoice greatly. But I ask you whether we are now wise and happy? or do we as yet only tend to that, that it may come to be in us?

E. I think we rather tend toward it.

A. Whence then do you understand the things which you cried out that you enjoyed as true and sure; and do you concede that this pertains to wisdom? Or is any fool able to know wisdom?

E. As long as he is a fool he can not.

A. Then you are already wise or else do not yet know wisdom.

E. I am not yet wise, but neither would I say that I am a fool in so far as I know wisdom; since these things which I know are certain and I can not deny that they pertain to wisdom.

A. Tell me, I ask, whether you will not grant that he who is not just is unjust; and he who is not prudent is imprudent; and he who is not temperate is intemperate or can anything be doubted in respect to these?

E. I grant that a man when he is not just is unjust; and I make the same reply too of the prudent and the temperate man.

A. Why then is he not a fool when he is not wise?

E. This too I grant that when any one is not wise he is a fool.

A. Well then which of these are you?

E. Whichever of them you may call me; I do not yet dare to call myself wise; and from the things which I have granted, I see that it follows that I should not hesitate to call myself a fool.

A. Then the fool knows wisdom. For he would not, as has already been said, be sure to wish to be wise, and he would not have to wish it if there did not cling to his mind a notion of wisdom, like the notion of those things, concerning which you replied when questioned one after the other, which pertain to wisdom itself, in the knowledge of which you were rejoiced.

E. It is as you say.

CHAPTER XVI

Wisdom Shows Itself along the Way to Its Earnest Seekers, Namely, in Numbers Impressed in Each Thing.

41.

A. What else therefore do we do when we apply ourselves to be wise, except bring in a measure all our soul, with as much alacrity as we can, to that which we touch with the mind, and place it there and fasten it durably, that it may no longer enjoy things private to it which it has involved in passing things, but having removed all the conditions of times and places, it may apprehend what is always one and the same? For just as all the life of the body is the soul, so the happy life of the soul is God. While we do this, even to the time when we may complete it, we are on the way. And consider whether this, that it is granted to enjoy these true and certain goods, even though as yet they flash forth on this dark route, is what has been written of wisdom in respect to what it does to its lovers when they come to it and seek it; for it has been said, "It shows itself to them joyfully along the ways and runs forward to them with all foreknowledge."[1] "Whithersoever you turn it speaks to you by certain marks which it has impressed upon its works, and it recalls you when you fall down among exterior things to the very forms of exterior things which are within: so that you may see that whatever delighted you in the body and allured you through the bodily senses, is numbered, and you may inquire whence it is, and you may return within yourself and understand that you can not approve or disapprove of what you perceive by the senses of the body unless you have in yourself certain laws of beauty, to which you refer whatever you feel is beautiful without.

42.

Look upon the sky and the earth and the sea and whatsoever flashes in them or above them or crawls beneath them or flies or swims; they have forms, because they have numbers: take that from them, they will be nothing. Therefore, from what are they, except from number: seeing that being pertains to them in so far as they are numbered? And human artificers too have numbers of all corporeal forms in art,

---

[1] *Book of Wisdom* 6:17.

to which they fit their works, and they move their hands and instruments in fashioning, until that which is formed outside is borne back to that light of numbers which is within, and until it can receive its consummation, so far as that is possible, and in order that by way of the interpreting sense it may please that internal judge who gazes upon the heavenly numbers. Ask in the next place, what moves the arms of the artificer himself; it will be a number, for they are moved likewise according to number. And if you withdraw work from the hands, and the intention of fashioning from the soul, and if the motion of the limbs be turned to delight, that will be called a dance. Ask then, what it is that pleases in a dance; number will answer you: behold it is I. Now look upon the beauty of the formed body; numbers are held fast in place. Look upon the beauty of mobility in the body; numbers are poured forth in time. Go into the art whence these proceed; seek in it time and space; it never will be; nowhere will it be: nevertheless number lives in it: nor is its region of spaces nor its age of days; and yet when they who wish to make themselves artists apply themselves to learning the art, they move their body through places and times, and even their mind through times: certainly with the passage of time they become more skilled. Transcend then the mind of the artist too that you may see the eternal number; then wisdom will flash forth to you from the very interior seat and from the secret place itself of truth; and if that should beat back your still too languid glance, turn the eye of your mind into that way, where wisdom showed itself joyfully. But remember that you have broken the vision which you may seek forth again when you are stronger and sounder.

43.

Alas, those who abandon you as a leader and wander from your footsteps, who love, instead of you, your beckonings and forget what you beckon for, O wisdom, most sweet light of the cleansed mind! For you do not cease to give us the sign of what you are and how much you are; and your beckonings are all the embellishment of creatures. For the artist too in a measure beckons to the spectator of his work from the very beauty of the work, not to remain fixed there wholly, but to run over with his eyes the species of the fabricated body in such wise that he may return in love to him who fabricated it. They, however, are like

men who love instead of you that which you make, who when they hear some eloquent wise man, listen too much to the sweetness of his voice and the structure of the well placed syllables, and lose the high importance of the thoughts of which these words sound only the signs. Alas, those who turn themselves from your light, and cling in delight to the shadow of it! For, turning their backs, so to speak, to you, they are fastened firmly in carnal work as in their own shadows, and notwithstanding they still, even there, derive what delights them from the circumfulgence of your light. But when the shadow is loved, it makes the eye of the soul too languid and too weak to prefer your sight. Because of this, more and more is man darkened, while he pursues more willingly anything that more tolerably exempts the weak. Wherefore, he begins to lack the power of seeing that which is supremely, and he begins to think evil whatever fails unforeseen, or attracts him though unworthy, or tortures him when acquired, because such a thing deserves his aversion rightly, and anything that is just, could not be evil.

44.

Therefore, if you have looked upon anything mutable, you can not grasp it by the sense of the body or by the consideration of the mind, unless it is held firmly by some form of numbers, and if they are removed, it falls back again into nothing; do not doubt that there is some eternal and immutable form in order that these mutable things may not be cut short, but may be, as it were, carried with measured movements and with a separate variety of forms through certain turns of time; and this form is neither contained in and, as it were, diffused through space, nor strengthened and varied in times; by it all mutable things can be formed and fulfill their genus and perform their numbers of places and times.

CHAPTER XVII

Every Good and Every Perfection is from God.

45.

For every mutable thing must also be susceptible of being formed or formable. Moreover, as we call that mutable which can be changed, so we should call that formable which can be formed. But no thing can form itself, because no thing can give itself that which it has not, and assuredly a thing is formed that it may have form. Wherefore if each thing has some form, there is no need that it receive that which it has; but if it does not have form, it can not receive from itself that which it does not have. Therefore no thing, as we have said, can form itself. But what more may we say of the mutability of body and mind? For enough has been said above. It so happens that body and mind are formed by a certain immutable and ever remaining form. To which form it has been said, "you will change them and they will be changed; but you yourself are the same and your years will not end."[1] The prophetic speech used "years without end" for "eternity." Of this form it has been said again that, persevering in itself, it renews all things.[2] Hence too, it is understood that all things are governed by providence. For if all things which are, will be, provided no form has been taken away, then the immutable form itself, by which all mutable things subsist that they may be fulfilled and governed by the numbers of their forms, is their providence; for things would not be, if it were not. Therefore, whoever, inspecting and considering the whole creation, takes the way to wisdom, he sees wisdom reveal herself to him joyfully along the way and run to him in all foreknowledge: and he burns the more readily to go that way, as the way itself is beautiful because of that which he is consumed to attain.

46.

If, however, you should find some other class of creatures beside that which is and does not live, and that which is and lives but does not understand, and that which is and lives and understands, then have the courage to say that there is some good which is not from God. These three, in fact, can be designated by only two names, if they are called body and life, because both that which only lives and does not understand (such is the life of animals) and that which understands (such is the life of men) is very rightly called life. However these two, namely, body and life, which surely are classed as creatures (for the life of the Creator himself is spoken of too, and that is the supreme life): these two creatures therefore, body and life, since they are *formable*, as the above remarks have pointed out, and since they would slip back into nothing should they lose their form entirely, show sufficiently that they subsist by that form which is always of this sort. Wherefore, no amount of good whatsoever, as great or as small as you will, could be except from God. For what can there be in creatures greater than intelligent life or what less than body? Howeversomuch they are wanting and howeversomuch they incline not to be, nevertheless something of form remains to them that they may in some way be. Still whatever form remains to any deficient thing is from that form which knows no deficiency, and which does not permit the motions of deficient or of successful things to go beyond the laws of their numbers. Whatever, therefore, is encountered praiseworthy in the nature of things, whether it be judged worthy of slight or full praise, must be referred to the most excellent and ineffable praise of the Creator: unless you have something to oppose to this. . . .

STUDY QUESTIONS: AUGUSTINE, ON FREE WILL

1. Why did God give us free will, when He knew it would make it possible for us to sin?
2. Why does God judge a sin, even though He knew in advance that it would happen?
3. What aspect of our own nature allows us to infer the existence of God?
4. What is the understanding?
5. When we are in a room together looking at, say, an apple, do we all see, touch, feel, and sense the same object?
6. How do we see colors?
7. How does Augustine distinguish "internal" from "external" sense?

---

[1] *Psalms* 101:27, 28 (or in some translations 102:26, 27).

[2] *Book of Wisdom* 7:27.

8. What makes it possible for many minds to see the same thing?
9. What are numbers? What is their significance?
10. What is wisdom?
11. What is the one light of wisdom that we all have in common?
12. How are wisdom and number related?
13. What is the one thing that can make us happy?
14. How does wisdom show itself?

CONFESSIONS

In the *Confessions* Augustine describes his own final and most dramatic conversion to Christianity, inspired by nothing more and nothing less than the desire to be happy, to which the Aristotelian concept of our desire to know is itself subordinate. Even knowledge is a desire based on the desire to be happy (e.g., knowledge is power and power makes me happy). Still under the influence both of the Manichaean doctrine that salvation comes from ascetic living and the philosophical minimalism of the Stoics and Skeptics, Augustine concludes that we can best achieve salvation by turning away from the world and its numerous pleasures, neither in the abstract and detached way of the Stoics nor in the belief-free disinterestedness of the Skeptics. Augustine's way is predicated on the mind's coming to understand, as in the philosophy of his Platonic predecessors, that what we call "the world" is not the real world but only our idea, a representation. Likewise, what you call your "self" is also but an idea, or representation, in your mind and not the real you. In this way Augustine argues that the Stoics were falsely caught up in reaction to what is not real and the Skeptics were caught up arguing against the reality of the appearances and that both were blinded by their inability to see beyond both the external and internal world of appearances, which he calls *God*.

The following passages illustrate the way in which Augustine argues for the existence of a supreme, higher being, what he calls "God," of which what we call "reality" is but an image or imperfect representation. His main question is this: with what mental faculty can we know God? Is it by perception? By conception? How? The problem, ultimately, is a variation of the age old philosophical problem of how the mind can reach beyond itself to something other than itself, in this case, the ultimate ground of all being. In the process, Augustine launches into what is probably one of the first introspective psychological analyses of awareness, consciousness, language, and memory. His approach is both analytic—explicating the concepts available for thinking about such things—and phenomenologica—explicating the structure of experience itself. His purpose is to provide a theory as to what it is about the mind's concepts and the nature of experience that allow us the mind to reach beyond itself. This is something that *idealists* with deny and thus, in that sense, Augustine provides a thoroughly *realist* methodology that remains influential throughout virtually all subsequent Christian thought.

Augustine, from *The Confessions of St. Augustine*, translated by E. B. Pusey (New York: Collier and Son, 1909).

BOOK X

Let me know Thee, O Lord, who knowest me: let me know Thee, as I am known. Power of my soul, enter into it, and fit it for Thee, that Thou mayest have and hold it without spot or wrinkle. This is my hope, therefore do I speak; and in this hope do I rejoice, when I rejoice healthfully. Other things of this life are the less to be sorrowed for, the more they are sorrowed for: and the more to be sorrowed for, the less men sorrow for them. For behold, Thou lovest the truth, and he that doth it, cometh to the light. This would I do in my heart before Thee in confession: and in my writing, before many witnesses.

And from Thee, O Lord, unto whose eyes the abyss of man's conscience is naked, what could be hidden in me though I would not confess it? For I should hide Thee from me, not me from Thee. But now, for that my groaning is witness, that I am displeased with myself, Thou shinest out, and art pleasing, and beloved, and longed for: that I may be ashamed of myself, and renounce myself, and choose Thee, and neither please Thee nor myself, but in Thee. To Thee therefore, O Lord, am I open, whatever I am: and with what fruit I confess unto Thee, I have said. Nor do I it with words and sounds of the flesh, but with the words of my soul, and the cry of the thought which Thy ear knoweth. For when I am evil, then to confess to Thee is nothing else than to be displeased with myself; but when holy, nothing else than not to ascribe it to myself: because Thou, O Lord, blessest the godly, but first Thou justifieth him when ungodly. My confession then, O my God, in Thy sight, is made silently, and not silently. For in sound, it is silent: in affection, it cries aloud. For neither do I utter any thing right unto men, which Thou hast not before heard from me: nor dost Thou hear any such thing from me, which Thou hast not first said unto me.

What then have I to do with men, that they should hear my confessions—as if they could heal all my infirmities—a race, curious to know the lives of others, slothful to amend their own? Why seek they to hear from me what I am: who will not hear from Thee what themselves are? And how know they, when from myself they hear of myself, whether I say true; seeing no man knows what is in man, but the spirit of man which is in him? But if they hear from Thee of themselves, they cannot say, "The Lord lieth." For what is it to hear from Thee of themselves, but to know themselves? And who knoweth and saith, "It is false," unless himself lieth? But because charity believeth all things (that is, among those whom knitting unto itself it maketh one), I also, O Lord, will in such wise confess unto Thee, that men may hear, to whom I cannot demonstrate whether I confess truly; yet they believe me, whose ears charity openeth unto me.

But do Thou, my inmost Physician, make plain unto me what fruit I may reap by doing it. For the confessions of my past sins, which Thou hast forgiven and covered, that Thou mightest bless me in Thee, changing my soul by Faith and Thy Sacrament, when read and heard, stir up the heart, that it sleep not in despair and say "I cannot," but awake in the love of Thy mercy and the sweetness of Thy grace, whereby whoso is weak, is strong, when by it he became conscious of his own weakness. And the good delight to hear of the past evils of such as are now freed from them, not because they are evils, but because they have been and are not. With what fruit then, O Lord my God, to Whom my conscience daily confesseth, trusting more in the hope of Thy mercy than in her own innocence, with what fruit, I pray, do I by this book confess to men also in Thy presence what I now am, not what I have been? For that other fruit I have seen and spoken of. But what I now am, at the very time of making these confessions, divers desire to know, who have or have not known me, who have heard from me or of me; but their ear is not at my heart where I am, whatever I am. They wish then to hear me confess what I am within: whither neither their eye, nor ear, nor understanding can reach; they wish it, as ready to believe—but will they know? For charity, whereby they are good, telleth them that in my confessions I lie not: and she in them, believeth me.

But for what fruit would they hear this? Do they desire to joy with me, when they hear how near, by Thy gift, I approach unto Thee? And to pray for me, when they shall hear how much I am held back by my own weight? To such will I discover myself. For it is no mean fruit, O Lord my God, that by many thanks should be given to Thee on our behalf, and Thou be by many entreated for us. Let the brotherly mind love in me what Thou teachest is to be loved, and lament in me what Thou teachest is to be lamented. Let a brotherly, not a stranger, mind, not that of the strange children, whose mouth talketh of vanity, and their right hand is a right hand of iniquity, but that brotherly mind which when it approveth, rejoiceth for me, and when it disapproveth me, is sorry for me: because whether it approveth or disapproveth, it loveth me. To such will I discover myself: they will breathe freely at my good deeds, sigh for my ill. My good deeds are Thine appointments, and Thy gifts: my evil ones are my offences, and Thy judgments. Let them breathe freely at the one, sigh at the other: and let hymns and weeping go up into Thy sight, out of the hearts of my brethren, Thy censers. And do Thou, O Lord, be pleased with the incense of Thy holy temple, have mercy upon me according to Thy great mercy for Thine own name's sake; and no ways forsaking what Thou hast begun, perfect my imperfections.

This is the fruit of my confessions of what I am, not of what I have been, to confess this, not before Thee only, in a secret exultation with trembling, and a secret sorrow with hope: but in the ears also of the believing sons of men, sharers of my joy, and partners in my mortality, my fellow citizens, and fellow pilgrims, who are gone before, or are to follow on, companions of my way. These are Thy servants, my brethren, whom Thou willest to be Thy sons: my masters, whom Thou commandest me to serve, if I would live with Thee, of Thee. But this Thy Word were little did it only command by speaking, and not go before in performing. This then I do in deed and word, this I do under Thy wings; in over great peril, were not my soul subdued unto Thee under Thy wings, and my infirmity known unto Thee. I am a little one, but my Father ever liveth, and my Guardian is sufficient for me. For He is the same who begat me, and defends me: and Thou Thyself are all my good: Thou, Almighty. Who are with me, yea, before I am with Thee. To such then whom Thou commandest me to serve will I discover, not what I have been, but what I now am and what I yet am. But neither do I judge myself. Thus therefore I would be heard.

For Thou, Lord, dost judge me: because, although no man knoweth the things of a man, but the spirit of a man which is in him, yet is there something of man, which neither the spirit of man that is in him, itself knoweth. But Thou, Lord, knowest all of him, Who hast made him. Yet I, though in Thy sight I despise myself, and account myself dust and ashes; yet know I something of Thee, which I know not of myself. And

truly, now we see through a glass darkly, not face to face as yet. So long therefore as I be absent from Thee, I am more present with myself than with Thee; and yet know I Thee that Thou art in no ways passible; but I, what temptations I can resist, what I cannot, I know not. And there is hope, because Thou art faithful, Who wilt not suffer us to be tempted above that we are able; but wilt with the temptation also make a way to escape, that we may be able to bear it. I will confess then what I know of myself, I will confess also what I know not of myself. And that because what I do know of myself, I know by Thy shining upon me: and what I know not of myself, so long know I not it, until my darkness be made as the noonday in Thy countenance.

Not with doubting, but with assured consciousness, do I love Thee, Lord. Thou hast stricken my heart with Thy word, and I loved Thee. Yea also heaven, and earth, and all that therein is, behold, on every side they bid me love Thee; nor cease to say so unto all, that they may be without excuse. But more deeply wilt Thou have mercy on whom Thou wilt have mercy, and wilt have compassion on whom Thou hast had compassion: else in deaf ears do the heaven and the earth speak Thy praises. But what do I love, when I love Thee? Not beauty of bodies, nor the fair harmony of time, nor the brightness of the light, so gladsome to our eyes, nor sweet melodies of varied songs, nor the fragrant smell of flowers, and ointments, and spices, not manna and honey, not limbs acceptable to embracements of flesh. None of these I love, when I love my God: and yet I love a kind of light, and melody, and fragrance, and meat, and embracement when I love my God, the light, melody, fragrance, meat, embracement of my inner man: where there shineth unto my soul what space cannot contain, and there soundeth what time beareth not away, and there smelleth what breathing disperseth not, and there tasteth what eating dimisheth not, and there clingeth what satiety divorceth not. This is it which I love when I love my God.

And what is this? I asked the earth, and it answered me, "I am not He"; and whatsoever are in it confessed the same. I asked the sea and the deeps, and the living creeping things, and they answered, "We are not thy God, seek above us." I asked the moving air: and the whole air with his inhabitants answered, "Anaximenes was deceived, I am not God." I asked the heavens, sun, moon, stars, "Nor (say they) are we the God whom thou seekest." And I replied unto all the things which encompass the door of my flesh: "Ye have told me of my God, that ye are not He: tell me something of Him." And they cried out with a loud voice, "He made us." My questioning them, was my thoughts on them: and their form of beauty gave the answer. And I turned myself unto myself, and said to myself, "Who art thou?" And I answered, "A man." And behold, in me there present themselves to me soul, and body, one without, the other within. By which of these ought I to seek my God? I had sought Him in the body from earth to heaven, so far as I could send messengers, the beams of mine eyes. But the better is the inner, for to it as presiding and judging, all the bodily messengers reported the answers of heaven and earth, and all things therein, who said, "We are not God, but He made us." These things did my inner man know by the ministry of the outer: I the inner knew them; I, the mind, through the senses of my body. I asked the whole frame of the world about my God; and it answered me, "I am not He, but He made me."

Is not this corporeal figure apparent to all whose senses are perfect? Why then speaks it not the same to all? Animals small and great see it, but they cannot ask it: because no reason is set over their senses to judge on what they report. But men can ask, so that the invisible things of God are clearly seen, being understood by the things that are made; but by love of them, they are made subject unto them: and subjects cannot judge. Nor yet do the creatures answer such as ask, unless they can judge; nor yet do they change their voice (i.e., their appearance), if one man only sees, another seeing asks, so as to appear one way to this man, another way to that, but appearing the same way to both, it is dumb to this, speaks to that; yea rather it speaks to all; but they only understand, who compare its voice received from without, with the truth within. For truth saith unto me, "Neither heaven, nor earth, nor any other body is thy God." This, their very nature saith to him that saith them: "They are a mass: a mass is less in a part thereof than in the whole." Now to thee I speak, O my soul, thou art my better part: for thou quickenest the mass of my body, giving it life, which no body can give to a body: but thy God is even unto thee the Life of thy life.

What then do I love, when I love my God? Who is He above the head of my soul? By my very soul will I ascend to Him. I will pass beyond that power whereby I am united to my body, and fill its whole frame with life. Nor can I by that power find my God: for so horse and mule that have no understanding might find Him: seeing it is the same power, whereby even their bodies live. But another power there is, not that only whereby I animate, but that too whereby I imbue with sense my flesh, which the Lord hath framed for me: commanding the eye not to hear, and the ear not to see: but the eye, that through it I should see, and the ear, that through it I should hear; and to the other senses severally, what is to each their own peculiar seats and offices: which, being divers, I the one mind, do through them enact. I will pass beyond this power of mind also: for this also have the horse, and mule, for they also perceive through the body.

I will pass then beyond this power of my nature also, rising by degrees unto Him Who made me. And I come to the fields and spacious palaces of my memory, where are the treasures of innumerable images, brought into it from things of all sorts perceived by the senses. There is stored up, whatsoever besides we think, either by enlarging or diminishing, or any other way varying those things which the sense hath come to: and whatever else hath been committed and laid up, which forgetfulness hath not yet swallowed up and buried. When I enter there, I require what I will to be brought forth, and something instantly comes; others must be longer sought after, which are fetched, as it were, out of some inner receptacle; others rush out in troops, and while one thing is desired and required, they start forth, as who should say, "Is it perchance I?" These I drive away with the hand of my heart, from the face of my remembrance: until what I wish for be unveiled, and appear in sight, out of its secret place. Other things come up readily, in unbroken order, as they are called for: those in front making way for the following; and as they make way, they are hidden from sight, ready to come when I will. All which takes place when I repeat a thing by heart.

There are all things preserved distinctly and under general heads, each having entered by its own avenue: as light, and all colors and forms of bodies by the eyes; by the ears all sorts of sounds; all smells by the avenue of the nostrils; all tastes by the mouth; and by the sensation of the whole body, what is hard or soft; hot or cold; or rugged; heavy or light; either outwardly or inwardly to the body. All these does that great harbor of the memory receive in her numberless secret and inexpressible windings, to be forthcoming, and brought out at need; each entering in by his own gate, and there laid up. Nor yet do the things themselves enter in; only the images of the things perceived are there in readiness, for thought to recall. Which images, how they are formed, who can tell, though it doth plainly appear by which sense each hath been brought in and stored up? For even while I dwell in darkness and silence, in my memory I can produce colors, if I will, and discern betwixt black and white, and what others I will: nor yet do sounds break in and disturb the image drawn in by my eyes, which I am reviewing, though they also are there, lying dormant, and laid up, as it were, apart. For these too I call for, and forthwith they appear. And though my tongue be still, and my throat mute, so can I sing as much as I will; nor do those images of colors, which notwithstanding be there, intrude themselves and interrupt, when another store is called for, which flowed in by the ears. So the other things, piled in and up by the other senses, I recall at my pleasure. Yea, I discern the breath of lilies from violets, though smelling nothing: and I prefer honey to sweet wine, smooth before rugged, at the time neither tasting nor handling, but remembering only.

These things do I within, in that vast court of my memory. For there are present with me, heaven, earth, sea, and whatever I could think on therein, besides what I have forgotten. There also meet I with myself, and recall myself, and when, where, and what I have done, and under what feelings. There be all which I remember, either on my own experience, or other's credit. Out of the same store do I myself with the past continually combine fresh and fresh likenesses of things which I have experienced, or, from what I have experienced, have believed: and thence again infer future actions, events and hopes, and all these again I reflect on, as present. "I will do this or that," say I to myself, in that great receptacle of my mind, stored with the images of things so many and so great, "and this or that will follow." "O that this or that might be!" "God avert this or that!" So speak I to myself: and when I speak, the images of all I speak of are present, out of the same treasury of memory: nor would I speak of any thereof, were the images wanting.

Great is this force of memory, excessive great, O my God; a large and boundless chamber! Who ever sounded the bottom thereof? Yet is this a power of mine, and belongs unto my nature: nor do I myself comprehend all that I am. Therefore is the mind too straight to contain itself. And where should that be, which it containeth not of itself? Is it without it, and not within? How then doth it not comprehend itself? A wonderful admiration surprises me, amazement seizes me upon this. And men go abroad to admire the heights of mountains, the mighty billows of the sea, the broad tides of rivers, the compass of the ocean, and the circuits of the stars, and pass themselves by: nor wonder that when I spake of all these things, I did not see them with mine eyes, yet could not have spoken of them, unless I then actually saw the mountains, billows, rivers, stars which I had seen, and that ocean which I believe to be, inwardly in my memory, and that, with the same vast spaces between, as if I saw them abroad. Yet did not I by seeing draw them into myself, when with mine eyes I beheld them; nor are they themselves with me, but their images only. And I know by what sense of the body each was impressed upon me.

Yet not these alone does the immeasurable capacity of my memory retain. Here also is all, learned of the liberal sciences and as yet unforgotten: removed as it were to some inner place, which is yet no place: nor are they the images thereof, but the things themselves. For, what is literature, what the art of disputing, how many kinds of questions there be, whatsoever of these I know, in such manner exists in my memory, as that I have not taken in the image, and left out the thing, or that it should have sounded and passed away like a voice fixed on the ear by that impress, whereby it might be recalled, as if it sounded, when it no longer sounded; or as a smell while it passes and evaporates into air affects the sense of smell, whence it conveys into the memory an image of itself, which remembering, we renew, or as meat, which verily in the belly hath now no taste, and yet in the memory still in a manner tasteth; or as any thing which the body by touch perceiveth, and which when removed from us, the memory still conceives. For those things are not transmitted into the memory, but their images only are with an admirable swiftness caught up, and stored as it were in wondrous cabinets, and thence wonderfully by the act of remembering, brought forth.

But now when I hear that there be three kinds of questions, "Whether the thing be? What it is? Of what kind it is?" I do indeed hold the images of the sounds of which those words be composed, and that those sounds, with a noise passed through the air, and now are not. But the things themselves which are signified by those sounds, I never reached with any sense of my body, nor ever discerned them otherwise than in my mind: yet in my memory have I laid up not their images, but themselves. Which how they entered into me, let them say if they can; for I have gone over all the avenues of my flesh, but cannot find by which they entered. For the eyes say, "If those images were colored, we reported of them." The ears say, "If they sound, we gave knowledge of them." The nostrils say, "If they smell, they passed by us." The taste says, "Unless they have a savour, ask me not." The touch says, "If it have not size, I handled it not; if I handled it not, I gave no notice of it." Whence and how entered these things into my memory? I know not how. For when I learned them, I gave not credit to another man's mind, but recognized them in mine: and approving them for true, I commended them to it, laying them up as it were, whence I might bring them forth when I willed. In my heart then they were, even before I learned them, but in my memory they were not. Where then? Or wherefore, when they were spoken, did I acknowledge them, and said, "So is it, it is true," unless that they were already in the memory, but so thrown back and buried as it were in deeper recesses, that had not the suggestion of another drawn them forth I had perchance been unable to conceive of them?

Wherefore we find, that to learn these things whereof we imbibe not the images by our senses, but perceive within by themselves, without images, as they are, is nothing else, but by conception, to receive, and by marking to take heed that those things which the memory did before contain at random and unarranged, be laid up at hand as it were in that same memory where before they lay unknown, scattered and neglected, and so readily occur to the mind familiarized to them. And how many things of this kind does my memory hear which have been already found out, and as I said, placed as it were at hand, which we are said to have learned and come to know which were I for some short space of time to cease to call to mind, they are again so buried, and glide back, as it were, into the deeper recesses, that they must again, as if new, be thought out thence, for other abode they have none; but they must be drawn together again, that they may be known; that is to say, they must as it were be collected together from their dispersion: whence to word "cogitation" is derived. For *cogo* (collect) and *cogito* (re-collect) have the same relation to each other as *ago* and *agito*, *facio* and *factito*. But the mind hath appropriated to itself this word (cogitation), so that, not what is "collected" any how, but what is "recollected," that is, brought together, in the mind. is properly said to be cogitated, or thought upon.

The memory containeth also reasons and laws innumerable of numbers and dimensions, none of which hath any bodily sense impressed; seeing they have neither color, nor sound, nor taste, nor smell, nor touch. I have heard the sound of the words whereby when discussed they are denoted: but the sounds are other than the things. For the sounds are other in Greek than in Latin; but the things are neither Greek, nor Latin, nor any other language. I have seen the lines of architects, the very finest, like a spider's thread; but those are still different, they are not the images of those lines which the eye of flesh showed me: he knoweth them, whosoever without any conception whatsoever of a body, recognizes them within himself. I have perceived also the numbers of the things with which we number all the senses of my body; but those numbers wherewith we number are different, nor are they the images of these, and therefore they indeed are. Let him who seeth them not, deride me for saying these things, and I will pity him, while he derides me.

All these things I remember, and how I learnt them I remember. Many things also most falsely objected against them have I heard, and remember; which though they be false, yet is it not false that I remember them; and I remember also that I have discerned betwixt those truths and these falsehoods objected to them. And I perceive that the present discerning of these things is different from remembering that I oftentimes discerned them, when I often thought upon them. I both remember then to have often understood these things; and what I now discern and understand, I lay up in my memory, that hereafter I may remember that I understand it now. So then I remember also to have remembered; as if hereafter I shall call to remembrance, that I have now been able to remember these things, by the force of memory shall I call it to remembrance.

The same memory contains also the affections of my mind, not in the same manner that my mind itself contains them, when it feels them: but far otherwise, according to a power of its own. For without rejoicing I remember myself to have joyed; and without sorrow do I recollect my past sorrow. And that I once feared, I review without fear: and without desire call to mind a past desire. Sometimes, on the contrary, with joy do I remember my fore-past sorrow, and with sorrow, joy. Which is not wonderful, as to the body; for mind is one thing, body another. If I therefore with joy remember some past pain of body, it is not so wonderful. But now seeing this very memory itself is mind (for when we give a thing in charge, to be kept in memory, we say, "See that you keep it in mind"; and when we forget, we say, "It did not come to my mind," and, "It slipped out of my mind," calling the memory itself the mind); this being so, how is it that when with joy I remember my past sorrow, the mind hath joy, the memory hath sorrow; the mind upon the joyfulness which is in it, is joyful, yet the memory upon the sadness which is in it, is not sad? Does the memory perchance not belong to the mind? Who will say so? The memory then is, as it were, the belly of the mind, and joy and sadness, like sweet and bitter food: which, when committed to the memory, are as it were passed into the belly, where they may be stowed, but cannot taste. Ridiculous it is to imagine these to be alike; and yet are they not utterly unlike.

But, behold, out of my memory I bring it, when I say there be four perturbations of the mind, desire, joy, fear, sorrow; and whatsoever I can dispute thereon, by dividing each into its subordinate species, and by defining it, in my memory find I what to say, and thence do I bring it; yet am I not disturbed by any of these perturbations, when by calling them to mind, I remember them; yea, and before I recalled and brought them back, they were there: and therefore could they, by recollection, thence be brought. Perchance, then, as meat is by chewing the cud brought up out of the belly, so by recollection these out of the memory. Why then does not the disputer, thus recollecting, taste in the mouth of his musing the sweetness of joy, or the bitterness of sorrow? Is the comparison unlike in this, because not in all respects like? For who would willingly speak thereof, if so oft as we name grief or fear, we should be compelled to be sad or fearful? And yet could we not speak of them,

did we not find in our memory, not only the sounds of the names according to the images impressed by the senses of the body, but notions of the very things themselves which we never received by any avenue of the body, but which the mind itself perceiving by the experience of its own passions, committed to the memory, or the memory of itself retained, without being committed unto it.

But whether by images or no, who can readily say? Thus, I name a stone, I name the sun, the things themselves not being present to my senses, but their images to my memory. I name a bodily pain, yet it is not present with me, when nothing aches: yet unless its image were present to my memory, I should not know what to say thereof, nor in discoursing discern pain from pleasure. I name bodily health; being sound in body, the thing itself is present with me; yet, unless its image also were present in my memory, I could by no means recall what the sound of this name should signify. Nor would the sick, when health were named, recognize what were spoken, unless the same image were by the force of memory retained, although the thing itself were absent from the body. I name numbers whereby we number; and not their images, but themselves are present in my memory. I name the image of the sun, and that image is present in my memory. For I recall not the image of its image, but the image itself is present to me, calling it to mind. I name memory, and I recognize what I name. And where do I recognize it, but in the memory itself? Is it also present to itself by its image, and not by itself?

What, when I name forgetfulness, and withal recognize what I name? Whence should I recognize it, did I not remember it? I speak not of the sound of the name, but of the thing which it signifies: which if I had forgotten, I could not recognize what that sound signifies. When then I remember memory, memory itself is, through itself, present with itself; but when I remember forgetfulness, there are present both memory and forgetfulness; memory whereby I remember, forgetfulness which I remember. But what is forgetfulness, but the privation of memory? How then is it present that I remember it, since when present I cannot remember? But if what we remember we hold it in memory, yet, unless we did remember forgetfulness, we could never at the hearing of the name recognize the thing thereby signified, then forgetfulness is retained by memory. Present then it is, that we forget not, and being so, we forget. It is to be understood from this that forgetfulness when we remember it, is not present to the memory by itself but by its image: because if it were present by itself, it would not cause us to remember, but to forget. Who now shall search out this? Who shall comprehend how it is?

Lord, I, truly, toil therein, yea and toil in myself: I am become a heavy soil requiring over much sweat of the brow. For we are not now searching out the regions of heaven, or measuring the distances of the stars, or enquiring the balancings of the earth. It is I myself who remember. I the mind. It is not so wonderful, if what I myself am not, be far from me. But what is nearer to me than myself? And to, the force of mine own memory is not understood by me; though I cannot so much as name myself without it. For what shall I say, when it is clear to me that I remember forgetfulness? Shall I say that that is not in my memory, which I remember? Or shall I say that forgetfulness is for this purpose in my memory, that I might not forget? Both were most absurd. What third way is there? How can I say that the image of forgetfulness is retained by my memory, not forgetfulness itself, when I remember it? How could I say this either, seeing that when the image of any thing is impressed on the memory, the thing itself must needs be first present, whence that image may be impressed? For thus do I remember Carthage, thus all places where I have been, thus men's faces whom I have seen, and things reported by the other senses; thus the health or sickness of the body. For when these things were present, my memory received from them images, which being present with me, I might look on and bring back in my mind, when I remembered them in their absence. If then this forgetfulness is retained in the memory through its image, not through itself, then plainly itself was once present, that its image might be taken. But when it was present, how did it write its image in the memory, seeing that forgetfulness by its presence effaces even what it finds already noted? And yet, in whatever way, although that way be past conceiving and explaining, yet certain am I that I remember forgetfulness itself also, whereby what we remember is effaced.

Great is the power of memory, a fearful thing, O my God, a deep and boundless manifoldness; and this thing is the mind, and this am I myself. What am I then, O my God? What nature am I? A life various and manifold, and exceeding immense. Behold in the plains, and caves, and caverns of my memory, innumerable and innumerably full of innumerable kinds of things, either through images, as all bodies; or by actual presence, as the arts; or by certain notions or impressions, as the affections of the mind, which, even when the mind doth not feel, the memory retaineth, while yet whatsoever is in the memory is also in the mind—over all these do I run. I fly; I dive on this side and on that, as far as I can, and there is no end. So great is the force of memory, so great the force of life, even in the mortal life of man.

BOOK XI

Lord, since eternity is Thine, art Thou ignorant of what I say to Thee? Or dost Thou see in time, what passeth in time? Why then do I lay in order before Thee so many relations? Not, of a truth, that Thou mightest learn them through me, but to stir up mine own and my readers' devotions towards Thee, that we may all say, Great is the Lord, and greatly to be praised. I have said already; and again will say, for love of Thy love do I this. For we pray also, and yet Truth hath said, Your Father knoweth what you have need of, before you ask. It is then our affections which we lay open unto Thee, confessing our own miseries, and Thy mercies upon us, that Thou mayest free us wholly, since Thou hast begun, that we may cease to be wretched in ourselves, and be blessed in Thee; seeing Thou hast called us, to become poor in spirit, and meek, and mourners, and hungering and athirst after righteousness, and merciful, and pure in heart, and peace-makers. See, I have told Thee many things, as I could and as I would, because Thou first wouldest that I should confess unto Thee, my Lord God. For Thou art good, for Thy mercy endureth for ever.

But how shall I suffice with the tongue of my pen to utter all Thy exhortations, and all Thy terrors, and comforts, and guidances, whereby Thou broughtest me to preach Thy Word, and dispense Thy Sacrament to Thy people? And if I suffice to utter them in order, the drops of time are precious with me; and long have I burned to meditate in Thy law, and therein to confess to Thee my skill and unskillfulness, the daybreak of Thy enlightening, and the remnants of my darkness, until infirmity be swallowed up by strength. And I would not have aught besides steal away those hours which I find free from the necessities of refreshing my body and the powers of my mind, and of the service which we owe to men, or which though we owe not, we yet pay.

O Lord my god, give ear unto my prayer, and let Thy mercy hearken unto my desire; because it is anxious not for myself alone, but would serve brotherly charity; and Thou seest my heart, that so it is. I would sacrifice to Thee the service of my thought and tongue; do Thou give me, what I may offer Thee. For I am poor and needy, Thou rich to all that call upon Thee; Who, inaccessible to care, carest for us. Circumcise from all rashness and all lying both my inward and outward lips: let Thy Scriptures be my pure delights; let me not be deceived in them, nor deceive out of them. Lord, hearken and pity, O Lord my God, Light of the blind, and Strength of the weak; yea also Light of those that see, and Strength of the strong; hearken unto my soul, and hear it crying out of the depths. For if Thine ears be not with us in the depths also, whither shall we go? Whither cry? The day is Thine, and the night is Thine; at Thy beck the moments flee by. Grant thereof a space for our meditations in the hidden things of Thy law, and close it not against us who knock. For not in vain wouldest Thou have the darksome secrets of so many pages written; nor are those forests without their harts which retire therein and range and walk; feed, lie down, and ruminate. Perfect me, O Lord, and reveal them unto me. Behold, Thy voice is my joy; Thy voice exceedeth the abundance of pleasures. Give what I love: for I do love; and this hast Thou given: forsake not Thy own gifts, nor despise Thy green herb that thirsteth. Let me confess unto Thee whatsoever I shall find in Thy books, and hear the voice of praise, and drink in Thee, and meditate on the wonderful things out of Thy law; even from the beginning, wherein Thou madest the heaven and the earth, unto the everlasting reigning of Thy holy city with Thee.

Lord, have mercy on me, and hear my desire. For it is not, I deem, of the earth, not of gold and silver, and precious stones, or gorgeous apparel, or honors and offices, or the pleasures of the flesh, or necessaries for the body and for this life of our pilgrimage: all which shall be added unto those that seek Thy kingdom and Thy righteousness. Behold, O Lord my God, wherein is my desire. The wicked have told me of delights, but not such as Thy law, O Lord. Behold,

wherein is my desire. Behold, Father, behold, and see and approve; and be it pleasing in the sight of Thy mercy, that I may find grace before Thee, that the inward parts of Thy words be opened to me knocking. I beseech by our Lord Jesus Christ Thy Son, the Man of Thy right hand, the Son of man, whom Thou hast established for Thyself, as Thy Mediator and ours, through Whom Thou soughtest us, not seeking Thee, but soughtest us, that we might seek Thee,— Thy Word, through Whom Thou madest all things, and among them, me also:— Thy Only-Begotten, through Whom Thou calledst to adoption the believing people, and therein me also:— I beseech Thee by Him, who sitteth at Thy right hand, and intercedeth with Thee for us, in Whom are hidden all the treasures of wisdom and knowledge. These do I seek in Thy books. Of Him did Moses write; this saith Himself; this saith the Truth.

I would hear and understand, how "In the Beginning Thou madest the heaven and earth." Moses wrote this, wrote and departed, passed hence from Thee to Thee; nor is he now before me. For if he were, I would hold him and ask him, and beseech him by Thee to open these things unto me, and would lay the ears of my body to the sounds bursting out of his mouth. And should he speak Hebrew, in vain will it strike on my senses, nor would aught of it touch my mind; but if Latin, I should know what he said. But whence should I know, whether he spake truth? Yea, and if I knew this also, should I know it from him? Truly within me, within, in the chamber of my thoughts, Truth, neither Hebrew, nor Greek, nor Latin, nor barbarian, without organs of voice or tongue, or sound of syllables, would say, "It is truth," and I forthwith should say confidently to that man of Thine, "thou sayest truly." Whereas then I cannot enquire of him, Thee, Thee I beseech, O Truth, full of Whom he spake truth, Thee, my God, I beseech, forgive my sins; and Thou, who gavest him Thy servant to speak these things, give to me also to understand them.

Behold, the heavens and the earth are; they proclaim that they were created: for they change and vary. Whereas whatsoever hath not been made, and yet is, hath nothing in it, which before it had not: and this it is, to change and vary. They proclaim also, that they made not themselves; "therefore we are, because we have been made; we were not therefore, before we were, so as to make ourselves." Now the evidence of the thing, is the voice of the speakers. Thou therefore, Lord, madest them; who art beautiful, for they are beautiful; who art good, for they are good; who art, for they are; yet are they not beautiful nor good, nor are they, as Thou their Creator art; compared with Whom, they are neither beautiful, nor good, nor are. This we know, thanks be to Thee. And our knowledge, compared with Thy knowledge, is ignorance.

But how didst Thou make the heaven and the earth? And what the engine of Thy so mighty fabric? For it was not as a human artificer, forming one body from another, according to the discretion of his mind, which can in some way invest with such a form, as it seeth in itself by its inward eye. And whence should he be able to do this, unless Thou hadst made that mind? And he invests with a form what already existeth, and hath a being, as clay, or stone, or wood, or gold, or the like. And whence should they be, hadst not Thou appointed them? Thou madest the artificer his body, Thou the mind commanding the limbs, Thou the matter whereof he makes any thing; Thou the apprehension whereby to take in his art, and see within what he doth without; Thou the sense of his body; whereby, as by an interpreter, he may from mind to matter, convey that which he doth, and report to his mind what is done; that it within may consult the truth, which presideth over itself, whether it be well done or no. All these praise Thee, the Creator of all. But how dost Thou make them? How, O God, didst Thou make heaven and earth? Verily, neither in the heaven, nor in the earth, didst Thou make heaven and earth; nor in the air, or waters, seeing these also belong to the heaven and the earth; nor in the whole world didst Thou make the whole world; because there was no place where to make it, before it was made, that it might be. Nor didst Thou hold any thing in Thy hand, whereof to make heaven and earth. For whence shouldest Thou have this, which Thou hadst not made, thereof to make any thing? For what is, but because Thou art? Therefore Thou spokest, and they were made, and in Thy Word Thou madest them.

But how didst Thou speak? In the way that the voice came out of the cloud, saying, This is my beloved Son? For that voice passed by and passed away, began and ended; the syllables sounded and passed away, the second after the first, the third after the second, and so forth in order, until the last after the rest, and silence after the last. Whence it is abundantly clear and plain that the motion of a creature expressed it, itself temporal, serving Thy eternal will. And these Thy words, created for a time, the outward ear reported to the intelligent soul, whose inward ear lay listening to Thy Eternal Word. But she compared these words sounding in time, with that Thy Eternal Word in silence, and said "It is different, far different. These words are far beneath me, nor are they, because they flee and pass away; but the Word of my Lord abideth above me for ever." If then in sounding and passing words Thou saidst that heaven and earth should be made, and so madest heaven and earth, there was a corporeal creature before heaven and earth, by whose motions in time that voice might take his course in time. But there was nought corporeal before heaven and earth; or if there were, surely Thou hadst, without such a passing voice, created that, whereof to make this passing voice, by which to say, Let the heaven and the earth be made. For whatsoever that were, whereof such a voice were made, unless by Thee it were made, it could not be at all. By what Word then didst Thou speak, that a body might be made, whereby these words again might be made?

Thou callest us then to understand the Word, God, with Thee God, Which is spoken eternally, and by It are all things spoken eternally. For what was spoken was not spoken successively, one thing concluded that the next might be spoken, but all things together and eternally. Else have we time and change; and not a true eternity nor true immortality. This I know, O my God, and give thanks. I know, I confess to Thee, O Lord, and with me there knows and blesses Thee, whoso is not unthankful to assure Truth. We know, Lord, we know; since inasmuch as anything is not which was, and is, which was not, so far forth it dieth and ariseth. Nothing then of Thy Word doth give place or replace, because It is truly immortal and eternal. And therefore unto the Word coeternal with Thee Thou dost at once and eternally say all that Thou dost say; and whatever Thou sayest shall be made is made; nor dost Thou make, otherwise than by saying; and yet are not all things made together, or everlasting, which Thou makest by saying.

Why, I beseech Thee, O Lord my God? I see it in a way; but how to express it, I know not, unless it be, that whatsoever begins to be, and leaves off to be, begins then, and leaves off then, when in Thy eternal Reason it is known, that it ought to begin or leave off; in which Reason nothing beginneth or leaveth off. This is Thy Word, which is also "the Beginning, because also It speaketh unto us." Thus in the Gospel He speaketh through the flesh; and this sounded outwardly in the ears of men; that it might be believed and sought inwardly, and found in the eternal Verity; where the good and only Master teacheth all His disciples. There, Lord, hear I Thy voice speaking unto me; because He speaketh us, who teacheth us; but He that teacheth us not, though He speaketh, to us He speaketh not. Who now teacheth us, but the unchangeable Truth? for even when we are admonished through a changeable creature, we are but led to the unchangeable Truth; where we learn truly, while we stand and hear Him, and rejoice greatly because of the Bridegroom's voice, restoring us to Him, from Whom we are. And therefore the Beginning, because unless It abided, there should not, when we went astray, be whither to return. But when we return from error, it is through knowing; and that we may know, He teacheth us, because He is the Beginning, and speaking unto us.

In this Beginning, O God, hast Thou made heaven and earth, in Thy Word, in Thy Son, in Thy Power, in Thy Wisdom, in Thy Truth: wondrously speaking, and wondrously making. Who shall comprehend? Who declare it? What is that which gleams through me, and strikes my heart without hurting it; and I shudder and kindle? I shudder, inasmuch as I unlike it; I kindle, inasmuch as I am like it. It is Wisdom, Wisdom's self which gleameth through me; severing my cloudiness which yet again mantles over me, fainting from it, through the darkness which for my punishment gathers upon me. For my strength is brought down in need, so that I cannot support my blessings, that Thou, Lord, Who hast been gracious to all mine iniquities, shalt heal all my infirmities. For Thou shalt also redeem my life from corruption, and crown me with loving kindness and tender mercies, and shalt satisfy my desire with good things, because my youth shall be renewed like an eagle's. For in hope we are saved, wherefore we through patience wait for Thy promises. Let him that is able, hear Thee inwardly discoursing out of Thy oracle: I will boldly cry out, How wonderful are Thy works, O Lord, in Wisdom hast Thou made them all; and this Wisdom is the Beginning, and in that Beginning didst Thou make heaven and earth.

Lo, are they not full of their old leaven, who say to us, "What was God doing before He made heaven and earth? For if (say they) He were unemployed and wrought not, why does He not also henceforth, and for ever, as He did heretofore? For did any new motion arise in God, and a new will to make a creature, which He had never before made, how then would that be a true eternity, where there ariseth a will, which was not? For the will of God is not a creature, but before the creature; seeing nothing could be created, unless the will of the Creator had preceded. The will of God then belongeth to His very Substance. And if aught have arisen in God's Substance, which before was not, that Substance cannot be truly called eternal. But if the will of God has been from eternity that the creature should be, why was not the creature also from eternity?"

Who speak thus, do not yet understand Thee, O Wisdom of God, Light of souls, understand not yet how the things be made, which by Thee, and in Thee are made; yet they strive to comprehend things eternal, whilst their heart fluttereth between the motions of things past and to come, and is still unstable. Who shall hold it, and fix it, that it be settled awhile, and awhile catch the glory of that everfixed Eternity, and compare it with the times which are never fixed, and see that it cannot be compared; and that a long time cannot become long, but out of many motions passing by, which cannot be prolonged altogether; but that in the Eternal nothing passeth, but the whole is present; whereas no time is all at once present; and that all time past, is driven on by time to come, and all to come followeth upon the past; and all past and to come, is created, and flows out of that which is ever present? Who shall hold the heart of man, that it may stand still, and see how eternity ever still-standing, neither past nor to come, uttereth the times past and to come? Can my hand do this, or the hand of my mouth by speech bring about a thing so great?

See, I answer him that asketh, "What did God before He made heaven and earth?" I answer not as one is said to have done merrily (eluding the pressure of the question), "He was preparing hell (saith he) for pryers into mysteries." It is one thing to answer enquiries, another to make sport of enquirers. So I answer not; for rather had I answer, "I know not," what I know not, than so as to raise a laugh at him who asketh deep things and gain praise for one who answereth false things. But I say that Thou, our God, art the Creator of every creature: and if by the name "heaven and earth," every creature be understood; I boldly say, "that before God made heaven and earth, He did not make any thing." For if He made, what did He make but a creature? And would I knew whatsoever I desire to know to my profit, as I know, that no creature was made, before there was made any creature.

But if any excursive brain rove over the images of forepassed times, and wonder that Thou the God Almighty and All-creating and All-supporting, Maker of heaven and earth, didst for innumerable ages forbear from so great a work, before Thou wouldest make it; let him awake and consider, that he wonders at false conceits. For whence could innumerable ages pass by, which Thou madest not, Thou the Author and Creator of all ages? Or what times should there be, which were not made by Thee? Or how should they pass by, if they never were? Seeing then Thou art the Creator of all times, if any time was before Thou madest heaven and earth, why say they that Thou didst forego working? For that very time didst Thou make, nor could times pass by, before Thou madest those times. But if before heaven and earth there was no time, why is it demanded, what Thou then didst? For there was no "then," when there was no time.

Nor dost Thou by time, precede time: else shouldest Thou not precede all times. But Thou precedest all things past, by the sublimity of an ever-present eternity; and surpassest all future because they are future, and when they come, they shall be past; but Thou art the Same, and Thy years fail not. Thy years neither come nor go; whereas ours both come and go, that they all may come. Thy years stand together, because they do stand; nor are departing thrust out by coming years, for they pass not away; but ours shall all be, when they shall no more be. Thy years are one day; and Thy day is not daily, but To-day, seeing Thy Today gives not place unto tomorrow, for neither doth it replace yesterday. Thy Today, is Eternity; therefore didst Thou beget The Coeternal,

to whom Thou saidst, This day have I begotten Thee. Thou hast made all things; and before all times Thou art: neither in any time was time not.

At no time then hadst Thou not made any thing, because time itself Thou madest. And no times are coeternal with Thee, because Thou abidest; but if they abode, they should not be times. For what is time? Who can readily and briefly explain this? Who can even in thought comprehend it, so as to utter a word about it? But what in discourse do we mention more familiarly and knowingly, than time? And, we understand, when we speak of it; we understand also, when we hear it spoken of by another. What then is time? If no one asks me, I know: if I wish to explain it to one that asketh, I know not: yet I say boldly that I know, that if nothing passed away, time past were not; and if nothing were coming, a time to come were not; and if nothing were, time present were not. Those two times then, past and to come, how are they, seeing the past now is not, and that to come is not yet? But the present, should it always be present, and never pass into time past, verily it should not be time, but eternity. If time present (if it is to be time) only cometh into existence, because it passeth into time past, how can we say that either this is, whose cause of being is, that it shall not be; so, namely, that we cannot truly say that time is, but because it is tending not to be?

And yet we say, "a long time" and "a short time"; still, only of time past or to come. A long time past (for example) we call a hundred years since; and a long time to come, a hundred years hence. But a short time past, we call (suppose) often days since; and a short time to come, often days hence. But in what sense is that long or short, which is not? For the past, is not now; and the future, is not yet. Let us not then say, "it is long"; but of the past, "it hath been long"; and of the future, "it will be long." O my Lord, my Light, shall not here also Thy Truth mock at man? For that past time which was long, was it long when it was now past, or when it was yet present? For then might it be long, when there was, what could be long; but when past, it was no longer; wherefore neither could that be long, which was not at all. Let us not then say, "time past hath been long": for we shall not find, what hath been long, seeing that since it was past, it is no more, but let us say, "that present time was long"; because, when it was present, it was long. For it had not yet passed away, so as not to be: and therefore there was, what could be long; but after it was past, that ceased also to be long, which ceased to be.

Let us see then, Thou soul of man, whether present time can be long: for to thee it is given to feel and to measure length of time. What wilt thou answer me? Are a hundred years, when present, a long time? See first, whether a hundred years can be present. For if the first of these years be now current, it is present, but the other ninety and nine are to come, and therefore are not yet, but if the second year be current, one is now past, another present, the rest to come. And so if we assume any middle year of this hundred to be present, all before it, are past; all after it, to come; wherefore a hundred years cannot be present. But see at least whether that one which is now current, itself is present; for if the current month be its first, the rest are to come; if the second, the first is already past, and the rest are not yet Therefore, neither is the year now current present: and if not present as a whole, then is not the year present. For twelve months are a year; of which whatever by the current month is present; the rest past, or to come. Although neither is that current month present: but one day only; the rest being to come, if it be the first; past, if the last; if any of the middle, then amid past and to come.

See how the present time, which alone we found could be called long, is abridged to the length scarce of one day. But let us examine that also; because neither is one day present as a whole. For it is made up of four and twenty hours of night and day: of which, the first hath the rest to come; the last hath them past; and any of the middle hath those before it past, those behind it to come. Yea, that one hour passeth away in flying particles. Whatsoever of it hath flown away, is past; whatsoever remaineth, is to come. If an instant of time be conceived, which cannot be divided into the smallest particles of moments, that alone is it, which may be called present. Which yet flies with such speed from future to past, as not to be lengthened out with the least stay. For if it be, it is divided into past and future. The present hath no space. Where then is the time, which we may call long? Is it to come? Of it we do not say, "it is long"; because it is not yet, so as to be long; but we say, "it will be long." When therefore will it be? For if even then, when it is

yet to come, it shall not be long (because what can be long, as yet is not), and so it shall then be long, when from future which as yet is not, it shall begin now to be, and have become present, that so there should exist what may be long; then does time present cry out in the words above, that it cannot be long.

And yet, Lord, we perceive intervals of times, and compare them, and say, some are shorter, and others longer. We measure also, how much longer or shorter this time is than that; and we answer, "This is double, or treble; and that, but once, or only just so much as that." But we measure times as they are passing, by perceiving them; but past, which now are not, or the future, which are not yet, who can measure? Unless a man shall presume to say, that can be measured, which is not. When then time is passing, it may be perceived and measured; but when it is past, it cannot, because it is not.

I ask, Father, I affirm not: O my God, rule and guide me. "Who will tell me that there are not three times (as we learned when boys, and taught boys), past, present, and future; but present only, because those two are not? Or are they also; and when from future it becometh present, doth it come out of some secret place; and so, when retiring, from present it becometh past? For where did they, who foretold things to come, see them, if as yet they be not? For that which is not, cannot be seen. And they who relate things past, could not relate them, if in mind they did not discern them, and if they were not, they could no way be discerned. Things then past and to come, are."

Permit me, Lord, to seek further. O my hope, let not my purpose be confounded. For if times past and to come be, I would know where they be. Which yet if I cannot, yet I know, wherever they be, they are not there as future, or past, but present. For if there also they be future, they are not yet there; if there also they be past, they are no longer there. Wheresoever then is whatsoever is, it is only as present. Although when past facts are related, there are drawn out of the memory, not the things themselves which are past, but words which, conceived by the images of the things, they, in passing, have through the senses left as traces in the mind. Thus my childhood, which now is not, is in time past, which now is not: but now when I recall its image, and tell of it, I behold it in the present, because it is still in my memory. Whether there be a like cause of foretelling things to come also; that of things which as yet are not, the images may be perceived before, already existing, I confess, O my God, I know not. This indeed I know, that we generally think before on our future actions, and that that forethinking is present, but the action whereof we forethink is not yet, because it is to come. Which, when we have set upon, and have begun to do what we were forethinking, then shall that action be; because then it is no longer future, but present.

Which way soever then this secret fore-perceiving of things to come be; that only can be seen, which is. But what now is, is not future, but present. When then things to come are said to be seen, it is not themselves which as yet are not (that is, which are to be), but their causes perchance or signs are seen, which already are. Therefore they are not future but present to those who now see that, from which the future, being foreconceived in the mind, is foretold. Which fore-conceptions again now are; and those who foretell those things, do behold the conceptions present before them. Let now the numerous variety of things furnish me some example. I behold the day-break, I foreshow, that the sun, is about to rise. What I behold, is present; what I foresignify, to come; not the sun, which already is; but the sun-rising, which is not yet. And yet did I not in my mind imagine the sun-rising itself (as now while I speak of it), I could not foretell it. But neither is that day-break which I discern in the sky, the sun-rising, although it goes before it; nor that imagination of my mind; which two are seen now present, that the other which is to be may be foretold. Future things then are not yet: and if they be not yet, they are not; and if they are not, they cannot be seen; yet foretold they may be from things present, which are already, and are seen.

Thou then, Ruler of Thy creation, by what way dost Thou teach souls things to come? For Thou didst teach Thy Prophets. By what way dost Thou, to whom nothing is to come, teach things to come; or rather of the future, dost teach things present? For, what is not, neither can it be taught. Too far is this way of my ken: it is too mighty for me, I cannot attain unto it; but from Thee I can, when Thou shalt vouchsafe it, O sweet light of my hidden eyes.

What now is clear and plain is, that neither things to come nor past are. Nor is it properly said, "there be three times, past, present, and to come": yet perchance it might be properly said, "there be three times: a present of things past, a present of things present, and a present of things future." For these three do exist in some sort, in the soul, but otherwhere do I not see them; present of things past, memory; present of things present, sight; present of things future, expectation. If thus we be permitted to speak, I see three times, and I confess there are three. Let it be said too, "there be three times, past, present, and to come": in our incorrect way. See, I object not, nor gainsay, nor find fault, if what is so said be but understood, that neither what is to be, now is, nor what is past. For but few things are there, which we speak properly, most things improperly; still the things intended are understood.

I said then even now, we measure times as they pass, in order to be able to say this time is twice so much as that one: or, this is just so much as that; and so of any other parts of time, which be measurable. Wherefore, as I said, we measure times as they pass. And if any should ask me, "How knowest thou?" I might answer, "I know, that we do measure, nor can we measure things that are not; and things past and to come, are not." But time present how do we measure, seeing it hath no space? It is measured while passing, but when it shall have passed, it is not measured; for there will be nothing to be measured. But whence, by what way, and whither passes it while it is a measuring? Whence, but from the future? Which way, but through the present? Whither, but into the past? From that therefore, which is not yet, through that, which hath no space, into that, which now is not. Yet what do we measure, if not time in some space? For we do not say, single, and double, and triple, and equal, or any other like way that we speak of time, except of spaces of times. In what space then do we measure time passing? In the future, whence it passeth through? But what is not yet, we measure not. Or in the present, by which it passes? But no space, we do not measure; or in the past, to which it passes? But neither do we measure that, which now is not.

My soul is on fire to know this most intricate enigma. Shut it not up, O Lord my God, good Father; through Christ I beseech Thee, do not shut up these usual, yet hidden things, from my desire, that it be hindered from piercing into them; but let them dawn through Thy enlightening mercy, O Lord. Whom shall I enquire of concerning these things? And to whom shall I more fruitfully confess my ignorance, than to Thee, to Whom these my studies, so vehemently kindled toward Thy Scriptures, are not troublesome? Give what I love; for I do love, and this hast Thou given me. Give, Father, Who truly knowest to give good gifts unto Thy children. Give, because I have taken upon me to know, and trouble is before me until Thou openest it. By Christ I beseech Thee, in His Name, Holy of holies, let no man disturb me. For I believed, and therefore do I speak. This is my hope, for this do I live, that I may contemplate the delights of the Lord. Behold, Thou hast made my days old, and they pass away, and how, I know not. And we talk of time, and time, and times, and times, "How long time is it since he said this"; "how long time since he did this"; and "how long time since I saw that"; and "this syllable hath double time to that single short syllable." These words we speak, and these we hear, and are understood, and understand. Most manifest and ordinary they are, and the self-same things again are but too deeply hidden, and the discovery of them were new.

I heard once from a learned man, that the motions of the sun, moon, and stars, constituted time, and I assented not. For why should not the motions of all bodies rather be times? Or, if the lights of heaven should cease, and a potter's wheel run round, should there be no time by which we might measure those whirlings, and say, that either it moved with equal pauses, or if it turned sometimes slower, otherwhiles quicker, that some rounds were longer, other shorter? Or, while we were saying this, should we not also be speaking in time? Or, should there in our words be some syllables short, others long, but because those sounded in a shorter time, these in longer? God, grant to men to see in a small thing notices common to things great and small. The stars and lights of heaven, are also for signs, and for seasons, and for years, and for days; they are: yet neither should I say, that the going round of that wooden wheel was a day, nor yet he, that it was therefore no time.

I desire to know the force and nature of time, by which we measure the motions of bodies, and say (for example) this motion is twice as long as that. For I ask, seeing "day" denotes not the stay only of the sun upon the earth (according to which day is one thing, night another); but also its whole circuit from east to east again; according to which we say, "there passed so many days," the night being included when we say, "so many days," and the nights not reckoned apart—seeing then a day is completed by the motion of the sun and by his circuit from east to east again, I ask, does the motion alone make the day, or the stay in which that motion is completed, or both? For if the first be the day; then should we have a day, although the sun should finish that course in so small a space of time, as one hour comes to. If the second, then should not that make a day, if between one sunrise and another there were but so short a stay, as one hour comes to; but the sun must go four and twenty times about, to complete one day. If both, then neither could that be called a day; if the sun should run his whole round in the space of one hour; nor that, if, while the sun stood still, so much time should overpass, as the sun usually makes his whole course in, from morning to morning. I will not therefore now ask, what that is which is called day; but, what time is, whereby we, measuring the circuit of the sun, should say that it was finished in half the time it was wont, if so be it was finished in so small a space as twelve hours; and comparing both times, should call this a single time, that a double time; even supposing the sun to run his round from east to east, sometimes in that single, sometimes in that double time. Let no man then tell me, that the motions of the heavenly bodies constitute times, because, when at the prayer of one, the sun had stood still, till he could achieve his victorious battle, the sun stood still, but time went on. For in its own allotted space of time was that battle waged and ended. I perceive time then to be a certain extension. But do I perceive it, or seem to perceive it? Thou, Light and Truth, wilt show me.

Dost Thou bid me assent, if any define time to be "motion of a body?" Thou dost not bid me. For that no body is moved, but in time, I hear; this Thou sayest; but that the motion of a body is time, I hear not; Thou sayest it not. For when a body is moved, I by time measure, how long it moveth, from the time it began to move until it left off? And if I did not see whence it began; and it continue to move so that I see not when it ends, I cannot measure, save perchance from the time I began, until I cease to see. And if I look long, I can only pronounce it to be a long time, but not how long; because when we say "how long," we do it by comparison; as, "this is as long as that," or "twice so long as that," or the like. But when we can mark the distances of the places, whence and whither goeth the body moved, or his parts, if it moved as in a lathe, then can we say precisely, in how much time the motion of that body or his part, from this place unto that, was finished. Seeing therefore the motion of a body is one thing, that by which we measure how long it is, another; who sees not, which of the two is rather to be called time? For and if a body be sometimes moved, sometimes stands still, then we measure, not his motion only, but his standing still too by time; and we say, "it stood still, as much as it moved"; or "it stood still twice or thrice so long as it moved"; or any other space which our measuring hath either ascertained, or guessed; more or less, as we use to say. Time then is not the motion of a body.

And I confess to Thee, O Lord, that I yet know not what time is, and again I confess unto Thee, O Lord, that I know that I speak this in time, and that having long spoken of time, that very "long" is not long, but by the pause of time. How then know I this, seeing I know not what time is? Or is it perchance that I know not how to express what I know? Woe is me, that do not even know, that I know not. Behold, O my God, before Thee I lie not: but as I speak, so is my heart. Thou shalt light my candle; Thou, O Lord my God, wilt enlighten my darkness.

Does not my soul most truly confess unto Thee, that I do measure times? Do I then measure, O my God, and know not what I measure? I measure the motion of a body in time: and the time itself do I not measure? Or could I indeed measure the motion of a body how long it were, and in how long space it could come from this place to that, without measuring the time in which it is moved? This same time then, how do I measure? Do we by a shorter time measure a longer, as by the space of a cubit, the space of a rood? For so indeed we seem by the space of a short syllable, to measure the space of a long syllable, and to say that this is double the other. Thus measure we the spaces of stanzas, by the spaces of the verses, and the spaces of the verses, by the spaces of the feet, and the spaces of the feet, by the spaces of the syllables, and the spaces of long, by the space of short syllables; not measuring by pages (for then we measure spaces, not times); but when we utter the words and they pass by, and we say "it is a long stanza, because composed of so many verses; long verses, because consisting of so many feet; long feet, because prolonged by so many syllables; a long syllable because double to a short one. But neither do we this way obtain any certain measure of time; because it may be, that a shorter verse, pronounced more fully, may take up more time than a longer, pronounced hurriedly. And so for a verse, a foot, a syllable. Whence it seemed to me, that time is nothing else than protraction; but of what, I know not; and I marvel, if it be not of the mind itself? For what, I beseech Thee, O my God, do I measure, when I say, either indefinitely "this is a longer time than that," or definitely "this is double that"? That I measure time, I know; and yet I measure not time to come, for it is not yet; nor present, because it is not protracted by any space; nor past, because it now is not. What then do I measure? Times passing, not past? For so I said.

Courage, my mind, and press on mightily. God is our helper, He made us, and not we ourselves. Press on where truth begins to dawn. Suppose, now, the voice of a body begins to sound, and does sound, and sounds on, and list, it ceases; it is silence now, and that voice is past, and is no more a voice. Before it sounded, it was to come, and could not be measured, because as yet it was not, and now it cannot, because it is no longer. Then therefore while it sounded, it might; because there then was what might be measured. But yet even then it was not at a stay; for it was passing on, and passing away. Could it be measured the rather, for that? For while passing, it was being extended into some space of time, so that it might be measured, since the present hath no space. If therefore then it might, then, to, suppose another voice hath begun to sound, and still soundeth in one continued tenor without any interruption; let us measure it while it sounds; seeing when it hath left sounding, it will then be past, and nothing left to be measured; let us measure it verily, and tell how much it is. But it sounds still, nor can it be measured but from the instant it began in, unto the end it left in. For the very space between is the thing we measure, namely, from some beginning unto some end. Wherefore, a voice that is not yet ended, cannot be measured, so that it may be said how long, or short it is; nor can it be called equal to another, or double to a single, or the like. But when ended, it no longer is. How may it then be measured? And yet we measure times; but yet neither those which are not yet, nor those which no longer are, nor those which are not lengthened out by some pause, nor those which have no bounds. We measure neither times to come, nor past, nor present, nor passing; and yet we do measure times.

"Deus Creator omnium," this verse of eight syllables alternates between short and long syllables. The four short then, the first, third, fifth, and seventh, are but single, in respect of the four long, the second, fourth, sixth, and eighth. Every one of these to every one of those, hath a double time: I pronounce them, report on them, and find it so, as one's plain sense perceives. By plain sense then, I measure a long syllable by a short, and I sensibly find it to have twice so much; but when one sounds after the other, if the former be short, the latter long, how shall I detain the short one, and how, measuring, shall I apply it to the long, that I may find this to have twice so much: seeing the long does not begin to sound, unless the short leaves sounding? And that very long one do I measure as present, seeing I measure it not till it be ended? Now his ending is his passing away. What then is it I measure? Where is the short syllable by which I measure? Where the long which I measure? Both have sounded, have flown, passed away, are no more; and yet I measure, and confidently answer (so far as is presumed on a practiced sense) that as to space of time this syllable is but single, that double. And yet I could not do this, unless they were already past and ended. It is not then themselves, which now are not, that I measure, but something in my memory, which there remains fixed.

It is in thee, my mind, that I measure times. Interrupt me not, that is, interrupt not thyself with the tumults of thy impressions. In thee I measure times; the impression, which things as they pass by cause in thee, remains even when they are gone; this it is which still present, I measure, not the things which pass by to make this impression. This I measure, when I measure times. Either then this is time, or I do not measure times. What when we measure silence, and say that this silence hath held as long time as did that voice? Do we not stretch out our thought to the measure of a voice, as if it sounded, that so we may be able to report of the intervals of silence in a given space of time? For though both voice and tongue be still, yet in thought we go over poems, and verses, and any other discourse, or dimen-

sions of motions, and report as to the spaces of times, how much this is in respect of that, no otherwise than if vocally we did pronounce them. If a man would utter a lengthened sound, and had settled in thought how long it should be, he hath in silence already gone through a space of time, and committing it to memory, begins to utter that speech, which sounds on, until it be brought unto the end proposed. Yea it hath sounded, and will sound; for so much of it as is finished, hath sounded already, and the rest will sound. And thus passeth it on, until the present intent conveys over the future into the past; the past increasing by the diminution of the future, until by the consumption of the future, all is past.

But how is that future diminished or consumed, which as yet is not? Or how that past increased, which is now no longer, save that in the mind which enacteth this, there be three things done? For it expects, it considers, it remembers; that so that which it expecteth, through that which it considereth, passeth into that which it remembereth. Who therefore denieth, that things to come are not as yet? And yet, there is in the mind an expectation of things to come. And who denies past things to be now no longer? And yet is there still in the mind a memory of things past. And who denieth the present time hath no space, because it passeth away in a moment? And yet our consideration continueth, through which that which shall be present proceedeth to become absent. It is not then future time, that is long, for as yet it is not: but a long future, is "a long expectation of the future," nor is it time past, which now is not, that is long; but a long past, is "a long memory of the past."

I am about to repeat a Psalm that I know. Before I begin, my expectation is extended over the whole; but when I have begun, how much soever of it I shall separate off into the past, is extended along my memory: thus the life of this action of mine is divided between my memory as to what I have repeated, and expectation as to what I am about to repeat; but "consideration" is present with me, that through it what was future, may be conveyed over, so as to become past. Which the more it is done again and again, so much the more the expectation being shortened, is the memory enlarged: till the whole expectation be at length exhausted, when that whole action being ended, shall have passed into memory. And this which takes place in the whole Psalm, the same takes place in each several portion of it, and each several syllable; the same holds in that longer action, whereof this Psalm may be part; the same holds in the whole life of man, whereof all the actions of man are parts; the same holds through the whole age of the sons of men, whereof all the lives of men are parts.

But because Thy loving-kindness is better than all lives, behold, my life is but a distraction, and Thy right hand upheld me, in my Lord the Son of man, the Mediator betwixt Thee, The One, and us many, many also through our manifold distractions amid many things, that by Him I may apprehend in Whom I have been apprehended, and may be recollected from my old conversation, to follow The One, forgetting what is behind, and not distended but extended, not to things which shall be and shall pass away, but to those things which are before, not distractedly but intently, I follow on for the prize of my heavenly calling, where I may hear the voice of Thy praise, and contemplate Thy delights, neither to come, nor to pass away. But now are my years spent in mourning. And Thou, O Lord, art my comfort, my Father everlasting, but I have been severed amid times, whose order I know not; and my thoughts, even the inmost bowels of my soul, are rent and mangled with tumultuous varieties, until I flow together into Thee, purified and molten by the fire of Thy love.

And now will I stand, and become firm in Thee, in my mould, Thy truth; nor will I endure the questions of men, who by a penal disease thirst for more than they can contain, and say, "What did God before He made heaven and earth?" Or, "How came it into His mind to make any thing, having never before made any thing?" Give them, O Lord, well to bethink themselves what they say, and to find, that "never" cannot be predicated, when "time" is not. This then that He is said "never to have made"; what else is it to say, than "in 'no have made?" Let them see therefore, that time cannot be without created being,

and cease to speak that vanity. May they also be extended towards those things which are before; and understand Thee before all times, the eternal Creator of all times, and that no times be coeternal with Thee, nor any creature, even if there be any creature before all times.

O Lord my God, what a depth is that recess of Thy mysteries, and how far from it have the consequences of my transgressions cast me! Heal mine eyes, that I may share the joy of Thy light. Certainly, if there be mind gifted with such vast knowledge and foreknowledge, as to know all things past and to come, as I know one well-known Psalm, truly that mind is passing wonderful, and fearfully amazing; in that nothing past, nothing to come in after-ages, is any more hidden from him, than when I sung that Psalm, was hidden from me what, and how much of it had passed away from the beginning, what, and how much there remained unto the end. But far be it that Thou the Creator of the Universe, the Creator of souls and bodies, far be it, that Thou shouldest in such wise know all things past and to come. Far, far more wonderfully, and far more mysteriously, dost Thou know them. For not, as the feelings of one who singeth what he knoweth, or heareth some well-known song, are through expectation of the words to come, and the remembering of those that are past, varied, and his senses divided—not so doth any thing happen unto Thee, unchangeably eternal, that is, the eternal Creator of minds. Like then as Thou in the Beginning knewest the heaven and the earth, without any variety of Thy knowledge, so madest Thou in the Beginning heaven and earth, without any distinction of Thy action. Whoso understandeth, let him confess unto Thee; and whoso understandeth not, let him confess unto Thee. Oh how high art Thou, and yet the humble in heart are Thy dwelling-place; for Thou raisest up those that are bowed down, and they fall not, whose elevation Thou art.

STUDY QUESTIONS: AUGUSTINE, *CONFESSIONS*

1. How do we recognize the image of God in ourselves?
2. In asking whether the Earth, the trees, the sea, etc., are God, what exactly is Augustine asking? And why does he deny that the answer is yes? How does he know this? What is his reasoning?
3. What does Augustine claim he loves, when he loves God?
4. Does Augustine apply his method of doubt to the love of God? Why?

5. What is the role of memory with regard to questions of faith and God?
6. What is God's relationship to time and space? Why is this a "most intricate enigma?"
7. How does Augustine define time? How does he define space?
8. What is the nature of the relationship between time, space and the mind (consciousness)?"
9. Where is the future, in relation to the present? Where is the past?
10. Does Augustine think God hears him? Understands him? Sees him?
11. Is God's consciousness like ours, or different?
12. What is Augustine's view of change? Why do things that God made change? Do they change in ways that God foreordains?
13. How does God speak, according to Augustine?
14. How does memory function in his inquiry?

Philosophical Bridges: The Influence of Augustine

Augustine deeply influenced many philosophers after him, most notably Descartes and Kant, especially regarding the nature and possibility of self-knowledge. His original argument against the skeptics, according to whom we cannot know ourselves with certainty, is that even if you doubt everything still, nevertheless, the act of doubting itself requires thought and a thinker and therefore affirms your existence. With his emphasis on doubt as being the noble path, paved with the best arguments of the skeptics, toward knowledge, Augustine not only anticipates Descartes' famous "I think, therefore I am," but providesz a secure place for education using the ancient Greek rudiments of scientific method. With regard to religious thought, his establishment of the principle of the will to believe, in opposition, or supplemental to, reason, remains a vastly inspirational theme not just for religious philosophers but secular ones as well, as for instance William James' profoundly influential "The Will to Believe" attests.

BIBLIOGRAPHY

GENERAL
Primary
King, P., *Against the Academics and The Teacher*, trans., Hackett, 1995

Bettenson, H., *City of God*, trans., Penguin, 1984

Baxter, J. H., *Saint Augustine: Select Letters*, ed., Harvard University Press, 1930

Secondary
Brown, P., *Augustine of Hippo, A Biography*, Fabor and Fabor, 1990

Chadwick, H., *Augustine*, Oxford University Press, 1986

Gilson, E., *The Christian Philosophy of St. Augustine*, Random House, 1960

Kaye, S. and Thomson, P., *On Augustine*, Wadsworth, 2001

Kirwan, C., *Augustine*, Routledge, 1989

Kretzman, N., *The Cambridge Companion to Augustine*, Cambridge University Press, 2001

O'Connell, R., *St. Augustine's Early Theory of Man, A.D. 386–391*, Harvard University Press, 1968

O'Daly, G., *Augustine's Philosophy of Mind*, University of California Press, 1987

O'Donnell, J. J., *Augustine: A New Biography*, Ecco, 2005

Rist, J. M., *Augustine: Ancient Thought Baptized*, Cambridge University Press, 1996

SECTION III

→ THE EARLY MEDIEVALS →

PROLOGUE

Philosophy in the early medieval period is characterized by what has since come to be known as *scholasticism*. The term comes from *doctores scholastici*, itself derived from *scholazein*, meaning "to have leisure or spare time," but which came to signify "devotion to pupil and master." It came to signify those who taught the liberal arts or theology in the cloister and cathedral schools throughout Christendom. Influenced by Greek rationality, Scholasticism evolved into a highly developed method and system of thought.

Scholastic philosophy had its roots in the ancient world. But whereas the philosophy of the ancient Greeks, which it emulated—albeit through the highly filtered influence of the few remaining works of Plato and Aristotle that had not been burned or banned—was inspired by a highly iconoclastic tradition in which each philosopher sought to develop a unique system virtually independent from all others, the scholastics sought to build a common philosophy that was part of a unified "Christian society." The purpose was, in effect, to suppress iconoclasm, not so much to suppress individuals, but rather, to transcend individual difference among separate nations and societies to which individual thinkers belonged. In other words, the motives were to achieve unification among different peoples through a collective system of beliefs. In this way, scholastic reasoning arguably became the corporate product of social thought, guided by obedience to authority (either mediated by ancient texts, or through immediate revelation, or some combination thereof).

During this time the practice of philosophy thus became codified by traditional forms of thought guided by "revealed" Christian dogma under the auspices of the church. Philosophy during this period became both subjugated to and suppressed by theology. However, the theology under which philosophy now operated had itself unfolded and evolved from within the philosophical framework established by Augustine, the most important dominant thinker in early Christian thought. Philosophy, in other words, became an important force in the subsequent development of theology, both in the Judeo-Christian and Muslim traditions.

The first philosopher of this new period was Boethius (approx. 480–524). Although primarily a commentator on Aristotle and Cicero (106–43 BCE)—the great Roman scholar who defended the classical principles throughout the various social upheavals that ended unraveling the republic—it was Boethius who provided many of the definitions and axioms that provided a foundation for the scholastic method. The first truly great philosopher of this era, however, was John Scotus Erigena (approx. 825–870), followed by Anselm (1033–1109), Abelard (Abailard, 1079–1142), Hildegard of Bingen (1098–1179) and John of Salisbury (1120–1180), all exemplars of scholasticism comprising this section.

Boethius (470–525)

Biographical History

Boethius was a leading Roman philosopher, scholar, and court official. He has often been described as the last Roman philosopher and the first scholastic. Born to a prominent political family, as a young man he probably went to Athens to study philosophy (historians dispute whether it was Athens). During his lifetime Boethius translated all of Aristotle's major works on logic, including the *Prior Analytics*, *Posterior Analytics*, *Topics* and *Sophistical Refutations*. He wrote what became the standard medieval textbook on logic, an introduction to *the Categories* of Aristotle.

Upon his return to Rome, Boethius embarked on a political career; he became consul in 510 and in 522 was appointed Master of Offices in the Emperor's court. As an official in the court of the Gothic king Theodoric, Boethius held some of the highest political offices until he was accused of conspiring against the king. Apparently he had been in favor of Justin I, the eastern emperor, but the official charge was that of practicing magic, a common complaint against philosophers at the time. Within a year he was tried and found guilty of treason. He wrote his *Consolation of Philosophy* in the last year of his life, while in prison awaiting execution. He was beheaded.

Boethius' works on mathematics, logic, music, and theology were read and admired throughout the Middle Ages; his *Consolation* was the most widely read and translated book after the Bible.

Philosophical Overview

Although influenced by Seneca and the Stoics, Boethius was highly critical of Epicurus and the Stoics, holding that the highest good is happiness, not pleasure. The neo-Platonic and Stoic elements in his thinking are clearly evident in all his extant writings, as is his deep and eclectic knowledge of virtually all areas of inquiry; he wrote scholarly works on arithmetic, geometry, music, astronomy, logic, ethics, and theology. His translations of Plato and Aristotle show a refined understanding of the categorical and hypothetical syllogisms, the concept of definition and analysis, universals, and the methods of rhetoric all of which he applies with great skill in his works.

COMMENTARIES ON THE ISAGOGE OF PORPHYRY
Boethius

Porphyry (approx. 232–304 BCE) was a student of Plotinus. Best known for his adaptation of Airstotle's logic to the neo-Platonic philosophy of the time, he originated what is known as the "Tree of Porphyry," a method of classification by division that came to be used by many philosophers throughout the Middle Ages.

Boethius' commentaries on Porphyry's *Isagoge* are not really commentaries in the ordinary sense. Only one page of Porphyry's text is the source of the commentary, a remark about the importance of logic. Boethius spends most of the book embellishing this one key point and filling in the details, the most important of which concerns the problem of universals. Since then, the problem of universals has became a leading bone of contention among philosophers. Do universals exist independently of the mind? Plato thought yes; in his view, the ideas (or forms) existed independently of the mind. They are abstract, meaning "not in space and time." (Think of "abstract art," which tries to depict not objects as they exist perceived in space and time, such as tables, chairs, and people but, rather, non-concrete, abstract structures.) Aristotle thought that universals did not exist independently of the mind or of the discrete, individual, concrete objects we perceive. The term "man," for instance, does not signify anything that exists above and beyond the individuals who fall under that category (concept). Who was right? Or was there the possibility of some sort of compromise, even synthesis?

The term *universal* means, literally, that which applies throughout the entire universe. Again, in Plato's view, ideas (the forms) were universals. For Aristotle, a universal is simply a term that can be predicated of many, such as "man" or "horse." According to subsequent medieval realists who followed Plato, universals were entities whose being is independent of the mind or perception. For medieval nominalists, who followed Aristotle, a universal is a general notion (concept) that has no reality independently of the mind. Now, most scholastics thought of universals as "second substances." In his work, Porphyry explicitly avoids having to address the problem of whether terms signifying genera and species exist outside the mind. It is this central problem that Boethius tackles head-on. He argues that one cannot avoid the problem by any sort of mere verbal maneuvers. What is most important about his contribution is not just the answers and conclusions he draws from the debate but how he goes about trying to solve this apparently insolvable problem. The terms in which he poses the problem would set the tone for subsequent discussions throughout the rest of the Middle Ages.

BOOK I.

1. This second task of exposition, which I have undertaken, will clarify the course of my translation, for I am afraid I have fallen victim in my translation to the fault of the faithful interpreter, in that I have rendered every word, expressed or implied, with a word. The reason for the present undertaking is that in these writings, in which knowledge of things is sought, there must be expressed, not a charm of translucent style, but the uncorrupted truth. It seems to me that I shall have accomplished a great deal to this end if books of philosophy should be composed in the Latin language by painstaking and complete translation, until nothing more were missing from the literature of the Greeks. And since the most excellent good of philosophy has been related with human souls, the exposition must begin with the powers of the human soul itself that it may proceed in some sequence and order. There is a triple power of the soul to be found in animated bodies. Of these, one power supports the life for the body, that it may arise by birth and subsist by nourishment; another lends judgment to perception; the third is the foundation for the strength of the mind and for reason. Of these, it is the function of the first to be at hand for creating, nourishing, and sustaining bodies, but it will exercise no judgment of reason or of sense. This power is possessed by herbs and trees and anything that is fixed, rooted to the earth. But the second is composite and conjoined: taking over to itself the first and making it part of itself, it is further able to form a varied and multiform judgment of things. For every animal who

Boethius, from *The Second Edition of the Commentaries on the Isagoge of Porphyry* translated by Richard McKeon in Richard McKeon, ed., *Selections from Medieval Philosophers*, vol. 1, Charles Scribners Sons, 1929, pp. 70–99.

has the power of sense, is also born, and nourished, and sustained. But the senses are different and rise in number as far as five; consequently anything that is only nourished, does not also perceive, but anything that can perceive is proved also to have the first power of the soul subject to it, that is, the power to be born and nourished. Moreover, all beings that possess sense grasp not only the forms of things by which they are bombarded, when the sensible body is present, but also retain the images of the forms known by sense even when the sense is withdrawn and when the sensible objects are removed; and they build up memory; and each animal, as he is able to, preserves these images a longer or a shorter time. But they take on these confused and unevident imaginations, so that they can make nothing from the conjunction and composition of their imaginations. And for this reason they can remember, to be sure, but not all things equally, for when oblivion has come upon the memory they can not recollect or recall it. Moreover, there is no knowledge of the future by these imaginations. But the third power of the soul, which carries with it the prior powers of nourishing and of perceiving, and which uses them as slaves and servants, is constituted completely in reason, and it is occupied in the very firm conception of present things, or in the understanding of absent things, or in the investigation of unknown things. This power is present in the human genus alone, which not only receives sensations and perfect and unconfused imaginations, but also explains and confirms by the full act of understanding, what the imagination has supplied. Consequently, as has been said, those things which it comprehends subject to the senses do not alone suffice this divine nature for knowledge, but besides, it can put names conceived by the imagination on insensible and absent things, and it also opens to the imposition of words that which it comprehends by way of understanding. Moreover, it is proper to that nature to investigate unknown things by means of those known to it and to wish to know of each single thing, not only whether it is, but also what it is, and how it is, and even why it is. Only the nature of man, as has been said, has received this power of the threefold soul. The power of this soul does not lack the movements of intelligence, for it exercises the power of reason itself in the following four respects. It

inquires of a thing *whether* it is, or if it has determined that it is, it has doubts concerning *what* it is. But if it has the knowledge of both of these by reason, it searches out *how* any particular thing is, and investigates the other changes of accidents in it; having learned these things, it also inquires and traces out by reason *why* it is thus.

2. Therefore, since the activity of the human soul is such that it is always occupied in the comprehension of present things, or in the understanding of absent things, or in the investigation and discovery of unknown things, there are two problems in which the power of the reasoning soul extends all its care: one, that it know the natures of things by a sure method of inquiry, and the other, that that which moral gravity may later perform, may come to be known beforehand. In investigating these matters there must necessarily be many things which may lead the inquiring mind not a little from progress along the right road, as happened in many points to Epicurus, who thinks the world consists of atoms and who measures virtue by pleasure. It is clear, moreover, that this happened to him, and to others, because they thought, through inexperience in logical argument, that everything they comprehended in reasoning occurred also in things themselves. This surely is a great error; for in reasoning it is not as in numbers. For in numbers whatever has come out in computing the digits correctly, must without doubt also eventuate in the things themselves, so that if by calculation there should happen to be a hundred, there must also be a hundred things subject to that number. But this does not hold equally in argumentation; nor, in fact, is everything which the evolution of words may have discovered held fixed in nature too. Wherefore, it was inevitable that they fall into error who, having cast aside the art of argument, made diligent search into the nature of things. For unless one has learned first the science that shows which reasoning holds to the true path of argument, and which holds to the path like to the truth, and unless one has learned to recognize what is trustworthy and what can be suspected, the uncorrupted truth of things can not be found by reasoning. Therefore, since the ancients often fell into a great many errors and brought together in argumentation many doctrines false and contrary to each other, and since it seemed impossible that this was done in order that, having come to contrary conclusions concerning the same thing, both conclusions which reasoning disagreeing with itself had formed should be true, and since it was ambiguous which line of though should be believed, it seemed proper to consider the true and whole nature of argumentation itself first, and when that was known, what was discovered or what had been comprehended truly by argument could then be understood too. Hence, started the knowledge of the logical discipline, which so contrives the modes of arguing and the ways of distinguishing reasoning themselves, that one can recognize what reasoning is now false, and now again true, what reasoning is always false, what never false. The power of this discipline, moreover, must be considered to be twofold, one in finding, the other in judging. This Cicero, too, expresses clearly in the book whose title is the *Topics*, saying:

> Although all reason suited to discourse has two parts, one of discovering, the other of judging, the prince of both, it seems to me, was Aristotle. The Stoics, however, exerted themselves in only one, for they pursued the ways of judging carefully in the science which they call dialectic, but they left aside the whole art of discovering, which is called topic, and which was more excellent in use and certainly prior in order of nature. But since there is the greatest utility in both and since we think to pursue both if there will be leisure, we shall begin from that which is first.

Since, therefore, the fruit of this consideration is so great, the whole attention of the mind must be given to this so very ingenious discipline, that we may be able, having been made steady in our first steps in the truth of arguing, to come easily to a sure comprehension of things themselves.

3. And since we have already stated what the beginning of the logical discipline is, the next question seems to follow: whether logic is absolutely a definite part of philosophy or, as others hold, an apparatus or instrument by which philosophy seizes on the knowledge and nature of things. I see that these opinions concerning this matter are diametrically opposed. For those who think the logical consideration a part of philosophy, use approximately the following arguments, saying, that philosophy doubt-

less has speculative and practical parts; the question concerning this third rational part is whether it is to be asserted to be a part: but it can not be doubted that it too is part of philosophy. For just as the investigation of philosophy alone is concerned with natural and other questions which are classed under the speculative part, and again as only philosophy deliberates concerning moral and other questions which fall under the practical part, so too only philosophy judges of this part of the inquiry, that is, concerning these questions which are subjects of logic. But if the speculative and practical are parts of philosophy because philosophy alone treats of them, then by the same reason logic will be part of philosophy, since this matter of arguing falls under philosophy alone. But then they say: since philosophy is concerned with these three, and since the subject matters distinguish the practical and speculative considerations, because the latter inquires concerning the nature of things, and the former concerning morals, there is no doubt that the logical discipline is distinct from the natural and the moral by the characteristic of its subject matter. For the consideration of logic is of propositions and syllogisms and other subjects of this sort, and neither that part of philosophy which speculates, not of discourse, but of things, nor the practical part which watches over morals, can take care of that too. But if philosophy consists in these three, that is, speculative, practical, and rational, which are set off from each other by their separate and triple ends, since the speculative and the practical are said to be parts of philosophy, there is no doubt that the rational, too, may be demonstrated to be part of philosophy.

Those on the other hand who think it is not a part but an instrument of philosophy, urge approximately the following arguments. They say, there is no end of logic similar to the end of the speculative and practical parts. For each of these is turned to its proper end, the speculative to work out the knowledge of things, and the practical to perfect morals and institutions; nor is the one referred to the other. The end of logic, however, can not be absolute, but is drawn and bound up in a certain manner with the other two parts. For what is there in the logical discipline which should be desired for its own worth; or was not the practise of this art undertaken for the investigation of things? For to know how an argumentation is to be concluded, or what is true, and what similar to the true, tends obviously to this, that this science of reasons is referred either to a knowledge of things or to discovering those things which produce happiness, having led to the exercise of morality. And, therefore, since the end of the speculative and the end of the practical parts are their own and certain, whereas the end of logic is referred to the other two parts, it is clear that logic is not a part of philosophy but rather an instrument. There are, of course, many more arguments which may be stated on either part, of which it suffices that we have noted strictly these which have been stated.

We settle this controversy, however, with the following reasoning. We say that surely nothing prevents the same logic from serving at the same time the function of part and of instrument. For since it retains its own end, and this end is considered by philosophy only, it must be asserted to be a part of philosophy, but since that end of logic, which philosophy alone contemplates, promises its aid to the other parts of philosophy, we do not deny that it is the instrument of philosophy; but the end of logic is the discovery and judgment of reasons. Obviously it will not seem strange that the same thing should be called a part and a kind of instrument, if we turn our mind to the parts of the body, for something is done by them, so that we use them as a manner of instruments, and yet they hold the place of parts in the whole body. For the hand is for touching, the eyes for seeing, and the other parts of the body seem to have each a proper function. But still if the utility of the whole body be considered, these, which no one would deny are also parts, are judged to be certain instruments of the body. So too the logical discipline is a part of philosophy, since philosophy alone is mistress of it, but it is an instrument too because by it the sought-for truth of philosophy is investigated.

4. But since I have explained, so far as succinct brevity has permitted me, the beginning of logic and what logic itself should be, I must now say a little concerning this book which I have undertaken here to expound. For in the title Porphyry proposes that be write an introduction to the *Categories* of Aristotle. I shall explain briefly what the value of this introduction is, or for what it prepares the mind of the reader. For Aristotle composed the book which is entitled *On the Ten Categories* with this intention, that he might embrace with a small number of genera the infinite diversities (which could not be encompassed in knowledge) of things, and so, that which could not come under discipline because of its number exceeding comprehension, might be made subject to the mind and to knowledge, as has been said, by the small number of the genera. Therefore, he considered that there are ten genera of all things, that is, one substance and nine accidents, which are quality, quantity, relation, place, time, action, passion, situation, and condition; and since they were the supreme genera and no other genus could be placed above them, all the multitude of things must necessarily be found to be species of these ten genera. These genera are divided from each other by all differences, and they seem to not have anything common except only the name, since all are predicated to be. Certainly substance is, quality is, quantity is, and the verb *is* is predicated commonly of all the others, but that is not their one common substance or nature, but only their name. Consequently the ten genera discovered by Aristotle are divided from each other by all differences. But things which are disjoined by any differences must necessarily have some peculiar property which maintains them in singular and solitary form. A property, moreover, is not the same as an accident. For accidents can appear or disappear, but properties are so implanted that apart from the things of which they are properties they could not be. Since these facts are so, and since Aristotle had found ten genera of things, which the mind seized in understanding or the disputant brought forth in speaking—for whatever we grasp by the understanding we divulge to another by word—it came about that he was led for the understanding of the ten categories to the treatments of these five predicables, namely, genus, species, difference, property and accident. Of *genus*, indeed, because we must first learn what genus is, to be able to recognize that those ten which Aristotle placed before other things are genera; and the knowledge of *species* is extremely valuable for the ability to recognize what the species of any genus is. For if we understand what species is, we are not encumbered by error and thrown into confusion. It can often happen, in fact, that through ignorance of species we may place the species of quantity in relation, and classify the species of some first genus under some other genus, and in this way a promiscuous and indistinguishable confusion of things may be made. Lest this happen it should be known beforehand what the nature of species is. Not only is it important that the nature of species be known, that we may not interchange the species of prior genera with each other, but also that we may know how to choose in any single genus the species proximate to the genus, to the end that we may not say that animal is directly the species of substance instead of body, or man of body instead of animated body. Certainly the knowledge of *differences* holds an extremely important place in these things. For who of us would learn to distinguish quality at all from substance, or the other genera from each other, if we did not see their differences? But how can we distinguish their differences if we do not know what difference itself is? Nor is it only this error which the ignorance of difference spreads over us, but it also takes away all judgment of species. For differences inform all species, and if difference is not known, the species too can not be known. But how can it happen that we be able to recognize any difference at all if we absolutely do not know what the significance of that word is? Moreover, in the next instance, so great is the usefulness of *property* that Aristotle investigated carefully the properties of each of the categories. Who would understand what the properties are before he learns at all what a property is? Nor is this knowledge valuable only in those properties which are stated by single words, as risible of man, but also in those which are employed in the place of definition. For all properties include the subject thing in a certain term of description, which too I shall take up more suitably in its place. Who furthermore can doubt how much the knowledge of *accident* aids, when he sees in ten categories nine natures of accident? How shall we judge that they are accidents, if we absolutely do not know what accident is, since certainly the knowledge of neither differences nor property would be had if we do not hold the nature of accident by most solid consideration? For it could happen that through ignorance accident might be set in the place of difference or property; this, definitions show, is also extremely defective, for although definitions themselves are composed out of differences, and

although they are made of any property, nevertheless they do not seem to admit accident.

Since, therefore, Aristotle brought together the genera of things, which contained under them species truly diverse, which species would never be diverse, if they were not separated by differences, and since he reduced all things to substance and accident, and accident to the other nine categories, and since he followed through for the most part the properties of some of the categories; he taught concerning these categories themselves, what genus was, what species, what difference, what that accident was, of which we have just had to speak, or what property, which he passed by as known. Lest, therefore, those who come to the *Categories* of Aristotle should be ignorant of what any one of these which have been mentioned above signifies, Porphyry wrote this book on the knowledge of these five predicables that having examined and having considered what each single one of these, which were set forth above, designated, the understanding might learn more easily the things which were set forth by Aristotle.

5. This is the intention of this book, which, Porphyry intimated in the very expression of the title, he had written as an introduction to the *Categories*. But although the intention of this book is turned to this one thing, nevertheless, the utility of it is not simple, but multiplex and extended very broadly. This, too, Porphyry notes in the beginning of this book, saying:

> Since it is necessary, Chrysaor, to know what genus is, and what difference is, and species, and property, and accident, as well for that doctrine of categories which is in Aristotle as for the imposition of definitions and in general for those things which are in division or demonstration, I shall try briefly, in this useful contemplation of such things, to approach as if in on introductory manner those things which have been said by the ancients, making a compendious rendering for you, abstaining from the more lofty questions, but interpreting in an ordinary manner the more simple.

The utility of this book is spread in a fourfold direction. For it is of great use to readers for that to which its intention is directed and also for other things; although these are beyond the intention, a utility no less because of that accrues to readers from them. For by means of this work one has ready knowledge of the categories, and one has the whole imposition of definitions, and the right understanding of divisions, and the most true conclusion of demonstrations. These things, the more difficult and arduous they are, the more they require in the reader a more perspicacious and diligent mind. It must be remarked, however, that this is true of all books. For, if it is known first what the intention is, the amount of utility which can arise thence is judged too; and although many other things besides, as it happens, may follow from a book of this sort, nevertheless, it seems to have that utility nearest, to which its intention is turned, as is shown by the very book which we have taken up. Since its intention is to prepare an easy understanding of the categories, there is no doubt that this is shown to be its principal utility, although definition, division, and demonstration are no lesser associates, of which certain principles are here suggested to us. The whole meaning, indeed, is of this sort: "*Since*," he says, "a knowledge of genus, species, difference, property, and accident is useful to the *Categories* of Aristotle and to its doctrine, and also to the imposition of definitions, to division and demonstration, I shall attempt briefly," he says, "by making a compendious rendering of the things which have been said broadly and diffusely by the ancients, to lay open that which is the useful and richest knowledge of these things." Nor, in fact, would it be compendious if the whole work were not bound together by brevity. And seeing that he was writing an introduction, "I shall avoid," he says, "the more lofty questions willingly, but I shall interpret in an ordinary manner the more simple," that is, I shall treat the obscurities of the more simple questions by holding to a kind of conjectural reasoning in them.

The whole sentiment of this introduction is such as to attract the mind of the beginner both by an extremely rich utility and by facility. But it seems proper to point out what else there is which the loftiness of the words conceals. The word *necessary* in the Latin tongue, like ἀναγκαῖον in Greek has several meanings. For when Cicero says that some one is his relation, and when we say that it is necessary that we go down to the forum, in which word a certain utility is signified, we speak according to different meanings. Still another meaning is the one in which we say that it is necessary that the sun be moved, that is, it is nec-

essary. That first meaning, however, must be passed over, for it is wholly unrelated to this necessary of which Porphyry speaks here. But the last two are of such sort that they seem to war with each other as to which will hold the signification in the place in which Porphyry says, "Since it is necessary, Chrysaor"; for, as has been said, the word *necessary* means both utility and necessity. They seem, moreover, both to fit in this place. For it is both useful in the highest degree for these things which were spoken of above, to investigate genus and species and the others; and the necessity is of the highest, since unless these things are known first, those for which they are prepared, can not be known. For neither can the categories be learned without a knowledge of genus and species, nor does definition ignore genus and difference, and it will appear how useful this treatise is in the others, when the investigation will turn to division and demonstration. But although these five which must be examined here must necessarily be known before those things for which they are prepared, nevertheless the word *necessary* is not used here by Porphyry in a meaning in which he would want necessity and not rather utility to be signified. For the statement itself and the context of words indicate this by the clearest reason to the understanding. Nor indeed does anyone use a reason that he may say that some necessity is referred to something else. For necessity is through itself, but utility is always referred to that for which it is useful, as is the case here. He says, in fact, "since it is necessary, Chrysaor, for that doctrine of categories which is in Aristotle." If, therefore, we understand this necessary as useful, and if we change it to that very word, saying: since it is useful, Chrysaor, to that doctrine of categories which is in Aristotle, to know what genus is and the rest, the order of words will be correct; but if we change it to *necessary* and if we say: since it is necessary, Chrysaor, for that doctrine of categories which is in Aristotle, to know what genus is and the rest, the order of words does not accord with right understanding. Wherefore there is no need to delay longer here. For although it is of the highest necessity that, if these things are ignored, one can not arrive at those things for which this treatise is intended, still the word necessary is used here not as of necessity, but rather of utility.

6. Now, although the subject has been touched on above, still we shall estimate briefly what profit the knowledge of genus, species, difference, property, and accident is to the categories. For Aristotle stated in the *Categories* ten genera of things which were predicated of all others that whatever could come to have meaning, if it held full meaning, would be subjected to each of those genera of which Aristotle treats in the book which is entitled *On the Ten Categories*. But for it to be referred to something as to a genus, is as if one were to place a species under a genus. Certainly this can in no way be done without knowledge of species, nor assuredly can the species themselves be understood in respect to what they are, or rather in respect to the genus of which they are, unless their differences are known. But if the nature of differences is unknown, what the differences of each single species are, will be ignored completely. Therefore, it must be recognized that if Aristotle treats of genera in the *Categories*, the nature of genera must also be known; an understanding of species also accompanies the knowledge of this. But when this is known, what difference is can not be ignored, since there are many things in the same book which absolutely no understanding will open up unless the reader bring to it a very great learning of genus and species and difference, as when Aristotle himself says, "Things of diverse genera, and not of genera placed subalternately, are diverse as to species and are differences," which can not be understood if these things are not known. But Aristotle also searches out in most diligent investigation the property of each one of the categories, so that when he says after many questionings, that the "property of substance is that remaining itself the same in number it is susceptible of contraries," or again that, "it is the property of quantity, that only in it may the equal and the unequal be spoken of," and "the property of quality," similarly, "that we state according to it that something is like or unlike something else," and in the others in the same manner, as, what the property of the contrary is, what the property according to the relation of opposition is, what the properties of privation and condition, of affirmation and negation are. In these he treats, as if for those already learned and scientific, what the nature of property is; if any one should be ignorant of it, he would enter in vain into the questions which are taken up concerning these things. Moreover, it is already clear that accident occupies a very large part of the categories, since it is applied generally as the proper name to nine categories.

7. And it is clear from these considerations how great the utility of this book is in regard to the categories. What he says concerning the *imposition of definitions* can surely be understood easily, if first a division of the principles of substance is made. One principle of substance is affirmed in description, and another in definition. But that principle which is in description, brings out a certain characteristic of the thing, the principle of whose substance it brings forth, and it not only informs that which it reveals with a characteristic, but it itself becomes the property which must also enter into definition; if any one wishes to state the principle of quantity, he may properly say: quantity is that according to which equals and unequals are spoken of. Just as, therefore, he placed the character of quantity in the principle of quantity and that whole principle is proper to quantity itself, so the description brings out the characteristic, and the description itself is made proper to it. On the other hand, the definition does not bring out properties, but is itself made proper. For the definition reveals substance, joins genus to differences, and, reducing to one species which it defines those things which are per se common and of many, it makes them equal. Consequently, the knowledge of property is useful to description, since only the characteristic is brought out in description, and it is itself made proper: so too in the case of definition, but for definition one needs the genus, which is affirmed first, and the species to which that genus is proper, and differences by which, when they have been joined to genus, the species is defined. . . .

8. This book is surely so useful for the making of *division*, that, apart from the knowledge of the things which are investigated one after the other in this book, partition would be made by chance rather than by reason. This however will be manifest if we divide division itself, that is, if we separate the name of division into that which it signifies. For there is division of genus into species, as when we say, "of color some is white, some black, and some medium." Again there is division whenever a word signifying many things is examined, and whenever it is shown how many there are which are signified by it, as if one were to say, "the word dog signifies many things, this barking and four-legged animal, and a celestial constellation, and a marine beast," which are all separated from each other by definition. Moreover, a thing is said to be divided whenever a whole is separated into its proper parts, as when we say, "house is part foundations, part walls, part roof." And we call this triple division "substantial partition." There is, however, another division which is said to be "accidental." This too is done in three ways: when we divide accident into subjects, as when I say, "of goods there are some in mind and some in body;" or again when we divide subject into accidents, as "of bodies there are some white, some black, and some of medium color;" or finally when we separate accident into accidents, as when we say, "of liquids some are white, some black, and some of medium color," or again "of white things some are hard, some liquid, and some soft." . . . this can in no manner be done without a knowledge of genera or without a knowledge of differences, which must be assumed in the division of species. It is manifest therefore how great the utility of this book is for this division which at first approach treats of genus and species and differences. Furthermore, the second substantial division into the meanings of a word, is not unconnected with the utility of this book. For in one way it will be possible to know whether a word whose division we wish to make, seems to be equivocal or a genus, and that is, if the things which it signifies are defined. And if the things which are under the common name are included by a definition, it is necessary that they be species and it be their common genus. But if those things which the stated word designates, can not be brought together in one definition, no one doubts that the word is equivocal or that it is not common to the things of which it is predicated as genus, inasmuch as those things which it signifies subordinate to it, can not be comprehended according to the common word by one definition. If therefore it is made manifest by definition, what is genus and what is equivocal word, and if definition runs through genera and differences, can anyone doubt that the authority of this book is equally very valuable in this form of division? In the next place, how is that substantial division, which is into the parts of the whole, distinguished, and how will one avoid thinking it rather to be a division of genus into species, if genus, and species, and differences, and their meanings are not treated before the principle of the discipline? Why, in fact, should one not say that the foundations, walls, and roof are the species of house rather than the parts? But since it happens that the name of the genus can fit wholly in every single species, whereas the name of the whole can not accord with every one of its parts, it becomes clear that the division of genus into species is one thing, and the division of the whole into parts another. The name of the genus, however, is shown to accord with each one of the species by the fact that both man and horse are individually called animals. But it is not customary for the roof or the walls or the foundations to be called singly by the name of house, but when the parts have been joined, then they take on rightly the name of the whole. In the next place, concerning accidental division, no one is unaware that if accident is unknown, and if the meaning of genus and of differences is unknown, it can easily happen that the accident may be separated into subjects as genus is divided into species, and finally ignorance will mix shamefully all this order of division.

9. And since we have shown of what profit this book is for division, we shall speak now of *demonstration*, lest he who has toiled with watchful care and sagacious labor in this so very great discipline, should be brought to a standstill because of arduous and difficult obstacles. For demonstration, that is, a sure inference of reason concerning any thing inquired about, is made from things known prior naturally, from agreements, from first principles, from cause, from necessary things, from things subsisting through themselves. But genera are naturally prior to their proper species, for species flow from genera. Moreover, it is clear that species are prior naturally to the things subordinate to them, whether the latter be species or individuals. But whatever things are prior, are known before and are known better than those which follow naturally. In fact, a thing is said to be first and to be known in two manners, namely, with respect to us and with respect to nature. For those things are more known to us which are nearest to us, as individuals, next species, finally genera; but by nature, conversely, those things are more known which are least proximate to us. And therefore the more distantly genera are removed from us, the more lucid, and naturally known, they will be. Substantial differences, now, are those which we recognize to be present through themselves in the things which are being demonstrated. A knowledge of genera and differences, however, must come first, that in any particular discipline it may be known what are the

appropriate principles of the thing which is demonstrated. That these necessary principles moreover are those which we call genera and differences, no one doubts who understands that without genus and difference species can not be. For genera and differences are the causes of species. Species are, in fact, for this reason, that their genera and differences are, which when placed in demonstrative syllogisms are the causes not only of the thing but also of the conclusion, which the last Resolutorii[1] will state more fully.

Since therefore it is extremely useful to determine all this by definition, and separate it by division, and prove it by demonstration, but since that can not be understood or done without a knowledge of those things which will be examined in this book, who will ever be able to doubt that this book is the greatest aid of all logic, without which the other aids which have great force in logic, can afford no approach to the doctrine?

10. But Porphyry remembered that he was writing an introduction, and he does not depart from the form of treatment which is the manner of instruction. He says in fact that "he abstains from the knots of the more lofty questions, but resolves the simple ones with ordinary interpretation." Moreover he sets down what the loftier questions are which he promises to put aside, thus:

> At present, he says, I shall refuse to say concerning genera and species whether they subsist or whether they are placed in the naked understandings alone or whether subsisting they are corporeal or incorporeal, and whether they are separated from sensibles or placed in sensibles and in accord with them. Questions of this sort are most exalted business and require very great diligence of inquiry.

I pass over, he says, the loftier questions, lest by pouring them intemperately into the mind of the reader I disturb his beginnings and first efforts. But lest he should make the reader wholly negligent, and lest the reader think that nothing more is hidden than what he had said, he adds the very thing whose question be promised he would put off pursuing, that he might spread no confusion before the reader by treating of these things obscurely and completely, and

yet that the reader, strengthened by knowledge, might recognize what could be inquired into rightly. The questions, however, concerning which he promises to be silent are extremely useful and secret and have been tried by wise men but have not been solved by many. The first of them is of this sort. The mind, whatever it understands, either conceives by understanding and describes to itself by reason that which is established in the nature of things, or else depicts to itself in vacant imagination that which is not. It is inquired therefore of which sort the understanding of genus and of the rest is: whether we understand species and genera as we understand things which are and from which we derive a true understanding, or whether we deceive ourselves, since we form for ourselves, by the empty cogitation of the mind, things which are not. But even if it should be established that they are, and if we should say that the understanding of them is conceived from things which are, then another greater, and more difficult question would occasion doubt, since the most grave difficulty is revealed in distinguishing and understanding the nature of genus itself. For since it is necessary that everything which is, be either corporeal or incorporeal, genus and species will have to be in one of these. Of what sort then will that which is called genus be, corporeal or incorporeal? Nor in fact can attention be turned seriously to what it is, unless it is known in which of these classes it must be placed. But even when this question has been solved, all ambiguity will not be avoided. For there remains something which, should genus and species be called incorporeal, besets the understanding and detains it, demanding that it be resolved, to wit, whether they subsist in bodies themselves, or whether they seem to be incorporeal subsistences beyond bodies. Of course, there are two forms of the incorporeal, so that some things can be outside bodies and perdure in their incorporeality separated from bodies, as God, mind, and soul; but others, although they are incorporeal, nevertheless can not be apart from bodies, as line, or surface, or number, or particular qualities, which, although we pronounce them to be incorporeal because they are not at all extended in three dimensions, nevertheless are in bodies in such fashion that they can not be torn from them or separated, or if they have been

---

[1]For example, *The Posterior Analytics*.

separated from bodies, they in no manner continue to be. These questions although they are difficult, to the point that even Porphyry for the time refused to solve them, I shall nevertheless take up, that I may neither leave the mind of the reader uneasy, nor myself consume time and energy in these things which are outside the sequence of the task I have undertaken. First of all I shall state a few things concerning the ambiguity of the question, and then I shall attempt to remove and untie that knot of doubt.

Genera and species either are and subsist or are formed by the understanding and thought alone. But genera and species can not be. This moreover is understood from the following considerations. For anything that is common at one time to many can not be one; indeed, that which is common is of many, particularly when one and the same thing is completely in many things at one time. Howsoever many species indeed there are, there is one genus in them all, not that the individual species share, as it were, some part of it, but each of them has at one time the whole genus. It follows from this that the whole genus, placed at one time in many individuals, can not be one; nor in fact can it happen that, since it is wholly in many at one time, it be one in number in itself. But if this is so, no genus can possibly be one, from which it follows that it is absolutely nothing; for everything which is, is because it is one. And the same thing may properly be said of species. Yet if there are genus and species, but they are multiplex and not one in number, there will be no last genus, but it will have some other genus superposed on it, which would include that multiplicity in the word of its single name. For as the genera of many animals are sought for the following reason, that they have something similar, yet are not the same, so too, since the genus, which is in many and is therefore multiplex, has the likeness of itself, which is the genus, but is not one, because it is in many, another genus of this genus must likewise be looked for, and when that has been found, for the reason which has been mentioned above, still a third genus is to be sought out. And so reason must proceed in *infinitum,* since no end of the process occurs. But if any genus is one in number, it can not possibly be common to many. For a single thing, if it is common, is common by parts, and then it is not common as a whole, but the parts of it are proper to individual things, or else it passes at differ-

ent times into the use of those having it, so that it is common as a servant or a horse is; or else it is made common to all at one time, not however that it constitute the substance of those to which it is common, but like some theatre or spectacle, which is common to all who look on. But genus can be common to the species according to none of these modes; for it must be common in such fashion that it is in the individuals wholly and at one time, and that it is able to constitute and form the substance of those things to which it is common. For this reason, if it is neither one, because it is common, nor many, because still another genus must be sought for that multitude, it will be seen that genus absolutely is not, and the same conclusion must be applied to the others. But if genera and species and the others are grasped only by understandings, since every idea is made either from the subject thing as the thing is constituted itself or as the thing is not constituted—for an idea can not be made from no subject—if the idea of genus and species and the others comes from the subject thing as the thing itself is constituted which is understood, then they are not only placed in the understanding but are placed also in the truth of things. And again it must be sought out what their nature is which the previous question investigated. But if the idea of genus and the rest is taken from the thing not as the thing is constituted which is subject to the idea, the idea must necessarily be vain, which is taken from the thing but not as the thing is constituted; for that is false which is understood otherwise than the thing is. Thus, therefore, since genus and species neither are, nor, when they are understood, is the idea of them true, it is not uncertain that all this must be set forth relative to the care which is needed for investigating concerning the five predicables aforementioned, seeing that the inquiry is neither concerning the thing which is, nor concerning that of which something true can be understood or adduced.

11. This for the present is the question with regard to the aforementioned predicables, which we solve, in accord with Alexander, by the following reasoning. We say that it is not necessary that every idea which is formed from a subject but not as the subject itself is constituted, seem false and empty. For false opinion, but not understanding, is in only those ideas which are made by composition. For if any one composes and joins by the understanding that which nature does not suffer to be joined, no one is unaware that that is false, as would be the case should one join by the imagination horse and man and construct a centaur. But if it be done by division and by abstraction, the thing would not be constituted as the idea is, yet for all that, the idea is still not in the least false; for there are many things which have their being in others, from which either they can not at all be separated, or if they should be separated they subsist by no reason. And in order that this be shown to us in a well-known example, the line is something in a body, and it owes to the body that which it is, namely, it retains its being through body. Which is shown thus: if it should be separated from body, it does not subsist; for who ever perceived with any sense a line separated from body? But when the mind receives from the senses things confused and intermingled with each other, it distinguishes them by its own power and thought. For sense transmits to us, besides bodies themselves, all incorporeal things of this sort which have their being in bodies, but the mind which has the power to compound that which is disjoined and to resolve that which is composite, so distinguishes the things which are transmitted by the senses, confused with and joined to bodies, that it may contemplate and see the incorporeal nature in itself and without the bodies in which it is concrete. For the characteristics of incorporeal things mixed with bodies are diverse even when they are separated from body. Genera, therefore, and species and the others are found either in incorporeal things or in those which are corporeal. And if the mind finds them in incorporeal things, it has in that instance an incorporeal understanding of a genus, but if it has perceived the geners, and species of corporeal things, it bears off, as is its wont, the nature of incorporeals from bodies, and beholds it alone and pure as the form itself is in itself. So when the mind receives these incorporeals intermixed with bodies, separating them, it looks upon them and contemplates them. No one, therefore, may say that we think about the line falsely because we seize it by the mind as if it were outside bodies, since it can not be outside bodies. For not every idea which is taken from subject things otherwise than the things are themselves constituted, must be considered to be false, but, as has been said above, that only is false which does this by composition, as when one thinks, joining man and

horse, that there is a centaur: but that which accomplishes it by divisions, and abstractions, and assumptions from the things in which they are, not only is not false, but it alone can discover that which is true with respect to the characteristic of the thing. Things of this sort therefore are in corporeal and sensible things, but they are understood without sensible things, in order that their nature can be perceived and their characteristic comprehended. Since genera and species are thought, their likeness, therefore, is gathered from the individuals in which they are, as the likeness of humanity is gathered from individual men unlike each other, which likeness conceived by the mind and perceived truly is made the species; again when the likeness of these diverse species is considered, which can not be except in the species themselves or in the individuals of the species, it forms the genus. Consequently, genera and species are in individuals, but they are thought universals; and species must be considered to be nothing other than the thought collected from the substantial likeness of individuals unlike in number, and genus the thought collected from the likeness of species. But this likeness when it is in individual things is made sensible, when it is in universals it is made intelligible; and in the same way when it is sensible, it remains in individuals, when it is understood, it is made universal. Therefore, they subsist in sensibles, but they are understood without bodies. For there is nothing to prevent two things which are in the same subject from being different in reason, like a concave and a convex line, which things, although they are defined by diverse definitions and although the understanding of them is diverse, are nevertheless always found in the same subject; for it is the same line which is convex and concave. So too for genera and species, that is, for singularity and universality, there is only one subject, but it is universal in one manner when it is thought, and singular in another when it is perceived in those things in which it has its being.

Once these distinctions are made, therefore, the whole question, I believe, is solved. For genera and species subsist in one manner, but are understood in another; and they are incorporeal, but they subsist in sensible things joined to sensible things. They are understood, to be sure, as subsisting through themselves and not as having their being in others. Plato, however, thinks that genera, and species, and the rest not only are understood as universals, but also are and subsist without bodies; whereas Aristotle thinks that they are understood as incorporeal and universal, but subsist in sensibles; we have not considered it proper to determine between their opinions, for that is of more lofty philosophy. But we have followed out the opinion of Aristotle very diligently for this reason, not in the least because we approved of it, but because this book has been written for the *Categories*, of which Aristotle is the author.

12. *This, however, I shall now try to show you, how the ancients treated probably of the categories and the predicables, and of the ancients most of all the peripatetics.*

Having passed by these questions which he [Aristotle] said were too lofty, he seeks an ordinary treatment of this introductory work, but lest the very omission of these questions by him be adduced as a defect, he set down how each of the suggested subjects is to be treated, and he makes announcement beforehand of the authority of every one on whom he relied when he undertook the work. Since be promises a moderateness of treatment, having removed the difficulty of obscurity, he invites the mind of the reader; but that his mind may acquiesce and listen silently to what will be said, he establishes what is said on the authority of the peripatelies. And therefore be says he will treat *probably* of these, that is, of genera and species concerning which he had raised the questions above, and of the predicables, that is, of differences, properties, and accidents. *Probably*, however, means *similarly to the true*, and *probably* in Aristotle and in Boethius and Alexander. Porphyry too has used that word in many places in that meaning, which we have omitted in translation . . . to be interpreted as if we were to say *rationally*. For the following meaning seemed by far better and more true: that he promised to speak probably, that is, not beyond the imagination of beginners and of readers, which is proper for an introduction. For since the secret of the more lofty doctrine would be remote from the minds of unlearned men, an introduction ought to be such that it is not beyond the imagination of beginners. And, therefore, we have interpreted it better, it seems to us, as *probably* than as *rationally*. He says, moreover, that the ancients had investigated concerning the same things, but that he followed most of all the treatment which the peripateties under the leadership of Aristotle left, so that the whole investigation is in accordance with the *Categories*.

STUDY QUESTIONS: BOETHIUS, *COMMENTARIES ON THE ISAGOGE OF PORPHYRY*

1. How do we grasp the forms of things? How do our images relate to the forms?
2. What is the "third power" of the soul?
3. What is the main activity of the soul?
4. What is Boethius' view of Epicurus' atoms?
5. Why is knowledge of differences important?
6. What does Boethius mean by *demonstration*? How is it achieved and what is its *significance*?
7. How does Boethius characterize the difference between Plato and Aristotle regarding genera and species?

CONSOLATION OF PHILOSOPHY

Written in alteration between verse and prose, the *Consolation of Philosophy* is a dialogue between the author and Philosophy, who appears to him in the guise of a beautiful, majestic woman. It begins with a condemnation of the views of the Stoics and the Epicureans; Philosophy proclaims that throughout its long history there have been but a handful of true philosophers, the most important of which are Socrates, Plato, and Aristotle. After giving a summary of Plato's *Timaeus* in verse she elaborates a vast, essentially Platonic metaphysics.

The book was written while Boethius was in prison awaiting execution. Its serene tone has evoked comparisons with the last of the four dialogues concerning Plato's trial, the *Phaedo*, in which Socrates drank the infamous hemlock bravely and without fear. Before his execution Socrates addressed his colleagues with his final commentaries on life, death, and the nature of philosophy. Centuries later, Boethius now awaits the same fate.

Our selection is from the fifth and final book. Here Philosophy slowly and carefully explains to Boethius how a fully determined, eternal world created by an all-knowing God is nevertheless compatible both with the existence of evil (of which Boethius is no doubt the victim) and human free will.

Here she made an end and was for turning the course of her speaking to the handling and explaining of other subjects. Then said I: "Your encouragement is right and most worthy in truth of your name and weight. But I am learning by experience what you just now said of Providence; that the question is bound up in others. I would ask you whether you think that chance exists at all, and what you think it is?"

Then she answered, "I am eager to fulfil my promised debt, and to shew you the path by which you may seek your home. But these things, though all-expedient for knowledge, are none the less rather apart from our path, and we must be careful lest you become wearied by our turnings aside, and so be not strong enough to complete the straight journey."

"Have no fear at all thereof," said I. "It will be restful to know these things in which I have so great a pleasure; and when every view of your reasoning has stood firm with unshaken credit, so let there be no doubt of what shall follow."

"I will do your pleasure," she made answer, and thus she began to speak:

"If chance is defined as an outcome of random influence, produced by no sequence of causes, I am sure that there is no such thing as chance, and I consider that it is but an empty word, beyond shewing the meaning of the matter which we have in hand. For what place can be left for anything happening at random, so long as God controls everything in order? It is a true saying that nothing can come out of nothing. None of the old philosophers has denied that, though they did not apply it to the effective principle, but to the matter operated upon—that is to say, to nature; and this was the foundation upon which they built all their reasoning. If anything arises from no causes, it will appear to have risen out of nothing. But if this is impossible, then chance also cannot be any-

thing of that sort, which is stated in the definition which we mentioned."

"Then is there nothing which can be justly called chance, nor anything 'by chance'?" I asked. "Or is there anything which common people know not, but which those words do suit?"

"My philosopher, Aristotle, defined it in his *Physics* shortly and well-nigh truly."

"How?" I asked.

"Whenever anything is done with one intention, but something else, other than was intended, results from certain causes, that is called chance: as, for instance, if a man digs the ground for the sake of cultivating it, and finds a heap of buried gold. Such a thing is believed to have happened by chance, but it does not come from nothing, for it has its own causes, whose unforeseen and unexpected coincidence seem to have brought about a chance. For if the cultivator did not dig the ground, if the owner had not buried his money, the gold would not have been found. These are the causes of the chance piece of good fortune, which comes about from the causes which meet it, and move along with it, not from the intention of the actor. For neither the burier nor the tiller intended that the gold should be found; but, as I said, it was a coincidence, and it happened that the one dug up what the other buried. We may therefore define chance as an unexpected result from the coincidence of certain causes in matters where there was another purpose. The order of the universe, advancing with its inevitable sequences, brings about this coincidence of causes. This order itself emanates from its source, which is Providence, and disposes all things in their proper time and place.

"In the land where the Parthian, as he turns in flight, shoots his arrows into the pursuer's breast, from the rocks of the crag of Achæmenia, the Tigris and

Euphrates flow from out one source, but quickly with divided streams are separate. If they should come together and again be joined in a single course, all, that the two streams bear along, would flow in one together. Boats would meet boats, and trees meet trees torn up by the currents, and the mingled waters would together entwine their streams by chance; but their sloping beds restrain these chances vague, and the downward order of the falling torrent guides their courses. Thus does chance, which seems to rush onward without rein, bear the bit, and take its way by rule."

Philosophy asserts the existence of free will.

"I have listened to you," I said, "and agree that it is as you say. But in this close sequence of causes, is there any freedom for our judgment, or does this chain of fate bind the very feelings of our minds too?"

"There is free will," she answered. "Nor could there he any reasoning nature without freedom of judgment. For any being that can use its reason by nature, has a power of judgment by which it can without further aid decide each point, and so distinguish between objects to be desired and objects to be shunned. Each therefore seeks what it deems desirable, and flies from what it considers should be shunned. Wherefore all who have reason have also freedom of desiring and refusing in themselves. But I do not lay down that this is equal in all beings. Heavenly and divine beings have with them a judgment of great insight, an imperturbable will, and a power which can effect their desires. But human spirits must be more free when they keep themselves safe in the contemplation of the mind of God; but less free when they sink into bodies, and less still when they are bound by their earthly members. The last stage is mere slavery, when the spirit is given over to vices and has fallen away from the possession of its reason. . . . by yielding to these passions and consenting to them, men increase the slavery which they have brought upon themselves, and their true liberty is lost in captivity. But God, looking upon all out of the infinite, perceives the views of Providence, and disposes each as its destiny has already fated for it according to its merits: 'He looketh over all and heareth all'.

"Homer with his honeyed lips sang of the bright sun's clear light; yet the sun cannot burst with his fee-

ble rays the bowels of the earth or the depths of the sea. Not so with the Creator of this great sphere. No masses of earth can block His vision as He looks over all. Night's cloudy darkness cannot resist Him. With one glance of His intelligence He sees all that has been, that is, and that is to come. He alone can see all things, so truly He may be called the Sun."

Then said I, "Again am I plunged in yet more doubt and difficulty."

Boethius cannot reconcile God's foreknowledge with man's free will.

"What are they," she asked, "though I have already my idea of what your trouble consists?"

"There seems to me," I said, "to be such incompatibility between the existence of God's universal foreknowledge and that of any freedom of judgment. For if God foresees all things and cannot in anything be mistaken, that, which His Providence sees will happen, must result. Wherefore if it knows beforehand not only men's deeds but even their designs and wishes, there will be no freedom of judgment. For there can neither be any deed done, nor wish formed, except such as the infallible Providence of God has foreseen. For if matters could ever so be turned that they resulted otherwise than was foreseen of Providence, this foreknowledge would cease to be sure. But, rather than knowledge, it is opinion which is uncertain; and that, I deem, is not applicable to God. And, further, I cannot approve of an argument by which some men think that they can cut this knot; for they say that a result does not come to pass for the reason that Providence has foreseen it, but the opposite rather, namely, that because it is about to come to pass, therefore it cannot be hidden from God's Providence. In that way it seems to me that the argument must resolve itself into an argument on the other side. For in that case it is not necessary that that should happen which is foreseen, but that that which is about to happen should be foreseen; as though, indeed, our doubt was whether God's foreknowledge is the certain cause of future events, or the certainty of future events is the cause of Providence. But let our aim be to prove that, whatever be the shape which this series of causes takes, the fulfilment of God's foreknowledge is necessary, even if this knowledge may not seem to induce the necessity for the occurrence of future events. For instance, if a man sits down, it must be that the opinion, which conjectures that he is sitting, is true; but conversely, if the opinion concerning the man is true because he is sitting, he must be sitting down. There is therefore necessity in both cases: the man must be sitting, and the opinion must be true. But he does not sit because the opinion is true, but rather the opinion is true because his sitting down has preceded it. Thus, though the cause of the truth of the opinion proceeds from the other fact, yet there is a common necessity on both parts. In like manner we must reason of Providence and future events. For even though they are foreseen because they are about to happen, yet they do not happen because they are foreseen. None the less it is necessary that either what is about to happen should be foreseen of God, or that what has been foreseen should happen; and this alone is enough to destroy all free will.

"Yet how absurd it is that we should say that the result of temporal affairs is the cause of eternal foreknowledge! And to think that God foresees future events because they are about to happen, is nothing else than to hold events of past time to be the cause of that highest Providence. Besides, just as, when I know a present fact, that fact must be so; so also when I know of something that will happen, that must come to pass. Thus it follows that the fulfilment of a foreknown event must be inevitable.

"Lastly, if anyone believes that any matter is otherwise than the fact is, he not only has not knowledge, but his opinion is false also, and that is very far from the truth of knowledge. Wherefore, if any future event is such that its fulfilment is not sure or necessary, how can it possibly be known beforehand that it will occur? For just as absolute knowledge has no taint of falsity, so also that which is conceived by knowledge cannot be otherwise than as it is conceived. That is the reason why knowledge cannot lie, because each matter must be just as knowledge knows that it is. What then? How can God know beforehand these uncertain future events? For if He thinks inevitable the fulfilment of such things as may possibly not result, He is wrong; and that we may not believe, nor even utter, rightly. But if He perceives that they will result as they are in such a manner that He only knows that they may or may not occur,

equally, how is this foreknowledge, this which knows nothing for sure, nothing absolutely? How is such a foreknowledge different from the absurd prophecy which Horace puts in the mouth of Tiresias: 'Whatever I shall say, will either come to pass, or it will not'?[1] How, too, would God's Providence be better than man's opinion, if, as men do, He only sees to be uncertain such things as have an uncertain result? But if there can be no uncertainty with God, the most sure source of all things, then the fulfilment of all that He has surely foreknown, is certain. Thus we are led to see that there is no freedom for the intentions or actions of men; for the mind of God, foreseeing all things without error or deception, binds all together and controls their results And when we have once allowed this, it is plain how complete is the fall of all human actions in consequence. In vain are rewards or punishments set before good or bad, for there is no free or voluntary action of the mind to deserve them; and what we just now determined was most fair, will prove to be most unfair of all, namely to punish the dishonest or reward the honest, since their own will does not put them in the way of honest or dishonesty, but the unfailing necessity of development constrains them. Wherefore neither virtues nor vices are anything, but there is rather an indiscriminate confusion of all deserts. And nothing could be more vicious than this; since the whole order of all comes from Providence, and nothing is left to human intention, it follows that our crimes, as well as our good deeds, must all be held due to the author of all good. Hence it is unreasonable to hope for or pray against aught. For what could any man hope for or pray against, if an undeviating chain links together all that we can desire? Thus will the only understanding between God and man, the right of prayer, be taken away. We suppose that at the price of our deservedly humbling ourselves before Him we may win a right to the inestimable reward of His divine grace: this is the only manner in which men can seem to deal with God, so to speak, and by virtue of prayer to join ourselves to that inaccessible light, before it is granted to us; but if we allow the inevitability of the future, and believe that we have no power, what means shall we have to join ourselves to the Lord of all, or how can we cling to Him? Wherefore, as you sang but a little

---

[1]Horace, *Satires*, II. v. 59.

while ago, the human race must be cut off from its source and ever fall away.

"What cause of discord is it breaks the bonds of agreement here? What heavenly power has set such strife between two truths? Thus, though apart each brings no doubt, yet can they not be linked together. Comes there no discord between these truths? Stand they for ever sure by one another? Yes, 'tis the mind, overwhelmed by the body's blindness, which cannot see by the light of that dimmed brightness the finest threads that bind the truth. But wherefore burns the spirit with so strong desire to learn the hidden signs of truth? Knows it the very object of its careful search? Then why seeks it to learn anew what it already knows? If it knows it not, why searches it in blindness? For who would desire aught unwitting? Or who could seek after that which is unknown? How should he find it, or recognize its form when found, if he knows it not? And when the mind of man perceived the mind of God, did it then know the whole and parts alike? Now is the mind buried in the cloudy darkness of the body, yet has not altogether forgotten its own self, and keeps the whole though it has lost the parts. Whosoever, therefore, seeks the truth, is not wholly in ignorance, nor yet has knowledge wholly; for he knows not all, yet is not ignorant of all. He takes thought for the whole which he keeps in memory, handling again what he saw on high, so that he may add to that which he has kept, that which he has forgotten."

Philosophy tries to shew how they may be reconciled.

Then said she, "This is the old plaint concerning Providence which was so strongly urged by Cicero when treating of Divination,[1] and you yourself have often and at length questioned the same subject. But so far, none of you have explained it with enough diligence or certainty. The cause of this obscurity is that the working of human reason cannot approach the directness of divine foreknowledge. If this could be understood at all, there would be no doubt left. And this especially will I try to make plain, if I can first explain your difficulties.

"Tell me why you think abortive the reasoning of those who solve the question thus; they argue that foreknowledge cannot be held to be a cause for the necessity of future results, and therefore free will is not in any way shackled by foreknowledge. Whence do you draw your proof of the necessity of future results if not from the fact that such things as are known beforehand cannot but come to pass? If, then (as you yourself admitted just now), foreknowledge brings no necessity to bear upon future events, how is it that the voluntary results of such events are bound to find a fixed end? Now for the sake of the argument, that you may turn your attention to what follows, let us state that there is no foreknowledge at all. Then are the events which are decided by free will, bound by any necessity, so far as this goes? Of course not. Secondly, let us state that foreknowledge exists, but brings no necessity to bear upon events; then, I think, the same free will will be left, intact and absolute. 'But,' you will say, 'though foreknowledge is no necessity for a result in the future, yet it is a sign that it will necessarily come to pass.' Thus, therefore, even if there had been no foreknowledge, it would be plain that future results were under necessity; for every sign can only shew what it is that it points out; it does not bring it to pass. Wherefore we must first prove that nothing happens but of necessity, in order that it may be plain that foreknowledge is a sign of this necessity. Otherwise, if there is no necessity, then foreknowledge will not be a sign of that which does not exist. Now it is allowed that proof rests upon firm reasoning, not upon signs or external arguments; it must be deduced from suitable and binding causes. How can it possibly be that things, which are foreseen as about to happen, should not occur? That would be as though we were to believe that events would not occur which Providence foreknows as about to occur, and as though we did not rather think this, that though they occur, yet they have had no necessity in their own natures which brought them about. We can see many actions developing before our eyes; just as chariot drivers see the development of their actions as they control and guide their chariots, and many other things likewise. Does any necessity compel any of those things to occur as they do? Of course not. All art, craft, and intention would be in vain, if everything took place by compulsion. Therefore, if things have no necessity for coming to pass when they do, they cannot have any necessity to be about to come to pass before they do. Wherefore there are things

---

[1] Cicero, *De Divinatione*, II.

whose results are entirely free from necessity. For I think not that there is any man who will say this, that things, which are done in the present, were not about to be done in the past, before they are done. Thus these foreknown events have their free results. Just as foreknowledge of present things brings no necessity to bear upon them as they come to pass, so also foreknowledge of future things brings no necessity to bear upon things which are to come.

"But you will say that there is no doubt of this too, whether there can be any foreknowledge of things which have not results bounden by necessity. For they do seem to lack harmony: and you think that if they are foreseen, the necessity follows; if there is no necessity, then they cannot be foreseen; nothing can be perceived certainly by knowledge, unless it be certain. But if things have uncertainty of result, but are foreseen as though certain, this is plainly the obscurity of opinion, and not the truth of knowledge. For you believe that to think aught other than it is, is the opposite of true knowledge. The cause of this error is that every man believes that all the subjects, that he knows, are known by their own force or nature alone, which are known; but it is quite the opposite. For every subject, that is known, is comprehended not according to its own force, but rather according to the nature of those who know it. Let me make this plain to you by a brief example: the roundness of a body may be known in one way by sight, in another way by touch. Sight can take in the whole body at once from a distance by judging its radii, while touch clings, as it were, to the outside of the sphere, and from close at hand perceives through the material parts the roundness of the body as it passes over the actual circumference. A man himself is differently comprehended by the senses, by imagination, by reason, and by intelligence. For the senses distinguish the form as set in the matter operated upon by the form; imagination distinguishes the appearance alone without the matter. Reason goes even further than imagination; by a general and universal contemplation it investigates the actual kind which is represented in individual specimens. Higher still is the view of the intelligence, which reaches above the sphere of the universal, and with the unsullied eye of

the mind gazes upon that very form of the kind in its absolute simplicity. Herein the chief point for our consideration is this: the higher power of understanding includes the lower, but the lower never rises to the higher. For the senses are capable of understanding naught but the matter; imagination cannot look upon universal or natural kinds; reason cannot comprehend the absolute form; whereas the intelligence seems to look down from above and comprehend the form, and distinguishes all that lie below, but in such a way that it grasps the very form which could not be known to any other than itself. For it perceives and knows the general kind, as does reason; the appearance, as does the imagination; and the matter, as do the senses, but with one grasp of the mind it looks upon all with a clear conception of the whole. And reason too, as it views general kinds, does not make use of the imagination nor the senses, but yet does perceive the objects both of the imagination and of the senses. It is reason which thus defines a general kind according to its conception: man, for instance, is an animal, biped and reasoning. This is a general notion of a natural kind, but no man denies that the subject can be approached by the imagination and by the senses, just because reason investigates it by a reasonable conception and not by the imagination or senses. Likewise, though imagination takes its beginning of seeing and forming appearances from the senses yet without their aid it surveys each subject by an imaginative faculty of distinguishing, not by the distinguishing faculty of the senses.

"Do you see then, how in knowledge of all things, the subject uses its own standard of capability, and not those of the objects known? And this is but reasonable, for every judgment formed is an act of the person who judges, and therefore each man must of necessity perform his own action from his own capability and not the capability of any other.

"In days of old the Porch at Athens[1] gave us men, seeing dimly as in old age, who could believe that the feelings of the senses and the imagination were but impressions on the mind from bodies without them, just as the old custom was to impress with swift-running pens letters upon the surface of a waxen tablet which bore no marks before. But if the

---

[1]Zeno, of Citium (342-270 BCE), the founder of the Stoa school, taught in the Stoa Pockile, whence the name of the school. The following lines refer to their doctrine of presentations and impressions.

mind with its own force can bring forth naught by its own exertions; if it does but lie passive and subject to the marks of other bodies; if it reflects, as does, forsooth, a mirror, the vain reflections of other things; whence thrives there in the soul an all-seeing power of knowledge? What is the force that sees the single parts, or which distinguishes the facts it knows? What is the force that gathers up the parts it has distinguished, that takes its course in order due, now rises to mingle with the things on high, and now sinks down among the things below, and then to itself brings back itself, and, so examining, refutes the false with truth? This is a cause of greater power, of more effective force by far than that which only receives the impressions of material bodies. Yet does the passive reception come first, rousing and stirring all the strength of the mind in the living body. When the eyes are smitten with a light, or the ears are struck with a voice's sound, then is the spirit's energy aroused, and, thus moved, calls upon like forms, such as it holds within itself, fits them to signs without and mingles the forms of its imagination with those which it has stored within.

Human reasoning, being lower than divine intelligence, can at best only strive to approach thereto.

"With regard to feeling the effects of bodies, natures which are brought into contact from without may affect the organs of the senses, and the body's passive affection may precede the active energy of the spirit, and call forth to itself the activity of the mind; if then, when the effects of bodies are felt, the mind is not marked in any way by its passive reception thereof, but declares that reception subject to the body of its own force, how much less do those subjects, which are free from all affections of bodies, follow external objects in their perceptions, and how much more do they make clear the way for the action of their mind? By this argument many different manners of understanding have fallen to widely different natures of things. For the senses are incapable of any knowledge but their own, and they alone fall to those living beings which are incapable of motion, as are sea shell-fish, and other low forms of life which live by clinging to rocks; while imagination is granted to animals with the power of motion, who seem to be affected by some desire to seek or avoid certain things. But reason belongs to the human race alone, just as the true intelligence is God's alone. Wherefore that manner of knowledge is better than others, for it can comprehend of its own nature not only the subject peculiar to itself, but also the subjects of the other kinds of knowledge. Suppose that the senses and imagination thus oppose reasoning, saying, 'The universal natural kinds, which reason believes that it can perceive, are nothing; for what is comprehensible to the senses and the imagination cannot be universal: therefore either the judgment, of reason is true, and that which can be perceived by the senses is nothing; or, since reason knows well that there are many subjects comprehensible to the senses and imagination, the conception of reason is vain, for it holds to be universal what is an individual matter comprehensible to the senses.' To this reason might answer, that 'it sees from a general point of view what is comprehensible to the senses and the imagination, but they cannot aspire to a knowledge of universals, since their manner of knowledge cannot go further than material or bodily appearances; and in the matter of knowledge it is better to trust to the stronger and more nearly perfect judgment.' If such a trial of argument occurred, should not we, who have within us the force of reasoning as well as the powers of the senses and imagination, approve of the cause of reason rather than that of the others? It is in like manner that human reason thinks that the divine intelligence cannot perceive the things of the future except as it conceives them itself. For you argue thus: 'If there are events which do not appear to have sure or necessary results, their results cannot be known for certain beforehand: therefore there can be no foreknowledge of these events; for if we believe that there is any foreknowledge thereof, there can exist nothing but such as is brought forth of necessity.' If therefore we, who have our share in possession of reason, could go further and possess the judgment of the mind of God, we should then think it most just that human reason should yield itself to the mind of God, just as we have determined that the senses and imagination ought to yield to reason.

"Let us therefore raise ourselves, if so be that we can, to that height of the loftiest intelligence. For there reason will see what it cannot of itself perceive, and that is to know how even such things as have uncertain results are perceived definitely and for certain by foreknowledge; and such foreknowledge will not be mere opinion, but rather the single and direct form of the highest knowledge unlimited by any finite bounds.

"In what different shapes do living beings move upon the earth! Some make flat their bodies, sweeping through the dust and using their strength to make therein a furrow without break; some flit here and there upon light wings which beat the breeze, and they float through vast tracks of air in their easy flight. 'Tis others' wont to plant their footsteps on the ground, and pass with their paces over green fields or under trees. Though all these thou seest move in different shapes, yet all have their faces downward along the ground, and this doth draw downward and dull their senses. Alone of all, the human race lifts up its head on high, and stands in easy balance with the body upright, and so looks down to spurn the earth. If thou art not too earthly by an evil folly, this pose is as a lesson. Thy glance is upward, and thou dost carry high thy head, and thus thy search is heavenward: then lead thy soul too upward, lest while the body is higher raised, the mind sink lower to the earth.

Philosophy explains that God's divine intelligence can view all things from its eternal mind, while human reason can only see them from a temporal point of view.

"Since then all that is known is apprehended, as we just now shewed, not according to its own nature but according to the nature of the knower, let us examine, so far as we lawfully may, the character of the divine nature, so that we may be able to learn what its knowledge is.

"The common opinion, according to all men living, is that God is eternal. Let us therefore consider what is eternity. For eternity will, I think, make clear to us at the same time the divine nature and knowledge.

"Eternity is the simultaneous and complete possession of infinite life. This will appear more clearly if we compare it with temporal things. All that lives under the conditions of time moves through the present from the past to the future; there is nothing set in time which can at one moment grasp the whole space of its lifetime. It cannot yet comprehend tomorrow; yesterday it has already lost. And in this life of today your life is no more than a changing, passing moment. And as Aristotle[1] said of the universe, so it is of all that is subject to time; though it never began to be, nor will ever cease, and its life is co-extensive with the infinity of time, yet it is not such as can be held to be eternal. For though it apprehends and grasps a space of infinite lifetime, it does not embrace the whole simultaneously; it has not yet experienced the future. What we should rightly call eternal is that which grasps and possesses wholly and simultaneously the fulness of unending life, which lacks naught of the future, and has lost naught of the fleeting past; and such an existence must be ever present in itself to control and aid itself, and also must keep present with itself the infinity of changing time. Therefore, people who hear that Plato thought that this universe had no beginning of time and will have no end, are not right in thinking that in this way the created world is co-eternal with its creator. For to pass through unending life, the attribute which Plato ascribes to the universe is one thing; but it is another thing to grasp simultaneously the whole of unending life in the present; this is plainly a peculiar property of the mind of God.

"And further, God should not be regarded as older than His creations by any period of time, but rather by the peculiar property of His own single nature. For the infinite changing of temporal things tries to imitate the ever simultaneously present immutability of His life: it cannot succeed in imitating or equaling this, but sinks from immutability into change, and falls from the single directness of the present into an infinite space of future and past. And since this temporal state cannot possess its life completely and simultaneously, but it does in the same manner exist for ever without ceasing, it therefore seems to try in some degree to rival that which it cannot fulfil or represent, for it binds itself to some sort of present time out of this small and fleeting moment; but inasmuch as this temporal present bears a certain appearance of that abiding present, it somehow makes those, to whom it comes, seem to be in truth what they imitate. But since this imitation could not

---

[1]Aristotle, *De Caelo*, 1.

be abiding, the unending march of time has swept it away, and thus we find that it has bound together, as it passes, a chain of life, which it could not by abiding embrace in its fulness. And thus if we would apply proper epithets to those subjects, we can say, following Plato, that God is eternal, but the universe is continual.

"Since then all judgment apprehends the subjects of its thought according to its own nature, and God has a condition of ever-present eternity, His knowledge, which passes over every change of time, embracing infinite lengths of past and future, views in its own direct comprehension everything as though it were taking place in the present. If you would weigh the foreknowledge by which God distinguishes all things, you will more rightly hold it to be a knowledge of a never-failing constancy in the present, than a foreknowledge of the future. Whence Providence is more rightly to be understood as a looking forth than a looking forward, because it is set far from low matters and looks forth upon all things as from a lofty mountain-top above all. Why then do you demand that all things occur by necessity, if divine light rests upon them, while men do not render necessary such things as they can see? Because you can see things of the present, does your sight therefore put upon them any necessity? Surely not. If one may not unworthily compare this present time with the divine, just as you can see things in this your temporal present, so God sees all things in His eternal present. Wherefore this divine foreknowledge does not change the nature or individual qualities of things: it sees things present in its understanding just as they will result some time in the future. It makes no confusion in its distinctions, and with one view of its mind it discerns all that shall come to pass whether of necessity or not. For instance, when you see at the same time a man walking on the earth and the sun rising in the heavens, you see each sight simultaneously, yet you distinguish between them, and decide that one is moving voluntarily, the other of necessity. In like manner the perception of God looks down upon all things without disturbing at all their nature, though they are present to Him but future under the conditions of time. Wherefore this foreknowledge is not opinion but knowledge resting upon truth, since He knows that a future event is,

though He knows too that it will not occur of necessity. If you answer here that what God sees about to happen, cannot but happen, and that what cannot but happen is bound by necessity, you fasten me down to the word necessity, I will grant that we have a matter of most firm truth, but it is one to which scarce any man can approach unless he be a contemplator of the divine. For I shall answer that such a thing will occur of necessity, when it is viewed from the point of divine knowledge; but when it is examined in its own nature, it seems perfectly free and unrestrained. For there are two kinds of necessities; one is simple: for instance, a necessary fact, 'all men are mortal'; the other is conditional; for instance, if you know that a man is walking, he must be walking: for what each man knows cannot be otherwise than it is known to be; but the conditional one is by no means followed by this simple and direct necessity; for there is no necessity to compel a voluntary walker to proceed, though it is necessary that, if he walks, he should be proceeding. In the same way, if Providence sees an event in its present, that thing must be, though it has no necessity of its own nature. And God looks in His present upon those future things which come to pass through free will. Therefore if these things be looked at from the point of view of God's insight, they come to pass of necessity under the condition of divine knowledge; if, on the other hand, they are viewed by themselves, they do not lose the perfect freedom of their nature. Without doubt, then, all things that God foreknows do come to pass, but some of them proceed from free will; and though they result by coming into existence, yet they do not lose their own nature, because before they came to pass they could also not have come to pass.

"'What then,' you may ask, 'is the difference in their not being bound by necessity, since they result under all circumstances as by necessity, on account of the condition of divine knowledge?' This is the difference, as I just now put forward: take the sun rising and a man walking; while these operations are occurring, they cannot but occur: but the one was bound to occur before it did; the other was not so bound. What God has in His present, does exist without doubt; but of such things some follow by necessity, others by their authors' wills. Wherefore I was justified in saying that if these things be regarded from the view of divine knowledge, they are necessary, but if they are viewed by themselves, they are perfectly free from all ties of necessity: just as when you refer all, that is clear to the senses, to the reason, it becomes general truth, but it remains particular if regarded by itself. 'But,' you will say, 'if it is in my power to change a purpose of mine, I will disregard Providence, since I may change what Providence foresees.' To which I answer, 'You can change your purpose, but since the truth of Providence, knows in its present that you can do so, and whether you do so, and in what direction you may change it, therefore you cannot escape that divine foreknowledge: just as you cannot avoid the glance of a present eye, though you may by your free will turn yourself to all kinds of different actions.' 'What?' you will say, 'can I by my own action change divine knowledge, so that if I choose now one thing, now another, Providence too will seem to change its knowledge?' No; divine insight precedes all future things, turning them back and recalling them to the present time of its own peculiar knowledge. It does not change, as you may think, between this and that alternation of foreknowledge. It is constant in preceding and embracing by one glance all your changes. And God does not receive this ever-present grasp of all things and vision of the present at the occurrence of future events, but from His own peculiar directness. Whence also is that difficulty solved which you laid down a little while ago, that it was not worthy to say that our future events were the cause of God's knowledge. For this power of knowledge, ever in the present and embracing all things in its perception, does itself constrain all things, and owes naught to following events from which it has received naught. Thus, therefore, mortal men have their freedom of judgment intact. And since their wills are freed from all binding necessity, laws do not set rewards or punishments unjustly. God is ever the constant foreknowing overseer, and the ever-present eternity of His sight moves in harmony with the future nature of our actions, as it dispenses rewards to the good, and punishments to the bad. Hopes are not vainly put in God, nor prayers in vain offered: if these are right, they cannot but be answered. Turn therefore from vice: ensue virtue: raise your soul to upright hopes: send up on high your prayers from this earth. If you would be honest, great is the necessity enjoined upon your goodness, since all you do is done before the eyes of an all-seeing Judge."

STUDY QUESTIONS: BOETHIUS, CONSOLATION OF PHILOSOPHY

1. How does philosophy define "chance?" How does she compare it to Aristotle's?
2. Does Philosophy believe in free will? Why?
3. What is the problem, according to Boethius, between God's foreknowledge and human free will?
4. How does Philosophy reconcile human free will with divine foreknowledge?
5. What is the difference between the way God sees and the way human see?
6. Is God older than the universe, according to Philosophy?

Philosophical Bridges: The Influence of Boethius

Boethius' works on mathematics, logic, music, and theology were read, studied, and admired throughout the Middle Ages; his *Consolation of Philosophy* was the most widely read and translated book after the Bible. His continues to inspire philosophers and theologians to this day, albeit mainly through his influential translations of Plato and Aristotle. His refinement of the categorical and hypothetical syllogisms has become a staple of logic, as have his contributions to our understanding of the methods of analysis (the division of concepts), along with his precise definition of the term *definition* itself. His approach to the problem of universals influenced scholars throughout the Middle Ages, regardless whether they agreed with him or took issue with his theory.

JOHN SCOTUS ERIGENA (APPROX. 800–877)

Biographical History

Very little is known about the personal life of this great Irish philosopher and theologian. His name, "Erigena," (also spelled "Eriugena") stems from Erin, the ancient name for Ireland, which is also the meaning of his middle name, "Scotus" (also spelled "Scottus"), because in the 9th century the Irish were called "Scots." He is known to have worked at the court of Charles the Bald, the West Frankish king, where he translated the works of Denis the Psudo-Dionysus (Denis the Areopagite). He wrote commentaries also on Boethius, providing also a glossary of terms that subsequent thinkers followed.

Philosophical Overview

One of the first and greatest original thinkers of the Scholastic era, John Scotus Erigena's initial contribution was to bring attention to the works of Denis the Pseudo-Dionysus (the Areopagite) and providing a very influential glossary to Boethius' *opuscule sacra*. Erigena blended natural philosophy (which eventually, after the modern era, would come to be called physics) with semi-pantheistic ideas. Pantheism is the view, dating back to some of the most ancient religions and cults, that everything—the entire universe and everything and everyone in it—is God. Erigena tried to provide a balance between human rationalism and divine revelation, saying that the church and revelation outrank reason, but reason nevertheless takes precedent over human authorities, be they secular or religious. Thus Erigena says that while to question "divine" authority would obviously be sacrilegious, to question the human authorities *interpreting* divine authority as revealed, say, in divine scripture, is fair game, since humans are prone to error; this, he points out, is revealed by the fact that so many church authorities disagree about so many things!

Erigena's epistemology is based on a tripartite division of the mind's faculties for knowing. First is sense, or perception, which itself has two functions, one "internal" and one "external." The external sense receives impressions of how things appear; the internal sense perceives the nature of things. The faculty of reason (*logos*) examines the nature and cause of created things. The faculty of the intellect contemplates God. The intellect, which is superior to reason, is however not independent from reason, and when the two are in accord this he calls "right" or "true" reason. Intellectual understanding (*nous*), is itself an emanation within us of the divine light; knowledge is ultimately the result of mysterious divine illumination.

According to Erigena, reality—the whole of nature—can be divided into four categories:

1. that which creates but is uncreated (God)
2. that which is created and creates (us)
3. nature created but not creating (matter)
4. nature that is not created and does not create (also God).

Erigena argues that (2) and (4) are the domain of the intelligible (us) and the sensible (the world around us), where as (1) and (4) are God at the beginning and the end of everything that is, was, and will be. Intelligible creatures like ourselves, which are created and creating, are the primordial causes operating in the world, what he calls *copula munidi*, "links of the universe." Our souls, which are divine and whose existence is derived directly from God, are co-eternal with the world but do not exist in space and time. The world itself evolves through an infinite series of theophanies, manifestations of God.

ON THE DIVISION OF NATURE
John Scotus Erigena

In this work Erigena asks the perennial metaphysical question: what is the nature of the connection between thought and things, mind and reality? This itself requires an epistemology, a method of acquiring knowledge. We cannot know what anything is by studying an individual thing. We must, as Plato originally argued, know the idea. Just as the true natures of triangles, squares, and circles are revealed not in individual geometric figures, but in the eternal forms of mathematics, so too with all things, including ourselves. The main difference is that we are intellectual ideas who exist eternally in the mind of God and so what we are is what God knows of us: *to be*, in that sense, is *to be intelligible*.

The selection begins with the question of why God created human beings and why he gave us a dual nature, simultaneously both divine and animalistic, a synergy of angel and beast. In so far as we are made in God's image, why are we not angels? The method of inquiry is what the division of nature itself is. It begins with a single unique principle revealed by metaphysical analysis and then applied to the many. It ends with God, who because he is himself not an essence, does not know himself. This is one of the mystical Latin incantations, practiced by mystics and occultists for centuries thereafter: *Deus itaque nescit se, quid est, quia non est quid.*

BOOK IV, CHAPTERS 7–9

7. *Disciple*. But still the question remains, why did God create man, whom he wished to make in his image and likeness, a creature in the genus of animals? Surely it would seem more glorious for man, since he had been elected to be partaker of the supernal sign beyond all animals, and sharer with the celestial essences in which no consubstantiality with terrestial animals is permitted, to be created free from all animality. For the celestial essences are not loaded with terrestial bodies, nor do they use corporeal senses for knowledge of sensible things. For they do not receive phantasies from without, but know within themselves the reasons of the things which they see. So too the soul does not see outside itself what it perceives, but it sees within by phantasies which angels

do not undergo. Although Plato defines angel as a rational and immortal animal, we must not include in the sure speculations on natures that which we can not prove by the authority of the Holy Scriptures and of the holy fathers, since such inclusion is rash. On the other hand, the fact that Saint Augustine does not deny, but asserts that the highest angels have spiritual bodies in which they appear often, in no way compels us to believe that celestial substances are animals, especially since a harmony and an inseparable joining of celestial and incorruptible bodies to angelic spirits does not make an animal, but a connection of terrestial and corruptible bodies to souls, rational or irrational, with sense mediating between body and soul, does. For, if the exterior sense is present in angelic bodies and understandings, what prevents

Scoti, from *De Divisione Naturae, Liber Quartus*, ch. 7–9, in J. P. Migne, *Patrolgia Latina*, vol. 122, col. 762–781.

us from saying, as it pleased Plato to say, that they are animals composed of body and soul, with sense mediating and understanding vivifying? And if that is so, why are they not to be counted in the genus of animals? But man, even, if he had not sinned, would be animal. Certainly it is not sin but nature which made an animal of man, for no authority holds that the transgressing angels are animals. This would follow definitely from such an argument. Yet the future felicity which is promised to holy men is announced to be no other than an equality with the angelic nature, perfect and lacking in nothing. But what wise man would believe sanely that the future transmutation of man will be as if from an inferior animal to a superior one, from a terrestrial animal to a celestial one, from a temporal to an eternal, from a mortal to an immortal, from a miserable to a happy, rather than that all the things which in this life are understood or perceived in holy men in common with other animals are transferred by a certain ineffable mutation into that essence celestial and incommunicable and lacking in all animality, because that was to happen to man too if he did not sin? Wherefore, then, was man created in the genus of animals, which were produced of earth, in which genus he will not remain always? For, when this world of which man is an animal part shall have perished, all that is animal in man will perish with it and in it. For true reason does not permit that the whole suffer destruction and yet parts of it be saved from destruction. Besides, if all the world with all its parts will be destroyed, I do not sufficiently see how or where man, in so far as he is part of the world, will remain after the world. And because of this I am insistent in asking that you undo the knots of this question.

Master. You demand a very lofty physical theory of human creation, and you compel us to draw out our discussion to much greater length. It would suffice for me to answer you briefly when you ask why God should have created man, whom he proposed to make in his own image, in the genus of animals, that he wished so to fashion him that there would be a certain animal in which he manifested his own express image. But whoever asks why he wished that, asks the causes of the divine will, to ask which is too

presumptuous and arrogant. *For who hath known the sense of the Lord?*[1] Yet, if I say this, you will perhaps be silent ungratefully, and you will think that we can conclude nothing with respect to the pure and the perfect. I shall not, therefore, say why he willed, because that is beyond all understanding, but I shall say, as he himself has permitted, what he has willed to do. He has made all creation, visible and invisible, in man since the whole spread of created nature is understood to be in him. For although it is still unknown how much the first creation of man after the transgression is in defect of the eternal light, nevertheless there is nothing naturally present in the celestial essences which does not subsist essentially in man. For there is understanding and reason, and there is naturally implanted the ground reason [*ratio*] of possessing a celestial and angelic body, which after the resurrection will appear more clearly than light both in the good and the evil. For it will be common to all human nature to rise again in eternal and incorruptible spiritual bodies. "It is sown," he[2] says, "an animal body; it is raised a spiritual body." All this sensible world is fashioned in man. There is no part of it to be found, whether corporeal or incorporeal, which does not subsist created in man, which does not perceive, which does not live, which is not incorporated in him. Do not think of the corporeal size in man; consider rather the natural power, especially since you see even in the human body the pupil of the eye, which subsists with the greatest power although it is the most minute in quantity of all the members. If, therefore, God did not create man in the genus of animals, or certainly, if He did not place the whole nature of all animals in man, how would all creation, visible and invisible, be comprehended in Him? And we can therefore say rationally that God wished to place man in the genus of animals for this reason, that He wished to create every creature in Him. But, if you ask me why He wished to create every creature in Him, I answer that He wished to make him in His image and likeness, so that, as the principal example surpasses all by the excellence of essence, so His image would excel all things of creation in dignity and grace. I confess, however, that I ignore completely why He wished to make man espe-

---

[1]Romans 11:34.

[2]Paul, I Corinthians 15:44.

cially in His image before other creatures visible and invisible.

Disc. You have in my judgment answered the question why God wished to make man in the genus of animals sufficiently and reasonably. Nevertheless, I still ask this, how were all things created in man and how do they subsist in him—according to essence alone or according to accidents alone, or according to all things that are considered in the whole creation, that is, according to essence, species, difference, and property, and all that is understood concerning them?

Mast. How I shall solve that question reasonably does not occur to me easily. For, if I say according to essence alone, you will reply rightly that then all things are only in so far as they subsist essentially, and the other things which are understood concerning essence or substance are not to be counted in the number of the whole of things, and they are not at all. And if that is so, you will ask me whence those things are, then, which are understood concerning the essence of things. If I answer that they have been made by God, you will say: why, then, are they not included in the whole of things which is made in man? If I say they were not made by God, you will reply that then they are not; for if they were, they would not be from any other cause than from the cause of all things which is God. And if I grant that those things which are understood concerning essences are not in the number of things because they are not from God, you will say forthwith: how, then, are they understood? For everything which is not from God can in no manner be understood because it is not in any manner. If I say that not only the essences but also all things which are understood naturally concerning them are from God and are to be numbered in the parts of the whole, there is no doubt but that I shall be compelled to choose one of the following two alternatives—either that the entire whole of things has not been fashioned in man, if only the essences have been made in him; or the entire whole of things, that is, the essences and whatsoever is perceived about them and in them, has been fashioned in man. And if I say that not a part of the whole, that is, substances, but the complete whole has been set up in man, you will follow after with a most weighty question, saying that then irrationality has been made in him, and bestiality, quadrapedality, volatility, and all the differences of diverse animals

and of other things, and the species too, and the properties, and the accidents, and innumerable other things which seem to be far removed from human nature, to such an extent that if it were certain that they are present in man, he would rightly be judged not to be man but a very disgraceful monster.

Disc. You have heaped up the difficulty of the question, and you have with a kind of deliberation opposed to yourself whatever would be opposed by another; and by this means you will either clear up the question or you will pass it by as abstruse and go on to another, which will seem very incongruous indeed.

Mast. Let us try then to examine it in some way, lest it lie wholly intact for the time.

Disc. You will not be able to satisfy me otherwise.

Mast. Do you think that everything which is known by the understanding and reason or which is imagined by the bodily sense, can in a certain manner be created and produced in him who understands and perceives?

Disc. It seems to me that it can. Indeed I think that the species of sensible things and the quantities and qualities which I attain by corporeal sense are in a certain way created in me; for, when I imprint the phantasies of them in memory, and when I treat of them within myself, divide, compare, and, as it were, collect them into a kind of unity, I perceive a certain knowledge of things which are outside me being produced in me. In the same way I understand that there arise and are made in me, when I seek them out earnestly, certain ideas like intelligible species, of the intelligibles within, which I contemplate with the mind alone, as, for example, the ideas of the liberal disciplines. But what there is between the knowledge and the things themselves, of which the knowledge is, I do not see clearly.

Mast. What does it seem to you? Are things and the ideas of things, which are made in the soul, of the same nature or different?

Disc. Of different natures. For how can the corporeal species, of, for example, a certain animal, or herb, or tree, and the idea of it which is produced in an incorporeal nature be of one single nature? For the same reason how can the intelligible species of any discipline and the idea of it be made of one single nature?

Mast. If, then, they are of different genera or natures, and not of the same, tell me, I ask, which of them do you judge must be set down as the more excellent of them; are things of a more exalted nature than their own ideas; or are ideas themselves more exalted than things?

Disc. I should have said that visible species are of a better nature than their ideas, if Saint Augustine did not state the following opinion in the ninth book *On the Trinity* in the eleventh chapter:

> Since, he says, we learn bodies through the sense of the body, some likeness of bodies is made in our mind; this is phantasy in memory. For bodies themselves are not at all in the mind when we reflect on them, but only their likenesses. Nevertheless, the imagination of the body in the mind is better than the species of the body, inasmuch as it is in a better nature, that is, in vital substance, such as the mind. However, I do not dare to say that intelligible things are better than their idea which is in the soul.

Reason teaches, to be sure, that that which understands is better than that which is understood. For, if the knowledge of all things subsists in the divine wisdom, I should pronounce this knowledge of all things, not rashly, to be incomparably better than all things of which it is the knowledge. And if that is so, such an order, I believe, proceeds from the divine providence through all creation, that not only every nature which comprehends the idea of the thing following it, is better and superior, but also, because of the dignity of the nature in which it is, the idea itself excels greatly that of which it is the idea. And by this fact I should say more easily that the idea of intelligible things is more ancient than the intelligible things themselves.

Mast. You would perhaps be right in saying that if what is formed is more excellent than what forms.

Disc. Why do you oppose that?

Mast. Because the idea of the arts which is in the soul seems to be formed from the arts themselves. But if you established by very sure reason that the idea was not formed from the arts, but the arts from the idea, your reasoning would perhaps start out rightly.

Disc. Did we not prove a moment ago that everything which understands is more excellent than that which is understood?

Mast. That was proved.

Disc. Tell me then, whether the expertness of the mind understands the discipline or the discipline understands the expertness.

Mast. I do not doubt that the discipline is understood by the mind. But if I say that the same discipline is learned by the expertness itself in the same way as it is learned by the mind of which it is the expertness, I fear lest I seem to assert that the mind and its expertness are two different outgrowths in ideas of the discipline, and not one and the same essence in which the knowledge of the discipline is present naturally. If, however, the mind and its expertness are not two different things but one and the same, true reason teaches (I am forced to admit) that everything which is understood by the mind is understood too by its expertness, and it follows necessarily that mind and expertness, or certainly the expert mind, is of a more excellent nature than that discipline which it understands, if understandings are more ancient than things understood. If, on the other hand, I say that the discipline itself is the expertness of the expert mind, the consequence will be either that the expert mind and the expert discipline are two particular understandings, one of the other, and understood one by the other, and by this attaining to an equal dignity of nature, or else the mind and its expertness and the discipline, which it understands and by which it is understood, must be granted to be of one and the same essence. But which of these must be held does not yet appear clearly.

Disc. Perhaps it will appear when we enter upon the right way of reasoning, God leading.

Mast. Let us seek therefore the more carefully; and first tell me. I pray, whether the nature of the mind in which there is the expertness of the discipline, is simple or not.

Disc. I think that it is simple. For it is incorporeal, intellectual, and for that reason it necessarily lacks all composition.

Mast. You think rightly. Do you think then that something is accidental to it which is not naturally present in its essence?

Disc. I think so. For I see many things are accidental to it. For example, it is moved temporally, although it is not itself time. Expertness of disciplines is accidental to it: for it is now recognized as expert, now as inexpert, now disciplined, now undisciplined, now wise, now foolish, now erring when it considers irrationally, now entering upon the way of reason rightly, and many things of this sort.

Mast. Therefore, the expertness of a discipline or the discipline itself is not present in it naturally, but they appear in it extrinsically by accidents.

Disc. I should not dare to say that. For it is not likely that God should have created in His own image and likeness a mind in which there were not implanted naturally expertness and discipline; otherwise it would not be a mind but a kind of brute and irrational life. For, I think, one would not say rightly that man was made in the image of God according to accident and not according to substance, especially since we see that understanding and reason are present in the mind substantially.

Mast. Therefore, they are not accidental to it, but are present naturally.

Disc. I should not say that inconsiderately, I believe. For although the mind seems to be born inexpert and unwise, which occurs through the transgression of the divine command, in which it was forgetful both of itself and of its Creator, nevertheless, it is able, when it has been reformed by the rules of doctrine, to find in itself its God and itself and its expertness and discipline and all things which subsist naturally in it, illuminated by the grace of its Redeemer.

Mast. It remains, therefore, to consider in what manner expertness and the discipline are present in the mind: whether as natural qualities, which are called powers, like species of wisdom and science which it perceives in the repercussion of the divine ray; or whether as the substantial parts of which the mind consists, so that it is a kind of trinity of one essence: mind, learning, and art.

Disc. I should believe it was what you stated last; for it seems to me a kind of substantial and connatural trinity.

Mast. Accordingly the mind understands both its expertness and its discipline, and it is understood by its expertness and its discipline, not with respect to what it is, but that it is; for otherwise it will not be a coessential and coequal trinity.

Disc. I would not deny that, since reason compels me to grant that it is so.

Mast. Consider then whether they are formed by each other or by some other nature superior to them.

Disc. If the Catholic faith did not teach and if truth did not assent that this trinity is set up and formed and understood by a superior nature, I should not inconsiderately reply that they are perhaps formed by themselves or that surely they are their own principal form; as it is, of course. I do not doubt, since the superior is itself that from which all things are formed, by which they begin to be formed, and turned toward which the things which are or can be turned to it are formed, that the trinity too of the mind is formed by the same nature.

Mast. To hesitate about that would be extremely stupid. Consequently only the divine mind possesses in itself, formed by itself and to itself, the true idea of the human mind, of expertness and of discipline.

Disc. Nothing could be considered more true.

Mast. Do you think the human mind is one thing and the idea of it in the mind of the one forming it and knowing it another?

Disc. That can not be. For I understand the substance of the entire man to be no other than his idea in the mind of the artificer who knew all things in himself before they were made; and that very knowledge is the true and only substance of those things which are known, since they subsist formed most perfectly in it eternally and immutably.

Mast. We can then define man thus: man is a certain intellectual idea formed eternally in the divine mind.

Disc. That is an extremely true and a very well-tested definition of man; and not only of man but also of all things which are formed in the divine wisdom. Nor do I fear them who define man, not as he is understood to be, but by those things which are understood about him, saying that man is a rational mortal animal capable of sense and discipline; and what is more wonderful, they call this definition substantial [*usiadis*] whilst it is not substantial but taken extrinsically about substance from those things which are accidental to substance through generation. But the idea of man in the divine mind is nothing of these. There, indeed, it is simple, nor can it be called this or that, standing above all definition and collection of parts, for only that it is is predicated of it, but not what it is. For that alone is indeed a true substantial [*usiadis*] definition, which affirms only that it is but negates that it is anything in particular [*quid esse*].

Mast. Does it seem to you that there is a kind of notion in man of all the sensible and intelligible things which the human mind can understand?

Disc. That seems clearly the case; and indeed man is understood to be most of all through the circumstance that it has been given to him to have an idea of all things which were either created equally with him or which he was instructed to govern. For how should the mastery be given to man of things of which he had no idea? Indeed his mastery would go astray if he were ignorant of that which he ruled. The holy Scripture indicates that to us most clearly, saying, "therefore having formed out of the ground every beast of the field and every bird of the heavens, the Lord God brought them unto Adam to see what he would call them: and whatsoever Adam called every living soul, that was the name of it."[1] It says, to "see," that is to understand what he would call them. For, if he did not understand, how would he be able to call them rightly? Whereas each that he called, is its very name [*nomen*], that is, it is the idea itself [*notio*] of the living soul.

Mast. What is there astonishing then, if the idea of things which the human mind possesses because the idea was created in it, be understood as the substance of the very things of which it is the idea, that is, in the likeness of the divine mind in which the idea of the whole created universe is the incommunicable substance of that whole? Just as we call the idea of all things which are understood and are perceived by the corporeal sense in the whole of things, the substance of the things which fall under the understanding or the sense, so shall we also say that the idea of the differences and properties and natural accidents are the differences themselves and the properties and the accidents?

Disc. Undoubtedly.

Mast. Irrationality therefore was created in the mind, and every species, and every difference, and the property of irrationality itself, and all things which are learned naturally concerning it, since there is an idea formed in it of all these and of things similar. I have spoken of things *similar* because of the things which the nature of things contains in addition to animals, such as the elements of the world, the genera

and species of grasses too and of woods, the quantities, and qualities, and still others multiplied through innumerable differences. True knowledge of all of these is implanted in human nature, although its presence is as yet concealed from the soul itself until it is restored to its pristine integrity, in which it will understand very purely the magnitude and beauty of the image fashioned in it, and nothing will shut it off from the things which are fashioned in it, encompassed as it will be by divine light and turned to God, in whom it will contemplate all things perspicuously. Or did the magnificent Boethius mean something else to be understood when he says?

> Wisdom is the comprehension of the truth of things which are and which draw as by lot their immutable substance. But we say that those things are which do not grow by any increase, and are not diminished by any with drawing, nor changed by any variations, but with the endeavor and resources of their own nature preserve themselves always in their own power. These are qualities, quantities, forms, magnitudes, smallnesses, equalities, conditions, acts, dispositions, places, times, and whatever is in any way found joined to bodies: they are themselves incorporeal in nature and thrive by reason of the immutable substance, but they are changed through participation of the body and pass into changeable inconstancy through contact with the variable thing.

And where do you understand these things to subsist except in their ideas in the mind of the wise man? For where they are understood, there they are, and as a matter of fact they are nothing more than their being understood [*imo vero intellectus sui sunt*].

Disc. The solution of the present questions requires a multiple exposition, and an innumerable crowd of different questions do not cease to flow forth on all sides, while it is being resolved, as from a kind of infinite fountain; consequently the figure of Herculean Hydra may with perfect justice be applied to it, of which as many heads grow again as are cut off, so that a hundred bubble forth for one cut off, symbolizing human nature, which is a Hydra, that is, a

---

[1]Genesis 2:19.

kind of multiplex fountain of infinite profundity, into which who besides Hercules, that is, virtue, is able to look? "For no one knoweth what things are in man, save the spirit of the man which is in him."[1] Accordingly, if that interior idea which is in the human mind constitutes the substance of the things of which it is the idea, it follows that the very idea by which man knows himself may be considered his substance.

Mast. That follows by all means. For we said that the human mind, its idea by which it knows itself, and the discipline by which it learns itself that it may know itself, subsist as one and the same essence.

Disc. Then what shall we say? Do you remember a little while ago we deduced the pure definition of man, saying, man is a certain intellectual idea formed eternally in the divine mind? And, if that is so, how may that idea by which man knows himself be his substance, if the aforesaid definition has not been made improperly?

Mast. Surely not improperly, for the definition which says that a certain idea eternally made in the divine mind is the substance of man, is true. And what we say now, namely, that the knowledge by which the human mind knows itself is substantially in man, is not stated irrationally. For each creature is considered in one fashion in the word of God, in which all things have been made, and in another fashion in himself. Therefore Saint Augustine in his *In Hexæmeron* says:

> In one fashion, the things which are made by it are under it, in another fashion the things which it is are in it. Since the understanding of all things in the divine mind is the substance of all things, it is, in fact, all things. For the knowledge by which an intellectual and rational creature understands himself in himself is, as it were, a kind of second substance of him, by which he knows only that he knows, and is, and wills, but not what he is. And the former substance, constituted in the wisdom of God, is eternal and immutable, but the latter is temporal and mutable; the former precedes, the latter follows; the former is primordial and causal, the latter resulting and causative; the former contains all things

universally, the latter, so far as is allotted by the superior, comprehends particularly the things subject to it by knowledge; the latter was produced from the former and it will return again into it.

And I do not speak now of that superessential substance which through itself is God and the unique cause of all things, but of that substance which in the beginning was made causally in the wisdom of God, the effect of which is this substance which we determined, on rather which the natural order of things established, in the second place.

Disc. We must, therefore, comprehend two substances of man, one general in the primordial causes, the other special in the effects of those causes.

Mast. I should not have said two but one understood doubly. For in one fashion, the human substance is perceived through its creation in intellectual causes, in the other by its generation in effects. In the former free from all mutability, in the latter liable to mutability; in the former, simple and absolved from all accidents, it escapes all consideration and understanding, in the latter it puts on a kind of composition of quantities and qualities and other things which are understood of it, and by that composition it has the consideration of the mind. Accordingly one and the same thing is spoken of as double because of the double observation of it, but it still preserves its incomprehensibility on all sides, in causes, I say, and in effects, that is, whether naked in its simplicity or endowed with accidents. For in all these, it comes under no created understanding or any sense, nor with respect to what it is, is it understood by itself.

Disc. Why is it, then, since you have spoken of it for a long time now, that the human mind has the idea by which it knows itself, and the discipline by which it learns itself, and now you assert on the other hand that it can be known neither by itself not by any other creature?

Mast. Reason teaches that both are true: that the human mind assuredly knows itself and does not know itself. For it knows that it is, but it does not know what it is. And through this circumstance, as we have taught in the previous books, the image of

---

[1] I Corinthians 2:11.

God is shown most of all to be in man. For as God is comprehensible in that one deduces from creation that He is, and is incomprehensible because what He is can be comprehended by no understanding, human or angelic, nor even by Himself because He is not a *what,* but is superessential: so it is given to the human mind to know only this, that it is, but it is in no way granted to it to know what it is; and, what is even more to be wondered at and more beautiful to those who contemplate themselves and their God, the human mind is more to be praised in its ignorance than in its knowledge. For it is more praiseworthy for it not to know what it is than for it to know that it is, just as the negation of the divine nature pertains better and with greater fitness to the praise of the divine nature than the affirmation of it: and it is wiser not to know than to know that, the ignorance of which is true wisdom, and which is known better by not knowing. The divine likeness in the human mind, therefore, is recognized most clearly in that it is known only to be; but what it is is not known; and, to put it thus, in it we deny that it is anything and affirm only that it is. Nor is this void of reason. For if it were known to be some certain thing, it would be circumscribed certainly in something and, by that fact, it would not express in itself wholly the image of its Creator who is entirely uncircumscribed and is understood in nothing because he is infinite, above all that is said and understood, superessential.

Disc. How then has every creature been made in the idea of man, which idea does not know itself with respect to what it is, and how is this taken for great praise of it, and as its mark of superiority in that it is confined by no finite substance?

Mast. On the contrary, that every creature has been created substantially in man may be deduced likewise by very cogent argument. For of all things that are, substance can in no way be defined with respect to what it is, according to Gregory, the theologian, who investigates concerning such things, taking issue with those who deny that the word of God is superessential, and who contend that it is comprised in some substance and therefore is not above all things but is contained within the number of all, and who insist that the substance of the Son be separated from

the substance of the Father. Accordingly, just as the divine essence in whose image it was made is infinite, so too that human determination is limited by no certain end. But, from the things which are understood concerning it, that is, from times, places, differences, properties, quantities, qualities, relations, conditions, positions, actions, passions, it is understood only to be, but what it is never understood. And thence may be understood that there is no other subsistence of any creature than that reason according to which it has been set in the primordial causes in the word of God, and therefore what it is can not be defined, because it exceeds all substantial definition. It is defined, however, by its circumstances, which occur to it, as it proceeds into its appropriate species by generation, whether intelligible or sensible.

8. *Disc.* The Holy Scripture and reason itself both assert that human and angelic nature are either the same or very similar. For both man and angel are called, and are, intellectual and rational creatures. And, if they agree so between them, it must be inquired not improperly, why every creature is seen created in man but not in the angel.

Mast. Not without cause, I believe. For, we see not a few things in man which authority does not teach nor reason understand to subsist in the angel, as this animal body, which the Holy Scripture testifies was joined to the human soul even before sin, and also the corporeal fivefold exterior sense and the fantasies of sensible things which are formed in the human soul by it, and then too the perplexity and fretful difficulty of ratiocination in inquiring the natures of things, and further the laborious ingenuity in discerning virtues and vices, and many more of that sort. No man rightly numbered among the wise would deny that it is clear that the angelic essence lacks all these and is nevertheless present in the nature of things. For all this, Augustine would seem to have taught that angels perceive, in the eighth book *On the City of God,* chapter seven,[1] where he praises the virtue of contemplation of the great philosophers who

> saw that every species in every mutable thing, by which it is whatever it is, in whatever manner and quality its nature is, can only be from him

---
[1] The reference should be to chapter 6.

who is truly because he is immutably. And because of this, whether we consider the body of the whole world, the figures, qualities, and the motion ordered and the elements disposed from heaven to earth, and whatever bodies are in them; or whether we consider all life whether the life which nourishes and maintains, as in trees, or the life which has these functions and also perceives, as in animals, or the life which has these functions and also understands, as in men, or the life which does not require the nutritive support, but only maintains, perceives, and understands, as in angels: all these can only be from him who is absolutely.

I should believe, however, that he spoke of the interior sense. So who does not know that the celestial essence does not share in many parts of nature and in many motions which inhere naturally in human nature? True reason testifies likewise that it has no knowledge of things which neither are inherent in it, that is, in celestial substance, as substance, nor happen to it as accident. For although angels are said to administer this world and every corporeal creature, they must in no manner be thought to need corporeal senses, or local or temporal motions or visible apparitions to accomplish that. Moreover, all the things which are accidental to us because of a deficiency of our nature, subject still to the variations of places and times, are judged rightly not to be accidental to angels by a defect of their power. For when they transmute their spiritual and invisible bodies into visible forms that they may appear to the senses of mortals visibly, locally, temporally, this accident does not occur to them because of themselves but because of men to whom they are present and declare the divine mysteries. For they do not see locally by sense nor is it an accident of theirs to know temporally what will be done in the administration of things, inasmuch as they are eternally above all time and place in the contemplation of truth in which they see at once the causes of the administration of things. And do not think that I say these things concerning all celestial essences, but only of the more excellent orders, which are always about God and to which there is no ignorance save that of the divine darknesses which exceed all understanding. In fact, the lowest order which is properly called angelic,

through which the higher orders administer whatever the divine providence commands by divine revelations to be done in the human mind or in other parts of this world, is not yet absolved of all ignorance, and so, as Saint Dionysius the Areopagite says most subtly in the book *On the Celestial Hierarchy*, "it is taught by the higher orders, and it is conducted into a knowledge of divine mysteries which are loftier than it." Moreover, we are commanded, not irrationally, to believe and understand that every visible and invisible creature was created in man alone, since there is no substance created which is not understood to be in him; no species, or difference, or property, or natural accident is found in the nature of things which either is not inherent in him naturally or the knowledge of which can not be in him; and the very knowledge of things, which are contained within him, is better than the things of which it is knowledge to the extent that the nature in which it is formed is better. Every rational nature however is set by right reason before every irrational and sensible nature since it is nearer to God. Wherefore, too, the things of which knowledge is inherent in human nature are understood not inconsistently to subsist in their ideas. For where they undergo their knowledge better, there they must be judged to exist more truly. Furthermore, if the things themselves subsist more truly in their ideas than in themselves, and if the ideas of them are naturally present in man, then they were created universally in man. The return of all things into man will doubtless prove this in its time. For by what reason would they return into him if they did not possess a certain connatural kinship in him and if they did not proceed in a certain manner from him? Concerning this return we have promised to speak in its proper place.

Disc. Although these things seem extremely difficult since they go beyond the mode of simple doctrine, nevertheless, considered speculatively by reason, they agree wholly with the breadth of understanding of human creation, and they very usefully establish, as we may say not inaccurately, that man was not produced in the genus of animals, but rather every genus of animals was produced in man from earth, that is, from the solidity of nature, and not only every genus of animal but indeed the whole created universe was made in man, so that what truth said, may be understood truly of man: "Preach the gospel to the whole creation";[1] again the Apostle: "the whole creation groaneth and travaileth in pain together until now."[2] But let him to whom these things seem too abstruse and deeply incredible, if he is inexpert of all the natural disciplines which are called liberal, let him either be silent or learn, but not combat incautiously these things which be is not able to understand; if he is learned, he will see clearly (to offer him an example of one of them) that geometrical figures do not subsist naturally in themselves but in the reasons of that very discipline of which they are figures. For since the triangular thing which is seen by the bodily sense in some matter, is surely a kind of sensible imagination of that which is present in the mind, he will understand the triangle itself which subsists in the mind apt to discipline, and he will weigh with unbiased judgment which is the more excellent, the figure of the triangle or the triangle itself of which it is the figure. And be will find, if I am not mistaken, that that figure is truly a figure, but a false triangle, whereas that triangle which subsists in the discipline is the cause of the figure itself and is the true triangle. And I do not speak of the triangle of fantasy [i.e. the triangle perceived by sense] which descends from the mind through the memory into the senses and through the senses into sensible figures, nor of that triangle which, on the other hand, is imprinted from the sensible figure through the corporeal sense on the memory, but that very triangle which remains uniformly in the discipline itself where line and angle are at once and at the same place, nor is the line in one place, the angle in another, the middle here, the extreme there, here a sign, there the spaces of sides from the sign, here the spaces of angles, there a point from which lines begin and in which, by the junctures of the sides, angles are formed, but all these things are one, in one and the same idea aforesaid of the mind of the geometer, and all are understood in each and each in all and they are united in the understanding itself because the understanding is the substantial reason of all that it understands and from it the formula of geometrical bodies are specified. And what we have said of the triangle is to be understood of other figures too, angular, or circular, or oblique, whether in planes or in solids, inasmuch as all these subsist in one and the same reason in their ideas in the mind which is expert and apt to discipline. If, therefore, geometrical bodies, whether they be formed in fantasies of memory or in some sensible matter, subsist in their rational ideas, lacking all fantasy and all matter, above all that which is perceived by bodily sense or fashioned in memory: what is there astonishing then that natural bodies, composed from the qualities of the elements of the world, should subsist in that nature in which there is the idea of them, especially since all things which are perceived concerning bodies are incorporeal? For the species in which they are contained are incorporeal. That quantities and qualities are similarly intelligible of nature and proceed from the intellectual reasons of vital substance seems doubtful to no wise man.

9. *Mast.* Whoever shall have considered the natures of things intently will find immediately that they are so constituted.

Disc. Accordingly, now that these things have been discussed, it may be asked, not improperly, how every creature is formed in man, since man is said to have been made after the creation of all. If, therefore, the whole visible and invisible universe was created before him, as the divine story tells, and one reads of the creation of no creature after him, by what reason can we perceive every creature to have been fashioned in man? For, if any one should say that the whole creation was fashioned twice, first specially in itself, but second generally in man, I should not believe that that would accord easily with reason, because if it is so, man will not have a substance proper to him, but will be, as it were, a kind of composition of many things, or rather indeed of the whole creation previously made, and a single multiplex cumulation by different forms. But what is even more grave, if the whole creation whether visible or invisible has been made most perfectly in itself (and indeed since the creator is perfect and more than perfect, it is credible that he should have made no imperfect things), how could it have taken on a second perfection of its creation, as it were, in man, who was

---

[1] Mark 16:15.

[2] Romans 8:22.

created last in the divine operations? And, if this is so, God did not make man out of nothing in his own image, but He made him of those things which had been made before him. But if any one should say the human body had not been made from nothing but from something earthly, namely mud, what would be said of the more perfect making of man, which was set without doubt in the soul and in the spiritual body in the first creation, which, that is the soul, we believe to have been made from the divine breath, or rather to have been made the divine breath, not from some thing, but out of nothing?

Mast. I see that this question is involved in a great deal of obscurity and requires a diversified skill for its solution. But lest we pass it over utterly untouched, we shall attempt to contemplate it in some way as the interior beam of the divine light shall have disposed. And first say, I ask, whether intelligible things or sensible things are prior to the mind which understands them or to the sense by which they are perceived.

Disc. I should say, not improperly, that where there is one thing which understands and another which is understood, and where that which understands is of a better nature than that which is understood, the thing understood or perceived is preceded by the understanding soul or the perceiving sense. I should not say, however, that the things which understand themselves are prior to themselves in so far as they can understand themselves. For where the thing and the knowledge of it are one, I do not see what precedence can be made. For I know that I am, nevertheless the knowledge of me does not precede me because I am not one thing and the knowledge by which I know myself another; and, if I did not know that I am, I would not ignore that I do not know that I am: and therefore, whether I shall have known or not have known that I am, I shall not lack knowledge; for it will remain for me to know my ignorance. And, if each being that can know that it does not know itself, can not ignore that it is, in that if it were not at all, it would not know that it does not know itself: it follows that absolutely everything is which knows that it is or knows that it does not know that it is. If anyone however is so far sunk in ignorance that he neither knows that he is nor perceives that he does not know that he is, I should say that either such a

one is absolutely not a man or is wholly annihilated. We have sufficiently established likewise in the reasons which have been given above that the following two activities are present in the human soul at the same time and inseparably and always: to know and not to know. For the soul knows that it is a rational and intellectual nature; it does not know, however, what intellect itself and reason itself are.

Mast. Then, were you not, before you know or did not know that you were?

Disc. No; for I received at the same time being and knowledge that I am and understanding that I do not know myself in the sense of knowing what I am.

Mast. Tell me, when does a man receive knowledge of himself: in that creation in which all men were made universally in the primordial causes before secular times, or in the generation in which in the order of times, known and predefined by God alone, he proceeds into this life?

Disc. In both, I judge; in one generally and hidden in causes, but in the other specially and manifestly in effects. For in that primordial and general creation of all human nature, no one knows himself specially nor begins to have proper knowledge of himself; for a single and general knowledge of all things is there, and known to God alone. For, therein, all men are one and that one assuredly made in the image of God, in whom all were created. Just as, indeed, all forms or species which are contained in one genus, do not as yet fall under the understanding or the sense, known through differences and properties, but subsist as a kind of unity not yet divided until each one receives intelligibly or sensibly its property and difference in individual species: so in the community of human nature no one discerns by proper knowledge either himself or his consubstantials before he has proceeded into this world at his times appointed in accordance with the eternal reasons.

Mast. Why, then, does not everyone know himself as soon as he has arrived through generation into this world?

Disc. I should say, not without justification, that the penalty of the transgression of nature is shown in that. For, if man had not sinned, he would certainly not have fallen into so profound ignorance of himself; just as he would not have suffered the ignominious generation from the two sexes in the likeness of irrational animals, as the wisest of the greek theologians affirm with most certain reasons. For he who alone was born into the world without sin, namely the Redeemer of the world, at no time and at no place endured such an ignorance, but as soon as he was conceived and born, he understood both himself and all things, and he was able to speak and teach, not only because he was the wisdom of the Father, which nothing escapes, but also because he had taken on uncontaminated humanity in order to purge the contaminated; not because he received another nature beyond that which he restored, but because he alone remained in it uncontaminated and preserved for the remedy of the wound of tainted nature in the most secret reasons of himself. For human nature perished entirely in all men except him in whom alone it remained incorruptible. And, indeed, he is the greatest example of grace, not because he was freed of any part of the guilt of human nature, but because he alone of all men with no antecedent merit was joined in a unity of substance to the word of God, in whom all the elect, partaking of the plenitude of his grace, are made sons of God and participants of the divine substance.

Mast. There was then present in human nature a power of having most perfect knowledge of itself if it had not sinned?

Disc. Nothing is more probable. The fall of human nature was surely the greatest and the most miserable, to forfeit the knowledge and wisdom implanted in it and to slip into profound ignorance of itself and its creator, even though the desire for the beatitude which it had lost be understood to have remained in it after the fall: this desire would in no way have remained in it, if it had completely ignored itself and its God.

Mast. Therefore the most perfect knowledge, both of itself and its creator, was implanted in it naturally before sin, so far as the knowledge of the creature can comprehend both itself and its cause?

Disc. I think it was not otherwise than that. For how would it be an image if it differed in something from that of which it is an image, except in the relation of subject, concerning which we spoke in the preceding books, when we inquired concerning the prototype, that is, concerning the principal example and its image, saying that God Himself is the principal example, subsisting through Himself, by Himself,

in Himself, and created or formed or altered by none, but the image of Him, which is man, created by Him, is not through itself nor does it subsist by itself nor in itself; but from Him, whose image he is, man receives being in accordance with nature and divine being [*Deus esse*] by dispensation of grace; and likewise all the rest which are predicated of God, can be predicated of His image, but of God essentially, of the image only by participation? For the image is both goodness and good by participation of the supreme goodness and the supreme good, of which it is the image, and also eternal and eternity by participation of the eternal and the eternity from which it has been formed; and again omnipotence by participation of the omnipotence by which it was fashioned and to which in turn it is specificated. For if human nature had not sinned, and if it had clung immutably to that which formed it, it would assuredly be omnipotent. For whatever it wished to be done in the nature of things, would necessarily be done, as long in any case as it wished nothing other done than that which it understood its creator wished to be done; and in turn, it would understand the will of its creator, absolutely omnipotent and immutable, provided it adhered wholly to Him and did not leave Him, lest it should be dissimilar to Him, and it would understand the other predicates which can be understood or thought or predicated with right reason of God and His image.

Mast. If, therefore, a perfect knowledge was present in human nature before sin, both of itself and of its creator, what is there astonishing that one understood of it reasonably that it had a most full knowledge of natures similar to itself, such as the celestial essences, and of essences inferior to itself, such as this world with its reasons which fall under the understanding, and that at the present time human nature still has this in possibility alone and in actuality in the highest men?

Disc. Clearly that will not be astonishing to those who understand, but true and probable.

Mast. It is great and true praise of human nature and most of all of Him who willed to create it thus. Wherefore, in the same way, the following must be accepted too of His understanding and knowledge. For just as the creative wisdom which is the word of God saw all things which were made in it before they were made, and the very sight of things which were seen before they were made is true and immutable and eternal essence, so too the created wisdom which is human nature knew all things which were made in it before they were made, and that very knowledge of the things which were known before they were made is true and unquestioned essence. Accordingly, the very idea of the creative wisdom is understood rightly to be the first and causal essence of all creation and the knowledge of the created wisdom subsists as a second essence and effect of the higher knowledge. And what we have said of the first and causal essence, established in the knowledge of the creative wisdom, and of the second and effective essence, which is asserted, not improperly, to subsist in the human soul, must be understood in the same way without hesitation of all things which are discerned about the essence of the whole creation. For the right consideration of nature declares that everything which is established in the human understanding with respect to the substances of things, proceeds from that very idea of the creative wisdom through the created wisdom. And will respect to essences there are established sensible species, quantities, qualities, places, times, and such things without which the essence can not be understood. Wherefore, all that we wish to teach may be concluded briefly thus: just as the understanding of all things which the Father made in his one-begotten word is the essence of them and the determination of all that is understood of essence naturally, so the knowledge of all things which the word of the Father created in the human soul is the essence of them and the subject of all the things which are discerned concerning it naturally. And, just as the divine understanding precedes all and is all, so the intellectual understanding of the soul precedes all that it knows and is all that it foreknows, so that all things subsist in the divine understanding causally and in the human understanding effectually. Not that the essence of all things, as we have often said, is one thing in the word and another in man, but that the mind observes one and the same thing in one fashion subsisting in eternal causes and in another fashion understood in effects; for in the first it exceeds all understanding, but in the second it is understood,

from the things which are considered concerning it, only to be; in neither, however, is it permitted to a created understanding to know what it is. For, if it could be known, it would not entirely express in itself the image of its creator who is known only to be from those things of which He is the principle and cause and founder, but what He is escapes all sense and understanding.

Disc. Therefore, no creature whether visible or invisible precedes the creation of man—not in time, not in place, not in dignity, not in origin, not in eternity, and, simply, in no manner of precedence: for in knowledge itself and dignity, but not in time and place, the creation of man precedes those things which were created with it and in it and below it; and it was concreated with those to which it is equal with a condignity of nature, namely, to celestial essences. For it is itself a partaker of celestial and intellectual essence; assuredly it was written of angelic and human essence: "Who made the heavens in the understanding,"[1] as if it were said openly: who made the intellectual heavens. Wherefore, it becomes difficult to understand, if man were concreated substantially with the angelic essences, how all visible and invisible things were made in him. For it does not seem to agree with reason that he should have the beginning of his creation together with the celestial powers and that they should have been created in him.

Mast. If you should examine intently the reciprocal joining and unity of intellectual and rational natures, you will find certainly both that the angelic essence is established in the human and the human in the angelic. For in everything that the pure understanding knows very perfectly, it is made and it becomes one with it. So great indeed was the community of human and angelic nature and so great would it be made if the first man had not sinned, that the two would become one. That, even now, begins to be done among the uppermost men of which number are the first in heaven. And the angel, moreover, is made in man through the understanding of the angel which is in man, and man in the angel through the understanding of man constituted in the angel. For he, as I have said, who understands purely, is made in that which he understands. Accordingly, the intellectual

---

[1]Psal. 135: 5 (or 136: 5); *in intellectu* is usually rendered in English, *by wisdom*.

and the rational angelic nature was made in the intellectual and rational human nature in the same manner as the human was made in the angelic by the reciprocal knowledge by which angel understands man and man angel. Nor is that strange. For while we discuss, each of us is made into the other. Since, in fact, when I understand what you understand, I am made your understanding and in a certain ineffable way I have been made into you. In the same way, when you understand purely what I understand clearly, you have been made my understanding and from two understandings one has been made, formed from that which we both sincerely and unhesitatingly understand. For instance, to use the example of numbers, you understand that the number six is equal to its parts, and I understand the same; and I understand that you understand it, just as you too understand that I understand it. Our two understandings are made one, formed by the number six, and by that process I am created in you and you are created in me. For we are not one thing and our understandings another, but our true and supreme essence is the understanding made specific in the contemplation of truth. The apostolic word, moreover, when it forbids our intellectual part to cherish visible forms, saying, "be not fashioned according to this world,"[1] teaches that the understanding can be conformed not only to natures coessential to it, but also to natures inferior when it understands or perceives them by loving them. Consequently, by reason of this reciprocal intelligence, it is said, not without foundation in fact, both that the angel is created in man and man in the angel, and it can not rightly be believed or understood that the angel proceeds man by any law of creation or by any manner of precedence, although, as many insist, the prophetic narrative pronounces the creation of the angelic nature first and of human nature later. For it is not credible as Saint Augustine points out in the eleventh book of the *City of God* that the Holy Scripture should have been completely silent in the works of the six primordial and intelligible days concerning the creation of the celestial powers, but either in the very first line of *Genesis,* where it was written, "in the beginning God created the heavens and the earth,"[2] their creation is brought forward under the name of the heavens, or a little later when is says, "And God said, let there be light: and there was light."[3] For, in one or the other place, the aforesaid father affirms that the angelic creation was manifested and most particularly in the second. In the first, to be sure, he asserts that under the appellation "the heavens" the making of the whole invisible creation in unformed matter is signified rather than the formation specially of the angelic nature. But in that which was written, "let there be light: and there was light," he asserts unhesitatingly that the formation of celestial essences was described; although he introduced the meaning of others who believe that there is in this divine precept the constitution of a certain primitive light, sensible and local in the upper parts of the world; but he attacks this meaning most acutely in his *In Hexæmeron.* When, however, it is said, "and God divided the light from the darkness. And God called the light Day, and the darkness Night,"[4] he wants that to be understood in two ways: for either, by the word "light" the formation of the angelic creature in its proper species, and by the word "darkness" the unshapeliness, preceding in origin not in time, of that nature as yet imperfect, or else by the division of the light from the darkness was signified the segregation and difference of that angelic part which clung immutably to its creator, foreknowing beatitude by virtue of its obedience, from that part which did not stand in truth but was precipitated as a penalty of its pride into the darkness of ignorance of its future fall and eternal misery. But, if anyone wishes to know more fully this double explanation of the most divine master, let him read it carefully in the words of the master himself in his *In Hexæmeron* and in the above-mentioned volume *On the City of God:* to insert these explanations in this little discussion of ours seems to me superfluous since they are detailed and clear to all.

---

[1] Romans 12:2.

[2] Genesis 1:1.

[3] Genesis 1:3.

[4] Genesis 1: 4–5.

Disc. Go on; for the opinions of the holy fathers need not be brought in, especially if they are known to most people, except where the gravest necessity requires that reasoning be fortified for those who, since they are untrained in reasoning, yield to authority more than to reason. . . .

STUDY QUESTIONS: ERIGENA, ON *THE DIVISION OF NATURE*

1. Why do we have animal natures? How is our divine soul related to our animal nature?
2. What is the understanding? What is its function?
3. Why is that which understands better than that which is understood?
4. Why does the mind understand *that* it is, but not *what* it is?
5. What is man? How does he define humanity?
6. What is wisdom?
7. Erigena quotes both Augustine and Boethius. What does he think of their ideas and how does he use them?
8. Do the intelligible (sensible) things exist prior to being perceived? Why?
9. How did creation result from the mind of God?

Philosophical Bridges: Erigena's Influence

Erigena's extraordinarily detailed glossary of terms, because it was the standard reference for subsequent medieval thinkers, alone would have assured his influence throughout the Middle Ages. But Erigena's contribution and influence was much broader. First, his work helped make possible the eventual integration of what was then called natural philosophy and has since come to be called physics, with the philosopher's understanding of the indirect, representational nature of perception. Second, his insistence that the mind's ability to reason logically and the systematic, empirical study of nature must be brought together in concordance with metaphysical principles, even though they may be purely theological in origin and derivation, set the tone for virtually all subsequent discussions of metaphysics, not just in later medieval thought but up through the modern era and Immanuel Kant. Erigena's focus on and fourfold division of nature itself provided the backdrop for the subsequent division of labor among the knowledge-seeking enterprise that would eventually come to be called science.

ANSELM (1033–1109)

Biographical History

Anselm was born high up in the Italian Alps, in the old Roman town of Piedmont. His father, a famous and wealthy nobleman, expected him to join the ranks. But as soon as he was old enough Anselm left home to travel throughout Europe as a wondering scholar and beggar. In Normandy, Benedictine monks took him in and he joined their monastery at Bec, where he remained. He studied philosophy and theology and soon became the favorite pupil of Lanfranc, who when he became archbishop of Canterbury chose Anselm as the new Abbott. When Lanfranc died, in 1093, he recommended that his best former student succeed him and so Anselm became Archbishop of Canterbury.

Philosophical Overview

Anselm, like the Greek philosophers whom he devoutly admired, was prolific. He wrote three theological works, *Molologion, Proslogion,* and *Cur Deus Homo (Why God Became Man)*, a groundbreaking work on semantics (*De Grammatico*), a treatise on truth (*De Veritate*), and another on freedom (*De Libertate Arbitrii*). His final, unfinished work, *On Power and Powerlessness, Possibility and Impossibility, Necessity and Liberty*, is an attempt to explain how it is possible that the soul should ever come into existence. When Anselm found out he was dying, he wrote: "If it is His will I shall gladly obey, but if He should prefer me to stay with you just long enough to solve the question of the origin of the soul which I have been turning over in my mind, I would gratefully accept the chance, for I doubt whether anybody else will solve it when I am gone."

Unlike Augustine, who insisted that God cannot be known by reason, Anselm uses Aristotelian logic, the arguments of Boethius, and a combination of neo-Platonist ideas, to argue that the existence of God can be proved and thus known by purely rational means.

Anselm's philosophy is inspired by a combination of Plato's metaphysics and Augustine's neo-Platonic reinterpretation of Christian dogma. A question that puzzled many thinkers, before and since, is this: *How* did God *create* the world and make it *real?* Why is the world not merely a *dream* in the mind of God? If the world in but a dream in the mind of God, it has no independent existence. This would imply pantheism—the view that the world and everything in it is the living God—which is incompatible with the orthodox Christian doctrine of metaphysical duality requiring a fundamental distinction between "things that are God" and "things that are not God."

Anselm was one of the first philosophers to use linguistic analysis to solve philosophical problems. His *De Veritate (On Truth)* provided subsequent thinkers with three different senses of the concept of "truth." In *De Libertate Arbitrii (On Free Will)*, he defines the concept of free will in an analytically fruitful manner, providing the necessary and sufficient conditions for the concept of free will.

PROSLOGION, "THE ONTOLOGICAL ARGUMENT"
Anselm

In *Proslogion*, Anselm originates his famous ontological argument for the existence of God. He quotes from Psalms 14:1, "The fool has said in his heart, there is no God." His proof relies on the meaning of the term, "God," which includes existence, such that to deny the existence of God would be an outright self-contradiction.

Anselm argues that only a fool would be so ignorant of logic as to contradict himself in this way. In other words, Anselm claims that the proposition, "God exists," can be derived logically from the very meaning of the word "God." What is meant by "God?" The concept of God is not just that of some being superior to us. Since God is conceived as the creator of all, God must be greater than any of God's creations. Anselm thus defines God in terms of the *greatest* conceivable being, "a greater than which" cannot be conceived. His argument can then be summarized along the following lines:

> "God" is the greatest conceivable being, a greater than which cannot be conceived.
> Existence is greater than nonexistence.
> Therefore, God exists.

Suppose someone claims that there is no God. The proposition, "God does not exist," then means something like this: "A being that cannot be conceived as anything other than existing does not exist." Or, one could interpret it as follows: "A being that exists necessarily does not exist." In either case one is uttering a self-contradictory proposition. To deny the existence of God is therefore the worst and lowliest form of logical error, namely, self-contradiction.

To better understand the logical depth of Anselm's thinking one must understand the medieval distinction between an idea that exists in reality—*in re*—and an idea that exists only in conception—*in intellectu*. If some concept, "X" includes the predicate "greatest," X must exist *in re*, not just *in intellectu*, since to exist in reality is far greater than to exist merely in conception. A supreme or perfect X exists *in re*. Thus for instance "Being" or "Reality" have, *necessarily, existence in actuality* not just *in concept*, that is merely *in intellectu*, in God's mind.

Another Benedictine monk, Gaunilo, Anselm's contemporary from the Abbey of Marmoutier near Tours, conjectured the first rejoinder to Anselm's ontological argument. Gaunilo claimed, quite explicitly on behalf of "the fool," that Anselm's proof does not work. The reason it fails is twofold:

1. we cannot properly form the concept of a necessarily existent being because nothing in experience can provide the basis for such a concept,
2. we can imagine perfect things defined as "perfect" but that in fact do not exist, such as a perfect island.

PREFACE

After I had published, at the solicitous entreaties of certain brethren, a brief work (*Monologium*) as an example of meditation on the grounds of faith, in the person of one who investigates, in a course of silent reasoning with himself, matters of which he is ignorant; considering that this book was knit together by the linking of many arguments, I began to ask myself whether there might be found a single argument which would require no other for its proof than itself alone; and alone would suffice to demonstrate that God truly exists, and that there is a supreme good requiring nothing else, which all other things require for their existence and well-being; and whatever we believe regarding the divine being.

Although I often and earnestly directed my thought to this end, and at some times that which I sought seemed to be just within my reach, while again it wholly evaded my mental vision, at last in despair I was about to cease, as if from the search for a thing which could not be found. But when I wished to exclude this thought altogether, lest, by busying my mind to no purpose, it should keep me from other thoughts, in which I might be successful; then more and more, though I was unwilling and shunned it, it began to force itself upon me, with a kind of importunity. So, one day, when I was exceedingly wearied with resisting its importunity, in the very conflict of my thoughts, the proof of which I had despaired offered itself, so that I eagerly embraced the thoughts which I was strenuously repelling.

Thinking, therefore, that what I rejoiced to have found, would, if put in writing, be welcome to some readers, of this very matter, and of some others, I have written the following treatise, in the person of one who strives to lift his mind to the contemplation of God, and seeks to understand what he believes. In my judgment, neither this work nor the other, which I mentioned above, deserved to be called a book, or to bear the name of an author; and yet I thought they ought not to be sent forth without some title by which they might, in some sort, invite one into whose hands they fell to their perusal. I accordingly gave each a title, that the first might be known as, *An*

Anselm, from *Proslogion* translated by Sidney Norton Deane, Open Court 1926. Preface, chs. 1–8.

Example of Meditation on the Grounds of Faith, and its sequel as, *Faith Seeking Understanding*. But, after, both had been copied by many under these titles, many urged me, and especially Hugo, the reverend Archbishop of Lyons, who discharges the apostolic office in Gaul, who instructed me to this effect on his apostolic authority—to prefix my name to these writings. And that this might be done more fitly, I named the first, *Monologium*, that is, *A Soliloquy*; but the second, *Proslogium*, that is, *A Discourse*.

CHAPTER 1

Exhortation of the mind to the contemplation of God—it casts aside cares, and excludes all thoughts save that of God, that it may seek Him. Man was created to see God. Man by sin lost the blessedness for which he was made, and found the misery for which he was not made. He did not keep this good when he could keep it easily. Without God it is ill with us. Our labors and attempts are in vain without God. Man cannot seek God, unless God himself teaches him: nor find him, unless he reveals himself. God created man in His image, that he might be mindful of Him, think of Him, and love Him. The believer does not seek to understand, that he may believe, but he believes that he may understand: for unless he believed he would not understand.

Up now, slight man! Flee, for a little while, thy occupations; hide thyself, for a time, from thy disturbing thoughts. Cast aside, now, thy burdensome cares, and put away thy toilsome business. Yield room for some little time to God, and rest for a little time in Him. Enter the inner chamber of thy mind, shut out all thoughts save that of God, and such as can aid thee in seeking Him; close thy door and seek Him. Speak now, my whole heart! Speak now to God, saying, I seek thy face; thy face, Lord, will I seek (*Psalms* xxvii. 8). And come thou now. O Lord my God, teach my heart where and how it may seek thee, where and how it may find thee.

Lord, if thou art not here, where shall I seek thee, being absent? But if thou art everywhere, why do I not see thee present? Truly thou dwellest in unapproachable light. But where is unapproachable light, or how shall I come to it? Or who shall lead me to that light and into it, that I may see thee in it? Again, by what marks, under what form, shall I seek thee? I

have never seen thee, O Lord, my God; I do not know thy form. What, O most high Lord, shall this man do, an exile far from thee? What shall thy servant do, anxious in his love of thee, and cast out afar from thy face? He pants to see thee, and thy face is too far from him. He longs to come to thee, and thy dwelling-place is inaccessible. He is eager to find thee, and knows not thy place. He desires to seek thee, and does not know thy face. Lord, thou art my God, and thou art my Lord, and never have I seen thee. It is thou that hast made me, and hast made me anew, and hast bestowed upon me all the blessing I enjoy; and not yet do I know thee. Finally, I was created to see thee, and not yet have I done that for which I was made.

O wretched lot of man, when he hath lost that for which he was made! O hard and terrible fate! Alas, what has he lost, and what has he found? What has departed, and what remains? He has lost the blessedness for which he was made, and has found the misery for which he was not made. That has departed without which nothing is happy, and that remains which, in itself, is only miserable. Man once did eat the bread of angels, for which he hungers now; he eateth now the bread of sorrows, of which he knew not then. Alas! for the mourning of all mankind, for the universal lamentation of the sons of Hades! He choked with satiety, we sigh with hunger. He abounded; we beg. He possessed in happiness, and miserably forsook his possession; we suffer want in unhappiness, and feel a miserable longing, and alas! We remain empty.

Why did He not keep for us, when He could so easily, that whose lack we should feel so heavily? Why did He shut us away from the light, and cover us over with darkness? With what purpose did He rob us of life, and inflict death upon us? Wretches that we are, whence have we been driven out; whither are we driven on? Whence hurled? Whither consigned to ruin? From a native country into exile, from the vision of God into our present blindness, from the joy of immortality into the bitterness and horror of death. Miserable exchange of how great a good, for how great an evil! Heavy loss, heavy grief, heavy all our fate!

But alas! Wretched that I am, one of the sons of Eve, far removed from God! What have I undertaken? What have I accomplished? Whither was I striving? How far have I come? To what did I aspire? Amid what thoughts am I sighing? I sought blessings, and lo! Confusion. I strove toward God, and I stumbled on myself. I sought calm in privacy, and I found tribulation and grief, in my inmost thoughts I wished to smile in the joy of my mind, and I am compelled to frown by the sorrow of my heart. Gladness was hoped for, and lo! A source of frequent sighs!

And thou too, O Lord, how long? How long, O Lord, dost thou forget us; how long dost thou turn thy face from us? When wilt thou look upon us, and hear us? When wilt thou enlighten our eyes, and show us thy face? When wilt thou restore thyself to us? Look upon us, Lord; hear us, enlighten us, reveal thyself to us. Restore thyself to us, that it may be well with us—thyself, without whom it is so ill with us. Pity our toilings and strivings toward thee since we can do nothing without thee. Thou dost invite us; do thou help us. I beseech thee, O Lord, that I may not lose hope in sighs, but may breathe anew in hope. Lord, my heart is made bitter by its desolation; sweeten thou it, I beseech thee, with thy consolation. Lord, in hunger I began to seek thee; I beseech thee that I may not cease to hunger for thee. In hunger I have come to thee; let me not go unfed. I have come in poverty to the rich, in misery to the compassionate; let me not return empty and despised. And if, before I eat, I sigh, grant, even after sighs, that which I may eat. Lord, I am bowed down and can only look downward; raise me up that I may look upward. My iniquities have gone over my head; they overwhelm me; and, like a heavy load, they weigh me down. Free me from them; unburden me, that the pit of iniquities may not close over me.

Be it mine to look up to thy light, even from afar, even from the depths. Teach me to seek thee, and reveal thyself to me, when I seek thee, for I cannot seek thee, except thou teach me, nor find thee, except thou reveal thyself. Let me seek thee in longing, let me long for thee in seeking; let me find thee in love, and love thee in finding. Lord, I acknowledge and I thank thee that thou hast created me in this thine image, in order that I may be mindful of thee, may conceive of thee, and love thee; but that image has been so consumed and wasted away by vices, and obscured by the smoke of wrong-doing, that it cannot achieve that for which it was made, except thou renew it, and create it anew. I do not endeavor, O Lord, to penetrate thy sublimity, for in no wise do I compare my understanding with that; but I long to understand in some degree thy truth, which my heart believes and loves. For I do not seek to understand that I may believe, but I believe in order to understand. For this also I believe—that unless I believed, I should not understand.

CHAPTER II

Truly There is a God, Although the Fool Hath Said in His Heart, There is No God.

And so, Lord, do thou, who dost give understanding to faith, give me, so far as thou knowest it to be profitable, to understand that thou art as we believe; and that thou art that which we believe. And indeed, we believe that thou art a being than which nothing greater can be conceived. Or is there no such nature, since the fool hath said in his heart, there is no God? (Psalms xiv 1). But, at any rate, this very fool, when he hears of this being of which I speak—a being than which nothing greater can be conceived—understands what he hears, and what he understands is in his understanding; although he does not understand it to exist.

For, it is one thing for an object to be in the understanding, and another to understand that the object exists. When a painter first conceives of what he will afterwards perform, he has it in his understanding but he does not yet understand it to be, because he has not yet performed it. But after he has made the painting, he both has it in his understanding, and he understands that it exists, because he has made it.

Hence, even the fool is convinced that something exists in the understanding, at least, than which nothing greater can be conceived. For, when he hears of this, he understands it. And whatever is understood, exists in the understanding. And assuredly that, than which nothing greater can be conceived, cannot exist in the understanding alone. For, suppose it exists in the understanding alone: then it can be conceived to exist in reality; which is greater.

Therefore, if that, than which nothing greater can be conceived, exists in the understanding alone, the very being, than which nothing greater can be conceived, is one, than which a greater can be conceived. But obviously this is impossible. Hence, there is doubt that there exists a being, than which nothing greater can be conceived, and it exists both in the understanding and in reality.

CHAPTER III

And it assuredly exists so truly, that it cannot be conceived not to exist. For, it is possible to conceive of a being which cannot be conceived not to exist; and this is greater than one which can be conceived not to exist. Hence, if that, than which nothing greater can be conceived, can be conceived not to exist, it is not that, than which nothing greater can be conceived. But this is an irreconcilable contradiction. There is, then, so truly a being than which nothing greater can be conceived to exist, that it cannot even be conceived not to exist, and this being thou art, O Lord, our God.

So truly, therefore, dost thou exist, O Lord, my God, that thou canst not be conceived not to exist; and rightly. For, if a mind could conceive of a being better than thee, the creature would rise above the Creator; and this is most absurd. And, indeed, whatever else there is, except thee alone, can be conceived not to exist. To thee alone, therefore, it belongs to exist more truly than all other beings, and hence in a higher degree than all others. For, whatever else exists does not exist so truly, and hence in a less degree it belongs to it to exist. Why, then, has the fool said in his heart, there is no God (*Psalms* xiv. 1), since it is so evident, to a rational mind, that thou dost exist in the highest degree of all? Why except that he is dull and a fool?

CHAPTER IV

But how has the fool said in his heart what he could not conceive; or how is it that he could not conceive what he said in his heart? Since it is the same to say in the heart, and to conceive.

But, if really, nay, since really, he both conceived, because he said in his heart; and did not say in his heart, because he could not conceive; there is more than one way in which a thing is said in the heart or conceived. For, in one sense, an object is conceived, when the word signifying it is conceived; and in another, when the very entity, which the object is, is understood.

In the former sense, then, God can be conceived not to exist, but in the latter, not at all. For no one who understands what fire and water are can conceive fire to be water, in accordance with the nature of the facts themselves, although this is possible according to the words. So, then, no one who understands what God is can conceive that God does not exist; although he says these words in his heart, either without any or with some foreign signification. For God is that than which a greater cannot be conceived. And he who thoroughly understands this assuredly understands that this being so truly exists, that not even in concept can it be nonexistent. Therefore, he who understands that God so exists cannot conceive that he does not exist.

I thank thee, gracious Lord, I thank thee; because what I formerly believed by thy bounty, I now so understand by thine illumination, that if I were unwilling to believe that thou dost exist, I should not be able not to understand this to be true.

CHAPTER V

What art thou, then, Lord God, than whom nothing greater can be conceived? But what art thou, except that which, as the highest of all beings, alone exists through itself, and creates all other things from nothing? For whatever is not this is less than a thing which can be conceived of. But this cannot be conceived of thee. What good, therefore, does the supreme Good lack, through which every good is? Therefore, thou art just, truthful, blessed, and whatever it is better to be than not to be. For it is better to be just than not just; better to be blessed than not blessed.

CHAPTER VI

But, although it is better for thee to be sensible, omnipotent, compassionate, passionless, than not to be these things, how art thou sensible, if thou art not a body: or omnipotent, if thou hast not all powers; or at once compassionate and passionless? For if only corporeal things are sensible, since the senses encompass a body and are in a body, how art thou sensible, although thou art not a body, but a supreme spirit, who is superior to body? But, if feeling is only cognition, or for the sake of cognition—for he who feels obtains knowledge in accordance with the proper functions of his senses; as through sight, of colors; through taste, of flavors—whatever in any way cognizes is not inappropriately said, in some sort, to feel.

Therefore, O Lord, although thou art not a body yet thou art truly sensible in the highest degree in respect of this, that thou dost cognise all things in the highest degree; and not as an animal cognises, through a corporeal sense.

CHAPTER VII

But how art thou omnipotent, if thou art not capable of all things? Or, if thou canst not be corrupted, and canst not lie, nor make what is true false—as, for example, if thou shouldst make what has been done not to have been done, and the like—how art thou capable of all things? Or else to be capable of these things is not power, but impotence. For, he who is capable of these things is capable of what is not for his good, and of what he ought not to do, and the more capable of them he is, the more power have adversity and perversity against him; and the less has he himself against these.

He, then, who is thus capable is so not by power, but by impotence. For, he is not said to be able because he is able of himself, but because his impotence gives something else power over him. Or, by a figure of speech, just as many words are improperly applied, as when we use "to be" for "not to be," and "to do" for what is really not to do, "or to do nothing." For, often we say to a man who denies the existence of something, "it is as you say it to be," though it might seem more proper to say, "it is not, as you say it is not." In the same way, we say, "this man sits just as that man does." or, "this man rests just as that man does"; although to sit is not to do anything, and to rest is to do nothing.

So, then, when one is said to have the power of doing or experiencing what is not for his good, or what he ought not to do, impotence is understood in the word power. For, the more he possesses this power, the more powerful are adversity and perversity against him, and the more powerless is he against them.

Therefore, O Lord, our God, the more truly art thou omnipotent, since thou art capable of nothing through impotence, and nothing has power against thee.

CHAPTER VIII

But how art thou compassionate, and, at the same time, passionless? For, if thou art passionless, thou dost not feel sympathy, and if thou dost not feel sympathy, thy heart is not wretched from sympathy for the wretched; but this it is to be compassionate. But if thou art not compassionate, whence cometh so great consolation to the wretched? How, then, art thou compassionate and not compassionate, O Lord, unless because thou art compassionate in terms of our experience, and not compassionate in terms of thy being.

Truly, thou art so in terms of our experience, but thou art not so in terms of thine own. For, when thou beholdest us in our wretchedness, we experience the effect of compassion, but thou dost not experience the feeling. Therefore, thou art both compassionate, because thou dost save the wretched, and spare those who sin against thee, and not compassionate because thou art affected by no sympathy for wretchedness.

IN BEHALF OF THE FOOL

An Answer to the Argument of Anselm by Gaunilo, a Monk of Marmoutier

. . . if it should be said that a being which cannot be even conceived in terms of any fact, is in the understanding. I do not deny that this being is, accordingly, in my understanding. But since through this fact it can in no ways attain to real existence also, I do not yet concede to it that existence at all, until some certain proof of it shall be given.

For he who says that this being exists, because otherwise the being which is greater than all will not be greater than all, does not attend strictly to what he is saying. For I do not yet say, no, I even deny or doubt that this being is greater than any real object. Nor do I concede to it any other existence than this (if it should be called existence) which it

"In Behalf of the Fool," *An Answer to the Argument of Anselm by Guanilo, a Monk of Marmoutier,* with Anselm's response, translated by Sidney Norton Deane, Open Court 1926.

has when the mind, according to a word merely heard, tries to form the image of an object absolutely unknown to it.

How, then, is the veritable existence of that being proved to me from the assumption, by hypothesis, that it is greater than all other beings? For I should still deny this, or doubt your demonstration of it, to this extent, that I should not admit that this being is in my understanding and concept even in the way in which many objects whose real existence is uncertain and doubtful, are in my understanding and concept. For it should be proved first that this being itself really exists somewhere; and then, from the fact that it is greater than all, we shall not hesitate to infer that it also subsists in itself.

For example: it is said that somewhere in the ocean is an island, which, because of the difficulty, or rather the impossibility, of discovering what does not exist, is called the lost island. And they say that this island has an inestimable wealth of all manner of riches and delicacies in greater abundance than is told of the Islands of the Blest; and that having no owner or inhabitant, it is more excellent than all other countries, which are inhabited by mankind, in the abundance with which it is stored.

Now if someone should tell me that there is such an island, I should easily understand his words, in which there is no difficulty. But suppose that he went on to say, as if by a logical inference, "you can no longer doubt that this island which is more excellent than all lands exists somewhere, since you have no doubt that it is in your understanding. And since it is more excellent not to be in the understanding alone, but to exist both in the understanding and in reality, for this reason it must exist. For if it does not exist, any land which really exists will be more excellent than it; and so the island already understood by you to be more excellent will not be more excellent."

If a man should try to prove to me by such reasoning that this island truly exists, and that its existence should no longer be doubted, either I should believe that he was jesting, or I know not which I ought to regard as the greater fool: myself, supposing that I should allow this proof; or him, if he should suppose that he had established with any certainty the existence of this island. For he ought to show first that the hypothetical excellence of this island exists as a real and indubitable fact, and in no wise as any unreal object, or one whose existence is uncertain, in my understanding.

ANSELM'S REPLY

But, you say, it is as if one should suppose an island in the ocean, which surpasses all lands in its fertility, and which, because of the difficulty, or rather the impossibility, of discovering what does not exist, is called a lost island; and should say that there can be no doubt that this island truly exists in reality, for this reason, that one who hears it described easily understands what he hears.

Now I promise confidently that if any man shall devise anything existing either in reality or in concept alone (except that than which a greater cannot be conceived) to which he can adapt the sequence of my reasoning, I will discover that thing, and will give him his lost island, not to be lost again.

But it now appears that this being than which a greater is inconceivable cannot be conceived not to be, because it exists on so assured a ground of truth; for otherwise it would not exist at all.

Hence, if anyone says that he conceives this being not to exist, I say that at the time when he conceives of this either he conceives of a being than which a greater is inconceivable, or he does not conceive at all. If he does not conceive, he does not conceive of the nonexistence of that of which he does not conceive. But if he does conceive, he certainly conceives of a being which cannot be even conceived not to exist. For if it could be conceived not to exist, it could be conceived to have a beginning and an end. But this is impossible.

He, then, who conceives of this being conceives of a being which cannot be even conceived not to exist; but he who conceives of this being does not conceive that it does not exist; else he conceives what is inconceivable. The nonexistence, then, of that than which a greater cannot be conceived is inconceivable.

STUDY QUESTIONS: ANSELM, PROSLOGION

1. What are the premises of Anselm's ontological argument?
2. How did the proof come to him?
3. What is the difference between an object existing in the understanding, and understanding that the object exists? Is this distinction important to the argument? Why?
4. Why is it greater to exist than not to exist?
5. What is the significance of Guanilo's objection using the example of the lost island?
6. What is Anselm's response to Guanilo? Are you persuaded by it? Who do you think wins the debate, and why?
7. Compare Guanilo's criticism of Anselm's argument with Kant's (in his *Critique of Pure Reason*): "If we think in a thing every feature of reality except one, the missing reality is not added by my saying that the defective thing exists . . . since otherwise what exists would be something different from what I thought. When, therefore, I think a being as the supreme reality, without any defect, the question still remains whether it exists or not." How do the criticisms differ? Which is better? How might Anselm try to respond to Kant? Who do you think wins that one?
8. Could you make an ontological argument for the existence of the devil?

Philosophical Bridges: Anselm's Influence

Anselm signaled the metaphysical sea change from the Augustinian view that ultimate reality, up to and including God, cannot be known by reason nor by experience, to the view which found its culmination in Aquinas, namely, that using Aristotelian logic to perfect reason buttressed by empirical insights the mind can know everything there is to know about everything, up to and including the nature of reality and God. In that sense, Anselm was the bridge between Augustine and Aquinas. His use of linguistic analysis on behalf of intractable philosophical conundrums continues to be a staple of philosophical technique for solving apparently unsolvable problems. His ontological argument for the existence of God, which Anselm originated, continues to inspire theologians and philosophers alike, up to the present day.

Peter Abelard (1079–1142)

Biographical History

French philosopher and theologian Peter Abelard (Latin name Petrus Abaelardus, French Pierre Abailard or Abélard) was born in Brittany, south of the Loire. After studying logic at Loches and Paris, he taught briefly at Melun and Corbeil before returning to Paris where a dispute with his former master, Guillaume de Champeaux, made him a controversial but famous figure: he got Guillaume to admit that he was wrong and Abelard right about the nature of universals. He took further study at Anselm of Laon's school, where also he had severe arguments with virtually all the masters teaching there. He ended up teaching logic and theology at the famous Notre Dame, where the canon Fulbert beseeched him to tutor his beautiful and brilliant niece Heloise. They fell madly in love, held secret liaisons at Notre Dame and around Paris, finally getting married—this was kept secret, even when their child was born. This so enraged Fulbert that he had Abelard castrated. Heloise became a nun.

Abelard entered the monastery of St. Denis, named after the pseudo-Dionysus (Areopagite), but soon got in trouble for arguing that Denis should never have been made a saint and that therefore the monastery that was now his home should never have been thus named. But his fame as a logician and debater were by now legendary, and he was given his own school in Paraclete (Le Paraclet, a lovely French village near Nogent-sur-Seine), which was eventually inherited by Heloise and her fellow nuns. When Abelard was made abbot of St. Gildas de Ruys in Brittany, he tried to get rid of the greed and corruption of the monks under him who, as a result, tried unsuccessfully to have him murdered. But Abelard, who had been born into a family famed for its warriors, was himself skilled with the sword. Unable to kill him, new charges were brought against him, regarding his theological views, and at the council of Sens the pope agreed that Abelard should be condemned. But Abelard went to meet his accusers, debating openly with their leader Bernard of Clairvaux, who lost the debate and promptly rescinded the charges.

Philosophical Overview

Abelard was a rationalist who believed that pure reason could ascend to true knowledge, both in the natural and supernatural realms. But reason alone could not provide understanding; for this, faith was required. The works which he most closely studied, and which had the greatest influence on him, were Aristotle's *Categories* and *On Interpretation*, Plato's *Timaeus* (the only Platonic dialogue then available), Porphyry's *Isagoge* and all the works of Boethius. Like John Scotus Erigena, Abelard argued that scripture and the works of the church fathers should be not just studied but questioned, and questioned deeply, because human beings were fallible. He was in many ways a skeptic, and argued like one, up to the point when there was conflict between sacred texts and reason; in that case, reason should give way to faith. But because his logical techniques of analysis were so powerful, his enemies saw his methods as heretical, for they led the mind to see clear conflict between scripture and reason and then asked the thinker to stop thinking and to believe what the scripture says; this was seen as itself too dangerous, even subversive.

His analysis of the logical and grammatical functions of universals in language influenced all subsequent philosophers and heralded the philosophy of language as a philosophical discipline in its own right. His reduction of human motives to intentional action brought into ethical disputes the notion that what mattered in whether an act is right or wrong is not the consequences of the act but the intention under which the actor conceived the act.

ETHICS, OR THE BOOK CALLED "KNOW THYSELF"
Peter Abelard

What makes an act good? There have throughout philosophy's long history been two sorts of moral theories, which can be categorized into *consequentialist* and *nonconsequentialist* (also known as *deontological*, from *deontos*, meaning rule-based). According to consequentialist moral theories, an act is good or right in so far as it leads to good consequences.

Aristotle's virtue ethics, for instance, is a prime example: the act is good in so far as it leads to a good result, namely, the attainment of rationality, virtue, and excellence. According to nonconsequentialist moral theories, an act is right or good in so far as it is done in accordance with some rule or principle, independently of the consequences. The ten commandments, for instance, would be a classic example (the great eighteenth century German philosopher Immanuel Kant's theory, with its *categorical imperative,* would be a more recent version). Now, what Abelard here argues uniquely is that what matters is neither the result nor the rule but, rather, the *intention.* A good intention is, as he says, a "good-in-itself," that is, a good independent of anything else such as consequences. It is an intrinsic (rather than instrumental) value. Since the source of intention is the conscience, sin is the result of actions done against one's conscience. Here, anticipating in some ways the views of philosophers such as most notably Kant regarding the human will, Abelard conceives conscience not as an "after the fact" psychological sensation resulting from one's actions, but a guiding principle that leads a good person to act rightly.

The logical force of his famous rhetoric that got Abelard into so much trouble and enraged pious people is well evident here. He argues, for instance, that those who persecuted Christ, such as the Roman soldiers, sinned in *act* but not in *intention,* since they were intending to do good; more than that, had they acted against their own conscience and not prosecuted Christ as they had been taught (and believed) they had to do, their sin would have been even greater!

CHAPTER IX

God and Man United in Christ Are Not Something Better than God Alone

Now let us go back to the previous point, to the statement that good added to good produces something better than either of them is by itself. You must guard against being led to say that Christ, that is, God and man joined together in a person, is something better than the divinity of Christ or even his humanity—or, in other words, than God himself united to man, or man himself assumed by God. Certainly, it is agreed that in Christ both the man who is assumed and the God who assumes him are good, and each substance can be understood only as good, just as in individual men both the corporeal and the incorporeal substance are good, though the goodness of the body has no bearing on the worth or merit of the soul. But in fact who will dare to prefer the whole which is called Christ—namely, God and man together—or any number of things at all, to God, as though anything could be better than He, who is both the highest good and the source from whom all things receive whatever good they possess? It is true that, in order to carry out something, some things seem to be so necessary that God cannot do it without them, as aids or even primordial causes. Nevertheless, whatever the greatness of things may be, nothing can be said to be better than God. For although a number of good things is established, so that goodness may be found in many things, it does not happen in consequence that goodness is greater, any more than the fact that many are filled with knowledge, or that the number of sciences is increasing, necessitates an increase in each person's knowledge, so that it becomes greater than before. So also, since God is good in Himself and creates countless things which neither exist nor are good save through Him, goodness is found in many through Him, so that the number of good things is greater; no goodness, however, can be preferred to or equated with His goodness. Goodness, it is true, exists in man, and goodness in God, and though the substances or natures in which goodness is to be found are diverse, there is nothing whose goodness can

Abailard, from *Ethics, or the Book Called "Know Thyself,"* edited and translated by Eugene R. Fairweather, *The Library of Christian Classics, Volume X, A Scholastic Miscellany: Anselm to Ockham,* Philadelphia: The Westminster Press 1956, pp. 288–297.

be preferred to or equated with the divine goodness; thus nothing is to be called better (that is, a greater good) than God, or even equally good.

CHAPTER X

A Multitude of Goods Is Not Better than One Good

But it does not seem that a plurality of goodnesses or of good things can be found in act plus intention. For when intention is called good and activity is called good—as springing from good intention—only the goodness of the intention is referred to; nor does the term "good" retain the same sense, so that we can speak of many "goods." For example, when we say that a man is simple and a saying simple, we do not on that account concede that there are many "simples," since the word "simple" is being applied in two different ways. Let no one, therefore, force us to admit, when good work is added to good intention, that good is superadded to good as if there were several goods, in proportion to which the reward ought to be increased; as has been stated, we cannot correctly say that these are many goods, when the term "good" cannot possibly be fittingly applied to them in the same way.

CHAPTER XI

A Deed Is Good Because of Good Intention

We say, in fact, that an intention is good, that is, right in itself, but that an action is good, not because it acquires any kind of goodness in itself, but because it comes from a good intention. It follows from this that the same thing may be done by the same man at different times, and yet that the action may sometimes be called good, sometimes bad, because of a difference of intention, and thus its relation to good and evil seems to be altered. The same thing happens to the proposition, "Socrates is seated," or rather to our understanding of its truth or falsity, because at one moment Socrates is sitting, at another he is standing.

Now Aristotle says that this alteration with respect to truth and falsity happens in this way in these propositions, not because they themselves, when they are changed with respect to truth and falsehood, undergo anything by a change of themselves, but because the subject-matter, namely, Socrates, is moved in himself—that is, changes from sitting to standing, or conversely.[1]

CHAPTER XII

On What Grounds an Intention Is Called Good

There are those, however, who think that an intention is good or right, whenever someone believes that he is acting well, and that what he is doing is pleasing to God. This was the case with those who persecuted the martyrs, to whom the truth refers in the Gospel: "The hour cometh, that whosoever killeth you will think that he doeth a service to God."[2] The apostle expresses sympathy with the ignorance of such people, when he says: "I bear them witness, that they have a zeal of God, but not according to knowledge."[3] That is to say, they do these things, which they believe to be pleasing to God, with great fervor and longing, but because they are deceived in this zeal or eagerness of mind their intention is erroneous, nor is the eye of their heart single, so as to see clearly—that is, to preserve itself from error. Thus the Lord, when he distinguished deeds according to a right or not-right intention, carefully called the mind's eye (or intention) "single" and, as it were, pure from uncleanness, so that it could see clearly, or on the contrary he called it "darksome," when he said, "If thine eye be single, they whole body shall be lightsome."[4] This means that if your intention is right, the whole mass of deeds springing from it, which can be seen in the manner of corporeal things, will be worthy of light (that is, good), and contrariwise. Thus intention is not to be called good simply because it seems good, but because it really is what it is thought to be—as, for example, when it believes that what it is

[1]Cf. Aristotle, *De interpret.*, 12 (21^b 10–15).

[2]John 16:2.

[3]Rom. 10:2.

[4]Matt. 6:22.

aiming at is pleasing to God, and in addition is not deceived at all in its judgment. Otherwise the very infidels would have good works, just as we do, since they, no less then we ourselves, believe that they are saved—or, if you will, please God—by their works.

CHAPTER XIII

Sin Is Only That Which Is Done Against Conscience

If anyone asks, nonetheless, whether those who persecuted the martyrs or Christ sinned in that which they believed to be pleasing to God, or whether they could let pass without sin that which they thought should in no ways be let pass, certainly, in terms of our previous description of sin as contempt of God, or consent to that to which one believes that consent should not be given, we cannot say that they sinned in this, or that ignorance of anything, or even disbelief itself (in which no one can be saved), is sin. For those who do not know Christ, and on that account reject the Christian faith, because they believe that it is contrary to God, can hardly be said to show contempt of God in what they do for God's sake, and for that reason think that they do well—especially since the apostle says, "If our heart do not reprehend us, we have confidence before God,"[1] as if he were to say, Where we do not violate our own conscience, it is in vain that we fear being found guilty of sin before God. Yet if the ignorance of such men is not to be imputed for sin in any way, how is it that the Lord himself prays for those who crucify him, saying: "Father, forgive them, for they know not what they do"?[2] Or how is it that Stephen, taught by this example, entreats for those who are stoning him, saying, "Lord, lay not this sin to their charge"?[3] For it does not seem that forgiveness should be granted, if no sin

has gone before, nor does forgiveness normally mean anything but the remission of the penalty deserved by sin. Besides, Stephen clearly calls what sprang from ignorance "sin."

CHAPTER XIV

In How Many Ways the Term "Sin" Is Used

But to reply to the objections more fully, one should know that the term "sin" is used in different ways. Properly, however, sin means actual contempt for God or consent to evil, as we mentioned above.[4] From this little children are exempt, as well as the naturally simple-minded. Since these have no merits, because they lack reason, nothing can be imputed to them for sin, and they are saved by the sacraments alone. A victim offered for sin is also called "sin," as when the apostle speaks of Jesus Christ as having been "made sin."[5] The penalty of sin is also called "sin" or a "curse,"[6] as when we say that sin is forgiven, meaning that the penalty is remitted, and that the Lord Jesus "bore our sins,"[7] meaning that he endured the penalty for our sins, or the penalties springing from them. But when we say that young children have "original sin," or that we all, as the apostle says, sinned in Adam,[8] this amounts to saying that our punishment or the sentence of our condemnation takes its rise from his sin. The actual works of sin, also, or whatever we do not rightly know or will, we sometimes call "sins." For what does it mean for anyone to have committed sin, except that he has put his sin into effect? Nor is this strange, since conversely we refer to sins themselves[9] as deeds, as in the statement of Athanasius, when he says: "They shall give account for their own deeds. And they that have done good will go into life eternal, they that have done evil into eternal fire." For

---

[1] I John 3:21.

[2] Luke 23:34.

[3] Acts 7:60.

[4] Cf. Ch. III (Cousin, II, 596 ff.).

[5] II Cor. 5:21.

[6] Cf. Gal. 3:13.

[7] I Peter 2:24.

[8] Cf. Rom. 5:12.

[9] That is, intentions.

what does "for their own deeds" mean? Does it mean that judgment will only be returned for the intentions that were carried out in action, so that he who has more deeds to point to will receive a greater recompense? Does it mean that he who was unable to put his intention into effect will be exempt from condemnation, like the devil who did not obtain in effect what he had anticipated in desire?[1] It cannot mean this. "For their own deeds," then, refers to their consent to the things which they decided to carry out, that is, to the sins which with the Lord are reckoned as deeds done, since he punishes them as we punish deeds.

Now when Stephen speaks of the "sin" which the Jews were committing against him in ignorance, he means by "sin" the very penalty which he was suffering on account of the sin of our first parents (just as the term is applied to other penalties from the same source), or else he is referring to their unjust action in stoning him. he asked indeed that it should not be charged to them, or, in other words, that they should not be punished bodily on its account. For here God often punishes some persons corporally, when no fault of theirs requires it, and yet not without cause—as, for instance, when he sends afflictions to the just with a view to their purification or testing, or when he permits some to be afflicted, so that afterward they may be delivered and he may be glorified for the benefit he has conferred. This happened in the case of the blind man, of whom he himself said: "Neither hath this man sinned, nor his parents; but that the works of God should be made manifest in him."[2] Who will deny, either, that innocent children are sometimes imperiled or afflicted along with wicked parents, by the fault of the latter—as in the case of the men of Sodom[3] and of a good many other peoples—so that greater terror may be inspired in the wicked by the wider extension of punishment? It was

because he had carefully noted this that blessed Stephen prayed that "sin" (that is to say, the punishment he was enduring at the hands of the Jews, or that which they were wrongly doing) should not be charged to them, or, in other words, that they should not be punished physically because of it.

The Lord was also of this mind, when he said, "Father, forgive them,"[4] meaning, Do not avenge, even by physical punishment, this that they are doing against me. Such revenge could, in fact, have reasonably been taken, even if no fault of theirs had gone before, so that others who saw it, or even they themselves, might learn from the punishment that they had not acted rightly in this matter. But it was fitting for the Lord, by this example of his own prayer, to encourage us supremely to foster the virtue of patience and display the highest love, so that he should display to us in deed what he himself had taught us by word of mouth—namely, to pray also for our enemies.[5] Therefore, when he said, "Forgive," this did not refer to any previous fault or contempt of God which they had in this matter, but had to do with the reasonableness of imposing a penalty, which, as we have said, could follow with good cause, even without any previous fault. This happened to the prophet who was sent against Samaria and by eating did what the Lord had forbidden. Since he did not presume to do anything in contempt of God, but was deceived by another prophet, he incurred death in his innocence, not so much from any guilty fault as from the actual doing of the deed.[6] God indeed, as blessed Gregory recalls, sometimes changes his sentence, but never his purpose.[7] That is to say, he often determines that what for some reason he had planned to command or to threaten shall not be carried out. But his purpose remains fixed, or, in other words, what in his own resolution he plans to do never lacks efficacy. He did

---

[1]That is, equality with God.

[2]John 9:3.

[3]Cf. Gen., ch. 19.

[4]Luke 23:34.

[5]Cf. Matt. 5:44.

[6]Cf. III Kings 13:24 (A. V., I Kings 13:24).

[7]Cf. Gregory the Great, *Moral. in Iob*, XVI, 37:46 (*PL*, 75, 1144).

not, we know, adhere to what he had enjoined on Abraham concerning the sacrifice of his son,[1] or to his threat against the Ninevites,[2] and thus, as we have said, he changed his sentence. So the aforesaid prophet, whom he had forbidden to take food on his journey, believed that his sentence had been changed, and indeed that he would certainly be in the wrong if he did not listen to the other prophet, who claimed that he had been sent by the Lord for the very purpose of refreshing his weariness with food. He did this, therefore, without blame, since he was resolved to avoid blame. Nor did sudden death harm him, when it delivered him from the tribulations of this present life, while it was a profitable warning to many, since they saw a just man thus punished without fault, and observed the fulfillment in him of that which is elsewhere addressed to the Lord: "Thou, O God, forasmuch as thou art just, orderest all things justly, since him also who deserveth not to be punished thou dost condemn."[3] This means: Thou dost condemn, not to eternal but to bodily death. For some, such as children, are saved without merits, and attain to eternal life by grace alone. Similarly, it is not absurd that some should endure bodily penalties which they have not deserved; this is certainly the case with young children who die without the grace of baptism, and are condemned to bodily as well as to eternal death. Many innocent persons, moreover, suffer affliction. What is strange, then, in the fact that those who crucified the Lord could reasonably incur temporal punishment by that unjust action, as we have said, even though ignorance excuses them from blame? It was for this reason that he said, "Forgive them"—in other words, do not bring upon them the penalty which, as we have said, they could not unreasonably incur.

Moreover, if what they did through ignorance, or even the ignorance itself, is not properly called "sin" (that is, contempt of God), this applies to disbelief as well, even though the latter necessarily shuts off the entrance to eternal life from adults who have the use of reason. In fact, it is enough for eternal damnation not to believe the gospel, to be ignorant of Christ, not to receive the sacraments of the Church, even though this is done not so much by malice as by ignorance. Concerning such persons the truth also says, "he that doth not believe is already judged,"[4] while the apostle declares, "he who knows not shall not be known."[5] But when we say that we sin unwittingly—that is, that we do something which is not fitting—by "sin" we mean, not contempt, but the action. For the philosophers also equate sinning with doing or saying something in an unfitting way, even though there is nothing here that seems to have any bearing on an offense against God. Thus Aristotle, when he spoke of the faulty attribution of relations (in Ad aliquid[6]), said: "But sometimes the relation will not seem to be reciprocal, unless it is attributed appropriately to that which is mentioned. For if he sins[7] in making the attribution, as in speaking of the 'wing of a bird,'" If, therefore, in this way we describe as "sin" everything that we do badly, or that we possess contrary to our salvation, then we shall certainly call "sins" both unbelief and ignorance of the things that must necessarily be believed for salvation, even though no contempt for God is in evidence. I think, nevertheless, that sin, properly speaking, is that which can never happen without blame. But ignorance of God, or disbelief, or actual deeds which are not done rightly, can occur without blame. For suppose that someone does not believe the gospel of Christ, because the proclamation has not reached him, as the text of the apostle indicates: "how shall they believe him, of whom they

---

[1]Cf. Gen., ch. 22.

[2]Cf. Jonah, ch. 4.

[3]Cf. Wisdom of Solomon 12:15, which actually says the opposite.

[4]John 3:18.

[5]I Cor. 14:38.

[6]The title refers to the beginning of the chapter in the not very literal translation Abailard was using; the reference is to Categ., 7 (6ᵇ36–7ᵃ4).

[7]Peccet.

have not heard? And how shall they hear without a preacher?"[1] In that case, what blame can be attributed to him because he does not believe? Cornelius did not believe in Christ until Peter had been sent to him and had instructed him concerning this. Moreover, even though he previously knew and loved God by natural law, and so merited to be heard for his prayer, and to have his alms accepted by God, nevertheless, if by any chance he had departed from this light before he believed in Christ, we should not dare to make him any promise of life, however great his good works seemed. Nor should we number him with the faithful, but rather with unbelievers, no matter how great the zeal for salvation which had possessed him.[2] Indeed, many of God's judgments are an abyss. Sometimes he draws those who resist, or at least are less concerned for their salvation, and repels those who present themselves, or at least are more ready to believe—all by the deepest counsel of his dispensation. For thus he rejected him who offered himself: "Master, I will follow thee whithersoever thou shalt go."[3] But when another excused himself on the ground of the solicitude he felt for his father, he did not tolerate this dutiful excuse of his, even for an hour.[4] Again, in rebuking the stubbornness of cities, he said, "woe to thee, Chorazin, woe to thee, Bethsaida, for if in Tyre and Sidon had been wrought the miracles that have been wrought in you, they had long ago done penance in sackcloth and ashes."[5] You see, he tendered them not only his own preaching, but also a display of miracles, even though he already knew that they were not going to be believed. But as for the other cities of the Gentiles, though he was aware that they were ready to receive the faith, he did not deem them worthy of a visit from himself. And yet, when some of their citizens perished, deprived of the word of preaching—even though they were prepared to accept it—how can we blame them for that, when we see that it did not happen by any negligence

of theirs? Nevertheless, we say that this their disbelief, in which they died, was enough to condemn them, although the cause of this blindness in which the Lord abandoned them is less clear to us.[6] Perhaps if anyone finds the cause in their sin, committed without guilt, it will be permitted, since he finds it absurd that they should be condemned without any sin at all.

Nonetheless, as we have often indicated, we think that the term "sin" can properly be applied to guilty negligence alone, and that this cannot exist in anyone, of any age whatever, without his deserving to be condemned. But I do not see how not believing in Christ, which is certainly a matter of disbelief, ought to be imputed as a fault to young children, or to those to whom belief in Christ has not been proclaimed. Nor do I see how blame attaches to anything that is done by invincible ignorance, when we have not even been able to foresee it—for instance, if someone kills a man with an arrow because he does not see him in a wood, while he intends to shoot at wild beasts or birds. Nonetheless, we say that he sins, but through ignorance, just as we sometimes admit that we sin, not only in consent but also in thought. But in this case we do not use the term properly, as equivalent to fault, but apply it loosely to that which it is not at all fitting for us to do, whether it is done by error or by negligence, or in any other unfitting way. This, then, is what it means to sin by ignorance: not to bear any blame, but to do what does not befit us—to sin in thought, that is, by willing what it is not at all fitting for us to will, or in speech or in act, that is, by saying or doing what should not be said or done, even if all these things happen to us involuntarily and by our ignorance. Thus, we may also say that those who persecuted Christ or his people, whom they thought they ought to persecute, sinned in act. Nevertheless, they would have sinned more grievously if they had spared them against their own conscience.

---

[1] Rom. 10:14.

[2] Cf. Acts 10:1 f.

[3] Matt. 8:19.

[4] Cf. Matt. 8:21 f.

[5] Matt. 11:21.

[6] Note the authentically Augustinian attitude.

STUDY QUESTIONS: ABELARD, *ETHICS, OR THE BOOK CALLED "KNOW THYSELF"*

1. Is anything better than God? Why?
2. What makes an act good? Why?
3. How does Abelard distinguish good intention from bad intention?
4. What is sin?
5. What is the significance of the different sorts of sins?
6. What does Abelard mean when he says that "many of God's judgments are an abyss?"

THE GLOSSES OF PETER ABELARD ON PORPHYRY

In this commentary and elaboration of the philosophy of Boethius, Abelard follows
Boethius in distinguishing three different but related aspects of philosophy: speculative,
concerned with metaphysical speculation on the nature and knowledge of reality; moral,
concerned with right action; and rational, concerned with arguments and logic. He then
proceeds to comment on Porphyry, Plotinus' greatest pupil, who blended Aristotelian logic
with neo-Platonic philosophy. In so doing Abelard integrates Boethius', Aristotle's, and
Plato's ideas into a rigorous method of logical analysis and construction of persuasive arguments adaptable, in principle, to any topic.

We may open our introduction to logic by examining something of the characteristic property of logic in its genus which is *philosophy.* Boethius says that not any knowledge whatever is philosophy, but only that which consists in the greatest things; for we do not call all wise men philosophers, but only those whose intelligence penetrates subtle matters. Moreover, Boethius distinguishes three species of philosophy, *speculative,* which is concerned with speculation on the nature of things; *moral,* for the consideration of the honorableness of life; *rational,* for compounding the relation of arguments, which the Greeks call logic. However, some writers separated logic from philosophy and did not call it, according to Boethius, a part of philosophy, but an instrument, because obviously the other parts work in logic in a manner, when they use its arguments to prove their own questions. As, if a question should arise in natural or moral speculation, arguments are derived from logic. Boethius himself holds against them that there is nothing to prevent the same thing from being both an instrument and a part

of a single thing, as the hand is both a part and an instrument of the human body. Logic moreover seems itself often its own instrument when it demonstrates a question pertaining to itself by its own arguments, as for example, "man is the species of animal." It is none the less logic, however, because it is the instrument of logic. So too it is none the less philosophy because it is the instrument of philosophy. Moreover, Boethius distinguishes it from the other two species of philosophy by its proper end, which consists in compounding arguments. For although the physicist compounds arguments, it is not physics but only logic which instructs him in that.

He noted too in regard to logic that it was composed of and reduced to certain rules of argumentation for this reason, namely, lest it lead inconstant minds into error by false inferences, since it seems to construct by its reasons what is not found in the nature of things, and since it seems often to infer things contrary in their conditions, in the following manner: "Socrates is body, but body is white, therefore

Abaelard from *Philosophische Schriften, herausgegeben von Dr. Bernhard Geyer, I Die Logica "Ingredientibus," in Beiträge zur Geschichte der Philosophie des Mittelalters, Band XXI, Heft I,* pp. 1–32.

The Glosses of Peter Abailard on Porphyry, edited and translated by Richard McKeon, New York: Charles Scribners Sons 1929, pp. 208–258.

Socrates is white." On the other hand, "Socrates is body, but body is black, therefore Socrates is black."

Moreover, in writing logic the following order is extremely necessary that since arguments are constructed from propositions, and propositions from words, he who will write logic perfectly, must first write of simple words, then of propositions, and finally devote the end of logic to argumentations, just as our prince Aristotle did, who wrote the *Categories* on the science of words, the *On Interpretation* on the science of propositions, and the *Topics* and the *Analytics* on the science of argumentations.

Porphyry himself moreover as the very statement of the title shows, prepares[1] this introduction for the *Categories* of Aristotle, but later he himself shows that it is necessary to the whole art. The *intention* of it, the *matter*, the *manner of treatment*, the *utility* or the *part of dialectic to which the present science is to be subordinated*, will now be distinguished briefly and precisely.

The *intention* is particularly to instruct the reader in the *Categories* of Aristotle, that he may be able to understand more easily the things that are there treated. This makes necessary the treatment of the five subjects which are its materials, namely genus, species, difference, property, and accident. He judged the knowledge of these to be particularly useful to the *Categories* because the investigation is concerning them in almost the whole course of the *Categories*. That which we spoke of as five, however, can be referred to the words, genus, species, and the others, and also in a certain sense to the things signified by them. For he appropriately makes clear the significance of these five words which Aristotle uses, lest one be ignorant, when one has come to the *Categories*, of what is to be understood by these words; and he is able, moreover, to treat of all the things signified by these words, as if of five things, since, although they are infinite taken singly, inasmuch as genera are infinite and likewise species and the others, nevertheless as has been said, all are considered as five, because all are treated according to five characteristics, all genera according to what constitutes genera, and the others in the same way, for in this same way the eight parts of speech are considered according to their eight characteristics, although taken singly they are infinite.

The *manner of treatment* here is the following: having first distinguished the natures of each singly in separate treatments of them, he proceeds then for further knowledge of them to their common properties and characteristics.

Its *utility*, as Boethius himself teaches, is principally as it is directed to the *Categories*. But it is spread in four directions which we shall disclose more carefully later when he himself takes it up.

If the parts of logic have first been distinguished carefully, it is seen at once what is the part through which the science of the present work leads to logic. On the authority of Cicero and Boethius there are two parts of which logic is composed, namely, the science of *discovering* arguments and of *judging* them, that is, of confirming and proving the arguments discovered. For two things are necessary to one who argues, first to find the arguments by which to argue, then if any should criticize the arguments as defective or as insufficiently firm to be able to confirm them. Wherefore Cicero says that discovery is by nature prior. The present science, however, is concerned with both parts of logic, but most of all with discovery, and it is a part of the science of discovering. For how can an argument be deduced from genus or species or the others, if the things which are here treated are not known? Wherefore, Aristotle himself introduces the definition of the predicables into the *Topics*, when he treats of their places, as Cicero likewise does in his *Topics*. But since an argument is confirmed from the same considerations from which it is discovered, this science is not unrelated to judgment. For, as an argument is derived from the nature of genus and species, so, once derived, it is confirmed from the nature of genus and species. For considering the nature of species in man, so far as it is related to animal, I find at once from the nature of the species the argument for proving animal. But if any one should criticize the argument, I show that it is suitable immediately by indicating the nature of the species and the genus in both, so that from the same conditions of the terms the argument may be found and when it has been found it may be confirmed. . . .

There are some nevertheless who separate this science [i.e. the *Isagoge*] and the science of the categories and of the divisions and of definitions and even of propositions completely from discovery and judg-

---

[1] See above, p. 77.

ment, nor do they count it in any sense among the parts of logic, although, for all that, they think such subjects are necessary to the whole of logic. But authority as well as reason seems contrary to them. For Boethius *On the Topics of Cicero* asserts a double division of dialectic, both parts of which so include each other reciprocally that they each comprise the whole of dialectic. The first part is through the science of discovery and judgment; the second through the science of division, definition and collection. He reduces each of these to the other so that in the science of discovery (which is one of the two divisions of the above classification) he includes also the science of division or definition, for the reason that arguments are deduced from divisions as well as from definitions. Wherefore the science of genus and of species or of the others may also be adapted for a similar reason to discovery. Boethius himself says that the treatise on the *Categories* comes first among the books of Aristotle for those beginning logic. From this it is apparent that the *Categories*, in which the reader has his introduction to logic, are not to be separated from logic, particularly since the distinction of the categories supplies the greatest strength to the argumentation, since the nature, to which each thing pertains or does not pertain, can be established by it. The peculiar study of propositions [i.e. the *On Interpretation*] likewise is not unrelated to that of arguments, since it proves now this, now that, as contrary or contradictory or opposed in any other manner whatever. Therefore, since all treatises of logic converge to the end of logic, that is to argumentation, we separate the knowledge of none of them from logic.

Having examined these things let us begin the literal commentary.

Since it is necessary, etc. He places first an introduction concerning the subject matter of which he will write, in which he indicates the subject matter itself and gives assurance of the utility of the book and promises that he will write in an introductory manner concerning that which philosophers have judged rightly of these things. There are however three accustomed meanings of the word *necessary*, since it is sometimes used to mean *inevitable*, as, *it is necessary that substance is not quality*; sometimes to mean *useful*, as, *to go to the forum*, and sometimes to mean *determined*, as, *that man will die some time*. The first two meanings of necessary obviously are of such

sort that they seem to contend with each other with respect to which of them can be taken more properly here. For it is both the highest necessity to know these things first that one may proceed to others, since without the former the latter can not be known, and it is an obvious utility. If however any one should consider seriously the context, he will decide that *useful* is meant more properly than *inevitable*. For since Porphyry supplies the thing for which he says it is necessary, as if intending some sort of relation to something else, he suggests the meaning of utility. For useful, has reference to something else; inevitable is so called because of itself.

Construe it thus: it is necessary, that is, useful, to know what genus is, etc., that is, what the characteristics of each are. This is shown in their definitions which are assigned not according to their substance but according to their accidental properties, since the name of genus and the name of the others do not designate substance but accident. Wherefore we interpret that *what* according to property rather than substance. *As well for that, etc.* He brings forward four points in which he shows a fourfold utility, as we noted above, namely, categories, definitions, divisions, demonstrations, that is, arguments, which demonstrate the question proposed. *Which*, that is, the knowledge of categories, *is in Aristotle*, that is, is contained in his treatise. For a book is sometimes designated by the name of its author, as for example Lucan. *And for the imposition of definitions*, that is, for imposing and compounding definitions. *And in general.* Likewise these five predicables are useful *for those things which are in division and demonstration*, that is, in argumentation. And since it is necessary, that is, it is useful to so many things to know these things, *I shall try to approach what has been said by the ancients, making a rendering for you*, that is, a treatise, concerning the contemplation of such things, that is, concerning the consideration of these five predicables, I say a *compact* rendering, that is, moderately short. This he explains immediately, saying: *briefly* and *as in an introductory manner*. For too much brevity may introduce too great obscurity, according to that saying of Horace: *I labor to be brief, I become obscure.* Therefore lest the reader be distrustful because of brevity or lest he be confused because of prolixity, he promises to write in an introductory manner. But, how this work may be of use as well to the categories as to the other three subjects, Boethius himself states carefully enough, but still let us touch on it briefly.

And first let us show how each of the treatments of these five predicables is proper to the categories. Knowledge of *genus* pertains to the categories because Aristotle there sets forth the ten supreme genera of all things, in which categories he comprehends the infinite meanings of the names of all things: but how they are the genera of other things can not be known, unless it is preceded by a knowledge of genera. The knowledge of *species* likewise is not unrelated to the categories; without that knowledge there can be no knowledge of genus; for since they are relative to each other they draw their essence and knowledge from each other. Wherefore it is necessary to define one by the other, as Porphyry himself states. *Difference*, too, which when joined to the genus completes the species, is necessary to distinguishing species as well as to distinguishing genus: in stating the division of the genus, the difference shows the signification of that which the species contains. Many things, moreover, are brought forth by Aristotle in the *Categories* where these three, genus, species, and difference, are taken up; if they were not first known those further conclusions could not be understood. One of these is the rule: *things of diverse genera* etc. The knowledge of *property* too is of help because Aristotle himself speaks of the properties of the categories, as when he says that the property of substance is that *since it is one and the same in number*, etc. Therefore, lest the nature of property be ignored at that later point, it must be demonstrated now. Still this must be noted, that Porphyry treats only of the properties of the most special species, whereas Aristotle investigates the properties of genera; but nevertheless the nature of those properties is made clear through the similarity of these for the properties of genera are described in the same way as the properties of species, namely, that the property belongs only to that one species, to every individual of that species, and at all times. Who will doubt the extent to which the knowledge of *accident* is valuable to the categories, when he finds in nine of the categories only accidents? Besides Aristotle frequently and earnestly seeks out the properties of those things which are *in the subject*, that is, of accidents, to which especially pertains the treatment of accident. The knowledge of accident is also profitable to the distinguishing of difference or property, because difference and property will not be known perfectly if the distinction of accident is not had.

Now, however, let us show how the same five predicables are valuable for *definitions*. Definition, of course, is either substantial or it is description. Substantial, on the one hand, which is only of species, uses genus and differences, and therefore the treatment of genus as well as of difference or species is valuable to it. But description is frequently derived from accidents. Wherefore knowledge of accident is particularly valuable to it. Knowledge of property moreover is generally present in all definitions which have a likeness to property in this respect, that they too are converted with that which is defined.

The five predicables also are so necessary to *divisions* that without a knowledge of them division is made by chance rather than by reason. This assertion must be tested in connection with the several divisions. There are three kinds of essential division, namely, division of genus, of whole, and of word; again, three kinds of accidental division, namely, when the accident is divided into subjects, or the subjects into accidents, or the accident into accidents. The division of genus is sometimes made into species, and sometimes into differences asserted for species. Wherefore genus as well as species and difference is needed for that division; and the same three contribute to the distinction of the division of whole and of word, which might be confused with the divisions of genus, if the nature of the genus were not first known, as for example, that the entire genus is predicated univocally of each species, whereas the whole is not predicated singly of the parts composing it, and the word which has multiplex applications is not adapted to its divisions univocally. The predicables are therefore also extremely useful for the division of equivocal words for the following reason, that they were useful for definitions, for from definitions it is known what is equivocal or what is not. For the accidental division likewise, the knowledge of accident, by which such division is constituted, is necessary, and the other predicables too are valuable for making the distinction of that division, otherwise we should divide genus into species or difference, as we divide accident into subjects.

The knowledge of the five predicables, as we have stated above, is obviously valuable too for discovering *argumentations* or for confirming them once they have been discovered. For we find arguments and we confirm them, when they have been found, according to the nature of genus and of species or the others. Boethius moreover in this place calls them the five seats of syllogisms, against which statement it might be said that we do not accept places [*topoi*] in the perfect combination of syllogisms. But certainly that special word is used loosely instead of the genus, that is, speaking of syllogism instead of argumentation, otherwise Boethius would lessen the utility if he directed this knowledge only to syllogisms and not generally to all argumentations, which are similarly called demonstrations by Porphyry. Moreover, in a certain sense it is possible to assign places in the perfect combination of syllogisms, not that they belong to syllogisms *per se*, but because they too can be adduced as evidence of syllogisms in that they afford confirmation of enthymemes which are deduced from syllogisms. Now, however, that these things have been stated concerning utility, let us return to the literal interpretation.

From the more lofty questions. He states further how he will preserve the introductory manner, namely, by abstaining from difficult questions and from questions involved in obscurity and by treating in an ordinary way the more simple ones. Nor is it without meaning that he says in an *ordinary way*: for a thing may be easy in itself and still not be treated lucidly.

At present concerning genera. He states definitely what those more lofty questions are, although he does not resolve them. And the cause is stated for both actions, namely, that he should pass over inquiring into them and nevertheless should make mention of them. For he does not treat of them for this reason, because the uncultivated reader is not able to inquire into them or perceive them. But on the other hand he mentions them lest he make the reader negligent. For if he had ignored them entirely, the reader, thinking there was absolutely nothing more to be inquired concerning them, would disdain altogether the inquiry into them. There are then three questions, as Boethius says, secret and very useful and tried by not a few philosophers, but solved by few. The *first* is as

follows, namely, whether genera and species subsist or are placed in the naked understandings alone, etc., as if he were to say: whether they have true being or whether they consist in opinion alone. The *second* is, if they are conceded to be truly, whether they are corporeal essences or incorporeal, and the *third* is whether they are separated from sensibles or are placed in them. For the species of incorporeal beings are two, in that some incorporeal beings, such as God and the soul, can subsist in their incorporeality apart from sensibles, and others are in nowise able to be beyond the sensible objects in which they are, as line cannot be found except in a body. These questions, however, he passes over in this fashion, saying: *at present I shall refuse to say concerning genera and species this, whether they subsist, etc., or whether subsisting they are corporeal or incorporeal, or whether,* when they are said to be incorporeal, they should be separated from *sensibles, etc., and in accord with them.* This last can be taken in different ways. For it can be taken this way as if to say: I will refuse to make the three assertions stated above concerning them and certain other statements in accord with these, that is, these three questions. In the same way, other questions which are difficult can be brought up concerning them, such as, the question of the common cause of the imposition of universal nouns, namely, what is that cause in virtue of which different things agree, or again the question of the understanding of universal nouns, in which no particular thing seems to be conceived, nor does the universal word seem to deal with any such particular thing, and many other difficult questions. We are able so to expound the words, *and in accord with them* that we may add a fourth question, namely, whether genera and species, so long as they are genera and species, must have some thing subject to them by nomination, or whether, if the things named were destroyed, the universal could still consist of the meaning only of the conception, as this noun *rose* when there is not a single rose to which it is common. But we shall investigate these questions more carefully later.

Now, however, let us follow the introduction literally. Note that when Prophyry says: *at present,* that is, in the present treatise, he intimates in a way that the reader may expect these questions to be solved elsewhere. *Most exalted business.* He states the reason for which he abstains here from these questions, namely, because to treat them is very exalted with respect to the reader who may not be able to attain to them in order to determine this business now. *And requiring greater diligence of inquiry,* for although the author is able to solve it, the reader is not able to inquire into it. Greater diligence of inquiry, I say, than yours. *This, however.* Having stated these things concerning which he is silent, he states those which he does treat of, namely, that which the *ancients,* not in age but in comprehension, *concluded probably,* that is, with verisimilitude, that is in which all have agreed and there was no dissension, *concerning these things,* to wit, genus and species *and of the* other three *things mentioned.* For in resolving the aforesaid questions some are of one opinion and others of another. Wherefore Boethius records that Aristotle held that genera and species subsist only in sensibles but are understood outside them, whereas Plato held not only that they were understood without sensibles but that they actually were separate. *And of these the ancients,* I say, and *most of all the peripatetics,* that is, part of these ancients; he calls dialecticians or a kind of argumentators the peripatetics.

Note likewise that the functions which are proper to introductions can be distinguished in this introduction. For Boethius says *On the Topics of Cicero: every introduction which is intended to compose the reader, as is said in the* Rhetoric, *seizes on benevolence or prepares, attention or produces docility.* For it is proper that any one of the three or several at the same time be present in every introduction; but two are to be noted in this introduction, docility when he sets forth the material, which is those five predicables, and attention when he commends the treatise for a fourfold utility in that which the ancients advanced as the doctrine of these, or when he promises the style of an introduction. But benevolence is not necessary here where there is no knowledge hateful to one who seeks the treatment of it by Porphyry.

Let us return now, as we promised, to the above stated questions, and inquire carefully into them, and solve them. And since it is known that genera and species are universals and in them Porphyry touches on the nature of all universals generally, let us inquire here into the common nature of universals by studying these two [genus and species], and let us inquire also whether they apply only to *words* or to *things* as well.

In the *On Interpretation* Aristotle defines the universal as "that which is formed naturally apt to be predicated of many;" Porphyry moreover defines the particular, that is, the individual as "that which is predicated of only one." Authority seems to ascribe the universal as much to things as to words; Aristotle himself ascribes it to things since he asserted immediately before the definition of universal: "however, since of things some are universals, and others are singulars, I call that universal which is formed to be predicated of many, and that singular which is not." Likewise Porphyry himself, when he said species are made of genus and difference, located them in the nature of things. From which it is manifest that things themselves are contained in the universal noun.

Nouns too are called universals. Wherefore, Aristotle says, "genus determines quality with respect to substance; for it signifies how each thing is." And Boethius in the book *On Divisions* says: "it is, however, extremely useful to know this, that the genus is in a certain manner the single likeness of many species, and that likeness displays the substantial agreement of them all." Yet "to signify" or "to display" pertains to words; but "to be signified applies to things. And again he says: "the designation of a noun is predicated of many nouns, and is in a certain manner a species containing under itself individuals." However, it is not properly called species since a noun is not substantial but accidental, but it is decidedly a universal since the definition of the universal applies to it. Hence, it follows that words are universals whose function it is to be predicates of propositions.

Since it would seem, then, that things as well as words are called universal, it must be inquired how the universal definition can be applied to things. For it seems that no thing, nor any collection of things, is predicated of many things taken one by one, which is required as the characteristic of the universal. For although this people or this house or Socrates may be predicated of all their parts at the same time, still no one says that they are universals, since the predication of them does not apply to each of the several individuals or parts. And one thing is predicated of many much less properly than a collector of things. Let us hear, therefore, how either one thing or a collection of things is called universal, and let us state all the opinions of all thinkers.

Certain philosophers, indeed, take the universal thing thus: in things different from each other in form they set up a substance essentially the same; this is the material essence of the individuals in which it is, and it is one in itself and diverse only through the forms of its inferiors. If these forms should happen to be taken away, there would be absolutely no difference of things, which are separated from each other only by a diversity of forms, since the matter is in essence absolutely the same. For example, in individual men, different in number, [i.e. in the different individuals of the species man] there is the same substance of man, which here is made Plato through these accidents, there Socrates through those. To these doctrines Porphyry seems to assent entirely when he says, "by participation in the species many men are one but in particulars the one and common is many." And again he says, "individuals are defined as follows, that each one of them consists of properties the collection of which is not in another." Similarly, too, they place in the several animals different in species one and essentially the same substance of animal, which they make into diverse species by taking on diverse differences, as if from this wax I should first make the statue of a man, then the statue of a cow, by accommodating the diverse forms to the essence which persists wholly the same. This, however, is of importance, that the same wax does not constitute the statues at the same time, as is possible in the case of the universal, namely, that the universal is common, Boethius says, in such a way that the same universal is at the same time entirely in the different things of which it constitutes the substance materially; and although it is universal in itself, the same universal is individual through forms advening, without which it subsists naturally in itself; and apart from them it in no sense exists actually; for it is universal in nature but individual in actuality, and it is understood incorporeal and not subject to sense in the simplicity of its universality, but the same universal subsists in actuality, corporeal and sensible through accidents: and according to the same authority, Boethius, individuals subsist and universals are understood.

This is one of two opinions. Although authorities seem to agree very much upon it, physics is in every manner opposed to it. For if what is the same

essentially, although occupied by diverse forms, exists in individual things, it is necessary that one thing which is affected by certain forms be another thing which is occupied by other forms, so that the animal formed by rationality, is the animal formed by irrationality, and so the rational animal is the irrational, and thus contraries would be placed in the same thing at the same time; but they are in no wise contrary when they come together in the same essence, just as whiteness and blackness would not be contrary if they occurred at the same time in this one thing, although the thing itself were white from one source and black from another, just as it is white from one source and hard from another, that is, from whiteness and from hardness. For things that are diverse by contrariness can not be inherent at the same time in the same thing, like relatives and most others. Wherefore, Aristotle in his chapter on Relativity [in the *Categories*] demonstrates that great and small, which he shows to be present at the same time in the same thing in diverse respects, can not be contraries because they are present in the same thing at the same time.

But perhaps it will be said according to that opinion that rationality and irrationality are no less contrary because they are found thus in the same thing, namely, in the same genus or in the same species, unless, that is, they be joined in the same individual. That, too, is shown thus: rationality and irrationality are truly in the same individual because they are in Socrates. But since they are in Socrates at the same time, it is proved that they are in Socrates and in an ass at the same time. But Socrates and the ass are Socrates. And Socrates and the ass are indeed Socrates, because Socrates is Socrates and the ass, since obviously Socrates is Socrates and Socrates is the ass. That Socrates is the ass is shown as follows according to this opinion: whatsoever is in Socrates other than the forms of Socrates, is that which is in the ass other than the forms of the ass. But whatever is in the ass other than the forms of the ass, is the ass. Whatever is in Socrates other than the forms of Socrates, is the ass. But if this is so, since Socrates is himself that which is other than the forms of Socrates, then Socrates is himself the ass. The truth of what we assumed above, namely, that whatever is in the ass other than the forms of the ass is the ass, we may indicate as follows, for neither are the forms of the ass the ass, since then accidents would be substance, nor are the matter and the forms of the ass taken together the ass, since then it would be necessary to say that body and not body were body.

There are those who, seeking an escape from this position, criticize only the words of the proposition, "the rational animal is the irrational animal," but not the opinion, saying that the animal is both, but that that is not shown properly by these words "the rational animal is the irrational animal," because clearly although it is one and the same thing, it is called rational for one reason and irrational for another, that is, from opposite forms. But surely, then, there is no opposition in those forms which would adhere absolutely in these things at the same time, nor do critics criticize the following propositions, "the rational animal is the mortal animal" or "the white animal is the walking animal," because the animal is not mortal in that it is rational, nor does it walk in that it is white, but these propositions they hold as entirely true because the same animal has both forms at the same time although under a different aspect. Otherwise they would say that no animal is man since nothing is man in that it is animal.

Furthermore, according to the position of the above stated doctrine there are only ten essences of all things, that is, the ten generalissima, because in each one of the categories only one essence is found, and that is diversified only through the forms of subordinated classes, as has been said, and without them the essence would have no variety. Therefore, just as all substances are the same at bottom, so all qualities are the same, and quantities, etc. through the categories. Since, therefore, Socrates and Plato have in themselves things of each of the categories, and since these things are at bottom the same, all the forms of the one are forms of the other, which are not essentially different in themselves, just as the substances in which they inhere are not different, so that, for example, the quality of the one is the quality of the other for both are quality. They are therefore no more different because of the nature of qualities than because of the nature of substance, because the essence of their substance is one as is likewise that of qualities. For the same reason quantity, since it is the same,

does not make a difference nor do the other categories. For which reason there can be no difference because of forms, which are not different from each other, exactly as substances are no different from each other.

Moreover, how should we explain the plurality of things under substance if the only diversity were of forms while the subject substance remained at bottom the same? For we do not call Socrates many in number because of the imposition of many forms.

That position can not stand, moreover, by which it is held that individuals are made up by the accidents of themselves. For if individuals draw their being from accidents, obviously the accidents are prior naturally to the individuals, as differences are prior to the species they draw into being. For as man is made distinct by the formation of difference, so they speak of Socrates from the imposition of accidents. Whence Socrates can not be without accidents, nor man without differences. Therefore, Socrates is not the basis of accidents as man is not the basis of differences. If, however, accidents are not in individual substances as in subjects, surely they are not in universals. For whatever things are in second substances as in subjects, he shows are likewise universally in first substances as in subjects. Whence, consequently, it is manifest that the opinion in which it is held that absolutely the same essence subsists at the same time in diverse things, lacks reason utterly.

Therefore others are of another opinion concerning universality, and approaching the truth more closely they say that individual things are not only different from each other in forms, but are discrete personally in their essences, nor is that which is in one in any way to be found in another whether it be matter or form; nor even when the forms have been removed can things subsist less discrete in their essences because their personal discreteness (according to which of course this is not that) is not determined by forms but is the diversity itself of essence, just as the forms themselves are diverse one from the other in themselves; otherwise the diversity of forms would proceed *in infinitum*, so that it would be necessary that still other forms be made the basis of the diversity of any forms. Porphyry noted such a difference between the most comprehensive genus and the ultimate species, saying, "further, species would never become the highest genus and genus would never become the ultimate species." as if he were to say: this is the difference between them, that the essence of the one is not the essence of the other. So too the distinction of categories is not effected through some forms which make it, but through the diversification of their very essence. But since they hold all things are so diverse from each other that none of them participates with another in either the same matter essentially or the same form essentially, and yet, they cling to the universality of things, they reconcile these positions by saying that things which are discrete are one and the same not *essentially* but *indifferently*, as they say individual men, who are discrete in themselves, are the same in man, that is, they do not differ in the nature of humanity, and the same things which they call individual according to discreteness, they call universal according to *indifference* and the agreement of similitude.

But here, too, there is disagreement. For some hold that the universal thing is only in a collection of many. They in no manner call Socrates and Plato species in themselves, but they say that all men collected together are that species which is man, and all animals taken together that genus which is animal, and thus with the others. Boethius seems to agree with them in this. "Species must be considered to be nothing other than the thought collected from the substantial likeness of individuals, and genus from the likeness of species." For since he says the "collected likeness" he indicates a collecting of many. Otherwise they would not have in the universal thing a predication of many things or a content of many things, nor would universals be fewer than individuals.

There are others, moreover, who say that the species is not only men brought together, but also the individuals in that they are men, and when they say that the thing which is Socrates is predicated of many, it is to be taken figuratively as if they were to say: many are the same as he, that is, agree with him, or else he agrees with many. According to the number of things they posit as many species as there are individuals and as many genera, but according to the likeness of natures they assign a smaller number of universals than individuals. Certainly all men are at one time many in themselves by personal discreteness and one by the similitude of humanity; and with

respect to discreteness and with respect to likeness the same are judged to be different from themselves, as Socrates, in that he is a man, is divided from himself in that he is Socrates. Otherwise the same thing could not be its own genus or species unless it should have some difference of its own from itself, since things that are relatives must at least in some one respect be opposed one to the other.

Now, however, let us first invalidate the opinion which was set down above concerning collection, and let us inquire how the whole collection of men together, which is called one species, has to be predicated of many that it may be universal, although the whole collection is not predicated of each. But if it be conceded that the whole is predicated of different things by parts, in that, namely, its individual parts are accommodated to themselves, that has nothing to do with the community of the universal, all of which, as Boethius says, must be in each individual, and it is in this point that the universal is distinguished from the type of community which is common by its parts, as for example a field of which the different parts belong to different men.

Further, Socrates would in the same way be predicated of many because of his many different parts, so that he would himself be a universal. Even more, it would be proper that any group of many men taken together be called universal, and the definition of the universal or even of the species would be adapted to them in the same way, so that the whole collection of men would then include many species. In the same way we should call any collection of bodies or spirits one universal substance with the result that, since the whole collection of substances is one generalissimum, if any one substance be removed and the others remain, we should have to maintain that there are many generalissima in substances. But perhaps it should be said that no collection which is included in the generalissimum, is generalissimum. But I still object that when one substance has been taken from substances, if the residual collection is not the generalissimum and nevertheless remains universal substance, it is necessary that this be a species of substance and have a coequal species under the same genus. But what can be opposite to it, since either the species of substance is contained entirely in it, or else it shares the same individuals with it, as rational animal, mortal animal? Even more. Every universal is naturally prior to its own individuals. But a collection of any things is an integral whole to the individuals of which it is composed and is naturally posterior to the things from which it is composed. Further. Between the integer and the universal Boethius sets up this difference in the *On Divisions*, that the part is not the same as the whole, but the species is always the same as the genus. But how will the whole collection of men be able to be the multitude of animals?

It remains for us now to attack those who call single individuals, in that they agree with others, universal, and who grant that the same individuals are predicated of many things, not as they may be the many essentially, but because the many agree with them. But if it is the same to be predicated of many as to agree with many, how do we say that an individual is predicated of only one, since clearly there is no thing which agrees with only one thing? How too is a difference made between universal and particular by *being predicated of many*, since in exactly the same way in which man agrees with many, Socrates too agrees with many? Surely man, in so far as he is man and Socrates in so far as he is man agree with others. But neither man, in so far as he is Socrates nor Socrates in so far as he is Socrates agrees with others. Therefore, that which man has, Socrates has and in the same way.

Further, since the thing is granted to be absolutely the same, namely, the man which is in Socrates and Socrates himself, there is no difference of the one from the other. For no thing is itself different from itself at the same time because it has whatsoever it has in itself and in absolutely the same manner. Whence Socrates, at once white and a grammarian, although he has different things in himself, is not nevertheless by that fact different from himself since he has the same two and in absolutely the same manner. Indeed he is not a grammarian in another manner from himself nor white in another manner, just as white is not other than himself nor grammarian other than himself. Moreover how can this, which they say, be understood, that Socrates agrees with Plato in man, since it is known that all men differ from each other as well in matter as in form? For if Socrates agrees with Plato in the thing which is man,

but no other thing is man except Socrates himself or another, it is necessary that he agree with Plato either in himself or in another. But in himself he is rather different from him; with respect to another it is concluded likewise that he is not another. There are, however, those who take agree in man negatively, as if it were said: Socrates does not differ from Plato in man. But this likewise can be said, that he does not differ from him in stone, since neither of them is stone. And so no greater agreement between them is noted in man than in stone, unless perchance some proposition precede it, as if it were stated thus: they are man because they do not differ in man. But this can not stand either, since it is utterly false that they do not differ in man. For if Socrates does not differ from Plato in the thing which is man, he does not differ from him in himself. For if he differs in himself from Plato, but he is himself the thing which is man, certainly he differs from him also in the thing which is man.

Now, however, that reasons have been given why things can not be called universals, taken either singly or collectively, because they are not predicated of many, *it remains to ascribe universality of this sort to words alone*. Just as, therefore, certain nouns are called appellative by grammarians and certain nouns proper, so certain simple words are called by dialecticians *universals*, certain words *particulars*, that is, individuals. A *universal* word, however, is one which is apt by its invention to be predicated singly of many, as this noun man which is conjoinable with the particular names of men according to the nature of the subject things on which it is imposed. A *particular* word is one which is predicable of only one, as *Socrates* when it is taken as the name of only one. For if you take it equivocally, you make it not a word, but many words in signification, because according to Priscian many nouns obviously may coincide in a single word. When, therefore, the universal is described to be that which is predicated of many, the *that which*, which is used, indicates not only the simplicity of the word as regards discreteness of expression but also the unity of meaning as regards discreteness of equivocals. . . .

Having shown, however, what is accomplished by the phrase *that which* above in the definition of the universal, we should consider carefully two more phrases which follow, namely, *to be predicated* and *of many*.

To be predicated is to be conjoinable to something truly by the declarative function of a substantive verb in the present [tense], as *man* can be joined truly to different things by a substantive verb. Verbs such as *he runs* and *he walks* likewise when predicated of many have the power of substantive verbs to join as a copula joins. Whence Aristotle says in the second section of the *On Interpretation*: *these verbs in which 'is' does not occur, as to run or to walk do the same when so affirmed as if 'is' were added.* And again he says: *there is no difference in the expressions, man walks and man is walking.*

That he says, *of many*, however, brings together names according to the diversity of things named. Otherwise Socrates would be predicated of many when it is said: *this man is Socrates, this animal is, this white, this musician.* These names although they are different in the understanding, nevertheless have precisely the same subject thing.

Note, moreover, that the conjoining involved in *construction* to which *grammarians* direct their attention is one thing; the conjoining of *predication* which *dialecticians* consider another: for as far as the power of construction is concerned, *man* and *stone* are properly conjoinable by *is*, and any nominative cases, as *animal* and *man*, in respect to making manifest a meaning but not in respect to showing the status of a thing. The conjoining involved in *construction* consequently is good whenever it reveals a perfect sentence, whether it be so or not. But the conjoining involved in *predication*, which we take up here, pertains to the nature of things and to demonstrating the truth of their status. If anyone should say *man is a stone*, he has not made a proper construction of man and stone in respect to the meaning he wished to demonstrate, but there has been no fault of grammar; and although so far as the meaning of the proposition is concerned, this stone is predicated of man, to whom clearly it is construed as predicated (as false categories too have their predicated term), still in the nature of things stone is not predicable of man. We merely note here the great force of this predication while defining the universal.

It seems, then, that the universal is never quite the appellative noun, nor the particular the proper noun, but they are related to each other as that which exceeds and that which is exceeded. For the appellative and proper contain not only the nominative cases but also the oblique cases, which do not have to be predicated, and therefore they are excluded in the definition of the universal by *to be predicated*; these oblique cases, moreover, because they are less necessary to the proposition (which alone, according to Aristotle, is the subject of the present speculation, that is, of dialectic consideration, and assuredly the proposition alone compounds argumentations), are not taken by Aristotle himself in any sense into the nouns, and he himself does not call them nouns but the cases of nouns. But just as it is not necessary that all appellative and proper nouns be called universals or particulars, so also conversely. For the universal includes not only nouns but also verbs and infinite nouns, to which, that is, to infinite nouns, the definition of the appellative which Priscian gives does not seem to apply.

However, now that a definition of universal and of particular has been assigned to words, let us inquire carefully into the property of universal words especially. Questions have been raised concerning these universals, for there are very grave doubts concerning their meaning, since they seem neither to have any subject thing nor to constitute a clear meaning of anything. Universal nouns seemed to be imposed on no things whatsoever, since obviously all things subsisted in themselves discretely and, as has been shown, did not agree in anything, according to the agreement of which thing the universal nouns could be imposed. Consequently, since it is certain that universals are not imposed on things according to the difference of discreteness of things, for they would then be not common, but particular; and again since universals could not name things as they agree in some thing, for there is no thing in which they agree, universals seem to derive no meaning from things, particularly since they constitute no understanding of any thing. Wherefore, in the *On Divisions*, Boethius says that the word "man" gives rise to doubt of its meaning because when it has been heard, "the understanding of the person hearing is carried off by many changing things and is betrayed into errors. For unless some one define the word, saying: 'all men walk' or at least 'certain men,' and should characterize this man if he happens to walk, the understanding of the person hearing does not have anything to understand reasonably." For since "man" is imposed upon individuals for the same reason, because namely they are rational mortal animals, that very community of imposition is an impediment which prevents any one man being understood in it, as on the contrary in this name *Socrates* the proper person of only one man is understood, and therefore it is called a particular. But in the common name which is *man,* not Socrates himself nor any other man nor the entire collection of men is reasonably understood from the import of the word, nor is Socrates himself, as certain thinkers hold, specified by that word, even in so far as he is man. For even if Socrates alone be sitting in this house, and if because of him alone this proposition is true: "a man sits in this house," nevertheless in no ways is the subject transferred by the name of man to Socrates, except in so far as he is also man, otherwise sitting would rationally be understood from the proposition to inhere in him, so that it could be inferred clearly from the fact that a man sits in this house, that Socrates sits in it. In the same way, no other man can be understood in this noun *man,* nor can the whole collection of men since the proposition can be true of only one. Consequently, man or any other universal word seems to signify no one thing since it constitutes the meaning of nothing. But it seems that there can not be a meaning which does not have a subject thing which it conceives. Whence, Boethius says in the *Commentary:* "Every idea is made either from the subject thing, as the thing is constituted or as it is not constituted. For an idea can not be made from no subject." Wherefore, universals seem wholly unrelated to signification.

But this is not so. For they signify in a manner different things by nomination, not however by forming a conception arising from different things but only pertaining to each of them. Just as this word "man" names individual things for a common reason, namely that they are men, because of which it is called universal, and also forms a certain conception which is common, not proper, that is, pertaining to the individuals of which it conceives the common likeness.

But now let us inquire carefully into these things which we have touched upon briefly, namely, "what

that common cause by which the universal word is imposed is, and what the conception of the understanding of the common likeness of things is, and whether the word is called common because of a common cause in which the things agree or because of a common conception or because of both at once."

And first we should consider the "common cause." Individual men, discrete from each other in that they differ in respect to properties no less in essences than in forms (as we noted above when we were inquiring into the physics of a thing) are united nevertheless in that they are men. I do not say that they are united in man, since nothing is man except a discrete thing, but in being man. But "to be man" is not the same as man nor any thing, if we should consider it very carefully, as "not to be in the subject" is not any thing, nor is it anything "not to undergo contrariety" or "not to undergo more and less"; in these nevertheless Aristotle says all substances agree. For since, as we have demonstrated above, there can be no agreement in fact, if that by which there is an agreement between any things, be taken in this way, that it is not any thing, so Socrates and Plato are alike in being man as horse and ass are alike in not being man, in which way both horse and ass are called non-man. Consequently for different things to agree is for the individuals to be the same or not to be the same, as to be man or white or not to be man and not to be white. It seems, however, that we must avoid considering the agreement of things according to that which is not anything (as if we were to unite in nothing things which are) since we say, in fact, that this and that agree in the status of man, that is, in that they are men. But we understand nothing other than that they are men, and in this they do not differ in the least, in this, I say, that they are men, although we appeal to no essence. We call it the status itself of man to be man, which is not a thing and which we also called the common cause of imposition of the word on individuals, according as they themselves agree with each other. Often, however, we call those things too by the name of cause which are not any thing, as when it is said: he was lashed because he does not wish to appear in court. He does not wish to appear in court, which is stated as cause, is no essence. We can also call the status of man those things themselves, established in the nature of man, the common likeness of which he who imposed the word conceived.

Having shown the signification of universals, namely, relative to things by nomination, and having set forth the cause of their common imposition, let us now show *what are the understandings of universals* which they constitute.

And let us first distinguish generally the nature of all understandings.

Although, then, the senses as well as the understandings are of the soul, this is the difference between them, that the senses are exercised only through corporeal instruments and perceive only bodies or what are in bodies, as sight perceives the tower and its visible qualities. The understanding, however, as it does not need a corporeal instrument, so it is not necessary that it have a subject body to which it may be referred, but it is satisfied with the likeness of things which the mind constructs for itself, into which it directs the action of its intelligence. Wherefore if the tower should be destroyed and removed, the sense which acted on it perishes, but the understanding remains in the likeness of the thing preserved in the mind. However, just as the sense is not the thing perceived to which it is directed, so neither is the understanding the form of the thing which it conceives, but the understanding is a certain action of the soul by which it is called intelligent or understanding, but the form to which it is directed is a certain imaginary and fictional thing, which the mind constructs for itself when it wishes and as it wishes, like those imaginary cities which are seen in dreams, or that form of the projected building which the artist conceives as the figure and exemplar of the thing to be formed, which we can call neither substance nor accident.

Nevertheless, there are those who call that form the same as the understanding, as they call the building of the tower, which I conceive while the tower is not there and which I contemplate, lofty and square in the spacious plain, the same as the understanding of the tower. Aristotle seems to agree with them, when he calls, in the *On Interpretation*, those passions of the soul which they call the understandings, the likenesses of things.

We, on the other hand, call the image the likeness of the thing. But there is nothing to prevent the understanding also being called in a sense a likeness, because obviously it conceives that which is properly called the likeness of the thing. But we have said, and well, that it is different from the image. For I ask whether that squareness and the loftiness is the true form of the understanding which is formed to the likeness of the quantity and the composition of the tower. But surely true squareness and true loftiness are present only in bodies, and neither an understanding nor any true essence can be formed from a fictional quality. It remains, therefore, that just as the quality is fictional, a fictional substance is subject to it. Perhaps, moreover, the image in a mirror too, which seems to be the subject of sight, can be said truly to be nothing, since obviously the quality of a contrary color appears often in the white surface of the mirror.

The following question, however, can be raised, when the soul perceives and understands the same thing at the same time, as when it discerns a stone, whether then the understanding too deals with the image of the stone or whether the understanding and the sense at the same time have to do with the stone itself. But it seems more reasonable that the understanding has no need of the image when there is present to it the truth of the substance. If, moreover, anyone should say where there is sense there is no understanding, we should not concede that. For it often happens that the mind perceives one thing and understands another, as is apparent to those who study well, who, while they look at the things present to the open eyes, nevertheless think of other things concerning which they write.

Now that the nature of understandings has been examined generally, let us distinguish between the understandings of universals and particulars. These are separated in that that which is of the universal noun, conceives a common and confused image of many things, whereas that which the particular word generates, holds to the proper and as it were the particular form of one thing, that is, restricts itself to only one person. Whence when I hear *man* a certain figure arises in my mind which is so related to individual men that it is common to all and proper to none. When, however, I hear *Socrates* a certain form arises in my mind, which expresses the likeness of a certain person. Whence, by this word *Socrates*, which generates in the mind the proper form of one person, a certain thing is specified and determined, but by *man*, the understanding of which rests in the common form of all men, that very community leads to confusion, lest we should not understand any one in particular. Wherefore, *man* is rightly said to signify neither Socrates nor any other man, since none is specified by the meaning of the word, although nevertheless it names particulars. *Socrates*, on the other hand, must not only name a certain particular, but also determine the subject thing.

But the question is raised, then, since we said earlier that according to Boethius every idea has a subject thing, how this applies to the ideas of universals. But it must be noted surely that Boethius introduces this statement in the Sophist argument by which he shows that the idea of universals is vain. Whence there is nothing to prevent that the statement is not proved in truth; whence avoiding falsity he shows the reasons of other writers. We can, moreover, refer to, as the thing subject to the understanding, either the true substance of the thing, as when it is at one with the sense, or else the conceived form of any thing whatsoever, that is, when the thing is absent, whether that form be common as we have said or proper; common, I say, with respect to the likeness of many which it retains although it is still considered in itself as one thing. For thus, to show the nature of all lions, one picture can be made representing what is proper to no one of them, and on the other hand another can be made suitable to distinguish any one of them, which would bring out certain individual characteristics, as if it were painted limping, or mutilated, or wounded by the spear of Hercules. Just as, therefore, one figure of things is painted common, another particular, so too, are they conceived one common, another proper.

However, with respect to that form to which the understanding is directed, it is a matter of doubt, not unintelligently, whether the word too signifies the form. This seems to be firmly established by authority as well as by reason. . . .

For Priscian in the first book of *Constructions*, after he had stated first the common imposition of universals on individuals, seemed to have a certain other meaning of universals, namely, a meaning of common form, saying: *with respect to the general and special forms of things, those which are constituted in the divine mind intelligibly before they were produced in bodies, are suited to demonstrate the genera or species of the nature of things.* For the question in this place is of God, as of an artist about to compose something, who preconceives in his mind the exemplary form of the thing to be composed; he works to the likeness of this form which is said to go into the body when the true thing is composed in its likeness. This common conception, however, is well ascribed to God, but not to man, because those general works or special states of nature are proper to God, not to the artist; as man, soul, or stone are proper to God, but house or sword to man. Whence the latter, house or sword, are not works of nature, as are the former, nor are words of them of substance, but of accident, and therefore they are neither genera nor are they species. Therefore, conceptions of this sort by abstraction are ascribed well to the divine mind but not to the human mind, because men who learn things only through the senses, scarcely ever or never ascend to simple understanding of this sort, and the exterior sensuality of accidents prevents them from conceiving the natures of things purely. God, however, to whom all things which he created are known through themselves and who knows them before they are, distinguishes the individual states among them, and sense is no impediment to him who alone has only true understanding. Whence it happens that men have, in those things which have not been touched by the sense, opinion rather than understanding as we learn from experience itself. For, when we have thought of some city which we have not seen we discover when we have come to it that we had thought it to be otherwise than it is.

So likewise I think we have opinion of the intrinsic forms which do not come to the senses, such as rationality and mortality, paternity, sitting. Any names of any existent things, on the other hand, generate, so far as is in them, understanding rather than opinion, because their inventor intended that they be imposed according to some natures or properties of things, although even he was not able to think out thoroughly the nature or the property of the thing. Priscian, however, calls these common conceptions general or special, because general or special nouns describe them in one way or another to us. He says that the universals themselves are as proper nouns to these conceptions, which, although they are of confused meaning with respect to the essences named, direct the mind of the auditor to that common conception immediately, just as proper nouns direct the attention to the one thing which they signify. Porphyry, too, when he says that some ideas are constituted from matter and form, and some to the likeness of matter and form, seems to have understood this conception, since he says to the likeness of matter and form, of which more will be said in its proper place. Boethius likewise, when he says that the thought collected from the likeness of many things is genus or species, seems to have understood the same common conception. Some insist that Plato was of this opinion too, namely that he called those common ideas which he places in *nous*, genera or species. In this perhaps Boethius records that he dissented from Aristotle when he says that Plato wanted genera and species and the others not only to be understood universals, but also to be and to subsist without bodies, as if to say that he understood as universals those common conceptions which he set up separated from bodies in *nous*, not perhaps taking the universal as the common predication, as Aristotle does, but rather as the common likeness of many things. For that latter conception seems in no wise to be predicated of many as a noun is which is adapted singly to many.

That he says Plato thinks universals subsist without sensibles, can be resolved in another manner so that there is no disagreement in the opinions of the philosophers. For what Aristotle says to the effect that universals always subsist in sensibles, he said only in regard to actuality, because obviously the nature which is animal which is designated by the universal name and which according to this is called universal by a certain transference, is never found in actuality except in a sensible thing, but Plato thinks that it so subsists in itself naturally that it would retain its being when not subjected to sense, and according to this the natural being is called by the universal name. That, consequently, which Aristotle denies with respect to actuality, Plato, the investigator of physics, assigns to natural aptitude, and thus there is no disagreement between them.

Moreover, now that *authorities* have been advanced who seem to build up by universal words

common concepts which are to be called forms, *reason* too seems to assent. For what else is it to conceive forms by nouns than to signify by nouns? But certainly since we make forms diverse from understandings, there arises now besides thing and understanding a third thing which is the signification of nouns. Although authority does not hold this, it is nevertheless not contrary to reason.

Let us, then, set forth what we promised above to define, namely, whether the community of universal words is considered to be because of a common cause of imposition or because of a common conception or because of both. There is nothing to prevent that it be because of both, but the common cause which is taken in accordance with the nature of things seems to have greater force.

Likewise we must define that which we noted above, namely, that "the conceptions of universals are formed by abstraction, and we must indicate how we may speak of them alone, naked and pure but not empty."

And first concerning "abstraction." In relation to abstraction it must be known that matter and form always subsist mixed together, but the reason of the mind has this power, that it may now consider matter by itself; it may now turn its attention to form alone; it may now conceive both intermingled. The two first processes, of course, are by abstraction; they abstract something from things conjoined that they may consider its very nature. But the third process is by conjunction. For example, the substance of this man is at once body and animal and man and invested in infinite forms; when I turn my attention to this in the material essence of the substance, after having circumscribed all forms, I have a concept by the process of abstraction. Again, when I consider only corporeity in it, which I join to substance, that concept likewise (although it is by conjunction with respect to the first, which considered only the nature of substance) is formed also by abstraction with respect to other forms than corporeity, none of which I consider, such as animation, sensuality, rationality, whiteness.

Conceptions of this sort through abstraction seemed perhaps false and vain for this reason, that they perceive the thing otherwise than it subsists. For since they are concerned with matter by itself or form separately, and since nonetheless neither of these sub-sists separately, they seem obviously to conceive the thing otherwise than it is, and therefore to be empty. But this is not so. For if one understands otherwise than the thing is constituted, in such manner that one considers it manifestly in such a nature and prop-erty as it does not have, certainly that understanding is empty. But that is not what is done in abstraction. For, when I consider this man only in the nature of substance or of body, and not also of animal or of man or of grammarian, obviously I understand nothing except what is in that nature, but I do not consider all that it has. And when I say that I consider only this one among the qualities the nature has, the *only* refers to the attention alone, not to the mode of subsisting, otherwise the understanding would be empty. For the thing does not have only it, but it is considered only as having it. And still in a certain sense it is said to be understood otherwise than it is, not in another state than it is, as has been said above, but otherwise, in that the mode of understanding is other than the mode of subsisting. For this thing is understood sepa-rately from the other, not separated from it, although it does not, notwithstanding, exist separately; and mat-ter is perceived purely and form simply, although the one is not purely and the other is not simply, so that manifestly that purity or simplicity is reduced to the understanding and not to the subsistence of the thing, so that they are of course modes of understand-ing and not of subsisting. The senses, moreover, often operate in different ways with composite things, so that if a statue is half of gold and half of silver, I can discern separately the gold and the silver which are joined together, that is, examining now the gold, now the silver by itself, looking separately upon things which are conjoined, but not looking upon them as separated, in that they are not separated. So too the understanding considers separately by abstraction, but does not consider as separated, otherwise it would be empty.

Nevertheless, perhaps such a conception too could be good which considers things which are con-joined, as in one manner separated and in another manner conjoined, and conversely. For the conjunc-tion of things as well as the division can be taken in two ways. For we say that certain things are conjoined to each other by some likeness, as these two men in

that they are men or grammarians, and that certain things are conjoined by a kind of apposition and aggregation, as form and matter or wine and water. The conception in question conceives things which are so joined to each other as divided in one manner, in another conjoined. Whence Boethius ascribes the following power to the mind, that it can by its reason both compound that which was disjoined and resolve that which is composite, departing nevertheless in neither from the nature of the thing, but only per-ceiving that which is in the nature of the thing. Oth-erwise it would not be reason, but opinion, that is if the understanding should deviate from the state or the thing. . . .

But the following question arises concerning the *providence* of the artist, whether it is empty when he holds in mind the form of a work still future, seeing that the thing is not yet constituted so. But if we grant that, we are forced to say that likewise the providence of God is empty, which he had before the creation of his work. But if one says this with respect to the effect, namely, that what he foresees would not eventuate actually as he foresees, then it is false that the providence was empty. If on the other hand one says that it was empty for this rea-son, that it did not yet agree with the future state of the thing, we are disinclined to the evil words but we do not object to the opinion. For it is true that the future state of the world was not yet materially, when he disposed it intelligibly as future still. Never-theless, we are not accustomed to call empty the thought or the providence of any thing except that which lacks effect, nor do we say that we think in vain except those thoughts which we will not accomplish actually. Consequently, modifying the words we should say that the providence is not empty which does not think in vain, but conceives things which are not yet materially as if they sub-sisted, which is natural to all providences. Obviously thought concerning future things is called provi-dence; thought concerning past things memory; con-cerning present things understanding proper. If, however, any one says that he is deceived who thinks of providing for the future state as for the one now existing, he is rather himself deceived in think-ing that such an one must be said to be deceived. For, to be sure, he who foresees for the future is not deceived, unless he should think it is already as he foresees. Nor, in fact, does the conception of a non-existent thing lead to deception, but rather the faith added to it. For even though I think of a rational crow, if I do not believe it, I am not deceived. So too the provident person is not deceived, in that he does consider that that which he thinks as existing does not now exist thus, but as he thinks of it now he sets it as present in the future. Surely every conception of the mind is as of the present. So if I should consider Socrates in that he was a boy or in that he will be an old man, I join boyhood or old age to him, as it were in the present, because I consider him at present in a past or future property. Nevertheless, no one says that this memory is empty because what it conceives as present it considers in the past. But there will be a fuller investigation of this in relation to the *On Interpretation*.

In the case of God it is decided even more rationally that his substance, which alone is immutable and simple, is varied by no conceptions of things or any other forms. For although the custom of human speech presumes to speak of the creator as of creatures, since of course it calls him either provident or intelligent, still nothing in him should be understood or can be diverse from him, that is, neither his understanding nor any other form. And consequently any question concerning the understanding with respect to God is superfluous. And to speak the truth more expressly, it is nothing other for him to foresee the future than for him, who is true reason in himself, not to be in darkness concerning the future.

Now, however, that many things have been shown concerning the nature of abstraction, let us return to the "conception of universals" which must always be formed by abstraction. For when I hear "man" or "whiteness" or "white," I do not recall from the meaning of the noun all the natures or properties which are in the subject things, but from *man* I have only the conception although confused, not discrete, of animal and rational mortal, but not of the later accidents as well. For the conceptions of individuals, too, are formed by abstraction, when namely, it is said: this substance, this body, this animal, this man, this whiteness, this white. For by "this man" I consider only the nature of man but related to a certain subject, whereas by *man* I consider that same nature

simply in itself not related to any one. Wherefore the understanding of universals is rightly spoken of as alone and naked and pure, that is, alone from the senses, because it does not perceive the thing as sensual, and naked in regard to the abstraction of all and of any forms, and pure with respect to discreteness because no thing whether it be matter or form, is designated in it; in this latter respect we ealied a conception of this sort confused above.

Consequently, *having examined these things, let us proceed to the resolution of the question concerning genera and species proposed by Porphyry*, which we can do easily now that the nature of all universals has been shown.

The first question, then, was to this effect, whether genera and species subsist, that is, signify something truly existent, or are placed in the understanding alone etc., that is, are located in empty opinion without the thing; like the following words, chimera and goat-stag which do not give rise to a rational understanding.

To this it must be replied that in truth they signify by nomination things truly existent, to wit, the same things as singular nouns, and in no ways are they located in empty opinion; nevertheless, they consist in a certain sense in the understanding alone and naked and pure, as has been determined. There is nothing, however, to prevent one who states the question from taking some words in one way in inquiry and one who solves it from taking them in another way in solution, as if he who solves the question were to say: you ask whether they are placed in the understanding alone, etc. This you can take in the manner (which is the true one) which we discussed above. And the words can be taken in absolutely the same sense on both sides, by the resolver and by the inquirer, and then it is made a single question not by opposition of the prior members of two dialectical questions, to wit, these: whether they are or are not, and again whether they are placed in the sole and naked and pure understanding or not.

The same can be said in the second question which is as follows: whether subsisting they are corporeal or incorporeal, that is, when they are conceded to signify subsistences whether they signify subsistences which are corporeal or subsistences which are incorporeal. Certainly everything that is, as Boethius says, is either corporeal, or incorporeal; that is, we take these words corporeal and incorporeal for substantial body and non-body, or for that which can be perceived by the corporeal sense, such as man, wood, whiteness, or that which can not, such as soul, justice. Corporeal likewise can be taken for discrete, as if the following were inquired; since universals signify subsistences, whether they signify them discrete or not discrete. For he who investigates the truth of the thing well, considers not only what can be said truly, but everything that can be stated in opinion. Whence even though it be certain to some that nothing subsists except the discrete, nevertheless because there can be the opinion that there might be other subsistences, it is inquired not without reason concerning them too. And this last meaning of corporeal seems to fall in better with the question; namely, that the question be raised concerning discrete and indiscrete. But perhaps when Boethius says that everything that is is either corporeal or incorporeal, the incorporeal seems superfluous since no existing thing is incorporeal, that is, non-discrete. Nor does that which comes to mind in relation to the order of the questions seem to afford any help, unless perhaps in this respect, that as corporeal and incorporeal divide subsistences in another sense, so too it seems they divide them in this sense, as if the inquirer were to say: I see that of existing things some are called corporeal and others incorporeal, which of these shall we say are the things signified by universals? To which the reply is made: in a certain sense corporeal things, that is, things discrete in their essence, and incorporeal with respect to the designation of the universal noun because obviously universals do not name discretely and determinately, but confusedly, as we have set forth sufficiently above.[28] Whence the universal names themselves are called both corporeal with respect to the nature of things and incorporeal with respect to the manner of signification, because although they name things which are discrete, nevertheless they do not name them discretely and determinately.

The third question, of course, whether they are placed in sensibles, etc., follows from granting that they are incorporeal, because obviously the incorporeal taken in a certain manner is divided by being and

by not being in the sensible, as we have also noted above.[29] And universals are said to subsist in sensibles that is to signify an intrinsic substance existing in a thing which is sensible by its exterior forms, and although they signify this substance which subsists actually in the sensible thing, yet they demonstrate the same substance naturally separated from the sensible thing, as we determined above in relation to Plato. Wherefore Boethius says that genera and species are understood, but are not, outside sensible things, in that obviously the things of genera and species are considered with respect to their nature rationally in themselves beyond all sensuality, because they can truly subsist in themselves even when the exterior forms by which they come to the senses have been removed. For we grant that all genera or species are in sensual things. But because the understanding of them was said to be always apart from sense, they seemed in no wise to be in sensible things. Wherefore it was inquired rightly whether they could ever be in sensibles, and it is replied with respect to some of them that they are, but in such fashion that, as has been said, they continue to be naturally beyond sensuality.

We can however take corporeal and incorporeal in the second question as sensible and insensible, in order that the order of questions may be more appropriate; and since the understanding of universals was said to be only from sense, as has been said, it was asked properly, whether universals were sensible or insensible; and since it is answered that some of them are sensible with respect to the nature of things, and that the same are insensible with respect to the mode of signifying, because obviously they do not designate the sensible things which they name in the same manner as they are perceived, that is as discrete, and sense does not discover them by demonstration of them, it remained a question whether universals named sensible things only or whether they also signified something else; to which it is replied that they signify both sensible things and at the same time that common conception which Priscian ascribes particularly to the divine mind.

And in accord with them. With respect to that which we understand here as the fourth question, as we noted above, the following is the solution, that we in no ways hold that universal nouns are, when, their things having been destroyed, they are not predicable of many things inasmuch as they are not common to any things, as for example the name of the rose when there are no longer roses, but it would still, nevertheless, be significative by the understanding, although it would lack nomination; otherwise there would not be the proposition: there is no rose.

Questions, moreover, were raised properly concerning universal words, but none concerning singular words, because there was no such doubt concerning the meaning of singular words. For their mode of signifying accorded well with the status of things. As things are discrete in themselves, so they are signified by words discretely, and the understanding of them refers to a definite thing, which reference universals do not have. Besides although universals did not signify things as discrete, they did not seem on the other hand to signify things as agreeing, since, as we have also shown earlier, there is no thing in which they agree. Consequently, since there was so much doubt concerning universals, Porphyry chose to treat of universals alone, excluding singulars from his intention as clear enough in themselves, although for all that, he sometimes treats of them in passing because of other things.

It must be noted, however, that although the definition of the universal or of the genus or the species includes only words, nevertheless these nouns are often transferred to their things, as when it is said that species is made up of genus and difference, that is, the thing of the species from the thing of the genus. For when the nature of words is examined with respect to signification, it is question sometimes of words and sometimes of things, and frequently the names of the latter and the former are transferred reciprocally. For this reason most of all, the ambiguous treatment of logic as well as grammar leads many, who do not distinguish clearly the property of the imposition of nouns or the abuse of transference, into error by the transference of nouns.

Boethius, moreover, makes this confusion by transferences in the *Commentaries* most of all and particularly in connection with the inquiry into these questions, so that it may even seem right to pass by the inquiry into what it is that he calls genera and species. Let us run over his questions briefly and let us apply ourselves, as is necessary, to the aforesaid

opinion. In the investigation of the questions here that he may resolve the problem better, he first throws it into confusion by some sophistical questions and reasons, that he may teach us later to free ourselves from them. And he sets forth such difficulty that all concern with and investigation of genera and species must be put off, as if to say, that clearly the words genera and species can not be said to be that which they seem, either with respect to the signification of things or with respect to the understanding. He shows this with respect to the signification of things in that no universal thing, whether single or multiplex, is ever found, that is, no thing predicable of many, as he himself shows carefully and as we have proved above. Moreover, he first establishes that there is no one universal thing and therefore no genus nor species, saying: everything that is one is one in number, that is, discrete in its own essence; but genera and species which must be common to many things can not be one in number and therefore can not be one. But since some one may say against this assumption that genera and species are one in number in the sense of one that is common, he offers such an one the following refutation, saying: each thing one in number in the sense that it is common either is common through its parts or whole through the succession of times or whole in the same time, but in such ways that it does not constitute the substances of those things to which it is common. He removes at once all such modes of community from genus as well as from species, saying that they on the other hand are common in such a way that they are in the same time whole in each and constitute the substance of each of their particulars. For universal names are not participated in by the different things, which they name, by parts, but they are the names, whole and entire, of singulars at the same time. They can likewise be said to constitute the substances of the things to which they are common either in that they signify by transference things which constitute other things, as for example animal names something in horse or in man which is the matter of them or even of men subordinated to it, or else in that they are said to make up the substance, because they come in a certain manner into the knowledge of the things because of which they are said to be substantial to them, seeing that *man* denotes all that which is animal and rational and mortal.

Moreover, after Boethius shows with respect to a simple thing that it is not universal, he proves the same with respect to a multiple thing showing that clearly the species or genus is not a multitude of discrete things, and he destroys the opinion by which some one may say that all substances collected together are the genus *substance* and all men the species which is *man*, as of the following were stated: if we assert that each genus is a multitude of things agreeing substantially, still every such multitude will have naturally another above it, and that again will have another and so *ad infinitum,* which is inconsistent. Consequently, it has been shown that universal names do not seem to be universal with respect to the signification of things, whether of a simple or of a multiple thing, since obviously they signify no universal thing, that is, nothing predicable of many.

Therefore he argued also that they should not be said to be universals with respect to the signification of understanding, because he shows sophistically that

it is a vain understanding, because clearly, since it is by abstraction, it is constituted otherwise than the thing subsists. He resolves sufficiently and we have resolved carefully the knot of this sophism. He did not think the other part of the argumentation, by which he shows that nothing is universal, needed limitation, since it was not Sophist. For he takes a thing as thing, not as word, because clearly the common word, since it is in itself as it were a single thing in essence, is common by nomination in the appellation of many; according to this appellation clearly and not according to its essence it is predicable of many. *Nevertheless,* the multitude of things themselves is the cause of the universality of the noun, because as we have stated above only that which contains many is universal; yet the universality which the thing confers upon the word, the thing does not have in itself, inasmuch as the word does not have meaning because of the thing and inasmuch as a noun is called appellative with respect to the multitude of things, even though we do not say that things signify or that they are appellative.

STUDY QUESTIONS: ABELARD, *THE GLOSSES OF PETER ABELARD ON PORPHYRY*

1. What are the three "species" of the "genus" philosophy?
2. Why did Aristotle write the *Categories, On Interpretation,* the *Topics,* and *Analytics?*
3. What is the science of discovering arguments versus the science of judging arguments, and how are the two related?
4. What is the "double division" of dialectic?
5. What is the relationship between knowledge of species and the categories?
6. How does Aristotle define universals? What is Abelard's view of this?
7. Are words and things called universals, or just words? What is the significance?
8. What does Abelard think is the point of Aristotle's chapter on Relativity in the *Catgories?*
9. What are species? Give an example.
10. What is the nature of all understandings that can be generally distinguished as such?

Philosophical Bridges: Abelard's Influence

Abelard's logical analysis of language and grammar in general, and, in particular, the grammatical function of universals, influenced virtually all subsequent thought on the subject. The philosophy of language as a discipline in its own right, to be studied not merely as an aid to understanding the nature and structure of language but as a means of inquiry into the nature both of thought and reality, owes much to the philosophical results of his astute technical skills of linguistic and logical analysis. In the domain of ethics, his original arguments that what matters is not the consequences of some particular act, but rather, the intentions of the actor considered independently of their consequences, inspired many subsequent non-consequentialist moral philosophers throughout the ages, such as Immanuel Kant.

HILDEGARD OF BINGEN (1098–1179)

Biographical History

German abbess Hildegard of Bingen was born at Böckelheim, near Spanheim, Germany, to a noble family. As a young child she experienced extraordinary, mystical visions, even before entering the Bendictine cloister of Disibodemberg at the age of 8, where she was educated and eventually became prioress (1136). She drew attention not only because of her visions but also because of her unusual ability to understand difficult and controversial passages; at the cloisters, one of the few places at the time where women could get equal education and even assume positions of leadership, she became a devoted and very influential nun of the Benedictine order. At the age of 38 she was named abbess of the convent. Upon recommendation of the Archbishop of Mainz, Hildegard went on to record her visions in written form; in the years 1141–1150 she produced her main written work, the *Scivias*, from which the following reading is taken.

Extremely outspoken, courageous, and original in her opinions, Hildegard's advice was widely sought after not only among leaders of the clergy and royalty alike but also among the common people, who found her a lucid and eloquent teacher. She worked on behalf of social justice and reform and was a very popular preacher throughout the Rhine river valley, for which she earned her nickname "Sibyl of the Rhine."

In her mid-forties she began to set her liturgical poetry to music. When a Parisian magister, Odo, heard her songs, he urged her to combine them into compositions that could be performed publically; the result, her "Symphony of the Harmony of Heavenly Revelations" (*Symphonia Harmoniae Caelestium* Revelationum) contains over sixty antiphons, responsories, and hymns for each feast of the liturgical year, virtually unmatched in scale—only Peter Abelard (see previous section) attempted such a grand musical expression. Her extraordinary attempts to sonically choreograph explicit philosophical themes, such as her antiphons on divine foreknowledge and divine wisdom, are unparalleled by composers of her time, as is her attempt at musical expression of cosmology in her equally extraordinary but rarely performed *Liber Divinorum Operum*, which she composed in 1163–73. Lyrically inventive, Hildegard creates a diverse harmony of voices and instruments designed to produce states of rapture and ecstasy in the listener while evoking peace and balance between mind and body, in essence, a spiritual healing through sound. While there have been other equally or more gifted composers musically, what makes her works unique is that she is a writer first, and her mystical imagery of love and transcendence of language, while to a degree explainable in exposition, must be heard to be appreciated. Listeners will be shocked by her rhapsodic invention, the strangeness and even violence of her unique and almost universally unrecognized genius.

Philosophical Overview

Hildegard's outspokenness was legendary and downright shocking at the time, for a man or a woman. During a time when many were imprisoned for heresy or burned at the stake, here is what Hildegard wrote in a letter to Pope Anastasius IV, "so it is, O man, that you who sit in the chief seat of the Lord, hold him in contempt when you embrace evil, since you do not reject but kiss it, by silently tolerating it in depraved men."[1] Although most of her non-visionary writings were commentaries on monastic life, including revising and explaining the rules of the Benedictine order to which she belonged, and commentaries on the scriptures, she produced medical works that showed rare scientific sophistication for their day. Her view of the relationship between God, the world, and humanity, expressed in her visions, contains detailed elaborations on the various parts of the soul integrating the senses with the intellect on the one hand, and the will with reason on the other, in ways that anticipate developments by subsequent medieval and modern philosophers.

But no mere words can possibly do justice to the extraordinary gifts this philosopher provides for anyone willing not just to read but to learn to listen to her immortal works, a woman whose unique vision of the human soul as *symphonic* (*symphonialis*) in nature has yet to be fully understood and appreciated.

SCIVIAS
Hildegard of Bingen

Scivias begins with a startling vision of the human embryo in a woman's womb, how and when the soul enters it, and how the soul is related to and guides the subsequent development of the physical body. Moral and spiritual development are one, determined through the "three paths" open to a person, which we are each free to choose. The intellect is not the soul but joined to it as "arm is to body," and the will that drives the soul is likened to the heart. Reason guides the soul, but reason must in turn be guided by the intellect and the will because reason by itself is neither bad nor good. The senses are not to be shunned but also should be integrated into both earthly and mystical knowledge.

This work, of which this brief selection, unaccompanied by music, can barely do justice, culminates with Hildegard's expressed vision in which the individual soul bears witness to the end of time and the beginning of eternity, in which destruction and creation are one.

BOOK I, VISION FOUR

16: An Infant Is Vivified in the Womb and Confirmed by a Soul on Leaving It

And you see the image of a woman who has a perfect human form in her womb. This means that after a woman has conceived by human semen, an infant with all its members whole is formed in the secret chamber of her womb. And behold! *By the secret design of the Supernal Creator that form moves with vital motion;* for, by God's secret and hidden command and will, fitly and rightly at the divinely appointed time, the infant in the maternal womb receives a spirit, and shows by the movements of its body that it lives, just as the earth opens and brings forth the flowers of its use when the dew falls on it. *So that a fiery globe which has no human lineaments possesses the heart of that form:* that is, the soul, burning with a fire of profound knowledge, which discerns whatever is within the circle of its understanding, and, without the form of human members, since it is not corporeal or transitory like a human body, gives strength to the heart

---

[1]Hildegard of Bingen, from *Mystical Writings*, edited by Fiona Bowie and Oliver Davies, translated by Robert Carver, Crossroads, 1990, p. 134.

and rules the whole body as its foundation, as the firmament of heaven contains the lower regions and touches the higher. *And it also touches the person's brain:* for in its powers it knows not only earthly but also heavenly things, since it wisely knows God: *and it spreads itself through all the person's members:* for it gives vitality to the marrow and veins and members of the whole body, as the tree from its root gives sap and greenness to all the branches. *But then this human form, in this way vivified, comes forth from the woman's womb, and changes its color according to the movement the globe makes in that form;* which is to say that after the person has received the vital spirit in the maternal womb and is born and begins his actions, his merits will be according to the works his soul does with the body, for he will put on brightness from the good ones and darkness from the evil ones.

17: How the Soul Shows Its Powers According to the Powers of the Body

The soul now shows its powers according to the powers of the body, so that in a person's infancy it produces simplicity, in his youth strength, and in adulthood, when all the person's veins are full, it shows its strongest powers in wisdom; as the tree in its first shoots is tender and then shows that it can bear fruit, and finally, in its full utility, bears it. But then in human old age, when the marrow and veins start to incline to weakness, the soul's powers are gentler, as if from a weariness at human knowledge; as when winter approaches the sap of the tree diminishes in the branches and the leaves, and the tree in its old age begins to bend.

18: A Person Has Three Paths Within Himself

But a person has within himself three paths. What are they? The soul, the body and the senses; and all human life is led in these. How? The soul vivifies the body and conveys the breath of life to the senses; the body draws the soul to itself and opens the senses: and the senses touch the soul and draw the body. For the soul gives life to the body as fire gives light to darkness, with two principal powers like two arms, intellect and will; the soul has arms not so as to move itself, but so as to show itself in these powers as the sun shows itself by its brilliance. Therefore. O human, who are not just a bundle of marrow pay attention to scriptural knowledge!

19: On the Intellect

The intellect is joined to the soul like an arm to the body. For as the arm, joined to the hand with its fingers, branches out from the body, so the intellect, working with the other powers of the soul, by which it understands human actions, most certainly proceeds from the soul. For before all the other powers of the soul it understands whatever is in human works, whether good or evil, so that through it, as through a teacher, everything is understood: for it sifts things as wheat is purified of any foreign matter, inquiring whether they are useful or useless, lovable or hateful, pertinent to life or death. Thus, as food without salt is tasteless, the other powers of the soul without intellect are insipid and undiscerning. But the intellect is also to the soul as the shoulder is to the body, the very core of the other powers of the soul; as the bodily shoulder is strong, so it understands the divinity and the humanity in God, which is the joint of the arm, and it has true faith in its work, which is the joint of the hand, with which it chooses among the various works wisely as if with fingers. But it does not work in the same way as the other powers of the soul. What does this mean?

20: On the Will

The will activates the work, and the mind receives it, and the reason produces it. But the intellect understands the work, knowing good and evil, just as the angels, who have intellect, love good and despise evil. And where the heart is in the body, there the intellect is in the soul, exercising its power in that part of the soul as the will does in another part. How? Because the will has great power in the soul. How? The soul stands in a corner of the house, that is, by the prop of the heart, like a man who stands in a corner of his house, so that looking through the whole house he may command all its contents, lifting his right arm to point out what is useful in the house and turning to the east. Thus the soul should do, looking along the streets of the body toward the rising sun. Thus it puts its will, like a right arm, as the support of the veins and marrow and the movement of the whole body; for the will does every work, whether it be good or bad.

21: Analogy of Fire and Bread

For the will is like a fire, baking each deed as if in a furnace. Bread is baked so that people may be nourished by it and be able to live. So too the will is the strength of the whole work, for it starts by kneading it and when it is firm adds the yeast and pounds it severely; and, thus preparing the work in contemplation as if it were bread, it bakes it in perfection by the full action of its ardor, and so makes a greater food for humans in the work they do than in the bread they eat. A person stops eating from time to time, but the work of his will goes on in him until his soul leaves his body. And in whatever differing circumstances the work is performed, whether in infancy, youth, adulthood, or bent old age, it always progresses in the will and in the will comes to perfection.

22: How in the Will's Tabernacle All Powers Are Activated and Come Together

But the will has in the human breast a tabernacle: the mind. upon which the intellect and that same will and a sort of force of the soul all breathe in strength. And all these are activated and come together in the same tabernacle. How? If anger arises, gall is produced and brings the anger to its height by filling the tabernacle with smoke. If wicked delight rises up, the flame of lust touches its structure, and so the wantonness that pertains to that sin is elevated and in that tabernacle united with it. But there is another, lovely kind of joy, which is kindled in that tabernacle by the Holy Spirit, and the rejoicing soul receives it faithfully and perfects good works in the desire of heaven. And there is a kind of sadness that engenders in the tabernacle, out of those humors that surround the gall, the sloth which produces disdain, obduracy, and stubbornness in people and depresses the soul, unless the grace of God comes quickly to rescue it.

But since in that tabernacle there occur contrary conditions. it is often disturbed by hatred and other deadly emotions, which kill the soul and try to lay it waste in perdition. But when the will wills, it can move the implements in the tabernacle and in its burning ardor dispose of them, whether they are good or evil. But if these implements please the will, it bakes its food there and offers it to people to enjoy. So in that tabernacle a great throng of good and evil things arises, like an army gathered in some place of assembly: when the commander of an army arrives, if the army pleases him he accepts it, but if it displeases him he orders it to disband. The will does the same. How? If good or evil arises in the breast, the will either carries it out or ignores it.

23: On the Reason

But both in the intellect and in the will reason stands forth as the loud sound of the soul, which makes known every work of God or Man. For sound carries words on high, as the wind lifts the eagle so that it can fly. Thus the soul utters the sound of reason in the hearing and the understanding of humanity, that its powers may be understood and its every work brought to perfection. But the body is the tabernacle and support of all the powers of the soul, since the soul resides in the body and works with the body, and the body with it, whether for good or for evil.

24: On the Senses

It is the senses on which the interior powers of the soul depend, so that these powers are known through them by the fruits of each work. The senses are subject to these powers, since they guide them to the work, but the senses do not impose work on the powers, for they are their shadow and do what pleases them. The exterior human being awakens with senses in the womb of his mother before he is born, but the other powers of the soul still remain in hiding. What is this? The dawn announces the daylight; just so the human senses manifest the reason and all the powers of the soul. And as on the two commandments of God hang all the law and the prophets, so also on the soul and its powers depend the human senses. What does this mean?

The law is ordained for human salvation, and the prophets show forth the hidden things of God; so also human senses protect a person from harmful things and lay bare the soul's interior. For the soul emanates the senses. How? It vivifies a person's face and glorifies him with sight, hearing, taste, smell, and touch, so that by this touch he becomes watchful in all things. For the senses are the sign of all the powers of the soul, as the body is the vessel of the soul. What does this mean? A person is recognized by his face, sees with his eyes, hears with his ears, opens his mouth to speak, feels with his hands, walks with his feet; and so the senses are to a person as precious stones and as a rich treasure sealed in a vase. But as the treasure within is known when the vase is seen, so also the powers of the soul are inferred by the senses.

25: That the Soul Is the Mistress and the Flesh the Handmaid

The soul is the mistress, the flesh the handmaid. How? The soul rules the body by vivifying it and the body is ruled by this vivification, for if the soul did not vivify the body it would fall apart and decay. But when a person does an evil deed and the soul knows it, it is as bitter for the soul as poison is for the body when it knowingly takes it. But the soul rejoices in a sweet deed as the body delights in sweet food. And the soul flows through the body like sap through a tree. What does this mean? By the sap, the tree grows green and produces flowers and then fruit. And how is this fruit matured? By the air's tempering. How? The sun warms it, the rain waters it, and thus by the tempering of the air it is perfected. What does this mean? The mercy of God's grace, like the sun, will illumine the person, the breath of the Holy Spirit, like the rain, will water him, and so discernment, like the tempering of the air, will lead him to the perfection of good fruits.

26: Analogy of a Tree to the Soul

The soul in the body is like sap in a tree, and the soul's powers are like the form of the tree. How? The intellect in the soul is like the greenery of the tree's branches and leaves, the will like its flowers, the mind like its bursting first fruits, the reason like the perfected mature fruit, and the senses like its size and shape. And so a person's body is strengthened and sustained by the soul. Hence, O human, understand what you are in your soul, you who lay aside your good intellect and try to liken yourself to the brutes.

STUDY QUESTIONS: HILDEGARD, *SCIVIAS*

1. When does the soul enter the body?
2. How are the powers of the soul related to the powers of the body?
3. What are the three paths each person has within him or herself?
4. What is the intellect? How is it related to the will?
5. What is the point of the analogy between fire and bread?
6. What role do the senses play?
7. What is the function of reason?
8. What is the significance of the tree analogy?

Philosophical Bridges: Hildegard's Influence

The work for which Hildegard earned her nickname "Sibyl of the Rhine" continued to inspire people for many centuries after her death. Her philosophy, while mainly on the periphery since the Middle Ages, has had a growing influence more recently, inspired and augmented, in part, by the rediscovery of her extraordinary musical works that over the past several decades have begun to attract a global audience. The growing interest in medieval mysticism and music is a direct result of the discovery of the immortality of works created by geniuses such as Hildegard, who found not just solace and survival throughout the so-called dark ages but flourished, finding extraordinary ways to voice her wisdom. Today she has finally come to be recognized as one of the most gifted creative personalities of the Middle Ages. Her enormous collected works of music and poetry, *The Symphony of the Harmony of Celestial Revelations*, which she composed and revised throughout her life, have only recently begun to be performed and recorded by some of the world's leading contemporary musicians. Among contemporary composers of a philosophical persuasion she inspires many, including the legendary Lithuanian genius Arvo Pärt.

Here is Hildegard's vision of herself, in her own words, of who and what she was, how she understood the source of her extraordinary talent: "Listen: there was once a king sitting on his throne. Around him stood great and wonderfully beautiful columns ornamented with ivory, bearing the banners of the king with great honor. Then it pleased the king to raise a small feather from the ground and he commanded it to fly. The feather flew, not because of anything in itself but because the air bore it along. Thus am I . . . a feather on the breath of God."

JOHN OF SALISBURY (1115–1180)

Biographical History

John of Salisbury was born in Old Salisbury, Wiltshire. Educated in France at various cathedral schools in Paris, including with Peter Abelard in Chartres, he joined the papal court, then served as the secretary to Thomas Becket, archbishop of Canterbury. King Henry II was suspicious of his views regarding ecclesiastical independence. During the time that John fell into disfavor he produced his two main works, *Metalogicon* and *Policraticus*, both written in 1159. The latter was dedicated to Thomas Becket and may well have influenced him into becoming a champion of ecclesiastical rights. In 1163 King Henry sent John into exile to France. John returned after Becket and the King reconciled. After Becket's assassination John acted as literary executor of Becket's correspondence. Near the end of his life he became bishop of Chartres, France.

Philosophical Overview

John of Salisbury viewed education in general, and philosophy and theology in particular, as having become overly compartmentalized. He sought a return to the sort of eclectic broadness of the ancient Greek genius. Specialization in any one area, as he saw it, was not the path toward attainment of excellence but a carefully and subtly coercive form of intellectual imprisonment, designed by the papal administration to constrain the development of individual philosophical, moral, and spiritual achievement. For instance in his *Metalogicon* John argues that logic must go hand in hand with literary education, lest the learned be seduced by literature without benefit of clarity of argument and logical demonstration. He uses as an example Aristotle's writings, and provides the first thorough analysis of the whole of Aristotle's works within the scholastic era, which influenced subsequent scholars' interpretations.

He argues for a surprisingly modern, middle-of-the-road, moderate skepticism in which knowledge requires withholding assent from doubtful propositions while affirming the probable. In this way one can avoid dogmatic error while allowing for the possibility of new knowledge which is always, at best, probable. His careful analyses of the leading views of the time are a model of scholarly criticism, illustrating what is good or insightful about some particular theory while showing the flaws, in such as way as to provide fodder for subsequent debates with a clear sense that there was always room for improvement in philosophy, that disagreements and refinements did not proclude knowledge but on the contrary, made advances possible.

METALOGICON
John of Salisbury

In this work John broadly defends logic, grammar, and rhetoric against critics who claim it leads either to skepticism or sophism. He argues for a return to the logic of Aristotle, especially the *Prior* and *Posterior Analytics*. Logic, in his view, must be liberated from its purely theoretical contemplations and applied to critical thinking in the sciences, where it can help provide a rigorous foundation for all knowledge. His tripartite division of logic into demonstration, dialectic, and sophistry was widely used to train students to be versatile thinkers in virtually any subject that came before them; the idea was that a sound reasoner could reach the best conclusions on any topic by separating what is mere illusion or sophistry from what is probable and more certain, while always leaving an open mind for revising one's former opinions. His innovative emphasis on probability, as presented in Aristotle's *Topics*, became part of the standard curriculum.

Here, again in a surprisingly contemporary tone, John begins by criticizing his fellow instructors for being overly narrow in their analyses of texts. The problem is that, first, by emphasizing their own interpretations over other readers, they are eliminating the essential aspect of understanding that comes from having multiple, often differing, points of view. Second, by focusing on poetic and rhetorical persuasion at the expense of logical development, instructors weaken students' critical abilities to think for themselves. Third, by being obscure, they pander to each other's learned eccentricities, instead of focusing on the simplicity and clarity that true understanding in any discipline requires.

With regard to the debate on universals, instead of joining the vehement debates of the time with a theory of his own, John once again reverts to an analysis of Aristotle's view, offering a theory in which universals are useful fictions.

BOOK II

Chapter 17: In What a Pernicious Manner Logic Is Sometimes Taught: and the Ideas of Moderns About [the Nature of] Genera and Species

To show off their knowledge, our contemporaries dispense their instruction in such a way that their listeners are at a loss to understand them. They seem to have the impression that every letter of the alphabet is pregnant with the secrets of Minerva. They analyze and press upon tender ears everything that anyone has ever said or done. Falling into the error condemned by Cicero, they frequently come to be unintelligible to their listeners more because of the multiplicity than the profundity of their statements. "It is indeed useful and advantageous for disputants," as Aristotle observes, " to take cognizance of several opinions on a topic." From the mutual disagreement thus brought into relief, what is seen to be poorly

John of Salisbury, from *The Metalogicon of John Salisbury: A Twelfth-Century Defense of the Verbal and Logical Arts of the Trivium*, Book II. Chapter 17, translated by Daniel D. McGarry, University of California Press. 1955.

stated may be disproved or modified. Instruction in elementary logic does not, however, constitute the proper occasion for such procedure. Simplicity, brevity, and easy subject matter are, so far as is possible, appropriate in introductory studies. This is so true that it is permissible to expound many difficult points in a simpler way than their nature strictly requires. Thus, much that we have learned in our youth must later be amended in more advanced philosophical studies. Nevertheless, at present, all are here [in introductory logical studies] declaiming on the nature of universals and attempting to explain, contrary to the intention of the author, what is really a most profound question, and a matter [that should be reserved] for more advanced studies. One holds that universals are merely word sounds, although this opinion, along with its author Roscelin, has already almost completely passed into oblivion. Another maintains that universals are word concepts, and twists to support his thesis everything that he can remember to have ever been written on the subject. Our Peripatetic of Pallet, Abelard, was ensnared in this opinion. He left many, and still has, to this day, some followers and proponents of his doctrine. They are friends of mine, although they often so torture the helpless letter that even the hardest heart is filled with compassion for the latter. They hold that it is preposterous to predicate a thing concerning a thing, although Aristotle is author of this monstrosity. For Aristotle frequently asserts that a thing is predicated concerning a thing, as is evident to anyone who is really familiar with his teaching. Another is wrapped up in a consideration of acts of the [intuitive] understanding, and says that genera and species are nothing more than the latter. Proponents of this view take their cue from Cicero and Boethius, who cite Aristotle as saying that universals should be regarded as and called "notions." "A notion," they tell us, "is the cognition of something, derived from its previously perceived form, and in need of unravelment." Or again [they say]: "A notion is an act of the [intuitive] understanding, a simple mental comprehension." They accordingly distort everything written, with an eye to making acts of [intuitive]understanding or "notions" include the universality of universals. Those who adhere to the view that universals are things have various and sunday opinions. One, reasoning from the fact that everything which exists is singular in number, concludes that either the universal is numerically one, or it is nonexistent. But since it is impossible for things that are substantial to be nonexistent, if those things for which they are substantial exist, they further conclude that universals must be essentially one with particular things. Accordingly, following Walter of Mortagne, they distinguish [various] states [of existence], and say that Plato is an individual in so far as he is Plato; a species in so far as he is a man; a genus of a subaltern [subordinate] kind in so far as he is an animal; and a most general genus in so far as he is a substance. Although this opinion formerly had some proponents, it has been a long time since anyone has asserted it. Walter now upholds [the doctrine of] ideas, emulating Plato and imitating Bernard of Chartres, and maintains that genus and species are nothing more nor less than these, namely, ideas. "An idea," according to Seneca's definition, "is an eternal examplar of those things which come to be as a result of nature." And since universals are not subject to corruption, and are not altered by the changes that transform particular things and cause them to come and go, succeeding one another almost momentarily, ideas are properly and correctly called "universals." Indeed, particular things are deemed incapable of supporting the substantive verb, [i.e., of being said "to be"]. Since they are not at all stable, and disappear without even waiting to receive names. For they vary so much in their qualities, time, location, and numerous different properties, that their whole existence seems to be more a mutual transition than a stable status. In contrast, Boethius declares, "we say that things 'are' when they may neither be increased nor diminished, but always continue as they are, firmly sustained by the foundations of their own nature." These [foundations] include their quantities, qualities, relations, places, times, conditions, and whatever is found in a way united with bodies. Although these adjuncts of bodies may seem to be changed, they remain immutable in their own nature. In like manner, although individuals [of species] may change, species remain the same. The waves of a stream wash on, yet the same flow of water continues, and we refer to the stream as the same river. Whence, the statement of Seneca, which, in fact, he has borrowed from another, "in one sense it is true that we may descend twice into the same river, although in another sense this is not so." These "ideas," or "exemplary forms," are the original plans of all things. They may neither be decreased nor augmented; and they are so permanent and perpetual, that even if the whole world were to come to an end, they could not perish. They include all things, and, as Augustine seems to maintain in his book *On Free Will*, their number neither increases nor diminishes, because the ideas always continue on, even when it happens that [particular] temporal things cease to exist. What these men promise is wonderful, and familiar to philosophers who rise to the contemplation of higher things. But as Boethius and numerous other authors testify, it is utterly foreign to the mind of Aristotle. For Aristotle very frequently opposes this view, as is clear from his books. Bernard of Chartres and his followers labored strenuously to compose the difference between Aristotle and Plato. But I opine that they arrived on the scene too late, so that their efforts to reconcile two dead men, who disagree as long as they were alive and could do so, were in vain. Still another, in his endeavor to explain Aristotle, places universality in "native forms," as does Gilbert, Bishop of Poitiers, who labors to prove that "native forms" and universals are identical. A "native form" is an example of an original [exemplar]. It [the native form, unlike the original] inheres in created things, instead of subsisting in the divine mind. In Greek it is called the *idos*, since it stands in relation to the idea as the example does to its exemplar. The native form is sensible in things that are perceptible by the senses; but insensible as conceived in the mind. It is singular in individuals, but universal in all [of a kind]. Another, with Joscelin, bishop of Soissons, attributes universality to collections of things, while denying it to things as individuals. When Joscelin tries to explain the authorities, he has his troubles and is hard put, for in many places he cannot bear the gaping astonishment of the indignant letter. Still another takes refuge in a new tongue, since he does not have sufficient command of Latin. When he hears the words "genus" and "species," at one time he says they should be understood as universals, and at another that they refer to the *maneries* [ways, modes, or manners] of things. I know not in which of the authors he has found this term or this distinction, unless perhaps he has dug it out of lists of abstruse and obsolete words, or it is an item of jargon [in the baggage] of present-day doctors. I am further at a loss to see what it can mean here, unless it refers to collections of things, which would be the same as Joscelin's view, or to a universal thing, which, however, could hardly be called a *maneries*. For a *maneries* may be interpreted as referring to both [collections and universals], since a number of things, or the status in which a thing of such and such a type continues to exist may be called a *maneries*. Finally, there are some who fix their attention on the status of things, and say that genera and species consist in the latter.

STUDY QUESTIONS: JOHN OF SALISBURY, *METALOGICON*

1. Is mutual disagreement, in John's view, good or bad?
2. What is it about those who teach the nature of universals that most bothers John? What is his view of universals?
3. Is John more critical of Plato and Aristotle or of their interpreters? Why?
4. What does John think of Augustine's *On Free Will*?
5. What are *maneries*?

POLICRATUS

In the massive volume *Policratus*, John provides a fascinating and innovative theory of ethics and politics. Here John of Salisbury outlines the progressive political and theological views that got him in trouble with King Henry.

Like Peter Abelard, John foregoes theoretical analysis in favor of examples that test our meanings and intuitions. In this way he expresses some of his more radical ideas in a way that often makes it difficult to know what he actually intends because he considers all the sides of various opposing positions. Some have criticized him in this regard on grounds that he is vague and noncommittal, but his intention is that the reader should make up his or her own mind, that the main value of the analysis is not so much to force a conclusion as to force one to the point of having to decide on the best solution.

In any case, there are some clear conclusions to John's arguments. For instance, he claims that a true prince should never be a tyrant and impose his will on the people. Not everyone is equal but everyone is equally obliged to follow the law. Thus even rulers, though they are not always explicitly obliged to obey all laws, are therefore bound to act under the law in the interest of justice, equity, and to preserve peace. Like Aristotle, he views virtue in terms of moderation in all things. Although he argues, in the end, for the supremacy of the church over the king, his innovative and original arguments rely as much on rational self-interest on the part of the rulers as divine providence.

PROLOGUE

The expression of the truth is unquestionably a difficult undertaking, and it is very frequently spoiled by the assault of the darkness of error or by the carelessness of the one who tries to express it. For when things are unknown, who rightly ponders what is true? However, the knowledge of things, in so far as it does not direct the ways of the disdainful, sharpens the stings of justice for the punishment of the transgressor. The first step, therefore, in philosophizing is to discuss the genera and the properties of things, so that one may prudently learn what is true in individual things, and the second step is that each should faithfully follow whatever truth has shone upon him. Now this paved route of those who philosophize is open only to the man who cries out from the realm of falsehood into the liberty by which those whom the truth has delivered are made free and, serving the Spirit, withdraw their necks from the yoke of wickedness and injustice. For "where the Spirit of" God "is, there is liberty," while the fear which is servile and consents to vices banishes the Holy Spirit. Moreover, it is the Spirit who speaks righteousness in the sight of princes and feels no shame, and who sets the poor in spirit above, or at least on a level with, kings, and teaches those whom he makes to cleave to him to speak and do the truth. But he who will not hear or

speak the truth is a stranger to the Spirit of truth. But no more of this. Now let us hear in what respect a tyrant differs from a prince.

CHAPTER I

The Difference Between a Prince and a Tyrant, and What a Prince Is

This, then, is the sole (or at least the greatest) difference between a tyrant and a prince, that the latter conforms to the law, and rules the people, whose servant he believes himself to be, by its judgment. Also, when he performs the duties of the commonwealth and undergoes its burdens, he claims for himself the first place by privilege of law, and is set before others in so far as universal burdens hang over the prince, while individuals are bound to individual concerns. On this account, the power over all his subjects is rightly conferred on him, so that in seeking and accomplishing the welfare of each and all, he may be self-sufficient and the state of the human commonwealth may be best disposed, while one is the member of another. In this, indeed, we follow nature, the best guide for living, which arranged all the senses of its microcosm—that is, its little world, man—in the head, and subjected all the members to the latter so that they all are rightly moved, as long as they follow

John of Salisbury, from on "genus" and "property," cf. Aristotle, *Topica*, I, 5–6 (101^{b}36–103^{a}5); summary in W. D. Ross, *Aristotle* (3rd ed., Methuen, London, 1937), 57.

John of Salisbury, from *The Policraticus (An Excerpt from the Fourth Book)*, edited and translated by Eugene R. Fairweather, *The Library of Christian Classics, Volume X, A Scholastic Miscellany: Anselm to Ockham*, Philadelphia: The Westminster Press 1956, pp. 247–260.

the decision of a sound head. Therefore, the princely crown is exalted and shines with privileges as many and as great as it has believed to be necessary for itself. And this is done rightly, because nothing is more beneficial for the people than for the prince's necessity to be met—when his will is not opposed to justice, to be sure. Therefore (as many define him) the prince is the public ruler and a kind of image of the divine Majesty on earth. Beyond doubt, it is shown that something great in the way of divine power dwells in princes, when men submit their necks to their nods and very often fearlessly yield their necks to be smitten, and each for whom he is a matter of dread fears him by divine instigation. I do not think that this could happen, save by the act of the divine pleasure. For all power is from the Lord God, and it has been with him always, and is with him eternally. Therefore, what the prince can do comes from God in such a way that the power does not depart from the Lord, but he exercises it by a hand that is subject to him, and that follows in all things the instruction of his clemency or justice. Thus "he that resisteth the power resisteth the ordinance of God," with whom rests the authority to confer it and (when he wills) to take it away or lessen it. For when a mighty one decides to rage against his subjects, this involves not just himself but also the divine dispensation, by which those who are subject to it are punished or vexed for God's good pleasure. So, for instance, during the depredations of the Huns, Attila was asked, by the devout bishop of a certain city, who he was, and replied, "I am Attila, the scourge of God." It is written that, when the bishop had reverenced the divine Majesty in him, he said, "Welcome to the servant of God," and, repeating, "Blessed is he that cometh in the name of the Lord," opened the doors of the church and admitted the persecutor, and through him attained to the palm of martyrdom. For he did not dare to shut out the scourge of God, knowing as he did that it is the beloved son that is scourged, and that the very power of the scourge comes from the Lord alone. If, then, the power is to be reverenced in this way by the good, even when it brings misfortune to the elect, who will not revere it? After all, it was instituted by the Lord "for the punishment of evildoers, and for the praise of the good," and it serves the laws with the

readiest devotion. For, as the emperor says, it is a statement worthy of the majesty of the ruler that the prince should acknowledge that he is bound by laws, because the authority of the prince depends on the authority of the law, and it is certainly a greater thing for the realm when sovereignty is set under the laws, so that the prince understands that nothing is permitted to him if it is at variance with justice and equity.

CHAPTER II

What Law Is, and that the Prince, Although He Is Released from the Obligations of Law, Is Still the Bondservant of Law and Equity, and Bears a Public Character, and Sheds Blood Blamelessly

Princes should not think that anything is taken away from them in all this, unless they believe that the statutes of their own justice are to be preferred to the justice of God, whose justice is justice forever, and his law equity. Besides, as legal experts affirm, equity is the fitness of things, which makes everything equal by reason and desires equal laws for unequal things; it is equitable toward all and assigns to each what belongs to him. But law is its interpreter, in so far as the will of equity and justice has been made known to it. Therefore, Chrysippus claimed that law has power over all things human and divine, and on that account is superior to all goods and evils and is the chief and guide of things and men alike. Papinian, a really great expert in the law, and Demosthenes, the powerful orator, seem to uphold the law and to subject the obedience of all men to it, inasmuch as in truth all law is the device and gift of God, the doctrine of wise men, the corrector of inclinations to excess, the settlement of the state, and the banishment of all crime, so that all who are engaged in the whole world of political affairs must live according to it. Thus, all are closely bound by the necessity of maintaining the law, unless there may perhaps be someone to whom license seems to have been conceded for wickedness. Nevertheless, the prince is said to be released from legal obligations, not because evil actions are allowed him, but because he should be one who cherishes equity, not from fear of punishment but from love of justice, and in everything puts others's advantage before his personal desires. But who will speak of the desires of the prince in connection with public business, since in this area he is permitted to desire nothing for himself save what law or equity suggests or the nature of the common welfare determines? For in these things his will ought to have the effect of a judgment, and it is quite right that what pleases him in such matters should have the force of law, in so far as his sentence is not in disagreement with the intention of equity. "Let my judgment," the psalmist says, "come forth from thy countenance; let thine eyes behold the thing that is equitable," for an uncorrupt judge is he whose sentence is the image of equity, because of assiduous contemplation. The prince, then, is the servant of the public welfare and the bondservant of equity, and in that sense plays a public role, because he both avenges the injuries and losses of all and punishes all crimes with impartial justice. Moreover, his rod and staff, applied with wise moderation, bring the agreements and the errors of all into the way of equity, so that the spirit rightly gives thanks to the princely power, when it says, "Thy rod and thy staff, they have comforted me." It is true also that his shield is strong, but it is the shield of the weak and it effectively intercepts the darts aimed at the innocent by the malicious. His function also is of the utmost benefit to those who have the least power, and is most strongly opposed to those who desire to do harm. Therefore, "he beareth not the sword in vain," when he sheds blood by it, but blamelessly, so that he is not a man of blood, but often kills men without thereby incurring the name or the guilt of a homicide. For if the great Augustine is to be believed, David was called a "man of blood," not because of his wars but on account of Uriah. And it is nowhere written that Samuel was a man of blood or a homicide, even though he slew Agag, the very rich king of Amalek. In fact, the princely sword is the "sword of the dove," which strives without animosity, smites without fury, and, when it goes into combat, conceives no bitterness whatsoever. For, just as the law proceeds against crimes without any hatred of persons, so the prince also punishes offenders most rightly, not by any impulse of anger but by the decision of a mild law. For though the prince may seem to have his own "lectors," we should believe that in fact he is his only (or

his foremost) lictor, but that it is lawful for him to smite by the hand of a substitute. For if we consult the Stoics, who diligently search out the origins of names, we shall learn that he is called a "lictor"—as it were, a "striker of the law"—inasmuch as it pertains to his office to smite him who, in the law's judgment, is to be smitten. On this account also, when the guilty were threatened with the sword, it used to be said in ancient days to the officials by whose hand the judge punished evildoers, "comply with the decision of the law," or "fulfill the law," so that the mildness of the words might in fact modify the sadness of the event.

CHAPTER III

That the Prince Is the Servant of Priests and Beneath Them, and What It Means to Carry Out the Princely Office Faithfully

The prince, therefore, receives this sword from the hand of the Church, even though, to be sure, the latter does not possess the sword of blood. Nevertheless, she does possess it as well, but makes use of it by the hand of the prince, to whom she has conceded the power of keeping bodies under restraint, although she has retained authority in spiritual matters for her pontiffs. Thus the prince is in fact the servant of the priesthood, and exercises that part of the sacred duties which seems unworthy of the hands of the priesthood. For while every duty imposed by the sacred laws is a matter of religion and piety, the function of punishing crimes, which seems to constitute a kind of image of the hangman's office, is lower than others. It was on account of this inferiority that Constantine, the most faithful emperor of the Romans, when he had convoked the council of priests at Nicaea, did not dare to take the first place or mingle with the assemblies of the presbyters, but occupied the lowest seat. Indeed, he reverenced the conclusions which he heard approved by them as if he supposed that they proceeded from the judgment of the divine Majesty. As for the written accusations, stating the offenses of the priests, which they had drawn up against one another and presented to the emperor, he received them and put them away, still unopened, in his bosom. Moreover, when he had recalled the council to charity and concord, he said that it was unlawful for him (as a man, and as one who was subject to the judgment of priests) to consider the cases of the gods, who can be judged by God alone. And he committed the books which he had received to the fire, without looking at them, because he was afraid to disclose the crimes or vices of the fathers, lest he bring on himself the curse of Ham, the rejected son, who failed to cover what he should have respected in his father. For the same reason, he is said (in the writings of Nicholas, the Roman Pontiff) to have stated, "truly, if with my own eyes I had seen a priest of God, or anyone who had been clothed in the monastic habit, committing sin, I should have spread out my cloak and covered him, lest he be seen by anyone." Theodosius also, the great emperor, when he was suspended from the use of the regalia and the badges of sovereignty by the bishop of Milan, because of a crime that was real enough, but not quite that serious, patiently and solemnly did the penance imposed on him for homicide. Certainly, to appeal to the testimony of the doctor of the Gentiles, he who blesses is greater than he who is blessed, and he who possesses the authority to confer a dignity surpasses in the privilege of honor him on whom the dignity itself is conferred. Besides, according to the very nature of law, it pertains to the same person to will and not to will, and it is he who has the right to confer who also has the right to take away. Did not Samuel bring sentence of deposition against Saul on account of his disobedience, and substitute the lowly son of Jesse for him in the highest place in the kingdom? But if he who is set up as prince has faithfully performed the function he received, he is to be shown great honor and great reverence, in proportion to the superiority of the head over all the members of the body. Now he performs his task faithfully when, mindful of his rank, he remembers that he bears in himself the totality of his subjects, and knows that he owes his own life not to himself but to others, and as it were distributes it among them with due charity. He owes his entire self, then, to God, most of himself to his fatherland, much to his kinsfolk and neighbors, and least (but still something) to strangers. He is debtor, then, to the wise and the unwise, to the small and the great. In fact, this concern is common to all who are set over others, both to those who bear the care of spiritual things and to those who exercise worldly jurisdiction.

On this account we read of Melchizedek, who is the first king and priest referred to in Scripture—not to mention, for the present, the mystery by which he prefigures Christ, who was born in heaven without a mother and on earth without a father—we read, I say, that he had neither father nor mother. It is not that he lacked either, but that flesh and blood do not by their nature bring forth kingship and priesthood, since in the creation of either respect of parents should not carry weight without regard for meritorious virtue, but the wholesome desires of faithful subjects should have priority. Thus, when anyone reaches the pinnacle of either kingship or priesthood, he should forget the affection of the flesh and do only what the welfare of his subjects demands. Let him be, therefore, the father and husband of his subjects, or, if he knows a more tender affection, let him practice it; let him strive to be loved more than he is feared, and let him show himself to them in such a light that out of sheer devotion they may put his life before their own and reckon his safety to be a kind of public life. Then everything will go well with him, and if need be a few guards will prevail by their obedience against countless enemies. For "love is strong as death," and a wedge which the cords of love hold together is not easily broken.

When the Dorians were about to fight with the Athenians, they consulted oracles about the outcome of the battle. "The reply was that they would win unless they killed the king of the Athenians. When the war began, care for the king was the first order given to the soldiers. At that time Codrus was king of the Athenians. When he learned of the response of the god and the orders of the enemy, he changed his kingly garments and, bearing fagots on his neck, entered the enemy's camp. There in a crowd of his opponents he was slain by a soldier, whom he had struck with his sickle. When the king's body was recognized, the Dorians withdrew without a battle. And in this way the Athenians were delivered from war by the virtue of their chief, who offered himself to death for the preservation of the fatherland."

Again, Lycurgus in his kingdom established decrees which set the people in obedience to their chiefs and the chiefs to the justice of their commanders. "He abolished the use of gold and silver and the source of all crimes." He gave to the senate the care of the laws, and to the people the power of electing the senate. He decreed that a maiden "should be married without a dowry, so that wives and not money should be chosen. He intended that the greatest honor should correspond closely . . . with the age of the old—nor in fact does old age have a more honored place anywhere on earth." Finally, "in order to give eternity to his laws, he bound the citizens by an oath not to change anything in his laws before he returned . . . . Then he set out for Crete, and lived there as a perpetual exile, and when he was dying he ordered his bones to be thrown into the sea, lest, if they were taken home, the Spartans might think that they were released from the obligation of their oath and might abrogate his laws."

I use these examples more freely, because I find that the apostle Paul made use of them when he preached to the Athenians. The illustrious preacher strove to impress "Jesus Christ, and him crucified" on their minds in such a way that he might teach them, by the example of the Gentiles, that the deliverance of many had come about through the shame of the cross. But he also convinced them that these things came about only by the blood of the just and of those who carried on the magistracy of the people. Besides, no one could be found who was sufficient for the deliverance of all—namely, of Jews and Gentiles— save him to whom the Gentiles were given for an inheritance and for whose possession the whole earth was fore-ordained. Now he affirmed that this could only be the Son of Almighty God, since apart from God no one has subdued all nations and lands. There- fore, while he preached the shame of the cross, so that little by little the folly of the Gentiles should be made void, he gradually lifted up the word of faith and the language of his preaching to the word of God and the wisdom of God and even to the very throne of the divine Majesty, and, lest the power of the gospel should become worthless through the weak- ness of the flesh, because of the stumbling block of the Jews and the folly of the Gentiles, he expounded the works of the Crucified, which were also supported by the testimony of public opinion, since it was agreed by all that God alone could do these things. But because public opinion often tells many lies on both sides, he assisted opinion itself, because his dis- ciples did greater things, as, for instance, when the sick were healed from any sickness whatever by the

shadow of a disciple. But why many things? He over- threw the subtleties of Aristotle, the acuteness of Chrysippus, and the snares of all the philosophers, when he rose from the dead.

It is in everyone's mouth that the Decii, Roman commanders, devoted themselves for their armies. Julius Caesar also said: "A commander who does not try to be esteemed by his soldiers does not know how to arm a soldier, does not know that the humanity of a general in an army tells against the enemy." Caesar never said to his soldiers, "go thither," but always said, "come," for he used to say that labor shared with the commander seems less to soldiers. Moreover, accord- ing to the same author, bodily pleasure is to be avoided, for he used to say that men's bodies are wounded by swords in war, by pleasures in peace. For the conqueror of the nations had thought that pleas- ure could most easily be overcome by flight, because he who had subdued the nations was tied up in the coils of Venus by a shameless woman.

CHAPTER IV

That It Is Certain, by the Authority of Divine Law, that the Prince Is Subject to the Law of Justice

But why do I appeal to examples borrowed from the Gentiles, even though they are so numerous, when anyone can be urged more suitably by laws than by examples to do what must be done? But lest you sup- pose that the prince himself is wholly free from laws, listen to the law which the "great king over all the earth," who is "terrible" and "who taketh away the spirit of princes," imposes on princes. "When thou art come," he says, "into the land, which the Lord God will give thee, and possessest it, and shalt say: 'I will set a king over me, as all nations have that are round about'; thou shalt set him whom the Lord thy God shall choose out of the number of they brethren. Thou mayest not make a man of another nation king, that is not thy brother. And when he is made king, he shall not multiply horses to himself, nor lead back the people into Egypt, being lifted up with the number of his horsemen, especially since the Lord hath com- manded you to return no more the same way. He shall not have many wives, that may take possession of his mind, nor immense sums of gold and silver. But after he is raised to the throne of his kingdom, he shall copy out to himself the Deuteronomy of this law in a volume, taking the copy of the priests of the Levitical tribe, and he shall have it with him, and shall read it all the days of his life, that he may learn to fear the Lord his God, and keep his words and ceremonies, that are commanded in the law, and that his heart be not lifted up with pride over his brethren, nor decline to the right or to the left, that he and his son may reign a long time over Israel." I ask, is he bound by no law, whom that law restrains? Certainly this is a divine law, and cannot be relaxed with impunity. If they are prudent, each of its words is thunder in the ears of princes. I say nothing of the election and the form required in the creation of a prince; consider with me for a little while the rule of living which is prescribed for him. When, it reads, he who professes himself to be the brother of the whole people by religious worship and charitable affection is set up, he shall not multiply horses to himself, since a large number of these would make him oppressive to his subjects. Now to multiply horses means to gather together more horses than necessity requires, for the sake of vainglory or some other fault. For "much" and "little", if we follow the chief of the Peripatetics, refer to the decrease or excess of legitimate quantity in particular genera of things. Will he, then, be permitted to multiply dogs or birds of prey or savage beasts or any natural monsters whatever, when he is told that the number of horses—which are necessary for warfare and the requirements of the whole of life—must be of a legitimate quantity? There was no need for mention to be made in the law of actors and mimes, jesters and prostitutes, procurers and human monsters of this kind (which a prince ought to exterminate, and not to foster); indeed, the law does not simply exclude all these abominations from the prince's court, but also turns them out of the people of God. By the term "horses" we are to understand the necessary use of a complete household and all its equipment; whatever amount of this a concern for necessity or utility demands is legitimate. The useful and the virtuous must, however, be equated, and government be chosen by the virtuous. For already in ancient times it was the view of the philosophers that no opinion was more pernicious than the opinion of those who separate the useful from the virtuous, and that the truest and most beneficial judgment was that the virtuous and the useful are altogether convertible.

Plato, as the histories of the Gentiles relate, when he had seen Dionysius, the tyrant of Sicily, surrounded by his bodyguards, said, "what great evil have you done, that you need so many to guard you?" This certainly is unnecessary for a prince, who so attaches the affections of all to himself by his services that any subject will risk his head for him when dangers threaten, since at the urging of nature the members are wont to risk themselves for the head, and "skin for skin and all that a man hath he will" lay down "for his life."

The text [of Deuteronomy] goes on: "nor lead back the people into Egypt, being lifted up with the number of his horsemen." For everyone who is set in a high place is to exercise the greatest diligence, lest he corrupt his inferiors by his example and his misuse of things, and by way of pride or luxury lead back the people to the darkness of confusion. For it often happens that subjects imitate the vices of their superiors, because the people strive to be conformed to the magistrate, and each and every one readily desires that in which he sees that another is distinguished. There is a celebrated passage of the distinguished poet, in which he states the thoughts and words of Theodosius the Great:

"If you order and decree anything to be held in common, First submit to what is ordered; then the people becomes More observant of the right, nor does it refuse to accept it, When it sees the lawgiver himself obey it. The nation Is ordered by the king's example, nor can ordinances Affect human inclinations as does the life of a ruler. The inconstant multitude always changes with the prince."

Now the means of individuals are far from equal to the resources of all. Each man dips into his own coffers, but the ruler draws on the public chest or treasury; if this by any chance fails, recourse is had to the means of individuals. But it is necessary for each private person to be satisfied with his own. If these prove to have been reduced, he who just now desired the ruler's renown is ashamed of the obscurity of his own disorder, mean as he is in his poverty. On this account thrift in the use of public goods was imposed by decree on the rulers of the Spartans, even though it is permissible by common right to make use of an inheritance or of something acquired by good fortune.

STUDY QUESTIONS: JOHN OF SALSIBURY, *POLICRATUS*

1. What is the main difference between a tyrant and a prince?
2. How should power be distributed within a state? Between church and state?
3. What is the law? From where does the law originate?
4. Is a prince (or king) obliged to follow the law? Why?
5. What is the nature of the relationship between the supreme ruler and the law?
6. How should interests of law, equity, justice, and peace enter into a supreme ruler's deliberations?
7. Is a prince the servant of priests? Why?

Philosophical Bridges: John of Salisbury's Influence

Among his contemporaries, John of Salisbury inspired many important figures, most notably, Thomas Becket, to seek ecclesiastical rights, for which he argued vehemently. Part of what inspired John sparked the same flame in subsequent thinkers, namely, a return to the eclectic vision of the great ancient Greek philosophers such as Aristotle. Many subsequent philosophers, especially during the Renaissance and throughout the modern era, culminating with polymaths such as René Descartes (see his *Rules for the Direction of the Mind*), drew inspiration from his call to a broad and balanced education in which logic and mathematics are balanced with literature and art.

Philosophical Bridges: The Early Medieval Influence

The writings of the early medieval philosophers provided a foundation for the Scholasticism that would embrace all intellectual, artistic, philosophical, and theological activities carried on in medieval schools as taught by its proponents, called *doctores scholastici*. Whereas ancient Greek philosophy was essentially the work by and for individuals, the Scholastics tried to develop philosophy as part of a "Christian society" whose purpose, in turn, was to transcend both individuals and nations. The corporate product of social thought, Scholastic reasoning required obedience to authority as espoused by traditional forms of thought strictly codified within "revealed" Christian religion. One could say that, as a result, philosophy was during this time subjugated to theology and controlled by the authoritarian hierarchy of the church. On the other hand, one could also say that the activity of philosophy came under the protection of the church. Although it was not practiced outside the church, the advances in thought made by these early medieval thinkers are profound in their own right and influential to this day.

Subsequent thinkers disagreed vehemently over the various early medieval arguments for the existence of God. But in many cases this had less to do with the notion of God than with the logical structures and techniques of the arguments, as the conceptual tools of metaphysics and language. Some, such as Descartes, Spinoza, Leibniz, and Hegel, took a Platonic or neo-Platonic realistic view of universals, according to which the role of essences is primary and materialism secondary. They thus all accepted, for instance, some form of Anselm's original version of the ontological argument. Others, for instance, Aquinas, Hume, and Kant, under the influence of Aristotelian nominalism, dismissed it. Most recently, similar sorts of arguments have been adduced by scientists using these same concepts, developed by the early medievals, on behalf not of God but of the universe itself. According to one version of the so-called "Anthropic-Cosmological Principle," the existence of the universe is logically necessary, as is our own existence.

BIBLIOGRAPHY

GENERAL

Armstrong, D. M., ed., *The Cambridge History of Later Greek and Early Medieval Philosophy*, Cambridge University Press, 1967

Brantl, G., *Catholicism*, George Braziller, 1962

Clebsch, W., *Christianity in European History*, Oxford, 1979

DeWulf, M., *History of Mediaeval Philosophy*, Dover, 1952

Fremantle, A., *The Age of Belief: The Medieval Philosophers*, New American Library, 1954

Gilson, E., *History of Christian Philosophy in the Middle Ages*, Random House, 1955

Harris, S., ed., *Misconceptions About the Middle Ages*, Routledge, 2007

Marenbon, J., *Early Medieval Philosophy (480–1150)*, Routledge & Kegan-Paul, 1983

Marenbon, J., *Medieval Philosophy: An Historical and Philosophical Introduction*, Routledge, 2006

Szarmach P. E., *An Introduction to the Medieval Mystics of Europe*, State University of New York Press, 1984

Underhill, E., *Mysticism: A Study in the Nature and Development of Man's Spiritual Consciousness*, Methuen, 1930

BOETHIUS
Primary

The Consolation of Philosophy, translated by W. V. Cooper, J. M. Dent, 1902

Secondary

Barrett, H. M., *Boethius: Some Aspects of His Times and Work*, Cambridge University Press, 1940

Chadwick, H., *Boethius: The Consolations of Music, Logic, Theology, and Philosophy*, Clarendon Press, 1981

Gibson, M., ed., *Boethius, His Life, Thought, and Influence*, Blackwell, 1981

Patch, H. R., *The Tradition of Boethius: A Study of His Importance in Medieval Culture*, Oxford University Press, 1935

Reiss, E., *Boethius*, Twayne, 1982

JOHN SCOTUS ERIGENA
Primary

Periphyseon: On the Division of Nature, edited and translated by M. L. Uhfelder, Macmillan Library of the Liberal Arts, 1976

Secondary

Bett, H., *Johannes Scotus Eriugena: A Study in Mediaeval Philosophy*, Russell and Russell, 1964

Moran, D., *The Philosophy of John Scotus Eriugena: A Study of Idealism in the Middle Ages*, Cambridge University Press, 1989

O'Meara, J., *Eriugena*, Clarendon Press, 1988

ANSELM
Primary

Anselm of Canterbury—the Major Works, eds. B. Davies and G. R. Evans, Oxford 1998

Monologion and Proslogion With the Replies of Gaunilo and Anselm, translated by T. Williams, Hackett 1996

St. Anselm: Basic Writings, translated by S. N. Deane, 1902, reprinted Open Court, 1962

Secondary

Barnes, J., *The Ontological Argument*, Macmillan, 1972

Evans, G. R., *Anselm and Talking About God*, Oxford University Press, 1978

Haight, D. and M., "An Ontological Argument for the Devil," *The Monist*, 1970

Harshorne, C., *Anselm's Discovery*, Open Court, 1965

Hopkins, J., *A Companion to the Study of St. Anselm*, University of Minnesota Press, 1972

Kolak, D., *In Search of God: The Language and Logic of Belief*, Wadsworth, 1994

Kolak, D., *In Search of Myself: Life, Death and Personal Identity*, Wadsworth, 1999

Leftow, B., ed., *The Cambridge Companion to Anselm*, Cambridge University Press, 2005

Plantinga, A., ed. *The Ontological Argument from St. Anselm to Contemporary Philosophers*, Doubleday, 1965

Plantinga, A. and Kolak, D., "Philosophy, the Bible and God: A Dialog," in *The Experience of*

Philosophy, 6th ed., Oxford University Press, 2005, and in *Questioning Matters*, D. Kolak, ed., McGraw Hill, 2000

Southern, R. W., *Saint Anselm: A Portrait in a Landscape*, Cambridge University Press, 1990

ABELARD
Primary
Ethics, translated by D. E. Luscombe, Clarendon Press, 1971

The Letters of Abelard and Heloise, translated by B. Radice, Penguin Classics, 1974

Secondary
Lloyd, R. B., *Peter Abelard: The Orthodox Rebel*, Latimer House, 1947

Marenbon, J., *The Philosophy of Peter Abelard*, Cambridge University Press, 1997

McCabe, J. *Peter Abelard*, Books for Libraries Press, 1971

Tweedale, M. M., *Abailard on Universals*, North Holland, 1976

HILDEGARD OF BINGEN
Primary
Mystical Writings, edited by Fiona Bowie and Oliver Davies, translated by R. Carver, Crossroads, 1990

Secondary
Dronke, P., *Women Writers of the Middle Ages*, Cambridge University Press, 1984

Flanagan, S., *Hildegard of Bingen, 1098–1179: A Visionary Life*, Routledge, 1989

Waithe, M. E., *A History of Women Philosophers, Volume II: Medieval, Renaissance and Enlightenment Women Philosophers, 500–1600*, Kluwer Academic (now Springer), 1989

JOHN OF SALISBURY
Primary
The Metalogicon of John Salisbury: A Twelfth-Century Defense of the Verbal and Logical Arts of the Trivium, translated by D. D. McGarry, University of California Press, 1955

Secondary
Liebeschutz, H., *Mediaeval Humanism in the Life and Writings of John of Salisbury*, Warburg Institute, University of London, 1950

Webb, C. C. J., *John of Salisbury*, Methuen, 1932

SECTION IV

→ ISLAMIC AND JEWISH → PHILOSOPHY

PROLOGUE

Two centuries after the fall of the Roman Empire, in the early part of the sixth century, the philosophical schools founded a thousand years earlier by Plato and Aristotle in Athens were closed. With Greek learning denounced by papal authorities as pagan heresies, philosophers were imprisoned or killed and the practice of what today we would call philosophy was outlawed in most of Europe. Some philosophers escaped with their banished classical and ancient Greek texts to Persia, where these works were translated into Syriac and Arabic and began to influence Islamic and Jewish thinkers.

During the coming centuries, while Orthodox Christendom ruled Europe with an iron fist, the philosophies of the ancients, especially Plato and Aristotle, not only survived but continued to evolve across the Mediterranean. New schools of philosophy arose in Alexandria, Syria, and Persia, where libraries were filled with translations of all the major Greek texts forbidden in Europe. When the Arabs conquered Spain, they brought these works back into Europe and thereby, in an ironic twist, Islamic philosophers rekindled within Europe the flame of the golden age of Greece. Two of the most important of Islamic philosophers of the time, Avicenna (Ibn Sina) and Averroës (Ibn Rushd), were both thought to be followers mainly of Aristotle. In reality, their thought and writings were a mix of Platonic and Aristotelian ideas which they learned from an influential neo-Platonic works such as *The Theology of Aristotle*, which was itself based mainly on Plotinus' *Enneads*.

At the same time, the great Jewish philosopher Maimonides—a contemporary of Averroës' born in Córdova, Spain—produced a synthesis of both systems in what generally is regarded as one of the greatest philosophical works of the Middle Ages: *Dalalat al-Ha'rin* (*Guide for the Perplexed*, 1190).

167

AVICENNA (IBN SINA, 980–1037)

Biographical History

The great—many would say greatest—Persian, or Iranian, philosopher Avicenna was born in Afshana, near Bocchara (Bukhara), in Turkistan. He studied the works of Porphyry, Euclid, Ptolemy, Plato, and Aristotle, along with the Koran, with a distinct eye for the art of healing; he practiced mainly not as a theoretical philosopher but as a physician. His first works were his medical *Canon* and his *Healing*, the latter which was an encyclopedic synthesis of logic, metaphysics, physics, philosophy, and medicine, which influenced scholars on both continents. He became a renowned teacher and personal physician to Persian kings and princes, and his works were standard fare well into the seventeenth century. He was a prolific writer, with over a hundred manuscripts, many of which were lost in 1030 during the fall of Isfahan, when the conquering Ghaznawids burned philosophers' works.

Philosophical Overview

Avicenna led the first and arguably greatest revival of classical Greek thought in the Islamic world. His main influences were Plato, as interpreted by the neo-Platonists, and even more so Aristotle, whom he and his students regarded as the greatest philosopher of all time. His distinctly Aristotelian metaphysics had a tripartite division of universals, which exist *ante res* in the mind of God, *in rebus* in individual particulars, and *post res* in the human mind. His interpretation of the logical and ontological forms of universals became the standard for medieval Aristotelians on both sides of the Mediterranean.

Avicenna, like Aristotle, views metaphysics as the science of being, based on an elaborate synthesis of neo-Platonic theory of emanation (see the section on Plotinus) and insights weaned from his own highly intuitive, introspective, empirical psychology. The idea is based on a distinction between the Aristotelian division between possible being, which exists through, by, or in virtue of something else other than itself, and necessary being, which exists through, by, or in virtue of its own essence. Only in God are essence and existence identical. The human mind is capable of knowing this because being itself consists of a series of intelligences whose essence as such is understandable, knowable, meaningful, orderly, logical, and communicable by an immediate act of intuition. The intelligences structure the ultimate reality both of the internal and external worlds and are accessible to individual human intelligence through philosophical contemplation. The active intelligence that illuminates the human mind is one and the same in all of human beings. But, as in the view of Aquinas in contrast to Averroës, Avicenna argues that the "potential intellect" in which the individual human psyche exists also survives death as such, which is in line both with Mohammedan and Christian ethics.

ESSAY ON THE SECRET OF DESTINY

Nearly all philosophers writing about God as conceived in the Judeo-Christian and Islamic traditions have had to grapple with the question of evil. How could God, the greatest and most perfect, all-knowing, all-good being, create a world with evil in it? Isn't evil a flaw in creation? How then can we conceive of the creator as perfect, if the world thus created by God is imperfect? Would not a perfect being create a perfect world, a utopia? In this selection, Avicenna takes this issue head-on. First, after arguing that the soul, though immortal, is vulnerable to punishment and reward for its actions, he argues that the existence of evil in a world created by a perfect being is not only possible, but necessary. He develops his view emphasizing ideas derived from Plato and Aristotle, whom he calls, simply and reverently, "the Sage."

In the name of God, the Merciful, the Compassionate.

Someone asked the eminent *Shaykh* Abū Alī b. Sīnī (may God the Exalted have mercy on him) the meaning of the Sūfī saying. "He who knows the secret of destiny is an atheist." In reply he stated that this matter contains the utmost obscurity, and is one of those matters which may be set down only in enigmatic form and taught only in a hidden manner, on account of the corrupting effects its open declaration would have on the general public. The basic principle concerning it is found in a Tradition of the Prophet (God bless and safeguard him): "Destiny is the secret of God: do not declare the secret of God." In another Tradition, when a man questioned the Prince of the Believers. "Alī (may God be pleased with him)," he replied. "Destiny is a deep sea: do not sail out on it." Being asked again he replied. "It is a stony path: do not walk on it." Being asked once more he said. "It is a hard ascent: do not undertake it." The shaykh said: Know that the secret of destiny is based upon certain premises, such as the world order, the report that there is Reward and Punishment, and the affirmation of the resurrection of souls.

The first premise is that you should know that in the world as a whole and in its parts, both upper and earthly, there is nothing which forms an exception to the facts that God is the cause of its being and origination and that God has knowledge of it, controls it, and wills its existence: it is all subject to His control, determination, knowledge, and will. This is a general and superficial account, although in these assertions we intend to describe it truly, not as the theologians understand it; and it is possible to produce proofs and demonstrations of that. Thus, if it were not that this world is composed of elements which give rise to good

and evil things in it and produce both righteousness and wickedness in its inhabitants, there would have been no completion of an order for the world. For if the world had contained nothing but pure righteousness, it would not have been this world but another one, and it would necessarily have had a composition different from the present composition; and likewise if it had contained nothing but sheer wickedness, it would not have been this world but another one. But whatever is composed in the present fashion and order contains both righteousness and wickedness.

The second premise is that according to the ancients, Reward is the occurrence of pleasure in the soul corresponding to the extent of its perfection, while Punishment is the occurrence of pain in the soul corresponding to the extent of its deficiency. So the soul's abiding in deficiency is its "alienation from God the Exalted," and this is "the curse," "the Penalty," "wrath," and "anger," and pain comes to it from that deficiency; while its perfection is what is meant by [God's] "satisfaction" with it, its "closeness" and "nearness" and "attachment." This, then, and nothing else is the meaning of "Reward" and "Punishment" according to them.

The third premise is that the resurrection is just the return of human souls to their own world: this is why God the Exalted has said, "O tranquil soul, return to your Lord satisfied and satisfactory."

These are summary statements, which need to be supported by their proper demonstrations.

Now, if these premises are established, we say that the apparent evils which befall this world are, on the principles of the Sage, not purposed for the world—the good things alone are what is purposed, the evil ones are a privation, while according to Plato

Avicenna, from "Essay on the Secret of Destiny," translated by George F. Hourani, in John F. Wippel and Allan B. Wolter, eds., *Medieval Philosophy* (The Free Press, New York, 1969). pp. 229–232. Originally published in the *Bulletin of the School of Oriental and African Studies* (University of London). Vol. 29. PII. 1966. pp. 31–33. Reprinted by permission.

both are purposed as well as willed; and that the commanding and forbidding of acts to responsible beings, by revelation in the world, are just a stimulant to him of whom it was foreknown that there would occur in him the commandments, or (in the case of a prohibition) a deterrent to him of whom it was foreknown that he would refrain from what is forbidden. Thus the commandment is a cause of the act's proceeding from him of whom it is foreknown that it will proceed, and the prohibition is a cause of intimidation to him who refrains from something bad because of it. Without the commandment the former would not have come to desire the act: without the prohibition the latter would not have been scared. It is as if one were to imagine that it would have been possible for 100 percent of wickedness to befall in the absence of any prohibition, and that with the presence of the prohibitions 50 percent of wickedness has befallen, whereas without prohibitions 100 percent would have befallen. Commandments must be judged in the same way: had there been no commandments nothing of righteousness would have befallen, but with the advent of the commandments 50 percent of righteousness has occurred.

As for praise and blame, these have just two objects. One is to incite a doer of good to repeat the like act which is willed to proceed from him; the second is to scare the one from whom the act has occurred from repeating the like of it, and that the one from whom that act has occurred will abstain from doing what is not willed to proceed from him, though it is in his capacity to do it.

It is not admissible that Reward and Punishment should be such as the theologians suppose: chastise-ment of the fornicator, for example, by putting him in chains and shackles, burning him in the fire over and over again, and setting snakes and scorpions upon him. For this is the behavior of one who wills to slake his wrath against his enemy, through injury or pain which he inflicts on him out of hostility against him; and that is impossible in the character of God the Exalted, for it is the act of one who wills that the very being who models himself on him should refrain from acts like his or be restrained from repeating such acts. And it is not to be imagined that after the resurrection there are obligations, commandments, and prohibitions for anyone, so that by witnessing Reward and Punishment they should be scared or refrain from what is proscribed to them and desire what is commanded to them. So it is false that Reward and Punishment are as they have imagined them.

As for the penalties ordained by the divine Law for those who commit transgressions, it has the same effect as the prohibitions in serving as a restraint upon him who abstains from transgression, whereas without it it is imaginable that the act might proceed from him. There may also be a gain to the one who is subject to penalty, in preventing him from further wickedness, because men must be bound by one of two bonds, either the bond of the divine Law or the bond of reason, that the order of the world may be completed. Do you not see that if anyone were let loose from both bonds the load of wickedness he would commit would be unbearable, and the order of the world's affairs would be upset by the dominance of him who is released from both bonds? But God is more knowing and wiser.

STUDY QUESTIONS: AVICENNA, *ESSAY ON THE SECRET OF DESTINY*

1. Would someone who believed in destiny have to be an atheist? Why?
2. According to Avicenna, did God create everything in the world?
3. How are rewards and punishments determined?
4. What contains both righteousness and wickedness?
5. What happens to souls upon the resurrection? Where do they go?
6. What is the divine Law?
7. Should one inflict great violence upon one's enemies? Why?
8. What is "the secret of destiny?" Why is this secret important regarding the question of the existence of God?
9. Why are reward and punishment not as we imagine them?

CONCERNING THE SOUL

In "Concerning the Soul," directly inspired by Aristotle's *On the Soul*, Avicenna distinguishes the different faculties of the soul, defined in terms of their various creative functions. God did not create the world directly, according to Avicenna, but through intermediary intelligences, conceived as different levels of being; thus creation in his view is a joint venture between God and the active intellect, which gave rise to the material world. He explains the Aristotelian distinction between the motive and perceptive faculties of the soul, the active and passive intellect, and how they give rise to human emotion.

He explains the ephemeral and representational nature of perception, how the eye, light, and seeing are involved in experience, and then shows how universals and intuition make rational knowledge possible using syllogistic logic. He asks the puzzling question of how one soul can be distinguished from another, independently of any body. He argues that numerical identity between souls existing as such in numerically distinct bodies is impossible, a position that Averroës will subsequently endeavor to refute.

CHAPTER 1: THE VEGETATIVE SOUL

When the element are mixed together in a more harmonious way, that is in a more balanced proportion than in the cases previously mentioned, other beings also come into existence out of them due to the powers of the heavenly bodies. The first of these are plants. Now some plants are grown from seed and set aside a part of the body bearing the reproductive faculty, while others grow from spontaneous generation without seeds.

Since plants nourish themselves they have the faculty of nutrition. And because it is of the nature of plants to grow, it follows that they have the faculty of growth. Again, since it is the nature of certain plants to reproduce their like and to be reproduced by their like, they have a reproductive faculty. The reproductive faculty is different from the faculty of nutrition, for unripe fruits possess the nutritive but not the reproductive faculty: just as they possess the faculty of growth, but not that of reproduction. Similarly, the faculty of nutrition differs from that of growth. Do you not see that decrepit animals have the nutritive faculty but lack that of growth?

The nutritive faculty transmits food and replaces what has been dissolved with it: the faculty of growth increases the substance of the main structural organs in length, breadth, and depth, not haphazard but in such a way that they can reach the utmost perfection of growth. The reproductive faculty gives the matter the form of the thing: it separates from the parent body a part in which a faculty derived from its origin inheres and which, when the matter and the place which are prepared to receive its activity are present, performs its functions.

It will be evident from the foregoing that all vegetable, animal, and human functions are due to faculties over and above bodily functions, and even over and above the nature of the mixture itself.

After the plant comes the animal, which emerges from a compound of elements whose organic nature is much nearer to the mean than the previous two and is therefore prepared to receive the animal soul, having passed through the stage of the vegetable soul. And so the nearer it approaches the mean the greater is its capacity for receiving yet another psychic faculty more refined than the previous one.

The soul is like a single genus divisible in some way into three parts. The first is the vegetable soul, which is the first entelechy of a natural body possessing organs in so far as it is reproduced, grows, and

Avicenna, from *Concerning the Soul from Avicenna's Psychology*, translated by Fazlur Rahman (London: Geoffrey Cumberlege, Oxford University Press, 1952). Reprinted by permission of Oxford University Press.

assimilates nourishment. Food is a body whose function it is to become similar to the nature of the body whose food it is said to be, and adds to that body either in exact proportion or more or less what is dissolved.

The second is the animal soul, which is the first entelechy of a natural body possessing organs in so far as it perceives individuals and moves by volition.

The third is the human soul, which is the first entelechy of a natural body possessing organs in so far as it acts by rational choice and rational deduction, and in so far as it perceives universals.

The vegetable soul has three faculties. First, the nutritive faculty which transforms another body into a body similar to that in which it is itself present, and replaces what has been dissolved. Secondly, the faculty of growth which increases every aspect of the body in which it resides, by length, breadth, and depth in proportion to the quantity necessary to make it attain its perfection in growth. Thirdly, the reproductive faculty which takes from the body in which it resides a part which is potentially similar to it and acts upon it with the help of other similar bodies, generating and mixing them so as to render that part actually similar to the body (to which it had been only potentially similar).

CHAPTER 2: THE ANIMAL SOUL

The animal soul, according to the primary division, has two faculties—the motive and the perceptive. The motive faculty again is of two kinds: either it is motive insofar as it gives an impulse, or insofar as it is active. Now the motive faculty, insofar as it provides the impulse, is the faculty of appetence. When a desirable or repugnant image is imprinted on the imagination of which we shall speak before long, it rouses this faculty to movement. It has two subdivisions: one is called the faculty of desire which provokes a movement (of the organs) that brings one near to things imagined to be necessary or useful in the search for pleasure. The second is called the faculty of anger, which impels the subject to a movement of the limbs in order to repulse things imagined to be harmful or destructive, and thus to overcome them. As for the motive faculty in its active capacity, it is a power which is distributed through the nerves and muscles, and its function is to contract the muscles and to pull the tendons and ligaments towards the starting point

of the movement, or to relax them or stretch them so that they move away from the starting point.

The perceptive faculty can be divided into two parts, the external sense and the internal sense. The external senses are the five or eight senses. One of them is sight, which is a faculty located in the concave nerve; it perceives the image of the forms of colored bodies imprinted on the vitreous humor. These forms are transmitted through actually transparent media to polished surfaces. The second is the sense of hearing, which is a faculty located in the nerves distributed over the surface of the earhole; it perceives the form of what is transmitted to it by the vibration of the air which is compressed between two objects, one striking and the other being struck, the latter offering it resistance so as to set up vibrations in the air which produce the sound. This vibration of the air outside reaches the air which lies motionless and compressed in the cavity of the ear, moving it in a way similar to that in which it is itself moved. Its waves touch that nerve, and so it is heard.

The third sense is that of smell, a faculty located in the two protuberances of the front part of the brain which resemble the two nipples of the breasts. It perceives the odor conveyed to it by inhaled air, which is either mixed with the vapor in the air or is imprinted on it through qualitative change in the air produced by an odorous body.

The fourth sense is that of taste, a faculty located in the nerves distributed over the tongue, which perceives the taste dissolved from bodies touching it and mingling with the saliva it contains, thus producing a qualitative change in the tongue itself.

The fifth sense is that of touch, which is a faculty distributed over the entire skin and flesh of the body. The nerves perceive what touches them and are affected when it is opposed to them in quality, and changes are then wrought in their constitution or structure.

Probably this faculty is not one species but a genus including four faculties which are all distributed throughout the skin. The first of them judges the opposition between hot and cold; the second that between dry and moist; the third that between hard and soft; and the fourth that between rough and smooth. But their coexistence in the same organ gives the false impression that they are essentially one.

The forms of all the sensibles reach the organs of sense and are imprinted on them, and then the faculty of sensation perceives them. This is almost evident in touch, taste, smell, and hearing. But concerning sight, a different view has been maintained, for some people have thought that something issues from the eye, meets the object of sight, takes its form from without—and that this constitutes the act of seeing. They often call the thing which according to them issues from the eye, light.

But true philosophers hold the view that when an actually transparent body, that is, a body which has no color, intervenes between the eye and the object of sight, the exterior form of the colored body on which light is falling is transmitted to the pupil of the eye and so the eye perceives it.

This transmission is similar to the transmission of colors by means of light being refracted from a colored thing and giving its color to another body. The resemblance is not complete, however, for the former is more like an image in a mirror.

The absurdity of the view that light issues from the eye is shown by the following consideration. What emanates is either a body or a non-body. If it is not a body it is absurd to attribute motion and change of place to it, except figuratively in that there may be a power in the eye which transforms the air and other things it encounters into some sort of quality, so that it may be said that this quality "came out of the eye." Likewise, it is absurd to hold the view that it is a body, because if so then either:

1. it will remain intact, issuing from the eye and reaching to the sphere of the fixed stars. In this case there will have emerged from the eye, despite its smallness, a conical body of immense size, which will have compressed the air and repulsed all the heavenly bodies, or it will have traversed an empty space. Both these views are manifestly absurd, or

2. it will be dispersed, diffused and split up. In that case the percipient animal will of necessity fell something being detached from him and then dispersed and diffused: also, he will perceive the spots where that ray falls to the exclusion of the spots where it does not fall, so that he will only partially perceive the body, sensing some points here and there but missing the major part, or

3. this emanating body is united with the air and the heavens and becomes one with them, so that the uniform whole is like one organ of the animal. In this case, the uniform whole in its entirety will possess

sensation. This is a most peculiar change indeed! It follows necessarily that if many eyes cooperate, it will be more powerful. Thus, a man when in the company of others would have keener sight than when alone, for many people can effect a more powerful change than a single person. Again, this emanating body will necessarily be either simple or composite, and its composite nature will also be of a particular kind. Its motion then must be either voluntary or natural. But we know that this movement is not voluntary and by choice, although the opening and closing of the eyelids are voluntary. The only remaining alternative is that the movement is natural. But the simple natural movement will be only in one direction, not in many; and so the composite movement will also be, according to the dominant element, only in one direction, not in many. But it is not so with this movement according to those who support the theory of the "issuing body."

Again, if the sensed object is seen through the base of the conical emanating body which touches it, and not through the angle, it will necessarily follow that the shape and magnitude of the object perceived at a distance will also be perceptible as well as its color. This is because the percipient subject comes in contact with it and encompasses it. But if it is perceived through the angle, I mean the section between the vitrium and the hypothetical cone, then the remoter the object, the smaller will be the angle and also the common section, and consequently the form imprinted on it will also be smaller and will be so perceived. Sometimes the angle will be so small that the object will fail to be perceived and so the form will not be seen at all.

As for the second part, namely that the emanating something is not a body but an accident or a quality, this "changing" or "being changed" will inevitably be more powerful with the increase of the percipient subjects. In that case, the same absurdity which we mentioned before will arise. Again, the air will either be merely a medium of transmission or percipient in itself. If it is only a medium of transmission and not percipient, then, as we maintain, perception takes place in the pupil of the eye and not outside it. But if the percipient is the air, then the same absurdity which we have already mentioned will be repeated; and it will necessarily follow that whenever there is commotion or disturbance in the air, sight will be distorted with the renewal of "change" and the renewed action of the percipient in perceiving one thing after another, just as when a man runs in calm air his perception of minute things is confused. All this shows that sight is not due to something issuing from us towards the sensed object. It must, therefore, be due to something coming towards us from the sensed object; since this is not the body of the object, it must be its form. If this view were not correct, the creation of the eye with all its strata and humors and their respective shape and structure would be useless.

CHAPTER 4: THE RATIONAL SOUL

The human rational soul is also divisible into a practical and a theoretical faculty, both of which are equivocally called intelligence. The practical faculty is the principle of movement of the human body, which urges it to individual actions characterized by deliberation and in accordance with purposive considerations. This faculty has a certain correspondence with the animal faculties of appetite, imagination, and estimation, and a certain dual character in itself. Its relationship to the animal faculty of appetite is that certain states arise in it peculiar to man by which it is disposed to quick actions and passions such as shame, laughter, weeping, etc. Its relationship to the animal faculty of imagination and estimation is that it uses that faculty to deduce plans concerning transitory things and to deduce human arts. Finally, its own dual character is that with the help of the theoretical intelligence it forms the ordinary and commonly accepted opinions concerning actions, as, for instance, that lies and tyranny are evil and other similar premises which, in books of logic, have been clearly distinguished from the purely rational ones. This faculty must govern all the other faculties of the body in accordance with the laws of another faculty which we shall mention, so that it should not submit to them but that they should be subordinated to it, lest passive dispositions arising from the body and derived from material things should develop in it. These passive dispositions are called bad morals. But far from being passive and submissive this faculty must govern the other bodily faculties so that it may have excellent morals.

It is also possible to attribute morals to the bodily faculties. But if the latter predominate they are in an active state, while the practical intelligence is in a passive one. Thus, the same thing produces morals in both. But if the practical intelligence predominates, it is in an active state while the bodily faculties are in a passive one, and this is morals in the strict sense (even so there would be two dispositions or moral characters); or character is only one with two different relationships. If we examine them more closely the reason why morals are attributed to this faculty is that the human soul, as will be shown later, is a single substance which is related to two planes—the one higher and the other lower than itself. It has special faculties which establish the relationship between itself and each plane: the practical faculty which the human soul possesses in relation to the lower plane, which is the body, and its control and management; and the theoretical faculty in relation to the higher plane, from which it passively receives and acquires intelligibles. It is as if our soul has two faces: one turned towards the body and it must not be influenced by any requirements of the bodily nature; and the other turned towards the higher principles, and it must always be ready to receive from what is there in the Higher Plane and to be influenced by it. So much for the practical faculty.

CHAPTER 6: HOW THE RATIONAL SOUL ACQUIRES KNOWLEDGE

The acquisition of knowledge, whether from someone else or from within oneself, is of various degrees. Some people who acquire knowledge come very near to immediate perception, since their potential intellect which precedes the capacity we have mentioned is the most powerful. If a person can acquire knowledge from within himself, this strong capacity is called "intuition." It is so strong in certain people that they do not need great effort, or instruction and actualization, in order to make contact with the active intelligence. But the primary capacity of such a person for this is so powerful that he might also be said to possess the second capacity: indeed, it seems as though he knows everything from within himself. This is the highest degree of this capacity. In this state, the material intelligence must be called "Divine Spirit." It belongs to the genus of *intellectus in habitu*, but is so lofty that not all people share it. It is not unlikely, indeed, that some of these actions attributed to the "Divine Intelligence" because of their powerful and lofty nature overflow into the imagination which symbolizes them in sense imagery and words in the way which we have previously indicated.

What proves this is the evident fact that the intelligible truths are acquired only when the middle term of a syllogism is obtained. This may be done in two ways: sometimes through intuition, which is an act of mind by which the mind itself immediately perceives the middle term. This power of intuition is quickness of apprehension. But sometimes the middle term is acquired through instruction, although even the first principles of instruction are obtained through intuition, since all knowledge can be reduced ultimately to certain intuitive principles handed down by those who first accepted them to their students.

It is possible that a man may find the truth within himself, and that the syllogism may be effected in his mind without any teacher. This varies both quantitatively and qualitatively; quantitatively, because some people possess a greater number of middle terms which they have discovered themselves; and qualitatively, because some people find the term more quickly than others. Now since these differences are unlimited and always vary in degrees of intensity, and since their lowest point is reached in men who are wholly without intuition, so their highest point must be reached in people who possess intuition regarding all or most problems, or in people who have intuition in the shortest possible time. Thus, there might be a man whose soul has such an intense purity and is so firmly linked to the rational principles that he blazes with intuition, that is with the receptivity of inspiration coming from the active intelligence concerning everything. So the forms of all things contained in the active intelligence are imprinted on his soul either all at once or nearly so, not that he accepts them merely on authority but on account of their logical order which encompasses all the middle terms. For beliefs accepted on authority concerning those things which are known only through their causes possess no rational certainty. This is a kind of prophetic inspiration, indeed its highest form and the one most fitted to be called Divine Power; and it is the highest human faculty.

The Hierarchy of Faculties

It should be seen how some of these faculties govern others. You will find the acquired intellect to be the governor whom all the rest serve. It is the ultimate goal. The *intellectus in habitu* serves the *intellectus in actu,* and is in turn served by the material intellect with all its capacities. The practical intellect serves them all, for attachment to the body, as will shortly become clear, exists for the sake of the perfection and purification of the theoretical intellect, and the practical intellect governs this relationship. It is served by the faculty of estimation which, in its turn, is served by two faculties: an anterior and a posterior. The posterior conserves what is brought to it by estimation, while the anterior is the totality of animal faculties. The faculty of representation is served by two faculties of different origins: the appetitive faculty serves it by obeying it, for the representative faculty impels the appetitive to movement, and the faculty of imagination serves it by accepting the combination and separation of its images. In their turn, those two are the governors of two groups. The faculty of imagination is served by *fantasia* or *sensus communis,* which is itself served by the five senses, while the appetitive faculty is served by desire and anger. These last two are served by the motive faculty distributed through the muscles. Here the animal faculties come to an end.

The animal faculties in their entirely are served by the vegetable faculties, of which the reproductive is the first in rank and the highest one. The faculty of growth serves the reproductive, and the nutritive faculty serves them both. The four "natural" faculties—of digestion, retention, assimilation, and excretion—are subservient to all these. The digestive faculty is served on the one hand by the retentive and the assimilative, and on the other by the excretive. The four physical qualities serve these, with cold subservient to heat, while dryness and moisture serve them both. This is the last degree of the faculties.

CHAPTER 12: CONCERNING THE TEMPORAL ORIGIN OF THE SOUL

We say that human souls are of the same species and concept. If they existed before the body, they would either be multiple entities or one single entity. But it is impossible for them to be either the one or the other, as will be shown later, therefore, it is impossible for them to exist before the body. We now begin with the explanation of the impossibility of its numerical multiplicity and say that the mutual difference of the souls before bodies is either due to their quiddity and form; or to the element and matter which is multiple in space, a particular part of which each matter occupies; or to the various times peculiar to every soul when it becomes existent in its matter; or to the causes which divide their matter. But their difference is not due to their quiddity or form, since their form is one, therefore their difference is due to the recipient of the quiddity or to the body to which the quiddity is specifically related. Before its attachment to the body the soul is quiddity pure and simple; thus it is impossible for one soul to be numerically different from another, or for the quiddity to admit of essential differentiation. This holds absolutely true in all cases; for the multiplicity of the species of those things whose essences are pure concepts is only due to the substrata which receive them and to what is affected by them, or due only to their times. But when they are absolutely separate, that is when the categories we have enumerated are not applicable to them, they cannot be diverse. It is, therefore, impossible for them to have any kind of diversity or multiplicity among them. Thus, it is untrue that before they enter bodies souls have numerically different essences.

I say that it is also impossible for souls to have numerically one essence, for when two bodies come into existence two souls also come into existence in them. Then either:

1. these two souls are two parts of the same single soul, in which case one single thing which does not possess any magnitude and bulk would be potentially divisible. This is manifestly absurd according to the principles established in physics, or

2. a soul which is numerically one would be in two bodies. This also does not require much effort to refute.

It is thus proved that the soul comes into existence whenever a body does so fit to be used by it. The body which thus comes into being is the kingdom and instrument of the soul. In the very disposition of the substance of the soul which comes into existence together with a certain body—a body, that is to say, with the appropriate qualities to make it suitable to receive the soul which takes its origin from the first principles—there is a natural yearning to occupy itself with that body, to use it, control it, and

be attracted by it. This yearning binds the soul specially to this body, and turns it away from other bodies different from it in nature so that the soul does not contact them except through it. Thus, when the principle of its individualization, namely, its peculiar dispositions, occurs to it, it becomes an individual. These dispositions determine its attachment to that particular body and form the relationship of their mutual suitability, although this relationship and its condition may be obscure to us. The soul achieves its first entelechy through the body; its subsequent development, however, does not depend on the body but on its own nature.

But after their separation from their bodies the souls remain individual owing to the different matters in which they had been, and owing to the times of their birth and their different dispositions due to their bodies which necessarily differ because of their peculiar conditions.

CHAPTER 13: THE SOUL DOES NOT DIE WITH THE DEATH OF THE BODY: IT IS INCORRUPTIBLE

We say that the soul does not die with the death of the body and is absolutely incorruptible. As for the former proposition, this is because everything which is corrupted with the corruption of something else is in some way attached to it. And anything which in some way is attached to something else is either coexistent with it or posterior to it in existence or prior to it, this priority being essential and not temporal. If, then, the soul is so attached to the body that it is coexistent with it, and this is not accidental but pertains to its essence, then they are essentially interdependent. Then neither the soul nor the body would be a substance; but in fact they are substances. And if this is an accidental and not an essential attachment, then, with the corruption of the one term only the accidental relationship of the other term will be annulled, but its being will not be corrupted with its corruption. If the soul is so attached to the body that it is posterior to it in existence, then, in that case, the body will be the cause of the soul's existence. Now the causes are four; so either the body is the efficient cause of the soul and gives it existence, or it is its receptive and material cause—maybe by way of composition as the elements are for the body or by way of simplicity as bronze is for the statue—or the body is the soul's formal or final cause. But the body cannot be the soul's efficient cause, for body, as such, does not act; it acts only through its faculties. If it were to act through its essence, not through its faculties, every body would act in the same way. Again, the bodily faculties are all of them either accidents or material forms, and it is impossible that either accidents or forms subsisting in matter should produce the being of a self-subsisting entity independent of matter or that of an absolute substance. Nor is it possible that the body should be the receptive and material cause of the soul, for we have clearly shown and proved that the soul is in no way imprinted in the body. The body, then, is not "informed" with the form of the soul, either by way of simplicity or composition so that certain parts of the body are composed and mixed together in a certain way and then the soul is imprinted in them. It is also impossible that the body should be the formal or the final cause of the soul, for the reverse is the more plausible case.

Thus, the attachment of the soul to the body is not the attachment of an effect to a necessary cause. The truth is that the body and the temperament are an accidental cause of the soul, for when the matter of a body suitable to become the instrument of the soul and its proper subject comes into existence, the separate causes bring into being the individual soul, and that is how the soul originates from them. This is because it is impossible to bring arbitrarily into being different souls without any specific cause. Besides, the soul does not admit of numerical multiplicity, as we have shown. Again, whenever a new thing comes into being, it must be preceded by a matter which is prepared to receive it or to have a relationship with it, as has been shown in the other sciences. Again, if an individual soul were to come into being without an instrument through which it acts and attains perfection, its being would be purposeless: but there is nothing purposeless in nature. In truth, when the suitability and preparation for such a relationship exist in the instrument, it becomes necessary that such a thing as a soul should originate from the separate causes.

But if the existence of one thing necessitates the existence of another, the corruption of the former does not necessarily entail that of the latter. This happens only where its very being subsists through or in that thing. Many things originating from other things survive the latter's corruption; when their being does not subsist in them, and especially when they owe their existence to something other than what was merely preparatory for the emanation of their being. And the being of the soul does in fact emanate from something different from the body. Thus, when the soul owes its being to that other thing and only the time of its realization to the body, its being would be independent of the body which is only its accidental cause; it cannot then be said that they have a mutual relationship which would necessitate the body preceding the soul as its necessary cause.

Let us turn to the third division which we mentioned in the beginning, namely, that the attachment of the soul to the body might be in the sense that the soul is prior to the body in existence. Now in that case the priority will be either temporal as well as essential, and so the soul's being could not possibly be attached to the body since it precedes the body in time, or the priority will be only essential and not temporal, for in time the soul will not be separate from the body. This sort of priority means that when the prior entity comes into existence, the being of the posterior entity must follow from it. Then the prior entity cannot exist, if the posterior is supposed to be nonexistent. I do not say that the supposition of the nonexistence of the posterior necessitates the nonexistence of the prior, but that the posterior cannot be nonexistent except when first something has naturally happened to the prior which has made it nonexistent, too. Thus, it is not the supposition of the nonexistence of the posterior entity which necessitates the nonexistence of the prior, but the supposition of the nonexistence of the prior itself, for the posterior can be supposed to be nonexistent only after the prior itself has ceased to exist. This being so, it follows that the cause of nonexistence must occur in the substance of the soul necessitating the body's corruption along with it, and that the body cannot be corrupted through a cause special to itself. But in fact the corruption of the body does take place through a cause special to itself, namely, through changes in its composition and its temperament. Thus, it is false to hold that the soul is attached to the body as essentially prior to it, and that at the same time the body is indeed corrupted through a cause in itself: so no such relationship subsists between the two.

This being so, all the forms of attachment between the body and the soul have proved to be false and it only remains that the soul, in its being, has no relationship with the body but is related with other principles which are not subject to change or corruption.

As for the proposition that the soul does not admit of corruption at all, I say that there is another conclusive reason for the immortality of the soul. Everything which might be corrupted through some cause has in itself the potentiality of corruption and, before corruption, has the actuality of persistence. But it is absurd that a single thing in the same sense should possess both, the potentiality of corruption and the actuality of persistence: its potentiality of corruption cannot be due to its actual persistence, for the concept of potentiality is contrary to that of actuality. Also, the relation of this potentiality is opposed to the relation of this actuality, for the one is related with corruption, the other with persistence. These two concepts, then, are attributable to two different factors in the concrete thing. Hence, we say that the actuality of persistence and the potentiality of corruption may be combined in composite things and in such simple things as subsist in composite ones. But these two concepts cannot come together in simple things whose essence is separate. I say in another absolute sense that these two concepts cannot exist together in a simple thing whose essence is unitary. This is because everything which persists and has the potentiality of corruption also has the potentiality of persistence, since its persistence is not necessary. When it is not necessary, it is possible; and possibility is of the nature of potentiality. Thus, the potentiality of persistence is in its very substance. But, of course, it is clear that the actuality of persistence of a thing is not the same as its potentiality of persistence. Thus, its actuality of persistence is a fact which happens to the body which has the potentiality of persistence. Therefore, that potentiality does not belong to something actual but to something of which actual existence is only an accident and does not constitute its real essence. From this it necessarily follows that its being is composed of a factor the possession of which gives actual existence to it (this factor is the form in every concrete existent), and another factor which attains this actual existence but which in itself has only the potentiality of existence (and this factor is the matter in the concrete existent).

So if the soul is absolutely simple and is not divisible into matter and form, it will not admit of corruption. But if it is composite, let us leave the composite and consider only the substance which is its matter. We say either that matter will continue to be divisible and so the same analysis will go on being applied to it and we shall then have a regress *ad infinitum*, which is absurd; or this substance and base will never cease to exist. But if so, then our present discourse is devoted to this factor which is the base and origin and not to the composite thing which is composed of this factor and some other. So it is clear that everything which is simple and not composite, or which is the origin and base of the composite thing, cannot in itself possess both the actuality of persistence and the potentiality of corruption. If it has potentiality of corruption, it cannot possibly have the actuality of persistence, and if it has the actuality of persistence and existence, it cannot have the potentiality of corruption. Obviously, then, the substance of the soul does not have the potentiality of corruption. Of those things which come to be and are corrupted, the corruptible is only the concrete composite. The potentiality of corruption and of persistence at the same time does not belong to something which gives unity to the composite, but to the matter which potentially admits of both contraries. So the corruptible composite as such possesses neither the potentiality of persistence nor that of corruption, let alone both. As to the matter itself, it either has persistence not due to any potentiality, which gives it the capacity for persistence—as some people think—or it has persistence through a potentiality which gives it persistence, but does not have the potentiality of corruption; this latter being something which it acquires. The potentiality of corruption of simple entities which subsist in matter is due to matter and is not in their own substance. The argument which proves that everything which comes to exist passes away on account of the finitude of the potentialities of persistence and corruption is relevant only to those things whose being is composed of matter and form. Matter has the potentiality that this form may persist in it, and at the same time the potentiality that this form may cease to exist in it. It is then obvious that the soul is absolutely incorruptible. This is the point which we wanted to make, and this is what we wanted to prove.

STUDY QUESTIONS: AVICENNA, *CONCERNING THE SOUL*

1. How are the animal soul, the human soul, and the vegetable soul related?
2. What does Avicenna mean by "faculties?"
3. What are the different parts of the soul? How are they related?
4. How does Avicenna use Aristotle (whom he calls, "The Sage") to justify his argument regarding evil?
5. What does Avicenna mean by saying that it is possible to attribute morals to the bodily faculties? How are they related to the practical faculties?
6. What is an intuition? What is the role of intuition with regard to knowledge acquisition?
7. What is the difference between the motive and perceptive faculties of the animal soul? What is their relative importance?
8. How does Avicenna explain the relationship between the eye, light, and seeing?
9. Why is it impossible for two souls to have numerically one essence? How are Avicenna's arguments for this view similar to Aquinas? How are they different?
10. What is his argument that one soul cannot be simultaneously in two bodies?
11. Why is the soul immortal?
12. How are soul and body related?
13. Is the soul composite or indivisible? Why? What is the significance of this?

THE NATURE OF UNIVERSALS AND THE ESSENCES OF THINGS

In this selection Avicenna discusses the notion of universals that has puzzled philosophers since Plato and Aristotle started the debate. He shows that the term "universal" has three distinct senses: a term that is in fact predicated of many actual things, for example, "human being," a term that *may* be predicated of many things, regardless of whether they exist, or, "seven-sided house," and a term where nothing prevents its being predicated of many things, such as "sun." The latter example is particularly interesting, since during Avicenna's time it was thought there was but one sun—yet he seems to derive from purely logical analysis the possibility that there may be many suns! The term "intention" that Avicenna uses, variously translated from the Latin (in which this work was disseminated throughout European schools in the twelfth century) as "intention," "knowledge," and "meaning," refers to what is in the mind at the moment when it is contemplating any object or word and makes knowledge possible. The idea is that since the mind cannot attend to anything *immediately* it must achieve knowledge by *mediation*. Words, thoughts, ideas, and images thus function variously as intentions. The nineteenth-century philosopher Franz Brentano (1838–1907) has been called a neo-Scholastic in part because he revived the importance of the term *intention* that has influenced philosophers throughout the twentieth century. He too gives "three modes" of intentionality, reminiscent of Avicenna's innovative clarification of Aristotle's notions.

Avicenna, from "The Nature of Universals," translated by Martin Tweedale, from *Basic Issues in Medieval Philosophy*, ed. Richard N. Bosley and Martin Tweedale, Orchard Park, NY: Broadview Press, 1999, pp. 401–403.

I say, then, that 'universal' has three senses: (1) Something is called universal because it is actually predicated of many items, for example *human being*. (2) An intention is called universal when it is possible for it to be predicated of many, even if none of these items actually exist, for example, the intention of a seven-sided house. This is universal because its nature can be predicated of many; it is not necessary that those many items exist nor even some one of them. (3) An intention is called universal when nothing prevents its being thought to be predicated of many, because if something did prevent [its being predicated of many] it would prevent this by a cause by which this is proven. Sun and earth are examples, for so far as the idea of them is concerned the fact that sun and earth are thought does not prevent its being possible for their intention to be found in many. This is only prevented if we bring in an argument by which it may be known that this is impossible. And then this will be impossible because of an extrinsic cause, not because of the imagination of them.

All of these senses agree in this much: what is universal is something which in thought it is not impossible to predicate of many. The logical universal and whatever is similar to it must have this feature. Thus, a universal, just from being a universal, is something, and from being something to which universality happens to belong it is something else. Thus, one of the aforesaid terms is signified by 'universal' just because it has been made a universal, for, since it is *human being* or *horse*, the intention here, which is humanity or horseness will be something else outside the intention of universality.

For the definition of horseness is outside the definition of universality, and universality is not contained in the definition of horseness. Horseness has a definition which does not require universality; rather universality happens to belong to it. Consequently, horseness itself is just mere horseness. In itself it is neither many nor one, existent neither in sensibles nor in the soul, neither potential nor actual in such a way that this is contained within the essence of horseness; rather from the fact that it is mere horseness.

Animal can be considered on its own even though it exists with something other than itself, for its essence is with something other than itself. There-

fore, its essence belongs to it on its own. Its existing with something other than itself is something which happens to it or something which goes along with its nature, for example *this* animality and humanity. Therefore, this consideration precedes in being both the animal which is individual on account of its accidents, and the universal which is in these sensible items and is intelligible, just as the non-composite precedes the composite and as the part the whole. For from this being it is neither a genus nor a species nor an individual, nor one nor many; rather from this being it is merely *animal* and merely *human being*.

But doubtless being one or many goes along with this, since it is impossible for something to exist but not be one or the other of these, although they go along with it extrinsically.

Thus, just as *animal* in existing has many modes, so also in the intellect. In the intellect it is the abstracted form of *animal* in virtue of the abstraction we have talked of earlier, and in this mode it is said to be an intelligible form. And in the intellect the form of *animal* exists in such a way that in the intellect by one and the same definition it agrees with many particulars. On account of this, one form in the intellect will be related to a multiplicity, and in this respect it is universal. [It is a universal] because it is a single intention in the intellect whose comparison does not change no matter which animal you take, that is when you first represent the form of any of these in your imagination, if later the intellect strips away the accidents from its intention, you will acquire in the intellect this very form. Therefore, this form is what you acquire by stripping away from animality any individual imagination taken from its external existence, even though it does not have external existence, rather the imagination abstracts it. . . . Thus common things in a way have existence outside and in a way do not. But that a thing one and the same in number is predicated of many, that is predicated of this individual in such a way that this individual is it, and likewise this [other] individual, is obviously impossible.

THE ESSENCES OF THINGS (FROM AVICENNA'S LOGIC)

[An essence has two modes of existence, in the mind and in material singulars, also is just simply what it is apart from modes of existence. Avicenna, in effect, tries to have Plato's Forms without attributing a special eternal existence to them.]

The essences of things either are in the things themselves or are in the intellect. Thus, they have three relationships: one relationship of an essence exists in as much as the essence is not related to some third existence nor to what follows on it in virtue of its being such. Another is in virtue of its existing in these singulars. And another is in virtue of its existing in the intellect. And then there follow on it accidents which are distinctive of this sort of existence. For example, supposition [i.e. standing for things], predication, universality and particularity in predicating, essentiality and accidentality in predicating, and others which you will get to know later. But in the items which are outside there is no essentiality or accidentality at all; neither is there some complex or non-complex item, neither proposition not argument, nor anything else like these.

Let us take an example of a genus: *animal* is in itself something. And it is the same whether it is sensible or is apprehended in the soul by thought. But in itself it is neither universal nor singular. For if it were universal in itself in such a way that animality from the fact that it is animality is universal, no animal could possibly be singular; rather every animal would be universal. But if *animal* from the fact that it is *animal* were singular, it would be impossible for there to be more than one singular, viz. the very singular to which animality is bound, and it would be impossible for another singular to be an animal. . . .

Generality is called a logical genus, which means what is predicated of many items of different species in answer to the question 'What?' It does not express or designate something because it is *animal* or something else. Just as a white item is in itself something thought of, but that it is a human being or a stone is outside its idea but follows on that, and is thought to be one, so also the logical genus. But the natural genus is *animal* according as it is *animal*, which is suited to having the comparison of generality added to its idea. For when the idea is in the soul it becomes suited to having generality understood of it. Neither the idea of Socrates nor the idea of *human being* has this aptitude. . . .

But if some one of the species is a genus, it has this not from its generality which is above it, but from those items which are under it. But the natural genus attributes to that which is under it its name and definition from its own naturalness, that is from the fact, for example, that *animal* is *animal*, and not from the fact that it is a natural genus, that is something which once it has been thought of tends to become a genus from the fact that it is the way it is. For it is impossible that the latter [i.e. the genus] not have what is beneath the former [i.e. the species].

And generally when it is said that the natural genus gives to that which is under it its name and definition, this is not really true except by accident. For it does not give this from the fact that is a natural genus, just as also it did not give it its being a logical genus, since it gave it only a nature which is apt to be a natural genus. This nature by itself is not a natural genus just as it is not a logical genus.

But if a natural genus means only the primary nature on its own which is suited to generality, and natural genus is not understood as we understand it, then it is correct to say that a natural genus attributes its name and definition to that which is under it. And then *animal* is really a natural genus only because it is mere *animal*.

An individual does not become an individual until outside properties, either shared or unshared, are joined to the nature of the species and this or that particular matter is designated for it. However, it is impossible for properties apprehended by thought to be added to the species, no matter how many they are, because in the end they will not succeed in showing the individuating intention on account of which an individual is created in the intellect. For if you say that Plato is tall, a beautiful writer, and so on, no matter how many properties you add still they will not describe in the intellect the individuality of Plato. For it is possible that the intention which is composed from all of them is possessed by more than one item and shows you only that he exists, and is a pointing to the individual intention. For example, if we said that he is the son of this person and at a given time is a tall philosopher, [and] it happened at that time that no one else had those properties, and you happened to know this appearance, then you would know his individuality just as you would know that which is sensible if it were pointed out to you with a finger. For example, if Plato were pointed to at the third hour. For then his individuality would be determined for you, and this would be a case of pointing out his individuality to you. . . .

And the difference which there is between *human being* which is a species and *individual human being,* which latter is common not just in name but also by being predicated of many, is this: we say that the idea of *human being,* which is a species, is that it is *rational animal.* And what we say of *individual human being* is that that nature taken together with an accident which happens to belong to it is joined to some designated matter. It is just as though we said 'a certain human being,' that is 'some rational animal.' Thus, *rational animal* is more common than that, for sometimes it is in the species, sometimes in the individual, that is, in this one named item. For the species is *rational animal* just as the individual rational animal is rational animal.

STUDY QUESTIONS, AVICENNA, *UNIVERSALS*

1. What are the three senses of the term "universal?" How are they related? What do they have in common?
2. Is the definition of horseness inside or outside the definition of universality? Why?
3. Does the term "animal" have one or many modes?
4. Is the term "animal" something in and of itself? Why?
5. What is the difference between the species "human being" and an individual human being?

METAPHYSICS

Avicenna's *Metaphysics* forms the fourth part of his collected works: Logic, Physics, Mathematics, and Metaphysics. It was the translation of these works into Latin by Dominicus Gundissalinus (Gondisalvi) that led to the revival of Aristotle in the late twelfth and early thirteenth century. Here Avicenna provides an original upgrade of Aristotle's thesis of the necessary relation between essence and cause. What makes any particular thing exist? What is the cause of its being? *That* it is versus *why* it is—these are two different questions, it would seem, and the latter is the more fundamental. However, there must be some *necessary* aspect of that thing that makes it exist, otherwise it would never come to exist because this would require an infinite regress of contingent existences, each one requiring its own cause. And the necessarily existing being that makes any and all existence possible, according to Avicenna, is God.

18. ANALYSIS OF THE CONDITION OF BEING AS BEING NECESSARY AND BEING CONTINGENT

The being of that entity which has being, is either necessary in itself due to its own nature, or it is not necessary. The being of that which is not necessary in itself is either an impossibility or a contingency. Whatever is impossible in itself can never be realized as we indicated previously.

Consequently, it must be contingent due to itself and necessary due to the condition that its cause exists, whereas it is an impossibility due to the condition that its cause does not exist. One factor is its being, and another distinct factor is the condition of the existence or the nonexistence of a cause. When one considers its being-qua-being without any other conditions, it is neither a necessity nor an impossibility. When one considers that determined cause which is the condition for realizing its cause, it becomes a necessity, whereas it becomes an impossibility if one considers as its cause the condition of the nonrealization of its cause. Hence, if one considers number without regard to any conditions which are usually associated with it, its nature cannot be an impossibility, for as such it would never exist. But, if one regards the state of the number four which results from two times two, the result must be a necessity, for its non-realization as four is an impossibility. Hence, any existing entity, for which existence is not intrinsically necessary is contingent in itself. Therefore, this entity is a contingent being in itself and a non-contingent being with regard to something else. Its existence is not yet realized in such a manner that it must exist due to that reason. Since becoming an existent is a contingency, and since a contingency in itself is never realized because it has not come from a cause, it is necessary, therefore, that the contingency be realized by means of a cause so that it may become necessary to that cause as an existent. And that entity, or that existent, is of such a nature that its union with its cause is completed and that all its conditions are fulfilled when it becomes an existent. Furthermore, a cause becomes a cause due to its acting. Hence, a cause becomes a cause due to action when it must be active so that an effect may necessarily result from it.

19. FINDING THAT THE NECESSARY EXISTENT IS NOT ESSENTIALLY UNITED WITH ANYTHING

In Itself, the Necessary Existent cannot be united with any cause. Since its being is necessary in Itself without being caused, Its being cannot be due to a cause. Thus, It is not united with any cause. If Its being were not necessary without a cause, It would not be the Necessary Existent in Itself.

The necessary Existent cannot be united with something in a reciprocal union. If It were in a reciprocal relation with another entity, and if one were the cause of the other, each would then be prior to the other, and the being of each would henceforth be prior to that of the other. As its cause, therefore, the being of one would be posterior to that of the other. Consequently, its being would then be conditioned by another being which could be realized only posterior to its own realization. Therefore, its being could never be.

If two entities are not causes of each other, though one is necessarily related to the other, they are then simultaneous, being neither posterior nor prior to one another, as in the case of two (twin) brothers. The essence of each is either necessary in itself, or it is not necessary in itself. If one entity were

necessary in itself, the non-being of the other would not then constitute a harm to it. Thus, such a union between two necessary entities could not be possible. If the non-being of one entity would harm the existence of the other, it would not be necessary in itself, and, hence, it would be contingent in itself. Considered only by itself, the being of any contingent entity is not superior to its non-being. Consequently, its existence is caused by the existence of its cause, and its nonexistence is similarly due to the nonexistence of its cause. If it existed due to itself, then nothing but its intrinsic nature would be necessary for it to exist.

Therefore, there is a cause for the existence of any contingent being, and this cause is prior to it in essence. Accordingly, within the being of each one of the two entities (in the reciprocal relation) there must be a cause other than its companion to which it corresponds. One of the two cannot be prior to the other, for, like its companion, it is necessary on account of its cause, and unnecessary in itself without the cause. If one were a cause and the other an effect, essentially both would not be necessary.

From this reasoning we learn that the Necessary Existent does not have an element nor a part, because elements and parts are due to material causes as we have indicated.

For this reason, the Necessary Existent is not united with anything essentially.

20. FINDING THE NATURE OF CONTINGENT BEING

The existence of that which is contingent in itself is necessitated and can be realized by something other than itself. The meaning of 'the existence of something is realized due to the existence of another thing' can have two senses. Either something can bring something else into existence, as someone who builds a house, or the existence of something can be realized through another thing, as when the being of the patient (i.e., the thing made) subsists because of the being of the agent as the illumination from the sun subsists in the earth.

There is a general belief on the part of the people that a maker of something is he who actualizes the being of a thing which, once it is realized, will no longer depend on him. But they are misled by an invalid argument and an improper example. The argument they offer is the following: the being of that which already has been actualized is no longer in need of a cause for its being, because that which has already been made does not need to be remade. The example they use is this: once a house has been made by someone, it is no longer dependent on its maker. But the mistake in this reasoning is due to this fact: no one claims that a thing made is thereafter still in need of a maker. We do assert, however, that what is made continues lo be in need of a supporter. As regards the analogy of the house, the mistake in the reasoning is apparent, for the builder of the house is not actually the cause of the house, though he is responsible for the movement of wood to the place of the house. This condition, (namely, the transport of clay and wood) terminates after the builder, or the maker, of the house has left. The actual cause realizing the form of a house is the super-imposition of the elements which constitute the house and their intrinsic nature which necessitates the persistence of the house having that form. Though by itself each element has a downward movement, when the elements are retained, they stand as upholders of the house. Thus, the cause actualizing the form of the house is a synthesis of these two causes. As long as a house exists, these two causes exist also. It is to be noted that in this reasoning no causality is attributed to the builder. He is to be regarded as a cause only inasmuch as he gathers the elements constituting the house and constructs them so that they support the another. And when the cause (i.e., the builder) has disappeared the cause of a house cannot continue to exist as a cause. Consequently, the builder constructing the clay is in reality not the builder of the house, but only its apparent maker, as we stated previously. Likewise, a father is in reality not the maker of the son, but rather, his apparent maker, for nothing has come from him but a movement which led to the issue of the sperm. For this reason, the act in which the sperm partakes of the form of man is due to other factors related to the sperm. The actualization of the form of humanity is due to an existent, as will be known from forthcoming discussions.

Though we have discussed two mistakes in popular arguments, our discussion is still incomplete, for we should also know why the causal relationship can-not be otherwise. Any patient has two properties and any agent also has two properties. The first one is that the being of the patient is due to the maker, and the second is that the patient cannot be prior to the agent. Henceforth, the union between the patient and the agent is either due to the existence of the maker, to his nonexistence, or to both. But, obviously, the union cannot be realized due both to existence and to nonexistence. It can result only from one or the other. If we were to suppose that the agent did not exist, then its effect could obviously not be united with anything. And were it not united with something due to the fact that it exists, then it would not be united for any other reason. For the very reason that it exists, the patient has no choice but to be united with something else and to depend on this entity in order to persist.

That existent which is due to non-existence is an entity which cannot have a cause. Its suggested cause cannot exist, for if it existed, it would not be nonexistence. It is certainly possible for the patient not to exist, but the existence of that which is not posterior to nonexistence cannot exist. Thus, from that aspect that it is a being, the patient depends on the maker because its existence is due to this maker. However, from another aspect, that its existence is posterior to its nonexistence, it is not in need of a maker, for from this point of view it is necessary in itself. An entity that is dependent in respect to being cannot be independent since it is united with a cause. Other correct arguments can be upheld for this subject, but this discussion is sufficient.

As regards the maker (the agent), however, functioning as a cause is not due to its own making if we consider as an agent that entity from which something originates that did not exist previously. Being a cause is due to the fact that something is realized from it. The patient did not exist before because the agent was previously not a cause.

We have, then, asserted the existence of two conditions. The first is that the agent is not the cause of the existence of a thing, and the second is that it functions as a cause at a given time. The first condition is its non-causality rather than its causality, whereas the second condition is its causality. For example, someone can will the existence of an entity in order that it may be realized from the other entities whose existence depend on his will. Since there is a will as well as a capability on the part of the agent, that entity is actualized. When it is actualized, it is true that that entity is an existent whose causality is due to the realization of that which was willed. When the will is realized and that which is willed is realized posterior to its 'nonexistence', then the former has no influence on the latter because the object willed must be as it is. Consequently, the realization of something into an existent is due to the fact that its agent becomes a cause, and that its being is due to its causation. But one should note that being a cause is one thing, whereas becoming a cause is another thing. Likewise, that being is one state, whereas becoming an existent is a different state. Being a cause corresponds, therefore, to being, but not to becoming an existent.

If one means by an agent that by means of which something becomes an existent (due to itself), rather than that by means of which something that already is continues to exist, then being an agent is not being a cause but becoming a cause. Let us suppose, however, and this we regard as a correct interpretation, that being an agent meant one thing, and that becoming an agent meant something else. Hence, there will be no relation between the state of being an agent and the condition of becoming an existent, posterior to the nonexistence of the agent. Agentness would then have to correspond to being an existent because something existed due to another cause from which it was separated either permanently or only temporarily after becoming an existent. Although the patient would actually be different from the agent, 'being a cause' is commonly regarded as becoming an agent. Although people generally fail to distinguish between being an agent and becoming one, they believe, nonetheless, that being an agent cannot be separated from becoming an agent. From the context of this discussion it becomes evident, therefore, that the essence of an effect is not an actuality (i.e., its essence alone does not imply its existence) unless the cause exists. If the effect should persist, though that which is regarded as a cause would not exist, then that cause would have to be the cause for something other than the existence of that effect. It has also become evident that the agent is in reality that from which the being of the patient is realized separately from the essence of the agent,

for if the patient were a part of the agent's essence, then the latter would be a receptacle rather than a maker.

21. FINDING THAT THERE CANNOT BE A MULTIPLICITY IN THE NECESSARY EXISTENT

The Necessary Existent cannot contain a multiplicity as though it were composed of many elements, as a man's body consists of many parts. The Necessary Existent cannot have different kinds of parts, each standing by itself and forming a unit, such as wood and clay in a house. Nor can such parts be separate in idea but not in essence in the manner matter and form are 'separate' in natural bodies. Hence, the possibilities mentioned here are ruled out, for if any of them were accurate, then the Necessary Existent would have to be united with the causes as we explained before. Different properties cannot be contained in the Necessary Existent, for if Its essence were realized with such properties, they would be together as parts. If Its essence were realized and the properties were accidental, then they would subsist in the Necessary Existent for their essence due to another cause. Consequently, the Necessary Existent would be a receptacle. But from what we have asserted it has become evident that the Necessary Existent is not the receptacle in essence. It cannot, moreover, be the case that these attributes are due to the Necessary Existent Itself, for It would then be a receptacle. From one idea no more than one thing can be realized, for we have proved that whatever comes from a cause is not realized until it becomes necessary. Consequently, when one entity becomes a necessity from a single idea and another entity also becomes a necessity from the same idea, then something must become a necessity due to something else because of the nature of the former due to which something becomes a necessity. It becomes a necessity due to two reasons. One of these originates, for example, from this nature and this will, whereas the other comes from that nature and that will. Another duality is then placed into this context. Discourse would then be directed at this duality and the argument would start anew. Hence, there is no multiplicity in the Necessary Existent.

22. FINDING THAT THE CHARACTERISTIC 'NECESSARY EXISTENT' CANNOT BE APPLIED TO MORE THAN ONE ENTITY

We have found that if two entities were called 'Necessary Existent,' then without a doubt there would be a differentia or a distinguishing mark for each. We have also found that both the differentia and the distinguishing mark do not occur in the essence (reality) of that which is universal. Hence, the Necessary Existent is a Necessary Existent without that differentia and that distinguishing mark. If we imagine only the nonexistence of that differentia and that distinguishing mark, one of these two cases would follow. Either each would be like the Necessary Existent or each would not be like It. If they were like the Necessary Existent, they would be two different things without, however, the distinctions of differentia and distinguishing mark, which is impossible. If they were not like It, then having a differentia and a distinguishing mark would be an essential condition for the necessary existence of the Necessary Existent, and this condition would have to be the essence of the Necessary Existent. Thus, differentia and distinguishing mark would come under the common idea of essence, which is absurd. Indeed, if existence were other than essence, then this could be a legitimate alternative. But, for the Necessary Existent, existence is either due to essence or it is essence. Consequently, the Necessary Existent cannot be a duality in essence, in differentia, or in the distinguishing mark. For this reason, the 'Necessary Existent' cannot be a characteristic that is applied to two things. Yet we have found that a cause is contained in the elements of any universal idea. For this reason, the Necessary Existent is not universal. If It were a universal, It would be an effect, and would not, therefore, be different from being a contingent being, which is impossible according to our demonstration.

23. FINDING THAT THE NECESSARY EXISTENT IS NOT RECEPTIVE TO CHANGE AND THAT IT NECESSARILY PERSISTS IN EVERY MODE

Whatever is receptive to change is also receptive to a cause. It is in a given condition due to one cause, and in another condition due to another cause. Its being is not devoid of the property of 'being in union with these causes.' Thus, its being depends on 'being in union with' the object with which it is united. We have established, however, that the Necessary Existent is not in union (with any other entity). Consequently, the Necessary Existent is not receptive to change?

24. FINDING THAT THE ESSENCE OF THE NECESSARY EXISTENT CAN BE NO OTHER THAN EXISTENCE

That whose essence is other than existence is not the Necessary Existent. It has become evident that existence has an accidental meaning for that whose essence is other than existence. And it has also become evident that there is a cause for that which has an accidental idea (i.e., for that which has a contingent being). The cause of such a being is either the essence of that entity in which it subsists or something else.

The Necessary Existent cannot have an essence as the cause of Its existence for the following reasons. If such an essence should have being so that the existence of the Necessary Existent could be derived from it, or that this being were the cause of Its existence, then the being of the essence would have to be realized prior to itself. Since the second hypothesis could not be the reason for Its being, an inquiry into the first explanation would be legitimate. On the other hand, if the essence had no being, it could not be the cause of anything. For whatever does not exist is not the cause of the existence of anything. Thus, the essence of the Necessary Existent is not the cause of its existence. Its cause is, therefore, something else. Henceforth, there must be a cause for the existence of the Necessary Existent. The Necessary Existent must exist, therefore, due to something else. This, however, is impossible.

25. FINDING THAT THE NECESSARY EXISTENT IS NEITHER A SUBSTANCE NOR AN ACCIDENT

A substance is that whose essence does not exist in a subject when the substance exists. Furthermore, it is that which can be realized only in a subject matter. From this point of view, there is no doubt that a body is a substance, though one can doubt the actual existence of that body which is a substance until one knows whether or not it is in a subject. Hence, substance is that which has an essence, such as materiality, spirituality, humanity, and horseness. The condition of such an essence specifies that one does not know whether or not it has existence until its existence is realized in a subject. Whatever is of such a nature possesses an essence other than existence. Consequently, whatever has no essence other than existence is not a substance. And with regard to accidentality it is obvious that the Necessary Existent does not subsist in anything. Since the existence of the Necessary Existent is not related by way of correspondence or generically to the existence of other things, this essence is neither in the subject (due to the subject), as it is for humanity and what is other than humanity, nor is the idea of genus applied to it, since existence is applied to what is posterior and prior, having neither opposite nor genus. And whatever is not in a subject has neither posteriority nor priority. Accordingly, an existent which does not subsist in a subject cannot be a genus of things other than in the sense described previously, whereas substance is the genus of those things which are substances. The Necessary Existent is, therefore, not a substance. In brief, It is not in any category because existence is external to essence for each category, and hence it would only be an accidental addition to the essence of the Necessary Existent if the Necessary Existent belonged to a category. Existence, however, is the essence of the Necessary Existent. From our discussion it becomes evident that there is no genus for the Necessary Existent. Consequently, It does not have a differentia and, thus, It does not have a definition. Since it has neither a place nor a subject, it has no opposite and no species. It has neither companion nor resemblance. Finally, it has become evident that It does not have a cause. Hence, It is not receptive to change or to divisibility.

26. ANALYSIS OF THE POSSIBILITY THAT THE NECESSARY EXISTENT MAY HAVE MULTIPLE CHARACTERISTICS WITHOUT HAVING MULTIPLICITY IN ITS ESSENCE

There are four kinds of characteristics for things. One is that which is attributed to a body. It is an accidental characteristic which subsists in a substance although it is not united with another thing external to it. Another is that which is said of the color white. It is an accidental characteristic subsisting in a substance, although it is not united with another thing external to it. The third is that characteristic by which we describe the 'knower.' It is characteristic for a substance such as man, such that the aspect it contains is something external to the accidentality which brings about a union between that thing and other things. For example, there is a union between the knower and the known in which the form of knowledge is applied to the former. There is also the union between knowledge and things that are known. The fourth characteristic may be asserted of a 'father' and of 'being complete.' For the father has no characteristic as 'father-qua-father' other than being united with a child. Due to the existence of the child he is considered a father and is therefore made complete.

In addition to these four cases, there are characteristics for things which actually lack a characteristic. Such is true of inertness when it is applied to a rock. The assertion that inertness subsists in a rock is meaningless, except for its implication that living is impossible for that to which 'inertness' applies. Thus, there cannot be multiple characteristics for the Necessary Existent, whether they are essential or accidental. The case for the accidental characteristic which subsists in an essence is self-evident. Let us consider, for instance, the characteristic of union of these characteristics; the Necessary Existent has no alternative but to exist with many things just as all things must exist due to it. While these characteristics refer to positive features of the Necessary Existent, there are many other characteristics describing the Necessary Existent in terms of what it lacks. For example, the characteristic of unity is attributed to the Necessary Existent, whereas this characteristic actually means that It has no companion. In another case it is said that It contains neither constituent nor part. There is also mention of 'being eternal' which in reality means that its being has no beginning. Both of these characteristics are such that they do not imply multiplicity to the essence of the Necessary Existent. These characteristics refer essentially to nothing but (1) union, where 'union' is an idea in the intelligence rather than in the essence, or (2) negation and denial. In so doing they do not imply the existence of many characteristics, but rather an omission of many characteristics. Yet the term 'characteristic' induces the imagination to believe that there is a characteristic which subsists in essence. For example the characteristic 'a rich man' can be attributed to someone. This descriptive name is due to the existence of something else with which the person is united, but it is not a characteristic which refers to the essence of the person. The label a 'poor man' is applied to someone on account of the nonexistence of a thing, rather than on account of a characteristic which refers to his essence. Enough has been said on this topic.

27. FINDING THAT THE NECESSARY EXISTENT IS A UNITY IN REALITY AND THAT THE EXISTENCE OF ALL THINGS IS DUE TO IT

As we have stated, the Necessary Existent is in fact a unity, and all other things are non-necessary beings. Thus, they are contingent beings. All have a cause, and causes are infinite series. Accordingly, they either attempt to return to a primary cause, the Necessary Existent, or they return to themselves (i.e., the chain of causation is circular). For example, if A is the cause of B, B the cause of J, and J the cause of D, then D will be the cause of A. Taken together, therefore, this group will be a group of effects. Hence, it has become evident that there must be an external cause for them. The absurdity of the argument for the circularity of causes is also apparent in another proof. If D were the cause of A, then the effect of the effect of A, and the effect of the effect of the effect of A would be the effect of A. For the one thing, another thing would have to act both as cause and effect, which is impossible. Therefore, each effect must return to the Necessary Existent which is unique. Consequently, all effects and contingencies return to the one Necessary Existent.

28. FINDING THAT THE NECESSARY EXISTENT IS ETERNAL AND THAT ALL OTHER THINGS ARE TRANSITORY

In brief, the being of bodies (i.e., substances), accidents, and the categories is evident in this sensible world. And for all entities in this realm which belong to the ten categories, essence is different from existence. We have asserted that they are all contingent beings. And accident subsists in substances which are receptive to change. Matter and form, the components of bodies, are also constituents of the body. By its own nature, matter is incapable of action. The same holds true for form. We have also made the assertion that any entity having this nature is a contingent being which exists due to a cause, rather than due to its own nature. Being dependent means that the contingent being exists due to something other than itself. We have likewise asserted that the causes culminate in a Necessary Existent and that the Necessary Existent is one. It has become evident, therefore, that there is a primary entity in the world which is not in the world though the being of the world comes from It. Its existence, which is necessary, is due to Itself. In reality It is absolute being and absolute existence. All things exist due to It in the same manner as the light of the sun is due to itself, whereas the illumination all other things receive from the sun is accidental. This analogy would have been correct if the sun were the basis of its own illumination. This is not the case, however, because the illumination of the sun has a subject whereas the being of the Necessary Existent has no subject but stands by Itself.

STUDY QUESTIONS: AVICENNA, METAPHYSICS

1. How does Avicenna distinguish necessary being from contingent being?
2. What is a *cause*?
3. Why is the Necessary Existent not a *many* but a *one*?
4. What is God?
5. What is existence?
6. Is the Necessary Existent eternal? Why?

Philosophical Bridges: Avicenna's Influence

The revival of classical Greek philosophy in Persia (Iran) and throughout the Islamic world throughout the Middle Ages is in large part the result of Avicenna. His studies of Plato and Aristotle opened the door, not just in the Islamic world, but inspired philosophers throughout Europe, to understand the roots of the great ancient philosophical traditions and to take up the perennial questions anew. His interpretation of the logical and ontological forms of universals, particularly regarding their division into *ante res, in rebus,* and *post res* (in the mind of God, in individual things, and in human minds, respectively) became the philosophical standard throughout Europe and the Arabic world.

Avicenna's pioneering analysis of intention and intentionality was revived in the late nineteenth and early part of the twentieth century by the neo-Scholastic philosopher Franz Brentano, whose three modes of intentionality follows Avicenna's insights into Aristotle's original notions. It has been par for the course among contemporary philosophers ever since, especially in the philosophy of mind and philosophy of language, both in the phenomenological and analytic traditions.

Al-Ghazali (1058–1111)

A Biographical History

Al-Ghazali (Abu Hamid Muhammad ibn Muhammad Ghazali) was born in Tus, in what was then Chorasan, and is now Iran. He lived for several years in Syria and then taught in Baghdad, where he was appointed rector of the university in Nizamiya. His early works, commentaries on Al Farabi and Avicenna, focused on pointing out the various contradictions between the various philosophers and schools. He developed this into a scathing criticism of philosophy, his famous *Destructio Philosophorum.* As a teacher of Islamic law he defended the Sunni Muslim theologians against the philosophers in Baghdad. He spent the rest of his life as a Sufi mystic and building on the foundations of the great Sunni Muslim tradition.

Philosophical Overview

Al-Ghazali developed an eclectic, systematic philosophy as a middle road between neo-Platonic mysticism and Aristotelianism. Although he viewed philosophy mainly as a path toward theology, he was skeptical of the possibility of empirical knowledge; like Plato and Augustine, he viewed rational insight as the path to knowledge. Though his rational insight is itself, as according to many mystics—both Muslim and Christian—inspired directly by God, an inner illumination. Ordinary logic and reasoning led to ignorance.

He did however apply the tools of philosophy and the works of the philosophers as preparation for a theological understanding that transcended the world of appearances by making it possible for us to know God. In his famous *Incoherence of the Philosophers (Tahafut al-Falasifah),* he argues that, taken as a whole, what all the philosophers are saying is utter nonsense in virtue of the fact that they blatantly contradict each other. All philosophers are in his view utter idiots, blind to the fact that each other's opposing views as it were cancel each other out. This is as much true of the ancient Greeks, he argues, as of his contemporaries; even Avicenna (Ibn Sina) is not spared his wrath.

In many ways, his attacks have much affinity to the skeptical arguments of the great modern French philosopher Descartes, as well as the "antinomies" of reason developed by the great German eighteenth-century philosopher Immanuel Kant. One can even find echoes of this aspect of al-Ghazali's thought in some recent philosophical geniuses such as the great twentieth-century Austrian philosopher Wittgenstein that philosophy is itself a sort of intellectual disease, the result of cognitive errors arising from a misunderstanding of the nature and function of language. One might even say that, whereas Wittgenstein concludes "whereof one cannot speak, thereof be silent," al-Ghazali might want to say something like, "whereof one cannot speak, thereof turn to prayer and God."

THE INCOHERENCE OF THE PHILOSOPHERS
al-Ghazali

In this famous attack on philosophers and their methods, al-Ghazali begins by asserting that the heretics have gotten most of their inspiration from the great Greek philosophers in the Socratic tradition, especially Plato and Aristotle. Part of the problem is that the followers have not understood what the philosophers were saying; another is that they exaggerate the claims of what is possible to achieve using their various methods, be they empirical or rational.

It is quite startling to read his criticism of the translations of Plato and Aristotle available in Arabic; he claims that they are not just bad or unclear but distorted, with all sorts of cloudy or misleading interpretations. Most of the works of Plato and Aristotle known to us today are themselves translations of the Arabic translations.

The heretics in our times have heard the awe-inspiring names of people like Socrates, Hippocrates, Plato, Aristotle, etc. They have been deceived by the exaggerations made by the followers of these philosophers—exaggerations to the effect that the ancient masters possessed extraordinary intellectual powers; that the principles they have discovered are unquestionable; that the mathematical, logical, physical and metaphysical sciences developed by them are the most profound, that their excellent intelligence justifies their bold attempts to discover the hidden things by deductive methods; and that with all the subtlety of their intelligence and the originality of their accomplishments they repudiated the authority of religious laws, denied the validity of the positive contents of historical religions, and believed that all such things are only sanctimonious lies and trivialities.

When such stuff was dinned into their ears, and struck a responsive chord in their hearts, the heretics in our times thought that it would be an honor to join the company of great thinkers for which the renunciation of their faith would prepare them. Emulation of the example of the learned held out to them the promise of an elevated status far above the general level of common men. They refused to be content with the religion followed by their ancestors. They flattered themselves with the idea that it would do them honor not to accept even truth uncritically, but they had actually begun to accept falsehood uncritically. They failed to see that a change from one kind of intellectual bondage to another is only a self-deception, a stupidity. What position in this world of God can be baser than that of one who thinks that it is honorable to renounce the truth which is accepted on authority, and then relapses into an acceptance of falsehood which is still a matter of blind faith, unaided by independent inquiry? Such a scandalous attitude is never taken by the unsophisticated masses of men, for they have an instinctive aversion to following the example of misguided genius. Surely, their simplicity

From al-Ghazālī, *Tahāfut al-Falāsifah (The Incoherence of the Philosophers)*, translated by Sabih Ahmad Kamali (Lahore, Pakistan: Pakistan Philosophical Congress. 1963), pp. 1–5. Reprinted by permission.

is nearer to salvation than sterile genius can be, for total blindness is less dangerous than oblique vision.

When I saw this vein of folly pulsating among these idiots, I decided to write this book in order to refute the ancient philosophers. It will expose the incoherence of their beliefs and the inconsistency of their metaphysical theories. It will bring to light the flimsiest and the obscurest elements of their thought which will provide some amusement for, and serve as a warning to, the intelligent men. (I mean those things which they contributed to beliefs and opinions, and by virtue of which they thought they could be distinguished from the common men.)

Moreover, this book will set forth the doctrines of the ancient philosophers as those doctrines really are. This will serve the purpose of making it clear to the hidebound atheists of our day that every piece of knowledge, whether ancient or modern, is really a corroboration of the faith in God and in the Last Day. The conflict between faith and knowledge is related only to the details added to these two fundamental principles, the two recurring themes in the teachings of all the prophets—that is, divinely ordained persons the truth of whose mission is evident from the miracles they performed. It was only a few persons having irresponsible views and perverted minds who denied these principles. But in serious discussions no importance can be attached to such persons; and no notice ought to be taken of them. And they must be branded with diabolical perversity and stupid contumacy, so that their example may be a deterrent to people who tend to think that a vainglorious conversion to unoriginal heresy would be an indication of intelligence and good sense. This book is going to demonstrate that the ancient philosophers, whose followers the atheists in our day claim to be, were really untainted with what is imputed to them. They never denied the validity of the religious laws. On the contrary, they did believe in God, and did have faith in His messengers; although in regard to the minor details, they sometimes faltered and went astray, and caused others to go astray, from the even path. We propose to show how they slipped into error and falsehood. But our examination will not obscure their solid achievements which lie beneath the repulsive facade of their thought. Let God be the sustainer and the helper in the investigations we have undertaken.

Now to begin the book, we proceed to the prefaces which will presage the general trend of the discussion in this book.

PREFACE ONE

Let it be known that it would be tedious to dwell at length upon the differences among the philosophers themselves. For prolixity is their manner, and their disputes are too many, and their opinions are scattered, and their ways are divergent and devious. Therefore, we will confine our attention to the inconsistencies which are found in the theories of the premier philosopher who is called *the* Philosopher, or the First Teacher, for he systematized their sciences, and reformulated them, eliminating all that was redundant in the philosophers' opinions, and retaining only that which was close to the basic principles and tendencies of philosophical thought. This is Aristotle, who refuted all his predecessors—including his own teacher, whom the philosophers call the divine Plato. Having refuted Plato, Aristotle excused himself by saying: "Plato is dear to us. And truth is dear, too. Nay, truth is dearer than Plato."

We have related this story in order to show that in their own view there is nothing fixed and constant in the philosophers' position. They base their judgments on conjecture and speculation, unaided by positive inquiry and unconfirmed by faith. They try to infer the truth of their metaphysical theories from the clarity of the arithmetical and logical sciences. And this method sometimes carries conviction with the weak-minded people. But if their metaphysical theories had been as cogent and definite as their arithmetical knowledge is, they would not have differed among themselves on metaphysical questions as they do not differ on the arithmetical.

As far as the translators of Aristotle's works into Arabic are concerned, our problem is even more difficult. For the translations themselves have been subjected to interpolation and changes, which have necessitated further commentaries and interpretations. As a result, the translations are as much in dispute among the philosophers as the original works are. However, the most faithful—as Aristotle's translators—and the most original—as his commentators—among the philosophising Muslims are al-Fārābī Abū Naṣr, and

Ibn Sīna [Avicenna]. Therefore, we will confine our attention to what these two have taken to be the authentic expression of the views of their misleaders. For what they discarded and refused to follow must undoubtedly have been utterly useless, and should not call for an elaborate refutation.

Therefore, let it be known that we propose to concentrate on the refutation of philosophical thought as it emerges from the writings of these two persons. For otherwise, the scattered character of the philosophical theories should have to be reflected in a proportionately loose arrangement of our subject matter.

STUDY QUESTIONS: AL-GHAZALI, *THE INCOHERENCE OF THE PHILOSOPHERS*

1. According to al-Ghazali, did Socrates, Plato, and Aristotle have extraordinary mental powers, as it is often suggested? Why?
2. Why can't deduction lead to the discovery of what is not immediately evident to the senses?
3. What does al-Ghazali he mean by "intellectual bondage?"
4. What are the two fundamental principles that all the teachings of the prophets have in common?
5. What does al-Ghazali think of Aristotle's disagreement with Plato?

THE BOOK OF HOPE AND FEAR

In this work al-Ghazali constructs a clever "middle path" between what he takes to be the sum and substance of all the ancient philosophies, namely, the doctrine of the mean, and the teachings of the Sunni Muslim tradition. On the one hand is the despair philosophy offers, and on the other hand is the self-deceit of the blind believer indoctrinated into bad faith; between them lies hope, the true path of salvation. One can thus see in his exposition certain elements in common with later existentialists such as Kierkegaard and Sartre.

HOPE (FROM *THE BOOK OF HOPE AND FEAR*)

In the name of God, the merciful, the compassionate. Praise be to God whose loving kindness and reward are hoped for, whose strategems and punishment are feared, who keeps alive the hearts of His saints with the breath of hope in Him, so that He may urge them on with the kindnesses of His benefits to alight in His courtyard and to swerve from His house of tribulation which is the abode of His enemies. And with the lashes of threatening and His harsh upbraiding He has driven the faces of those who shun His presence towards the house of His reward and preferment; and he has blocked them from thwarting His leaders and becoming the butt of His wrath and vengeance by leading the different types of His creatures with

chains of violence and coercion, and reins of compassion and graciousness, to His garden. And the blessing be on Muhammad, master of His prophets and the most elect of His caliphs, and on his family and companions and relations.

To proceed. Hope and fear are two wings by means of which those who are brought near fly to every commendable station, and two mounts on which every steep ascent of the paths of the next world is traversed. And nothing but the reins of hope will lead to the vicinity of the merciful and the joy of the gardens the person who is distant from hoping and heavy with burdens, who is encompassed with what the heart abhors and with toils of members and limbs. And nothing shall avert from the fire of Gehenna and the painful punishment the person who

al-Ghazali, from *The Book of Fear and Hope*, translated by W. McKane, Leiden: E. J. Brill 1965, pp. 1–25.

is encompassed with the blandishments of lusts and the marvels of pleasures except the scourges of threatening and the assaults of violence. Consequently there is nothing for it but an exposition of the essence and merits of them both, as well as the way of arriving at a junction between the two of them, in spite of their polarity and mutual antipathy.

And we join the mention of them in a single book which is comprised of two parts, the first part concerning hope, and the second part fear. As for the first part it is made up of an exposition of the essence of hope and an exposition of its merit; and an exposition of the therapy of hope and the way in which hope is induced by it.

Exposition of the Essence of Hope

Know that hope is among the sum of the stations of the pilgrims and the states of the seekers. And the description *station* is given only when it is permanent and endures, and *state* only when transitoriness is hinted at. Just as yellow is divided into permanent such as the yellow of gold; transitory such as the yellow of fear; and what comes between these two like the yellow of a sick person. Similarly the attributes of the heart follow these divisions and whatever is not permanent is called a state, because it soon changes, and this is continually happening in any description of the heart.

We are dealing at present with the essence of hope. Hope also comprises state, knowledge, and deed. Knowledge is the cause which produces the state and the state decrees the deed. Hope is the comprehensive name of the three. Its exposition is that everything that confronts you is either what is abhorred or what is desired, and is divided into what is existent at the moment, what has existed in the past, and what is expected in the future. When what has existed in the past occurs to your mind, it is called remembering and recollecting; if what occurs to your mind is existent at the moment, it is called finding and tasting and perceiving. It is called finding because it is a state which you find for yourself. And, if the existence of something in the future occurs to your mind and prevails over your heart, it is called expectation and anticipation. If the thing expected is abhorred, with pain in the heart resulting from it, it is called fear and distress. If it is something desired, with pleasure and relief of

heart resulting from the expectation of it and the attachment of the heart to it and the occurrence of its existence to your mind, that relief is hope.

Hence, hope is the relief of the heart, because of the expectation of what it esteems desirable. But the desirable thing which is anticipated must have a cause, so, if the expectation of it is on account of the obtaining of the majority of the means to it, the name of hope in relation to it is justified. If that expectation is in spite of the defectiveness of the means and their disorder, the name of self-deceit and stupidity is more justified in relation to the expectation than that of hope. If the means are not specified either as existent or in mutual contradiction, the name of wishful thinking is more justified in relation to the expectation of it, because it is an expectation which is devoid of a cause. And, in any circumstance, the name of hope and fear does not apply to what is determined. For one does not say: I hope for the rising of the sun at the time of sunrise, and I fear its setting at the time of sunset, because that is determined. But one does say: I hope that the rain will fall and I fear lest it should be cut off.

And the spiritual directors teach that this present world is the field of the next world, and the heart is as the earth, and faith is as the seed in it, and obedience is conducive to the turning over of the earth and the cleansing of it and the digging of channels and the leading of waters to them; and the heart which is infatuated with this present world and submerged in it is like swampy ground in which the seed does not fructify. And the Day of Resurrection is the day of reaping, and no one reaps except what he has sown, and only he who has sown the seed of faith grows crops. Rarely is faith profitable in company with a vicious heart whose moral traits are tainted just as seed does not fructify in swampy soil. And it is fitting that the hope of the creature for pardon should equal the hope of the owner of the crops.

For everyone who seeks good ground and casts into it seed of first quality which is neither moldy nor worm-eaten, who thereafter furnishes it with what is necessary to it, that is, the conducting of water to it appropriate times; who then clears the ground of thorns and weeds and everything that obstructs the growth of the seed or makes it rot; who then sits down and expects from the bounty of God the warding off of thunderbolts and blights, until his crop is mature and he arrives at his goal—his expectation is called hope. And, if he scatters his seed in ground which is baked hard or swampy, which is so elevated that the water does not flow into it, and does not labor one whit in the preparation of the seed—if he then expects a harvest from it, his expectation is called stupidity and self-deceit, not hope. And, if he scatters seed in ground which is good but without water, and proceeds to wait for the waters of the rains where they neither prevail nor are cut off, his expectation is called wishful thinking and not hope. Therefore, the name of hope is legitimate only in relation to the expectation of a thing desired, all of whose means, which come within the choice of the creature, have been facilitated, and only what does not come within his choice remains, and this is the bounty of God in repelling birds and blights.

So when the creature sows the seed of faith and irrigates it with the water of obedience and cleanses the heart from the thorns of vicious moral traits and expects from the bounty of God his being established in that course until death and the virtue of the seal that gives access to pardon, such expectation as his is hope in its essence, commendable in itself, and giving him an incentive for perseverance and endurance, in accordance with the means of faith, in perfecting the means of pardon until death. If its preparation with the water of obedience is cut off from the seed of faith, or, if the heart is remiss, filled with moral delinquencies, and obstinately persists in seeking the pleasures of this world, and then expects pardon, its expectation is stupidity and self-deceit. [Muhammad] said: "the fool is he whose soul follows its passions and who desires of God the garden." And [God] said: "then there came after them a succession who have wasted the prayer and followed their lusts; so they shall meet error." And He said: "and there came after them a succession who inherited the Book, who lay hold on the chance gain of this present world and say: It will be forgiven us." And God condemned the owner of the garden, when he entered his garden and said, "I do not think that this will ever perish, nor do I think the hour is coming; and, if I am indeed taken back to my Lord, I shall surely find a better sphere than this."

Therefore, the creature who strives after obedience and recoils from disobedience is right to expect from the bounty of God the completion of blessing and blessing achieves completion only by the enter-

ing into the garden. As for the disobedient person, when he has repented and repaired all that was remiss through shortcoming, it is proper that he should hope to receive repentance. With regard to the reception of repentance, when he has come to abhor disobedience, when sin grieves him and virtue delights him, when he blames himself and reproves [evil] and desires repentance and yearns after it, it is proper that he should hope from God the advancement towards repentance because of his repugnance for disobedience; and his zeal for repentance is conducive to the cause which may give access to repentance.

And hope is only present after the consolidating of the means and for that reason He said, "but those who have believed and emigrated and striven in the way of God have hope of the mercy of God." His meaning is that these have a right to hope for the mercy of God. He did not intend by it that the existence of hope is exclusive to them, since others also may hope, but he has made exclusive to them the right to hope. As for him who obstinately perseveres in what God abhors, and does not upbraid himself because of it, and does not resolve on repentance and return, his hope of pardon is stupidity, like the hope of the person who has sown seed in swampy ground and made up his mind not to cultivate it by leading water to it and cleansing it of weeds.

Since you are acquainted with the essence of hope and its marks you know that it is a state which knowledge has produced through the setting in motion of the majority of the means, and this state produces zeal to persevere in the remainder of the means in accordance with what is possible. For the man whose seed is fine and whose land is good and who has abundance of water is entitled to his hope, and his legitimate hope will continually urge him towards the oversight of the ground and the cultivation of it and the clearing of all the weeds which grow on it. Thus, he will not be remiss in any detail of its cultivation until the time of harvest. This is because hope sets him at the opposite pole from despair, and despair inhibits cultivation. For whoever "knows" that the ground is swampy and that the water will not flow and the seed will not grow, will, doubtless, as a consequence, neglect the oversight of the land and toil in its cultivation.

Hope is a commendable thing, because it is a source of incentive, and despair is reprehensible and is the antithesis of hope, because it distracts from work. Fear is not the antithesis of hope, rather it is a companion to it, as its exposition will bring out. More, it is another source of incentive, impelling along the path of awe just as hope impels along the path of inclination. Hence, the state of hope produces sustained spiritual combat through actions, and perseverance in obedience, however fickle circumstances may be. Among its effects are finding pleasure in unbroken acceptance with God, contentment in private prayer with Him and fondness for deferring to Him. For these states must be manifest to everyone who hopes, whether king or commoner, and so how will that not be manifest to God? If it is not manifest, that will be a pointer to preclusion from the station of hope and descent into the pit of self-delusion and wishful thinking. This then is the exposition of the state of hope and how knowledge produces it and how action is produced from it.

Exposition of the Merit of Hope and the Inclination Towards It

Know that action on account of hope is of a higher order than action on account of fear, because the creatures who are nearest to God are those who love Him most, and love dominates hope. This is expressed by two kings, one of whom is served through fear of his punishment and the other through hope of his reward. For this reason what is desiderated, especially at the time of death, has to do with hope and optimism. [God] said: "do not despair of the mercy of God." Thus He proscribed the root of despair. And [it is recorded] in the traditions about Jacob that God revealed to him saying: "do you know why I parted Joseph from you? It was because you said: 'I am afraid that the wolf will eat him, while you are neglectful of him.' Why did you fear the wolf and not hope in me? And why did you have regard to the negligence of his brothers and did not have regard to my preserving him?"

Exposition of the Therapy of Hope and the Way in which the State of Hope Is Obtained from It and Becomes Dominant

Know that two types of persons have need of this therapy; either the person over whom despair has become dominant, so that he has neglected worship;

or the person over whom fear has become dominant, and who has been extravagant in his perseverance in worship, so that he has done injury to himself and his family. And these two examples of persons incline away from the equilibrium towards the two extremes of neglect and excess, and so they have need of the treatment which will restore them to the equilibrium.

For the person who is disobedient and self-deceived, who has wishful thoughts of God in company with his evasion of worship and his blind plunging into deeds of disobedience—the therapeutic properties of hope are, in his case, turned into lethal poisons, just as is the case with honey which is a cure for the person who is overcome by cold and a lethal poison to the person who is overcome by heat. More, in the case of the self-deluded person, only the therapeutic properties of fear can be employed and the means which excite it, and, for that reason, it is necessary that there should be one to preach to the people; one benevolently disposed who observes the incidence of diseases and treats every disease with its antidote and not with what it has excess of. For what is sought after is the equilibrium, and the goal with respect to all attributes and moral traits, and the optimum state of affairs, is their mean. And, when the mean transgresses upon one of the two extremes, it is treated with what returns it to the mean, not with what would increase its tendency away from the mean.

And the present time is one in which it is not expedient that the means of hope should be employed with most people. Yet an exaggerated employment of threatening, no less, will hardly return them to the highway of truth and the beaten tracks of rectitude. As for the mention of the means of hope it would cause them to perish and would destroy them totally. But when [the means of hope] are less burdensome to the heart and more pleasurable to the appetites, the goal of preaching is no more than to sway hearts [to hope] and make people speak in eulogies, whatever be the reason for their inclining to hope, so that the corrupt increase in corruption and the stubborn in their rebellion through procrastination.

Ali said, "the knowledgeable person is simply he who does not make people despair of the mercy of God and does not make them feel secure from the stratagems of God."

And we make mention of the means of hope in order that they may be employed in the case of the despairing person or the one who has been overcome by fear, according to the pattern of the book of God and the practice of His messenger. For both embrace hope and fear in union, since these two unite the means of healing with respect to different kinds of sick people, in order that the knowledgeable, who are the heirs of the prophets, may employ one or the other of them according to need, just as the discriminating physician would employ them and not the quack who supposes that everything that has therapeutic value will be salutary to every sick person, whatever may be his condition.

The state of hope becomes dominant by means of two things; the one is reflection, and the other the reciting of the verses [of the Koran] and traditions and reports. With respect to reflection a person reflects on all that we have mentioned concerning the different kinds of benefits in *The Book of Gratitude*, until he knows the kindnesses of the blessings of God to His creatures in this world, and the marvels of His wisdom which He has disposed in the constitution of human beings, so that He has furnished for them in this world all that is necessary to them for the maintenance of existence. For example, the means of sustenance and what is needful to them, such as fingers and nails, and what is adornment to them, such as the arching of the eyebrows and the variegation of the colors of the eyes, and the redness of the lips, and other such things by the loss of which the goal aimed at would not be impaired. Only they would miss thereby the attainment of beauty. Since the divine providence has not left His creatures deficient in the instances of these minutiae, so that He was not content for His creatures that accessories and refinements in respect of adornment and necessity should pass them by, how will He take pleasure in driving them to everlasting destruction?

Moreover, when He ran over mankind with the eye of a physician, He knew that most people have at their disposal the means of happiness in this world, so that they dislike the translation from this world through death. Even if it were reported that there was never a single instance of a person being chastised after death or that there was no gathering [for judgment], their distaste would not be nonexistent, unless, doubtless, because the means of grace were predominant. The person who wishes for death is simply a rarity, and then he does not wish for it

except in a rare circumstance, and an unexpected and unfamiliar contingency.

Since the condition of most people in this world is one in which well-being and security prevail, the practice of God does not find a substitute for them. The probability is that the affair of the next world is likewise, for the framer of this world and the next is One, and He is forgiving, merciful and kind to His creatures, having compassion on them. So, when due reflection is given to this, the means of hope are strengthened thereby.

And also included in reflection is the scrutiny of the wisdom of the law and its practice in respect of this-worldly benefits, and the aspect of mercy to the creatures which is in it, so that one of the gnostics used to consider the verse on incurring a debt in the Sura al-Baqra as among the most powerful of the means of hope. So it was said to [the gnostic]. And what is there of hope in it? So he said: this present world in its entirety is small, and the provision for mankind from it is small, and religion is small separated from His provision. And perceive how God revealed concerning it the longest verse (Koran ii, 282), that He might guide His creature in the way of being encompassed in the keeping of his religion. And how will his religion not keep him who will not give anything in exchange for it?

The second kind is the reciting of the verses and the traditions, and the material which has to do with hope is beyond definition. With regard to the verses, He said, "say: O my creatures who have been profligate against yourselves, do not despair of the mercy of God; surely God pardons sins altogether; He is the forgiving, the compassionate." And according to the recitation of the messenger of God: then do not fret, surely He is the forgiving, the compassionate. And He said: "and the angels celebrate the praise of their Lord, and ask pardon for those upon the earth." And He has recorded that He has prepared the fire for his enemies and has simply frightened His friends with it. So He said to them, "above them are overshadowings from the fire and below them are overshadowings; by means of that God threatens His servants." And He said, "and fear the fire prepared for unbelievers." And He said, "and I have warned you of a blazing fire; only the most reprobate who has been perfidious and turned renegade will roast in it." He said, "surely your Lord is forgiving to the people in spite of their wrongdoing."

These are the means by which the relief of hope is induced in the hearts of the fearful and despairing. And, as for the foolish and self-deluded, it is not expedient that they should hear anything of that; no, they are to hear what we shall cite of the means of fear. For the most of people are not made healthy except through fear, just as the bad servant and the naughty boy are not reformed except through the whip and the stick and speech with an explicit threat. But the opposite of that would block up against them the door of health with respect to religion and this world.

FEAR (FROM *THE BOOK OF HOPE AND FEAR*)

The Second Part of the Book Concerning Fear

In [this part] is the exposition of the essence of fear, and an exposition of its degrees, and an exposition of the divisions of the objects of fear; and an exposition of the merit of fear, and an exposition of whether fear or hope is the optimum, and an exposition of the therapy of fear, and an exposition of the meaning of the evil of the seal; and an exposition of the states of those among the prophets and the sound in faith who feared. And let us ask God for good success.

The Exposition of the Essence of Fear

Know that fear is an expression for the suffering of the heart and its conflagration by means of the anticipation of what is abhorred as a future contingency. And this has been made clear in the exposition of the essence of hope. And whoever is intimate with God, whose heart is ruled by truth and who lives in the present through his seeing the majesty of truth perpetually, no longer turns to the future and is possessed of neither fear nor hope. More, his state has become higher than fear or hope, for both of these are reins which preclude the soul from its excursions into laxness. Al-Wasiti has pointed to this in saying: fear is a veil between God and the creature. Again he said, "when the truth makes plain the things which are secret, there remains in them no residue for hope and fear."

And, in general, if the heart of the lover is distracted by fear of separation, while he is viewing his beloved, that would indicate a deficiency of vision, and the goal of the stations is simply constancy of vision. But, for the present, we are to discuss only the initial stations and so we shall say: the state of fear can also be classified in terms of knowledge, state, and action. With regard to knowledge, it is knowledge of the cause which leads to the thing which is abhorred. So that it is as if someone committed a crime against a king, then fell into his hands and feared that he would be put to death as an example, while pardon and escape were possibilities. But the suffering of his heart through fear is in proportion to the strength of his knowledge of the means which would lead to his being put to death, such as the enormity of his crime and the fact that the king in himself is rancorous, wrathful and revengeful, that he is surrounded by such as incite him to take vengeance and is isolated from such as would intercede with him in his case. And this man in his fear was destitute of any merit or virtue that might wipe out the trace of his crime with the king. Hence, the knowledge that these means are manifest is a cause of the strength of the fear and the rigour of the suffering of the heart.

And fear is faint in proportion to the weakness of those means. And it may be that fear does not derive from the crime which the person who fears has committed, but is because of the nature of the object feared. As, for example, the person who falls into the claws of the lion, for he fears the lion because of the nature of the lion itself, namely, that, for the most part, it is avid and violent in pouncing on its prey. Even if its pouncing on its prey were within the province of choice, it might seem to the person threatened by it to be due to inborn disposition. Similarly, the person who falls into the path of a torrent or into a blazing pit, for he fears the water because it is endowed by nature with the power of flowing and drowning and likewise fire is endowed with burning. And the knowledge of the means of the thing which is abhorred is the cause which initiates and fans the conflagration and suffering of the heart, and that conflagration is fear. And, similarly, fear of God may sometimes be due to knowledge of God and His attributes, that, if He destroyed the worlds, He would not care and no person would obstruct Him. And sometimes it may be due to the multitude of the sins of the creature through his committing deeds of disobedience; and sometimes it may be due to both of them together. And the strength of his fear will be in proportion to his knowledge of his own defects and his knowledge of the majesty of God and His self-subsistence, and that He will not be asked about what He does, while they will be asked. And the person most filled with fear in respect of His Lord is the man who has most knowledge of himself and his Lord. For that reason Muhammad said: I am the one who fears God most among you. And, likewise, God said: "only the knowledgeable among his creatures fear God."

Then, when knowledge is perfected, the majesty of fear and the conflagration of the heart are produced. Then the trace of the conflagration flows from the heart into the body and the members and the attributes. In the body by means of emaciation and pallidness and fainting and shrieking and weeping, and it may be that in this way bitterness is inhaled and it leads to death; or it goes up to the brain and rots the intelligence: or it intensifies in strength and produces despair and hopelessness.

In the members by restraining them from disobedience and binding them to deeds of obedience by repairing what is defective and making ready for the future. And for that reason it is said: the man who fears is not he who weeps and wipes his eyes; no, it is he who forsakes that on whose account he fears punishment. And Abu I-Qasim al-Hakim said, "whoever fears anything flees from it, and whoever fears God flees to Him." And it was said to Dhu 'l-Nun, "when is the creature a person who fears?" He said, "when he has brought himself down to the level of the sick man who is abstemious for fear that his sickness may be prolonged."

In the attributes by stifling the lusts and blackening the pleasures, so that the disobediences beloved by him become abhorrent, just as honey becomes abhorrent to the man who desires it, when he knows that there is poison in it. So the lusts are burned up by fear and the members are trained, and self-abasement and humility and submissiveness and lowliness obtain in the heart, and pride, rancour, and envy abandon it.

Moreover, he is absorbed with concern through his fear and his observing the peril of its sequel, and has no leisure for other than it. And he has no preoccupation but vigilance and self-examination and spiritual combat and conserving breaths and glances and reprehending the soul for the suggestions and footsteps and words [of Satan]. And his condition is that of the man who falls into the claws of a harmful lion.

And he does not know whether it will ignore him and he will escape, or it will pounce on him and he will perish. So he will be engrossed outwardly and inwardly with what he fears and there will be no room in him for anything else. This is the state of the person over whom fear has prevailed and gained the mastery—the state of the company of the Companions and Followers was thus. And the strength of vigilance and self-examination and spiritual combat is in proportion to the strength of fear which is the suffering of the heart and its conflagration. And the strength of fear is in proportion to the strength of knowledge of the majesty of God and of His attributes and His actions, and in proportion to the defects of the soul and the perils and terrors which confront it.

And the least of the degrees of fear whose trace is visible in actions is the blocking of access to the forbidden; and the restraint which excludes the forbidden is called abstinence. If its strength increases, it restrains from what directs at it the possibility of the forbidden and hence also from that whose forbiddenness is not a matter of certainty, and that is called piety, since piety is the forsaking of that which one suspects so as to arrive at what one does not suspect. And it may urge a person on to forsake what has no evil in it for fear of what has evil in it, and this is sincere piety. When fully consecrated worship is joined to it, the consequence is that one does not build what he does not inhabit nor gather what he does not eat, nor turn to this world, since he knows that it will abandon him nor expend a single breath except towards God.

This is sincerity and its owner is worthy to be named sincere. And piety enters into sincerity and abstinence into piety and chastity into abstinence, for it (chastity) is a specialized expression for being cut off from the determinism of lusts. Therefore, fear is effective in the members through restraint and perseverance, and it is in virtue of restraint that it is given the new name of chastity which is refraining from the determinism of lusts. And abstinence is higher than it, since it is more universal, because it is refraining from everything forbidden. And higher than it is piety, since it is the name for refraining from the sum of things forbidden and dubious. And beyond it is the name sincere and He who is brought near. And the course of the most ultimate rank in relation to what precedes it is from the most general to the most particular, for, when you have mentioned the most particular, you have mentioned the whole. As if you were saying: mankind, whether Arab or non-Arab, and Arab, whether Quraysh or non-Quraysh, and Quraysh, whether Hashimi or non-Hashimi, and Hashimi, whether Alid or non-Alid, and Alid, whether Hasani or Husayni; and, when you have mentioned, for example, that a man is Hasani, you have described him totally, and, if you describe him as Alid, you describe him by what is above him—what is more general than he. Similarly when I have said *sincere*, I have said that a man is pious, is abstemious, and is chaste. And there is no need for you to suppose that these numerous names point to numerous dissimilar meanings; for that would reduce you to confusion, just as confusion reigns over whoever seeks different meanings from linguistic variants, where the meanings have not followed the variants. So this is a pointer to the concert of the meanings of fear, and what surrounds it on the higher side, such as the knowledge which determines it, and on the lower side, such as the actions which derive from it through restraint and perseverance.

Exposition of the Degrees of Fear and Its Differentiation into Power and Weakness

Know that fear is commendable. Often it is supposed that all fear is commendable, and that the more powerful and frequent it is the more it is commendable. This is a fallacy. No, fear is the whip of God by which He drives His creatures towards perseverance in knowledge and action, so that by means of both of these they may obtain the rank of nearness to God. And what is most salutary for the beast is that it should not escape the whip, and thus with the boy, but that does not point to the conclusion that excessive beating is commendable. And likewise with fear; it has deficiency and equilibrium, and what is commendable is the equilibrium and the mean.

The person who is deficient in it is he who tends towards effeminate softness which alights on his mind, whenever he hears a verse from the Koran, and produces weeping, and the tears overflow and similarly when he sees a cause of terror. And, when that cause is absent from his attention, his heart returns to negligence. So this is a fear which is deficient, of little profit and feeble in utility; just like the slight stick with which the powerful riding-beast is beaten, which

gives it no serious pain and does not urge it on to the destination, nor is it salutary for its correction. Such is the fear of all men except the gnostics and the knowledgeable. And I do not mean by knowledgeable those who are stamped with the marks of scholars or are called by their names; for they, of all men, are the most distant from fear. No, I mean those who are knowledgeable concerning God and His days and His actions, and that is a thing whose existence is rare at the present time. And, for that reason, al-Fudayl b. 'Iyad said, "when it is said to you, 'Do you fear God?,' keep silence. For, if you say no, you are an unbeliever; and if you say yes, you are a liar." And he indicated by this that it is fear that restrains the members from deeds of disobedience and binds them to deeds of obedience, and whatever does not take effect in the members is no more than an impulse and a fleeting motion which does not deserve the name of fear.

The extremist is he whose fear is strong and transgresses the limit of the equilibrium, so that it goes out towards hopelessness and despair, and it again is reprehensible, because it stultifies action. Fear may also issue in sickness and weakness and depression and bewilderment and intellectual atrophy. The aim of fear is the same as the aim of the whip which is to incite to action. If it is otherwise, fear is imperfect, because it is deficient in its essence, since its product is ignorance and impotence. Ignorance, because one does not know the sequel of his affair; and, if he knew he would not be afraid, since the thing which is feared is that about which there is doubt. Impotence, because he is exposed to a forbidden thing which he is unable to repel. Therefore, fear is commendable in connection with human deficiencies, and only knowledge is commendable in itself and its essence, together with power and everything by which it is possible to describe God. And that by which it is not possible to describe God is not perfect in its essence and only becomes commendable in connection with a deficiency which is greater than it; just as the enduring of therapeutic pain is commendable, because it is milder than the pain of disease and death. And whatever issues in despair is reprehensible, and fear also may issue in disease, weakness, depression, bewilderment, and intellectual atrophy; it may even issue in death. All that is reprehensible and is to be likened to the beating which kills the boy and the whip which slays the riding-beast or makes it ill or breaks one of its limbs.

The messenger of God mentioned the means of hope and multiplied them simply in order that he might thereby treat the shock of excessive fear which leads to despair or one of these conditions, and all that is implied with respect to a condition. The commendable part of it is whatever leads to the goal which is intended by it, and whatever comes short of it or goes beyond it is reprehensible. The profit of fear is caution and abstinence and piety and spiritual combat and worship and reflection and recollection, and all the means that bring about union with God. And all of that requires life along with health of body and wholeness of intellect, and whatever impairs these means is reprehensible.

If you say: whoever fears and dies because of his fear is a martyr, and how can his state be reprehensible? Know that the meaning of his being a martyr is that he possesses a rank in virtue of his death through fear which he would not have attained had he died at that time through a cause other than fear. So that in connection with him it is meritorious, but in connection with the ordering of his survival and the prolongation of his life in obedience to God and the treading of His paths it is not meritorious. No, the person who is making a pilgrimage to God by the path of reflection, spiritual combat, and the ascent of the degrees of knowledge possesses at every instant the rank of martyr and martyrs. Were it otherwise the rank of a lad who is killed or the madman whom a lion mauls would be higher than the rank of a prophet or saint who dies a natural death, and this would be absurd. Nor is it proper that this should be supposed. No, the most valued of blessings is prolongation of life in obedience to God, and everything which annuls life or mind or health (for life is impaired when it is impaired) is a loss and deprivation in relation to some conditions, even if some parts of it should have merit in relation to the other conditions, just as martyrdom has merit in relation to what is below it, not in relation to the degree of the pious and the sincere. So, if fear does not effect action, its existence and nonexistence are alike, just as the whip which does not accelerate the movement of the riding-beast. And, if it is effective, it has degrees according as its effects are visible. For, if it is an incentive only to chastity, it is the refraining from the determinism of lusts, so that it possesses a degree. And, if it produces abstinence, it is higher (in degree). And the most ultimate of its

degrees is that it should produce the degrees of the sincere, which is that it should tear one away outwardly and inwardly from what is other than God, so that there remains in him no room for other than God, and this is the most ultimate of its commendable characteristics, and it is accompanied with preservation of health and mind. If it goes beyond this towards the atrophy of mind and health, it is sickness which must be treated, if there is an effectual treatment. And, if it were commendable, its treatment by hope and other means until it passes away would not be necessary. For this reason Sahl used to say to novices who persisted with fasting over a long period: keep your wits. God has never had a saint who was mentally deficient.

Exposition of the Divisions of Fear in Relation to the Object Which is Feared

Know that fear does not deserve the name except it concerns the expectation of what is abhorred, whether it is abhorred in its essence, such as fire, or because it leads to what is abhorred, as deeds of disobedience are abhorred, because they lead to what is abhorred in the next world; just as the invalid abhors the fruits which do him injury, because they lead to death. So everyone who fears is bound to picture to himself an abhorred thing from one of the two divisions, and the expectation of it grows powerful in his heart, so that his heart is burnt up through his terror of the abhorred thing.

And the station of those who fear is differentiated in accordance with the kind of abhorred things whose dread dominates their hearts. So there are those whose hearts are dominated by what is not essentially abhorred, but abhorred because of what is outside itself, such as those who are dominated by the fear of death before repentance or a fear of a deficiency of repentance and a breaking of the covenant; or the fear of a diminishing of strength so as not to fulfil the complete demands of God. Or the fear that the tenderness of the heart will pass away and that it will be replaced by hardness; or the fear of inclining away from uprightness; or the fear of the mastery of custom in the following of the familiar lusts; or the fear that God will entrust people to their good works in which they have put their trust, and which they have boasted about among God's creatures. Or the fear of taking God for granted by reason of the multitude of God's favors towards one; or the fear of being distracted from God by other than God; or the fear of being deceived by the regular succession of favors. Or the fear that the defections of one's obedience will be uncovered, where there is revealed to him from God what he did not take into the reckoning. Or the fear that people will persecute one with backstabbing, perfidy, dissimulation and premeditated thoughts of evil. Or the fear of one's lack of knowledge of what may happen in the remainder of one's life; or the fear of punishment being brought forward to this world and one's being disgraced before death. Or the fear of being deceived by the blandishments of this world; or the fear that God will scrutinize one's secret heart at a moment when one is heedless of Him. Or the fear of being sealed at death with the Seal of evil; or the fear of the predestination which has been predestined to one from all eternity.

And all these are things which the gnostics fear and there is that which is particularly advantageous to everyone, which is the treading of the path of caution so as to exclude what leads to the thing feared. And so, whoever fears the mastery of custom over him will persevere in weaning himself from custom. And whoever fears that God will scrutinize his secret heart occupies himself with the purifying of his heart from the whisperings of Satan. And thus, with the remainder of the divisions; and among those fears the one which most overcomes assurance is the fear of the seal, for its affair is full of danger. The highest of all the divisions and the one which gives best access to perfection of knowledge is the fear of predestination, because the seal follows from what has been predestined, and is a branch which springs from it in accordance with the interaction of many causes. So the seal makes manifest what the eternal decree has predestined in the essence of the book.

The relation of him who fears the seal to him who fears predestination is like that of two men in judgement of whom the king has signed a decree, the import of which might be their beheading or the assigning to them of a ministry. And the decree was not yet delivered to them and the heart of one was tied up with the circumstance of the delivery of the decree and its publication and what it would disclose; and the heart of the other was tied up with the circumstance of the decree of the king, its nature, and what it was that had passed through his mind at the moment of the decree, of mercy or of anger. And this was to turn towards the cause which is a higher activity than to turn towards what is a corollary. And, likewise, to turn towards the eternal decree in promulgating which the reed pen flowed is a higher activity than turning towards what is made manifest at the end.

The prophet pointed to this when he was in the pulpit and clenched his right hand and said, "this is the book of God in which He has written the people of the garden with their names and the names of their fathers of which there shall be no increase and no diminution." Then he clenched his left hand and said, "this is the book of God in which He has written the people of the Fire with their names and the names of their fathers of which there shall be no increase and no diminution." And let the people of bliss do the works of the people of woe, so that it is said it is as if they were numbered with them; more, they are identical with them. Then God will save them before death, even if it is in the time between two milkings of a she-camel. And let the people of woe do the works of the people of bliss, so that it is said it is as if they were numbered with them; more, they are identical with them. Then God will extract them before death, even if it is in the time between two milkings of a she-camel. He who is numbered among the blessed is so by the decree of God, as is the reprobate by the decree of God, and works are in the nature of seals. And this accords with the division of those who fear into the person who fears his disobedience and sin, and the one who fears God in person, because of His attributes and majesty and characteristics which, without a doubt, compel awe. So this fear is the highest in rank, and, for that reason, his fear endures, even if he enters into the obedience of the sincere. As for the other it is in the target area of self-deception, and the safest part of it is if one perseveres in obedience. So fear of disobedience is the fear of the sound in faith, and the fear of God is that of the unitarians and the sincere. It is the fruit of knowledge concerning God, and whoever knows Him and knows His attributes, knows from His attributes how He is worthy to be feared apart altogether from sin. More, if the disobedient person knew God as he ought to know Him, he would fear God and would not fear his disobedience. And were it not that He is to be feared in His person, He would not constrain him to disobedience and smooth its path for him and prepare its means, for the facilitating of the means of disobedience is alienation. And he has not committed disobedience prior to his (present) disobedience in virtue of which he deserves to be constrained to disobedience and to have access to its means. Nor is obedience preceded by merit in virtue of which favour is shown to him for whom obedience is made easy and the path of communion smoothed for him. For the disobedient person has had disobedience decreed to him whether he wills it or not; and thus with the obedient person. And He who exalts Muhammad to the highest Heaven irrespective of merit which he had acquired prior to its taking place, and abases Abu Jahl in the lowest hell irrespective of sin which he had committed prior to its taking place, is worthy to be feared for His attribute of majesty.

For whoever obeys God, obeys because the will to obedience has dominion over him and power comes to him, and, after the creation of the irrevocable will and the complete power, the action comes into being of necessity. And he who is disobedient is so because a powerful and irrevocable will has dominion over him, and the means and power come to him, and the action, in the wake of the will and the power, is of necessity. Would that I knew what it is that determines the preferment of this man and his being singled out through the dominion over him of the will to obedience, and what determines the abasement of that man and his alienation through the dominion over him of the impulses of disobedience, and how this is transferred to the creature! But, since the transfer goes back to the eternal decree, irrespective of sin or merit, fear of one who decrees as He wills and legislates as He desires is a resolution with every intelligent person. And beyond this meaning is the secret of predestination whose dissemination is not permissible.

And the understanding of the fear of Him in respect of His attributes is not possible except by parable. Were it not for the permission of the law, the person of insight would not have dared to mention it. So it has come down in the tradition: surely God revealed to David: fear me as you fear the harmful lion. And this is the parable which lets you understand what is the effect of the meaning, even if it does not acquaint you with its cause. For to be acquainted with its cause is to be acquainted with the secret of predestination, and He does not disclose that except

to His "people." And the conclusion to be drawn is that the lion is to be feared not because of the sin which you have previously committed against it, but because of its characteristics, its violence and rapaciousness and arrogance and awfulness, and because it does what it will and does not care. For, if it killed you, its heart would be untouched by compunction, and it would feel no pain at killing you. And, if it left you alone, it would not leave you out of pity for you or to preserve your breath. No, you are in its sight too insignificant for it to notice you, whether dead or alive. More, the killing of a thousand like you and the killing of a gnat are on one plane with it, since that does not impugn the animal kingdom or the power and rapaciousness attributed to it. And the parable has its highest application to God. Whoever knows Him knows with inward sight which is more powerful and trustworthy and transparent than outward sight. He speaks the truth in His saying: these to the garden and I do not care; and these to the fire and I do not care. And of the things which compel awe and fear knowledge that He is self-subsistent and that He does not care will suffice you.

As for the second class of those who fear, the thing abhorred is pictured within them, such as the image of the pangs of death and its rigours, or the interrogation of Munkar and Nakir, or the punishment of the grave, or the terror of the resurrection, or the awfulness of the halting-place before God and shame because of the drawing back of the veil, and the interrogation about the smallest details; or the fear of the bridge and its edge and the manner of crossing over it; or the fear of the fire and its shackles and terrors, or the fear of being banned from the garden, the house of bliss and the enduring kingdom, and from a diminution of degrees; or the fear of being veiled from God.

And all these means are abhorred in themselves and are, indubitably, to be feared. And the states of those who fear are differentiated according to them; and the highest of them in rank is the fear of alienation and of being veiled from God and this is the fear of the gnostics. And what comes before this is the fear of the practitioners and the sound in faith and the ascetics and the body of the people. He whose knowledge is not perfect and whose inner sight is not opened up does not feel the pleasure of union nor the pain of alienation and separation. When it is mentioned to him that the gnostic does not fear the fire but fears only the veil, he finds that inwardly repugnant, and marvels at it in his soul. And it may be that he would find repugnant the pleasure of looking at the face of God, the magnanimous one, were it not that the law precludes him from being repugnant to it. And his confessing it with the tongue derives from the compulsion of authority, and, were it otherwise, it would not be inwardly vouched for because he knows only the pleasure of the stomach, of sexual intercourse and of the eye (when he looks at colors and fair faces), and, in general, every pleasure in which the beasts are his associates. As for the pleasure of the gnostics they only attain to it, and its classification and exposition are forbidden to whoever is not a party to it. And whoever is a party to it himself possesses the insight, and so has no need that someone else should expound it to him. The fear of those who fear can be traced to these divisions. Let us ask God for good success through His magnanimity.

STUDY QUESTIONS: AL-GHAZALI, *THE BOOK OF HOPE AND FEAR*

1. How are hope and fear related?
2. What is the essence of hope?
3. What is the "therapy" of hope? What does it alleviate?
4. What is fear the expression of?
5. How are piety and sincerity related?
6. How is fear related to the object of fear?

Philosophical Bridges: al-Ghazali's Influence

In the Islamic world al-Ghazali is well known as one of the foundational figures of the great Sunni Muslim tradition. His skeptical attacks on the various views of different philosophers and philosophical traditions, and on philosophy itself, were themselves taken quite seriously by philosophers; his arguments have affinity to the skeptical attacks by Descartes, and even Wittgenstein and Kant's "antinomies" of reason are logical cousins of al-Ghazali's searing method of attack by comparative analysis of competing systems—each of which claims to be the correct path to truth and knowledge. Al-Ghazali's evocation of rational insight as a mystical path to truth is sympathetic with subsequent views of many mystics both in Christian and Muslim traditions. Certain aspects of his approach can even be found in the views of some recent existentialist thinkers, such as Kierkegaard and Sartre.

AVERROËS (1126–1198)

Biographical History

Averroës (Muhammad Ibn-Rushd) was born in Córdova, Spain. His father was a powerful and well known *qadi* (judge). As a young man Averroës studied philosophy, theology, law, medicine, and mathematics. Philosophy at the time under Islam enjoyed the protection of the ruling classes, who by and large were as enamored of the masterworks of Plato and Aristotle as their counterparts in Europe were revolted. The Islamic educational process required of students lengthy and original commentaries on the great books that at the time were banned in the adjoining Holy Roman Empire.

Although Averroës worked as a judge both in Seville and Córdova, philosophy was his true love and his obsession. According to one story, during a party attended by the Almohad prince Abū Ya'qub Yusuf, he got into a heated debate over the origin and nature of reality and its relation to the human mind. Apparently, Averroës's stand-up lecture on Aristotle's account of existence and the nature of the soul lasted all night until sunrise, with apparently no one falling asleep. The prince appointed him as his personal physician and commissioned Averroës to write an entire set of new commentaries, and Averroës spent the rest of his life doing so. Because of his radical criticism of the work of other commentators, claiming that they corrupted Aristotle's views by putting a theological spin to them, as soon as his priestly protector, Abū Ya'qub Yusuf, died, Averroës was accused of promoting the "pagan" philosophy of the ancients and thereby using philosophy to corrupt the Muslim faithful. As a result he spent his remaining years in Morocco, writing and teaching in exile.

Five centuries had passed since Justinian had tried to ban philosophy from Christendom; now it was Islam's turn. The caliph al-Mansur ordered all books on logic and metaphysics burned. He issued an edict that declared anyone who believed in reason, and that truth can be known rationally and independently of any divine revelation, a heretic. Eventually the war between the Christians and Muslims forced the Muslims out of Spain, but the censorship of Averroës by the orthodox Islamic rulers continued. Strange as it may seem, just as previous Islamic authorities welcomed works banned by their Christian enemies, the new, conquering Christians seized the works banned by the Muslims among which were translations of texts they themselves had once burned! Philosophy thus passed hands from one opposing religion to another and then back again, in what no doubt has to be one of the greatest historical ironies of all time.

Philosophical Overview

Averroës defended philosophy from various assaults by the Mohammedan orthodoxy, such is found in the widely read *Destruction of the Philosophers* by the theologian al-Ghazali, according to which all necessary truth is revealed in the Koran and therefore the activity of philosophy is unnecessary. Averroës was anything but timid or subtle about his defense: in his *Destruction of the Destruction*, he argues that all religious dogmas are at best philosophically derived truths falsely presented in allegorical form. Similarly, Averroës's *Tahafut al-Tahafut* (*The Incoherence of the Incoherence*) was a direct frontal response to al-Ghazali's attack on philosophy, *The Incoherence of the Philosophers*. Al-Ghazali criticized all philosophers, including and especially Avicenna, for advocating views that he saw as incompatible with religious faith (Avicenna would have disagreed). In his defense, Averroës attacks al-Ghazali's book in a very clever way, by showing point by point that one does not have to deny *any* of the doctrines of Islam to practice philosophy.

However, unlike just about all other philosophers of the time, be they Islamic, Jewish, or Christian, Averroës does not see philosophy's job as involving the reinterpretation of the ancient Greek texts so as to make them accord with the religion of the day. On the contrary. Averroës claims that all other commentators, including and especially the widely admired Avicenna, had corrupted the pure philosophy of Aristotle and Plato by rewriting their ideas from a theological point of view. He was thus a philosophical revolutionary, in the true sense of the word.

THE INCOHERENCE OF THE INCOHERENCE
Averroës

As we saw in the previous section, al-Ghazali claimed that taken together the philosophers are a bunch of incoherent idiots, who contradict each other into absurdity. Averroës, in this celebrated work, attacks al-Ghazali's attack on philosophers by arguing that al-Ghazali's book is itself incoherent. Averroës wrote the work as an imaginary dialogue between himself and al-Ghazali. But by no means does he belittle or distort al-Ghazali's arguments; rather, he puts them in the best light possible in order to refute them.

The debate begins with the question of whether the world had a beginning in time or is itself eternal. The nature of the soul and its immortality becomes the central issue, with Averroës arguing that we are all one numerically identical soul. His argument is that we are numerically different individual material beings but identical in form. (He uses the names "Zaid" and "Amr" the way we might use "Smith" and "Jones" to refer to any two nonspecific individuals).

The term "quiddity" comes up in the discussion. It means, literally, "what," and is used to refer to the being or entity of a thing that makes it exist and be what it is rather that some other thing.

The aim of this book is to show the different degrees of assent and conviction attained by the assertions in [Al-Ghazali's book] *The Incoherence of the Philosophers*, and to prove that the greater part has not reached the degree of evidence and of truth.

THE FIRST DISCUSSION

Concerning the Eternity of the World

al-Ghazali, speaking of the philosophers' proofs for the eternity of the world, says:

The philosophers say: It is impossible that the temporal should proceed from the absolutely Eternal. For it is clear—if we assume the Eternal existing without, for instance, the world proceeding from Him, then, at a certain moment, the world beginning to proceed from Him—that it did not proceed before, because there was no determining principle for its existence, but its existence was pure possibility. When the world begins in time, a new determinant either does or does not arise.

If it does not, the world will stay in the same state of pure possibility as before; if a new determinant does arise, the same question can be asked about this new determinant, why it determines now, and not before, and either we shall have an infinite regress or we shall arrive at a principle determining eternally.

I say:

This argument is in the highest degree dialectical and does not reach the pitch of demonstrative proof. For its premises are common notions, and common notions approach the equivocal, whereas demonstrative premises are concerned with things proper to the same genus. For the term 'possible' is used in an equivocal way of the possible that happens more often than not, of the possible that happens less often than not, and of the possible with equal chances of happening, and these three types of the possible do not seem to have the same need for a new determining principle. For the possible that happens more often than not is frequently believed to have its determining principle in itself, not outside, as is the case with the possible which has equal chances of happening and not happening. Further, the possible resides sometimes in the agent, that is the possibility of acting, and sometimes in the recipient, that is the possibility of receiving, and it does not seem that the

Averroës (Ibn Rushd), from *The Incoherence of the Incoherence (Tahāfut al-Tahāfut)*, translated by Simon Van Den Bergh, Unesco Collection of Great Works Arabic Series, London: Luzac & Co. Ltd., 1969, pp. 1–36 and 235–241.

necessity for a determining principle is the same in both cases. For it is well known that the possible in the recipient needs a new determinant from the outside; this can be perceived by the senses in artificial things and in many natural things too, although in regard to natural things there is a doubt, for in most natural things the principle of their change forms part of them. Therefore, it is believed of many natural things that they move themselves, and it is by no means self-evident that everything that is in motion has a mover and that there is nothing that moves itself. But all this needs to be examined, and the old philosophers have therefore done so. As concerns the possible in the agent, however, in many cases it is believed that it can be actualized without an external principle, for the transition in the agent from inactivity to activity is often regarded as not being a change which requires a principle; for example the transition in the geometer from non-geometrizing to geometrizing, or in the teacher from non-teaching to teaching.

Further, those changes which are regarded as needing a principle of change can sometimes be changes in substance, sometimes in quality, or in quantity, or in place. In addition, 'eternal' is predicated by many of the eternal-by-itself and the eternal-through-another. According to some, it is permissible to admit certain changes in the Eternal, for instance a new volition in the Eternal, according to the Karramites, and the possibility of generation and corruption which the ancients attribute to primary matter, although it is eternal. Equally, new concepts are admitted in the possible intellect although, according to most authors, it is eternal. But there are also changes which are inadmissible, especially according to certain ancients, though not according to others.

Then there is the agent who acts of his will and the agent which acts by nature, and the manner of actualization of the possible act is not the same for both agents, that is so far as the need for a new determinant is concerned. Further, is this division into two agents complete, or does demonstration lead to an agent which resembles neither the natural agent for the voluntary agent of human experience?

All these are multifarious and difficult questions which need, each of them, a special examination, both in themselves and in regard to the opinions the ancients held about them. To treat what is in reality a plurality of questions as one problem is one of the well-known seven sophisms, and a mistake in one of these principles becomes a great error by the end of the examination of reality.

Al-Ghazali says:

There are two objections to this. The first objection is to say: why do you deny the theory of those who say that the world has been created by an eternal will which has decreed its existence in the time in which it exists; that its nonexistence lasts until the moment it ceases and that its existence begins from the moment it begins; that its existence was not willed before and therefore did not happen, and that at the exact moment it began it was willed by an eternal will and therefore began? What is the objection to this theory and what is absurd in it?

I say:

This argument is sophistical: although it is not permissible for him to admit the possibility of the actual effect being delayed after the actual cause, and in a voluntary agent, after the decision to act, he regards it as possible that the effect should be delayed after the will of the agent. It is possible that the effect should be delayed after the will of the agent, but its being delayed after the actual cause is impossible, and equally impossible is its being delayed after a voluntary agent's decision to act. The difficulty is thus unchanged; for he must of necessity draw one of these two conclusions: either that the act of the agent does not imply in him a change which itself would need an external principle of change, or that there are changes which arise by themselves, without the necessity of an agent in whom they occur and who causes them, and that therefore there are changes possible in the Eternal without an agent who causes them. And his adversaries insist on these two very points: (1) that the act of the agent necessarily implies a change and that each change has a principle which causes it; (2) that the Eternal cannot change in any way. But all this is difficult to prove.

The Ash'arites are forced to assume either a first agent or a first act of this agent, for they cannot admit that the disposition of the agent, relative to the effect, when he acts is the same as his disposition, when he does not act. This implies, therefore, a new disposition or a new relation, and this necessarily either in the agent, or in the effect, or in both. But in this case, if we posit as a principle that for each new disposition there is an agent, this new disposition in the first agent will either need another agent, and then this first agent was not the first and was not on his own account sufficient for the act but needed another, or the agent of the disposition which is the condition of the agent's act will be identical with the agent of the act. Then this act which we regarded as being the first act arising out of him will not be the first, but his act producing the disposition which is the condition of the effect will be anterior to the act producing the effect. This, you see, is a necessary consequence, unless one allows that new dispositions may arise in the agents without a cause. But this is absurd, unless one believes that there are things which happen haphazardly and by themselves, a theory of the old philosophers who denied the agent, the falsehood of which is self-evident.

In al-Ghazali's objection there is confusion. For our expressions 'eternal will' and 'temporal will' are equivocal, indeed, contrary. The empirical will is a faculty which possesses the possibility of doing equally one of two contraries and then of receiving equally one of the two contraries willed. For the will is the desire of the agent towards action. When the agent acts, desire ceases and the thing willed happens, and this desire and this act are equally related to both the contraries. But when one says, "there is a Willer who wills eternally one of two contraries in Himself," the definition of the will is abandoned; we have transferred its nature from the possible to the necessary. If it is objected that in an eternal will the will does not cease through the presence of the object willed, (for as an eternal will has no beginning, there is no moment in it which is specially determined for the realization of the object willed), we answer: this is not obvious, unless we say that demonstrative proof leads to the existence of an agent endowed with a power which is neither voluntary nor natural, which, however, the Divine Law calls 'will,' in the same way as demonstrative proof leads to middle terms between things which seemed at first sight to be contrary, without being really so, as when we speak of an existence which is neither inside nor outside the world.

Al-Ghazali answers, on behalf of the philosophers: The philosophers say: This is clearly impossible, for everything that happens is necessitated and has its cause, and as it is impossible that there should

be an effect without a necessitating principle and a cause, so it is impossible that there should exist a cause of which the effect is delayed, when all the conditions of its necessitating, its causes and elements are completely fulfilled. On the contrary, the existence of the effect, when the cause is realized with all its conditions, is necessary, and its delay is just as impossible as an effect without a cause. Before the existence of the world there existed a Willer, a will, and its relation to the thing willed. No new willer arose, nor a new will, nor a new relation to the will—for all this is change. How then could a new object of will arise, and what prevented its arising before? The condition of the new production did not distinguish itself from the condition of the non-production in any way, in any mode, in any relation. On the contrary, everything remained as it was before. At one moment the object of will did not exist; everything remained as it was before, and then the object of will existed. Is not this a perfectly absurd theory?

I say:

This is perfectly clear, except for one who denies one of the premises we have laid down previously. But al-Ghazali passes from this proof to an example based upon convention, and through this he confuses this defence of the philosophers.

Al-Ghazali says:

This kind of impossibility is found not only in the necessary and essential cause and effect but also in the accidental and conventional. If a man pronounces the formula of divorce against his wife without the divorce becoming irrevocable immediately, one does not imagine that it will become so later. For he made the formula through convention and usage a cause of the judgement, and we do not believe that the effect can be delayed, except when the divorce depends on an ulterior event, for example on the arrival of tomorrow or on someone's entering the house, for then the divorce does not take place at once, but only when tomorrow arrives or someone enters the house; in this case the man made the formula a cause only in conjunction with an ulterior event. But as this event, the coming of tomorrow and someone's entering the house, is not yet actual, the effect is delayed until this future event is realized. The effect only takes place when a new event, that is entering the house or the arrival of tomorrow, has actually happened. Even if a man wanted to delay the effect after the formula, without making it dependent on an ulterior event, this would be regarded as impossible, although it is he himself who lays down the convention and fixes its modalities. If thus in conventional matters such a delay is incomprehensible and inadmissible, how can we admit it in essential, rational, and necessary causal relations? In respect of our conduct and our voluntary actions, there is a delay in actual volition only when there is some obstacle. When there is actual volition and actual power and the obstacles are eliminated, a delay in the object willed is inadmissible. A delay in the object willed is imaginable only in decision, for decision is not sufficient for the existence of the act; the decision to write does not produce the writing, if it is not, as a new fact, accompanied by an act of volition, that is an impulse in the man which presents itself at the moment of the act. If there is thus an analogy between the eternal Will and our will to act, a delay of the object willed is inadmissible, unless through an obstacle, and an antecedent existence of the volition is equally inadmissible, for I cannot will to get up tomorrow except by way of decision. If, however, the eternal Will is analogous to our decision, it does not suffice to produce the thing decided upon, but the act of creation must be accompanied by a new act of volition, and this brings us again to the idea of a change. But then we have the same difficulty all over again. Why does this impulse or volition or will or whatever you choose to call it happen just now and not before? There remain, then, only these alternatives: either something happening without a cause, or an infinite regress. This is the upshot of the discussion: there is a cause the conditions of which are all completely fulfilled, but notwithstanding this the effect is delayed and is not realized during a period to the beginning of which imagination cannot attain and for which thousands of years would mean no diminution; then suddenly, without the addition of any new fact, and without the realization of any new condition, this effect comes into existence and is produced. And this is absurd.

I say:

This example of divorce based on convention seems to strengthen the argument of the philosophers, but in reality it weakens it. For it enables the Ash'arites to

say: in the same way as the actual divorce is delayed after the formula of divorce till the moment when the condition of someone's entering the house, or any other, is fulfilled, so the realization of the world can be delayed after God's act of creation until the condition is fulfilled on which this realization depends, that is the moment when God willed it. But conventional things do not behave like rational. The Literalists, comparing these conventional things to rational, say: this divorce is not binding and does not become effective through the realization of the condition which is posterior to the pronouncement of the divorce by the divorcer, since it would be a divorce which became effective without connexion with the act of the divorcer. But in this matter there is no relation between the concept drawn from the nature of things and that which is artificial and conventional.

Then al-Ghazali says, on behalf of the Ash'arites:

The answer is: Do you recognize the impossibility of connecting the eternal Will with the temporal production of anything, through the necessity of intuitive thought or through a logical deduction, or, to use your own logical terminology, do you recognize the clash between these two concepts through a middle term or without a middle term? If you claim a middle term—and this is the deductive method—you will have to produce it, and if you assert that you know this through the necessity of thought, why do your adversaries not share this intuition with you? For the party which believes in the creation of the world in time through an eternal Will includes so many persons that no country can contain them and no number enumerate them, and they certainly do not contradict the logically minded out of obstinacy, while knowing better in their hearts. A proof according to the rules of logic must be produced to show this impossibility, as in all your arguments up till now there is only a presumption of impossibility and a comparison with our decision and our will; and this is false, for the eternal Will does not resemble temporal volitions, and a pure presumption of impossibility will not suffice without proof.

I say:

This argument is one of those which have only a very feeble persuasive power. It amounts to saying that one who claims the impossibility of delay in an effect, when its cause with all its conditions is realized, must assert that he knows this either by a syllogism or from first principles; if through a syllogism, he must produce it—but there is none; if from first principles, it must be known to all, adversaries and others alike. But this argument is mistaken, for it is not a condition of objective truth that it should be known to all. That anything should be held by all does not imply anything more than its being a common notion, just as the existence of a common notion does not imply objective truth.

Al-Ghazali answers on behalf of the Ash'arites:

If it is said, "we know by the necessity of thought that, when all its conditions are fulfilled, a cause without effect is inadmissible and that to admit it is an affront to the necessity of thought," we answer: "what is the difference between you and your adversaries, when they say to you, 'we know by the necessity of thought the impossibility of a theory which affirms that one single being knows all the universals, without this knowledge forming a plurality in its essence or adding anything to it, and without this plurality of things known implying a plurality in the knowledge'?" For this is your theory of God, which according to us and our science is quite absurd. You, however, say there is no analogy between eternal and temporal knowledge. Some of you acknowledge the impossibility involved, and say that God knows only Himself and that He is the knower, the knowledge and the known, and that the three are one. One might object: the unity of the knowledge, the knower, and the known is clearly an impossibility, for to suppose the Creator of the world ignorant of His own work is necessarily absurd, and the Eternal—who is far too high to be reached by your words and the words of any heretics—could, if He knows only Himself, never know His work.

I say:

This amounts to saying that the theologians do not gratuitously and without proof deny the admitted impossibility of a delay between the effect and its cause, but base themselves on an argument which leads them to believe in the temporal creation of the world, and that they therefore act in the same way as the philosophers, who only deny the well-known necessary plurality of knowledge and known, so far as it concerns their unity in God, because of a demonstration which, according to them, leads them to their theory about Him. And that this is still more true of those philosophers who deny it to be necessary that God should know His own work, affirming that He knows only Himself. This assertion belongs to the class of assertions whose contrary is equally false. For there exists no proof which refutes anything that is evidently true, and universally acknowledged. Anything that can be refuted by a demonstrative proof is only supposed to be true, not really true. Therefore, if it is absolutely and evidently true that knowledge and known form a plurality, both in the visible and in the invisible world, we can be sure that the philosophers cannot have a proof of this unity in God; but if the theory of the plurality of knowledge and known is only a supposition, then it is possible for the philosophers to have a proof. Equally, if it is absolutely true that the effect of a cause cannot be delayed after the causation and the Ash'arites claim that they can advance a proof to deny it, then we can be absolutely sure that they cannot have such a proof. If there is a controversy about questions like this, the final criterion rests with sound understanding which does not base itself on prejudice and passion, when it probes according to the signs and rules by which truth and mere opinion are logically distinguished. Likewise, if two people dispute about a sentence and one says that it is poetry, the other that it is prose, the final judgment rests with the sound understanding which can distinguish poetry from prose, and with the science of prosody. And as, in the case of metre, the denial of him who denies it does not interfere with its perception by him who perceives it, so the denial of a truth by a contradictory does not trouble the conviction of the men to whom it is evident. This whole argument is extremely inept and weak, and al-Ghazali ought not to have filled his book with such talk if he intended to convince the learned.

Drawing consequences which are irrelevant and beside the point, al-Ghazali goes on to say:

But the consequences of this argument cannot be overcome. And we say to them: how will you refute your adversaries, when they say the eternity of the world is impossible; for it implies an infinite number and an infinity of unities for the spherical revolutions, although they can be divided by six, by four, and by two. For the sphere of the sun revolves in one year, the sphere of Saturn in thirty years, and so Saturn's revolution is a thirtieth and Jupiter's revolution—for Jupiter revolves in twelve years—a twelfth of the sun's revolution. But the number of revolutions of Saturn has the same infinity as the revolutions of the sun, although they are in a proportion of one to thirty and even the infinity of the sphere of the fixed stars which turns round once in thirty-six thousand years is the same as the daily revolution which the sun performs in twenty-four hours. If your adversary says that this is plainly impossible, in what does your argument differ from his? And suppose it is asked: are the numbers of these revolutions even or uneven or both even and uneven or neither even nor uneven? If you answer, both even and uneven, or neither even nor uneven, you say what is evidently absurd. If, however, you say 'even' or 'uneven,' even and uneven become uneven and even by the addition of one unit and how could infinity be one unit short? You must, therefore, draw the conclusion that they are neither even nor uneven.

I say:

This too is a Sophistical argument. It amounts to saying: in the same way as you are unable to refute our argument for the creation of the world in time, that if it were eternal, its revolutions would be neither even nor uneven, so we cannot refute your theory that the effect of an agent whose conditions to act are always fulfilled cannot be delayed. This argument aims only at creating and establishing a doubt, which is one of the sophist's objectives.

But you, reader of this book, have already heard the arguments of the philosophers to establish the eternity of the world and the refutation of the Ash'arites. Now hear the proofs of the Ash'arites for their refutation and hear the arguments of the philosophers to refute those proofs in the wording of al-Ghazali.

If you imagine two circular movements in one and the same finite time and imagine then a limited part of these movements in one and the same finite time, the proportion between the parts of these two circular movements and between their wholes will be the same. For instance, if the circular movement of Saturn in the period which we call a year is a thirtieth of the circular movement of the sun in this period, and you imagine the whole of the circular movements

of the sun in proportion to the whole of the circular movements of Saturn in one and the same period, necessarily the proportion between their wholes and between their parts will be the same. If, however, there is no proportion between two movements in their totality, because they are both potential, that is they have neither beginning nor end but there exists a proportion between the parts, because they are both actual, then the proportion between the wholes is not necessarily the same as the proportion between the parts—although many think so, basing their proof on this prejudice. For there is no proportion between two magnitudes or quantities which are both taken to be infinite. When, therefore, the ancients believed that, for instance, the totality of the movements of the sun and of Saturn had neither beginning nor end, there could be no proportion between them, for this would have implied the finitude of both these totalities, just as this is implied for the parts of both. This is self-evident. Our adversaries believe that, when a proportion of more and less exists between parts, this proportion holds good also for the totalities, but this is only binding when the totalities are finite. For where there is no end there is neither 'more' nor 'less.' The admission in such a case of the proportion of more and less brings with it another absurd consequence, namely that one infinite could be greater than another. This is only absurd when one supposes two things actually infinite, for then a proportion does exist between them. When, however, one imagines things potentially infinite, there exists no proportion at all. This is the right answer to this question, not what al-Ghazali says in the name of the philosophers.

And through this are solved all the difficulties which beset our adversaries on this question, of which the greatest is that which is habitually formulated in this way: if the movements in the past are infinite, then no movement in the actual present can take place unless an infinite number of preceding movements is terminated. This is true, and acknowledged by the philosophers, once granted that the anterior movement is the condition for the posterior movement's taking place, that is once granted that the existence of one single movement implies an infinite number of causes. But no philosopher allows the existence of an infinite number of causes, as accepted by the materialists, for this would imply the existence of an effect without cause and a motion without mover.

But when the existence of an eternal prime mover had been proved, whose act cannot be posterior to his being, it followed that there could as little be a beginning for his act as for his being; otherwise his act would be possible, not necessary, and he would not be a first principle. The acts of an agent who has no beginning have a beginning as little as his existence, and therefore it follows necessarily that no preceding act of his is the condition for the existence of a later, for neither of them is an agent by itself and their sequence is accidental. An accidental infinite, not an essential infinite, is admitted by the philosophers; nay, this type of infinite is in fact a necessary consequence of the existence of an eternal first principle. And this is not only true for successive or continuous movements and the like, but even where the earlier is regarded as the cause of the later, for instance the human who engenders a human like himself. For it is necessary that the series of temporal productions of one individual human by another should lead upwards to an eternal agent, for whom there is no beginning either of his existence or of his production of human out of human. The production of one human by another *ad infinitum is* accidental, whereas the relation of before and after in it is essential. The agent who has no beginning either for his existence or for those acts of his which he performs without an instrument, has no first instrument either to perform those acts of his without beginning which by their nature need an instrument. But since the theologians mistook the accidental for the essential, they denied this eternal agent; the solution of their problem was difficult and they believed this proof to be stringent. This theory of the philosophers is clear, and their first master Aristotle has explained that, if motion were produced by motion, or element by element, motion and element could not exist. For this type of infinite the philosophers admit neither a beginning nor an end, and therefore one can never say of anything in this series that it has ended or has begun, not even in the past, for everything that has an end must have begun and what does not begin does not end. This can also be understood from the fact that beginning and end are correlatives. Therefore, one who affirms that there is no end of the celestial revolutions in the future cannot logically ascribe a beginning to them; for what has a beginning has an end and what has no end has no beginning, and the same relation exists between first

and last; that is, what has a first term has also a last term, and what has no first term has no last term, and there is in reality neither end nor beginning for any part of a series that has no last term, and what has no beginning for any of its parts has no end for any of them either. When, therefore, the theologians ask the philosophers if the movements which precede the present one are ended, their answer is negative, for their assumption that they have no beginning implies their endlessness. The opinion of the theologians that the philosophers admit their end is erroneous; for they do not admit an end for what has no beginning. It will be clear to you that neither the arguments of the theologians for the temporal creation of the world of which al-Ghazali speaks, nor the arguments of the philosophers which he includes and describes in his book, suffice to reach absolute evidence or afford stringent proof. And this is what we have tried to show in this book. The best answer one can give to him who asks where in the past is the starting-point of His acts, is: the starting point of His acts is at the starting point of His existence; for neither of them has a beginning.

And here is the passage of al-Ghazali in which he sets forth the defence of the philosophers against the argument built on the difference in speed of the celestial spheres, and his refutation of their argument.

Al-Ghazali says:

If one says, "the error in your argument consists in your considering those circular movements as an aggregate of units, but those movements have no real existence; for the past is no more and the future not yet. 'Aggregate' means units existing in the present, but in this case there is no existence."

Then he says to refute this:

We answer: number can be divided into even and uneven; there is no third possibility, whether for the numbered permanent reality, or for the numbered passing event. Therefore, whatever number we imagine, we must believe it to be even or uneven, whether we regard it as existent or nonexistent. If the thing numbered vanishes from existence, our judgement of its being even or uneven does not vanish or change.

This is the end of his argument. But this argument that the numbered thing must be judged as even or uneven, whether it exists or not—is only valid so that as it concerns external things or things in the soul that have a beginning and an end. For of the number which exists only potentially, that is which has neither beginning nor end, it cannot truly be said that it is even or uneven, or that it begins or ends; it happens neither in the past nor in the future, for what exists potentially falls under the law of nonexistence. This is what the philosophers meant when they said that the circular movements of the past and the future are nonexistent. The upshot of this question is: everything that is called a limited aggregate with a beginning and an end is so called either because it has a beginning and end in the world exterior to the soul, or because it is inside, not outside, the soul. Every totality, actual and limited in the past, whether inside or outside the soul, in necessarily either even or uneven. But an unlimited aggregate existing outside the soul cannot be usher than limited so far as it is represented in the soul; for the soul cannot represent unlimited existence. Therefore, also this unlimited aggregate, as being limited in the soul, can be called even or uneven; in so far, however, as it exists outside the soul, it can be called neither even nor uneven. Equally, past aggregates which are considered to exist potentially outside the soul, that is which have no beginning, cannot be called even or uneven unless they are looked upon as actual, that is as having beginning and end. No motion possesses totality or forms an aggregate, that is, is provided with a beginning or an end, except in so far as it is in the soul, as is the case with time. And it follows from the nature of circular movement that it is neither even nor uneven except as represented in the soul. The cause of this mistake is that it was believed that, when something possesses a certain quality in the soul, it must possess this quality also outside the soul, and, since anything that has happened in the past can only be represented in the soul as finite, it was thought that everything that has happened in the past must also be finite outside the soul. And as the circular movements of the future are regarded by the imagination as infinite; for it represents them as a sequence of part after part. Plato and the Ash'arites believed that they might be infinite, but this is simply a judgement based on imagination, not on proof. Therefore, those who believe—as many theologians have done—that, if the world is supposed to have begun, it must have an end, are truer to their principles and show more consistency.

Al-Ghazali says after this:

And we say moreover to the philosophers: according to your principles it is not absurd that there should be actual units, qualitatively differentiated, which are infinite in number; I am thinking of human souls, separated through death from their bodies. These are therefore realities that can neither be called even nor uneven. How will you refute the person who affirms that this is necessarily absurd in the same way as you claim the connection between an eternal will and a temporal creation to be necessarily absurd? This theory about souls is that which Avicenna accepted, and it is perhaps Aristotle's.

I say:

This argument is extremely weak. It says, in brief, "you philosophers need not refute our assertion that what is a logical necessity for you is not necessary, as you consider things possible which your adversaries consider impossible by the necessity of thought. That is to say, just as you consider things possible which your adversaries consider impossible, so you consider things necessary which your adversaries do not consider so. And you cannot bring a criterion for judging the two claims." It has already been shown in the science of logic that this is a weak rhetorical or sophistical kind of argument. The answer is that what we claim to be necessarily true is objectively true, whereas what you claim as necessarily absurd is not as you claim it to be. For this there is no other criterion than immediate intuitive apprehension, just as, when one person claims that a line is rhythmical and another denies it, the criterion is the intuition of sound understanding.

As for the thesis of a numerical plurality of immaterial souls, this is not a theory acknowledged by the philosophers; for they regard matter as the cause of numerical plurality and form as the cause of congruity in numerical plurality. And that there should be a numerical plurality without matter, having one unique form, is impossible. For in its description one individual can only be distinguished from another accidentally, as there is often another individual who participates in this description, but only through their matter do individuals differ in reality. And also this: the impossibility of an actual infinite is an acknowledged axiom in philosophical theory, equally valid for material and immaterial things. We do not know of any one who makes a distinction here between the spatial and the non-spatial, with the single exception of Avicenna. I do not know of any other philosopher who affirms this; it does not correspond with any of their principles, and it makes no sense. For the philosophers deny the existence of an actual infinite equally for material and for immaterial things, as it would imply that one infinite could be greater than another. Perhaps Avicenna wanted only to satisfy the masses, telling them what they were accustomed to hear about the soul. But this theory is far from satisfactory. For if there were an actual infinite, and if it were divided in two, the part would equal the whole; for example if there were a line or a number actually infinite in both directions, and if it were divided in two, both the parts and the whole would be actually infinite; and this is absurd. All this is simply the consequence of the admission of an actual and not potential infinite.

Al-Ghazali says:

If it is said, "the truth lies with Plato's theory of one eternal soul which is only divided in bodies and returns after its separation from them to its original unity," we answer: This theory is still worse, more objectionable and more apt to be regarded as contrary to the necessity of thought. For we say that the soul of Zaid is either identical with the soul of Amr or different from it; but their identity would mean something absurd, for everyone is conscious of his own identity and knows that he is not another, and, were they identical, their knowledge, which is an essential quality of their souls and enters into all the relations into which their souls enter, would be identical too. If you say their soul is unique and only divided through its association with bodies, we answer that the division of a unity which has no measurable volume is absurd by the necessity of thought. And how could the one become two, and indeed a thousand, and then return to its unity? This can be understood of things which have volume and quantity, like the water of the sea which is distributed into brooks and rivers and flows then back again into the sea, but how can that which has no quantity be divided? We seek to show by all this that the philosophers cannot shake the conviction of their adversaries that the eternal Will is connected with temporal creation, except by claiming its absurdity by the necessity of thought, and that therefore they are in no way different from the theologians who make the same claim against the philosophical doctrines opposed to theirs. And out of this there is no issue.

I say:

Zaid and Amr are numerically different, but identical in form. If, for example, the soul of Zaid were numerically different from the soul of Amr in the way Zaid is numerically different from Amr, the soul of Zaid and the soul of Amr would be numerically two, but one in their form, and the soul would posses another soul. The necessary conclusion is therefore that the soul of Zaid and the soul of Amr are identical in their form. An identical form inheres in a numerical, that is a divisible, multiplicity, only through the multiplicity of matter. If then the soul does not die when the body dies, or if it possesses an immortal element, it must, when it has left the bodies, form a numerical unity. But this is not the place to go deeper into this subject.

His argument against Plato is Sophistical. It says in short that the soul of Zaid is either identical with the soul of Amr or different from it; but that the soul of Zaid is not identical with the soul of Amr and that therefore it is different from it. But 'different' is an equivocal term, and 'identity' too is predicated of a number of things which are also called 'different.' The souls of Zaid and Amr are one in one sense and many in another; we might say, one in relation to their form, many in relation to their substratum. His remark that division can only be imagined of the quantitative is partially false; it is true of essential division, but not of accidental division, that is of those things which can be divided, because they exist in the essentially divisible. The essentially divisible is, for example, body; accidental division is, for instance, the division of whiteness, when the bodies in which it is present are divided, and in this way the forms and the soul are accidentally divisible, that is through the division of the substrate. The soul is closely similar to light: light is divided by the division of illuminated bodies, and is unified when the bodies are annihilated, and this same relation holds between soul and bodies. To advance such Sophistical arguments is dishonest; for it may be supposed that he is not a man to have overlooked the points mentioned. What he said, he said only to flatter the masses of his times, but how far removed is such an attitude from the character of those who seek to set forth the truth! But perhaps the man may be forgiven on account of the time and place in which he lived; and indeed he only proceeded in his books in a tentative way.

Since these arguments carry no evidence whatsoever, al-Ghazali says:

We want to show by all this that the philosophers cannot shake the conviction of their adversaries that the eternal Will is connected with temporal creation, by claiming its absurdity by the necessity if though, and that therefore they do not distinguish themselves from the theologians, who make the same claim against the philosophical doctrines opposed to theirs. And out of this there is no issue.

I say:

When someone denies a truth of which it is absolutely certain that it is such and such, there exists no argument by which we can come to an understanding with him; for every argument is based on known premises about which both adversaries agree. When each point advanced is denied by the adversary, discussion with him becomes impossible, but such people stand outside the pale of humanity and have to be educated. But for him who denies an evident truth, because of a difficulty which presents itself to him there is a remedy, truth, because he is lacking in intelligence, cannot be taught anything, nor can he be educated. It is like trying to make the blind imagine colors or know their existence.

Al-Ghazali says:

The philosophers may object: this argument (that the present has been preceded by an infinite past) can be turned against you. For God before the creation of the world was able to create it, say, one year or two years before He did, and there is no limit to His power; but He seemed to have patience and did not create. Then He created. Now, the duration of His inactivity is either finite or infinite. If you say finite, the existence of the Creator becomes finite; if you say infinite, a duration in which there is an infinite number of possibilities receives its termination. We answer: duration and time are, according to us, created, but we shall explain the real answer to this question when we reply to the second proof of the philosophers.

I say:

Most people who accept a temporal creation of the world believe time to have been created with it. Therefore his assertion that the duration of His inactivity was either limited or unlimited is untrue. For what has no beginning does not finish or end. And the opponent does not admit that the inactivity has any duration at all. What one has to ask them about the consequences of their theory is: is it possible, when the creation of time is admitted, that the term of its beginning may lie beyond the real time in which we live? If they answer that it is not possible, they posit a limited extension beyond which the Creator cannot pass, and this is, in their view, shocking and absurd. If, however, they concede that its possible beginning may lie beyond the moment of its created term, it may further be asked if there may not lie another term beyond this second. If they answer in the affirmative—and they cannot do otherwise—it will be said: Then we shall have here a possible creation of an infinite number of durations, and you will be forced to admit—according to your argument about the spherical revolutions—that their termination is a condition for the real age which exists since them. If you say what is infinite does not finish, the arguments you use about the spherical revolutions against your opponents your opponents will use against you on the subject of the possibility of created durations. If it is objected that the difference between those two cases is that these infinite possibilities belong to extensions which do not become actual, whereas the spherical revolutions do become actual, the answer is that the possibilities of things belong to their necessary accidents and that it does not make any difference, according to the philosophers, if they precede these things or are simultaneous with them, for of necessity they are the dispositions of things. If, then, it is impossible that before the existence of the present spherical revolution there should have been infinite spherical revolutions, the existence of infinite possible revolutions is equally impossible. If one wants to avoid these consequences, one can say that the age of the world is a definite quantity and cannot be longer or shorter than it is, in conformity with the philosophical doctrine about the size of the world. Therefore, these arguments are not stringent, and the safest way for him who accepts the temporal creation of the world is to regard time as of a definite extension and not to admit a possibility which precedes the possible; and to regard also the spatial extension of the world as finite. Only, spatial extension forms a simultaneous whole; not so time.

Al-Ghazali expounds a certain kind of argument attributed to the philosophers on this subject against the theologians when they denied that the impossibility of delay in the Creator's act after His existence is known by primitive intuition.

Al-Ghazali says:

How will you defend yourselves, theologians, against the philosophers, when they drop this argument, based on the necessity of thought, and prove the eternity of the world in this way, saying that times are equivalent so far as the possibility that the Divine Will should attach itself to them is concerned; for what differentiates a given time from an earlier or a later time? And it is not absurd to believe that the earlier or the later might be chosen when on the contrary you theologians say about white, black, movement, and rest that the white is realized through the eternal Will although its substrate accepts equally black and white. Why, then, does the eternal Will attach itself to the white rather than to the black, and what differentiates one of the two possibles from the other for connexion with the eternal Will? But we philosophers know by the necessity of thought that one thing does not distinguish itself from a similar except by a differentiating principle, for if not, it would be possible that the world should come into existence, having the possibility both of existing and of not existing, and that the side of existence, although it has the same possibility as the side of nonexistence, should be differentiated without a differentiating principle. If you answer that the Will of God is the differentiating principle, then one has to inquire what differentiates the Will, that is the reason why it has been differentiated in such or such way. And if you answer: one does not inquire after the motives of the Eternal, well, let the world then be eternal, and let us not inquire after its Creator and its cause, since one does not inquire after the motives of the Eternal! If it is regarded as possible that the Eternal should differentiate one of the two possibles by chance, it will be an extreme absurdity to say that the world is differentiated in differentiated forms which

might just as well be otherwise, and one might then say that this has happened by chance in the same way as you say that the Divine Will has differentiated one time rather than another or one form rather than another by chance. If you say that such a question is irrelevant, because it refers to anything God can will or decide, we answer that this question is quite relevant, for it concerns any time and is pertinent for our opponents to any decision God takes.

We answer: the world exists, in the way it exists, in its time, with its qualities, and in its space, by the Divine Will and will is a quality which has the faculty of differentiating one thing from another, and if it had not this faculty, power in itself would suffice. But, since power is equally related to two contraries and a differentiating principle is needed to differentiate one thing from a similar, it is said that the Eternal possesses besides His power a quality which can differentiate between two similars. And to ask why will differentiates one of two similars is like asking why knowledge must comprehend the knowable, and the answer is that 'knowledge' is the term for a quality which has just this nature. And in the same way, 'will' is the term for a quality the nature or rather the essence of which is to differentiate one thing from another.

The philosophers may object: The assumption of a quality the nature of which is to differentiate one thing from a similar one is something incomprehensible, nay even contradictory, for 'similar' means not to be differentiated, and 'differentiated' means not similar. And it must not be believed that two blacks in two substrates are similar in every way, since the one is in one place and the other in another, and this causes a distinction; nor are two blacks at two times in one substrate absolutely similar, since they are separated in time, and how could they therefore be similar in every way? When we say of two blacks that they are similar, we mean that they are similar in blackness, in their special relation to it, not absolutely. Certainly, if the substrate and the time were one without any distinction, one could not speak any more of two blacks or of any duality at all. This proves that the term 'Divine Will' is derived from our will, and one does not imagine that through our will two similar things can be differentiated. On the contrary, if someone who is thirsty has before him two cups of water, similar in everything in respect to his aim, it will not be possible for him to take either of them. No, he can only take the one he thinks more beautiful or lighter or nearer to his right hand, if he is right-handed, or act from some such reason, hidden or known. Without this the differentiation of the one from the other cannot be imagined.

I say:

The summary of what al-Ghazali relates in this section of the proofs of the philosophers for the impossibility of a temporal proceeding from an eternal agent is that in God there cannot be a will.

The philosophers could only arrive at this argument after granting to their opponents that all opposites—opposites in time, like anterior and posterior, as well as those in quality, like white and black—are equivalent in relation to the eternal Will. And also nonexistence and existence are, according to the theologians, equivalent in relation to the Divine Will. And having granted their opponents this premise, although they did not acknowledge its truth, they said to them: It is of the nature of will that it cannot give preponderance to one thing rather than to a similar one, except through a differentiating principle and a cause which only exist in one of these two similar things; if not, one of the two would happen by chance—and the philosophers argued for the sake of discussion, as if they had conceded that, if the Eternal had a will, a temporal could proceed from an eternal. As the theologians were unable to give a satisfactory answer, they took refuge in the theory that the eternal Will is a quality the nature of which is to differentiate between two similar things, without there being for God a differentiating principle which inclines Him to one of two similar acts; that the eternal Will is thus a quality like warmth which gives heat or like knowledge which comprehends the knowable. But their opponents, the philosophers, answered: It is impossible that this should happen, for two similar things are equivalent for the willer, and his action can only attach itself to the one rather than to the other through their being dissimilar, that is through one's having a quality the other has not. When, however, they are similar in every way and when for God there is no differentiating principle at all, His will will attach itself to both of them indifferently and, when this is the case—His will being the cause of His act—the act will not attach itself to the one rather than to the other, it will attach itself either to the

two contrary actions simultaneously or to neither of them at all, and both cases are absurd. The philosophers, therefore, began their argument, as if they had it granted to them that all things were equivalent in relation to the First Agent, and they forced them to admit that there must be for God a differentiating principle which precedes Him, which is absurd. When the theologians answered that will is a quality the nature of which is to differentiate the similar from the similar, in so far as it is similar, the philosophers objected that this is not understood or meant by the idea of will. They therefore appear to reject the principle which they granted them in the beginning. This is in short the content of this section. It waves the argument from the original question to the problem of the will; to shift one's ground, however, is an act of sophistry.

Al-Ghazali answers in defence of the theological doctrine of the Divine Will:

There are two objections: first, as to your affirmation that you cannot imagine this, do you know it by the necessity of thought or through deduction? You can claim neither the one nor the other. Your comparison with our will is a bad analogy, which resembles that employed on the question of God's knowledge. Now God's knowledge is different from ours in several ways which we acknowledge. Therefore it is not absurd to admit a difference in the will. Your affirmation is like saying that an essence existing neither outside nor inside the world, neither continuous with the world nor separated from it, cannot be understood, because we cannot understand this according to our human measure; the right answer is that it is the fault of your imagination, for rational proof has led the learned to accept its truth. How, then, will you refute those who say that rational proof has led to establishing in God a quality the nature of which is to differentiate between two similar things? And, if the word 'will' does not apply, call it by another name, for let us not quibble about words! We only use the term 'will' by permission of the Divine Law. It may be objected that by its conventional meaning 'will' designates that which has desire, and God has no desire, but we are concerned here with a question not of words but of fact. Besides, we do not even with respect to our human will concede that this cannot be imagined. Suppose two similar dates in front of a man who has a strong desire for them, but who is unable to take them both. Surely he will take one of them through a quality in him the nature of which is to differentiate between two similar things. All the distinguishing qualities you have mentioned, like beauty or nearness or facility in taking, we can assume to be absent, but still the possibility of the taking remains. You can choose between two answers: either you merely say that an equivalence in respect to his desire cannot be imagined—but this is a silly answer, for to assume it is indeed possible—or you say that if an equivalence is assumed, the man will remain for ever hungry and perplexed, looking at the dates without taking one of them, and without a power to choose or to will, distinct from his desire. And this again is one of those absurdities which are recognized by the necessity of thought. Everyone, therefore, who studies, in the human and the divine, the real working of the act of choice, must necessarily admit a quality the nature of which is to differentiate between two similar things.

I say:

This objection can be summarized in two parts: In the first al-Ghazali concedes that the human will is such that it is unable to differentiate one thing from a similar one, in so far as it is similar, but that a rational proof forces us to accept the existence of such a quality in the First Agent. To believe that such a quality cannot exist would be like believing that there cannot exist a being who is neither inside nor outside the world. According to this reasoning, will, which is attributed to the First Agent and to human beings, is predicated in an equivocal way, like knowledge and other qualities which exist in the Eternal in a different way from that in which they exist in the temporal, and it is only through the prescription of the Divine Law that we speak of the Divine Will. It is clear that this objection cannot have anything more than a dialectical value. For a proof that could demonstrate the existence of such a quality, that is a principle determining the existence of one thing rather than that of a similar, would have to assume things willed that are similar; things willed are, however, not similar, but on the contrary opposite, for all opposites can be reduced to the opposition of being and not being, which is the extreme form of opposition; and opposition is the contrary of similarity. The assumption of the theologians that the things to which the will attaches itself are

similar is a false one, and we shall speak of it later. If they say: we affirm only that they are similar in relation to the First Willer, who in His holiness is too exalted to possess desires, and it is through desires that two similar things are actually differentiated, we answer: as to the desires whose realization contributes to the perfection of the essence of the willer, as happens with our desires, through which our will attaches itself to the things willed—those desires are impossible in God; for the will which acts in this way is a longing for perfection when there is an imperfection in the essence of the willer; but as to the desires which belong to the essence of the things willed, nothing new comes to the willer from their realization. It comes exclusively to the thing willed, for instance, when a thing passes into existence from nonexistence, for it cannot be doubted that existence is better for it than nonexistence. It is in this second way that the Primal Will is related to the existing things, for it chooses for them eternally the better of two opposites, and this essentially and primally. This is the first part of the objection contained in this argument.

In the second part he no longer concedes that this quality cannot exist in the human will, but tries to prove that there is also in us, in the face of similar things, a will which distinguishes one from the other; of this he gives examples. For instance, it is assumed that in front of a man there are two dates, similar in every way, and it is supposed that he cannot take them both at the same time. It is supposed that no special attraction need be imagined for him in either of them, and that nevertheless he will of necessity distinguish one of them by taking it. But this is an error. For, when one supposes such a thing, and a willer whom necessity prompts to eat or to take the date, then it is by no means a matter of distinguishing between two similar things when, in this condition, he takes one of the two dates. It is nothing but the admission of an equivalence of two similar things; for whichever of the two dates he may take, his aim will be attained and his desire satisfied. His will attaches itself therefore merely to the distinction between the fact of taking one of them and the fact of leaving them altogether; it attaches itself by no means to the act of taking one definite date and distinguishing this act from the act of leaving the other (that is to say, when it is assumed that the desires for the two are equal); he does not prefer the act of taking the one to the act of taking the other, but he prefers the act of taking one of the two, whichever it may be, and he gives a preference to the act of taking over the act of leaving. This is self-evident. For distinguishing one from the other means giving a preference to the one over the other, and one cannot give a preponderance to one of two similar things in so far as it is similar to the other—although in their existence as individuals they are not similar since each of two individuals is different from the other by reason of a quality exclusive to it. If, therefore, we assume that the will attaches itself to that special character of one of them, then it can be imagined that the will attaches to the one rather than the other because of the element of difference existing in both. But then the will does not attach itself to two similar objects, in so far as they are similar. This is, in short, the meaning of al-Ghazali's first objection. Then he gives his second objection against those who deny the existence of a quality, distinguishing two similar objects from one another.

Al-Ghazali says:

The second objection is that we say: you in your system also are unable to do without a principle differentiating between two equals, for the world exists in virtue of a cause which has produced it in its peculiar shape out of a number of possible distinct shapes which are equivalent; why, then, has this cause differentiated some of them? If to distinguish two similar things is impossible, it is irrelevant whether this concerns the act of God, natural causality, or the logical necessity of ideas: Perhaps you will say: the universal order of the world could not be different from what it is; if the world were smaller or bigger than it actually is, this order would not be perfect, and the same may be asserted of the number of spheres and of stars. And perhaps you will say: the big differs from the small and the many from the few, in so far as they are the object of the will, and therefore they are not similar but different; but human power is too feeble to perceive the modes of Divine Wisdom in its determination of the measures and qualities of things; only in some of them can His wisdom be perceived, as in the obliquity of the ecliptic in relation to the equator, and in the wise contrivance of the apogee and the eccentric sphere. In most cases, however, the secret is not revealed, but the differences are known, and it is

not impossible that a thing should be distinguished from another, because the order of the world depends on it; but certainly the times are absolutely indifferent in relation to the world's possibility and its order, and it cannot be claimed that, if the world were created one moment later or earlier, this order could not be imagined; and this indifference is known by the necessity of thought.

We answer: although we can employ the same reasoning against your argument in the matter of different times, for it might be said that God created the world at the time most propitious for its creation, we shall not limit ourselves to this refutation, but shall assume, according to your own principle, a differentiation in two points about which there can be no disagreement: (1) the difference in the direction of spherical movement; (2) the definite place of the poles in relation to the ecliptic in spherical movement. The proof of the statement relating to the poles is that heaven is a globe, moving on two poles, as on two immovable points, whereas the globe of heaven is homogeneous and simple, especially the highest sphere, the ninth, which possesses no stars at all, and these two spheres move on two poles, the north and the south. We now say: of all the opposite points, which are infinite, according to you philosophers, there is no pair one could not imagine as poles. Why then have the two points of the north and south pole been fixed upon as poles and as immovable; and why does the ecliptic not pass through these two poles, so that the poles would become the opposite points of the ecliptic? And if wisdom is shown in the size and shape of heaven, what then distinguishes the place of the poles from others, so that they are fixed upon to serve as poles, to the exclusion of all the other parts and points? And yet all the points are similar, and all parts of the globe are equivalent. And to this there is no answer.

One might say: perhaps the spot in which the point of the poles is, is distinguished from other points by a special quality, in relation to its being the place of the poles and to its being at rest, for it does not seem to change its place or space or position or whatever one wishes to call it; and all the other spots of the sphere by turning change their position in relation to the earth and the other spheres and only the poles are at rest; perhaps this spot was more apt to be at rest than the others.

We answer: if you say so, you explain the fact through a natural differentiation of the parts of the first sphere; the sphere, then, ceases to be homogeneous, and this is in contradiction with your principle, for one of the proofs by which you prove the necessity of the globular shape of heaven, is that its nature is simple, homogeneous, and without differentiation, and the simplest shape is the globe; for the quadrangle and the hexagon and other figures demand a salience and a differentiation of the angles, and this happens only when its simple nature is added to. But although this supposition of yours is in contradiction with your own theory, it does not break the strength of your opponents' argument; the question about this special quality still holds good, namely, can those other parts accept this quality or not? If the answer is in the affirmative, why then is this quality limited to a few only of those homogeneous parts? If the answer is negative, we reply: the other parts, in so far as they constitute bodies, receiving the form of bodies, are homogeneous of necessity, and there is no justification for attributing this special quality to this spot exclusively on account of its being a part of a body and a part of heaven, for the other parts of heaven participate in this qualification. Therefore, its differentiation must rest on a decision by God, or on a quality whose nature consists in differentiating between two similars. Therefore, just as among philosophers the theory is upheld that all times are equivalent in regard to the creation of the world, their opponents are justified in claiming that the parts of heaven are equivalent for the reception of the quality through which stability in position becomes more appropriate than a change of position. And out of this there is no issue.

I say:

This means in brief that the philosophers must acknowledge that there is a quality in the Creator of the world which differentiates between two similars, for it seems that the world might have had another shape and another quantity than it actually has, for it might have been bigger or smaller. Those different possibilities are, therefore, equivalent in regard to the determination of the existence of the world. On the other hand, if the philosophers say that the world can have only one special shape, the special quantity of its bodies and the special number of them it actually

has, and that this equivalence of possibilities can only be imagined in relation to the times of temporal creation—since for God no moment is more suitable than another for its creation—they may be told that it is possible to answer this by saying that the creation of the world happened at its most propitious moment. But we, the theologians say, want to show the philosophers two equivalent things of which they cannot affirm that there exists any difference between them; the first is the particular direction of the spherical movement and the second the particular position of the poles, relative to the spheres; and any pair whatever of opposite points, united by a line which passes through the center of the sphere, might constitute the poles. But the differentiation of these two points, exclusive of all other points which might just as well be the poles of this identical sphere cannot happen except by a quality differentiating between two similar objects. If the philosophers assert that it is not true that any other place on the sphere might be the seat for these poles, they will be told: such an assertion implies that the parts of the spheres are not homogeneous and yet you have often said that the sphere is of a simple nature and therefore has a simple form, that is to say the spherical. And again, if the philosophers affirm that there are spots on the sphere which are not homogeneous, it will be asked how these spots came to be of a heterogeneous nature; is it because they are a body or because they are a celestial body? But the absence of homogeneity cannot be explained in this way. Therefore, al-Ghazali says just as among philosophers the theory is upheld that all times are equivalent in regard to the creation of the world, the theologians are justified in claiming that the parts of heaven are equivalent in regard to their serving as poles, and that the poles do not seem differentiated from the other points through a special position or through their being in an immovable place, exclusive of all other places. This then in short is the objection; it is, however, a rhetorical one, for many things which by demonstration can be found to be necessary seem at first sight merely possible. The philosophers' answer is that they assert that they have proved that the world is composed of five bodies: a body neither heavy nor light, i.e. the revolving spherical body of heaven and four other bodies, two of which are earth, absolutely heavy, which is the center of the revolving spherical body, and fire, absolutely light, which is seated in the extremity of the revolving sphere; nearest to earth is water, which is heavy relatively to air, light relatively to earth; next to water comes air, which is light relatively to water, heavy relatively to fire. The reason why earth is absolutely heavy is that it is furthest away from the circular movement, and therefore it is the fixed centre of the revolving body; the reason why fire is absolutely light is that it is nearest to the revolving sphere; the intermediate bodies are both heavy and light, because they are in the middle between the two extremes, that is the farthest point and the nearest. If there were not a revolving body, surely there would be neither heavy nor light by nature, and neither high nor low by nature, and this whether absolutely or relatively; and the bodies would not differ by nature in the way in which, for instance, earth moves by nature to its specific place and fire moves by nature to another place, and equally so the intermediary bodies. And the world is only finite, because of the spherical body, and this because of the essential and natural finiteness of the spherical body, as one single plane circumscribes it. Rectilinear bodies are not essentially finite, as they allow of an increase and decrease; they are only finite because they are in the middle of a body that admits neither increase nor decrease, and is therefore essentially finite. And, therefore, the body circumscribing the world cannot but be spherical, as otherwise the bodies would either have to end in other bodies, and we should have an infinite regress, or they would end in empty space, and the impossibility of both suppositions has been demonstrated. He who understands this knows that every possible world imaginable can only consist of these bodies, and that bodies have to be either circular—and then they are neither heavy nor light, or rectilinear—and then they are either heavy or light, that is either fire or earth or the intermediate bodies; that these bodies have to be either revolving, or surrounded by a revolving periphery, for each body either moves from, towards, or round the center; that by the movements of the heavenly bodies to the right and to the left all bodies are constituted and all that is produced from opposites is generated; and that through these movements the individuals of these four bodies never cease being in a continual production and corruption. Indeed, if a single one of these movements should cease, the order and proportion of this universe would disappear, for it is clear

that this order must necessarily depend on the actual number of these movements—for if this were smaller or greater, either the order would be disturbed, or there would be another order—and that the number of these movements is as it is, either through its necessity for the existence of this sublunary world, or because it is the best.

Do not ask here for a proof for all this, but if you are interested in science, look for its proof where you can find it. Here, however, listen to theories which are more convincing than those of the theologians and which, even if they do not bring you complete proof, will give your mind an inclination to lead you to proof through scientific speculation. You should imagine that each heavenly sphere is a living being, in so far as it possesses a body of a definite measure and shape and moves itself in definite directions, not at random. Anything of this nature is necessarily a living being; that is when we see a body of a definite quality and quantity move itself in space, in a definite direction, not at random, through its own power, not through an exterior cause, and move in opposite directions at the same time, we are absolutely sure that it is a living being, and we said only "not through an exterior cause" because iron moves towards a magnet when the magnet is brought to it from the outside—and besides, iron moves to a magnet from any direction whatever. The heavenly bodies, therefore, possess places which are poles by nature, and these bodies cannot have their poles in other places, just as earthly animals have particular organs in particular parts of their bodies for particular actions, and cannot have them in other places, for example the organs of locomotion, which are located in definite parts. The poles represent the organs of locomotion in animals of spherical form, and the only difference in this respect between spherical and non-spherical animals is that in the latter these organs differ in both shape and power, whereas in the former they only differ in power. For this reason it has been thought on first sight that they do not differ at all, and that the poles could be in any two points on the sphere. And just as it would be ridiculous to say that a certain movement in a certain species of earthly animal could be in any part whatever of its body, or in that part where it is in another species, because this movement has been localized in each species in the place where it conforms most to its nature, or in the only place where this animal can perform the movement, so it stands with the differentiation in the heavenly bodies for the place of their poles. For the heavenly bodies are not one species and numerically many, but they form a plurality in species, like the plurality of different individuals of animals where there is only one individual in the species. Exactly the same answer can be given to the question why the heavens move in different directions: that, because they are animals, they must move in definite directions, like right and left, before and behind, which are directions determined by the movements of animals, and the only difference between the movements of earthly animals and those of heavenly bodies is that in the different animals these movements are different in shape and in power, whereas in the heavenly animals they only differ in power. And it is for this reason that Aristotle thinks that heaven possesses the directions of right and left, before and behind, high and low. The diversity of the heavenly bodies in the direction of their movements rests on their diversity of species, and the fact that this difference in the directions of their movements forms the specific differentia of their species is something proper to them. Imagine the first heaven as one identical animal whose nature obliges it—either by necessity or because it is for the best—to move with all its parts in one movement from east to west. The other spheres are obliged by their nature to have the opposite movement. The direction which the body of the universe is compelled to follow through its nature is the best one, because its body is the best of bodies and the best among the moving bodies must also have the best direction. All this is explained here in this tentative way, but is proved apodictically in its proper place. This is also the manifest sense of the Divine Words, "there is no changing the words of God," and "there is no altering the creation of God." If you want to be an educated man, proceeding by proof, you should look for the proof of this in its proper place.

Now if you have understood all this, it will not be difficult for you to see the faults in al-Ghazali's arguments here about the equivalence of the two opposite movements in relation to each heavenly body and to the sublunary world. On first thoughts it might be imagined that the movement from east to west might also belong to other spheres besides the first, and that the first sphere might equally well move

from west to east. You might as well say that the crab could be imagined as having the same direction of movement as a human being. But, as a matter of fact, such a thought will not occur to you about humans and crabs, because of their difference in shape, whereas it might occur to you about the heavenly spheres, since they agree in shape. He who contemplates a product of art does not perceive its wisdom if he does not perceive the wisdom of the intention embodied in it, and the effect intended. And if he does not understand its wisdom, he may well imagine that this object might have any form, any quantity, any configuration of its parts, and any composition whatever. This is the case with the theologians in regard to the body of the heavens, but all such opinions are superficial. He who has such beliefs about products of art understands neither the work nor the artist, and this holds also in respect of the works of God's creation. Understand this principle, and do not judge the works of God's creation hastily and superficially, so that you may not become one of those about whom the Koran says: "say, shall we inform you of those who lose most by their works, those who erred in their endeavor after the life of this world and who think they are doing good deeds?" May God make us perspicacious and lift from us the veils of ignorance; indeed He is the bounteous, the generous! To contemplate the various actions of the heavenly bodies is like contemplating the kingdom of heaven, which Abraham contemplated, according to the words of the Koran: "thus did we show Abraham the kingdom of heaven and of the earth, that he should be of those who are sure." And let us now relate al-Ghazali's argument about the movements.

Al-Ghazali says:

The second point in this argument concerns the special direction of the movement of the spheres which move partially from east to west, partially in the opposite direction, whereas the equivalence of the directions in relation to their cause is exactly the same as the equivalence of the times. If it is said: if the universe revolved in only one direction, there would never be a difference in the configuration of the stars, and such relations of the stars as their being in trine, in sextile, and in conjunction would never arise, but the universe would remain in one unique position without any change; the difference of these relations, however, is the principle of all production in the world—we answer: our argument does not concern the difference in direction of movement; no, we concede that the highest sphere moves from east to west and the spheres beneath it in the opposite direction, but everything that happens in this way would happen equally if the reverse took place, that is if the highest sphere moved from west to east and the lower spheres in the opposite direction. For all the same differences in configuration would arise just as well. Granted that these movements are circular and in opposite directions, both directions are equivalent; why then is the one distinguished from the other, which is similar to it? If it is said: as the two directions are opposed and contrary, how can they be similar, we answer: this is like saying "since before and after are opposed in the existing world, how could it be claimed that they are equivalent?" Still, it is asserted by you philosophers that the equivalence of times, so far as the possibility of their realization and any purpose one might imagine in their realization is concerned, is an evident fact. Now, we regard it as equally evident that spaces, positions, situations, and directions are equivalent so far as concerns their receiving movement and any purpose that might be connected with it. If, therefore, the philosophers are allowed to claim that notwithstanding this equivalence they are different, their opponents are fully justified in claiming the same in regard to the times.

I say:

From what I have said previously, the speciousness of this argument and the way in which it has to be answered will not be obscure to you. All this is the work of one who does not understand the exalted natures of the heavenly bodies and their acts of wisdom for the sake of which they have been created, and who compares God's knowledge with the knowledge of ignorant man.

Al-Ghazali says:

If it is said: as the two directions are opposed and contrary, how can they be similar, we answer: this is like saying, "since before and after in the existing world are opposed, how could it be claimed that they are equivalent?" Still, it is asserted by you philosophers that the equivalence of times so far as the possibility of their realization, and any purpose one might imag-

ine in their realization is concerned, is an evident fact. Now, we regard it as equally evident that spaces, positions, situations, and directions are equivalent so far as concerns their receiving the movement and any purpose that might be connected with it.

I say:

The falsehood of this is self-evident. Even if one should admit that the possibilities of human existence and nonexistence are equivalent in the matter out of which humans have been created, and that this is a proof for the existence of a determining principle which prefers the existence of humans to their nonexistence, still it cannot be imagined that the possibilities of seeing and not seeing are equivalent in the eye. Thus, no one can claim that the opposite directions are equivalent, although he may claim that the substratum for both is indifferent, and that therefore out of both directions similar actions result. And the same holds good for before and after: they are not equivalent, in so far as this event is earlier and that event later; they can only be claimed to be equivalent so far as their possibility of existence is concerned. But the whole assumption is wrong: for essential opposites also need essentially opposite substrata and a unique substratum giving rise to opposite acts at one and the same time is an impossibility. The philosophers do not believe that the possibilities of a thing's existence and of its nonexistence are equivalent at one and the same time; no, the time of the possibility of its existence is different from the time of the possibility of its nonexistence, time for them is the condition for the production of what is produced, and for the corruption of what perishes. If the time for the possibility of the existence of a thing and the time for the possibility of its nonexistence were the same, that is to say in its proximate matter, its existence would be vitiated, because of the possibility of its nonexistence, and the possibility of its existence and of its nonexistence would be dependent only on the agent, not on the substratum.

Thus, he who tries to prove the existence of an agent in this way gives only persuasive, dialectical arguments, not apodictic proof. It is believed that Farabi and Avicenna followed this line to establish that every act must have an agent, but it is not a proof of the ancient philosophers, and both of them merely took it over from the theologians of our religion. In relation, however, to the temporal creation of the world—for him who believes in it—before and after cannot even be imagined, for before and after in time can only be imagined in relation to the present moment, and as, according to the theologians, there was before the creation of the world no time, how could there be imagined something preceding the moment when the world was created? A definite moment cannot be assigned for the creation of the world, for either time did not exist before it, or there was an infinite time, and in neither case could a definite time be fixed to which the Divine could attach itself. Therefore, it would be more suitable to call this book *Incoherence* without qualification rather than *The Incoherence of the Philosophers*, for the only profit it gives the reader is to make him incoherent.

Al-Ghazali says:

If, therefore, the philosophers are allowed to claim that, notwithstanding this equivalence, they are different, their opponents are fully justified in claiming the same in regard to times.

I say:

He wants to say: if the philosophers are justified in claiming a difference in the direction of movement, the theologians have the right to assert a difference in times, notwithstanding their belief in their equivalence. This is only a verbal argument, and does not refer to the facts themselves, even if one admits an analogy between the opposite directions and the different times, but this is often objected to, because there is no analogy between this difference in times and directions. Our adversary, however, is forced to admit that there is an analogy between them, because they are both claimed to be different, and both to be equivalent. These, therefore, are one and all dialectical arguments.

Al-Ghazali says:

The second objection against the basis of their argument is that the philosophers are told, "you regard the creation of a temporal being by an eternal as impossible, but you have to acknowledge it too, for there are new events happening in the world and they have causes. It is absurd to think that these events lead to other events *ad infinitum*, and no intelligent person can believe such a thing. If such a thing were possible, you need not acknowledge a creator and establish

a necessary being on whom possible existences depend. If, however, there is a limit for those events in which their sequence ends, this limit will be eternal and then indubitably you too acknowledge the principle that a temporal can proceed from an eternal being."

I say:

If the philosophers had introduced the eternal being into reality from the side of the temporal by this kind of argument, that is if they had admitted that the temporal, in so far as temporal, proceeds from an eternal being, there would be no possibility of their avoiding the difficulty in this problem. But you must understand that the philosophers permit the existence of a temporal which comes out of a temporal being *ad infinitum* in an accidental way, when this is repeated in a limited and finite matter when, for instance, the corruption of one of two things becomes the necessary condition for the existence of the other. For instance, according to the philosophers it is necessary that human should be produced from human on condition that the anterior human perishes so as to become the matter for the production of a third. For instance, we must imagine two humans of whom the first produces the second from the matter of a human who perishes; when the second becomes a human himself, the first perishes, then the second human produces a third human out of the matter of the first, and then the second perishes and the third produces out of his matter a fourth, and so we can imagine in two matters an activity continuing ad infinitum, without any impossibility arising. And this happens as long as the agent lasts, for if this agent has neither beginning nor end for his existence, the activity has neither beginning nor end for its existence, as it has been explained before. And in the same way you may imagine this happening in them in the past: when a human exists, there must before him have been a human who produced him and a human who perished, and before this second man a human who produced him and a human who perished, for everything that is produced in this way is, when it depends on an eternal agent, of a circular nature in which no actual totality can be reached. If, on the other hand, a human were produced from another human out of infinite matters, or there were an infinite addition of them, there would be an impossibility, for then there could arise an infinite matter and there could be an infinite whole. For if a finite whole existed to which things were added *ad infinitum* without any corruption taking place in it, an infinite whole could come into existence, as Aristotle proved in his *Physics*. For this reason the ancients introduce an eternal absolutely unchanging being, having in mind not temporal beings, proceeding from it in so far as they are temporal, but beings proceeding from it as being eternal generically, and they hold that this infinite series is the necessary consequence of an eternal agent, for the temporal needs for its own existence only a temporal cause. Now there are two reasons why the ancients introduce the existence of an eternal numerically unique being which does not suffer any change. The first is that they discovered that this revolving being is eternal, for they discovered that the present individual is produced through the corruption of its predecessor and that the corruption of this previous individual implies the production of the one that follows it, and that it is necessary that this everlasting change should proceed from an eternal mover and an eternal moved body, which does not change in its substance, but which changes only in place so far as concerns its parts, and approaches certain of the transitory things and recedes from certain of them, and this is the cause of the corruption of one half of them and the production of the other half. And this heavenly body is the being that changes in place only, not in any of the other kinds of change, and is through its temporal activities the cause of all things temporal; and because of the continuity of its activities which have neither beginning nor end, it proceeds from a cause which has neither beginning nor end. The second reason why they introduce an eternal being absolutely without body and matter is that they found that all the kinds of movement depend on spatial movement, and that spatial movement depends on a being moved essentially by a prime mover, absolutely immobile, both essentially and accidentally, for otherwise there would exist at the same time an infinite number of moved movers, and this is impossible. And it is necessary that this first mover should be eternal, or else it would not be the first. Every movement, therefore, depends on this mover and its setting things in motion essentially, not accidentally. And this mover exists simultaneously with each thing moved, at the time of its motion, for a mover existing before the thing moved—such as a human producing a human—sets in motion only accidentally, not essentially; but the mover who is the condition of a human's existence from the beginning of his production till its end, or rather from the beginning of his existence till its end, is the prime mover. And likewise its existence is the condition for the existence of all beings and the preservation of heaven and earth and all that is between them. All this is not proved here apodictically, but only in the way we follow here and which is in any case more plausible for an impartial reader than the arguments of our opponents.

If this is clear to you, you certainly are in no need of the subterfuge by which al-Ghazali in his argument against the philosophers tries to conciliate them with their adversaries in this matter; indeed these artifices will not do, for if you have not understood how the philosophers introduce an eternal being into reality, you have not understood how they settle the difficulty of the rise of the temporal out of the eternal; they do that, as we said, either through the medium of a being eternal in its essence but generable and corruptible in its particular movements, not, however, in its universal circular movement, or through the medium of what is generically eternal—that is has neither beginning nor end in it acts.

Al-Ghazali answers in the name of the philosophers:

The philosophers may say, "we do not consider it impossible that any temporal being, whatever it may be, should proceed from an eternal being, but we regard it as impossible that the first temporal should proceed from the eternal, as the mode of its procession does not differ from that which precedes it, either in a greater inclination towards existence or through the presence of some particular time, or through an instrument, condition, nature, accident, or any cause whatever which might produce a new mode. If this therefore is not the first temporal, it will be possible that it should proceed from the eternal, when another thing proceeds from it, because of the disposition of the receiving substratum, or because the time was propitious or for any other reason."

Having given this reply on the part of the philosophers, al-Ghazali answers it: this question about the actualization of the disposition, whether of the time and of any new condition which arises in it, still holds good, and we must either come to an infinite regress or arrive at an eternal being out of which a first temporal being proceeds.

I say:

This question is the same question all over again as he asked the philosophers first, and this is the same kind of conclusion as he made them draw then, namely that a temporal proceeds from an eternal, and having given as their answer something which does not correspond with the question, that is that it is possible that a temporal being should proceed from the Eternal without there being a first temporal being, he turns the same question against them again. The correct answer to this question was given above: the temporal proceeds from the First Eternal, not in so far as it is temporal but in so far as it is eternal, that is through being eternal generically, though temporal in its parts. For according to the philosophers an eternal being out of which a temporal being proceeds essentially is not the First Eternal, but its acts, according to them, depend on the First Eternal; that is the actualization of the condition for activity of the eternal, which is not the First Eternal, depends on the First Eternal in the same way as the temporal products depend on the First Eternal and this is a dependence based on the universal, not on individuals.

After this al-Ghazali introduces an answer of the philosophers, in one of the forms in which this theory can be represented, which amounts to this: a temporal being proceeding from an eternal can only be represented by means of a circular movement which resembles the eternal by not having beginning or end and which resembles the temporal in so far as each part of it is transient, so that this movement through the generation of its parts is the principle of temporal things, and through the eternity of its totality the activity of the eternal.

Then al-Ghazali argues against this view, according to which in the opinion of the philosophers the temporal proceeds from the First Eternal, and says to them: is this circular movement temporal or eternal? If it is eternal, how does it become the principle for temporal things? And if it is temporal, it will need another temporal being and we shall have an infinite regress. And when you say that it partially resembles the eternal, partially the temporal, for it resembles the eternal in so far as it is permanent and the tempo-

ral in so far as it arises anew, we answer: is it the principle of temporal things, because of its permanence, or because of its arising anew? In the former case, how can a temporal proceed from something because of its permanence? And in the latter case, what arises anew will need a cause for its arising anew, and we have an infinite regress.

I say:

This argument is Sophistical. The temporal does not proceed from it in so far as it is eternal, but in so far as it is temporal; it does not need, however, for its arising anew a cause arising anew; for its arising anew is not a new fact, but an eternal act, that is an act without beginning or end. Therefore its agent must be an eternal agent, for an eternal act has an eternal agent, and a temporal act a temporal agent. Only through the eternal element in it can it be understood that movement has neither beginning nor end, and this is meant by its permanence, for movement itself is not permanent, but changing.

THE EIGHTH DISCUSSION

Whether the First Cause Is Simple

> To refute their theory that the existence of the First is simple, namely that it is pure existence and that its existence stands in relation to no quiddity and to no essence, but stands to necessary existence as do other beings to their quiddity.

Al-Ghazali says:

There are two ways of attacking this theory. The first is to demand a proof and to ask how you know this, through the necessity of the intellect, or through speculation and not by immediate necessity; and in any case you must tell us your method of reasoning. If it is said that, if the First had a quiddity, its existence would be related to it, and would be consequent on this quiddity and would be its necessary attribute, and the consequent is an effect and therefore necessary existence would be an effect, and this is a contradiction, we answer: this is to revert to the source of the confusion in the application of the term 'necessary existence'; for we call this entity 'reality' or 'quiddity' and this reality exists, that is it is not nonexistent and is not denied, but its existence is brought into a relation with it, and if you like to call this 'consequent' and 'necessary attribute,' we shall not quibble about words, if you have once acknowledged that it has no agent for its existence and that this existence has not ceased to be eternal and to have no efficient cause; if, however, you understand by 'consequent' and 'effect' that it has an efficient cause, this is not true. But if you mean something else, this is conceded, for it is not impossible, since the demonstration proves only the end of a causal series and its ending in an existent reality; a positive quiddity, therefore, is possible, and there is no need to deny the quiddity.

If it is said: then the quiddity becomes a cause for the existence which is consequent on it, and the existence becomes an effect and an object of the act, we answer: The quiddity in temporal things is not a cause of their existence, and why should it therefore be the cause in the eternal, if you mean by 'cause,' the agent? But if you mean something else by it—namely that without which it could not be, let that be accepted, for there is nothing impossible in it; the impossibility lies only in the infinite causal series, and if this series only comes to a final term, then the impossibility is cancelled. Impossibility can be understood only on this point, therefore you must give a proof of its impossibility.

All the proofs of the philosophers are nothing but presumptions that the term has a sense from which certain consequences follow, and nothing but the supposition that demonstration has in fact proved a necessary existent with the meaning the philosophers ascribed to it. We have, however, shown previously that this is not true. In short, this proof of the philosophers comes down to the proof of the denial of attributes and of the division into genus and specific difference; only this proof is still more ambiguous and weak, for this plurality is purely verbal, for the intellect does allow the acceptance of one single existent quiddity. The philosophers, however, say that every existent quiddity is a plurality, for it contains quiddity and existence, and this is an extreme confusion; for the meaning of a single existent is perfectly understandable—nothing exists which has no essence, and the existence of an essence does not annul its singleness.

I say:

Al-Ghazali does not relate Avicenna's doctrine literally as he did in his book *The Aims of the Philosophers.*

For since Avicenna believed that the existence of a thing indicated an attribute additional to its essence, he could no longer admit that its essence was the agent of its existence out of the possibles; for then the thing would be the cause of its own existence and it would not have an agent. It follows from this, according to Avicenna, that everything which has an existence additional to its essence has an efficient cause, and since, according to Avicenna, the First has no agent, it follows necessarily that its existence is identical with its essence. And therefore al-Ghazali's objection that Avicenna assimilates existence to a necessary attribute of the essence is not true, because the essence of a thing is the cause of its necessary attribute and it is not possible that a thing should be the cause of its own existence, because the existence of a thing is prior to its quiddity. To identify the quiddity and the existence of a thing is not to do away with its quiddity, as al-Ghazali asserts, but is only the affirmation of the unity of quiddity and existence. If we regard existence as an accidental attribute of the existent, and it is the agent which gives possible things their existence, necessarily that which has no agent either cannot have an existence (and this is absurd), or its existence must be identical with its essence.

But the whole of this discussion is built on the mistake that the existence of a thing is one of its attributes. For the existence which in our knowledge is prior to the quiddity of a thing is that which signifies the true. Therefore, the question whether a thing exists, either (1) refers to that which has a cause that determines its existence, and in that case its potential meaning is to ask whether this thing has a cause or not, according to Aristotle at the beginning of the second chapter of the *Posterior Analytics;* or (2) it refers to that which has no cause, and then its meaning is to ask whether a thing possesses a necessary attribute which determines its existence. And when by 'existent' is meant what is understood by 'thing' and 'entity,' it follows the rule of the genus which is predicated analogically, and whatever it is in this sense is attributed in the same way to that which has a cause and to that which has none, and it does not signify anything but the concept of the existent, and by this is meant "the true," and if it means something additional to the essence, it is only in a subjective sense which does not exist outside the soul except potentially, as is also the case with the universal. And this is the way in which the ancient philosophers considered the First Principle, and they regarded it as a simple existent. As to the later philosophers in Islam, they stated that, in their speculation about the nature of the existent *qua* existent, they were led to accept a simple existent of this description.

The best method to follow, in my opinion, and the nearest to strict proof, is to say that the actualization of existents which have in their substance a possible existence necessarily occurs only through an actualizer which is in act, that is acting, and moves them and draws them out of potency into act. And if this actualizer itself is also of the nature of the possible, that is possible in its substance, there will have to be another actualizer for it, necessary in its substance and not possible, so that this sublunary world may be conserved, and the nature of the possible causes may remain everlastingly, proceeding without end. And if these causes exist without end, as appears from their nature, and each of them is possible, necessarily their cause, that is that which determines their permanence, must be something necessary in its substance, and if there were a moment in which nothing was moved at all, there would be no possibility of an origination of movement. The nexus between temporal existence and eternal can only take place without a change affecting the First through that movement which is partly eternal, partly temporal. And the thing moved by this movement is what Avicenna calls "the existence necessary through another," and this "necessary through another" must be a body everlastingly moved, and in this way it is possible that the essentially temporal and corruptible should exist in dependence on the eternal, and this through approach to something and through recession from it, as you observe it happen to transitory existents in relation to the heavenly bodies. And since this moved body is necessary in its substance, possible in its local movement, it is necessary that the process should terminate in an absolutely necessary existent in which there is no potency at all, either in its substance, or locally or in any of the other forms of movement; and that which is of this description is necessarily simple, because if it were a compound, it would be possible, not necessary, and it would require a necessary existent. And this method of proving it is in my opinion sufficient, and it is true.

However, what Avicenna adds to this proof by saying that the possible existent must terminate either in an existent necessary through another or in an existent necessary through itself, and in the former case that the necessary through another should be a consequence of the existent necessary through itself, for he affirms that the existent necessary through another is in itself a possible existent and what is possible needs something necessary—this addition, is to my mind superfluous and erroneous, for in the necessary, in whatever way you suppose it, there is no possibility whatsoever and there exists nothing of a single nature of which it can be said that it is in one way possible and in another way necessary in its existence. For the philosophers have proved that there is no possible whatsoever in the necessary; for the possible is the opposite of the necessary, and the only thing that can happen is that a thing should be in one way necessary, in another way possible, as they believed, for instance, to be the case with the heavenly body or what is above the body of the heavens, namely that it was necessary through its substance and possible in its movement and in space. What led Avicenna to this division was that he believed that the body of the heavens was essentially necessary through another, possible by itself, and we have shown in another place that this is not true. And the proof which Avicenna uses in dealing with the necessary existent, when this distinction and this indication are not made, is of the type of common dialectical notions; when, however, the distinction is made, it is of the type of demonstrative proof.

You must know further that the becoming of which the Holy Law speaks is of the kind of empirical becoming in this world, and this occurs in the forms of the existents which the Ash'arites call mental qualities and the philosophers call forms, and this becoming occurs only through another thing and in time, and the Holy Words, "have not those who have disbelieved considered that the heavens and the earth were coherent, and we have rent them," and the Divine Words, "then he straightened himself up to the sky which was smoke," refer to this. But as to the relation which exists between the nature of the possible existent and the necessary existent, this the Holy Law is silent, because it is too much above the understanding of the common man and knowledge of it is not necessary for his blessedness. When the Ash'arites affirm that the nature of the possible is created and has come into existence in time out of nothing (a notion which all the philosophers oppose, whether they believe in the temporal beginning of the world or not), they do not say this, if you consider the question rightly, on the authority of the law of Islam, and there is no proof for it. What appears from the Holy Law is the commandment to abstain from investigating that about which the Holy Law is silent, and therefore it is said in the Traditions: "the people did not cease thinking till they said: God has created this, but who has created God? And the Prophet said: when one of you finds this, this is an act of pure truth," and in another version: "when one of you finds this, let him read the verse of the Koran: say, He, God is one. And know that for the masses to turn to such a question comes from the whisperings of Satan and therefore the prophet said, this is an act of pure faith."

Al-Ghazali says:

The second way is to say that an existence without quiddity or essence cannot be conceived, and just as mere nonexistence, without a relation to an existent the nonexistence of which can be supposed, cannot be conceived, in the same way existence can be only conceived in relation to a definite essence, especially when it is defined as a single essence; for how could it be defined as single, conceptually differentiated from others, if it had not a real essence? For to deny the quiddity is to deny the real essence, and when you deny the real essence of the existent, the existent can no longer be understood. It is as if the philosophers affirmed at the same time existence and a nonexistent, which is contradictory. This is shown by the fact that, if it were conceivable, it would be also possible in the effects that there should be an existence without an essence, participating with the First in not having a real essence and a quiddity, differing from it in having a cause, whereas the First is causeless. And why should such an effect not be imagined? And is there any other reason for this than that it is inconceivable in itself? But what is inconceivable in itself does not become conceivable by the denial of its cause, nor does what is conceivable become inconceivable because it is supposed to have a cause. Such an extreme negation is the most obscure of their theories, although they believe indeed that they have proved what they say. Their doctrine ends in absolute negation, and indeed the denial of the quiddity is the denial of the real essence, and through the denial of this reality nothing

remains but the word 'existence,' which has no object at all when it is not related to a quiddity.

And if it is said, "its real essence is that it is the necessary, and the necessary is its quiddity," we answer, "The only sense of 'necessary' is 'causeless,'" and this is a negation which does not constitute a real essence; and the denial of a cause for the real essence presupposes the real essence, and therefore let the essence be conceivable, so that it can be described as being causeless; but the essence cannot be represented as nonexistent, since 'necessity' has no other meaning than 'being causeless.' Besides, if the necessity were added to the existence, this would form a plurality; and if it is not added, how then could it be the quiddity? For the existence is not the quiddity, and thus what is not added to the existence cannot be the quiddity either.

I say:

This whole paragraph is sophistry. For the philosophers do not assume that the First has an existence without a quiddity and a quiddity without an existence. They believe only that the existence in the compound is an additional attribute to its essence and it only acquires this attribute through the agent, and they believe that in that which is simple and causeless this attribute is not additional to the quiddity and that it has no quiddity differentiated from its existence; but they do not say that it has absolutely no quiddity, as he assumes in his objection against them. Having assumed that they deny the quiddity, which is false, al-Ghazali begins now to charge them with reprehensible theories.

He says:

If this were conceivable it would also be possible in the effects that there should be an existence without an essence, participating with the First in not having a real essence.

I say:

But the philosophers do not assume an existent absolutely without a quiddity, they only assume that it has not a quiddity like the quiddities of the other existents; and this is one of the sophistical fallacies, for the term 'quiddity' is ambiguous, and this assumption, and everything built upon it, is a sophistical argument, for the nonexistent cannot be described either by denying or by affirming something of it. And al-Ghazali, by fallacies of the kind perpetrated in this book, is not exempt from wickedness or from ignorance, and he seems nearer to wickedness than to ignorance—or should we say that there is a necessity which obliged him to do this?

As to his remark, that the meaning of 'necessary existent' is 'causeless,' this is not true, but our expression that it is a necessary existent has a positive meaning, consequent on a nature which has absolutely no cause, no exterior agent, and no agent which is part of it.

And as to al-Ghazali's words, "if the necessity were added to the existence, this would form a plurality; and if it is not added, how then could it be the quiddity? For existence is not the quiddity, and thus what is not added to the existence cannot be the quiddity either."

I say:

According to the philosophers necessity is not an attribute added to the essence, and it is predicated of the essence in the same way as we say of it that it is inevitable and eternal. And likewise if we understand by 'existence' a mental attribute, it is not an addition to the essence, but if we understand it as being an accident, in the way Avicenna regards it in the composite existent, then it becomes difficult to explain how the uncompounded can be the quiddity itself, although one might say perhaps, "in the way the knowledge in the uncompounded becomes the knower himself." If, however, one regards the existent as the true, all these doubts lose their meaning, and likewise, if one understands 'existent' as having the same sense as 'entity,' and according to this it is true that the existence in the uncompounded is the quiddity itself.

ABOUT THE NATURAL SCIENCES (FROM THE *TAHAFUT AL-TAHAFUT*)

The Denial of a Logical Necessity Between Cause and Effect

Al-Ghazali says:

According to us the connection between what is usually believed to be a cause and what is believed to be an effect is not a necessary connection; each of two things has its own individuality and is not the other, and neither the affirmation nor the negation, neither the existence nor the nonexistence of the one is implied in the affirmation, negation, existence, and nonexistence of the other, for example the satisfaction of thirst does not imply drinking, nor satiety eating, nor burning contact with fire, nor light sunrise, nor decapitation death, nor recovery the drinking of medicine, nor evacuation the taking of a purgative, and so on for all the empirical connexions existing in medicine, astronomy, the sciences, and the crafts. For the connection in these things is based on a prior power of God to create them in a successive order, though not because this connection is necessary in itself and cannot be disjoined—on the contrary, it is in God's power to create satiety without eating, and death without decapitation, and to let life persist notwithstanding the decapitation, and so on with respect to all connexions. The philosophers, however, deny this possibility and claim that that is impossible. To investigate all these innumerable connexions would take us too long, and so we shall choose one single example, namely the burning of cotton through contact with fire; for we regard it as possible that the contact might occur without the burning taking place, and also that the cotton might be changed into ashes without any contact with fire, although the philosophers deny this possibility. The discussion of this matter has three points.

The first is that our opponent claims that the agent of the burning is the fire exclusively; this is a natural, not a voluntary agent, and cannot abstain from what is in its nature when it is brought into contact with a receptive substratum. This we deny, saying the agent of the burning is God, through His creating the black in the cotton and the disconnection of its parts, and it is God who made the cotton burn and made it ashes either through the intermediation of angels or without intermediation. For fire is a dead body which has no action, and what is the proof that it is the agent? Indeed, the philosophers have no other proof than the observation of the occurrence of the burning, when there is contact with fire, but observation proves only a simultaneity, not a causation, and, in reality, there is no other cause but God. For there is unanimity of opinion about the fact that the union of the spirit with the perceptive and moving faculties in the sperm of animals does not originate in the natures contained in warmth, cold, moistness, and dryness, and that the father is neither the agent of the embryo through introducing the sperm into the uterus, nor the agent of its life, its sight and hearing, and all its other faculties. And although it is well known that the same faculties exist in the father, still nobody thinks that these faculties exist through him; no, their existence is produced by the First either directly or through the intermediation of the angels who are in charge of these events. Of this fact the philosophers who believe in a creator are quite convinced, but it is precisely with them that we are in dispute.

It has been shown that coexistence does not indicate causation. We shall make this still more clear through an example. Suppose that a man blind from birth, whose eyes are veiled by a membrane and who has never heard people talk of the difference between night and day, has the membrane removed from his eyes by day and sees visible things, he will surely think then that the actual perception in his eyes of the forms of visible things is caused by the opening of his eyelids, and that as long as his sight is sound and in function, the hindrance removed and the object in front of him visible, he will, without doubt, be able to see, and he will never think that he will not see, till, at the moment when the sun sets and the air darkens, he will understand that it was the light of the sun which impressed the visible forms on his sight. And for what other reason do our opponents believe that in the principles of existence there are causes and influences from which the events which coincide with them proceed, than that they are constant, do not disappear, and are not moving bodies which vanish from sight? For if they disappeared or vanished we should observe the disjunction and understand then that behind our perceptions there exists a cause. And out of this there is no issue, according to the very conclusions of the philosophers themselves.

The true philosophers were therefore unanimously of the opinion that these accidents and events which occur when there is a contact of bodies, or in general a change in their positions, proceed from the bestower of forms who is an angel or a plurality of angels, so that they even said that the impression of the visible forms on the eye occurs through the bestower of forms, and that the rising of the sun, the soundness of the pupil, and the existence of the visible object are only the preparations and dispositions which enable the substratum to receive the forms; and this theory they applied to all events. And this refutes the claim of those who profess that fire is the agent of burning, bread the agent of satiety, medicine the agent of health, and so on.

I say:

To deny the existence of efficient causes which are observed in sensible things is sophistry, and he who defends this doctrine either denies with his tongue what is present in his mind or is carried away by a sophistical doubt which occurs to him concerning this question. For he who denies this can no longer acknowledge that every act must have an agent. The question whether these causes by themselves are sufficient to perform the acts which proceed from them, or need an external cause for the perfection of their act, whether separate or not, is not self-evident and requires much investigation and research. And if the theologians had doubts about the efficient causes which are perceived to cause each other, because there are also effects whose cause is not perceived, this is illogical. Those things whose causes are not perceived are still unknown and must be investigated, precisely because their causes are not perceived; and since everything whose causes are not perceived is still unknown by nature and must be investigated, it follows necessarily that what is not unknown has causes which are perceived. The man who reasons like the theologians does not distinguish between what is self-evident and what is unknown, and everything al-Ghazali says in this passage is sophistical.

And further, what do the theologians say about the essential causes, the understanding of which alone can make a thing understood? For it is self-evident that things have essences and attributes which determine the special functions of each thing and through which the essences and names of things are differentiated. If a thing had not its specific nature, it would not have a special name nor a definition, and all things would indeed be one, not even one; for it might be asked whether this one has one special act or one special passivity or not, and if it had a special act, then there would indeed exist special acts proceeding from special natures, but if it had no single special act, then the one would not be one. But if the nature of oneness is denied, the nature of being is denied, and the consequence of the denial of being is nothingness.

Further, are the acts which proceed from all things absolutely necessary for those in whose nature it lies to perform them, or are they only performed in most cases or in half the cases? This is a question which must be investigated, since one single action-and-passivity between two existent things occurs only through one relation out of an infinite number, and it happens often that one relation hinders another. Therefore, it is not absolutely certain that fire acts when it is brought near a sensitive body, for surely it is not improbable that there should be something which stands in such a relation to the sensitive thing as to hinder the action of the fire, as is asserted of talc and other things. But one need not therefore deny fire its burning power so long as fire keeps its name and definition.

Further, it is self-evident that all events have four causes, agent, form, matter, and end, and that they are necessary for the existence of the effects—especially those causes which form a part of the effect, namely that which is called by the philosophers matter, by the theologians condition and substratum, and that which is called by the philosophers form, by the theologians psychological quality. The theologians acknowledge that there exist conditions which are necessary for the conditioned, as when they say that life is a condition of knowledge; and they equally recognize that things have realities and definitions, and that these are necessary for the existence of the existent, and therefore they here judge the visible and the invisible according to one and the same scheme. And they adopt the same attitude towards the consequences of a thing's essence, namely what they call "sign," as for instance when they say that the harmony in the world indicates that its agent possesses mind and that the existence of a world having a design indicates that its agent knows this world. Now intelligence is nothing but the perception of things with their causes, and in this it distinguishes itself from all the other faculties of apprehension, and he who denies causes must deny the intellect.

Logic implies the existence of causes and effects, and knowledge of these effects can only be rendered perfect through knowledge of their causes. Denial of cause implies the denial of knowledge, and denial of knowledge implies that nothing in this world can be really known, and that what is supposed to be known is nothing but opinion, that neither proof nor definition exist, and that the essential attributes which compose definitions are void. The man who denies the necessity of any item of knowledge must admit

that even this, his own affirmation, is not necessary knowledge.

As to those who admit that there exists, besides necessary knowledge, knowledge which is not necessary, about which the soul forms a judgement on slight evidence and imagines it to be necessary, whereas it is not necessary, the philosophers do not deny this. And if they call such a fact "habit," this may be granted, but otherwise I do not know what they understand by the term 'habit'—whether they mean that it is the habit of the agent, the habit of the existing things, or our habit to form a judgement about such things? It is, however, impossible that God should have a habit; for a habit is a custom which the agent acquires and from which a frequent repetition of his act follows, whereas God says in the Holy Book, "thou shalt not find any alteration in the course of God, and they shall not find any change in the course of God." If they mean a habit in existing things, habit can only exist in the animated; if it exists in something else, it is really a nature, and it is not possible that a thing should have a nature which determined it either necessarily or in most cases. If they mean our habit of forming judgements about things, such a habit is nothing but an act of the soul which is determined by its nature and through which the intellect becomes intellect. The philosophers do not deny such a habit; but "habit" is an ambiguous term, and if it is analysed, it means only a hypothetical act; as when we say, "So-and-so has the habit of acting in such-and-such a way," meaning that he will act in that way most of the time. If this were true, everything would be the case only by supposition, and there would be no wisdom in the world from which it might be inferred that its agent was wise.

And, as we said, we need not doubt that some of these existents cause each other and act through each other, and that in themselves they do not suffice for their act, but that they are in need of an external agent whose act is a condition of their act, and not only of their act but even of their existence. However, about the essence of this agent or of these agents the philosophers differ in one way although in another they agree. They all agree in this, that the First Agent is immaterial and that its act is the condition of the existence and acts of existents, and that the act of their agent reaches these existents through the inter-mediation of an effect of this agent which is different from these existents and which, according to some of them, is exclusively the heavenly sphere, whereas others assume besides this sphere another immaterial existent which they call the bestowed of forms.

But this is not the place to investigate these theories, and the highest part of their inquiry is this; and if you are one of those who desire these truths, then follow the right road which leads to them. The reason why the philosophers differed about the origin of the essential forms and especially of the forms of the soul is that they could not relate them to the warm, cold, moist, and dry, which are the causes of all natural things which come into being and pass away, whereas the materialists related everything which does not seem to have an apparent cause to the warm, cold, moist, and dry, affirming that these things originated through certain mixtures of those elements, just as colors and other accidents come into existence. And the philosophers tried to refute them.

Al-Ghazali says:

Our second point is concerned with those who acknowledge that these events proceed from their principles, but say that the disposition to receive the forms arises from their observed and apparent causes. However, according to them the events proceed from these principles not by deliberation and will, but by necessity and nature, as light does from the sun, and the substrata differ for their reception only through the differentiations in their disposition. For instance, a polished body receives the rays of the sun, reflects them and illuminates another spot with them, whereas an opaque body does not receive them; the air does not hinder the penetration of the sun's light, but a stone does; certain things become soft through the sun, others hard; certain things, like the garments which the fuller bleaches, become white through the sun, others like the fuller's face become black. The principle is, however, one and the same, although the effects differ through the differences of disposition in the substratum. Thus, there is no hindrance or incapacity in the emanation of what emanates from the principles of existence; the insufficiency lies only in the receiving substrata. If this is true, and we assume a fire that has the quality it has, and two similar pieces of cotton in the same contact with it, how can it be imagined that only one and not the other will be burned, as there is here no voluntary act? And

from this point of view they deny that Abraham could fall into the fire and not be burned notwithstanding the fact that the fire remained fire, and they affirm that this could only be possible through abstracting the warmth from the fire (through which it would, however, cease to be fire) or through changing the essence of Abraham and making him a stone or something on which fire has no influence, and neither the one nor the other is possible.

I say:

Those philosophers who say that these perceptible existents do not act on each other, and that their agent is exclusively an external principle, cannot affirm that their apparent action on each other is totally illusory, but would say that this action is limited to preparing the disposition to accept the forms from the external principle. However, I do not know any philosopher who affirms this absolutely; they assert this only of the essential forms, not of the forms of accidents. They all agree that warmth causes warmth, and that all the four qualities act likewise, but in such a way that through it the elemental fire and the warmth which proceeds from the heavenly bodies are conserved. The theory which al-Ghazali ascribes to the philosophers, that the separate principles act by nature, not by choice, is not held by any important philosophers; on the contrary, the philosophers affirm that that which possesses knowledge must act by choice. However, according to the philosophers, in view of the excellence which exists in the world, there can proceed out of two contraries only the better, and their choice is not made to perfect their essences—since there is no imperfection in their essence—but in order that through it those existents which have an imperfection in their nature may be perfected.

As to the objection which al-Ghazali ascribes to the philosophers over the miracle of Abraham, such things are only asserted by heretical Muslims. The learned among the philosophers do not permit discussion or disputation about the principles of religion, and he who does such a thing needs, according to them, a severe lesson. For whereas every science has its principles, and every student of this science must concede its principles and may not interfere with them by denying them, this is still more obligatory in the practical science of religion, for to walk on the path of the religious virtues is necessary for human being's existence, according to them, not in so far as he is human, but in so far as he has knowledge; and therefore it is necessary for every human to concede the principles of religion and invest with authority the human who lays them down. The denial and discussion of these principles denies human existence, and therefore heretics must be killed. Of religious principles it must be said that they are divine things which surpass human understanding, but must be acknowledged although their causes are unknown.

Therefore, we do not find that any of the ancient philosophers discusses miracles, although they were known and had appeared all over the world, for they are the principles on which religion is based and religion is the principle of the virtues; nor did they discuss any of the things which are said to happen after death. For if a person grows up according to the religious virtues he becomes absolutely virtuous, and if time and felicity are granted to him, so that he becomes one of the deeply learned thinkers and it happens that he can explain one of the principles of religion, it is enjoined upon him that he should not divulge this explanation and should say, "all these are the terms of religion and the wise," conforming himself to the Divine Words, "but those who are deeply versed in knowledge say, 'we believe in it, it is all from our Lord.'"

Al-Ghazali says:

There are two answers to this theory. The first is to say we do not accept the assertion that the principles do not act in a voluntary way and that God does not act through His will, and we have already refuted their claim in treating of the question of the temporal creation of the world. If it is established that the Agent creates the burning through His will when the piece of cotton is brought in contact with the fire, He can equally well omit to create it when the contact takes place.

I say:

Al-Ghazali, to confuse his opponent, here regards as established what his opponent refuses to admit, and says that his opponent has no proof for his refusal. He says that the First Agent causes the burning without an intermediary which He might have created in order that the burning might take place through the fire. But such a claim abolishes any perception of the existence of causes and effects. No philosopher doubts that, for instance, the fire is the cause of the burning which occurs in the cotton through the fire—not, however, absolutely, but by an external principle which is the condition of the existence of fire, not to speak of its burning. The philosophers differ only about the quiddity of this principle—whether it is a separate principle, or an intermediary between the event and the separate principle besides the fire.

Al-Ghazali says, on behalf of the philosophers:

But it may be said that such a conception involves reprehensible impossibilities. For if you deny the necessary dependence of effects or their causes and relate them to the will of their Creator, and do not allow even in the will a particular definite pattern, but regard it as possible that it may vary and change in type, then it may happen to any of us that there should be in his presence beasts of prey and flaming fires and immovable mountains and enemies equipped with arms, without his seeing them, because God had not created in him the faculty of seeing them. And a man who had left a book at home might find it on his return changed into a youth, handsome, intelligent, and efficient, or into an animal; or if he left a youth at home, he might find him turned into a dog; or he might leave ashes and find them changed into musk; or a stone changed into gold, and gold changed into stone. And if he were asked about any of these things, he would answer, "I do not know what there is at present in my house; I only know that I left a book in my house, but perhaps by now it is a horse which has soiled the library with its urine and excrement, and I left in my house a piece of bread which has perhaps changed into an apple tree." For God is able to do all these things, and it does not belong to the necessity of a horse that it should be created from a sperm, nor is it of the necessity of a tree that it should be created from a seed; no, there is no necessity that it should be created out of anything at all. And perhaps God creates things which never existed before; indeed, when one sees a man one never saw before and is asked whether this man has been generated, one should answer hesitantly, "it may be that he was one of the fruits in the market which has been changed into a man, and that this is that man." For God can do any possible thing, and this is possible, and one cannot avoid being perplexed by it; and to this kind of fancy one may yield *ad infinitum*, but these examples will do.

But the answer is to say: if it were true that the existence of the possible implied that there could not be created in man any knowledge of the non-occurrence of a possible, all these consequences would follow necessarily. But we are not at a loss over any of the examples which you have brought forward. For God has created in us the knowledge that He will not do all these possible things, and we only profess that these things are not necessary, but that they are possible and may or may not happen, and protracted habit time after time fixes their occurrence in our minds according to the past habit in a fixed impression. Yes, it is possible that a prophet should know in such ways as the philosophers have explained that a certain man will not come tomorrow from a journey, and although his coming is possible the prophet knows that this possibility will not be realized. And often you may observe even ordinary men of whom you know that they are not aware of anything occult, and can know the intelligible only through instruction, and still it cannot be denied that nevertheless their soul and conjecturing power can acquire sufficient strength to apprehend what the prophets apprehend in so far as they know the possibility of an event, but know that it will not happen. And if God interrupts the habitual course by causing this unusual event to happen this knowledge of the habitual is at the time of the interruption removed from their hearts and He no longer creates it. There is, therefore, no objection to admitting that a thing may be possible for God, but that He had the previous knowledge that although He might have done so He would not carry it out during a certain time, and that He has created in us the knowledge that He would not do it during that time.

I say:

When the theologians admit that the opposite of everything existing is equally possible, and that it is such in regard to the Agent, and that only one of these opposites can be differentiated through the will of the Agent, there is no fixed standard for His will either constantly or for most cases, according to which things must happen. For this reason the theologians are open to all the scandalous implications with which they are charged. For true knowledge is the knowledge of a thing as it is in reality. And if in

reality there only existed, in regard both to the substratum and to the Agent, the possibility of the two opposites, there would no longer, even for the twinkling of an eye, be any permanent knowledge of anything, since we suppose such an agent to rule existents like a tyrannical prince who has the highest power, for whom nobody in his dominion can deputize, of whom no standard or custom is known to which reference might be made. Indeed, the acts of such a prince will undoubtedly be unknown by nature, and if an act of his comes into existence the continuance of its existence at any moment will be unknown by nature.

Al-Ghazali's defence against these difficulties that God created in us the knowledge that these possibilities would be realized only at special times, such as at the time of the miracle, is not a true one. For the knowledge created in us is always in conformity with the nature of the real thing, since the definition of truth is that a thing is believed to be such as it is in reality. Therefore, if there is knowledge of these possibles, there must be in the real possibles a condition to which our knowledge refers, either through these possibles themselves or through the agent, or for both reasons—a condition which the theologians call habit. And since the existence of this condition which is called habit is impossible in the First Agent, this condition can only be found in the existents, and this, as we said, is what the philosophers call nature.

The same congruity exists between God's knowledge and the existents, although God's knowledge of existents is their cause, and these existents are the consequence of God's knowledge, and therefore reality conforms to God's knowledge. If, for instance, knowledge of Zaid's coming reaches the prophet through a communication of God, the reason why the actual happening is congruous with the knowledge is nothing but the fact that the nature of the actually existent is a consequence of the eternal knowledge, for knowledge as knowledge can only refer to something which has an actualized nature. The knowledge of the Creator is the reason why this nature becomes actual in the existent which is attached to it. Our ignorance of these possibles is brought about through our ignorance of the nature which determines the being or nonbeing of a thing. If the opposites in existents were in a condition of equilibrium, both in themselves and through their efficient causes, it would follow that they neither existed nor did not exist, or that they existed and did not exist at the same time, and one of the opposites must therefore have a preponderance in existence. And it is the knowledge of the existence of this nature which causes the actualization of one of the opposites. And the knowledge attached to this nature is either a knowledge prior to it, and this is the knowledge of which this nature is the effect, namely eternal knowledge, or the knowledge which is consequent on this nature, namely non-eternal knowledge. The attainment of the occult is nothing but the vision of this nature, and our acquisition of this knowledge not preceded by any proof is what is called in ordinary human beings a dream, and in prophets inspiration. The eternal will and eternal knowledge are the causes of this nature in existents. And this is the meaning of the Divine Words: "say that none in the heavens or on the earth know the occult but God alone." This nature is sometimes necessary and sometimes what happens in most cases. Dreams and inspiration are only, as we said, the announcement of this nature in possible things, and the sciences which claim the prognostication of future events possess only rare traces of the influences of this nature or constitution or whatever you wish to call it, namely that which is actualized in itself and to which the knowledge attaches itself.

Al-Ghazali says:

The second answer—and in it is to be found deliverance from these reprehensible consequences—is to agree that in fire there is created a nature which burns two similar pieces of cotton which are brought into contact with it and does not differentiate between them, when they are alike in every respect. But still we regard it as possible that a prophet should be thrown into the fire and not burn, either through a change in the quality of the fire or through a change in the quality of the prophet, and that either through God or through the angels there should arise a quality in the fire which limited its heat to its own body, so that it did not go beyond it, but remained confined to it, keeping, however, to the form and the reality of the fire, without its heat and influence extending beyond it; or that there should arise in the body of the person an attribute, which did not stop the body from being flesh and bone, but still defended it against the action of the fire. For we can see a man rub himself with talc

and sit down in a lighted oven and not suffer from it; and if one had not seen it, one would deny it, and the denial of our opponents that it lies in God's power to confer on the fire or the body an attribute which prevents it from being burnt is like the denial of one who has not seen the talc and its effect. For strange and marvelous things are in the power of God, many of which we have not seen, and why should we deny their possibility and regard them as impossible?

And also the bringing back to life of the dead and the changing of a stick into a serpent are possible in the following way: matter can receive any form, and therefore earth and the other elements can be changed into a plant, and a plant, when an animal eats it, can be changed into blood, then blood can be changed into sperm, and then sperm can be thrown into the womb and take the character of an animal. This, in the habitual course of nature, takes place over a long space of time, but why does our opponent declare it impossible that matter should pass through these different phases in a shorter period than is usual, and when once a shorter period is allowed there is no limit to its being shorter and shorter, so that these potencies can always become quicker in their action and eventually arrive at the stage of being a miracle of a prophet.

And if it is asked, "does this arise through the soul of the prophet or through another principle at the instigation of the prophet," we answer: does what you acknowledge may happen through the power of the prophet's soul, like the downpour of rain or the falling of a thunderbolt or earthquakes, does that occur through him or through another principle? What we say about the facts which we have mentioned is like what you say about those facts which you regard as possible. And the best method according to both you and us is to relate these things to God, either immediately or through the intermediation of the angels. But at the time these occurrences become real, the attention of the prophet turns to such facts, and the order of the good determines its appearance to ensure the duration of the order of religion, and this gives a preponderance to the side of existence. The fact in itself is possible, and the principle in God is His magnanimity; but such a fact only emanates from Him when necessity gives a preponderance to its existence and the good determines it, and the good only determines it when a prophet needs it to establish his prophetic office for the promulgation of the good.

And all this is in accordance with the theory of the philosophers and follows from it for them, since they allow to the prophet a particular characteristic which distinguishes him from common people. There is no intellectual criterion for the extent of its possibility, but there is no need to declare it false when it rests on a good tradition and the religious law states it to be true. Now, in general, it is only the sperm which accepts the form of animals—and it receives its animal potencies only from the angels, who according to the philosophers, are the principles of existents—and only a human being can be created from the sperm of a man, and only a horse from the sperm of a horse, in so far as the actualization of the sperm through the horse determines the preponderance of the analogous form of a horse over all other forms, and it accepts only the form to which in this way the preponderance is given, and therefore barley never grows from wheat or an apple from a pear. Further, we see that certain kinds of animal are only produced by spontaneous generation from earth and never are generated by procreation, for example worms, and some which are produced both spontaneously and by procreation, like the mouse, the serpent, and the scorpion, for their generation can come also from earth. Their disposition to accept forms varies through causes unknown to us, and it is not in human power to ascertain them, since those forms do not, according to the philosophers, emanate from the angels by their good pleasure or haphazard, but in every substratum only in such a way that a form arises for whose acceptance it is specially determined through its own disposition. These dispositions differ, and their principles are, according to the philosophers, the aspects of the stars and the different relative positions of the heavenly bodies in their movements. And through this the possibility is open that there may be in the principles of these dispositions wonderful and marvelous things, so that those who understand talismans through their knowledge of the particular qualities of minerals and of the stars succeed in combining the heavenly potencies with those mineral peculiarities, and make shapes of these earthly substances, and seek a special virtue for them and produce marvelous things in the world through them. And often they drive serpents and scorpions from a country, and sometimes bugs, and

they do other things which are known to belong to the science of talismans.

And since there is no fixed criterion for the principles of these dispositions, and we cannot ascertain their essence or limit them, how can we know that it is impossible that in certain bodies dispositions occur to change their phases at a quicker rhythm, so that such a body would be disposed to accept a form for the acceptance of which it was not prepared before, which is claimed to be a miracle? There is no denying this, except through a lack of understanding and an unfamiliarity with higher things and oblivion of the secrets of God in the created world and in nature. And he who has examined the many wonders of the sciences does not consider in any way impossible for God's power what is told of the wonders of the prophets.

Our opponents may say, "we agree with you that everything possible is in the power of God, and you theologians agree with us that the impossible cannot be done and that there are things whose impossibility is known and things which are known to be possible, and that there are also things about which the understanding is undecided and which it does not hold to be either impossible or possible. Now what according to you is the limit of the impossible? If the impossible includes nothing but the simultaneous affirmation and negation of the same thing, then say that of two things the one is not the other, and that the existence of the one does not demand the existence of the other. And say then that God can create will without knowledge of the thing willed, and knowledge without life, and that He can move the hand of a dead man and make him sit and write volumes with his hand and engage himself in sciences while he has his eye open and his looks are fixed on his work, although he does not see and there is no life in him and he has no power, and it is God alone who creates all these ordered actions with the moving of the dead man's hand, and the movement comes from God. But by regarding this as possible the difference between voluntary action and a reflex action like shivering is destroyed, and a judicious act will no longer indicate that the agent possesses knowledge or power. It will then be necessary that God should be able to bring about a change from one genus to another and transform the substance into an accident and knowledge into power and black into white and a voice into an odor, just as He is able to change the inorganic into an animal and a stone into gold, and it will then follow that God can also bring about other unlimited impossibilities."

The answer to this is to say that the impossible cannot be done by God, and the impossible consists in the simultaneous affirmation and negation of a thing, or the affirmation of the more particular with the negation of the more general, or the affirmation of two things with the negation of one of them, and what does not refer to this is not impossible and what is not impossible can be done. The identification of black and white is impossible, because by the affirmation of the form of black in the substratum the negation of the form of white and of the existence of white is implied; and since the negation of white is implied by the affirmation of black, the simultaneous affirmation and negation of white is impossible. And the existence of a person in two places at once is only impossible because we imply by his being in the house that he cannot be in another place, and it cannot be understood from the denial that he is in another place that he can be simultaneously both in another place and in the house. And in the same way by will is implied the seeking of something that can be known, and if we assume a seeking without knowledge there cannot be a will and we would then deny what we had implied. And it is impossible that in the inorganic knowledge should be created, because we understand by inorganic that which does not perceive, and if in the organic perception was created it would become impossible to call it inorganic in the sense in which this word is understood.

As to the transformation of one genus into another, some theologians affirm that it is in the power of God, but we say that for one thing to become another is irrational; for, if for instance, the black could be transformed into power, the black would either remain or not, and if it does not exist any more, it is not changed but simply does not exist any more and something else exists; and if it remains existent together with power, it is not changed, but something else is brought in relation to it, and if the black remains and power does not exist, then it does not change, but remains as it was before. And when we say that blood changes into sperm, we mean by it that this identical matter is divested of one form and invested with another; and it amounts to this, that one form becomes non-existent and another form comes into existence while the matter remains, and that two

forms succeed one another in it. And when we say that water becomes air through being heated, we mean by it that the matter which had received the form of the water is deprived of this form and takes another, and not the matter common to them but the attribute changes. And it is the same when we say that the stick is changed into a serpent or earth into an animal. But there is no matter common to the accident and the substance, nor to black and to power, nor to the other categories, and it is impossible for this reason that they should be changed into each other.

As to God's moving the hand of a dead man, and raising this man up, in the form of a living one who sits and writes, so that through the movement of his hand a well-ordered script is written, this in itself is not impossible as long as we refer events to the will of a voluntary being, and it is only to be denied because the habitual course of nature is in opposition to it. And your affirmation, philosophers, that, if this is so, the judiciousness of an act no longer indicates that the agent possesses knowledge is false, for the agent in this case is God; He determines the act and He performs it. And as to your assertion that if this is so there is no longer any difference between shivering and voluntary motion, we answer that we know this difference only because we experience in ourselves the difference between these two conditions, and we find thereby that the differentiating factor is power, and know that of the two classes of the possible the one happens at one time, the other at another; that is to say, we produce movement with the power to produce it at one time, and a movement without this power at another. Now, when we observe other movements than ours and see many well-ordered movements, we attain knowledge of the power behind them, and God creates in us all these different kinds of knowledge through the habitual course of events, through which one of the two classes of possibility becomes known, though the impossibility of the second class is not proved thereby.

I say:

When al-Ghazali saw that the theory—that with respect to everything things have no particular qualities and forms from which particular acts follow—is very objectionable, and contrary to common sense, he conceded this in this last section and replaced it by the denial of two points: first, that a thing can have these qualities but that they need not act on a thing in the way they usually act on it, for example fire can have its warmth but need not burn something that is brought near to it, even if it is usually burnt when fire is brought near to it; second, that the particular forms have not a particular matter in every object.

The first point can be accepted by the philosophers, for because of external causes the procession of acts from agents may not be necessary, and it is not impossible that for instance fire may sometimes be brought near cotton without burning it, when something is placed with the cotton that makes it non-inflammable, as al-Ghazali says in his instance of talc and a living being.

As to the point that matter is one of the conditions for material things, this cannot be denied by the theologians, for, as al-Ghazali says, there is no difference between our simultaneous negation and affirmation of a thing and our simultaneous denial of part of it and affirmation of the whole. And since things consist of two qualities, a general and a particular—and this is what the philosophers mean by the term *definition*, a definition being composed according to them of a genus and a specific difference—it is indifferent for the denial of an existent which of its two qualities is denied. For instance, since human being consists of two qualities, one being a general quality, that is to say, animality, and the second a particular, that is to say, rationality, human remains human just as little when we take away his animality as when we take away his rationality, for animality is a condition of rationality and when the condition is removed the conditioned is removed equally.

On this question the theologians and the philosophers agree, except that the philosophers believe that for particular things the general qualities are just as much a condition as the particular, and this the theologians do not believe; for the philosophers, for instance, warmth and moisture are a condition of life in the transient, because they are more general than life, just as life is a condition of rationality. But the theologians do not believe this, and so you hear them say, "for us dryness and moisture are not a condition of life." For the philosophers shape, too, is one of the particular conditions of life in an organic being; if not, one of two following cases might arise: either the special shape of the animal might exist without exercising any function, or this special shape might not

exist at all. For instance, for the philosophers the hand is the organ of the intellect, and by means of it man performs his rational acts, like writing and the carrying on of the other arts; now, if intelligence were possible in the inorganic, it would be possible that intellect might exist without performing its function, and it would be as if warmth could exist without warming the things that are normally warmed by it. Also, according to the philosophers, every existent has a definite quantity and a definite quality, and also the time when it comes into existence and during which it persists are determined, although in all these determinations there is, according to the philosophers, a certain latitude.

Theologians and philosophers agree that the matter of existents which participate in one and the same matter sometimes accepts one of two forms and sometimes its opposite, as happens, according to them, with the forms of the four elements, fire, air, water, and earth. Only in regard to the things which have no common matter or which have different matters do they disagree whether some of them can accept the forms of others—for instance, whether something which is not known by experience to accept a certain form except through many intermediaries can also accept this ultimate form without intermediaries. For instance, the plant comes into existence through composition out of the elements; it becomes blood and sperm through being eaten by an animal and from sperm and blood comes the animal, as is said in the Divine Words: "we created man from an extract of clay, then We made him a clot in a sure depository" and so on till His words "and blessed be God, the best of creators." The theologians affirm that the soul of a human being can inhere in earth without the intermediaries known by experience, whereas the philosophers deny this and say that, if this were possible, wisdom would consist in the creation of a human being without such intermediaries, and a creator who created in such a way would be the best and most powerful of creators; both parties claim that what they say is self-evident, and neither has any proof for its theory. And you, reader, consult your heart; it is your duty to believe what it announces, and this is what God—who may make us and you into persons of truth and evidence—has ordained for you.

But some of the Muslims have even affirmed that there can be attributed to God the power to combine the two opposites, and their dubious proof is that the judgment of our intellect that this is impossible is something which has been impressed on the intellect, whereas if there had been impressed on it the judgment that this is possible, it would not deny this possibility, but admit it. For such people it follows as a consequence that neither intellect nor existents have a well-defined nature, and that the truth which exists in the intellect does not correspond to the existence of existing things. The theologians themselves are ashamed of such a theory, but if they held it, it would be more consistent with their point of view than the contradictions in which their opponents involve them on this point. For their opponents try to find out where the difference lies between what as a matter of fact the theologians affirm on this point and what they deny, and it is very difficult for them to make this out—indeed they do not find anything but vague words. We find, therefore, that those most expert in the art of theological discussion take refuge

in denying the necessary connexion between condition and conditioned, between a thing and its definition, between a thing and its cause and between a thing and its sign. All this is full of Sophistry and is without sense, and the theologian who did this was Abū-l-Ma'ali.

The general argument which solves these difficulties is that existents are divided into opposites and correlates, and if the latter could be separated, the former might be united, but opposites are not united and correlates therefore cannot be separated. And this is the wisdom of God and God's course in created things, and you will never find in God's course any alteration. And it is through the perception of this wisdom that the intellect of man becomes intellect, and the existence of such wisdom in the eternal intellect is the cause of its existence in reality. The intellect, therefore, is not a possible entity which might have been created with other qualities, as Ibn Hazm imagined.

STUDY QUESTIONS: AVERROËS, *INCOHERENCE OF THE INCOHERENCE*

1. Does al-Ghazali believe that the world is eternal? Why?
2. What is the debate regarding whether God knows himself about?
3. Is the notion of the numerical plurality of forms the same as the notion of the numerical plurality of souls?
4. How does Averroës suggest the notion of the numerical identity of souls?
5. Is the soul divisible? Why?
6. What is the relationship between time and the creation of the world?
7. Does he think al-Ghazali is accurate in his rendition of Avicenna's philosophy? To which issue is this important?
8. What is the main mistake al-Ghazali makes with regard to his interpretation of Avicenna?
9. Is existence an attribute of a thing? What is Avicenna's position on this? Aristotle's? Al-Ghazali's? Averroës'?
10. What is the relationship between the concepts "necessary" and "causeless"?
11. Is there a logical necessity between cause and effect?
12. What is Averroës' view of miracles? Why did the ancient philosophers not discuss them as such?
13. What is the point of agreement between theologians and philosophers?

COMMENTARY ON "ON THE SOUL"

Like Aquinas, Averroës argues that the existence of God, along with complete knowledge of God's real nature, can be known directly through reason. However, according to Averroës, both philosophy and theology have a legitimate, albeit distinct, function. He explains this in terms of his three-tiered class division of human beings, modeled after the golden lie as espoused by Plato in *The Republic* (the lie that there are three distinct classes of souls: bronze, silver, and gold). Just like Plato's cave dwellers, the lowest form of soul, as embodied in the majority of people, is incapable of reasoning for itself. Most people, therefore, cannot comprehend philosophy. They need simple answers, forced by obedience to an orthodox religious dogma, into which priests indoctrinate them. The next class is more intelligent but also lives not by reason but by imagination. Such people do not accept dogma because it is taught but because they have justified it for themselves. The soul of the theologian comes from this second class. But theologians, too, are ultimately prejudiced because they seek justification only for commonly accepted beliefs or beliefs into which they themselves have been indoctrinated by others. Because truth requires complete impartiality from all orthodoxy, such theologians can never attain it. The third, highest, level of intelligence allows the soul to see that religion cannot provide knowledge of the truth. Only a few extraordinary individuals are sufficiently intelligent to discover directly for themselves the awesome truths that the rational theologians and the irrational believers can only go on seeking.

Averroës claims that true philosophers know this. They know that to know the truth you must come to it neither by faith nor by reasoning from premises accepted as true by faith, but rather on the basis of premises tested by experience and justified by logical reasoning. Moreover, there is the one most difficult of all truths, known only by a select few philosophers, such as Plato and Aristotle. This truth, as powerful as it is enigmatic, is that the active part of your mind is not a distinct and separately existing individual from anyone else's. You and I are the same, numerically identical unity. This, according to Averroës, is the greatest of all truths, hidden in the great tradition passed down from Plato and Aristotle: there is but one soul who is everyone, self-same and identical to the agent intellect, the mind of God.

Like Aristotle, Averroës argues against the individual immortality of that aspect of the soul that he and Aristotle call the passive intellect. Thus, like Avicenna, Averroës claims that the individual human intellect, illuminated into existence by God (the agent intellect), is itself but an emanation of God (the agent intellect). The passive intellect is brought into existence through interaction with the God via the active intellect. It does not survive death. The active intellect is immortal. It is numerically identical in all sentient beings. He argues that the active intellect is not a personal faculty but is itself an emanation of the agent intellect (God), with which it is numerically identical, one and the same being. It is the one, which individuates itself into the many, by illuminating into existence each and every manifestation of itself, as each and every human being.

Book III

TEXT 4

It is necessary, therefore, that if the intellect understands all things, it be not mixed, as Anaxagoras has said, in order that it may dominate, that is in order that it may understand. For if something were to appear in it, that which appears would prevent something foreign from appearing in it, since it is something other.

COMMENTARY

After Aristotle has set down that the material, receiving intellect must belong to the genus of passive powers, and, that in spite of this, it is not altered by the reception of that which it receives, for it is neither a body nor a power within a body, he provides a demonstration for this. And he says, "it is necessary, therefore, that, if the intellect understands." That is, it is necessary, therefore, that, if the intellect understands all those things which exist outside the soul, it be described—prior to its understanding—as belonging to the genus of passive, not active, powers, and it is necessary that it be not mixed with bodies, that is, that it be neither a body nor a power within a body, be it a natural or animate power, as Anaxagoras has said. Thereafter, Aristotle says, "in order that it may understand." That is, it is necessary that it be not mixed, in order that it may understand all things and receive them. For if it were mixed, then it would be either a body or a power within a body, and if it were one of these, it would have a form proper to itself, which form would prevent it from receiving some foreign form.

This is what he has in mind when he says, "For if something were to appear in it." That is, if the passive intellect were to have a form proper to itself, then that form would prevent it from receiving the various external forms, which are different from it. Thus, one must inquire into those propositions by means of which Aristotle shows these two things about the intellect, namely [1] that it belongs to the genus of passive powers, and [2] that it is not alterable, since it is neither a body nor a power within a body. For these two [propositions] are the starting point of all those things which are said about the intellect. As Plato said, the most extensive discussion must take place in the beginning; for the slightest error in the beginning is the cause of the greatest error in the end, as Aristotle says.

We say that conception by the intellect belongs in some way to a passive power, just as in the case of a sensory power perception by a sense belongs to a passive power, becomes clear through the following considerations. Now, the passive powers are movable by that to which they are related, while active powers move that to which they are related. And since it is the case that something moves something else only insofar as it exists in actuality and something is moved insofar as it exists in potentiality, it follows necessarily, that since the forms of things exist in actuality outside the soul, they move the rational soul insofar as it understands them, just as in the case of sensible things it is necessary that they move the senses insofar as they are things existing in actuality and that the senses are moved by them. Therefore, the rational soul must consider the forms which are in the imaginative faculty, just as the senses must inspect sensible things. And since it appears that the forms of external things move this power in such a way that the mind abstracts these forms from material things and thereby makes them the first intelligibles in actuality, after they had been intelligibles in potentiality—it appears from this that this soul [the intellect] is also active, not only passive. For insofar as the intelligibles move [the intellect], it is passive, but insofar they are moved by it, it is active. For this reason Aristotle states subsequently that it is necessary to posit in the rational soul two distinct powers, namely, an active power and a passive power. And he states clearly that each one of the rational soul's parts is neither generable nor corruptible. In the present discussion, however, he begins to describe the nature of this passive power, to the extent to which it is necessary in this exposition. Therefore, he states that this distinct power, namely, that which is passive and receptive, exists in the rational faculty.

That the substance which receives these forms can not be a body or a power in a body, becomes clear from the propositions of which Aristotle makes use in this discussion. One of these is that this substance [the material intellect] receives all material forms, and this is something well known about this intellect. The other is that everything which receives something else must necessarily be devoid of the nature of that which it receives and that its essence is not the same in species as the essence of that which it receives. For, if that which receives is of the same nature as that which is received, then something would receive itself and that which moves would be the same as that which is moved. Wherefore, it is necessary that the sense which receives color lacks color and the sense which receives sound lacks sound. And this proposition is necessarily true and there is no doubt about it. From these two propositions it follows that the substance which is called the material intellect does not have any of the material forms in its nature. And since the material forms are either a body or forms in a body, it is evident that the substance which is called material intellect is not a body or a form in a body. For this reason it is not mixed with matter in any way at all. And you should know that what he states is necessarily so, namely that, since it [the material intellect] is a substance, and since it receives the forms of material things or material forms, it does not have in itself a material form, that is, it is not composed of matter and form. Nor is it some one of the material forms, for the material forms are not separable from bodies. Nor, again, is it one of the first simple forms since these are separable from bodies, but it [the material intellect] does not . . . receive forms except as differentiated and insofar as they are intelligible in potentiality, not in actuality, that is, it must be related to the body in some way. Therefore, it is something different from form and from matter and from that which is composed of these. But whether this substance [the material intellect] has a proper form which is different in its being from the material forms has not yet been explained in this discussion. For the proposition which states that that which receives must be devoid of the nature of that which it receives is understood as referring to the nature of the species, not to the nature of its genus, and even less to the nature of something remote, and still less to the nature of something which is predicated according to equivocation. Thus, we say that in the sense of touch there exists something intermediate between the two contraries which it perceives, for contraries differ in species from intermediate things. Since this is the disposition of the material intellect, namely, that it is some existing thing, and that it is a power separate from body, and that it has no material form, it is clear that it is not passive [in the sense of being alterable] (for passive things, that is things which are alterable, are like material forms), and that it is simple, and separable from body, as Aristotle says. The nature of the material intellect is understood by Aristotle in this manner. We shall speak subsequently about the questions which he raised.

TEXT 5

And thus [the material intellect] has no other nature but that which is possible. Therefore, that part of the soul which is called intellect (and I call intellect that part by means of which we distinguish and think) is not something existing in actuality before it thinks.

COMMENTARY

After Aristotle has shown that the material intellect does not possess any of the forms of material things, he begins to define it in the following manner, and he says that it has no nature but the nature of the possibility for receiving the material intelligible forms. He states, "And thus the material intellect has no other nature." That is, that part of the soul which is called the material intellect has no nature and essence through which it exists (constituatur) insofar as it is material but the nature of possibility, for it is devoid of all material and intelligible forms.

Thereafter he says, "and I call intellect." That is, and I intend by *intellect* that faculty of the soul which is truly called intellect, not that faculty which is called intellect in a general sense, that is, the imaginative faculty (in the Greek language), but I intend that faculty by means of which we distinguish speculative things and by means of which we think about things to be done in the future. Thereafter he says, "it is not something existing in actuality before it thinks." That is, it is the definition of the material intellect that it is that which is in potentiality all the concepts (intentiones) of the universal material forms and it is not something in actuality before it understands them.

Since this is the definition of the material intellect, it is clear that it differs in respect to itself from prime matter in that it is in potentiality all the concepts of the universal material forms, while prime matter is in potentiality all these sensible forms, not as knowing and comprehending. And the reason why this nature, that is, the material intellect, distinguishes and knows, while prime matter does not distinguish or know, is that prime matter receives differentiated, that is, individual and particular forms, while the material intellect receives universal forms. And from this it is clear that this nature, that is, the material intellect, is not some individual thing, either a body or a power in a body, for if it were, it would receive the forms insofar as they are differentiated and particular, and if this were the case, then the forms existing in the material intellect would be intelligible in potentiality and thus this intellect would not distinguish the nature of the forms insofar as they are forms, and the case would be the same as that of a disposition for individual forms, whether they are spiritual or corporeal. Therefore, if this nature, which is called intellect, receives forms, it is necessary that it receives these forms in a manner of reception different from that according to which these matters receive the forms whose determination in prime matter is the determination of prime matter in respect to them. Therefore it is not necessary that there belong to the genus of those matters by which the form is determined as particular anything but prime matter. For if there were other matters in this genus, then the reception of forms in these matters would be of the same genus, for diversity in the nature of the receptacle produces a diversity in the nature of that which is received. This consideration moved Aristotle to affirm that this nature, that is, the material intellect, differs from the nature of matter and from the nature of form and from the nature of the composite.

All these things being as they are, it seems to me proper to write down what appears to me to be correct concerning this subject. And if that which appears to me to be correct will not be complete, let it be the starting point for something which can be completed. Now, I beg those brethren who see what has been written, that they write down their questions and perhaps in this way that which is true about this subject will be discovered, if I should not have discovered it. But should I have discovered what is true, as I think I have, then this truth will become clear through these questions. For truth, as Aristotle says, agrees with itself and bears witness to itself in every way.

As for the question stating: in what way are the speculative intelligibles generable and corruptible, while the intellect producing them and that receiving them are eternal (and what need would there be to posit an agent intellect and a receiving intellect were there not something that is generated)—this question would not arise would there not exist something which is the cause of the generation of the speculative intelligibles. But what has been said concerning the fact that these [speculative] intelligibles consists of two [principles], one of which is generated, the other of which is not generated is according to the course of nature. For, since conception by the intellect, as Aristotle says, is like perception by the senses—but perception by a sense is accomplished through two principles, one of which is that object through which sense perception becomes true (and this is the sensible outside the soul), and the other is that subject through which sense perception is an existing form (and this is the first actuality of the sense organ), it is likewise necessary that the intelligibles in actuality have two principles, one of which is the object through which they are true, namely, the forms which are the true images, the other one of which is that subject through which the intelligibles are one of the things existing in the world, and this is the material intellect. But there is no difference between sense and intellect except that the object through which sense-perception is true exists outside the soul, while the object through which conception by the intellect is true exists within the soul. As will be seen subsequently, this is what was said by Aristotle about this intellect.

This similarity exists in an even more perfect manner between the visible object which moves the sense of sight and the intelligible object which moves the intellect. For just as the visible object, which is color, moves the sense of sight only when through the presence of light it was made color in actuality after it had been color in potentiality, so also the imaginative forms move the material intellect only when they are made intelligibles in actuality after they had been intelligibles in potentiality. And for this reason (as will be seen later) it was necessary for Aristotle to posit an agent intellect, and this is the intellect which brings the imaginative forms from potentiality into actuality. Thus, just as the color which exists in potentiality is not the first actuality of that color which is the perceived form, while the subject which is actualized by this color is the sense of sight, so also the subject which is actualized by the intelligible object is not the imaginative forms which are intelligible in potentiality, but the material intellect is that subject which is actualized by the intelligibles. And the relation of the intelligible forms to the material intellect is as the relation of the form of color to the faculty of sight.

All these matters being as we have related, it is only necessary that the intelligibles in actuality, that is the speculative intelligibles, are generable according to the object through which they are true, that is, according to the imaginative forms, but not according to that subject through which they are one of the existing things, that is, according to the material intellect.

But the second question which states: in what way is the material intellect numerically one in all individual human beings, not generable nor corruptible, while the intelligibles existing in it in actuality (and this is the speculative intellect) are numbered according to the numeration of individual human beings, and generable and corruptible through the generation and corruption of individual human beings—this question is extremely difficult and one that has the greatest ambiguity.

If we posit that this material intellect is numbered according to the numeration of individual human beings, it follows that it is some individual thing, either a body or a power in a body. And if it were some individual thing, it would be the intelligible form in potentiality. But the intelligible form in potentiality is an object which moves the receiving intellect, not a subject which is moved. For, if the receiving subject were assumed to be some individual thing, it would follow, as we have said, that something receives itself, and this is impossible.

Even if we were to admit that it receives itself, it would necessarily follow that it receives itself insofar as it is diverse. And thus the intellectual faculty would be the same as the sensory faculty, and there would be no distinction between the existence of the form outside the soul and in the soul. For this individual matter receives the forms only as particulars and individuals. And this is one of the arguments which provide evidence that Aristotle was of the opinion that the material intellect is not an individual form.

On the other hand, were we to assert that the material intellect is not numbered according to the numeration of individual human beings, it would follow that its relation to all individual human beings who possess its ultimate perfection through generation would be the same. Whence, it would be necessary that if one of these individual human beings acquires some knowledge, this knowledge would be acquired by all of them. For, if the conjunction of these individual human beings with what is known occurs because of the conjunction of the material intellect with them, just as the conjunction of a human being with the sensory form occurs because of the conjunction of the first perfection of the sense organ with him who receives the sensory form (but the conjunction of the material intellect with all human beings who exist in actuality in their ultimate perfection at some given time must be one and the same conjunction, for there is nothing which would produce any difference in the relation of conjunction between the two who are conjoined)—if, I say, this is the case, it is necessary that if you acquire some knowledge, I will acquire the same knowledge, which is absurd.

And regardless whether you assert that the ultimate perfection which is generated in some individual human being—that is, that perfection through which the material intellect is joined to human beings and through which it is as a form separable from the subject to which it is joined—inheres in the intellect, if something like that should be the case, or whether you assert that this perfection belongs to one of the faculties of the soul or to one of the faculties of the body, each of these assumptions leads to an absurd conclusion.

Therefore, one must be of the opinion that if there exist some beings having a soul whose first perfection is a substance existing in separation from their subjects, as it is thought about the celestial bodies, it is impossible that there exist in each of their species more than one individual. For if there would exist in these, that is, in each of their species more than one individual, for example, in the body moved by the same mover, then the existence of these individuals would be unnecessary and superfluous, since their motion would result from the form which is one in number. For example, it is unnecessary that one sailor [captain] should have more than one ship at the same time, and it is likewise unnecessary that one artisan should have more than one instrument of the same kind.

This is the meaning of what was said in the first book of *De Caelo*, namely that, if there existed another world, there would have to exist another celestial body corresponding to a celestial body in this world. And if there existed another celestial body, it would have to have a motive force numerically different from the motive force of this celestial body, that is, the one existing in this world. If this were the case, then the motive force of the celestial body would be material and numbered through the numeration of the celestial bodies, since it is impossible that a motive force which is one in number should belong to two bodies which are different in number. Therefore, a craftsman does not use more than one instrument when only one action proceeds from him. And it is generally thought that necessarily absurd conclusions will follow from the assertion we have made, namely, that the intellect *in habitu* is one in number. Avempace enumerated most of these absurd conclusions in his Letter which he called *The Conjunction of the Intellect with Man*. Since this is so, of what sort is the road toward the solution of this difficult question?

We say that it is evident that a man is thinking in actuality only because of the conjunction of the intelligible in actuality with him. It is also evident that matter and form are joined to one another in such a way that something which is composed of them is a unitary thing and this is especially evident in the case of the conjunction of the material intellect and the intelligible form in actuality. For that which is composed of these [the material intellect and the intelligible form] is not some third thing different from them as is the case in respect to other beings composed of matter and form. Hence, the conjunction of the intelligible with man is only possible through the conjunction of one of these two parts with him, namely, that part which belongs to it [the intelligible] as matter or that part which belongs to it (namely, the intelligible) as form.

Since it is clear from the previously mentioned difficulties that it is impossible that the intelligible be joined to each individual human being and that it be numbered according their numeration through that part which is to it as matter, that is, through the material intellect, it remains that the conjunction of the intelligibles with us human beings takes place through the conjunction of the intelligible forms (and they are the imaginative forms) with us, that is, through that part which is in us in respect to them in some way like a form. And therefore the statement that a boy is potentially thinking can be understood in two ways. One of these is insofar as the imaginative forms which exist in him are intelligible in potentiality; the other is insofar as the material intellect, to whose nature it belongs to receive the concept of this imaginative form, is receptive in potentiality and joined to us in potentiality.

It is clear, therefore, that the first perfection of the intellect differs from the first perfection of the other faculties of the soul and that the term *perfection* is predicated of them in an equivocal fashion, and this is the opposite of what Alexander [of Aphrodisias] thought. For this reason Aristotle said in his definition of the soul that the soul is the first perfection of a natural organic body, for it is not yet clear whether a body is perfected by all faculties in the same way, or whether there is among them some faculty by which a body is not perfected, or, if it is perfected by it, it will be perfected in some other way.

Now the predisposition of the intelligibles which exists in the imaginative faculty is similar to the predispositions which exist in the other faculties of the soul, namely, the predisposition for the first perfec-

tions of the other faculties of the soul, insofar as each of these predispositions is generated through the generation of the individual in which it exists and destroyed through the destruction of this individual and, generally, this predisposition is numbered according to the numeration of that individual.

But the two kinds of predisposition differ in that the first kind, namely, the predisposition which exists in the imaginative forms, is a predisposition in a moving principle, while the second kind, namely that predisposition which exists for the first perfections of the other parts of the soul, is a predisposition in a recipient.

Because of the similarity between these two kinds of predispositions Avempace thought that the only predisposition for the production of the intelligible concept is the predisposition existing in the imaginative forms. But these two predispositions differ as earth and heaven. For one of them is a predisposition in a moving principle insofar as it is a moving principle, while the other is a predisposition in something moved insofar as it is moved and is a recipient.

Thus, one should hold the opinion which has already become clear to us from Aristotle's discussion, namely, that there are two kinds of intellect in the soul. One of these is the receiving intellect whose existence has been shown here, the other is the agent intellect and this is the one which causes the forms which are in the imaginative faculty to move the material intellect in actuality, after they had only moved it potentially, as will be clear further on from Aristotle's discussion. And these two kinds of intellect are not generable or corruptible. And the agent intellect is to the receiving intellect as form to matter, as will be shown later on.

Now Themistius was of the opinion that we are the agent intellect, and that the speculative intellect is nothing but the conjunction of the agent intellect with the material intellect. And it is not as he thought, but one must be of the opinion that there are three kinds of intellect in the soul. One of these is the receiving intellect, the second is the producing [agent] intellect, and the third is the produced [speculative] intellect. Two of these intellects are eternal, namely, the agent and receiving intellects, the third, however, is generable and corruptible in one way, eternal in another way.

Since as a result of this discussion we are of the opinion that the material intellect is a single one for all human beings and since we are also of the opinion that the human species is eternal, as has been shown in other places, it follows that the material intellect is never devoid of the natural principles which are common to the whole human species, namely, the first propositions and individual concepts which are common to all. For these inteligibles are one according to the recipient [the material intellect], and many according to the received form [the imaginative form].

Hence, according to the manner in which they are one, they are necessarily eternal; for existence does not depart from the received object, namely, the moving principle which is the form of the imaginative forms, and there is nothing on part of the recipient which prevents its reception. For generation and corruption belongs to them only according to the multitude which befalls them, not according to the manner according to which they are one. Therefore, when in respect to some individual human being, some knowledge of the things first known is destroyed through the destruction of the object through which it is joined to us and through which it is true, that is the imaginative form, it does not follow that this knowledge is destroyed absolutely, but it is only destroyed in respect to some individual human being. Because of this we can say that the speculative intellect is one in all human beings.

If one considers these intelligibles insofar as they exist absolutely, not in respect to some individual human being, they are truly said to be eternal, and it is not the case that they are known at one time and not known at another time, but they are known always. And that existence belongs to them as intermediate between absence of existence and permanent existence. For in accordance with the quantitative difference [according to the increase and decrease] which comes to the intelligibles from the ultimate perfection of human beings they are generable and corruptible, while insofar as they are one in number they are eternal.

This will be the case if it is not set down that the disposition in respect to the ultimate perfection in man is as the disposition in respect to the intelligibles which are common to all men, that is, that the world [worldly existence] is not devoid of such an individual existence. That this should be impossible is not obvious, but someone who affirms this must have an adequate reason and one that puts the mind at rest. For if

knowledge belongs in some proper fashion to human beings, just as the various kinds of crafts belong in some proper fashions to human beings, one should think that it is impossible that philosophy should be without any abode, just as one must be of the opinion that it is impossible that all the natural crafts should be without any abode. If some part of the earth lacks them, that is, these crafts, for example, the northern quarter of the earth, the other quarters will not lack them, since it is clear that they can have an abode in the southern part, just as in the northern.

Thus, perhaps, philosophy comes to be in the major portion of the subject at all times, just as man comes to be from man and horse from horse. According to this mode of existence the speculative intellect is neither generable nor corruptible.

In general, the case of the agent intellect which produces the intelligibles is the same as the case of the intellect which distinguishes and receives the intelligibles. For just as the agent intellect never ceases from generating and producing intelligibles in an absolute manner, even though some particular subject may be removed from this generation, so is it with the intellect that distinguishes.

Aristotle indicated this in the first treatise of this book [De Anima] when he said, "Conception and consideration by the intellect are differentiated, so that within the intellect something other is destroyed, while the intellect itself is not subject to destruction." Aristotle intends by "something other" the human imaginative forms. And he intends by "conception by the intellect" the reception which exists always in the material intellect, about which he intends to raise questions in the present treatise as well as in the former when he says, "And when it [the intellect] is set free . . . we do not remember, since this intellect is not passive, but the passive intellect is corruptible, and without it nothing thinks."

And by the "passive intellect" he intends the imaginative faculty, as will be shown later. Generally, this meaning seems to be remote, namely, that the soul, that is, the speculative intellect, should be immortal.

For this reason Plato said that the universals are neither generable nor corruptible and that they exist outside the mind. This statement is true in the sense that the intelligibles inhering in the speculative intellect are immortal, but false according to the sound of his words (and this is the sense which Aristotle labored to destroy in the *Metaphysics*). In general, in regard of the nature of the soul, there is something true in the probable propositions which attribute to the soul both kinds of existence, namely mortal and immortal, since it is impossible that probable propositions should be completely false. The ancients give an account of this and all the religious laws agree in this account.

The third question (namely, in what way is the material intellect some existing thing, while it is not one of the material forms nor prime matter) is answered as follows: one should be of the opinion that there are four kinds of existence. For just as sensible being is divided into form and matter, so also must intelligible being be divided into principles similar to these, that is into something similar to form and something similar to matter. This distinction is necessary for every incorporeal intellect which understands another, for if this distinction did not apply there would be no multiplicity in regard to the incorporeal forms. It has been shown in *First Philosophy* [that is, in the *Metaphysics*] that there exists no form absolutely free from potentiality except the first form which does not think anything outside itself, but its existence is its quiddity, but other forms are differentiated in respect to quiddity and existence in some way. Were there not this genus of beings which we know in the science of the soul, we could not think of multiplicity in the case of incorporeal beings, just as we would not know that incorporeal motive forces must be intellect, if we would not know the nature of the intellect.

This escaped many modern philosophers, so that they deny what Aristotle said in the eleventh treatise of the *First Philosophy*, namely, that it is necessary, that the incorporeal forms which move the celestial bodies are numbered according to the number of the celestial bodies. Therefore, knowledge about the soul is necessary for the knowledge of *First Philosophy*. It is necessary that the receiving intellect knows the intellect which exists in actuality. For if this intellect understands the material forms, it is more fitting that it understands immaterial forms, and that which it knows of the incorporeal forms, for example, of the agent intellect, does not hinder it from knowing the material forms.

But the proposition which states that a recipient must not have anything in actuality insofar as it receives is not said in an absolute fashion, but with the provision, that it is not necessary that the receiving intellect be not anything whatsoever in actuality, but only that it is not something in actuality in respect to that which it receives, as we have stated previously. Indeed, you should know that the relation of the agent intellect to the receiving intellect is as the relation of light to the transparent medium, and that the relation of the material forms to the receiving intellect is as the relation of color to the transparent medium. For just as light is the perfection of the transparent medium, so is the agent intellect the perfection of the material intellect. And just as the transparent medium is only moved by color and receives it when it is illuminated, so also the material intellect only receives the intelligibles which exist in it when the material intellect is perfected by the agent intellect and illuminated by it. And just as light makes color in potentiality exist in actuality, as a result of which it [color] can move the transparent medium, so also the agent intellect makes the intelligible forms in potentiality exist in actuality, as a result of which the material intellect receives them. In this manner one must understand about the material and agent intellect.

When the material intellect becomes joined insofar as it is perfected through the agent intellect, then we are joined with the agent intellect. And this disposition is called *acquisition* and *acquired intellect,* as will be seen later. The manner in which we have described the essence of the material intellect answers all the questions arising about our statement that this intellect is one and many. For if something which is known by me and by you were one in all respects, it would follow that, if I know something, you would also know it, and many other absurdities would also follow. And if we were to assert that the material intellect is many, it would follow that something known by me and by you is one in respect to species and two in respect to individual, and, thus, something known would possess something else known and this would go on to infinity. Thus, it will be impossible that a student learns from a teacher if the knowledge which exists in the teacher is not a force generating and producing the knowledge which is in the student, in the same manner as one fire produces another fire alike to it in species, which is absurd. The fact that something known by the teacher and the student is the same in this manner made Plato believe that learning is remembering. But if we assert that something known by me and by you is many in respect to that object according to which it is true, that is, in respect to the imaginative forms, and one in respect to the subject through which it is an existing intellect (and this is the material intellect), these questions are resolved completely.

STUDY QUESTIONS: AVERROËS, COMMENTARY ON "ON THE SOUL"

1. Why must the intellect understand all things?
2. What is Averroës' disagreement with Anaxagoras, and why?
3. How does Averroës differentiate the passive from the active intellect?
4. Is conception an active or passive power? Why?
5. What is the material intellect? How is it related to the active and the passive?
6. What does Averroës mean by substance?
7. How does Aristotle define the material intellect? What use does Averroës make of this?
8. What does Averroës mean by "intellect," and how does it differ from what Aristotle calls the imaginative faculty?
9. Does the material intellect exist before it thinks? How does this compare with Augustine's notion of self-existence? How does it compare with Descartes' "I think, therefore I am?"
10. What is the "receiving subject?" Why is this important? What function does it serve in Averroës' theory of the soul?
11. What is the speculative intellect?
12. What does Averroës mean by *perfection?* What is "first perfection?" How are these terms relevant to his concept of the soul?
13. What is Averroës' explanation of Plato's theory of universals as being eternal and existing outside the mind?
14. Why does the predicate "multiplicity" not apply to the soul?

Philosphical Bridges: The Influence of Averroës (Ibn Rushd)

Averroës was the first medieval philosopher who tried to liberate philosophy from theology by returning it to its pre-Christian origins in ancient Greece. Averroës' arguments against and criticisms of al-Ghazali amounted to a systematic defense of the Aristotelian philosophy through commentaries that purified it of its Stoic and neo-Platonic elements. Averroës did this so well that subsequent Scholastic writers referred to Averroës as "the Commentator," giving him the honorary title because he had no equal. Thomas Aquinas used Averroës' work as a constant source for his own commentaries on Aristotle, as well as in the writing of his *Summa contra Gentiles* (see the Aquinas section). The view of many subsequent theologians and philosophers that philosophy and theology each have a legitimate but distinct function owes much to Averroës' arguments.

Averroës' extraordinary view that the active intellect is numerically identical in all sentient beings—that in some deep metaphysical sense we are all one and the same entity—has influenced and inspired many, whether they accepted his vision or vehemently opposed it; Aquinas's *Against the Averroists* was instrumental in putting a prohibition, punishable by death, throughout Europe, against teaching this aspect of Averroës' philosophy. The church placed Averroës' view that all human beings are one on its infamous list of Forbidden

Propositions. Nevertheless, the Averroists—who also called themselves "Integral Aristotelians"—continued to teach in secret at the University of Paris and Oxford throughout the Middle Ages and beyond that the active intellect, as described in Averroës' *Commentary on On the Soul*, is itself numerically identical to the agent intellect, the one who individuates himself into the many by illuminating the passive intellects within individual human beings.

MAIMONIDES (1135–1204)

Biographical History

Maimonides (Moses ben Maimon) lived at the same time as Averroës and was born and raised in the same city—Córdova, Spain. He also came from a prominent family, in his case a Jewish one. At the age of 13, when the Almohads conquered Córdova and made life difficult for the Jews, he escaped with his family first to Morocco, then Palestine, and then finally in Fostat (old Cairo), Egypt. Like many prominent students of the time, he learned medicine, philosophy, and theology. His reputation as an extraordinary doctor earned him an appointment as royal physician to the king of Egypt. As a rabbi, his vast theological knowledge and philosophical agility earned him the position of *nagid*, head of the Egyptian Jewish community in Fostat.

Philosophical Overview

Maimonides produced a number of influential works, among them *Sharh al-Mishnah* (*Commentary on the Mishnah*); the Mishnah, also known as *Siraj* (*Luminary*, 1168); *Mishnah Torah* (*Code of Jewish Law, 1178*); and *Treatise on Resurrection* (1191). But his most famous and lasting philosophical work, generally regarded as one of the greatest philosophical works of the Middle Ages, *Dalalat al-Ha'rin* (*Guide for the Perplexed*, 1190), is generally regarded as one of the greatest works of philosophy of the Middle Ages. Just as Aquinas tries to make philosophy compatible with Christianity, and Avicenna tries to make philosophy compatible with Islam, Maimonides attempts to make room within Judaism for his brand of neo-Platonic Aristotelianism, as taught by Al-Farabi (Abū Nasr, 870–950) and Avicenna.

The very highest form of human knowledge, according to Maimonides, is metaphysics. The problem is that naked (uninterpreted) perception is blind, unaided reason uncomprehending, to the literally blinding truths of metaphysics. Unless one is philosophically prepared, metaphysics causes grave psychological and intellectual harm. Moreover, although religion and science are incapable of representing ultimate metaphysical truths, their function is to prepare us philosophically to attain true understanding of the world and ourselves.

Maimonides thus tries to reconcile not only religion with philosophy, but also science with metaphysics. These different ways of inquiry are each suited to different aspects of the human mind. They must all function together properly, until the mind is ready to attain full intellectual illumination through wisdom, which he defines as "consciousness of self." The way to attain this is through education, gradually, by moving the mind from the particular to the abstract. His method relies on faith, but only if and when reason fails;

otherwise, one defers always to reason. Only thus can mind transcend the limitations of the mind to attain thereby complete knowledge of itself and the world, and of the nature and role of God. "When you understand physics," he instructs his students, "you have entered the hall; and when, after completing the study of natural philosophy, you master metaphysics, you have entered the innermost court, and are with the king in the same palace."

Moreover, faith has a place not only in religion but also philosophy. By faith he does not mean the traditional acceptance of beliefs taught to you by authorities but, rather, the intuitive leap of faith that experience, when supported by reason, corresponds to reality. This truth cannot otherwise ever be known. He thus revamps traditional Christian, Muslim and Jewish forms of faith-based mystical knowledge of God as absolute unity, a one without form, indivisible, everywhere identical. He thus dismisses the Christian doctrine of the Trinity and of Christ as an embodiment of God as absurdities. In his view there can be no such relation between man, world and God, any more than there can be a relationship between the relative world of potentiality and absolute actuality. Because God has no positive attributes, to say anything at all about God, such as "God exists" or "God is One," is absurd. One would have to say, rather, that God exists without having the attribute of existence, that God is one without having the attribute of unity, and so on.

However, God is not nothing. The universe does not and cannot exist without God, of which the universe itself is but a reflection. Like God, the universe is one being, everywhere identical to itself, even while all its many parts are differentiated from each other. In that respect, the unity of the universe is like the unity of the body: the whole is not in any part thereof.

GUIDE FOR THE PERPLEXED
Maimonides

Like Aquinas' *Summa Theologica*, Maimonides' *Guide for the Perplexed* is written for philosophers and theologians, not the general public. Often it is obscure, apparently deliberately so. Metaphysics, according to Maimonides, is the highest level of human activity. He agrees with Averroës that that such lofty activity can be practiced only by a soul with a sufficiently active and high intellect. But whereas Averroës claims that different intellectual abilities among people is predetermined, Maimonides provides a startlingly modern philosophical pedagogy by which anyone can be raised, by proper teaching, through the various stages of intellectual ability, up to the very highest level. Such guidance can be provided by a good education, a bold idea that inspired theologians and philosophers alike throughout the ages.

The *Guide for the Perplexed*, dedicated to Maimonides' own favorite pupil, Iknin of Syria, is divided into three parts. In part one, he applies his *via negativa* (negative way) of discovering God's attributes. He criticizes Islamic theology by showing the circularity involved in the method of *kalam*, whereby propositions accepted in advance to be true are demonstrated to be true. In part two, he offers new proofs for the existence of God based on Aristotle's analysis of the relationship between matter in relation to Plato's theory of

Maimonides, from *Guide for the Perplexed*, translated by M. Friedländer (London: Routledge & Kegan Paul, 1904).

forms. In part three he considers the problems of determinism and free will, the problem of evil, the nature of rationality, and a compatiblist argument for reconciling reason and revelation. He argues that if the Bible is perfectly clear on some point against which no clear philosophical arguments can be made, we are obliged to accept the Bible. On the other hand, if the point seems dubious or there is a philosophical argument to the contrary, the biblical passage should be taken as allegory and interpreted according to reason. His arguments paved the way for the Jewish emphasis on reason over scripture.

Maimonides argues, perhaps surprisingly, that most people should not begin their studies with metaphysics. The problem is that the uneducated mind lacks the discipline required for accurate self-representation, and so the mind cannot come to know its own functioning, neither in the realm of perception nor in the conceptual realm. He compares trying to philosophize without proper training to trying to lift too heavy a weight or running too far in poor physical condition. Such activity is not only impossible but also harmful. This he calls the "mysteries of the Law" according to which ultimate truths about the universe must be kept secret from the masses and, therefore, never revealed in writing. If passed on at all it must be done, as Socrates argued philosophy itself must be done, by word of mouth, "*vivâ voce.*" Only when worthy students have demonstrated that they have attained the highest levels of intellectual maturity can the truth be to them revealed.

Know that for the human mind there are certain objects of perception which are within the scope of its nature and capacity; on the other hand, there are, amongst things which actually exist, certain objects which the mind can in no way and by no means grasp: the gates of perception are closed against it. Further, there are things of which the mind understands one part, but remains ignorant of the other; and when man is able to comprehend certain things, it does not follow that he must be able to comprehend everything. This also applies to the senses: they are able to perceive things, but not at every distance; and all other powers of the body are limited in a similar way. . . .

All this is applicable to the intellectual faculties of man. There is a considerable difference between one person and another as regards these faculties, as is well-known to philosophers. While one man can discover a certain thing by himself, another is never able to understand it, even if taught by means of all possible expressions and metaphors, and during a long period; his mind can in no way grasp it, his capacity is insufficient for it. This distinction is not unlimited. A boundary is undoubtedly set to the human mind which it cannot pass. There are things (beyond that boundary) which are acknowledged to be inaccessible to human understanding, and man does not show any desire to comprehend them, being aware that such knowledge is impossible, and that there are no means

of overcoming the difficulty; for example, we do not know the number of stars in heaven, whether the number is even or odd; we do not know the number of animals, minerals, or plants, and the like. There are other things, however, which man very much desires to know, and strenuous efforts to examine and to investigate them have been made by thinkers of all classes, and at all times. They differ and disagree, and constantly raise new doubts with regard to them, because their minds are bent on comprehending such things, that is to say, they are moved by desire; and every one of them believes that he has discovered the way leading to a true knowledge of the thing, although human reason is entirely unable to demonstrate the fact by convincing evidence. For a proposition which can be proved by evidence is not subject to dispute, denial, or rejection; none but the ignorant would contradict it, and such contradiction is called "denial of a demonstrated proof." Thus you find men who deny the spherical form of the earth, or the circular form of the line in which the stars move, and the like; such men are not considered in this treatise. This confusion prevails mostly in metaphysical subjects, less in problems relating to physics, and is entirely absent from the exact sciences. Alexander Aphrodisius said that there are three causes which prevent men from discovering the exact truth; first, arrogance and vainglory; secondly, the subtlety, depth, and difficulty of any subject which is being examined; thirdly, ignorance and want of capacity to comprehend what might be comprehended. These causes are enumerated by Alexander. At the present time there is a fourth cause not mentioned by him, because it did not then prevail, namely, habit and training. We naturally like what we have been accustomed to, and are attracted towards it. . . .

The same is the case with those opinions of man to which he has been accustomed from his youth; he likes them, defends them, and shuns the opposite views. This is likewise one of the causes which prevent men from finding truth, and which make them cling to their habitual opinions. . . .

You must consider, when reading this treatise, that mental perception, because connected with matter, is subject to conditions similar to those to which physical perception is subject. That is to say, if your eye looks around, you can perceive all that is within the range of your vision; if, however, you overstrain your eye, exerting it too much by attempting to see an object which is too distant for your eye, or to examine writings or engravings too small for your sight, and forcing it to obtain a correct perception of them, you will not only weaken your sight with regard to that special object, but also for those things which you otherwise are able to perceive: your eye will have become too weak to perceive what you were able to see before you exerted yourself and exceeded the limits of your vision.

The same is the case with the speculative faculties of one who devotes himself to the study of any science. If a person studies too much and exhausts his reflective powers, he will be confused, and will not be able to apprehend even that which had been within the power of his apprehension. For the powers of the body are all alike in this respect.

The mental perceptions are not exempt from a similar condition. If you admit the doubt, and do not persuade yourself to believe that there is a proof for things which cannot be demonstrated, or to try at once to reject and positively to deny an assertion the opposite of which has never been proved or attempt to perceive things which are beyond your perception, then you have attained the highest degree of human perfection. . . . If, on the other hand, you attempt to exceed the limit of your intellectual power, or at once to reject things as impossible which have never been proved to be impossible, or which are in fact possible, though their possibility be very remote, then you will . . . not only fail to become perfect, but you will become exceedingly imperfect. Ideas founded on mere imagination will prevail over you, you will incline toward defects, and toward base and degraded habits, on account of the confusion which troubles the mind, and of the dimness of its light, just as weakness of sight causes invalids to see many kinds of unreal images, especially when they have looked for a long time at dazzling or at very minute objects.

Respecting this it has been said, "Hast thou found honey? Eat so much as is sufficient for thee, lest thou be filled therewith, and vomit it" (Prov. xxv. 16).

How excellent is this simile! In comparing knowledge to food . . . the author of Proverbs mentions the sweetest food, namely, honey, which has the further property of irritating the stomach, and of causing sickness. He thus fully describes the nature of knowledge. Though great, excellent, noble, and perfect, it is injurious if not kept within bounds or not guarded properly; it is like honey which gives nourishment and is pleasant, when eaten in moderation, but is totally thrown away when eaten immoderately. Therefore, it is not said "lest thou be filled and loathe it," but "lest thou vomit it." . . .

It was not the object of the Prophets and our Sages in these utterances to close the gate of investigation entirely, and to prevent the mind from comprehending what is within its reach, as is imagined by simple and idle people, whom it suits better to put forth their ignorance and incapacity as wisdom and perfection, and to regard the distinction and wisdom of others as irreligion and imperfection, thus taking darkness for light and light for darkness. The whole object of the Prophets and the Sages was to declare that a limit is set to human reason where it must halt. . . .

You must know that it is very injurious to begin with this branch of philosophy, that is to say, Metaphysics; or to explain the sense of the similes occurring in prophecies, and interpret the metaphors which are employed in historical accounts and which abound in the writings of the Prophets. On the contrary, it is necessary to initiate the young and to instruct the less intelligent according to their comprehension; those who appear to be talented and to have capacity for the higher method of study, that is, that based on proof and on true logical argument, should be gradually advanced towards perfection, either by tuition or by self-instruction. He, however, who begins with Metaphysics, will not only become confused in matters of religion, but will fall into complete infidelity. I compare such a person to an infant fed with wheaten bread, meat and wine; it will undoubtedly die, not because such food is naturally unfit for the human body, but because of the weakness of the child, who is unable to digest the food, and cannot derive benefit from it. The same is the case with the true principles of science. They were presented in enigmas, dad in riddles, and taught by all wise men in the most mysterious way that could be devised, not because they contain some secret evil, or are contrary to the fundamental principles of the Law (as fools think who are only philosophers in their own eyes), but because of the incapacity of man to comprehend them at the beginning of his studies: only slight allusions have been made to them to serve for the guidance of those who are capable of understanding them. These sciences were, therefore, called Mysteries (sodoth), and Secrets of the Law (sitre torah), as we shall explain.

This also is the reason why "the Torah speaks the language of man," as we have explained, for it is the object of the Torah to serve as a guide for the instruction of the young, of women, and of the common people; and as all of them are incapable to comprehend the true sense of the words, tradition was considered sufficient to convey all truths which were to be established; and as regards ideals, only such remarks were made as would lead towards a knowledge of their existence, though not to a comprehension of their true essence. When a man attains to perfection, and arrives at a knowledge of the "Secrets of the Law," either through the assistance of a teacher or by self-instruction, being led by the understanding of one part to the study of the other, he will belong to those who faithfully believe in the true principles, either because of conclusive proof, where proof is possible, or by forcible arguments, where argument is admissible; he will have a true notion of those things which he previously received in similes and metaphors, and he will fully understand their sense. We have frequently mentioned in this treatise the principle of our Sages "not to discuss the Ma'aseh Mercabah even in the pres-

ence of one pupil, except he be wise and intelligent; and then only the headings of the chapters are to be given to him." We must, therefore, begin with teaching these subjects according to the capacity of the pupil, and on two conditions, first, that he be wise, that is, that he should have successfully gone through the preliminary studies, and secondly that he be intelligent, talented, clear-headed, and of quick perception, that is, "have a mind of his own" (mebin midda'ato), as our Sages termed it.

I will now proceed to explain the reasons why we should not instruct the multitude in pure metaphysics, or begin with describing to them the true essence of things, or with showing them that a thing must be as it is, and cannot be otherwise. This will form the subject of the next chapter; and I proceed to say—there are five reasons why instruction should not begin with Metaphysics, but should at first be restricted to pointing out what is fitted for notice and what may be made manifest to the multitude.

First Reason: the subject itself is difficult, subtle, and profound, "Far off and exceeding deep, who can find it out?" (Eccles. vii. 24). The following words of Job may be applied to it: "whence then cometh wisdom? And where is the place of understanding?" (Job xxviii. 20). Instruction should not begin with abstruse and difficult subjects. In one of the similes contained in the Bible, wisdom is compared to water, and amongst other interpretations given by our Sages of this simile, occurs the following: he who can swim may bring up pearls from the depth of the sea, he who is unable to swim will be drowned, therefore only such persons as have had proper instruction should expose themselves to the risk.

Second Reason: the intelligence of man is at first insufficient; for he is not endowed with perfection at the beginning, but at first possesses perfection only in potentiâ, not in fact. Thus it is said, "and man is born a wild ass" (Job xi. 12). If a man possesses a certain faculty in potentiâ, it does not follow that it must become in him a reality. He may possibly remain deficient either on account of some obstacle, or from want of training in practices which would turn the possibility into a reality. Thus it is distinctly stated in the Bible, "Not many are wise" (ib., xxxii. 9); also our Sages say, "I noticed how few were those who attained to a higher degree of perfection" (B. T. Succah 45a). There are many things which obstruct the path to perfection, and which keep man away from it. Where can he find sufficient preparation and leisure to learn all that is necessary in order to develop that perfection which he has *in potentiâ?*

Third Reason: the preparatory studies are of long duration, and man, in his natural desire to reach the goal, finds them frequently too wearisome, and does not wish to be troubled by them. Be convinced that, if man were able to reach the end without preparatory studies, such studies would not be preparatory but tiresome and utterly superfluous. Suppose you awaken any person, even the most simple, as if from sleep, and you say to him, Do you not desire to know what the heavens are, what is their number and their form; what beings are contained in them; what the angels are; how the creation of the whole world took place; what is its purpose, and what is the relation of its various parts to each other; what is the nature of the soul; how it enters the body; whether it has an independent existence, and if so, how it can exist independently of the body; by what means and to what purpose, and similar problems. He would undoubtedly say "Yes," and show a natural desire for the true knowledge of these things; but he will wish to satisfy that desire and to attain to that knowledge by listening to a few words from you. Ask him to interrupt his usual pursuits for a week, till he learns all this, he would not do it, and would be satisfied and contented with imaginary and misleading notions; he would refuse to believe that there is anything which requires preparatory studies and persevering research. . . .

The majority of scholars, that is to say, the most famous in science, are afflicted with this failing, that is to say, that of hurrying at once to the final results, and of speaking about them, without treating of the preliminary disciplines. Led by folly or ambition to disregard those preparatory studies, for the attainment of which they are either incapable or too idle, some scholars endeavour to prove that these are injurious or superfluous. On reflection the truth will become obvious.

The Fourth Reason is taken from the physical constitution of man. It has been proved that moral conduct is a preparation for intellectual progress, and that only a man whose character is pure, calm and steadfast, can attain to intellectual perfection; that is, acquire correct conceptions. Many men are naturally so constituted that all perfection is impossible; for example, he whose heart is very warm and is himself very powerful, is sure to be passionate, though he tries to counteract that disposition by training; he whose testicles are warm, humid, and vigorous, and the organs connected therewith are surcharged, will not easily refrain from sin, even if he makes great efforts to restrain himself. You also find persons of great levity and rashness, whose excited manners and wild gestures prove that their constitution is in disorder, and their temperament so bad that it cannot be cured. Such persons can never attain to perfection; it is utterly useless to occupy oneself with them on such a subject [as Metaphysics]. For this science is, as you know, different from the science of Medicine and of Geometry, and, from the reason already mentioned, it is not every person who is capable of approaching it. It is impossible for a man to study it successfully without moral preparation; he must acquire the highest degree of uprightness and integrity, "for the forward is an abomination to the Lord, but His secret is with the righteous" (Prov. iii. 32). Therefore it was considered inadvisable to teach it to young men; nay, it is impossible for them to comprehend it, on account of the heat of their blood and the flame of youth, which confuses their minds; that heat, which causes all the disorder, must first disappear; they must have become moderate and settled, humble in their hearts, and subdued in their temperament; only then will they be able to arrive at the highest degree of the perception of God, that is, the study of Metaphysics. . . .

Fifth Reason: man is disturbed in his intellectual occupation by the necessity of looking after the material wants of the body, especially if the necessity of providing for wife and children be superadded; much more so if he seeks superfluities in addition to his ordinary wants, for by custom and bad habits these become a powerful motive. Even the perfect man to whom we have referred, if too busy with these necessary things, much more so if busy with unnecessary things, and filled with a great desire for them—must weaken or altogether lose his desire for study, to which he will apply himself with interruption, lassitude, and want of attention. He will not attain to that for which he is fitted by his abilities, or he will acquire imperfect knowledge, a confused mass of true and false ideas. For these reasons it was proper that the study of Metaphysics should have been exclusively cultivated by privileged persons, and not entrusted to the common people. It is not for the beginner, and he should abstain from it, as the little child has to abstain from taking solid food and from carrying heavy weights.

Know that many branches of science relating to the correct solution of these problems; were once cultivated by our forefathers, but were in the course of time neglected, especially in consequence of the tyranny which barbarous nations exercised over us. Besides, speculative studies were not open to all men, as we have already stated (Introd. p. 2 and I. chap. xxxi.), only the subjects taught in the Scriptures were accessible to all. Even the traditional Law, as you are well aware, was not originally committed to writing, in conformity with the rule to which our nation generally adhered, "things which I have communicated to you orally, you must not communicate to others in writing." With reference to the Law, this rule was very opportune; for while it remained in force it averted the evils which happened subsequently, that is to say, great diversity of opinion, doubts as to the meaning of written words, slips of the pen, dissensions among the people, formation of new sects, and confused notions about practical subjects. The traditional teaching was in fact, according to the words of the Law, entrusted to the Great Tribunal, as we have already stated in our works on the Talmud.

Care having been taken, for the sake of obviating injurious influences, that the Oral Law should not be recorded in a form accessible to all, it was but natural that no portion of "the secrets of the Law" (*i.e., metaphysical problems*) would be permitted to be written down or divulged for the use of all men. These secrets, as has been explained, were orally communicated by a few able men to others who were equally distinguished. Hence, the principle applied by our teachers, "the secrets of the Law can only be entrusted to him who is a councilor, a cunning artificer, etc." The natural effect of this practice was that our nation lost the knowledge of those important disciplines. Nothing but a few remarks and allusions are to be found in the Talmud and the Midrashim, like a few kernels enveloped in such a quantity of husk, that the reader is generally occupied with the husk, and forgets that it encloses a kernel. . . .

Know that this Universe, in its entirety, is nothing else but one individual being; that is to say, the outermost heavenly sphere, together with all included therein, is as regards individuality beyond all question a single being like Said and Omar. The variety of its substances—I mean the substances of that sphere and all its component parts—is like the variety of the substances of a human being: just as, for example, Said is one individual, consisting of various solid substances, such as flesh, bones, sinews, of various humours, and of various spiritual elements. . . .

The living being as such is one through the action of its heart, although some parts of the body are devoid of motion and sensation, as, for example, the bones, the cartilage, and similar parts. The same is the case with the entire universe; although it includes many beings without motion and without life, it is a single being living through the motion of the sphere, which may be compared to the heart of an animated being. You must, therefore, consider the entire globe as one individual being which is endowed with life, motion, and a soul. This mode of considering the universe is, as will be explained, indispensable, that is to say, it is very useful for demonstrating the unity of God; it also helps to elucidate the principle that He who is One has created only *one* being.

Again, it is impossible that any of the members of a human body should exist by themselves, not connected with the body, and at the same time should actually be organic parts of that body, that is to say, that the liver should exist by itself, the heart by itself, or the flesh by itself. In like manner, it is impossible that one part of the Universe should exist independently of the other parts in the existing order of things as here considered. . . .

In man there is a certain force which unites the members of the body, controls them, and gives to each of them what it requires for the conservation of its condition, and for the repulsion of injury—the physicians distinctly call it the leading force in the body of the living being; sometimes they call it "nature." The Universe likewise possesses a force which unites the several parts with each other, protects the species from destruction, maintains the individuals of each species as long as possible, and endows some individual beings with permanent existence. Whether this force operates through the medium of the sphere or otherwise remains an open question. . . .

. . . [T]hese subjects belong to the mysteries of the Law. You are well aware how our Sages blame those who reveal these mysteries, and praise the merits of those who keep them secret, although they are perfectly clear to the philosopher. In this sense they explain the passage, "Her merchandise shall be for them that dwell before the Lord, to eat sufficiently" (Isa. xxiii. 18), which concludes in the original with the words *ve-li-me-kasseh 'atik*, that is, that these blessings are promised to him who hides things which the Eternal has revealed [to him], viz., the mysteries of the Law (Babyl. Talmud, '*Pesahim*' 119a). If you have understanding you will comprehend that which our Sages pointed out. They have clearly stated that the Divine Chariot includes matters too deep and too profound for the ordinary intellect. It has been shown that a person favored by Providence with reason to understand these mysteries is forbidden by the Law to teach them except *viva voce*, and on condition that the pupil possess certain qualifications, and even then only the heads of the sections may be communicated. This has been the cause why the knowledge of this mystery has entirely disappeared from our nation, and nothing has remained of it. This was unavoidable, for the explanation of these mysteries was always communicated *viva voce*, it was never committed to writing. Such being the case, how can I venture to call your attention to such portions of it as may be known, intelligible, and perfectly clear to me? But if,

on the other hand, I were to abstain from writing on this subject, according to my knowledge of it, when I die, as I shall inevitably do, that knowledge would die with me, and I would, thus, inflict great injury on you and all those who are perplexed [by these theological problems]. I would then be guilty of withholding the truth from those to whom it ought to be communicated, and of jealously depriving the heir of his inheritance. I should in either case be guilty of gross misconduct.

To give a full explanation of the mystic passages of the Bible is contrary to the Law and to reason; besides, my knowledge of them is based on reasoning, not on divine inspiration [and is therefore not infallible]. I have not received my belief in this respect from any teacher, but it has been formed by what I learned from Scripture and the utterances of our Sages, and by the philosophical principles which I have adopted. It is, therefore, possible that my view is wrong, and that I misunderstood the passages referred to. . . . Those, however for whom this treatise has been composed, will, on reflecting on it and thoroughly examining each chapter, obtain a perfect and clear insight into all that has been clear and intelligible to me. This is the utmost that can be done in treating this subject so as to be useful to all without fully explaining it. . . .

STUDY QUESTIONS: MAIMONIDES, *GUIDE FOR THE PERPLEXED*

1. What are the objects that the mind cannot grasp, and why?
2. What is the difference between mental perception and physical perception?
3. What is the limit of human reason? How is it set, and why?
4. What is metaphysics?
5. Why is metaphysics dangerous?
6. What is the purpose and function of the Torah?
7. What are the five reasons why learning should not begin with metaphysics?
8. What is the major flaw that afflicts most scholars and scientists?
9. In what sense is the universe one individual being?
10. What are the mystic passages of the Bible, and should they be explained? Why?

Philosophical Bridges: The Influence of Maimonides

Maimonides' idea that human intelligence is not preordained, but can be raised through proper education, had tremendous influence among Jewish thinkers ever since. This radical idea provided Christian Scholasticism with a great religious incentive toward a philosophically rigorous education. Albertus Magnus and Thomas Aquinas were deeply moved by his arguments. In subsequent centuries Maimonides' arguments as to how and why philosophical enlightenment was attainable not by birthright but thorough education, inspired Spinoza, Mendelssohn, and Leibniz.

One of the most important methodological innovations in the *Guide for the Perplexed* was Maimonides's further development of John Scotus Erigena's (810–877) method *via negativa* (literally, "the negative way"). This involved relating a thing's attributes not by stating its essence in positive terms but by what is left after the deficiency of all positive statements about its essence has been exhausted. This method *via negativa* can be used, according to Maimonides, to transcend the limitations of the human mind and attain knowledge of things beyond the direct reach of the senses or the intellect, such as God. Philosophers and theologians throughout the Middle Ages applied this method not only to questions of God, but also to reality, the self, and morality.

Philosophical Bridges: The Islamic and Jewish Influence

There are two different aspects of the influence of Islamic philosophy: one is to the Islamic world and the other, no less significant, to western philosophy. First it must again be said that were it not for the Islamic philosophers we would probably know next to nothing about the works of Plato and Aristotle. When Europe turned fundamentalist and burned the philosophy books, they were not just saved by the Islamic intellectual tradition thriving at the time but augmented with spectacularly insightful and original commentaries that have colored virtually all aspects of our understanding of those two great pillars of ancient wisdom.

Second, the Islamic influence on the world of Islam by the philosophers here discussed is far-reaching indeed. In many ways Avicenna did for Islam what Aquinas did for Christianity (or, contrapositively, for philosophy), namely, made philosophy in the tradition of Plato and Aristotle compatible within the religion of the day. His distinction between existence and essence in individual creatures, and the unity of existence and essence in God, became an integral part of medieval philosophical education that formed the basis for Thomas Aquinas' philosophy. Aquinas' theory of intelligences, derived from Aristotle, became the medieval religious doctrine of angels. The Dominican Albertus Magnus (1193–1280), who was mentor to Aquinas, incorporated many of Avicenna's principles and methods, which influenced him to formulate his notion of *intentio*. In Islamic thought, Avicenna provided the basis for the work of Averroës, who also argued for the unity of the active intellect, albeit in a way that both Islamic and Christian religious philosophers rejected because it did not carry individual differences beyond the grave, into a system of justified rewards and punishments in the next life.

Likewise in the case of the great Averroës, who saw himself as the philosophical counterpart not only of Avicenna but also the great Muslim theologian al-Ghazali. His lengthy, detailed, and original commentaries on all of Aristotle's works—including the *Metaphysics, Physics, Posterior Analytics, De Caelo,* and *De Anima*—as well as Plato's *Republic,* became the standard library of philosophy for centuries, influencing Islamic, Jewish, and Christian thinkers on both sides of the Mediterranean. His distinction between "revealed" theology and "natural" theology was a powerful philosophical tool used by many subsequent medieval philosophers to keep themselves out of trouble with the Christian counterparts of the orthodox Muslim authorities.

There is a radical Socratic force to his method, which won him as many critics as supporters, be they Islamic, Jewish or Christian, and not only during the Middle Ages but subsequently, even up to the present day. In his attempt to "cleanse" Aristotle of Stoic and neo-Platonic influences, Averroës provided such robust and detailed analysis of ancient Greek thought that subsequent Scholastic writers referred to him as "The Commentator." Even his Christian philosophical nemesis, Thomas Aquinas, used Averroës as a constant source not only for his own commentaries on Aristotle but also in the writing of *Summa contra Gentiles*. Averroës was an extremely important influence also on Aquinas' teacher, Albertus Magnus, as well as John of Salisbury and Roger Bacon.

In the case of Maimonides, his view that human intelligence is improved by proper education, influenced Jewish scholars and educators ever since and inspired Christian Scholasticism to create a philosophically rigorous education. That philosophical enlightenment was possible thorough education, inspired Spinoza, Mendelssohn, Leibniz and other philosophers ever since.

BIBLIOGRAPHY

GENERAL WORKS
Brown, E. G., *Arabian Medicine*, Cambridge University Press, 1921
De Boer, T. J., *The History of Philosophy in Islam*, translated by E. Jones, Dover, 1967
Fakhry, M., *A History of Islamic Philosophy*, Columbia University Press, 1970
Kolak, D., *I Am You: The Metaphysical Foundations For Global Ethics*, Kluwer Academic Publishers, 2004
Leeman, O., *An Introduction to Medieval Islamic Philosophy*, Cambridge University Press, 1985
Netton, I. R., *Muslim neo-Platonists*, George Allen & Unwin, 1982
Peters, F. E., *Aristotle and the Arabs: The Aristotelian Tradition in Islam*, New York University Press, 1968

AVICENNA
Primary
Avicenna on Theology, translated by A. A. Murray, 1951
The Life of Ibn Sina, translated by W. Gohlman, State University of New York Press, 1974
The "Metaphysica" of Avicenna, translated by P. Morewedge, Routledge & Kegan Paul, 1973

Secondary
Afnan, S. M., *Avicenna: His Life and Works*, George Allen & Unwin, 1958
Burrell, D., *Knowing the Unknowable God: Ibn-Sina, Maimonides*, University of Notre Dame Press, 1986
Corbin, H., *Avicenna and the Visionary Recital*, translated by W. R. Trask, Pantheon, 1960

Davidson, H., *Al-Farabi, Avicenna, and Averroës: Their Cosmologies, Theories of Active Intellect and Theories of the Human Intellect*, Oxford University Press, 1992
Goodman, L., *Avicenna*, Routledge, 1992

AL-GHAZALI
Primary
Freedom and Fulfillment: An Annotated Translation of al-Ghazali's al-Munqidh min al-Dalal and other Relevant Works of al-Ghazali, R. J. McCarty, Twayne, 1980

Secondary
Muslim Intellectual: A Study of al-Ghazali, W. M. Watt, University Press, 1963
Al-Ghazali and the Ash'arite School, R. M. Frank, Duke University Press, 1994

AVERROËS
Primary
Averroës' Middle Commentaries on Aristotle's Categories and De Interpretatione, translated, with notes and introductions by C. Butterworth, St. Augustine's Press, 1998
Tahafut al-Tahafut (The Incoherence of the Incoherence), translated by S. van den Bergh, Luzac, 1954
Aquinas, T., *On The Unity of the Intellect Against the Averroists*, translated by B. H. Zedler, Marquette University Press, 1968

Secondary
Davidson, H. *Al-Farabi, Avicenna, and Averroës: Their Cosmologies, Theories of Active Intellect and*

Theories of the Human Intellect, Oxford University Press, 1992

Kolak, D., *I Am You: The Metaphysical Foundations for Global Ethics*, Springer, 2004

Kogan, B., *Averroës and the Metaphysics of Causation*, State University of New York Press, 1985

Leaman, O., *Averroës and His Philosophy*, Oxford University Press, 1988

MAIMONIDES

Primary

Rambam: Readings in the Philosophy of Moses Maimonides, translated by L. E. Goodman, Viking Press, 1976

Minkin, J. S., *The World of Moses Maimonides, with Selections from His Writings*, Yoseloff, 1957

Secondary

Baron, S. W., ed., *Essays on Maimonides: An Octocennial Volume*, Columbia University Press, 1941

Heschel, J. A., *Maimonides: A Biography*, translated by J. Neugroschel, Farrar, Straus & Giroux, 1982

Kellner, M., *Dogma in Medieval Jewish Thought: From Maimonides to Abravanel*, Oxford University Press, 1986

Klein, C., *The Credo of Maimonides: A Synthesis*, Philosophical Library, 1958

Leaman, O., *Moses Maimonides*, Routledge, 1990

Melber, J., *The Universality of Maimonides*, Jonathan David, 1968

Ormsby, E., ed., *Moses Maimonides and His Time*, Catholic University Press, 1989

Weiss, R., *Maimonides' Ethics*, University of Chicago Press, 1991

SECTION V

◆ AQUINAS ◆

PROLOGUE

By the time Aquinas came upon the scene in the early part of the thirteenth century, the unprecedented revival of ancient Greek philosophy was in full swing. The works of Aristotle, which just a few decades earlier (1215) had been forbidden by the papal legate at Paris, were officially exonerated in 1231 by a commission appointed by Gregory IX. By the 1260s the ecclesiastical assemblies in charge of the schools allowed no deviation from the official Aristotelian doctrines. Thus, when Aquinas entered school, the ancient philosophers were being studied from Constantinople to Alexandria. The crusaders had brought back better and more accurate Greek copies of all the works of Plato, Aristotle, and other Greek masters, which excited scholars throughout Europe. Written commentaries on all the classic masterworks became the dominant way that new ideas and interpretations emerged.

The revival of ancient Greek wisdom was in full force. The new curriculum included Aristotle's *Organon of Logic*, Plato's *Meno* and *Timaeus*, along with the works of all the brilliant Muslim, as well as Jewish commentators discussed in the preceding section (Avicenna, al-Ghazali, Averroës, Maimonides). So profoundly inspirational and moving were the detailed commentaries of the Islamic philosophers that many in Europe feared that the ways of philosophy would surrender entirely to the Islamic protectors and that Europe, where the philosophy had originated more than a thousand years earlier, would have to play second fiddle.

The yearning to retake the philosophical helm was made all the more acute throughout Europe in part because of the tremendous wealth accumulated by commerce and advances in industry and agriculture. This economic growth lead to a groundswell of new universities, the liberation of communities and states, and the codification of canon law to form what has been called the "Renaissance" of the twelfth century, the most important new by-product of which was leisure. The great ideas of the ancients were discussed and elaborated on; children were taught at a young age the ways of Scholastic thought, both at universities and in medieval secondary schools. The Scholastic method of argument produced adults who sought ever greater education for their children. The arts and sciences were taught as part of Plato's forms, in which the mind aspired toward illumination and creativity. The liberal arts were in full swing.

It is against this illuminating backdrop that Aquinas entered the scene, ready to be heralded by the tumultuous and yearning masses as the genius of a new age in which philosophy would at long last return, awakened after the demise of Athens and the fall of Rome. The Second Dawn had begun.

AQUINAS (1225–1274)

Biographical History

Thomas Aquinas was born in Italy, in a small town between Rome and Naples, at the grand Roccasecca Castle of his father, the rich and powerful Count of Aquino. The thirteenth-century custom of parents giving their children to monasteries as *oblates*, meaning "offered up" to God, was usually normal when the parents were not only pious but also poor and with too many children. Aquinas's parents were wealthy; his father was a count. Even so, young Thomas was given to the monastery where he was educated, the Benedictine abbey at Monte Cassino, until the age of 14. He then went to the University of Naples.

Like Anselm before him, Aquinas rejected his father's plans for the aristocratic life of a nobleman. He wanted to chart his own course. To his father's horror, in 1244 he joined the Dominican order of mendicant friars whose ideal was complete poverty. He traveled through the countryside, begging for food and money for the Dominicans, while spreading the Gospel of Jesus. His father was appalled and begged Thomas to instead join the Benedictines; if you're going to live the religious life, his father pleaded, then do so not with the poor Dominican beggars but with the rich and powerful, prestigious order of the Benedictines, which was backed by corporate wealth. When Thomas wouldn't listen, his father had him locked up in the family castle, where he offered him all sorts of bribes, including a very beautiful prostitute. Thomas refused and instead with her help escaped.

Thomas ended up in France, where he studied philosophy and theology with one of the greatest Scholastic thinkers, fellow Dominican Albertus Magnus (1200–1280), called "Doctor Universalis" and "Albert the Great" because of his vast knowledge of both Greek and Islamic philosophy. Like his Islamic nemesis Averroës, Aquinas spent his formative philosophical years primarily in the study and interpretation of the works of Aristotle and the writing of scholarly commentaries on those works. In his later, more mature philosophical works, Aquinas developed a full-blown metaphysics involving both a theory of being and of essence that incorporated Aristotelian principles of cause and change, arguing against the Averroist doctrine of the unity of all souls. Aquinas became regent master (full professor) at the University of Paris. He taught there and in Italy for the rest of his life.

Philosophical Overview

The Dominicans weren't just poor; many regarded them as dangerous philosophical and religious radicals. The order's political troubles began when conservative university authorities in Paris accused the order of being Averroists (see the next section), who believed—quite contrary to received *orthodox* Christian doctrine—that all souls are one. This idea, besides being antithetical to the political agenda of the time, which required uncrossable class borders between the haves and the have nots, was a bone of contention between early Gnostic Christianity and its later Orthodox variant. Because history tends to be written by winners, that early radical aspect of Christian thought was repressed, especially during the top-down authoritarian times that so characterized the entire Middle Ages. Like the great neo-Platonist Plotinus before him, who interpreted Plato's teaching as leading to the summit that all souls are one, Averroës (see the next section) argued that personality, defined in terms of the "passive" aspect of the soul, is not immortal. It dies with the body. But the active part of your consciousness, the "active intellect," is not only immortal, but according to Averroës—which he derived using the arguments not of Plato but Aristotle—is numerically identical in all sentient beings. Everyone who has ever existed or will exist, including God, are one and the same entity. This idea, which arguably can be derived from the teachings of the ancient Greeks, from Pythagoras, Plato, and Aristotle—was declared heresy by the church, punishable by death. (As late as the start of the seventeenth century, renaissance philosopher Giordano Bruno was burned at the stake for professing it.)

Aquinas helped defend his fellow Dominicans against this heresy, with help, ironically, from another one of Averroës' doctrines—namely, that there are two very different notions of truth:

1. *"truth" as defined in logical terms by the use purely of human reason, and*
2. *"truth" defined in terms of direct revelation from God.*

The latter does not necessarily contradict or destroy the former but it does, as it were, trump it; if and when the two conflict, direct revelation is the "real" truth. Aquinas then goes on to argue that, since Christian dogma derives from views fundamentally antithetical to Averroës' monopsychism (the idea that all souls are one), its revealed truth trumps the rational arguments for the unity of mankind as espoused by Averroës and the so-called "internal Aristotelian" school of philosophy.

It is perhaps even more deeply ironic that Aristotle, whose works had been lost to the non-Arabic world for centuries, was the main ancient influence both on Aquinas and Averroës. Aristotle's return upon the scene from two opposing philosophical camps troubled many conservative Christian theologians, who feared that the Islamic philosophers had colored them with their own spins and interpretations through their detailed and often deeply illuminating commentaries. They worried that the ancient philosophy had been thus compromised or tainted. Aquinas would have none of that. Instead he openly agreed with his Islamic nemesis, Averroës, that Aristotle was without question the greatest philosopher ever. If Averroës could use Aristotle to justify Islam, Aquinas was ready and willing to use Aristotle to justify Christianity, to put the formerly faith-based doctrine on a new and philosophically secure intellectual foundation rooted in reason.

SUMMA CONTRA GENTILES
Aquinas

Using Aristotle's metaphysics, cosmology, epistemology, and ethics as his philosophical foundation, Aquinas explains how it is possible that your soul preserves your ego beyond the death of the body, with your personality intact. We can have our immortality and our individuality too: we are, according to Aquinas, metaphysical entities whose individuality is not limited to the physical borders within which during our lives we are bound. We are each immortal, numerically distinct, separately existing metaphysical entities.

This is a rather difficult and complex philosophical position to maintain. Aquinas not only maintained it, but to a great extent, originated it. Aristotle, who had made a taxonomy of everything, saw the categories as natural sets distinguished by unique, individual-defining characteristics. The *soul*, or *essence*, of something, then, is what makes the thing—say a horse, a plant, or pebble—belong to that category, which is what makes it what it is rather than some other thing. Thus the essence of humanity—the unique defining thing that makes us human rather than, say, a lower animal or vegetable—is, according to Aristotle, *rationality*. But this unique defining thing is not to any one of us unique. This is a very important point to understand because it explains the origin and basis of the "integral Aristotelian" interpretation of the soul, which is also in line with the interpretation of Plato that brilliant neo-Platonists, such as Plotinus, had also advocated, and which Averroës now made complete, coherent, and thus philosophically famous (or infamous).

Aquinas' contrary interpretation of Aristotle, put forth as commentaries on his friend William of Moerbeke's translations of Aristotle, are, however, no less astute than those of Averroës. The difference is no mere hair splitting; such arguments were, and are, the philosophical battlefields upon which the metaphysical struggle to understand the nature of the human soul unfolds. What Aquinas does to make Aristotelianism consistent with Christianity is philosophically quite clever; instead of arguing against the Averroist interpretation, Aquinas shows that reason (and here he draws inspiration from Augustine) is by itself unable to force either conclusion. In other words, the question of whether all souls are one, as Plotinus argued no less so than Averroës, cannot be decided without appeal to revelation from God, requiring faith. Thus, while Christian belief has it that God created the universe, Aristotle argued that the universe was eternal and uncreated. Aquinas, in a sense anticipating the Kantian antinomies, argues that *neither* the creation of the universe nor the eternity of the universe could be confirmed or denied directly by reason. We *need* revelation from God to know the truth. Similarly, instead of simply declaring Averroist monopsychism to be a false heresy, Aquinas argues that whether the individual human soul is mortal or immortal also cannot be settled by pure reason, nor can it be settled by experience; one needs direct revelation to know the truth. Aristotelian arguments against the immortality of the soul, according to Aquinas, only help make the point that without divine revelation there can be no knowledge. This clever line of argument is further developed in even more detail in his *On The Unity of the Intellect Against the Averroists*. Aquinas takes on the Averroist philosophy that all human beings share one and the same numerically identical intellect. This excited and pleased church leaders, yet at the same time, ironically, once again made the arguments of the philosophers part of the church's "proof" of the need for unphilosophical ways of knowing truth. Aquinas thus in his own way also firmly strengthened the role of philosophy within Christendom.

2.57 PLATO'S THEORY OF THE UNION OF THE INTELLECTUAL SOUL WITH THE BODY

. . . some have said that no subsistent intelligence can possibly be the form of a body. But because the nature of man himself seemed to give the lie to this statement, inasmuch as man is seen to be composed of an intellectual soul and a body, they have thought out various ways to save the nature of man and adjust their theory to fact. Plato, therefore, and his followers, laid it down that the intellectual soul is not united with the body as form with matter, but only as

---

Summa Contra Gentiles, selections, translated by Joseph Rickaby. Burns and Oates, London, 1905.

the mover is with the moved, saying that the soul is in the body as a sailor in his boat—thus the union of soul and body would be virtual contact only. But as such contact does not produce absolute oneness, this statement leads to the awkward consequence that man is not absolutely one, nor absolutely a being at all, but is a being only accidentally. To escape this conclusion, Plato laid it down that man is not a compound of soul and body, but that the soul using the body is man. This position is shown to be impossible: for things different in being cannot have one and the same activity. I call an activity one and the same, not in respect to the effect to which the activity is terminated, but as it comes forth from the agent. It is true that many men towing a boat make one action in respect of the thing done, which is one; but still on the part of the men towing there are many actions, as there are many different strains and exertions to haul the boat along; for as action is consequent upon form and power, it follows that where there are different forms and powers there must also be different actions. Now though the soul has a certain proper motion of its own, which it performs independently of the body, namely, the act of understanding, there are however other activities common to soul and body, namely, those of fear, anger, sensation, and the like; for these only come about by some change wrought in some definite part of the body; hence evidently they are conjoint activities of soul and body. Therefore, out of soul and body there must result one being, and the two cannot be distinct in being.

But this reasoning may be met by the following reply on behalf of Plato's view. There is no difficulty, it will be said, in mover and moved having the same act, notwithstanding their difference in being; for motion is at once the act of the moving force, from which it is, and the act of the thing moved, in which it is. Thus, then, in Plato's theory, the aforesaid activities may be common to soul and body, belonging to the soul as the moving force, and to the body as the thing moved. But this explanation cannot hold for the following reasons.

As the Philosopher proves sensation results by the sentient subject being moved or impressed by external sensible things—hence, a man cannot have a sensation without some external sensible thing, as nothing can be moved without a mover. The sensory organ, therefore, is moved and impressed in sensation, but that is by the external sensible object. What receives the impression is the sense, as is evident from this, that senseless things do not receive any such manner of impression from sensible objects. The sense, therefore, is the passive power of the sensory organ. The sentient soul, therefore, in sensation does not play the part of mover and agent, but is that principle in the subject impressed, in virtue of which the said subject lies open to the impression. But such a principle cannot be different in being from the subject impressed. Therefore, the sentient soul is not different in being from the animated body.

Though motion is the common act of moving force and object moved, still it is one activity to impart motion and another to receive motion; hence, the two categories of action and passion. If then in sensation the sentient soul stands for the agent, and the body for the patient, there will be one activity of the soul and another of the body. The sentient soul, therefore, will have an activity and proper motion of its own; it will have its own subsistence; therefore, when the body perishes, it will not cease to be. Thus, sentient souls, even of irrational animals, will be immortal, which seems improbable, although it is not out of keeping with Plato's opinion. But this will be matter of enquiry further on.

A body moved does not take its species according to the power that moves it. If, therefore, the soul is only united to the body as mover to moved, the body and its parts do not take their species from the soul. Therefore, when the soul departs, the body and the parts thereof will remain of the same species. But this is manifestly false, for flesh and bone and hands and such parts, after the departure of the soul, do not retain their own names except by a *façon de parler*, since none of these parts retains its proper activity, and activity follows species. Therefore, the union of soul and body is not that of mover with moved, or of a man with his dress.

If the soul is united with the body only as mover with moved, it will be in the power of the soul to go out of the body when it wishes, and, when it wishes, to reunite itself with the body. That the soul is united with the body as the proper form of the same, is thus proved. That whereby a thing emerges from potential to actual being, is its form and actuality. But by the soul the body emerges from potentiality to actuality, for the being of a living thing is its life. Moreover, the seed before animation is only potentially alive, and by the soul it is made actually alive: the soul, therefore, is the form of the animated body. Again, as part is to part, so is the whole sentient soul to the whole body. But sight is the form and actuality of the eye; therefore, the soul is the form and actuality of the body.

2.58 THAT VEGETATIVE, SENTIENT, AND INTELLIGENT ARE NOT THREE SOULS IN MAN

Plato lays it down that not one and the same soul is in us at once intelligent, sentient, and vegetative. In this view, granted that the sentient soul is the form of the body, it does not follow that any subsistent intelligence can be the form of a body. The untenableness of this position is thus to be shown.

Attributes of the same subject representing different forms are predicated of one another accidentally; thus, 'white' is said to be 'musical' accidentally, inasmuch as whiteness and music happen both to be in Socrates. If then the intelligent, sentient, and vegetative soul are different powers or forms in us, then the attributes that we have according to these forms will be predicated of one another accidentally. But according to the intelligent soul we are called 'men,' according to the sentient 'animals,' according to the vegetative 'living.' This then will be an accidental predication: 'man is an animal;' or 'an animal is a living creature.' But on the contrary these are cases of essential predication for man, as man, is an animal; and an animal, as an animal, is a living creature. Therefore, it is from the same principle that one is man, animal, and alive.

A thing has unity from the same principle whence it has being, for unity is consequent upon being. Since then everything has being from its form, it will have unity also from its form. If, therefore, there are posited in man several souls, as so many forms, man will not be one being, but several. Nor will the order of the forms to one another, one ensuing upon the other, suffice for the unity of man—for unity in point of orderly succession is not absolute unity; such unity of order in fact is the loosest of unities.

If man, as Plato held, is not a compound of soul and body, but is a soul using a body, either this is understood of the intelligent soul, or of the three souls, if there are three, or of two of them. If of three,

or two, it follows that man is not one, but two, or three, for he is three souls, or at least two. But if this is understood of the intelligent soul alone, so that the sentient soul is to be taken for the form of the body, and the intelligent soul, using the animate and sentient body, is to be man, there will still ensue awkward consequences, to wit, that man is not an animal, but uses an animal; and that man does not feel, but uses a thing that does feel.

Of two or three there cannot be made one without anything to unite them, unless one of them stands to the other as actuality to potentiality, for so of matter and form there is made one without any external bond to bind them together. But if in man there are several souls, they do not stand to one another as matter and form, but they are all supposed to be actualities and principles of action. If then they are to be united to make one man, or one animal, there must be something to unite them. This cannot be the body, since rather the body is made one by the soul; the proof of which fact is that, when the soul departs, the body breaks up. It must be some more formal principle that makes of those several entities one; this will be rather the soul than those several entities which are united by it. If this again has several parts, and is not one in itself, there must further be something to unite those parts. As we cannot proceed to infinity, we must come to something which is in itself one; and this of all things is the soul. There must, therefore, in one man, or one animal, be one only soul.

2.59 THAT THE POTENTIAL INTELLECT OF MAN IS NOT A SPIRIT SUBSISTING APART FROM MATTER

There were others who used another invention in maintaining the point that a subsistent intelligence cannot be united with a body as its form. They say that the intellect which Aristotle calls 'potential,' is a spiritual being, subsisting apart by itself, and not united with us as a form. And this they endeavor to prove from the words of Aristotle, who says, speaking of this intellect, that it is "separate, unmixed with body, simple and impassible," terms which could not be applied to it, they say, if it were the form of a body. Also from the argument by which Aristotle proves that because the potential intellect receives all impressions of sensible things, and is in potentiality to them all, it must be devoid of all to begin with, as the pupil of the eye, which receives all impressions of colors, is devoid of all color; because if it had of itself any color, that color would prevent other colors from being seen; nay, nothing would be seen except under that color; and the like would be the case of the potential intellect, if it had of itself any form or nature of sensible things, as it would have were it the form of any body, because, since form and matter make one, the form must participate to some extent in the nature of that whereof it is the form. These passages moved Averroës to suppose the potential intellect, whereby the soul understands, to be separate in being from the body, and not to be the form of the body. But because this intellect would have no connection with us, nor should we be able to understand by it unless it were somehow united with us, Averroës fixes upon a mode in which it is united with us, as he thinks, sufficiently. He says that an impression actually made in the understanding is a 'form' of the potential intellect, in the same way that an actually visible appearance, as such, is a 'form' of the visual faculty; hence, out of the potential intellect, and this form or impression actually made in the same, there results one being. With whatever being, therefore, this 'form' of the understanding is conjoined, the potential intellect is also conjoined with that being. But this 'form' is conjoined with us by means of the 'phantasm,' or image in the fantasy, which image is a sort of subject receiving in itself that 'form' of understanding.

It is easy to see how frivolous and impossible all this construction is. For what has understanding is intelligent; and that of which an intelligible impression is united with the understanding, is understood. The fact that an intelligible impression, united with a (foreign) understanding, comes somehow to be in man, will not render man intelligent; it will merely make him understood by that separately subsisting intelligence.

Besides, the impression actually in understanding is the form of the potential intellect, in the same way that the actual visible appearance is the form of the visual power, or eye. But the impression actually in understanding is to the phantasms as the actual visible appearance is to the colored surface, which is outside the soul. This similitude is used by Averroës, as

also by Aristotle. Therefore the supposed union of the potential intellect (by means of the intelligible form) with the phantasm that is in us will resemble the union of the visual power with the color that is in the stone. But this union does not make the stone see but be seen. Therefore, the aforesaid union does not make us understand, but be understood. But, plainly, it is properly and truly said that man understands; for we should not be investigating the nature of understanding were it not for the fact that we have understanding. The above mode of union is then insufficient.

The intellect in the act of understanding and the object as represented in understanding are one, as also the sense in the act of sensation and the object as represented in sense. But the understanding as apt to understand and its object as open to representation in understanding are not one, as neither is sense, so far as it is apt to have sensation, one with its object, so far as that is open to be represented in sensation. The impression made by the object, so far as it lies in images of the fantasy, is not any representation in the understanding. Only by undergoing a process of abstraction from such images does the impression became one with the intellect in the act of understanding. In like manner the impression of color is actually felt in sense, not as it is in the stone, but as it is in the eye. Now, on the theory of Averroës, the intelligible form, or impression in the understanding, only comes to be conjoined with us by finding a place in the images of our fantasy. Therefore it is not conjoined with us inasmuch as it is one with the potential intellect, being its form. Therefore it cannot be the medium whereby the potential intellect is conjoined with us, because, insofar as it is conjoined with the potential intellect, it is not conjoined with us; and insofar as it is conjoined with us, it is not conjoined with the potential intellect.

2.60 THAT MAN IS NOT A MEMBER OF THE HUMAN SPECIES BY POSSESSION OF PASSIVE INTELLECT, BUT BY POSSESSION OF POTENTIAL INTELLECT

Averroës endeavors to meet these arguments and to maintain the position aforesaid. He says accordingly that man differs from dumb animals by what Aristotle calls the 'passive intellect,' which is that 'cogitative power' (*vis cogitativa*) proper to man, in place whereof other animals have a certain 'estimative power' (*aestimativa*). The function of this 'cogitative power' is to distinguish individual ideas and compare them with one another, as the intellect, which is separate and unmixed, compares and distinguishes between universal ideas. And because by this cogitative power, along with imagination and memory, phantasms, or impressions of fantasy, are prepared to receive the action of the 'active intellect,' whereby they are made actual terms of understanding, therefore, the aforesaid cogitative power is called by the names of 'intellect' and 'reason.' Doctors say that it has its seat in the middle cell of the brain. According to the disposition of this power one man differs from another in genius, and in other points of intelligence; and by the use and exercise of this power man acquires the habit of knowledge. Hence, the passive intellect is the subject of the various habits of knowledge. And this passive intellect is in a child from the beginning; and by virtue of it he is a member of the human species before he actually understands anything. So for Averroës. The falsity and perverseness of his statements evidently appears.

Vital activities stand to the soul as second actualities to the first. Now the first actuality is prior in time to the second in the same subject, as knowledge is prior in time to learned speculation. In whatever being, therefore, there is found any vital activity, there must be some portion of soul standing to that activity as the first actuality to the second. But man has one activity proper to him above all other animals, namely that of understanding and reasoning. Therefore, we must posit in man some proper specific principle, which shall be to the act of understanding as the first actuality to the second. This principle cannot be the aforesaid 'passive intellect,' for the principle of the aforesaid activity must be "impassible and no ways implicated with the body," as the philosopher proves, whereas, evidently, quite the contrary is the case with the passive intellect. Therefore that cognitive faculty called the 'passive intellect' cannot possibly be the speciality that differentiates the human species from other animals.

2. An incident of the sensitive part cannot constitute a being in a higher kind of life than that of the sensitive part, as an incident of the vegetative soul does not place a being in a higher kind of life than the vegetative life. But it is certain that fantasy and

the faculties consequent thereon, as memory and the like, are incidents of the sensitive part. Therefore by the aforesaid faculties, or by any one of them, an animal cannot be placed in any higher rank of life than that which goes with the sentient soul. But man is in a higher rank of life than that. Therefore, the man does not live the life that is proper to him by virtue of the aforesaid 'cogitative faculty,' or 'passive intellect.'

The 'potential intellect' is proved not to be the actualization of any corporeal organ from this consideration, that the said intellect takes cognizance of all sensible forms under a universal aspect. Therefore no faculty, the activity of which can reach to the universal aspects of all corporeal forms, can be the actualization of any corporeal organ. But such a faculty is the will, for of all of the things that we understand we can have a will, at least of knowing them. And we also find acts of the will in the general; thus, as Aristotle says, we hate in general the whole race of robbers. The will then cannot be the actualization of any bodily organ. But every portion of the soul is the actualization of some bodily organ, except only the intellect properly so called. The will, therefore, belongs to the intellectual part, as Aristotle says. Now the will of man is not extrinsic to man, planted as it were in some separately subsisting intelligence, but is in the man himself; otherwise he would not be master of his own acts, but would be worked by the will of a spirit other than himself; those appetitive, or conative, faculties alone would remain in him, the activity whereof is conjoined with passion, to wit the irascible and concupiscible in the sentient part of his being, as in other animals, which are rather acted upon than act. But this is impossible: it would be the undoing of all moral philosophy and all social and political science. Therefore, there must be in us a potential intellect to differentiate us from dumb animals; the passive intellect is not enough.

A habit and the act proper to that habit both reside in the same faculty. But to view a thing intellectually, which is the act proper to the habit of knowledge, cannot be an exercise of the faculty called 'passive intellect,' but must properly belong to the potential intellect, for the condition of any faculty exercising intelligence is that it should not be an actualization of any corporeal organ. Therefore, the habit of knowledge is not in the passive intellect, but in the potential intellect.

Habitual understanding, as our opponent acknowledges, is an effect of the 'active intellect.' But the effects of the active intellect are actual representations in understanding, the proper recipient of which is the potential intellect, to which the active intellect stands related, as Aristotle says, "as art to material." Therefore, the habitual understanding, which is the habit of knowledge, must be in the potential intellect, not in the passive.

2.61 THAT THE AFORESAID TENET IS CONTRARY TO ARISTOTLE

Aristotle defines soul, "the first actuality of a natural, organic body, potentially alive"; and adds, "this definition applies universally to every soul." Nor does he, as the aforesaid Averroës pretends, put forth this latter remark in a tentative way, as may be seen from the Greek copies and the translation of Boethius. Afterwards in the same chapter he adds that there are "certain parts of the soul separable," and these are none other than the intellectual parts. The conclusion remains that the said parts are actualizations of the body.

Nor is this explanation inconsistent with Aristotle's words subjoined: "About the intellect and the speculative faculty the case is not yet clear: but it seems to be another kind of soul." He does not hereby mean to separate the intellect from the common definition of 'soul,' but from the peculiar natures of the other parts of soul: as one who says that fowls are a different sort of animal from land animals, does not take away from the fowl the common definition of 'animal.' Hence, to show in what respect he called it "another kind," he adds, "and of this alone is there possibility of separation, as of the everlasting from the perishable." Nor is it the intention of Aristotle, as the Commentator aforesaid pretends, to say that it is not yet clear whether intellect be soul at all, as it is clear of other and lower vital principles. For the old text has not, "nothing has been declared," or "nothing has been said", but "nothing is clear," which is to be understood as referring to the peculiar properties of intellect, not to the general definition (of soul). But if, as the commentator says, the word 'soul' is used not in the same sense of intellect and other varieties, Aristotle would have first distinguished the ambiguity and then made his definition, as his manner is; otherwise his argu-

ment would rest on an ambiguity, an intolerable procedure in demonstrative sciences.

Aristotle reckons 'intellect' among the 'faculties' of the soul. Also, in the passage last quoted, he names 'the speculative faculty.' Intellect, therefore, is not outside the human soul, but is a faculty thereof.

Also, when beginning to speak of the potential intellect, he calls it a part of the soul, saying; "concerning the part of the soul whereby the soul has knowledge and intellectual consciousness."

And still more clearly by what follows, he declares the nature of the potential intellect: "I call intellect that whereby the soul thinks and understands"; it is manifestly shown that the intellect is something belonging to the human soul.

The above tenet (of Averroës), therefore, is contrary to the mind of Aristotle and contrary to the truth; hence it should be rejected as chimerical.

2.62 AGAINST ALEXANDER'S OPINION CONCERNING THE POTENTIAL INTELLECT

Upon consideration of these words of Aristotle, Alexander determined the potential intellect to be some power in us, so that the general definition of soul assigned by Aristotle might apply to it. But because he could not understand how any subsistent intelligence could be the form of a body, he supposed the aforesaid faculty of potential intellect not to be planted in any subsistent intelligence, but to be the result of some combination of elements in the human body. Thus a definite mode of combination of the components of the human body puts a man in potentiality to receive the influence of the active intellect, which is ever an act, and according to him, is a spiritual being subsisting apart, under which influence man becomes actually intelligent. But that in man whereby he is potentially intelligent is the potential intellect; hence, it seemed to Alexander to follow that the potential intellect in us arises from a definite combination of elements. But this statement appears on first inspection to be contrary to the words and argument of Aristotle. For Aristotle shows (De anima, III, iv, 2–4) that the potential intellect is unmingled with the body, but that could not be said of a faculty that was the result of a combination of bodily elements. To meet this difficulty, Alexander says that the potential intellect is precisely the 'predisposition' which exists in human nature to receive the influence of the active intellect; and that this 'predisposition' is not any definite sensible nature, nor is it mingled with the body, for it is a relation and order between one thing and another. But this is in manifest disagreement with the mind of Aristotle, as the following reasons show.

Aristotle assigns these characteristics to the potential intellect: to be impressed by the intelligible presentation, to receive intelligible impressions, and to be in potentiality towards them (*De anima*): all which things cannot be said of any 'disposition,' but only of the subject predisposed. It is therefore contrary to the mind of Aristotle, that the mere 'predisposition' should be the potential intellect.

An effect cannot stand higher above the material order than its cause. But every cognitive faculty, as such, belongs to the immaterial order. Therefore, it is impossible for any cognitive faculty to be caused by a combination of elements. But the potential intellect is the supreme cognitive faculty in us; therefore, it is not caused by a combination of elements.

No bodily organ can possibly have a share in the act of understanding. But that act is attributed to the soul, or to the man; for we say that the soul understands, or the man through the soul. Therefore, there must be in man some principle independent of the body, to be the principle of such an act. But any predisposition, which is the result of a combination of elements, manifestly depends on the body. Therefore, no such predisposition can be a principle like the potential intellect, whereby the soul judges and understands.

But if it is said that the principle of the aforesaid operation in us is the intellectual impression actually made by the active intellect, this does not seem to suffice, because when man comes to have actual intellectual cognition from having had such cognition potentially, he needs to understand not merely by some intelligible impression actualizing his understanding, but likewise by some intellectual faculty as the principle of such activity. Besides, an impression is not in actual understanding except so far as it is purified from particular and material being. But this cannot happen so long as it remains in any material faculty, that is to say, in any faculty either caused by material principles or actualizing a material organ. Therefore, there must be posited in us some immaterial intellectual faculty, and that is the potential intellect.

2.64 THAT THE SOUL IS NOT A HARMONY

The maintainers of this view did not mean that the soul is a harmony of sounds, but a harmony of contrary elements, whereof they saw living bodies to be composed. The view is rejected for the following reasons.

You may find such a harmony in any body, even a mere chemical compound. A harmony cannot move the body, or govern it, or resist the passions, and neither can a temperament. Also a harmony, and a temperament also, admits of degrees. All these considerations go to show that the soul is neither harmony nor temperament.

The notion of harmony rather befits qualities of the body than the soul; thus, health is a harmony of humors: strength, of muscles and bones; beauty, of limb and color. But it is impossible to assign any components, the harmony of which would make sense, or intellect, or other appurtenances of the soul.

Harmony may mean either the composition itself or the principle of composition. Now, the soul is not a composition, because then every part of the soul would be composed of certain parts of the body, an arrangement which cannot be made out. In like manner, the soul is not the principle of composition, because to different parts of the body there are different principles of composition, or proportions of elements, which would require the several parts of the body to have so many several souls—one soul for bone, one for flesh, one for sinew, which is evidently not the case.

2.65 THAT THE SOUL IS NOT A BODY

Living beings are composed of matter and form—of a body, and of a soul which makes them actually alive. One of these components must be the form, and the other the matter. But a body cannot be a form, because a body is not in another as in its matter and subject. Therefore, the soul must be the form; therefore, it is not a body.

The act of understanding cannot be the act of anything corporeal. But it is an act of the soul. Therefore, the intellectual soul at least is not a body.

It is easy to solve the arguments whereby some have endeavored to prove that the soul is a body. They point such facts as these, that the son resembles the father even in the accidents of his soul, being generated from the father by severance of bodily substance; and that the soul suffers with the body, and is separated from the body, separation supposing previous bodily contact. Against these instances we observe that bodily temperament is a sort of predisposing cause of affections of the soul, that the soul suffers with the body only accidentally, as being the form of the body; also that the soul is separated from the body, not as touching from touched, but as form from matter, although there is a certain contact possible between an incorporeal being and the body, as has been shown earlier.

Many have been moved to this position by their belief that what is not a material body has no existence, being unable to transcend the imagination, which deals only with material bodies. Hence, this opinion is proposed in the person of the unwise: *the breath of our nostrils is smoke, and reason a spark in the beating of the heart* (Wisdom ii, 2).

2.66 AGAINST THOSE WHO SUPPOSE INTELLECT AND SENSE TO BE THE SAME

Sense is found in all animals, but animals other than man have no intellect, which is proved by this: that they do not work, like intellectual agents, in diverse and opposite ways, but just as nature moves them fixed and uniform specific activities, as every swallow builds its nest in the same way.

Sense is cognizant only of singulars, but intellect is cognizant of universals.

Sensory knowledge extends only to bodily things, but intellect takes cognizance of things incorporeal, as wisdom, truth, and the relations between objects.

No sense has reflex knowledge of itself and its own activity; the sight does not see itself, nor see that it sees. But intellect is cognizant of itself, and knows that it understands.

2.67 AGAINST THOSE WHO MAINTAIN THAT THE POTENTIAL INTELLECT IS THE FANTASY

Fantasy is found in other animals besides man, the proof of which is that, as objects of sense recede from sense, these animals still shun or pursue them. But intellect is not in them, as no work of intelligence appears in their conduct.

Fantasy is only of things corporeal and singular, but intellect, of things universal and incorporeal.

Intelligence is not the actualization of any bodily organ. But fantasy has a fixed bodily organ.

Hence it is said: *who teacheth us above the beasts of the earth, and above the fowls of the air instructeth us* (Job xxxv, 11); whereby we are given to understand that there is in man a certain cognitive power, above the sense and fancy that are in other animals.

2.68 HOW A SUBSISTENT INTELLIGENCE MAY BE THE FORM OF A BODY

Nor is the intellect, whereby man understands, a predisposition in human nature, as Alexander said; nor a temperament, as Galen; nor a harmony, as Empedocles.

There are two requisites for one thing to be the substantial form of another. One requisite is that the form be the principle of substantial being to that whereof it is the form—I do not mean the *effective*, but the *formal* principle, whereby a thing is and is denominated 'being.' The second requisite is that the form and matter should unite in one 'being'; namely, in that being wherein the substance so composed subsists. There is no such union of the effective principle with that to which it gives being. A subsistent intelligence, as shown earlier, is not hindered by the fact that it is subsistent from communicating its being to matter, and becoming the formal principle of the said matter. There is no difficulty in the identification of the being, in virtue of which the compound subsists, with the form itself of the said compound, since the compound is only through the form, and neither subsist apart.

It may be objected that a subsistent intelligence cannot communicate its being to a material body in such a way that there shall be one being of the subsistent intelligence and the material body, for things of different kinds have different modes of being, and nobler is the being of the nobler substance. This objection would be in point, if that being were said to belong to that material thing in the same way in which it belongs to that subsistent intelligence. But it is not so: for that being belongs to that material body as to a recipient subject raised to a higher state; while it belongs to that subsistent intelligence as to its principle and by congruence of its own nature.

In this way a wonderful chain of beings is revealed to our study. The lowest member of the higher genus is always found to border close upon the highest member of the lower genus. Thus some of the lowest members of the genus of animals attain to little beyond the life of plants, certain shellfish for instance, which are motionless, have only the sense of touch, and are attached to the ground like plants. Hence Dionysius says, "divine wisdom has joined the ends of the higher to the beginnings of the lower." Thus, in the genus of bodies we find the human body, composed of elements equally tempered, attaining to the lowest member of the class above it, that is, to the human soul, which holds the lowest rank in the class of subsistent intelligences. Hence, the human soul is said to be on the horizon and boundary line between things corporeal and incorporeal, inasmuch as it is an incorporeal substance and at the same time the form of a body.

Above other forms there is found a form, likened to the supramundane substances in point of understanding, and competent to an activity which is accomplished without any bodily organ at all; and this is the intellectual soul, for the act of understanding is not done through any bodily organ. Hence, the intellectual soul cannot be totally encompassed by matter, or immersed in it, as other material forms are: this is shown by its intellectual activity, wherein bodily matter has no share. The fact however that the very act of understanding in the human soul needs certain powers that work through bodily organs, namely, fantasy and sense, is a clear proof that the said soul is naturally united to the body to make up the human species.

2.69 SOLUTION OF THE ARGUMENTS ALLEGED TO SHOW THAT A SUBSISTENT INTELLIGENCE CANNOT BE UNITED WITH A BODY AS THE FORM OF THAT BODY

The arguments wherewith Averroës endeavors to establish his opinion do not prove that the subsistent intelligence is not united with the body as the form of the same.

The words of Aristotle about the potential intellect, that it is "impassible, unmixed, and separate," do not necessitate the admission that the intellectual substance is not united with the body as its form, giving it being. They are sufficiently verified by saying that the intellectual faculty, which Aristotle calls the 'speculative faculty.' is not the actualization of any organ, as exercising its activity through that organ.

Supposing the substance of the soul to be united in being with the body as the form of the body, while still the intellect is not the actualization of any organ, it does not follow that intellect falls under the law of physical determination, as do sensible and material things, for we do not suppose intellect to be a harmony, or function of any organ, as Aristotle says that sense is.

That Aristotle is saying that the intellect is 'unmingled' or 'separate,' does not intend to exclude it from being a part, or faculty, of the soul, which soul is the form of the whole body, is evident from this passage, where he is arguing against those who said that there were different parts of the soul in different parts of the body: "If the whole soul keeps together the body as a whole, it is fitting that each part of the soul should keep together some part of the body; but this looks like an impossibility, for it is difficult even to imagine what part of the body the intellect shall keep together, or how."

2.73 THAT THE POTENTIAL INTELLECT IS NOT ONE AND THE SAME IN ALL MEN

Hence, it is plainly shown that there is not one and the same potential intellect, belonging to all men who are and who shall be and who have been, as Averroës pretends.

It has been shown that the substance of the intellect is united with the human body and is its form. But it is impossible for there to be one form otherwise than of one matter. Therefore there is not one intellect for all men.

It is not possible for a dog's soul to enter a wolf's body, or a man's soul any other body than the body of a man. But the same proportion that holds between a man's soul and a man's body, holds between the soul of this man and the body of this man. It is impossible, therefore, for the soul of this man to enter any other body than the body of this man. But it is by the soul of this man that this man understands. Therefore there is not one and the same intellect of this man and of that.

A thing has being from that source from whence it has unity, for one and being are inseparable. But everything has being by its own form. Therefore, the unity of the thing follows the unity of the form. It is impossible, therefore, for there to be one form of different individual men. But the form of any individual man is his intellectual soul. It is impossible, therefore, for there to be one intellect of all men.

But if it is said that the sentient soul of this man is other than the sentient soul of that, and so far the two are not one man, though there be one intellect of both, such explanation cannot stand. For the proper activity of every being follows upon and is indicative of its species. But as the proper activity of an animal is to feel, so the proper activity of a man is to understand. As any given individual is an animal in that he has feeling, so is he a man by virtue of the faculty whereby he understands. But the faculty whereby the soul understands, or the man through the soul, is the potential intellect. This individual then is a man by the potential intellect. If then this man has another sentient soul than another man, but not another potential intellect, but one and the same, it follows that they are two animals, but not two men.

To these arguments the Commentator replies by saying that the potential intellect is conjoined with us through its own form, namely, through an intelligible impression, one subject of which is the phantasm existing in us, which differs in different men; and thus the potential intellect is multiplied in different men, not by reason of its substance, but by reason of its form.

The nullity of this reply appears by what has been shown earlier; that it would be impossible for any man to have understanding, if this were the only way in which the potential intellect were conjoined with us. But suppose that the aforesaid conjunction were sufficient to render man intelligent, still the said answer does not solve the arguments already alleged.

According to the above exposition, nothing belonging to intellect will remain multiplied as men are multiplied except only the phantasm, or impression in fantasy, and this very phantasm will not be multiplied as it is actually understood, because, as so understood, it is in the potential intellect, and has undergone abstraction of material conditions under the operation of the active intellect; whereas the phantasm, as a potential term of intelligence, does not transcend the grade of the sentient soul.

Still the objection holds, that this man will not be differentiated from that except by the sentient soul; and the awkward consequence follows that this man and that together do not make a plurality of men.

Nothing attains its species by what it is potentially, but by what it is actually. But the impression in fantasy, as multiplied in this man and that, has only a potentially intelligible being. Therefore that impression, as so multiplied, does not put any given individual in the species of 'intelligent animal,' which is the definition of 'man.' Thus it remains true that the specific ratio of 'man' is not multiplied in individual men.

It is the first and not the second perfection that gives the species to every living thing. But the impression in fantasy is a second perfection; and therefore not from that multiplied impression has man his species.

That which puts a man in the species of man must be something abiding in the same individual as long as he remains, otherwise the individual would not be always of one and the same species, but now of one species and now of another. But the impressions of fantasy do not remain always the same in the same man; new impressions come, and previous impressions perish. Therefore the individual man does not attain his species by any such impression; nor is it anything in the fantasy that conjoins him with the formal principle of his species, which is the potential intellect.

But if it is said that the individual does not receive his species by the phantasms themselves, but by the faculties in which the phantasms are, namely, the fantasy, the memory, and the *vis cogitativa* which is proper to man, and which in the *De anima*, III, v, Aristotle calls the 'passive intellect,' the same awkward consequences still follow.

Since the *vis cogitativa* operates only upon particulars, the impressions of which it puts apart and puts together, and further, since it has a bodily organ through which it acts, it does not transcend the rank of the sentient soul. But in virtue of his sentient soul, as such, man is not a man, but an animal. It still, therefore, remains true that the element, supposed to be multiplied in us, belongs to man only in his animal capacity.

The cogitative faculty, since it acts through an organ, is not the faculty whereby we understand. But the principle whereby we understand is the principle whereby man is man. Therefore no individual is man by virtue of the cogitative faculty, nor does man by that faculty essentially differ from dumb animals, as the Commentator pretends.

The cogitative faculty is united to the potential intellect, the principle of human intelligence, only by its action of preparing phantasms for the active intellect to render them actual terms of intelligence and perfections of the potential intellect. But this preliminary activity of the cogitative faculty does not always remain the same in us. Therefore, it cannot be the means whereby man is conjoined with the specific principle of the human species, or made a member of that species.

If the potential intellect of this and that man were numerically one and the same, the act of understanding would be one and the same in both which is an impossibility.

But if it is said that the act of understanding is multiplied according to the diversity of impressions in fantasy, that supposition cannot stand.

For the potential intellect understands a man, not as this individual man, but as man simply, according to the specific essence of the race. But this specific essence remains one, however much impressions in fantasy are multiplied, whether in the same man or in different men. Therefore no multiplication of phantasms can be the cause of multiplication of the act of understanding in the potential intellect, considering the same species; and thus we shall still have numerically one action in different men.

The proper subject in which the habit of knowledge resides is the potential intellect. But an accident, so long as it remains specifically one, is multiplied only by coming to reside in different subjects. If then the potential intellect is one in all men, any habit of knowledge specifically the same, say, the habit of grammar, must be numerically the same in all men, which is unthinkable.

But to this they say that the subject of the habit of knowledge is not the potential intellect, but the passive intellect and the cogitative faculty, which it cannot be.

For, as Aristotle shows in the *Ethics,* like acts engender like habits; and like habits reproduce like acts. Now, by the acts of the potential intellect there comes to be the habit of knowledge in us; and we are competent for the same acts by possession of the habit of knowledge. Therefore, the habit of knowledge is in the potential intellect, not in the passive.

Scientific knowledge is of demonstrated conclusions; and demonstrated conclusions, like their premises, are universal truths. Science, therefore, is in that faculty which takes cognizance of universals. But the passive intellect is not cognizant of universals, but of particular notions.

The error of placing the habit of scientific knowledge in the passive intellect seems to have arisen from the observation that men are found more or less apt for the study of science according to the several dispositions of the cogitative faculty and the fantasy.

But this aptitude depends on those faculties only as remote conditions, so it also depends on the complexion of the body, as Aristotle says that men of delicate touch and soft flesh are clever. But the proximate principle of the act of speculative understanding is the habit of scientific knowledge; for this habit must perfect the power of understanding to act readily at will, as other habits perfect the powers in which they are.

The dispositions of the cogitative faculty and the fantasy regard the object; they regard the phantasm, which is prepared by the efficiency of these faculties readily to become a term of actual understanding under the action of the active intellect. But habits do not condition objects; they condition faculties. Thus, conditions that take the edge off terrors are not the habit of fortitude; fortitude is a disposition of the conative part of the soul to meet terrors. Hence, it appears that the habit of knowledge is not in the passive but in the potential intellect.

If the potential intellect of all men is one, we must suppose that the potential intellect has always existed, if men have always existed, as Averroists suppose; and much more the active intellect, because agent is more honorable than patient, as Aristotle says. But if the agent is eternal, and the recipient eternal, the contents received must be eternal also. Therefore, the intellectual impressions have been from eternity in the potential intellect: therefore it will be impossible for it to receive afresh any new intellectual impressions. But the only use of sense and fantasy in the process of understanding is that intellectual impressions may be gathered from them. At this rate then neither sense nor fantasy will be needed for understanding; and we come back to the opinion of Plato, that we do not acquire knowledge by the senses, but are merely roused by them to remember what we knew before.

But to this the Commentator replies that intellectual presentations reside in a twofold subject: in one subject, from which they have everlasting being, namely, the potential intellect; in another subject, from which they have a recurring new existence, namely, the phantasm, or impression in fantasy. He illustrates this by the comparison of a sight presentation, which has also a twofold subject, the one subject being the thing outside the soul, the other the visual faculty. But this answer cannot stand.

For it is impossible that the action and perfection of the eternal should depend on anything temporal. But phantasms are temporal things, continually springing up afresh in us from the experience of the senses. Therefore the intellectual impressions, whereby the potential intellect is actuated and brought to activity, cannot possibly depend on phantasms in the way that visual impressions depend on things outside the soul.

Nothing receives what it has already got. But before any sensory experience of mine or yours there were intellectual impressions in the potential intellect, for the generations before us could not have understood had not the potential intellect been reduced to act by intellectual impressions. Nor can it be said that those impressions, formerly received in the potential intellect, have ceased to be, because the potential intellect not only receives, but keeps what it receives—hence, it is called the "place of ideas." Therefore, on this showing, no impressions from our phantasms are received in the potential intellect.

If the potential intellect receives no intellectual impressions from the phantasms that are in us, because it has already received them from the phantasms of those who were before us, then for the like reason we must say that it receives impressions from the phantasms of no generation of men, whom another generation has preceded. But every generation has been preceded by some previous generation, if the world and human society is eternal, as Averroists suppose. Therefore, the potential intellect never receives any impressions from phantasms; and from this it seems to follow that the potential intellect has no need of phantasms to understand. But we understand by the potential intellect. Therefore, neither shall we need sense and phantasm for our understanding, which is manifestly false and contrary to the opinion of Aristotle.

For the potential intellect, like every other substance, operates according to the mode of its nature. Now, according to its nature, it is the form of the body. Hence, it understands immaterial things, but views them in some material medium, as is shown by the fact that in teaching universal truths particular examples are alleged, in which what is said may be seen. Therefore, the need which the potential intellect has of the phantasm before receiving the intellectual impression is different from that which it has after the impression has been received. Before reception, it needs the phantasm to gather from it the intellectual impression, so that the phantasm then stands to the potential intellect as an object which moves it. But after receiving the impression, of which the phantasm is the vehicle, it needs the phantasm as an instrument or basis of the impression received. Thus by command of the intellect there is formed in the fantasy a phantasm answering to such and such an intellectual impression; and in this phantasm the intellectual impression shines forth as an exemplar in the thing exemplified, or as in an image.

If the potential intellect is one for all men and eternal, by this time there must have been received in it the intellectual impressions of all things that have been known by any men whatsoever. Then, as every one of us understands by the potential intellect—nay, as the act of understanding in each is the act of that potential intellect understanding—every one of us must understand all that has been understood by any other men whatsoever.

To this the Commentator replies that we do not understand by the potential intellect except insofar as it is conjoined with us through the impressions in our fantasy, and that these phantasms are not the same nor similar amongst all men. And this answer seems to be in accordance with the doctrine that has gone before; for, apart from any affirmation of the unity of the potential intellect, it is true that we do not understand those things, the impressions whereof are in the potential intellect, unless the appropriate phantasms are at hand. But that this answer does not altogether escape the difficulty, may be thus shown.

When the potential intellect has been actualized by the reception of an intellectual impression, it is competent to act of itself: hence, we see that, once we have got the knowledge of a thing, it is in our power to consider it again when we wish; nor are we at a loss for lack of phantasms, because it is in our power to form phantasms suitable to the consideration which we wish, unless there happens to be some impediment on the part of the organ, as in persons out of their mind or in a comatose state. But if in the potential intellect there are intellectual impressions of all branches of knowledge—as we must say, if that intellect is one and eternal—then the necessity of phantasms for the potential intellect will be the same as in his case who already has knowledge, and wishes to study and consider some point of that knowledge, for that also he could not do without phantasms. Since then every man understands by the potential intellect so far as it is reduced to act by intellectual impressions, so every man should be able on this theory to regard, whenever he would, all the known points of all sciences, which is manifestly false, for at that rate no one would need a teacher. Therefore, the potential intellect is not one and eternal.

2.74 OF THE OPINION OF AVICENNA, WHO SUPPOSED INTELLECTUAL FORMS NOT TO BE PRESERVED IN THE POTENTIAL INTELLECT

The above arguments against Averroës seem to be obviated by the theory of Avicenna. He says that intellectual impressions do not remain in the potential intellect except just so long as they are being actually understood. And this he endeavors to prove from the fact that forms are actually apprehended so long as they remain in the faculty that apprehends them; thus, in the act of perception both sense and intellect become identified with their objects; hence, it seems that whenever sense or intellect is united with its object, as having taken its form, actual apprehension, sensible or intellectual, occurs. But the faculties which preserve forms not actually apprehended, he says, are not the faculties that apprehend those forms, but storehouses attached to the said apprehensive faculties. Thus fantasy is the storehouse of forms apprehended by sense; and memory, according to him, is the storehouse of notions apprehended independently of sensation, as when the sheep apprehends the hostility of the wolf. The capacity of these faculties for storing up forms not actually apprehended comes from their having certain bodily organs in which the forms are received, such reception following close upon the (first) apprehension; and thereby the apprehensive faculty, turning to these storehouses, apprehends in act. But it is

acknowledged that the potential intellect is an apprehensive faculty, and has no bodily organ; hence, Avicenna concludes that it is impossible for intellectual impressions to be preserved in the potential intellect except so long as it is actually understanding. Therefore, one of three things, either

1. these intellectual impressions must be preserved in some bodily organ, or faculty having a bodily organ, or
2. they must be self-existent intelligible forms, to which our potential intellect stands in the relation of a mirror to the objects mirrored, or
3. whenever the potential intellect understands, these intellectual impressions must flow into it afresh from some separate agent.

The first of these three suppositions is impossible, because forms existing in faculties that use bodily organs are only potentially intelligible. The second supposition is the opinion of Plato, which Aristotle rejects. Hence Avicenna concludes that, whenever we actually understand, there flow into our potential intellect intellectual impressions from the active intellect, which he assumes to be an intelligence subsisting apart. If anyone objects against him that then there is no difference between a man when he first learns, and when he wishes to review and study again something which he has learnt before, he replies that to learn and con over again what we know is nothing else than to acquire a perfect habit of uniting ourselves with the active intelligence, so as to receive therefrom the intellectual form; and, therefore, before we come to reflect on and use our knowledge, there is in man a bare potentiality of such reception, but reflection on our knowledge is like potentiality reduced to act. And this view seems consonant with what Aristotle teaches, that memory is not in the intellectual but in the sensitive part of the soul. So it seems that the preservation of intellectual impressions does not belong to the intellectual part of the soul. But on careful consideration this theory will be found ultimately to differ little or nothing from the theory of Plato. Plato supposed forms of intellect to be separately existing substances, whence knowledge flowed in upon our souls; Avicenna supposes one separate substance, the active intellect, to be the source when knowledge flows in upon our souls. Now, it makes no matter for the acquirement of knowledge whether our knowledge is caused by one separate substance or by several. Either way it will follow that our knowledge is not caused by sensible things, the contrary of which conclusion appears from the fact that any one wanting in any one sense is wanting in acquaintance with the sensible objects of which that sense takes cognizance.

It is a novelty to say that the potential intellect, viewing the impressions made by singular things in the fantasy, is lit up by the light of the active intellect to know the universal, and that the action of the lower faculties, fantasy, memory, and cogitative faculty, fit and prepare the soul to receive the emanation of the active intellect. This, I say, is novel and strange doctrine, for we see that our soul is better disposed to receive impressions from intelligences subsisting apart, the further it is removed from bodily and sensible things: the higher is attained by receding from the lower. It is not, therefore, likely that any regarding of bodily phantasms should dispose our soul to receive the influence of an intelligence subsisting apart. Plato made a better study of the basis of his position, for he supposed that sensible appearances do not dispose the soul to receive the influence of separately subsisting forms, but merely rouse the intellect to consider knowledge that has been already caused in it by an external principle, and that from the beginning knowledge of all things intellectually knowable was caused in our souls by separately existing forms, or ideas; hence, learning, he said, was nothing else than recollecting.

Intellectual knowledge is more perfect than sensory. If, therefore, in sensory knowledge there is some power of preserving apprehensions, much more will this be the case in intellectual knowledge.

This opinion is contrary to the mind of Aristotle, who says that the potential intellect is "the place of ideas," which is tantamount to saying that it is a "storehouse" of intellectual impressions, to use Avicenna's own phrase.

The arguments to the contrary are easily solved. For the potential intellect is perfectly actuated about intellectual impressions when it is actually considering them: when it is not actually considering them, it is not perfectly actuated about them, but is in a condition intermediate between potentiality and actuality. As for memory, that is located in the sentient part of the soul, because the objects of memory fall under a definite time for there is no memory but of the past; and therefore, since there is no abstraction of its object from individualizing conditions, memory does not belong to the intellectual side of our nature, which deals with universals This however does not bar the potential intellect's preservation of intellectual impressions, which are abstracted from all particular conditions.

2.75 CONFUTATION OF THE ARGUMENTS WHICH SEEM TO PROVE THE UNITY OF THE POTENTIAL INTELLECT

Arg. 1. Apparently, every form that is specifically one and numerically multiplied, is individualized by its matter, for things specifically one and numerically many agree in form, and are distinguished according to matter. If then the potential intellect is multiplied according to number in different men, while it remains one in species, it must be multiplied in this and that man by matter—by the matter which is that man's body the form of which it is supposed to be. But every form, individualized by matter which it actuates, is a material form, for the being of everything must depend on that on which its individuation depends; for as general constituents are of the essence of the species, so individualizing constituents are of the essence of this individual. It follows, therefore, that the potential intellect is a material form, and consequently that it does not receive anything, nor do anything, except through a bodily organ, which is contrary to the nature of the potential intellect.

Reply. We confess that the potential intellect is specifically one in different men, and many according to number—waiving the point that the constituents of man are not put into genus and species for what they are in themselves, but for what they are as constituents of the whole. Still it does not follow that the potential intellect is a material form, dependent for its being on the body. For as it is specifically proper to the human soul to be united to a certain species of body, so any individual soul differs from any other individual soul, in number only, inasmuch as it is referable to numerically another body. Thus, human souls—and consequently the potential intellect, which is a faculty of the human soul—are individualized according to bodies, not that the individuation is caused by the bodies.

Arg. 2. If the potential intellect were different in this man and that, the impression understood would have to be numerically different in this man, while remaining one in species, for since the proper subject of impressions actually understood is the potential intellect, when that intellect is multiplied there must be a corresponding multiplication of intellectual impressions according to the number of different individuals. But the only impressions or forms which are the same in species and different in number are individual forms, which cannot be intellectual forms, because objects of intellect are universal, not particular. It is impossible, therefore, for the potential intellect to be multiplied in different individual men.

Reply. This second argument fails from neglecting to distinguish between that *whereby* we understand, and that *which* we understand. The impression received in the potential intellect is not to be taken for that *which* is understood. For as all arts and sciences have for their object matter things *which* are understood it would follow that the subject matter of all sciences was impressions on the potential intellect, which is manifestly false, for no science has anything to say to such mental impressions except psychology and metaphysics—though it is true that through those mental impressions there is known the whole content of all the sciences. Therefore, in the process of understanding, the intellectual impression received in the potential intellect is that *whereby* we understand, as the impression of color in the eye is not that *which* is seen, but that *whereby* we see. On the other hand, that *which* is understood is the nature of things existing outside the soul, as also it is things existing outside the soul that are seen with the bodily sight; for to this end were arts and sciences invented, that things might be known in their natures.

Still it does not follow that, if sciences are of universal truths, universals should subsist by themselves outside the soul, as Plato supposed. For though for the truth of knowledge it is necessary that the knowledge should answer to the thing, still it is not necessary that the mode of the knowledge and the mode of the thing should be the same: for properties that are united in the thing are sometimes known separately. Thus, one and the same thing is white and sweet; still sight takes cognizance only of the whiteness, and taste only of the sweetness. Thus, again intellect understands a line drawn in sensible matter apart from that sensible matter, though it might understand it also along with the sensible matter. This difference arises according to the diversity of intellectual impressions received in the intellect, which some times are the likeness of quantity only, sometimes of a sensible quantitative substance. In like manner also, though the nature of genus and species never exists except in concrete individuals, still the intellect understands the nature of genus and species without understanding the individualizing elements; and this is the meaning of understanding universals. And so these two positions are reconciled, that universals have no subsistence outside the soul; and yet that the intellect, understanding universals, understands things which are outside the soul.

The fact of the intellect understanding the nature of genus and species stripped of its individualizing elements, arises from the condition of the intellectual impression received in understanding, which impression is rendered immaterial by the active intellect, inasmuch as it is abstracted from matter and materializing conditions whereby a thing is individualized. And therefore the sentient faculties can take no cognizance of universals, since they cannot receive an immaterial form, seeing that they receive always in a bodily organ.

It is not, therefore, necessary that the intellectual impression of this and that intelligence should be numerically one, for it would follow thereupon that the act of understanding in them both was also numerically one, since activity follows form, which is the principle of species; but it is necessary, to the end that one object should be understood by both minds, that there should be a like impression of one and the same object in them both. And this is possible enough, although the intellectual impressions differ in number, for there is no difficulty in having different images of one thing; hence, the contingency of one thing being seen by several persons. There is nothing inconsistent then with the universalizing knowledge of the understanding in their being different intellectual impressions in different minds. Nor need it ensue, because these intellectual impressions are many in number and the same in species, that they are not actual but only potential terms of understanding, as is the case with other individual things. Mere individuality is not inconsistent with intelligibility, for we must admit the potential and active intellects themselves, if we may suppose the two to subsist apart, united to no body, but subsistent by themselves, to be individual beings and still intelligible. What is inconsistent with intelligibility is materiality: as is shown by this consideration, that for the forms of material things to become actually intelligible, abstraction has to be made from the particular matter in which they are lodged; and, therefore, in cases in which individuation is due to particular matter involving particular dimensions, the things so individualized are not actually intelligible. But where individuation is not due to matter, such individual things may without difficulty be actually intelligible. Now intellectual impressions, like all other forms, are individualized by their subject, which is the potential intellect; and since the potential intellect is not material, it does not stand in the way of the actual intelligibility of the impressions individualized by it.

But though we have said that the intellectual impression, received in the potential intellect, is not that which is understood, but that whereby we understand, still it remains true that by reflection the intellect understands itself and its own intellectual act and the impression whereby it understands. Its own intellectual act it understands in two ways—in one way, in particular, for it understands that it is now understanding; in another way, in general, inasmuch as it reasons about the said act. And likewise it understands intellect and the impression in intellect in two ways, by remarking that itself is and has an intellectual impression, which is particular knowledge; and by studying its own nature and the nature of the intellectual impression, which is knowledge of the universal. According to this latter way we treat intellect and the intelligible in science.

Arg. 3. The master transfuses the knowledge which he has into the scholar. Either then the knowledge transfused is the same in number, or different in number, though the same in species. The latter alternative seems impossible because it supposes the master to cause his own knowledge in the scholar in the same way that an agent causes its own form in another being, by generating a nature specifically like its own, which seems proper to material agents. It must be then that numerically the same knowledge is caused in the scholar that was in the master, which would be impossible, were there not one potential intellect of them both.

Reply. The saying that the knowledge in master and scholar is numerically one, is partly true and partly not; it is numerically one in point of the thing known, but not in point of the intellectual impressions whereby the thing is known, nor in point of the habit of knowledge itself. It is to be observed however that, as Aristotle teaches, there are arts in whose subject matter there is not any principle active in producing the effect of the art, as is clear in the building art, for in wood and stones there is no active power moving to the erection of a house, but only a passive aptitude. But there is an art in whose subject matter there is an active principle moving in the direction of the effect of the art, as is clear in the healing art; for in the sick subject, there is an active principle tending to health. And, therefore, the effect of the former kind of art is never produced by nature, but always by art, as every house is a work of art; but the effect of the latter kind is produced as well by art as by nature without art, for many are healed by the operation of nature without the art of medicine. In these things that can be done both by art and nature, art imitates nature: thus, if one is sick of a chill, nature heals him by warming him; hence, the physician also, if he is to cure him, heals him by warming. Similar is the case with the art of teaching, for in the pupil there is an active principle making for knowledge, namely, the understanding, and those primary axioms which are naturally understood; and, therefore, knowledge is acquired in two ways—without teaching, by a man's own finding out, and again by teaching. The teacher, therefore, begins to teach in the same way that the discoverer begins to find out, by offering for the consideration of the scholar elements of knowledge already possessed by him; because all education and all knowledge starts from pre-existing knowledge, drawing conclusions from elements already in the mind, and proposing sensible examples whereby there may be formed in the scholar's soul those impressions of fantasy which are necessary or intelligence. And because the working of the teacher from without would effect nothing, unless borne out by an internal principle of knowledge, which is within us by the gift of God, so it is said among theologians that man teaches by rendering the service of ministry, but God by working within; so, too, the physician is called nature's minister in healing.

A final remark: since the Commentator makes the passive intellect the residence of habits of knowledge, the unity of the potential intellect helps not at all to the numerical unity of knowledge in master and scholar, for certainly the passive intellect is not the same in different men, since it is an organic faculty. Hence, on his own showing, this argument does not serve his purpose.

2.76 THAT THE ACTIVE INTELLECT IS NOT A SEPARATELY SUBSISTING INTELLIGENCE, BUT A FACULTY OF THE SOUL

We may further conclude that neither is the active intellect one in all men, as Alexander and Avicenna suppose, though they do not suppose the potential intellect to be one in all men.

Plato supposed knowledge in us to be caused by Ideas, which he took to subsist apart by themselves. But clearly the first principle on which our knowledge depends is the active intellect. If, therefore, the active intellect is something subsisting apart by itself, the difference will be none, or but slight, between this opinion and that of Plato, which the Philosopher rejects.

If the active intellect is an intelligence subsisting apart, its action upon us will either be continual and uninterrupted, or at least we must say that it is not continued or broken off at our pleasure. Now its action is to make the impressions on our fantasy actual terms of intelligence. Either it will do this always or not always. If not always, still it will not do it at our discretion. Either we must be always in the act of understanding, or it will not be in our power actually to understand when we wish.

But it may be said that the active intellect, so far as with it lies, is always in action, but that the impressions in our fantasy are not always becoming actual terms of intelligence, but only when they are disposed thereto; and they are disposed thereto by the act of the cogitative faculty, the use of which is in our power; and, therefore, actually to understand is in our power; and this is why not all men understand the things whereof they have the impressions in their fantasy, because not all have at command a suitable act of the cogitative faculty, but only those who are accustomed and trained thereto.

But this answer does not appear to be altogether sufficient. That the impressions in fantasy are mar-

shaled by the cogitative faculty to the end that they may become actual terms of understanding and move the potential intellect, does not seem a sufficient account, if it be coupled with the supposition of the potential intellect being a separately subsistent intelligence. This seems to go with the theory of those who say that inferior agents supply only predispositions to final perfection, but that final perfection is the work of an extrinsic agency, which is contrary to the mind of Aristotle—for the human soul does not appear to be worse off for understanding than inferior natures are for their own severally proper activities.

In the nature of every cause there is contained a principle sufficient for the natural operation of that cause. If the operation consists in action, there is at hand an active principle, as we see in the powers of the vegetative soul in plants. If the operation consists in receiving impressions, there is at hand a passive principle, as we see in the sentient powers of animals. But man is the most perfect of all inferior causes; and his proper and natural operation is to understand, an operation which is not accomplished without a certain receiving of impressions, inasmuch as every understanding is determined by its object, nor again without action, inasmuch as the intellect makes potential into actual terms of understanding. There must, therefore, be in the nature of man a proper principle of both operations, to wit, both an active and a potential intellect, and neither of them must be separate in being from the soul of man.

If the active intellect is an intelligence subsisting apart, it is clearly above the nature of man. But any activity which a man exercises by mere virtue of a supernatural cause is a supernatural activity, as the working of miracles, prophecy, and the like effects, which are wrought by men in virtue of a divine endowment. Since then man cannot understand except by means of the active intellect, it follows, supposing that intellect a separately subsistent being, that to understand is not an operation proper and natural to man; and thus man cannot be defined as intellectual or rational.

No agent works except by some power which is formally in the agent as a constituent of its being. But the working both of potential and of active intellect is proper to man; for man produces ideas by abstraction from phantasms, and receives in his mind those ideas, operations which it would never occur to us to think of, did we not experience them in ourselves. The principles, therefore, to which these operations are attributable, namely, the potential and the active intellect, must be faculties formally existing in us.

A being that cannot proceed to its own proper business without being moved thereto by an external principle, is rather driven to act than acts of itself. This is the case with irrational creatures. Sense, moved by an exterior sensible object, makes an impression on the fantasy; and so in order the impression proceeds through all the faculties until it reaches those which move the rest. Now the proper business of man is to understand; and the prime mover in understanding is the active intellect, which makes intellectual impressions whereby the potential intellect is impressed; which potential intellect, when actualized, moves the will. If then the active intellect has a separate subsistence outside man, the whole of man's activity depends on an extrinsic principle. Man then will not be his own leader, but will be led by another; and thus will not be master of his own acts, nor deserve praise nor blame, and the whole of moral science and political society will perish—an awkward conclusion. Therefore, the active intellect has no subsistence apart from man.

2.77 THAT IT IS NOT IMPOSSIBLE FOR THE POTENTIAL AND THE ACTIVE INTELLECT TO BE UNITED IN THE ONE SUBSTANCE OF THE SOUL

Someone perhaps may think it impossible for one and the same substance, that of our soul, to be in potentiality to receive all intellectual impressions (which is the function of the potential intellect), and to actualize those impressions (which is the function of the active intellect); since nothing acts as it is in potentiality to receive, but only as it is in actual readiness to act. But, looking at the matter rightly, no inconvenience or difficulty will be found in this view of the union of the active and potential intellect in the one substance of the soul. For a thing may well be in potentiality in one respect and in actuality in another; and this we find to be the condition of the intellectual soul in its relation to phantasms, or impressions in fantasy. For the intellectual soul has something in actuality, to which the phantasm is in potentiality; and on the other hand the intellectual

soul is in potentiality to that which is actually found in the phantasms. For the substance of the human soul has the attribute of immateriality, but it is not thereby assimilated to this or that definite thing; and yet such assimilation is requisite for our soul to know this or that thing definitely, since all cognition takes place by some likeness of the object known being stamped on the knowing mind. Thus, the intellectual soul remains in potentiality, open to the reception of definite impressions in the likeness of things that come within our observation and knowledge, which are the natures of sensible things. These definite natures of sensible things are represented to us by phantasms, which, however, have not yet reached the stage of being objects of intellect, seeing that they are likenesses of sensible things under material conditions, which are individualizing properties, and besides they are in bodily organs. They are, therefore, not actual objects of understanding; and yet, since in the case of this man, whose likeness is represented by phantasms, it is possible to fix upon a universal nature stripped of all individualizing conditions, these phantasms are potentially intelligible. Thus, they have a potentially intelligible being, but an actually definite likeness to things, whereas in the intellectual soul, as we saw, the situation was the other way about. There is then in the intellectual soul a power exercising its activity upon phantasms, making them actual objects of understanding; this power of the soul is called the active intellect. There is also in the soul a power that is potentially open to definite impressions of sensible things; this power is the potential intellect.

But the intellectual soul does not lie open to receive impressions of the likenesses of things that are in phantasms in the way that the likeness exists in the phantasm, but according as those likenesses are raised to a higher stage, by being abstracted from individualizing material conditions and rendered actual objects, or terms, of understanding. And, therefore, the action of the active intellect upon the phantasms precedes their being received into the potential intellect; and thus the prime agency is not attributable to the phantasms, but to the active intellect.

There are some animals that see better by night than by day, because they have weak eyes, which are stimulated by a little light, but dazzled by much. And the case is similar with our understanding: hence, the little intellectual light that is natural to us is sufficient for us to understand with. But that the intellectual light natural to our soul is sufficient to produce the action of the active intellect, will be clear to any one who considers the necessity for positing such an intellect. Our soul is found to be in potentiality to intelligible objects as sense to sensible objects; for as we are not always having sensations, so we are not always understanding. These intelligible objects Plato assumed exist by themselves, calling them 'Ideas': hence, it was not necessary for him to posit any 'active intellect' rendering objects intelligible. But if this Platonic position were true, the absolutely better objects of intelligence should be better also relative to us, and be better understood by us, which is manifestly not the case— for things are more intelligible to us which are nigher to sense, though in themselves they are less excellent objects of understanding. Hence Aristotle was moved to lay down the doctrine, that the things which are intelligible to us are not any self-existent objects of understanding, but are gathered from objects of sense. Hence, he had to posit some faculty to do this work of making terms of understanding—that faculty is the active intellect. The active intellect, therefore, is posited to make terms of understanding proportionate to our capacity. Such work does not transcend the measure of intellectual light natural to us. Hence, there is no difficulty in attributing the action of the active intellect to the native light of our soul, especially as Aristotle compares the active intellect to light (*De anima*, III, v, 2).

2.79 THAT THE HUMAN SOUL DOES NOT PERISH WITH THE BODY

Every intelligent subsisting being is imperishable, but the human soul is an intelligent, subsisting being.

Nothing is destroyed by that which makes its perfection. But the perfection of the human soul consists in a certain withdrawal from the body, for the soul is perfected by knowledge and virtue—now, in knowledge there is greater perfection, the more the view is fixed on high generalizations, or immaterial things; while the perfection of virtue consists in a man's not following his bodily passions, but tempering and restraining them by reason. Nor is it of any avail to reply that the perfection of the soul consists in its separation from the body in point of activity, but to be separated from the body in point of being is

its destruction. For the activity of a thing shows its substance and being, and follows upon its nature; thus, the activity of a thing can only be perfected inasmuch as its substance is perfected. If then the soul is perfected in activity by relinquishing the body and bodily things, its substance cannot fail in being by separation from the body.

A natural craving cannot be in vain. But man naturally craves after permanent continuance, as is shown by this: that while existence is desired by all, man by his understanding apprehends existence, not in the present moment only, as dumb animals do, but existence absolutely. Therefore, man attains to permanence on the part of his soul, whereby he apprehends existence absolute and for all time.

Intelligible being is more permanent than sensible being. But the substratum of material bodies is indestructible, much more the potential intellect, the recipient of intelligible forms. Therefore, the human soul, of which the potential intellect is a part, is indestructible.

No form is destroyed except either by the action of the contrary, or by the destruction of the subject wherein it resides, or by the failure of its cause. Thus, heat is destroyed by the action of cold; by the destruction of the eye the power of sight is destroyed; and the light of the atmosphere fails by the failure of the sun's presence, which was its cause. But the human soul cannot be destroyed by the action of its contrary, for it has no contrary, since by the potential intellect the soul is cognitive and receptive of all contraries. Nor again by the destruction of the subject in which it resides, for it has been shown above that the human soul is a form not dependent on the body for its being. Nor lastly by the failure of its cause, for it can have no cause but one which is eternal, as will be shown. In no way, therefore, can the human soul be destroyed.

If the human soul is destroyed by the destruction of the body, it must be weakened by the weakening of the body. But the fact is that if any faculty of the soul is weakened by the body being weakened, that is only incidentally, inasmuch as that faculty of the soul stands in need of a bodily organ, as the sight is weakened by the weakening of the organ of sight, but only incidentally, as may be shown by this consideration: if any weakness fell essentially upon the faculty, the faculty would not be restored by the restoration of the organ; but now we see that however much the faculty of sight seems weakened, it is restored, if only the organ is restored. Since then the soul's faculty of understanding needs no bodily organ, the understanding itself is not weakened, neither essentially nor incidentally, either by old age or by any other weakness of body. But if in the working of the understanding there happens fatigue or hindrance through bodily weakness, this is not due to weakness of the understanding itself, but to weakness of other faculties that the understanding has need of, to wit, the fantasy, the memory, and the cogitative faculty.

The same is evidenced by the very words of Aristotle: "moving causes pre-exist, but formal causes are along with the things whereof they are causes; for when a man is well, then there is health. But whether anything remains afterwards, is a point to consider. In some cases there may well be something remaining: the soul is an instance, not the whole soul, but the intelligence; as for the whole soul remaining, that is perhaps an impossibility." Clearly then, in speaking of forms, he wishes to speak of the intellect, which is the form of man, as remaining after its matter, that is, the body. It is clear, also, that though Aristotle makes the soul a form, yet he does not represent it as nonsubsistent and consequently perishable, as Gregory of Nyssa imputes to him; for he excludes the intellectual soul from the general category of other forms, saying that it remains after the body and is a subsistent being.

Hereby is banished the error of the impious in whose person it is said: *we were born out of nothingness, and hereafter we shall be as though we had never been* (Wisd. ii, 2); in whose person again Solomon says: *one is the perishing of man and beast, and even is the lot of both: as man dies, so do beasts die; all breathe alike, and man hath no advantage over beasts* (Eccles iii, 19). That he does not say this in his own person, but in the person of the ungodly, is clear from what he says at the end, as it were drawing a conclusion: *till the dust return to the earth, from whence it came: and the spirit go back to the God who gave it* (Eccles xii, 7).

2.80, 81: ARGUMENTS OF THOSE WHO WISH TO PROVE THAT THE HUMAN SOUL PERISHES WITH THE BODY, WITH REPLIES TO THE SAME

Arg. 1. If human souls are multiplied according to the multiplication of bodies, as shown above then when the bodies perish, the souls cannot remain in their multitude. Hence, one of two conclusions must follow: either the human soul must wholly cease to be; or there must remain one soul only, which seems to suit the view of those who make that alone incorruptible which is one in all men, whether that be the active intellect alone, as Alexander says, or with the active also the potential intellect, as Averroës says.

Reply. Whatever things are necessarily in conjunction and proportion with one another, are made many or one together, each by its own cause. If the being of the one depends on the other, its unity or multiplication also will depend on the same; otherwise it will depend on some extrinsic cause. Form, then, and matter, must always be in proportion with one another, and conjoined by a certain natural tie. Hence, matter and form must vary together in point of multiplicity and unity. If then the form depends on the matter for its being, the multiplication of the form will depend on the matter, and so will its unity. But if the form is in no such dependence on the matter, then—though it will still be necessary for the form to be multiplied with the multiplication of the matter—the unity or multiplicity of the form will not depend on the matter. But it has been shown that the human soul is a form not dependent on matter for its being. Hence, it follows that, though souls are multiplied as the bodies which they inform are multiplied, still the fact of bodies being many cannot be the cause of souls being many. And, therefore, there is no need for the plurality of souls to cease with the destruction of their bodies.

Arg. 2. The formal nature of things is the cause of their differing in species. But if souls remain many after the perishing of their bodies, they must differ in species, since in souls so remaining the only diversity possible is one of formal nature. But souls do not change their species by the destruction of the body, otherwise they would be destroyed too, for all that changes from species to species is destroyed in the transition. Then they must have been different in species even before they parted from their bodies. But compounds take their species according to their form. So then individual men must differ in species, an awkward conclusion consequent upon the position that souls remain a multitude after their bodies are gone.

Reply. It is not any and every diversity of form that makes a difference of species. The fact of souls separated from their bodies making a multitude follows from their forms being different in substance, inasmuch as the substance of this soul is different from the substance of that. But this diversity does not arise from the souls differing in their several essential constitutions, but from their being differently commensurate with different bodies, for one soul is commensurate with one body and not with another. These commensurations remain in souls even when their bodies perish, as the substances of the souls also remain, not being dependent on their bodies for their being. For it is by their substances that souls are forms of bodies; otherwise they would be united with their bodies only accidentally, and soul and body would not make up an essential but only an accidental unity. But inasmuch as they are forms, they must be commensurate with their bodies. Hence, it is clear that their several different commensuratenesses remain in the departed souls, and consequently plurality.

Arg. 3. It seems quite impossible, on the theory of those who suppose the eternity of the world, for human souls to remain in their multitude after the death of the body. For if the world is from eternity, infinite men have died before our time. If then the souls of the dead remain after death in their multitude, we must say that there is now an actual infinity of souls of men previously dead. But actual infinity is impossible in nature.

Reply. Of supporters of the eternity of the world, some have simply allowed the impossibility, saying that human souls perish altogether with their bodies. Others have said that of all souls there remains one spiritual existence which is common to all—the active intellect according to some, or with the active also the potential intellect according to others. Others have supposed souls to remain in their multitude after their bodies; but, not to be obliged to suppose an infinity of souls, they have said that the same souls are united to different bodies after a fixed period; and this was the opinion of the Platonists, of which hereafter others, avoiding all the aforesaid answers, have maintained that there was no difficulty in the existence of an actual infinity of departed souls; for an actual infinity of things, not related to one another, was only an accidental infinity, in which they saw no difficulty; and this is the position of Avicenna and Algazel. Which of these was the opinion of Aristotle is not

expressly set down in his writings, although he does expressly hold the eternity of the world. But the last-mentioned opinion is not inconsistent with his principles: in the *Physics*, III, v, his argument against an actual infinity is confined to natural bodies, and is not extended to immaterial substances. Clearly, however, the professors of the Catholic faith can feel no difficulty on this point, as they do not allow the eternity of the world.

Arg. 5. It is impossible for any substance to exist destitute of all activity. But all activity of the soul ends with the body, as may be shown by simple enumeration. For the faculties of the vegetative soul work through bodily qualities and a bodily instrument; and the term of their activity is the body itself, which is perfected by the soul, is thereby nourished and developed, and comes to furnish the generative products. Also all the activities of the faculties of the sensitive soul are accomplished through bodily organs; and some of them are accompanied by (sensible) bodily change, as in the case of the passions. As for the act of understanding, although it is not an activity exercised through any bodily organ, nevertheless its objects are phantasms, which stand to it as colors to sight: hence, as sight cannot see without colors, so the intellectual soul cannot understand without phantasms. The soul also needs, for purposes of understanding, the faculties which prepare the phantasms to become actual terms of intellect, namely, the cogitative faculty and the memory, of which it is certain that they cannot endure without the body, seeing that they work through organs of the body. Hence Aristotle says that "the soul by no means understands without a phantasm," and that "nothing understands without the passive intellect," by which name he designates the cogitative faculty, "which is perishable" and that "we remember nothing" after death of the things that we knew in life. Thus, it is clear that no activity of the soul can continue after death, and, therefore, neither can its substance continue.

Reply. The assertion that no activity can remain in the soul after its separation from the body, we say, is incorrect, for those activities remain which are not exercised through organs, and such are understanding and will. As for activities exercised through bodily organs, as are the activities of the vegetative and sentient soul, they do not remain. But we must observe that the soul separated from the body does not understand in the same way as when united with the body, for everything acts according as it is. Now though the being of the human soul, while united with the body, is perfect, not depending on the body, still the body is a sort of housing to it and subject receptive of it. Hence, the proper activity of the soul, which is understanding, while independent of the body in this that it is not exercised through any bodily organ, nevertheless finds in the body its object, which is the phantasm. Hence, so long as the soul is in the body, it cannot understand without a phantasm, nor remember except by the cogitative and reminiscent faculty whereby phantasms are shaped and made available; and, therefore, this method of understanding and remembering has to be laid aside when the body is laid aside. But the being of the departed soul belongs to it alone without the body; hence, its intellectual activity will not be accomplished by regard to such objects as phantasms existing in bodily organs, but it will understand by itself after the manner of those intelligences that subsist totally apart from bodies, from which superior beings it will be able to receive more abundant influence in order to more perfect understanding.

We may see some indication of this even in living men. When the soul is hampered by preoccupations about its body, it is less disposed to understand higher things. Hence, the virtue of temperance, withdrawing the soul from bodily delights, helps especially to make men apt to understand. In sleep again, when men are not using their bodily senses, they have some perception of things to come, impressed upon them by superior beings, and attain to facts that transcend the measure of human reasonings. This is much more the case in states of syncope and ecstasy, as the withdrawal from the bodily senses is there greater. And

that is what one might expect, because, as has been pointed out above, the human soul being on the boundary line between corporeal and incorporeal substances, and dwelling as it were on the horizon of eternity and time, it approaches the highest by receding from the lowest. Therefore, when it shall be totally severed from the body, it will be perfectly assimilated to the intelligences that subsist apart, and will receive their influence in more copious streams. Thus then, though the mode of our understanding according to the conditions of the present life is wrecked with the wreck of the body, it will be replaced by another and higher mode of understanding.

But memory, being an act exercised through a bodily organ, as Aristotle shows, cannot remain in the soul after the body is gone; unless memory be taken in another sense for the intellectual hold upon things known before: this intellectual memory of things known in life must remain in the departed soul, since the intellectual impressions are indelibly received in the potential intellect. As regards other activities of the soul, such as love, joy, and the like, we must beware of a double meaning of the terms: sometimes they mean passions, or emotions, which are activities of the sensitive appetite, concupiscible or irascible, and as such they cannot remain in the soul after death, as Aristotle shows: Sometimes they mean a simple act of will without passion, as Aristotle says that, "the joy of God is one, everlasting, and absolute," and that, "in the contemplation of wisdom there is admirable delight"; and again he distinguishes the love of friendship from the love of passion. But as the will is a power that uses no bodily organ, as neither does the understanding, it is evident that such acts, inasmuch as they are acts of will, may remain in the departed soul.

STUDY QUESTIONS: AQUINAS, *SUMMA CONTRA GENTILES*

1. How are body and soul related? How does Aquinas distinguish Plato's view from Aristotle's (whom he calls not by name but "The Philosopher") regarding this question?
2. What is the difference between the "intellectual soul" and the "potential intellect?" How are they related?
3. How does Aquinas distinguish between the passive and active intellect? Which defines the human being, and why?
4. Which of Averroës' statements does Aquinas find not only "false" but "perverse," and why?
5. What does Aquinas mean by "harmony?" Why is the soul not in harmony?

6. Are "intellect" and "sense" the same? Why?
7. What is Aquinas' argument that the potential intellect is *not* one and the same in all human beings? What is Averroës' (whom he calls "The Commentator") argument to the contrary?
8. How does Aquinas use the arguments of Avicenna against Averroës?
9. Why does the human soul not perish with the body? Does Averroës agree? How does Aquinas argue for immortality?
10. What are Aquinas' arguments for the existence of God? Which are the most interesting or compelling and why?
11. What does Aquinas mean by "first cause?"
12. Does everything have a cause? Or are there some things that can exist without being caused by anything else? How does Aquinas establish his position on issues of causality?

SUMMA THEOLOGICA

Summa contra Gentiles, written between 1259 and 1264, is intended primarily for those who do not yet believe in God or Christianity. In it, Aquinas uses arguments without assuming in advance that God exists or that Christianity is based in truth. *Summa Theologica*, on the other hand, written between 1265 and 1274, is intended primarily for those who already believe and are Christians but who may come to doubt, or are unsure whether their beliefs are true. This is an extremely important point to keep in mind when one reads the famous "five proofs" for the existence of God, which are often (unfairly) criticized from a skeptical point of view. For skeptics, Aquinas designed the prior work; the latter speaks to those believers who may have lost their way.

THE FIRST WAY

The Argument from Change

The existence of God can be shown in five ways. The first and clearest is taken from the idea of motion. (1) Now it is certain, and our senses corroborate it, that some things in this world are in motion. (2) But everything which is in motion is moved by something else. (3) For nothing is in motion except in so far as it is in potentiality in relation to that towards which it is in motion. (4) Now a thing causes movement in so far as it is in actuality. For to cause movement is nothing else than to bring something from potentiality to actuality; but a thing cannot be brought from potentiality to actuality except by something which exists in actuality, as, for example, that which is hot in actuality, like fire, makes wood, which is only hot in potentiality, to be hot in actuality, and thereby causes movement in it and alters it. (5) But it is not possible that the same thing should be at the same time in actuality and potentiality in relation to the same thing, but only in relation to different things; for what is hot in actuality cannot at the same time be hot in potentiality, though it is at the same time cold in potentiality. (6) It is impossible, therefore, that in relation to the same thing and in the same way anything should both cause movement and be caused, or that it should cause itself to move. (7) Everything, therefore, that is in motion must be moved by something else. If, therefore, the thing which causes it to move be in motion, this too must be moved by something else, and so on. (8) But we cannot proceed to infinity in this way, because in that case there would be no first mover, and in consequence, neither would there be any other mover; for secondary movers do not cause movement except they be moved by a first mover, as, for example, a stick cannot cause movement unless it is moved by the hand. Therefore, it is

Thomas Aquinas, from *Summa Theologica*, translated by Laurence Shapcote (London: O. P. Benziger Brothers, 1911).

necessary to stop at some first mover which is moved by nothing else. And this is what we all understand God to be.

THE SECOND WAY

The Argument from Causation

The Second Way is taken from the idea of the efficient cause. (1) For we find that there is among material things a regular order of efficient causes. (2) But we do not find, nor indeed is it possible, that anything is the efficient cause of itself, for in that case it would be prior to itself, which is impossible. (3) Now it is not possible to proceed to infinity in efficient causes. (4) For if we arrange in order all efficient causes, the first is the cause of the intermediate, and the intermediate the cause of the last, whether the intermediate be many or only one. (5) But if we remove a cause the effect is removed; therefore, if there is no *first* among efficient causes, neither will there be a last or an intermediate. (6) But if we proceed to infinity in efficient causes there will be no first efficient cause, and thus there will be no ultimate effect, nor any intermediate efficient causes, which is clearly false. Therefore, it is necessary to suppose the existence of some first efficient cause, and this men call God.

THE THIRD WAY

The Argument from Contingency

The Third Way rests on the idea of the "contingent" and the "necessary" and is as follows: (1) Now we find that there are certain things in the Universe which are capable of existing and of not existing, for we find that some things are brought into existence and then destroyed, and consequently are capable of being or not being. (2) But it is impossible for all things which exist to be of this kind, because anything which is capable of not existing, at some time or other does not exist. (3) If, therefore, *all* things are capable of not existing, there was a time when nothing existed in the Universe. (4) But if this is true there would also be nothing in existence now; because anything that does not exist cannot begin to exist except by the agency of something which has existence. If, therefore, there was once nothing which existed, it would have been impossible for anything to begin to exist, and so nothing would exist now. (5) This is

clearly false. Therefore, all things are not contingent, and there must be something which is necessary in the Universe. (6) But everything which is necessary either has or has not the cause of its necessity from an outside source. Now it is not possible to proceed to infinity in necessary things which have a cause of their necessity, as has been proved in the case of efficient causes. Therefore, it is necessary to suppose the existence of something which is necessary in itself, not having the cause of its necessity from any outside source, but which is the cause of necessity in others. And this "something" we call God.

THE FOURTH WAY

The Argument from Degrees of Excellence

The Fourth Way is taken from the degrees which are found in things. (1) For among different things we find that one is more or less good or true or noble; and likewise in the case of other things of this kind. (2) But the words "more" or "less" are used of different things in proportion as they approximate in their different ways to something which has the particular quality in the highest degree—for example, we call a thing hotter when it approximates more nearly to that which is hot in the highest degree. There is, therefore, something which is true in the highest degree, good in the highest degree and noble in the highest degree; (3) and consequently there must be also something which has being in the highest degree. For things which are true in the highest degree also have being in the highest degree (see Aristotle, *Metaphysics*, 2). (4) But anything which has a certain quality of any kind in the highest degree is also the cause of all the things of that kind, as, for example, fire which is hot in the highest degree is the cause of all hot things (as is said in the same book). (5) Therefore, there exists something which is the cause of being, and goodness, and of every perfection in all existing things; and this we call God.

THE FIFTH WAY

The Argument from Harmony

The Fifth Way is taken from the way in which nature is governed. (1) For we observe that certain things which lack knowledge, such as natural bodies, work for an end. This is obvious, because they always, or at any rate very frequently, operate in the same way so as to attain the best possible result. (2) Hence, it is clear that they do not arrive at their goal by chance, but by purpose. (3) But those things which have no knowledge do not move towards a goal unless they are guided by someone or something which does possess knowledge and intelligence—for example, an arrow by an archer. Therefore, there does exist something which possesses intelligence by which all natural things are directed to their goal; and this we call God.

STUDY QUESTIONS: AQUINAS, *SUMMA THEOLOGICA*

1. What is the clearest argument for God, according to Aquinas? Why?
2. Is motion possible without a mover?
3. What does Aquinas mean by efficient cause?
4. How does Aquinas distinguish contingency from necessity?
5. Is everything contingent? Or are some things necessary?
6. What is the cause of being?
7. What is necessary in and of itself?
8. What sorts of things are goal-oriented?

ON BEING AND ESSENCE

"The Philosopher" mentioned in Aquinas's preface is, of course, Aristotle; "The Commentator" is the great Islamic philosopher Avicenna. Following Avicenna's contention that the intellect begins first with the concepts *being* and *essence*, Aquinas begins by defining his terms. Like Aristotle, Aquinas starts by distinguishing between *being through itself* as divided into ten genera and signifying the truth of propositions regardless of whether what is named in those propositions exists. But he then goes on to advance an original metaphysical system that goes well beyond the classical Greek notions and which paved the way for subsequent metaphysical developments in logic and philosophy as well as theology.

Aquinas' central concern throughout this work is the question of whether abstract terms such as "mankind," "human nature," and so on, have any reality in and of themselves, that is, over and above the language itself. In other words, are these merely words and phrases, denoting meanings within a language that has significance, as such, in the human mind only, or is there really such a thing as "human nature" that exists outside the mind and independently of the language? This groundbreaking essay *On the Problem of Universals* was written over a four-year period starting in 1252, when Aquinas was only 27.

PREFACE

A small error in the beginning of something is a great one at the end, as the Philosopher claims in the first book of his *On the Heavens*. Moreover, being and essence are what the intellect first conceives, as Avicenna maintains in the first book of his *Metaphysics*. Hence, we ought to state what the terms *essence* and *being* signify, how they are found in diverse things, and, finally, how they are related to logical intentions, namely, genus, species, and difference. We proceed in this way in order to avoid the errors which follow from being ignorant of being and essence, and to reveal their difficulty.

St. Thomas Aquinas, from *Selected Writings of St. Thomas Aquinas*, translated by Robert P. Goodwin (New York: Macmillan/Library of the Liberal Arts, 1965).

CHAPTER 1

Since a knowledge of simple things must be acquired from those that are complex, and since a knowledge of prior things must be acquired from those that are posterior—so that beginning with easier matters a discipline might more suitably proceed—we must, therefore, begin with the meaning of *being* and then take up the meaning of *essence*.

As the Philosopher states in the fifth book of the *Metaphysics*, it must be understood that *being through itself* is used in two ways. In one way it is divided into the ten genera. In another way it signifies the truth of propositions. The difference between these two is that, according to the latter way, *being* can be attributed to anything concerning which an affirmative proposition can be formed, even if it posits nothing in reality. In this way even privations and negations are called beings; for we say that an affirmation *is* opposed to a negation, and that blindness *is* in the eye. But in the former way, *being* can be said only of something which exists in reality. Accordingly, in the first way, blindness and things of this kind are not beings. Therefore, the term "essence" is not derived from *being* said in the second way, for, in this way, some things are said to be beings which do not have an essence, as is evident in privations. *Essence*, however, is derived from being said in the first way. Hence, the Commentator, in the same place, says that *being* used in the first way signifies the essence of a thing. As we have noted, because *being* used in this way is divided into ten genera, *essence* must signify something common to all natures, through which natures diverse beings are placed in diverse genera and species. Thus, for example, humanity is the essence of man, and so with others.

Moreover, that through which something is constituted in its proper genus or species is what is signified by the definition that declares what a thing is. Hence, philosophers have substituted the name "quiddity" for that of "essence." It is what the Philosopher frequently calls "the *what* a thing was to be," that is, that through which something is a certain kind of being. It is called *form*, moreover, inasmuch as "form" signifies the certitude of anything, as Avicenna says in the third book of his *Metaphysics*. It is also called by the name "nature," when the latter is understood according to the first of those four senses which

Boethius establishes in the book *De Duabus Naturis* is, when *nature* is said of anything that can be grasped intellectually in some way. For a thing is intelligible only through its definition and essence. Accordingly, the Philosopher, in the fifth book of the *Metaphysics*, states that every substance is a nature. Yet the term *nature*, taken in this sense, seems to signify the essence of a thing inasmuch as it possesses an ordering to its proper operations, since no thing is devoid of its proper operation. The term "quiddity," however, is used to signify the definition. But "essence" is used inasmuch as it designates that through which and in which a being has the act of existing.

But because being is asserted absolutely and primarily of substances, and secondarily and in a relative sense of accidents, it follows also that essence is truly and properly in substances, but is in accidents only in a certain way and in a qualified sense. Some substances indeed are simple, and some are composite. Essence is present in both, but it exists more truly and in a nobler way in simple substances, inasmuch as they have their acts of existing in a nobler way. For simple substances are the cause of composite ones—at least the first substance, God, is. However, because the essences of simple substances are more hidden from us, we must, therefore, begin with essences of composite ones, so that our study might proceed more suitably from easier things.

CHAPTER 2

In composite substances both the matter and the form are known, as soul and body are known in man. Moreover, neither one of them alone can be called essence. For it is clear that the matter alone of a thing is not its essence, because through its essence a thing both is knowable, and is established in a species and a genus. But matter is neither a principle of knowledge nor that by which something is determined in a genus or species. On the contrary, a thing is so determined by that by which it is in act. Nor can it be said that form alone is the essence of a composite substance, although some try to assert this.

From what we have said, it is evident that essence is that which is signified by the definition of a thing. Moreover, the definition of natural substances contains not only form, but also matter; otherwise there would be no difference between definitions in physics and in mathematics. Nor can it be said that matter is put in the definition of a natural substance as something added to its essence, or as a being outside of its essence, because this kind of definition is proper to accidents, which do not have a perfect essence. Hence, the definition of an accident must include its subject, which is outside its genus.

Clearly, then, essence includes matter and form. One cannot, however, say that essence signifies a relationship between matter and form, or something superadded to them, since this would necessarily be an accident or something extraneous to the thing; nor would the thing be known through it. None of these features is suitable for an essence. By form, which is the act of matter, matter is made a being in act and an individual substance. Hence, what is superadded does not make matter be in act without qualification, but rather makes matter be actually such, just as accidents do. For example, whiteness makes something be actually white. Accordingly, when such a form is acquired, one says that something is generated in a qualified way, not absolutely.

Consequently, in the case of composite substances, the term "essence" signifies the composite of matter and form. This, too, agrees with Boethius' commentary on the *Categories*, where he says that (ousia) signifies a composite. (Ousia) among the Greeks is the same as *essence* for us, as Boethius himself says in the book *De Duabus Naturis*. Avicenna also says that the quiddity of composite substances is itself a composition of form and matter. The Commentator also says in his comment on the seventh book of the *Metaphysics*, "the nature which species have in things that can be generated is a certain mean, that is, a composite of matter and form." Reason, too, agrees with this, because the existing of a composite substance is not simply the act of the form alone, nor of the matter alone, but of the composite itself. Moreover, essence is that according to which a thing is said to be. Hence it is necessary that an essence, by which a thing is denominated a being, be neither the form alone nor the matter alone, but both, although the form in its own way is the cause of this act of existing. We find the same thing in other things constituted by a plurality of principles, for a thing gets its name, not from one or another of these principles alone, but from what embraces both of them. This is evident in the case of flavors. Sweetness is caused by

the action of heat spreading moisture. Although heat, in this way, is the cause of sweetness, nevertheless a body is not called sweet because of heat, but because of flavor, which embraces both heat and moisture.

But, since the principle of individuation is matter, it might seem to follow that essence, which embraces in itself both matter and form simultaneously, is particular only and not universal. From this it would follow that universals would not have a definition, if essence is that which is signified by a definition. Accordingly, it should be known that matter in just any way is not held to be the principle of individuation. Only designated matter is. By *designated matter* I mean matter considered under determinate dimensions. This matter, however, is not included in the definition of a man insofar as he is a man, but would be included in the definition of Socrates, if Socrates had a definition. Undesignated matter, however, is included in the definition of man. We do not include in man's definition this bone or this flesh, but bone and flesh absolutely, which are the undesignated matter of man. Thus, it is evident that the essence of Socrates and the essence of man differ only in that one is designated and the other is not. Hence, the Commentator says in his commentary on the seventh book of the *Metaphysics*, "Socrates is nothing other than animality and rationality, which are his quiddity." So also the essence of a genus and of a species differ according as one is designated and the other not, although a different mode of designation is used in regard to this and to the preceding case, because the designation of an individual with respect to his species is through matter determined by dimensions, whereas the designation of a species with respect to its genus is through a constitutive difference taken from the form of the thing.

However, this determination or designation, which is in the species with respect to the genus, is not through something in the essence of the species that is in no way in the essence of the genus. Rather, whatever is in the species is in the genus in an undetermined fashion. For if *animal* were not the whole that is man, but only a part, *animal* would not be predicated of man, since no integral part is predicated of its whole.

How this occurs can be seen if we consider how *body*, understood as part of an animal, differs from *body* understood as a genus. For it is impossible for body to be a genus in the same way as it is an integral part. Therefore this term "body" is understood in many ways. Body is said to be in the genus substance inasmuch as it has a nature such that three dimensions can be designated in it. Indeed, these three designated dimensions themselves are body according as it is in the genus of quantity.

Moreover, it happens in things that what has one perfection may also possess a further perfection. This is evident in man, since he has both a sensitive nature and, beyond that, an intellectual nature. Similarly, to this perfection of having a form such that three dimensions can be designated in it, can be added another perfection, such as life or the like. It is possible, therefore, for this term "body" to signify a certain thing having such a form as there follows precisely and exclusively the capacity of having designated in it three dimensions. Hence, from this form no further perfection would follow. If something else were added, it would be outside the meaning of *body* so understood. In this way body is an integral and material part of an animal, because in this way soul will be extrinsic to what is signified by the term "body" and will be an addition to body itself, so that an animal will be constituted from these two, body and soul, as from parts.

The term "body" can also mean a certain something having a form such that three dimensions can be designated in it, whatever that form be, and whether or not a more ultimate perfection can arise from it. Body in this sense is the genus *animal* because nothing is understood in *animal* which is not contained implicitly in body. For the soul is not another form distinct from that through which three dimensions can be designated in that thing. Therefore, when it was said that body is such that it has a form according to which three dimensions can be designated in it, body was understood, no matter what form it possesses, whether it be animality, or rockness, or any other. Thus the form *animal* is contained implicitly in the form *body*, according as body is its genus. Such also is the relationship of animal to man. If "animal" names only a certain thing which has the perfection of sensing or being moved by a principle existing within it known in precision from any other perfection, then the addition of any further perfection would be related to animal as a part, and not as implicitly contained in the notion of animal. In this way *animal* would not be a genus. It is a genus insofar as it signi-

fies anything from whose form can arise sensation and motion, whatever that form be, whether a sensitive soul only, or a sensitive and rational one. Therefore, a *genus* signifies indeterminately that whole which is in the species, for it does not signify matter alone. *Difference* likewise signifies a whole and does not signify the form alone. A definition, too, signifies the whole, as does even the species. They do this, however, in various ways. A genus signifies the whole as a certain determination, designating what is material in the thing, exclusive of the determination proper to the form. Hence, genus is derived from matter, although it is not matter. This is evident from the fact that something is said to be a body from its perfection according to which three dimensions can be designated in it. This perfection is related materially to further perfection. On the other hand, a difference signifies the whole as a certain determination taken determinately from the form, without determinate matter being included in its primary notion. This is evident from the usage of "animate," or that which has a soul, for what this is, whether body or something else, is not determined. Accordingly, Avicenna says that genus is not understood in the difference as part of its essence, but only as a being outside its essence, just as a subject is contained in the understanding of properties. Therefore, too, the genus, properly speaking, is not predicated of the difference, as the Philosopher says in the third book of the *Metaphysics* and in the fourth book of the *Topics*, except perhaps in the way a subject is predicated of a property. But the definition or species includes both, namely, determinate matter, designated by the term "genus," and determinate form, designated by the term "difference."

On the basis of what we have just said, it is clear why genus, species, and difference are related proportionately to matter, form, and the composite in nature, although the former are not the same as the latter. The genus is not matter, but is taken from matter and signifies the whole; and the difference is not the form, but is taken from form as signifying the whole. Accordingly we say that a man is a rational animal, but not that he is composed of animal and rational, as we say that a man is composed of body and soul. For man is said to be composed of body and soul after the manner of a third thing that is constituted of two things, and identical with neither of them. For a man is neither a soul nor a body. However, if man is said to be composed in some way of animal and rational, it is not as a third thing from two other things, but as a third notion from two other notions. For the notion *animal* lacks the determination of a special form which expresses the nature of the thing, inasmuch as animal is matter with respect to the ultimate perfection. However, the notion of this difference, rational, consists in the determination of the special form. The notion of species or definition is constituted from these two notions. Therefore, just as the things which compose are not predicated of the thing composed of them, so neither are constitutive notions predicated of the notion constituted from them. For we do not say that a definition is "genus" or difference.

Although "genus" signifies the whole essence of the species, nevertheless it is not necessary that the diverse species in the same genus have the same essence. This is so because the unity of genus proceeds from its very indetermination or indifference. This is not to say, however, that what is signified by "genus" is numerically one nature in diverse species, to which nature some other thing which is the difference is added, determining it as the form determines matter which is numerically one. It is a question, rather, of "genus" signifying a certain form—not, however, this one or that one determinately. The difference expresses this determinately, and it is none other than the one signified indeterminately by the genus. And this is why the Commentator says in the twelfth book of the *Metaphysics* that prime matter is said to be one through the removal of all forms, whereas genus is said to be one through the community of the form signified. It is, therefore, evident that through the addition of the difference, which thereby removes that indetermination which was the cause of the unity of the genus, essentially diverse species remain.

Now because the nature of the species is, as we have stated, indeterminate with respect to the individual, as is the nature of a genus with respect to the species, it therefore follows that just as a genus, insofar as it is predicated of a species, implies (although indistinctly) in its signification everything determinate in the species, so also the species, as predicated of an individual, must signify (although indistinctly) all that is essentially in the individual. In this way the essence of Socrates is signified by the name "man."

Accordingly, *man* is predicated of Socrates. But if the nature of a species is signified in precision from designated matter, which is the principle of individuation, then it will be related to the individual after the manner of a part. In this way the essence of Socrates is signified by the term "humanity." For humanity signifies that whereby man is a man. But designated matter is not that whereby man is a man. Therefore, in no way is designated matter included among those things by which a man is a man. Hence, since humanity includes in its conception only those things by which a man is man, it is clear that designated matter is excluded or precluded from its signification. In addition, since a part is not predicated of the whole, so humanity is predicated of neither man nor Socrates. Accordingly, Avicenna says that the quiddity of a composite is not the composite of which it is the quiddity, even if the quiddity itself is a composite. Hence, although humanity is composite, it is nevertheless not identified with man. Indeed, it must be received in something, which is designated matter.

As has been said, the designation of a species with respect to the genus is through the form, and the designation of an individual with respect to the species is through the matter. Because of this the term signifying that whence the nature of the genus is taken, in precision from the determinate form perfecting the species, must signify the material part of the whole itself, as body is the material part of man. However, the term signifying that whence the nature of the species is taken in precision from designated matter, signifies the formal part.

Therefore, humanity is signified as a certain form, and is said to be the form of the whole—not, however, as something superadded to the essential parts, namely form and matter, as the form house is superadded to its integral parts, but rather as a form which is a whole, that is, a form embracing matter. It is, nevertheless, signified in precision from those things according to which matter is apt to be designated. In this way it is clear that the terms "man" and "humanity" signify the essence *man*, but in diverse ways, as has been said. For the term "man" signifies the essence *man* as a whole, inasmuch as it does not prescind from the designation of matter but contains it implicitly and in an indistinct way, just as genus was said to contain the difference. Accordingly, the term "man" is predicated of individuals.

The term "humanity," however, signifies the essence man as a part, since it contains in its signification only what is in man insofar as he is man, and prescinds from all designation of matter. Hence humanity cannot be predicated of individual men. On account of this, the term "essence" is sometimes predicated of a thing, as when it is said that Socrates is an essence, and sometimes it is denied of a thing, as when it is said that the essence of Socrates is not Socrates.

CHAPTER 3

Having seen, therefore, what is signified in composite substances by the term "essence," we should see how this term is related to the notions of genus, species, and difference. Inasmuch as what belongs to the character *genus, species,* or *difference* is predicated of this designated singular, it is impossible for the character *universal,* namely of a genus or species, to belong to an essence according as it is signified after the manner of a part, as by the term "humanity" or "animality." This is why Avicenna says that rationality is not a difference but the principle of a difference; and by the same token, humanity is not a species, nor is animality a genus. Similarly, it is not possible to say that the character *genus* and *species* is proper to the essence, where essence is a certain thing existing outside of the singulars, as the Platonists proposed; for then the genus and the species would not be predicated of this individual. One cannot say that Socrates is something separated from himself, nor can one say that what is separated aids in the cognition of this singular. Therefore, we are left with saying that the character *genus* or *species* belongs to an essence according as it is signified as the whole, as by the terms "man" or "animal," insofar as it implicitly and indistinctly contains all that is in the individual.

Nature or essence, understood in this sense, can be considered in two ways. One way is according to its own proper character. This is an absolute consideration of nature. In this way nothing is true of it except what is proper to it as such. Hence, the attribution to it of anything belonging to others would be false. As an example, *rational* and *animal,* and whatever else is included in man's definition, are proper to man as man. Neither white nor black, however, nor anything

else of this sort which is not in the notion of humanity, belongs to man as man. Accordingly, if the question arises whether the nature so considered can be said to be one or many, neither should be conceded, because each is extrinsic to the notion of humanity, and either can happen to it. For if plurality were included within its notion, the nature *man* could never be one, although it is one insofar as it is in Socrates. Similarly, if unity were included in its notion, then Socrates and Plato would be one and the same, and the nature could not be multiplied in many.

Nature can be considered, however, in another way: according to the act of existing which it has in this or that individual. When so considered, something is predicated of the nature accidentally, in virtue of that in which it exists; it is said, for example, that man is white because Socrates is white. The condition of being white, however, is not proper to man as man.

Now, this nature has two acts of existing: one in singular things, another in the soul. And according to each, accidents follow upon the aforesaid nature. In addition, the nature, in singulars, has many acts of existing according to the diversity of singulars. Yet according to the first consideration, that is, an absolute one, no act of existing is due the nature. For it is false to say that the essence of man, as man, has the act of existing in this singular inasmuch as, if it were proper to man as man to exist in this singular, man would never exist outside it. Similarly, if it pertained to a man as man not to exist in this singular, then man would never exist in this singular. But it is true to say that it is not proper to man as man to exist in this or that singular, or in a soul. It is, therefore, evident that the nature of man considered absolutely abstracts from every act of existing, but in such a way, however, that no act of existing is excluded by way of precision. Now it is this nature so considered which is predicated of all individuals.

Nevertheless, it cannot be said that the character *universal* belongs to nature so understood, because community and unity belong to the character *universal,* whereas neither of these belong to human nature considered absolutely. For if community were included in the notion of man, community would be found whenever humanity was found. But this is false, because in Socrates no community is found. On the contrary, whatever is in him is individuated. Similarly, it cannot be said that the character *genus* or species accrues to human nature according as it exists in individuals, because human nature in individuals does not possess such a unity as to be something that is one belonging to all, which the character *universal* demands. It remains, therefore, that the character species accrues to human nature as it exists in the intellect. For human nature itself exists in the intellect in abstraction from all individuating conditions. Thus it has a uniform relation to all individuals outside the soul, inasmuch as it is equally the similitude of all and leads to the cognition of all inasmuch as they are men. And since the nature has such a relationship to all individuals, the intellect forms the notion of species and attributes it to the nature. Hence, the Commentator says in the first book of the *De Anima* that it is the intellect which makes universality in things. Avicenna makes the same claim in his *Metaphysics*. Hence, although this nature existing in the intellect has the character *universal* inasmuch as it is compared to things which are outside of the mind, since it is the similitude of all of them, nevertheless, according as it exists in this or that intellect, it is a certain particular species understood by the intellect.

For this reason, the defect in the Commentator's reasoning in the third book of the *De Anima* is evident. He chose to conclude to the unity of an intellect for all men from the universality of the known form. This view is defective because the form is not universal according as it exists in the intellect, but inasmuch as it refers to things as their similitude. So also if there were one corporeal statue representing many men, that image or species of the statue would still be properly singular, since it would exist in this matter. It would, however, have the character *community*, inasmuch as it would be the common representation of many.

Since it belongs to human nature absolutely considered to be predicated of Socrates, and since the character *species* does not belong to it absolutely considered, but is among the accidents which follow upon it according as it exists in the intellect, therefore the term "species" is not predicated of Socrates, as in the sentence, "Socrates is a species." This would necessarily happen if the character *species* were proper to man according as it exists in Socrates, or according

to its absolute consideration, that is, as man. For whatever belongs to man as man is predicated of Socrates. To be predicated, however, belongs essentially to genus, since it is posited in the definition of genus. For predication is something which is accomplished by the action of the intellect composing and dividing, and has for its foundation in the real thing itself the unity of those things one of which is said of the other. Hence, the character *predicability* can be included in the nature of this kind of intention, that is, genus, which is similarly accomplished by an act of the intellect. Nonetheless, that to which the intellect attributes the intention *predicability*, composing it with another, is not the intention itself, *genus*. It is rather that to which the intellect attributes the intention *genus*, as the *what* that is signified by this term "animal."

It is evident, therefore, how an essence or nature is related to the character *species*, for the character *species* does not belong to essence or nature considered absolutely, nor is the character *species* one of the accidents which follow upon it according as it exists outside the soul, like whiteness or blackness. The character *species* is included among the accidents which follow upon it according as it exists in the intellect. The characters *genus* and *difference* also belong to nature so considered.

CHAPTER 4

It now remains for us to see the way in which essence is found in separated substances, namely, the soul, the intelligences, and the First Cause.

Although all hold that the first cause is simple, nevertheless certain men try to introduce a composition of form and matter into intelligences and the soul. Avicebron,[1] the author of the *Fons Vitae*, appears to be the originator of this position. This is contrary to the common views of the philosophers, for they call them substances separated from matter, and prove that they exist without any matter. The strongest argument for this position is from the power of understanding present in these substances. For we see that forms are actually intelligible only insofar as they are separated from matter and material conditions. Nor can they be made actually intelligible

---

[1]Ibn Gabirol (1021–1058), neo-Platonic philosopher.

except through the power of an intelligent substance according as they are received in this substance, and are effected through it. It is, therefore, necessary that every substance capable of intellectual understanding be completely free of matter such that it have no matter as part of itself, nor be like a form impressed on matter, as material forms are.

Nor can anyone maintain that not all matter impedes intelligibility, but that only corporeal matter does. If this impeding were of the nature of corporeal matter only, then matter would have to impede intelligibility because of its corporeal form, since matter is not called corporeal except insofar as it exists under a corporeal form. But this is impossible because, like other forms, even a corporeal form is actually intelligible when abstracted from matter. Hence, in no way whatsoever can there be a composition of form and matter in the soul or in an intelligence such that their essence would be understood in the same way as essence in corporeal substances. There is in them, however, a composition of form and act of existing. Wherefore, in the comment on the ninth proposition in the book *De Causis*,[2] it is said that an intelligence is something having form and an act of existing. Form is understood there as the simple quiddity or nature itself.

How this can be so is plain enough. Whatever things are related to each other in such a way that one causes the other to be, that thing which has the nature *cause* can have the act of existing without the other thing, but not vice versa. Such is the relation between matter and form, because form gives existence to matter. It is, therefore, impossible for matter to exist without some form, but it is not impossible for some form to exist without matter. For the form, as form, is not dependent upon matter. However, if some forms are found which can exist only in matter, this happens to them because of their distance from the first principle, which is first and pure act. Accordingly, those forms which are nearest to the first principle are forms subsisting of themselves without matter. As has just been said, form, according to every genus of form, may not need matter; and the intelligences are forms of this kind. Hence, it is not necessary that the essences or quiddities of these sub-

stances be other than the form itself. In this, therefore, the essences of composite substances and of simple substances differ, since the essence of a composite substance is not the form alone but includes both form and matter, whereas the essence of a simple substance is the form alone.

This accounts for two other differences. One is that the essence of composite substances can be signified as a whole or as a part. This occurs because of the designation of matter as has just been said. Therefore, not in just any way is the essence of a composite thing predicated of the composite thing itself. For it is not possible to say that a man is his quiddity. But the essence of a simple thing, which is its form, cannot be signified except as the whole, since there is nothing in the essence besides the form, as it were to receive the form. Therefore, in whatever way it is taken, the essence of simple substances is predicated of the simple substances. Accordingly, Avicenna says that "the quiddity of simple substances is the simple substance itself," inasmuch as there is nothing else receiving it.

The second difference is that the essences of composite things, inasmuch as they are received in designated matter, are multiplied according to the division of matter. It happens, therefore, that some are the same in species but different in number. But since the essence of simple substances is not received in matter, no such multiplication is possible. Therefore, among these substances there cannot be many individuals of the same species. Rather, there are as many species as there are individuals, as Avicenna expressly states.

Although substances of this kind are simply forms without matter, nonetheless they are not in every way simple, as pure acts are. They do have an admixture of potency, which is evident in the following way. Whatever is extraneous to the concept of an essence or quiddity is adventitious, and forms a composition with the essence, since no essence can be understood without those things which are its parts. On the other hand, every essence or quiddity can be understood without its act of existing being understood. I can understand what a man or phoenix is, and yet not know whether or not it exists in the nature of things. Therefore, it is evident that the act of existing is other than essence or quiddity. This is true, unless, perhaps,

---

[2]Containing various excerpts from *Elements of Theology* by neo-Platonist philosopher Proclus (410–485).

there is something whose quiddity is its very act of existing. This thing would have to be unique and primary, since it would be impossible for anything to be multiplied except by the addition of some difference, as the nature *genus* is multiplied into species; or by a form being received in diverse matters, as the nature *species* is multiplied in different individuals; or by one being absolute, and the other being received in something. For example, if there were a certain "separated" heat it would be distinct, in virtue of its very separation from the heat which is not separated. If, however, something is posited which is simply its own act of existing such that it would be subsistent existence itself, this existence cannot receive the addition of a difference, because then it would not be simply an act of existing, but an act of existing plus this certain form. Even less would it receive the addition of matter, because then it would not be subsistent existence, but material existence. Hence, there remains only one such thing that is its own act of existing. Accordingly, in anything other than it, the act of existing must necessarily be other than its quiddity or nature or form. Hence, among the intelligences, their acts of existing must be other than their forms. Therefore, it is said that intelligences are forms and acts of existing.

Whatever belongs to something is either caused by the principles of its nature, like risibility in man, or accrues to it from some extrinsic principle, like the light in the air, which is caused by the sun. It is impossible that the act of existing itself be caused by the form or quiddity—and by "caused" I mean as by an efficient cause—for then something would be the cause of itself and produce itself in existence, which is impossible. It is, therefore, necessary that everything whose act of existing is other than its nature have its act of existing from another. And because everything which exists through another is reduced to that which exists through itself, as to a first cause, there must be something which causes all things to exist, inasmuch as it is subsistent existence alone. Otherwise we would proceed to infinity in causes, since everything which is not a subsistent act of existing has a cause for its act of existing, as we have just said. It is evident, therefore, that an intelligence is a form and an act of existing, and that it has its act of existing from the First Being which is existence only; and this is the First Cause, God.

Everything that receives something from another is in potency with respect to what is received, and what is received in it is its act. Therefore, that quiddity or form which an intelligence is must be in potency with respect to the act of existing, which it receives from God. And that act of existing is received as an act. Thus, potency and act are found in intelligences, but not (except equivocally) matter and form. Hence, even *to suffer, to receive, to be subject to,* and all other things of this kind which seem proper to things in virtue of their matter, belong equivocally to intellectual and corporeal substances, as the Commentator states in his commentary on the third book of the *De Anima.* Likewise, because the quiddity of an intelligence is as has been said, the intelligence itself, its quiddity or essence, therefore, is itself that which is; and its act of existing, received from God, is that by which it subsists in the nature of things. Because of this, certain men contend that a substance of this kind is composed of that by which it is and that which it is, or as Boethius says, of what is and the act of existing.

Inasmuch as potency and act are found in intelligences, there will be no difficulty in discovering multitude among the intelligences. This would be impossible if there were no potency in them. Hence, the Commentator says in his commentary on the third book of the *De Anima* that if the nature of the possible intellect were unknown to us we could not find multitude in the separated substances. The distinction between them, therefore, is in accordance with the degree of potency and act, such that a superior intelligence which is nearer to the first being would have more act and less potency; and so on with the others. This terminates in the human soul, which holds the lowest grade among intellectual substances. Hence, its possible intellect is related to intelligible forms as prime matter, which holds the lowest grade among sensible beings, is related to sensible forms, as the Commentator says in his commentary on the third book of the *De Anima.* Accordingly, the Philosopher compares it to a writing tablet on which nothing is written, because it has a greater degree of potency than the other intelligible substances. The human soul, then, is so near to material things that the material thing is drawn to participate in its act of existing; thus from body and soul there results one act of existing in one composite, although that act of existing, insofar as it is the soul's, does not depend upon the body. Then, after that form which is the soul, there are other forms having more potency and having a greater propinquity to matter, to the extent that their acts of existing are not without matter. Among these, too, order and grade are found, all the way down to the primary forms of the elements, which are closest to matter. Hence, they have no operations except in accordance with the demands of their active and passive qualities, and of other qualities by which matter is disposed to form.

CHAPTER 5

From what has been seen previously, it is evident how essence is found in diverse things; for we found among substances a threefold mode of possessing an essence.

There is something, God, whose essence is its very act of existing. Accordingly, some philosophers argue that God does not have a quiddity or essence because His essence is nothing other than His act of existing. From this it follows that He is not in any genus, since everything that is in a genus necessarily has a quiddity distinct from its act of existing. This, in turn, follows from the fact that the quiddity or nature of a genus or species is not distinguished according to the character *nature* in those things of which there is a genus or species, but according to the act of existing which is diverse in diverse things. If we say that God is only an act of existing, we do not necessarily fall into the error of those who have stated that God is that universal existence by which each thing formally exists. The act of existing which God is is such that no addition can be made to it. Hence, by its very purity, His act of existing is distinct from every other act of existing. A comparable situation would be this: if there were a certain separated color, it would, by its very separation, be distinct from the color not separated. Wherefore, it is stated in the commentary on the ninth proposition of the book *De Causis* that the individuation of the first cause, which is only an act of existing, is through its pure goodness. However, just as the notion of existing in general does not include any addition, neither does it include any precision of addition; for if this were so, nothing in which something were added over and above the act of existing could be understood to exist. Similarly, even though He is only an act of existing, this does not necessitate

that He be deficient in other perfections and excellences. Indeed, God possesses the perfections which are in all genera, because of which He is said to be perfect without qualification, as the Philosopher and the Commentator state in the fifth book of the *Metaphysics*. He has these perfections, however, in a more excellent way than other things, because in Him they are one, while in other things they are diverse. This is so because all these perfections belong to Him according to His simple act of existing, just as, if someone were able to perform the operations of all the qualities in virtue of one quality, He would, in that one quality, have all qualities; so God possesses all perfections in His very act of existing.

Essence is found in a second way in created intellectual substances in which their essence is other than their acts of existing, although their essence is without matter. Hence, their acts of existing are not absolute, but received, and, therefore, limited and restricted to the capacity of the receiving nature. Nonetheless, their nature or quiddity is absolute and not received in any matter. Therefore, the book *De Causis* maintains that intelligences are infinite from below and finite from above. For they are limited as to their acts of existing, which are received from something higher. They are not limited from below, since their forms are not limited to the capacity of some matter receiving them. Hence, there is not found among such substances a multitude of individuals in one species, as has been said, except in the case of the human soul because of the body to which it is united. And although its individuation depends on the body as the occasion for its beginning, since it does not acquire an individuated act of existing except in the body whose act it is, nevertheless individuation would not necessarily cease if the body were removed. For since the human soul possesses absolutely the act of existing, which is individuated in being received, and from which union the soul is made the form of this body, that act of existing always remains individuated. Accordingly, Avicenna says that the individuation and the multitude of souls depend on the body as to its source, but not on the body as to its end. Moreover, inasmuch as quiddity in these substances is not identical with the act of existing, they can therefore be assigned a category; and because of this, genus, species, and differences are found in them, although the differences proper to them are hidden to us. Even in sensible things essential differences themselves are unknown. They are, therefore, signified through accidental differences which arise from essential ones, just as a cause is signified by its effect; for example, *biped* is proposed as the difference of man. However, the proper accidents of immaterial substances are unknown to us; hence, their differences cannot be signified by us either through themselves or through accidental differences.

One must realize, however, that genus and difference cannot be taken in the same way in these substances and in sensible substances. In sensible substances, genus is taken from what is material in the thing, whereas difference is taken from what is formal in it. Hence Avicenna says in the beginning of his book *De Anima* that form in things composed of matter and form "is the simple difference of what is constituted from it." This is so not because the form itself is the difference, but rather because it is the principle of the difference, as he states in his *Metaphysics*. Such a difference is called the simple difference, inasmuch as it is taken from that which is a part of the quiddity of the thing—that is, from the form. Moreover, since immaterial substances are simple quiddities, a difference in them cannot be taken from that which is a part of the quiddity, but from the whole quiddity. Therefore, in the beginning of the *De Anima*, Avicenna states that only species whose essence is composed of matter and form have a simple difference. Likewise among them the genus is taken from the whole essence, but in a different way. For one separated substance agrees with the others in immateriality; they differ from each other in grade of perfection according to their withdrawal from potency or approach to pure act. And, therefore, a genus among them is taken from what follows upon them inasmuch as they are immaterial, like intellectuality or something of that sort. Their difference, unknown to us, is taken from that which follows in them the grade of perfection.

These differences need not be accidental, because they are according to a greater and a lesser perfection, which do not diversify a species. For a grade of perfection in the reception of the same form does not diversify a species, like being more white or less white in participating in a whiteness of the same nature. A diverse grade of perfection in the participated forms or natures themselves does diversify a species, just as nature advances through grades from

plants to animals by way of certain things which are midway between animals and plants, according to the Philosopher in his eighth book of the *De Animalibus*.

The division of intellectual substances, moreover, need not always be through two genuine differences, because this cannot happen in all things, as the Philosopher says in the eleventh book of the *De Animalibus*.

The third way in which an essence is found is in substances composed of matter and form, wherein also the act of existing is received and limited inasmuch as they have it from another, and their nature or quiddity is received in designated matter. Therefore, they are limited from above and from below. Moreover, multiplication of individuals in one species is possible among them because of the division through designated matter. And how essence in these is related to logical intentions has been explained above.

CHAPTER 6

Having declared how essence is found in all substances, it now remains for us to see how essence is in accidents. As has been said, because essence is what is signified through a definition, accidents must have an essence in the same way that they have a definition. However, they have an incomplete definition, for they cannot be defined except by positing the subject in their definition. This is so because they do not, of themselves, have the act of existing independently of the subject, but, just as a substantial act of existing follows upon a composition of matter and form, so an accidental act of existing follows upon addition of an accident to a subject. Therefore, neither the substantial form itself, nor matter, has a complete essence because in the definition of substantial form one must include that of which it is the form. Thus, its definition is through the addition of something extrinsic to its class, as is the definition of an accidental form. In the definition of the soul, therefore, the natural philosopher, who considers the soul only insofar as it is the form of the physical body, includes body.

There is, however, this difference between substantial and accidental forms: just as a substantial form does not have through itself an absolute act of existing without that to which it is added, so neither does that to which it is added, namely, matter. Therefore, from their union arises that act of existing in which the thing subsists through itself, and from them is produced something that is one through itself. Hence, a certain essence results from their union. Thus, although form, when considered in itself, does not have the complete nature *essence*, nevertheless, it is part of a complete essence. On the other hand, that to which an accident is added is a being complete in itself, subsisting in its own act of existing, which act naturally precedes the added accident. Therefore, an added accident, from its union with that to which it is added, does not cause the act of existing in which the thing subsists and through which the thing is a being through itself; but it does cause a certain second existence, without which the subsisting thing can be understood to exist, as "first" can be understood without "second." Hence, from the union of accident and subject there is not produced something that is one through itself, but something that is accidentally one. And so from their union no distinctive essence results, as results from the union of form and matter. Because of this, an accident neither has the character of a complete essence, nor is part of a complete essence; rather, just as it is a being in a qualified sense, so it has an essence in a qualified sense.

Now what is said maximally and most truly in any genus is the cause of those which are posterior in that genus; for example, fire, which is at the extreme of heat, is the cause of heat in hot things, as is stated in the second book of the *Metaphysics*. Accordingly, substance, which is first in the genus *being*, having essence in the truest and fullest sense, must be the cause of accidents, which participate secondarily and in a qualified way in the character of being.

This happens in diverse ways, however. Inasmuch as the parts of a substance are matter and form, certain accidents follow principally upon the form; others, upon the matter. Moreover, there is some form whose act of existing does not depend upon matter, as the intellective soul. Matter, however, has the act of existing only through form. Hence, among the accidents which follow upon form, there is something that does not have any communication with matter, namely, understanding, which does not occur through a corporeal organ, as the Philosopher proves in the third book of the *De Anima*. Indeed, others

among those accidents following upon the form do have a communication with matter, as hearing and the like. No accident, however, follows upon the matter without a communication of the form.

There is, moreover, a certain diversity among those accidents which follow upon matter. Certain of them follow upon matter according to an order which they have to a special form; for example, in animals, male and female, whose diversity is reduced to matter, as is stated in the tenth book of the *Metaphysics*. Accordingly, if the animal form is removed, the aforesaid accidents do not remain, except in an equivocal sense. There are others which follow upon matter according to an order which they have to a general form. Hence, if the special form is removed, they nevertheless remain in it, like the blackness of an African's skin, which depends upon a mixture of the elements and not upon the soul. It, therefore, remains in it after death. And because each thing is individuated by matter but is located in a genus or species by its form, accidents which follow upon matter, therefore, are accidents of the individual, according to which individuals of the same species differ from each other. Accidents which follow the form, however, are proper attributes of the genus or species; hence, they are found in all participants in the nature of the genus or species. For example, risibility follows the form in man, since laughter arises from a certain knowledge in a man's soul.

One should understand likewise that accidents are caused sometimes by the essential principles according to a perfect act, like the heat in fire, which is always actually hot. Sometimes they are caused according to an aptitude only, with completion occurring by the action of an exterior agent; for example, lucency in the air, which is completed by a bright external body. Among these, the aptitude is an inseparable accident, whereas the complement, which comes from some principle which is outside the essence of the thing, or which does not enter into the constitution of the thing, will be separable, as being moved and the like.

It should be known, therefore, that in accidents, genus, species, and difference are understood differently from the way they are understood in substances. For in substances, something that is one through itself is brought about from substantial form and matter, with one certain nature resulting from their union, which properly is placed in the predicament *substance*. Therefore, in substances, concrete names which signify the composite are properly said to be in the genus, as a species or genus; for example, *man* or *animal*. However, neither the form nor the matter is in the predicament in this way except by reduction, as a principle is said to be in a genus. But something that is one through itself does not come about from the union of accident and subject. Hence, from their union there does not result any nature to which the intention *genus* or *species* can be attributed. Accordingly, accidental names said concretely, like *white* and *musical*, are not placed in a category, as species or genus are, except by reduction. They are placed in a category only according as they are signified abstractly, like *whiteness* or *music*.

In addition, because accidents are not composed of matter and form, genus in them cannot be taken from matter, nor difference from form, as in composite substances. Their first genus must be taken from the very mode of existing, according as *being* is said diversely, with certain priorities and posteriorities, of the ten genera of predicaments. Accordingly, quantity is called being inasmuch as it is the measure of a substance; quality, insofar as it is a disposition of a substance; and so on for the others, as the Philosopher says in the fourth book of the *Metaphysics*. On the other hand, differences in accidents are taken from the diversity of the principles by which they are caused. So, because proper attributes are caused by the proper principles of the subject, the subject, therefore, is included in their definition in place of a difference. This is true if they are defined in any absolute way, according as they are properly in a genus; for example, it is said that snubness is curvature of the nose. But the converse is true, if their definition is taken according as they are said concretely. Then a subject is placed in their definition as a genus, since then they would be defined after the manner of composite substances wherein the character genus is taken from matter. Accordingly, we say that a snub nose is a curved nose. The same is true if one accident is the principle of another accident, as action, passion, and quantity are the principles of relation. Therefore, in the fifth book of his *Metaphysics*, the Philosopher divides relation according to this. But because the proper principles of accidents are not always evident, we sometimes take the differences of accidents from their effects; for example, *contractive* and *expansive* are called differences of color, and are caused by the abundance or scarcity of light which produce diverse species of color.

It is evident, therefore, how essence is found in substances and in accidents, in composite substances and in simple substances, and how universal intentions of logic are found in all these. An exception was made, however, of the first principle, which is the ultimate in simplicity, and to which, because of its simplicity, the character *genus*, *species*, and consequently *definition*, does not belong. This brings us to the end and consummation of this discourse.

STUDY QUESTIONS: AQUINAS, *ON BEING AND ESSENCE*

1. What are the two different senses of the term "being?"
2. What does *quiddity* mean?
3. What are *forms*, in Aquinas' view?
4. Why does the definition of natural substances contain both form and matter?
5. What is the essential difference between truths in mathematics versus truths in physics?
6. What does Aquinas mean by *designated matter*?
7. How is the term *essence* related to the notions of *genus*, *species*, and *difference*?
8. How can we discover essence in separated substances (such as the soul, the intelligences, and the First Cause)?
9. When Avicenna says, "the quiddity of simple substances is the simple substance itself," what, according to Aquinas, does he mean?
10. What is the First Cause?
11. Why can essences be found in substances and in accidents but not in the first principle?

Philosophical Bridges: The Influence of Aquinas

Aquinas' influence on both philosophy and theology, especially within the Christian tradition, has been immense, deep, and profound. If Augustine was primarily a Platonist, and worked within the confines of the Platonic wisdom, Aquinas was without doubt primarily an Aristotelian, and worked within the confines of the Aristotelian wisdom.

From a socio-political point of view and given the extreme religious constraints of the time, by "purging" the works of those great ancient Greek thinkers of what were perceived by church leaders of the time of their "Islamic" elements (given that the texts were returned to Europe after the Islamic interpreters had had their way with them), Aquinas made philosophy not only acceptable but respectable to church leaders. As a result, room was made for the autonomous pursuit of philosophy within theology and beyond.

On a less abstract and more personal level, Aquinas made possible the subsequent development of human individuality and personality as a true causal force in the universe, which—with its emphasis on the primordial importance of the act of existing (*esse*)—influenced virtually all humanistic thinkers thereafter, even the existentialists up into the twentieth century, most notably Jacques Maritain (1882–1973). The idea that the power of human reason plays a central role in the pursuit of wisdom, and that the purpose of philosophy "is not to find out what men have thought, but what the truth of the matter is," liberated non-Scholastic scholarship by making all such "research" distinctly forward-looking. Aquinas' balance of faith with reason is not only accommodating to both and subtle, but it also inspired many subsequent thinkers to see that faith can and should in some way be liberating to reason. Christian humanism was the direct result.

BIBLIOGRAPHY

PRIMARY

A *Commentary on Aristotle's De Anima*, translated by R. Pasnau, Yale University Press, 1999

Aristotle on Interpretation: Commentary by St. Thomas and Cajetan (Peri Hermeneias), translated by J. T. Marquette University Press, 1962

Commentary on Aristotle's De Anima, Dumb Ox Books, 1994

Commentary on Aristotle's Metaphysics. Translated by J. P. Rowen, Dumb Ox Books, 1995

Commentary on Aristotle's Nicomachean Ethics, translated by C. I. Litzinger, Dumb Ox Books, 1993

Commentary on Aristotle's Physics, translated by R. J. Blackwell, Yale University Press, 1963

Commentary on the Posterior Analytics of Aristotle. Translated by F. R. Larcher, Magi Books, 1970

Disputed questions on virtue: Quaestio disputata de virtutibus in commune and Quaestio disputata de virtutibus cardinalibus, translated by R. McInerny, St. Augustine's Press, 1998

On the Power of God, translated by the Fathers of the English Dominican Providence, 3 vols, Burns, Oates & Washbourne, 1932–1934

On Truth, translated by R. W. Mulligan, J.V. McGlynn, and R. W. Schmidt, 3 vols., Henry Regnery Publishers, 1952–1954

Questions on the Soul, translated by J. H. Robb, Marquette University Press, 1984

Quodlibet Questions 1 and 2, translated by S. Edwards. Pontifical Institute of Medieval Studies, 1983

Selected Writings, translated by R. McInerny, Penguin, 1998

Summa Contra Gentiles, translated by A. C. Pegis, J. F. Anderson, V. J. Bourke, C. J. O'Neil, 5 vols., University of Notre Dame Press, 1975

Summa Theologiae, edited by T. Gilby and T. C. O'Brien, 60 vols., Blackfriars, 1964–1973

The Summa Theologica of St. Thomas Aquinas, translated by the Fathers of the English Dominican Providence, 3 vols, Benziger Brothers, 1948

SECONDARY

Boyle, L. E., *The Setting of the Summa Theologiae of Saint Thomas*, Pontifical Institute of Medieval Studies, 1982

Copleston, F. C., *Aquinas*, Penguin Books, 1955

Davies, B., *The Thought of Thomas Aquinas*, Clarendon Press, 1992

Inglis, J., *On Aquinas*, Wadsworth, 2002

Kenny, A., *Five Ways: St. Thomas Aquinas' Proofs of God's Existence*, Routledge & Kegan Paul, 1969

Kretzman, N. and Stump, E., eds., *The Cambridge Companion to Aquinas*, Cambridge University Press, 1993

Mackie, J. L., *The Miracle of Theism*, Oxford University Press, 1982.

Pegis, A., *Introduction to Saint Thomas Aquinas*, Modern Library, 1948

SECTION VI

THIRTEENTH CENTURY AND LATE MEDIEVAL PHILOSOPHERS

PROLOGUE

The second thousand years of philosophy, from Plato-inspired Augustine to Aristotle-inspired Aquinas, resulted in what is generally classified under the rubric of "Scholastic" philosophy. If ancient philosophy can be characterized as philosophical systems built by individuals (Pythagoras, Socrates, Plato, Aristotle), the great metaphysical systems that had been developed during the early and middle part of medieval times was by and large the corporate product of vast social networks each organized under a different religious order. The guiding light was tradition, revealed religion, and respect for authority. As a result, philosophical work was done under the auspices of theology, which set the standards and problems. In the thirteenth and fourteenth centuries, however, this so-called *via antiqua*—the ancient way—gradually gave way to what would be called *via moderna*—the modern way—led in large part by philosophers such as Roger Bacon, Bonaventure, John Duns Scotus, William of Ockham, Nicholas of Cusa, and Giordano Bruno, heralding the advent of modern thought and philosophy's return to the work of individuals.

ROGER BACON (APPROX. 1220–1292)

Biographical History

Roger Bacon was born to a wealthy aristocratic family in England; the place of his birth is unknown, though probably it was Ilchester in Somerset. His early education was the quadrivium, which then consisted of geometry, arithmetic, music, and astronomy; his favorite ancient figure, he said, was Aristotle, whose works he read at a young age (though which works we don't know). He spent much of his fortune buying all sorts of secret books and built laboratories where he experimented in all areas, though we have no records as to his actual research. He employed assistants and also savants, brilliant and eccentric (sometimes pathological) minds to help him in his quest to know everything. At the University of Paris he was well known for his stunning and detailed lectures on Aristotelian philosophy and science. This was all in his twenties; at around the age of 30 he returned to Oxford and met Robert Grosseteste (1168–1253), the world's greatest expert at the time on light and optics. Under Grosseteste's influence, Bacon branched out his studies to mathematics, optics, and astronomy.

Bacon was extremely critical of authority, which he saw as a way of oppressing people's native intelligence and propensity to discover for themselves what is true and actual. He wanted not only to achieve knowledge but to share it openly with everyone, and so he turned his energies to the writing of an encyclopedia that would contain all knowledge of all the sciences, including mathematics and philosophy. He organized the greatest minds and savants of the time to help him with the project, which the Church then ordered him not to publish. He appealed to Pope Clement IV, who agreed to see some of Bacon's writings; as a result, Bacon wrote his *Opus Majus*, *Opus Minus*, and *Opus Tertium* in an incredibly short time and sent them to Rome. But Clement died before he could finish reading it. Bacon was thrown into prison, where he continued to write until his death. Only parts of his massive encyclopedia were ever published, in three volumes, *Communia Naturalium*, the *Communia Mathematica*, and *Compendium Philosophiae*, on science, mathematics, and philosophy, respectively.

Philosophical Overview

The most significant aspect to Bacon's philosophy is his advocacy of the experimental method. At the time, the only experimentalists as such were astrologers and alchemists, the avatars of modern astronomy and chemistry. Many of their results and conclusions were erroneous, but the techniques they developed for the observation and codification of experience laid the foundation for the empirical methods of science that followed. Bacon, instead of disregarding their methods, sought to integrate them with a better eye toward the rational and conceptual analysis that philosophy and mathematics make available.

OPUS MAJUS
Roger Bacon

This work was a *persuasio*, a form of writing in which the author tries to persuade a religious authority, in this case the pope, of the merit of publishing some work, in this case the encyclopedia that would have made knowledge of science, mathematics, and philosophy available to the public. His *Opus Majus* includes instructions as to how to integrate experimental method with reason, and calls for educational reform in which students would be allowed not only to *question* authority but *test* the claims authorities make.

Bacon begins by outlining the major causes of error in our judgments concerning nature and ourselves. Wisdom is not just a rational or intellectual ability but something balanced by a keen eye for observation and experiment. He refers often to the secrets of

The Opus Majus of Roger Bacon, ed. by J. H. Bridges. London: Williams and Norgate, 1900, 3 vols

Roger Bacon, from *The Opus Majus*, translated by Richard McKeon in Richard McKeon, ed., *Selections from Medieval Philosophers*, Vol. 2, Charles Scribners Sons, 1929, pp. 7–110.

the sciences and the arts, because the techniques of experiment were widely regarded as the "dark arts," magic and demonology. His source is Aristotle, in whom he sees the perfect balance of reason and experience. Even what the scriptures say must be tested by reason and experience; to accept anything merely on faith, Bacon suggests, is itself contrary to the will of God and verges on sin. He argues that "the power of philosophy is not foreign to the wisdom of God." He urges Christians not to destroy the works of the philosophers but to learn from and study them.

The First Part of This Demonstration [1]

THE CAUSES OF ERROR

In which the four universal causes of all human ignorance are removed. There are four distinctions in this part, and in the first distinction there are four chapters. In the first chapter, after the intention of the whole demonstration has been stated, these four causes are criticized in general.

Chapter I

The perfect consideration of wisdom consists of two things, namely, in perceiving what is required for wisdom that it may be known best, and then, in perceiving how wisdom should be related to all things that they may be directed by it in proper ways. For by the light of wisdom (1) the Church of God is directed; (2) the commonwealth of the faithful is disposed; (3) the conversion of unbelievers is procured; and (4) by the excellence of wisdom those who are obstinate in evil can be curbed that they may be thrust far from the bounds of the Church more effectively than by the shedding of Christian blood. All matters, in fact, which need the guidance of wisdom are reduced to the above four, nor can wisdom be related to more. Wherefore, that this wisdom be known not only relatively but absolutely, I shall try here to present to Your Holiness, following the tenor of your recent letter, whatever I can at the present time in a probable demonstration, until a more certain and fuller writing is completed. But, since the subjects under consideration are weighty and uncommon, they demand for human frailty, grace, and favor. For according to the Philosopher in the seventh book of the *Metaphysics*,

those things which are of greatest understanding in themselves are of least apprehension to us. Indeed, enveloped truth is concealed in the depths and deposited in the abyss, as Seneca says in the seventh book on *Favors* and in the fourth of Natural questions; and Cicero says in the Hortensius that all our understanding is obstructed by many difficulties, since our understanding is related to what is most manifest in its own nature, as the eye of the owl and the eye of the bat are to the light of the sun (as the Philosopher says in the second book of the *Metaphysics*[2]) and as one deaf from birth is related to harmonic delights, as Avicenna says in the ninth book of the *Metaphysics*. Wherefore we are sufficiently impressed with the weakness of our own intellect in the investigation of truth, to want to remove, as much as possible, extraneous causes and occasions of error from the imperfection of our perception.

There are, indeed, four chief hindrances to the understanding of truth, which stand in the way of every man, however wise, and permit hardly any to arrive at the true title of wisdom; to wit, (1) the example of frail and unsuited authority, (2) the long duration of custom, (3) the opinion of the unlearned crowd, and (4) the concealment of one's own ignorance in the display of apparent wisdom. Every man is involved in these difficulties, every condition of man is held by them. For everyone in all the acts of life and study and every occupation uses three of the worst arguments to the same conclusion; namely, (1) this has been exemplified by our ancestors, (2) this is the custom, (3) this is the common belief: therefore, it must be held. But the opposite to the conclusion follows far better from the premises, as I shall prove in many instances by authority and experience and reason. But if these three arguments are

---

[1]Vol. I, pp. 1–8, and vol. III, pp. 1–8
[2]Aristotle, *Met.* II, 1, 993^b9–11.

sometimes refuted by the splendid power of reason, the fourth is always before the eyes or on the lips of every one to excuse his own ignorance; and although he knows nothing worth knowing, nevertheless what he knows he magnifies shamelessly so that he overwhelms and shatters the truth in the consolation of his unhappy stupidity. Moreover, all the evils of the human race come from these deadly plagues; for the most useful and the greatest and most beautiful instances of wisdom and the secrets of all the sciences and arts are ignored; but what is even worse, men blinded by the mist of these four arguments do not perceive their own ignorance, but cover and conceal it with all caution so that they find no remedy for it; and finally, what is worst of all, they think they are in the full light of truth when they are in the densest shadows of error; because of this they hold the most true to be in the bounds of falsity, the best to be of no value, the greatest to possess neither weight nor worth; and on the contrary they honor the most false praise the worst, extol the most vile, blind to the truth that all the brightness of wisdom is other than these, disdainful of what they can attain with great ease; and because of the greatness of their stupidity they spend most considerable labors, consume much time, pour out vast expenditures on things which are of no, utility or little and of no merit in the judgment of the wise man. Hence it is necessary that the violence and harm of these four causes of all evils be known in the beginning and be condemned and put off far from the consideration of wisdom. For where the first three of these causes dominate, no reason moves; no right judges; no law binds; the injunctions of religion have no place; the dictates of nature perish; the face of things is changed; order is confounded; vice prevails; virtue is extinguished; falsity reigns; truth is puffed away. And, therefore, nothing is more necessary to this consideration than the sure condemnation of these four causes of error by chosen arguments of wise men which shall not possibly be contradicted.

Since moreover the wise bring the first three together and condemn them at the same time and since the fourth requires a separate investigation because of its special stupidity, therefore, I shall try

first to disclose the harm of the three. But although authority is one of them, I speak in no wise of the solid and true authority which is bestowed by the judgment of God on the Church or which arises from the merit and dignity of some one among the saints and perfect philosophers and other wise men who are expert to the full measure of human possibility in the cultivation of wisdom; but I speak of that authority which many men seize upon violently in this world without the help of God, not from the merit of their wisdom, but because of their own presumption and their desire for fame; and I speak of the authority which the unlearned multitude grants (to its own destruction in the just judgment of God) to many. For according to the Scripture the hypocrite often rules because of the sins of the people; I speak, in fact, of those Sophistical authorities of the insensate multitude which are authorities in an equivocal sense, as a stone eye or a painted eye has the name of eye but not its power.

Chapter II

The sacred Scripture, moreover, reproves these three causes of error; the holy doctors condemn them; canon law forbids them; philosophy reprehends them. But for reasons touched upon before with reference to philosophic treatments and because the opinions of philosophers concerning these three are very little known, I shall treat principally of the philosophic opinions, Seneca, of course, in the second book of his *Letters* (near the end) condemns all three of these banes in a single phrase. He says, "among the causes of our ills is that we live according to model; we are not regulated by reason but are carried along by custom; that which we would not care to imitate if few were to do it, we do when many begin to do it rather because it is more frequent than because it is more honorable: and error holds the place of right among us when it has been made general."[1] The Philosopher moreover, attacking throughout his philosophy unworthy authority, asserts in the second book of the Metaphysics that the principal causes of human error are custom and the influence of the masses.[2] And again Seneca in the book on the *Happy Life* says, "no man errs for himself alone, but he is the cause and

---

[1] *Seneca lib, XX, Ep. S, ed. Haase.*

[2] *Meta, II, 3, 995a 3-6.*

author of another's error, and error transmitted from one to another turns us aside and throws us down and we perish by the examples of other men."[1] And in the second book on *Anger*, "because of the evil of custom, he says, vices which have grown with us are removed with difficulty."[2] And in the book on the *Happiness of Life* he contends against the opinion of the crowd,

> Nothing implicates us in greater evils than that we adapt ourselves to rumor and think those things best which have been received with great approval; nor do we live according to reason but according to likeness and precedent. Thence is that great heaping together of men rushing upon other men. For this befalls man in a great massacre, since people so press upon one another that no one falls without drawing another with him, and the first are the cause of destruction to those who follow. You may see this happen in every life.

And again he says in the same book, "the people, defenders of their own evil, stand against reason"; and further on, "human affairs are not so well ordered that the better pleases most"; and then follows, "the crowd is the worst argument."[3] And Cicero in the third of the Tusculan questions says, "when we have been handed over to school masters, we are so filled with a variety of errors, that truth yields to vanity, and nature itself yields to established opinion."[4] And he says in the *Lucullus*, "some, having accommodated themselves to a friend or having been captivated by only the speech of some one whom they have heard, judge of unknown things and into whatever art or discipline they are borne as by a tempest, they hold fast to that judgment as to a rock; most would rather err and defend the opinion which they had liked, than investigate without obstinacy what they say most

surely."[5] And because of the depravity of custom he asks in the first book on *Divine Nature*, "does it not shame him who speculates on nature, to seek from minds steeped in custom the testimony of truth?"[6] And against the opinion of the mob, he says in the introduction to the second book of *Disputations*, "philosophy is content with are judges, fleeing the multitude deliberately, and suspected and detested by it,"[7] and in the same second book he says, "all things which are done without publicity seem to me the more praiseworthy"[8] But other authors take up these three errors separately. For in the book of *Natural Questions* of Adalardus [Adelard of Bath], the question is raised concerning frail authority; "what else is authority of this sort than a halter? For surely as brute animals are led by any halter, and see neither whither nor why they are led, so this very authority leads not a few into danger, taken and bound in bestial credulity." And in the book on the *Eternity of the World* it is said, "he who has chosen one side of a question because of love of custom can not rightly distinguish true opinion." And Averroës at the end of the second book of the *Physics* says,

> Custom is the greatest cause in keeping us from many manifest things. Just as certain actions, although they are harmful, will he easy to the man accustomed to them and as, for that reason, he believes that they are useful, so when one has been accustomed to believe certain false statements from boyhood, that custom will be the cause of denying the truth, as some people have been so accustomed to eating poison that it has become a food for them.

And Averroës likewise holds in the second book of the *Metaphysics*, "when the opposites to principles have become well-known, they are more readily

---

[1] Seneca, *Dialog*, VII, 1.

[2] Seneca, *Dial*. IV, 18.

[3] Seneca, *Dial*. VII, 1 and 2.

[4] Cicero, *Tus. Disput*. III, 1, 2.

[5] Cicero, *Aeadom. Prior*. II, 3.

[6] *Do Deorum Natura*. I, 30.

[7] *Tusc. Disp*. II, 1, 4.

[8] *Ibid*. II, 26, 64.

received by the multitude and by those following the testimony of the many than the principles themselves." And Jerome in the Prologue to the fifth book on Jeremiah asserts that truth is content with few, and it is not terrified by a multitude, of enemies. John Chrysostom says likewise in his commentary on Matthew, that they have professed themselves stripped of truth who have armed themselves with multitude.

Chapter III

Whatever has been proved by authorities is determined even more certainly from the experience of any man. For we find in ourselves and in others that these three practices, embracing evils as they do in most instances, adhere very frequently to what is false. But, if occasionally they are found in connection with good and true things, they are almost always imperfect, and they contain but a weak degree of wisdom. As normally the daughter follows the deeds of the mother, the son those of the father, the slave those of the master, the subject those of the king, the subordinate those of the prelate, the disciple those of the master. Because it is customary for the sons of Adam to claim authority and to scatter their examples in the light. For all men, according to Aristotle in the fourth book of the *Ethics*, love their own deeds, as parents love their children, poets their measures, and so with the others. And for this reason many have used too much freedom in writing, and have not hesitated even to insinuate to depraved and bestial men the thought, why do you not fill up pages of paper? And why do you not write on the back of the sheet? These men are like a lame and purblind shepherd with many sheep which they are neither able nor know how to recall from wandering in the byways of falsity to the healthier pasturage of wisdom, and they are like birds who wish to fly without wings, presuming to the master's place before they are proficient in the grade of good disciple. They fall necessarily into so many errors that idlers comparing themselves to them [these bad workers] deem themselves happy, as, when many run a race, he whom hopelessness will not permit to run notwithstanding

that the prize seems precious to him, nevertheless counts himself happy in comparison to him who while racing falls into an unseen pit. And for that reason we see with enlightened faith that for one example of truth, in knowledge as in life, there are more than a thousand examples of falsity. The world indeed is full of examples of this sort, and one example of true perfection easily finds ten thousand imperfect. Nature, in fact, has formed for us in numbers the fitting illustration of perfection and imperfection. For a number is said to be perfect[1] the sum of whose divisors, added, equal the number itself, and there is only one such number beneath ten, namely six, and one between 10 and 100, namely 28, and one between 100 and 1000, namely 496, and one between 1,000 and 10,000, namely 8,128, and so on; and would that it were thus with men and that this was accorded to the human race! But this never was the case, neither in life nor in knowledge, nor will it ever be, even to the final destruction of sin, since not only is there the scarcity of those who are perfect in all virtue and knowledge, but of those who have arrived at the perfection of one virtue or knowledge. The first are and will be and have always been very rare. For they are the truly perfect, but of 10,000 men not one is found so perfect in either condition of life or profession of wisdom; would that there were of the second class of perfect men one in the first ten and so on, that the perfection of numbers might be preserved in men! But it is not thus, indeed it is found to be far otherwise. In the same way with respect to custom we prove by experience in our acts what has now been stated in examples of individuals. Let any one go over his life from his infancy, and he will find that in a great many of his acts he very easily transformed evils and falsenesses into custom. For in goods and in truths identity is mother of satiety for human frailty, and unfortunate man is delighted in the variety of useful things, according to the opinion of the authorities whom I brought forward in the beginning. But the contrary is true in the case of evils and falsenesses and things harmful to himself and others, for in most actions, except where special grace and divine privilege intervene in some perfect men, human corruption

---

[1]If $2^n - 1$ is a prime number, then $(2^n - 1)(2^n - 1)$ is a perfect number, as 6, 28, 496, 8,128, etc.

preserves carefully the things which are contrary to truth and salvation; nor is it affected with weariness in the continuance of sin, nor does it easily find loathing in things that are vain. But if one be devoted from youth to the truth of life and of knowledge, such an one retains imperfection in a great many of his actions and he is pleased in imperfection; perfection indeed saddens him more frequently, for it delights extremely few and most of all in the plenitude of virtues and science, and so it happens that youth seldom guards against error, and old age with the greatest difficulty ascends to perfection in any thing. Of the crowd moreover the judgment is the same. For the multitude of the human race has always erred in the truth of God, and only the small group of Christians has received it; and we know that the great mass of christians is imperfect, for the paucity of the saints shows that. Similarly in the case of philosophical doctrine, for the crowd has always lacked the wisdom of philosophy. The slight number of philosophers, in fact, declares that. And the ordinary run of those who philosophize has always remained imperfect. For of famous philosophers only Aristotle, together with his followers, has been called philosopher in the judgment of all wise men, since he ordered all the parts of philosophy so far as it was possible in his times, but still he did not come to the limit of wisdom, as will be made sufficiently manifest below. . . .

The Second Part of This Demonstration[1]

THE AFFINITY OF PHILOSOPHY WITH THEOLOGY

Chapter I

Having banished to infernal regions, then, the four general causes of all human ignorance and having removed them completely from this demonstration, I want in this second distinction to show that one wisdom is perfect and that it is contained in sacred letters; all truth has grown from the roots of this wisdom. I say, then, that either there is one science

the mistress of the others, namely theology (to which the rest are entirely necessary; and without the others it can not attain to its effect; their excellence it claims as its right; the rest of the sciences obey its nod and authority), or better, there is only one perfect wisdom which is contained wholly in the sacred Scriptures, to be explained by canon law and philosophy. Indeed, the exposition of the divine truth is had through these sciences. For, although it is spread out by sciences as if in the palm of the hand, yet of itself it brings all wisdom together in the grasp of the fist, for all wisdom was given by one God and to one world and for one end. Wherefore this wisdom divides unity by its triple comparison. The way of salvation is one, although there may be many steps; but wisdom is the way to salvation. Indeed, every consideration of man which is not of salvation is full of blindness and leads to the final gloom of hell; for which reason many wise men, famous in this world, have been damned, because they did not have the true wisdom but an apparent and false one, whence holding themselves wise they were made fools according to the Scripture. Augustine speaking of the sacred Scripture says in the second book on *Christian Doctrine,* "if there is truth elsewhere, it is found here; if there is evil, it is condemned here." And he wishes the Christian, wheresoever he may have found the truth, to understand it to be of his Lord, as was said in the beginning. The truth of Jesus Christ is the wisdom of the sacred Scriptures. Therefore, there is no truth elsewhere except the truth contained in that knowledge. Ambrose on the *Epistle to the Colossians* says, "all reason of celestial knowledge and of terrestrial creature is in him who is the head and author, so that he who knows him should seek nothing beyond, because he is perfect virtue and wisdom. Whatever is sought elsewhere, is found here perfectly." Since, therefore, the sacred Scriptures give us this wisdom, which is of Christ, it is manifest that all truth is included here. But if wisdom is so called elsewhere and if it is contrary to this, it will be erroneous, nor will it have anything save the name of wisdom; or if it is not said to be contrary, it is nevertheless diverse. But diversity, although it does not induce contrariety elsewhere,

---

[1]O. c., vol. I, pp. 33–44, and vol. III, pp. 36–53.

does here, as is evident from evangelical authority, "He who is not with me, is against me." So it is true of this wisdom that what is not bound to is, is proved to be against it, and therefore to be avoided by the Christian.

Chapter II

This moreover appears more clearly to one considering the division of the sciences. For if we attempt to separate the sciences one from the other we can not say that theology is not both the science of canon law and philosophy. For under one division of philosophy, namely moral science, which Aristotle called civil, is contained civil law, as will be noted below. Canon law, moreover, is named from the canonical Scriptures, not from others, as the name itself reveals. The books of the Old Testament are referred to as these canonical books, as is done many times in the ninth distinction of the first part of the *Decreta* and elsewhere. Or else canon law is called canonical, from that same word, namely canon; for *canon* in greek is translated by *regula* in latin, and canon law as well as divine law is acknowledged to transmit the mode of living according to rule. But canon law is founded wholly on the authority of Scripture and on its expositors, as is clearly evident throughout the whole body of the *Decretum* and the *Decretals*: for either the authorities of the expositors of sacred Scriptures, such as Augustine, Jerome, Gregory, Ambrose, Isidore, Cyprian, Hilary and others are cited in support of the ordinances of the canons, or the holy and supreme pontiffs bring forward authorities and examples of the New and Old Testaments in support of their decrees; and therefore this law is only the explication of the will of God in the Scriptures. Again, canon law is called ecclesiastical law, by which the church of God is ruled in spiritual matters, as well in its head as in its members. But Scripture gives utterance to nothing other than this guidance of the Church. Furthermore, the natural law is contained in the sacred Scripture, as is taught in the beginning of the *Decretum*; but whatever has been accepted in customs or comprehended in writings, if it should be contrary to natural law, must be held to be vain and invalid, as is stated in the first part, eighth section. Canon laws can not be different from divine law; indeed, they must be derived from the fountains of divine law; and common law is either divine or human. It is divine if it was proclaimed to the world by the understanding and spirit of God in his scripture; human if it was devised by the understanding of man. But it is clear that the church is ruled by the divine understanding and spirit and therefore by the divine law which is included in the sacred writings. and it is certain that the church is ruled by canon law. Wherefore this law is divine and must be drawn from the treasury of the sacred scriptures. And this is manifest to one considering the divisions of canon law. For it orders the degrees of ecclesiastical offices. or it determines the sacraments of God, or it discusses the questions of conscience, or it decides ecclesiastical cases. But the roots of all these matters and the upright trunk itself are to be found in the sacred Scriptures; the branches moreover are in the expositors of the Scriptures; but the leaves, flowers, and salvation-bringing fruit are to be found in the body of the canon. For the delightful embellishment of canonic discourse is likened to leaves according to the Scriptures, but the utility of flowers and fruit comprehends in its own metaphor the four above-stated parts. And therefore the canons are only the golden shoots of corn, and the sprigs, and the ripeness of grapes by virtue of their presentation of the Scripture. Since, therefore, things are so, canon law is contained in one body under the authority of the Scripture, as the body of a single tree is composed of roots and trunk, branches, flowers, and fruits.

Chapter III

It must be shown, however, both in general and in particular that the power of philosophy is not foreign to the wisdom of God, but is included in it. After this has been shown by authorities and examples and common reasons, it will then be explained more fully by taking up the four or five parts of philosophy within the range of each of the sciences and arts. For if Christians ought to seize from the philosophers as from unlawful possessors the useful things which are contained in their books, as I showed in the beginning by the opinion of Augustine, it is obvious that philosophy is wholly worthy of and proper to sacred truth. Augustine says again . . . that the philosophers did not themselves originate the gold and silver of philosophers, but that it was drawn, as it were, from certain metals of divine providence which are spread out everywhere; which he shows to have been prefigured, saying,

> As the egyptians had vessels and ornaments of gold and silver and clothing which that people departing from Egypt appropriated to itself as to a better use, so the doctrines of the gentiles contain liberal disciplines better suited to the use of truth and contain more useful moral precepts; and some points are found in these philosophers concerning even the worship of God himself; which gold, as it were, and silver of theirs, the Christian should take from them for good use in preaching the gospel.

And he explains this in all things subject to human treatment, which are moral, or historical, or artificial, or natural, or logical and grammatical. For as regards *morals* he says, "the clothing likewise of those men (that is certain institutions of men), if accommodated to human society which we can not dispense with in this life, properly have to be converted to Christian use." He says of the *historical*,

> The history of the gentiles helps us greatly in the understanding of the sacred books. For many things are sought by us, and frequently, by means both of the Olympiads and the names of the consuls; and ignorance of the consulship under which our Lord suffered causes many to err in thinking that our Lord suffered in the forty-sixth year of his life, because it was said by the jews that the temple was built in that number of years and because it was symbolically representative of the Lord's body.

And this is manifest in almost innumerable places in the New and Old Testament. Moreover, of other human considerations, as well of the *arts* as of *nature* he says, "of the other arts, however, by which something is manufactured or remains after the operation, as for example, a house, bench, vessel, and other objects of this sort, or medicine, or agriculture, and navigation, or of those arts whose only effect is the action, as of jumping, running, wrestling:" knowledge of these must be used in judgment lest we be wholly ignorant, of what the scripture would teach when it uses some figures from these arts, and we may take the *natural sciences* broadly that medical matters may be

included under them and what belongs to agriculture. For these latter sciences are based on natural things and are two of the eight principal natural sciences, as will be explained below. But in general he says of all the natural sciences. "That man would indeed perform a worthy task for the sacred scripture who would bring together the characteristics of times and of places, of stones and other inanimate things, of plants and animals." And in regard to the *logical* sciences he says, in the first book, that discipline of disputation is most valuable for all kinds of questions which must be examined and solved in the sacred writings. And elsewhere in the same book he says that there is a difference in the case of logic from that of the other sciences. For certain things which are necessary and very important for theology can be found in these latter sciences, but I do not see, he says, whether this can be done in the case of logic, since it is to be found, like nerves, throughout the whole text of the Scriptures. And in the third book, on the order of discipline, he says that no one should approach the sacred science without knowledge of the power of logic. Almost all of the second, third, and fourth books exhort us concerning the application of *grammatical* sciences to sacred things. And Jerome in his commentary on the *Epistle to Titus*, speaking of the utility of grammatical science in respect to theology, which is beyond that of many other sciences, says, "the doctrine of the grammarians can benefit life provided it be applied to better uses," concerning which many and important things must be said in what follows. But of *mathematics*, Cassiodorus says in his book on that science,

> When we turn over these four sciences, geometry, arithmetic, astronomy, music, with a careful mind, they whet perception, they cleanse away the filth of ignorance, and they lead, God granting, to that speculative contemplation; the holy fathers rightly urge that these four be read, since by them the appetite is in large part withdrawn from carnal things, and they make us desire that which we can contemplate with heart alone, the understanding aiding.

But these things will be shown abundantly in their proper place. And if such is the case in these sciences, much more forcefully are the *metaphysical* sciences in accord with divine utterances. For metaphysics occupies the place of one part of theology for philosophers, and it is called by them, together with moral philosophy, the divine science and physical theology, as is clear from the first and eleventh books of the *Metaphysics* of Aristotle and from the ninth and tenth books of the *Metaphysics* of Avicenna. For metaphysics takes up many things concerning God and the angels and divine subjects of this sort, and thus it is clear that the sacred Scripture claims the power of all wisdom. But not only does Augustine teach the above doctrines but he brings to mind that many saints have done this when he asks, "do we not see with how much gold Cyprian, most delectable doctor and most blessed martyr, went enriched out of Egypt, and Lactantius and Victorinus, Optatus, Hilary (to say nothing of those still living) and innumerable greeks, as indeed Moses himself, the most faithful servant of God had done before, of whom it was written that he was learned in all the wisdom of the Egyptians?"

Chapter IV

Not only the blessed Augustine but also other saints assert the same thing, and they show likewise that it was expressed figuratively, and they testify that the saints acted accordingly. For I think that Jerome should be called to be our great spokesman in the present instance, for he says,

But do you ask the reason that we sometimes place in our works examples drawn from secular literature and pollute the purity of the Church with the filth of the pagans? You are easily answered. You would never ask this if Cicero did not possess you wholly; you would never ask it if you read the sacred Scriptures, or if you pondered the commentators on them, with the exception of Vulcatius. For who does not know that in Moses and in the books of the prophets certain things are taken over from the books of the gentiles, and that Solomon proposed some questions

to the philosophers of Tyre and answered some? Wherefore he admonishes us at the beginning of the Proverbs to understand the discourses of wisdom and the subtleties of words, parables and obscure speech, the sayings of wise men, and the enigmas which belong properly to dialecticians and philosophers. But even the Apostle Paul used a verse of the poet Epimenides when he wrote to Titus, *"Cretans are always liars, evil beasts, idle bellies."*[1] In another letter likewise he sets down the verse of Menander, *"evil companionships corrupt good morals."*[2] Moreover, disputing before the Athenians on the hill of Mars, he calls Aratus to witness, *"for we too are his offspring;"*[3] which is the close in Greek of an heroic verse. And lest that should be too little, the leader of the Christian army, and invincible orator advancing the cause for Christ, turns even a chance inscription artfully into an argument of the faith. He had, indeed, learned from the true David to wrench the sword from the hands of the foe and to cut off the head of the very haughty Goliath with his own sword. He had read moreover in Deuteronomy a precept given in the speech of the Lord, that the head of the woman captive must be shaved, the eyebrows, all the hair and nails of her body must be cut off, and thus must she be taken in marriage. Why then is it strange if I too wish to make secular wisdom, because of its charm of speech and beauty of words, an israelite, from a handmaiden and slave? And if I cut and shave off whatever there is dead in her of idolatry, pleasure, error, lusts, and if united to her most pure body I beget of her servants to the Lord of Sabaoth, my labor is profitable in the household of Christ. Julian Augustus vomited forth on his parthian expedition seven books against Christ; if I shall attempt to write against him, am I to think that you will forbid me to beat back the mad dog with the doctrines of the philosophers and of the stoics, that is to say, with the club of Hercules?

[1] *Epistle of Paul to Titus* 1:11.

[2] *I Corinthians* 15:33.

[3] *Acts 17:28.*

And he [Jerome] brings to the proof of this the prophets themselves and all the famous doctors from the beginning of the Church who by the doctrines of the philosophers have urged on the princes and unbelievers the faith of Christ and have strengthened the faith in many ways. And Bede, in his commentary on the book of Kings, says that it is proper for Christians to take over to divine science as their own whatever is useful in the liberal sciences. Otherwise Moses and Daniel would not have suffered themselves to be instructed in the wisdom and letters of the Egyptians and the Chaldeans. Again he says in his book on the building of the temple that Solomon with his servants symbolize Christ, and Hiram with his servants symbolize the philosophers and wise men of the gentiles, so that the temple of God, that is the Church, was constructed not only by the apostolic wisdom but by the wisdom of the philosophers. And the Scripture says, "the servants of Hiram were more skillful in hewing wood than the servants of Solomon." Because, as Bede says in reference to this, the gentiles, when they had been converted from error and transformed to the truth of the Gospels, knew the errors of the gentiles better, and the more, certainly they knew them, the more; skillfully they learned to refute and dislodge them. Paul knew the Gospel, which he had learned by revelation, better; but Dionysius was better able to refute the false dogmas of Athens, the arguments of which, as well as similar errors, he had known from boyhood; and therefore Solomon says, "For you know that there is no man in my people who knows how to hew wood like the sidonians." These and many statements of this sort the Venerable Bede recounts and many other writers too, but let these suffice now.

Chapter V

The causes can be given why the saints state thus the point which we seek, and why they declare that it was prefigured, and why they announce that it was seized upon in effect by the saints. First, because the truth, wheresoever it be found, is judged to be of Christ, according to the opinions and authorities of Augustine mentioned above. In the second place, although the truth of philosophy is said in one manner to belong to philosophers, nevertheless that they might have this [the philosophic] truth, the divine light first poured into their minds and illumined them with additional light. For it lighteth every man that cometh into this world, as the scripture says; with which opinions the philosophers themselves agree. For they maintain that there is an active and possible intellect. The human soul is called possible by them, because of itself it is in potentiality with respect to the sciences and virtues, and receives them from another source. That which flows into our minds, illuminating them to knowledge and virtue, is called the active intellect, because although the possible intellect may be called active from the act of understanding, still if the active intellect be taken as they take it, it is the intellect which flows upon and illumines the possible intellect to knowledge of truth that is called the active intellect. And thus the active intellect, according to the ancient philosophers, is not a part of the soul, but is an intellective substance other than and separated in essence from the possible intellect. And since this point is necessary to the demonstration of my proposition, which is that philosophy exists through the influence of divine illumination, I wish to prove it conclusively; particularly since a great error has taken possession of the general run of philosophers in this matter, and likewise of the great mass of theologians, since what a man is in philosophy, that he is proved to be in theology. Al Farabi in fact says in his book *On the Understanding and the Understood* that the active intellect, which Aristotle spoke of in his third treatise on the soul, is not matter, but is a separated substance. And Avicenna teaches the same doctrine in the fifth book on the *Soul* and the ninth of the *Metaphysics*. Likewise the Philosopher himself says that the active intellect is separate from the possible, and unmixed. Again he holds that the active intellect is incorruptible with respect to being and substance, since he says that it differs from the possible in the possession of incorruption; but the possible is incorruptible with respect to substance and corruptible with respect to being, because of its separation. Therefore the active intellect will be incorruptible with respect to being and substance; wherefore it will not be part of the soul, since then it would be corrupted in respect to its being in body, when it was separated from the body; and he says that it is related to the possible as the artisan to his material and as the light of the sun to colors. The artisan, however, is outside the material in which he works and is separated from it in essence; in the same way the light of the sun expelling shadows from colors and other things, is separated from them in essence and comes from without. He says also that the active intellect knows all things, and is always in actuality, which is true neither of the rational soul nor of the angel, but of God alone. Again if it were part of the soul, the soul would then know the same thing through something active [agens] and be ignorant of it through something possible because the active is in actuality what the possible is in potentiality, as Aristotle maintains. Again a thing should be denominated rather from its more worthy part; therefore, the soul should be spoken of rather as knowing by the active intellect than as ignoring by the possible intellect before discovery and learning. If it be said that the active intellect, although it is part of the soul, is still not the actuality and form of the body as the possible intellect is, and that, therefore, man has the functions of the possible and not of the active intellect, this is contrary to the definition of the soul, in which it is stated that the soul is the actuality of the physical body. For if one part of the soul only is actuality because it is the form of the body, then it is wrongly made to differ from the whole soul both absolutely and simply through the actuality of the body, and, therefore, that part which is the actuality of the body should then be excluded, as Aristotle himself (when, in the beginning of the second book, he states that some parts of the soul are not only the actuality of the whole body, but of its parts, such as the sensitive and vegetative parts of the soul) excludes the intellect which he says is not the actuality and perfection of a part of the body, because it is not attached to an organ like the other parts of the soul. Again, to state this more expressly, Aristotle says that the intellect is in the body as a sailor is in a ship, since it is not bound to any part any more than the sailor is bound to the ship, although it is the actuality and perfection of the whole. The sailor, however, is not the perfection of the ship but only the mover. Moreover, the soul would then be composed of a separated substance and of a conjunct substance; but this is impossible. For the Intelligence or angel and the soul differ in species as unible or not unible,

and therefore the soul is not composed of something which is the actuality of the body and of something which is not. For one species is not composed of something of another opposite species. Since, therefore, the opinion stated here is in agreement with truth, and since the text of the Philosopher indicates it clearly, and since his greatest expositors state it in this form, and since these words active and possible have been taken from the Philosopher, not from the saints, it is far better, in accordance with the opinion of the Philosopher, to speak of the active intellect as a substance separated from the soul in essence. No one learned in philosophy, to be sure, is doubtful that this is his opinion; and in this, all the wise and learned men of the past are in agreement. For I twice saw and heard, at convocations of the University of Paris, the venerable priest, Master William, bishop of Paris, of blessed memory, declare in the presence of all, that the active intellect can not be part of the soul; and Master Robert, bishop of Lincoln, and brother Adam of the Marsh and elders of this sort supported this same opinion. How possible objections to this may be refuted will be made clear in the principal work, when natural questions are taken up. But lest some caviller arise on the side, alleging the doctrine by which the mass is deceived, I reply that although the following words are attributed to Aristotle, "but since in every nature there is something which acts and something else which suffers, so it is in the soul,"[1] this has been translated falsely many times and even more often obscurely. For although it is said in the third book on the Heavens and the World that the circle and the orbicular figure fill space, the statement is false, as those expert in the natural and geometrical sciences know, as Averroës demonstrates in the same place. And the statement made in the third book of the Meteorologics that the rainbow of the moon occurs only twice in 50 years, is false too. For experience teaches that whenever the moon is full, and there is rain, and the moon is not covered with clouds, the rainbow appears. And so many other things have been translated falsely, the cause of which will appear in the third part of this work when the question of faults of translators will be taken up; but a great many more passages have been

---

[1] De. An. III. c. 5, 430a 10–15.

translated obscurely and unintelligibly, so that any one of them might contradict some other. And in this place both faults occur or at least the second one, which I shall prove by Aristotle himself. For he says in the second book of the *Physics*, that matter does not coexist with the other causes in any single thing [i.e. a thing which is the same in number]: therefore, in no nature are there at the same time active cause and matter; therefore, not in the soul. If, therefore, the badly translated text be held to the letter, then it is wholly false and contrary to Aristotle elsewhere, and so great an author does not contradict himself. And however that may be, his statement in the second book of the *Physics* is true and conceded by all; therefore his statement in the third book on the *Soul* is falsely translated or is in need of exposition. For he intends nothing other than that two things, to wit, agent and matter, are required in the soul and in the operation of the soul, as in all nature. That is, in every operation of nature two things are needed, namely, an efficient cause and matter, and this is true, but the agent is always different than matter and outside it as regards substance, although it operates in it. Moreover, we can relieve this passage in still another way. For Aristotle in the fourth book of the *Physics* says that there are eight modes of being in anything, one of which is as the mover is in the moved, because the moving principle or the agent is in the matter moved with respect to its power, although not with respect to substance. And thus the agent is in every nature in which it operates and so it is in the soul. And thus in no manner does it follow that the active intellect is part of the soul as the run of people imagines; and this opinion is completely in accordance with the faith and confirmed by the saints, for all theologians know that Augustine says in the *Soliloquies* and elsewhere that the rational soul is subject to God alone in illuminations and in all important influences. And, although the angels may purify our minds and illumine them and stir them in many ways, and although they may be to our souls as stars are to the corporeal eye, nevertheless Augustine ascribes to God the principal influence, just as the flow of light falling through the window is ascribed to the sun, and the

angel is compared to one opening a window, according to Augustine in his gloss on the psalm, *"give me understanding."*[1] And what is more he holds in many places that we know no truth except in the uncreated truth and in the eternal laws, and this must be understood to mean at least effectively and by influence, although Augustine not only maintains this but intimates something else in his words, for which reason some have believed that he is thinking here of greater things, as is commonly known. All these things are evidence that the active principle illuminating and influencing the possible intellect is a separated substance, that is, God himself. Since, therefore, God has illumined the souls of those men in perceiving the truths of philosophy, it is manifest that their labor is not unrelated to divine wisdom.

Chapter VI

The third cause by which the wisdom of philosophy is reduced to divine wisdom, is not only that God enlightened their minds to acquire a knowledge of wisdom, but that they had wisdom from him and he has revealed, presented, and given it to them. For all wisdom is from the Lord God, as the authority of the Scripture holds, because, as the apostle says, "that which is known of God is manifest in them, for God manifested it unto them."[2] And Augustine says in the commentary on John, that God is warrant to them for wisdom, and that the greatest philosopher, Aristotle, in the *Book of Secrets*, asserts that all philosophy was manifestly given and revealed by God; and one of the greatest of philosophers, namely Cicero, asks in the first book of the Tusculan questions, "what is philosophy except, as Plato says, a gift and, as I believe, a discovery of God?" Whence he says also that even the poet does not pour forth a grave and full song without some heavenly instinct of mind. And Augustine in the eighth book of the *City of God* teaches and approves of what Socrates, the father of great philosophers, affirmed, that man can not know the causes of things except in the divine light and by the divine gift; and any one can prove for himself that nothing which is of the power of philosophy is discovered by man first. And I set down a very minor example: that

---

[1]*Psalms* 119:34, 73, 125, 144, 169.

[2]*Romans* 1:19.

although Porphyry's universals are explained almost sufficiently by him and are expounded elsewhere sufficiently in logic, and metaphysics, and natural philosophy, and perspective, nevertheless there is not a man so well prepared that it is not essential that he have teachers of many sorts, and that he listen and study for a long time before he knows the whole truth about universals. And almost no one learns sufficiently about them before death howsoever many doctors he have, which is evident by the discord of all in this subject, since some hold that universals are only in the soul, others only outside, others that they are in things with respect to being, but that in their status as universal they are in the soul. Avicenna shows in his commentary on Porphyry that Porphyry lacked the sixth universal [i.e. a sixth predicable] and that he made many false statements. If, therefore, every man is ignorant of these things, even though he study throughout his whole life in the books of the philosophers, and though he have illustrious teachers, he will much the more be ignorant of them and never discover the truth about them for himself without books and teachers. Wherefore it is necessary that the truth of philosophers was revealed to man from the beginning. If, moreover anyone, knowing howsoever much concerning universals, had delivered the book of Porphyry to oblivion as well as all things that are necessary for knowing universals, and if he were not able to have either books or teachers, it would be impossible for him ever to explain the truth of universals. I speak of universals with respect to their true being, as a metaphysician must consider them, not merely with respect to the childish doctrine of Porphyry and the considerations of logic. Wherefore, anyone can judge for himself that revelation is necessary in this part; and since these are childish and very slight matters, it will be much more evident in the whole wisdom of philosophy. But what is from God and what was revealed, set forth, and given, must be wholly in conformity with his wisdom.

Chapter VII

For the rest, the whole aim of philosophy consists in this, that through the knowledge of his creature, the creator be known, who is served on account of the reverence due his majesty and the benefits of creation and conservation and future felicity, in honorific worship and in beauty of morals and in honor of useful laws, that men may live in peace and justice in this life. For speculative philosophy rises to the knowledge of the creator from his creatures, and moral philosophy sets up the honor of morals, just laws, and the cult of God, and is usefully and magnificently persuasive concerning the future felicity so far as that is possible to philosophy. These things are certain to any one who runs through all the principal parts of philosophy, as that which follows will show. Since, therefore, these are all absolutely necessary to Christians and are wholly consonant with the wisdom of God, it is manifest that philosophy is necessary to the divine law and to the faithful who glory in it.

Chapter VIII

Again, all the saints and all the ancient wise men in their expositions take a literal sense from the natures of things and from their properties, that they may bring forth spiritual senses by appropriate adaptations and likenesses. Augustine declares this in the second book on *Christian Doctrine*, adducing an example from the word of the Lord speaking to his apostles, "Be ye wise as serpents and harmless as doves."[1] For the Lord intended by this, that the apostles and the apostolic men, like the serpent exposing its whole body in defense of its head, give themselves and theirs for Christ, who is their head, and for his faith. And for this reason every creature is placed in the Scripture either in itself or in its like, either in universal or in particular, from the heights of the heavens to their very ends, for, as God made creatures and Scripture, so he wished to place in the Scripture the things themselves which he had made for the understanding of its literal as well as its spiritual sense. But the whole intention of philosophy is only to work out the natures and properties of things. Wherefore, the power of all philosophy is contained in the sacred writings; and this is especially apparent in that the Scripture deals with creatures far more surely and far better and more truly than philosophic labor is able to work out. This may be shown, out of infinite examples, for the present in the rainbow. The Philosopher,

---

[1]*Matthew* 10:16.

Aristotle, disturbs us with his obscurities, nor are we able to understand through him anything that is proper; nor is that surprising since Avicenna, his chief imitator, the prince and leader of philosophy after him, confesses (as the Commentator says in connection with Aristotle's chapter on the rainbow in the third book of the *Meteors*) that he does not understand the nature of the rainbow very well. The cause of this is that the philosophers did not know the final cause of the rainbow; and having ignored the end, they do not know the things which lead to the end, because the end imposes a necessity on those things which are ordered to the end, *as* Aristotle holds in the second book of the *Physics*. But the final cause of the rainbow is the dissipation of aqueous vapor, as is manifest in the book of Genesis, whence in the apparition of the rainbow there is always a resolution of clouds into an infinity of drops. And the aqueous vapors are consumed in the air and in the sea and in the land, for one part of the rainbow falls into the spheres of water and earth. Moreover, the consumption of the aqueous vapor can not be through the rainbow except as the rays of the sun accomplish it, for by various reflections and refractions an infinity of rays are congregated, and the congregation of rays is the cause of the resolution and consumption of the waters, and for that reason the rainbow is generated by multiple reflections. For the rays can not be congregated except by fraction and reflection, as will be shown later in its proper place. From the Scripture, then, when it is said in Genesis, I shall set my bow in the clouds of heaven, that there may no more be a deluge over the earth,[1] the final cause of the rainbow itself is given, from which can be investigated the efficient cause and the mode of generating the rainbow. This mode was not known sufficiently to philosophers, as their books make manifest to us. And so it is with every creature. In fact, it is impossible for man to know the ultimate truth of the creature as it is employed in the Scripture, unless he shall have been especially illuminated by God. For creatures are employed there to bring forth the truths of grace and of glory, concerning which philosophers were ignorant, and therefore they did not attain to the most exalted power of the wisdom of creatures, such as the sacred Scripture contains in its

bowels. Whence all the excellence of philosophy reposes in the literal sense ornamented with the sacred mysteries of grace and of glory, as if wreathed in a manner of paintings and of most noble colors. . . .

THE KNOWLEDGE OF LANGUAGES

takes up the study of grammar which is the first of the five divisions of philosophy. The study of grammar, not only of Latin but of the languages from which Latin is derived, is important for eight reasons which Bacon discusses in detail:

1. The quality of one language can never be reproduced perfectly in translation in another.
2. Latin lacks many of the necessary words for things described by foreign authors.
3. The translator must be perfectly acquainted not only with his subject but with the two languages with which he deals.
4. There are vast omissions, as well as confused and corrupt passages, in the texts now possessed.
5. Allusions to foreign languages in writings of antiquity are not otherwise, to be understood.
6. The Latin text of the Scriptures is extremely corrupt and is becoming more so.
7. When the text is correct there is often obscurity in its interpretation.
8. Confusion arises from the circumstances that Latin grammar is formed on the model of Greek and Hebrew grammar.

The Fourth Part
of This Demonstration[1]

THE UTILITY OF MATHEMATICS

In which the power of mathematics in the sciences and in things and in the occupations of this world is shown.

First Distinction

The utility of mathematics in the physical arts and sciences; having three chapters.

---

[1]*Genesis* 9:13–15.

[1]O. c., vol I, pp. 97–111, and vol. III, p. 129.

Chapter I

Now that it has been shown that many very famous roots, of wisdom are dependent on the power of languages; and that through them there is entry into the wisdom: of the Latins, I wish to examine the foundations of that same wisdom as found in the great sciences in which there is special power with respect to other sciences and the things of this world. There are four great sciences, without which the other sciences can not be known nor a knowledge of things be had: if they are known, any one can advance in power of wisdom gloriously, without difficulty and labor, not only in human sciences but in divine. And the virtue of each one of them will be touched on, not only because of wisdom absolutely, but in respect to the other sciences mentioned above. The door and key of these sciences is mathematics, which the saints discovered at the beginning of the world as I shall show, and which has always been in the use of all the saints and wise men before all the other sciences. The neglect of it now for 30 or 40 years has wiped out all learning among the Latins. Since he who ignores it can not know the other sciences nor the things of this world, as I shall prove. And what is worse, men who are ignorant of it do not perceive their own ignorance, and, therefore, seek no remedy for it. And on the contrary, knowledge of this science prepares the mind and elevates it to a certified knowledge of all things, so that if one learns the roots of wisdom given in relation to it, and if one applies those roots rightly to the notions of the other sciences and of things, then one will be able to know all things which follow without error and without doubt and easily and powerfully. Without these roots of wisdom, on the other hand, neither the precedents nor the consequences can be known; whence they perfect and regulate things prior, as the end perfects and regulates the things which are related to the end, and they dispose and open the way to things that follow. To this I plan now to refer by authority and reason; and first in respect to human sciences and the things of this world, then in respect to divine science, and finally as they are related to the Church and the other three sciences.

Chapter II

In which it is proved by authority that every science requires mathematics.

As regards authority I proceed thus. Boethius says in the second prologue to the *Arithmetic* that, "if the inquirer lacks the four parts of mathematics. he can in no wise discover truth." And again, "without this speculation of truth no one is rightly trained." And even more he says, "who spurns these paths of wisdom, I declare to him he does not rightly philosophize." And once again, "it is known that whosoever has neglected these, has lost the doctrine of all wisdom." He likewise confirms this by the opinion of all men of importance, saying, "among all the men of early authority, who have flourished, with Pythagoras as leader, in the purer reason of the mind, it is held to be manifest that almost no one comes to the height of perfection in the disciplines of philosophy except only him to whom such nobility of knowledge is discovered by something like the quadrivium." And this is shown in particular by Ptolemy and by Boethius himself. Since, in fact, there are three essential modes of philosophy, as Aristotle says in the sixth book of the *Metaphysics*, mathematical, natural, and divine, the mathematical is of no little value for the understanding of the other two modes of knowledge, as Ptolemy teaches in the first chapter of the *Almagest* and which he himself shows there. And since the divine science is twofold, as is evident from the first book of the *Metaphysics*, namely, the first philosophy, which shows that God is, whose high properties it investigates, and civil science, which sets up the divine cult and expounds many things concerning God to the extent of the possibility of man, the same Ptolemy asserts and declares that mathematics is of great value to both of these. Whence Boethius at the end of the Arithmetic insists that mathematical means are to be found in civil affairs. He says, in fact, that

> the arithmetical mean is to be compared to a commonwealth which is ruled by a few, for this reason, that its greater proportion is in its lesser terms, and he says that the musical mean is a commonwealth of aristocrats, in that the greater proportionality is found in the greater terms. The geometrical mean is in a certain sense of the equalized democratic state: for its people are compounded in equal proportionality of all, whether in the lesser or in the greater terms. For there is among all a certain parity of mean conserving a proportional right of equality.

And Aristotle and his expositors teach in several places in morals that without proportional evaluations the commonwealth can not be ruled. But these means will be expounded when they are to be applied to the divine truths. Since, moreover, all the essential modes of philosophy, which make up more than forty sciences distinct one from the other, are reduced to these three: the authorities already cited are sufficient to be convincing of the worth of mathematics in respect to the essential modes of philosophy.

Further, the accidental modes of philosophy are grammar and logic. And that these sciences can not be known without mathematics is evident from Al Farabi in the book on the *Sciences*. For although grammar supplies to children that which pertains to speech and its properties in prose and meter and rhythm, none the less it does it childishly, and by the way of narration, not by causes nor by reasons. For it is the function of another science to give the causes for these things, namely, of that science which has to consider fully the nature of speech and that is music alone, of which the species and parts are many. For one deals with prose, and a second with meter, and a third is rhythmical, and a fourth is lyrical in singing. And there are more parts besides these. The prosaic part teaches the causes of all the elevations of speech in prose, with reference to differences of accents, and with reference to colons and commas and periods and others of this sort. The metrical part teaches all the reasons and causes of feet and meters. The rhythmical treats of every modulation and pleasing proportion of rhythms, because all these are certain kinds of song, although they are not as in the ordinary song. For *accentus* is spoken of as if *accantus*, derived from *accino, accinis*. Whence they pertain to music as Cassiodorus teaches in his *Music*, and Censorinus in his book on *Accent*, and so too with the other topics. Moreover, authors of music and books on that science testify to this. And Al Farabi agrees with them in the book on the *Division of the Sciences*. Therefore, grammar depends causally on music.

In the same way logic. For the end of logic is the composition of arguments which move the practical intellect to belief and to love of virtue and of future felicity, as has been shown before; and these are treated in the books of Aristotle on these arguments, as has been stated. But these arguments should have to do with the end of beauty, that the mind of man may be pulled to salubrious truths suddenly and without prevision, as is taught in those books. And Al Farabi teaches this most of all in relation to poetic argument, the words of which should be sublime and beautiful, and therefore with prose and metric and unusual rhythmic adornments, such as are suitable to the place and time and persons and material with which the demonstration is concerned. And thus Aristotle taught in his book on poetic argument [i.e. the *Poetics*] which the translator Hermann did not dare to turn into Latin because of the difficulty of the meters, which he did not understand, as he himself says in the prologue to the commentary of Averroës on that book. And, therefore, the end of logic depends on music. But the end is the most noble aspect in the thing, and it imposes necessity on whatever is related to the end, as Aristotle says in the second book of the *Physics*; nor do things which are ordered naturally to their end have their utility, except when they are related to their end, as is evident in each individual thing. And consequently the whole utility of logic arises from the relation of all logical arguments to arguments of this sort, and therefore since they depend on musical arguments, it is necessary that logic depend on the power of music. All these things are according to the opinion of Al Farabi in the book on the *Sciences*, and they are made clear similarly by Aristotle and Averroës in their books, although the Latins do not have the use of them. But the knowledge of logic depends on mathematics not only because of its end but because of its middle and heart, which is the book of the *Posterior* [*Analytics*], for that book teaches the art of demonstration. But the principles of demonstration can not be learned nor the conclusions nor the demonstration as a whole, nor can they be shown except in mathematical things, because there alone is demonstration true and forceful, as all know and as will be expounded later. Wherefore, it is necessary that logic depend on mathematics.

Likewise because of its beginning as well as because of its middle and its end. For the book of the *Categories* is the first book of logic according to Aristotle. But it is obvious that the category of quantity can not be known without mathematics. For only mathematics is constituted for the understanding of quantity. The categories of when and where, moreover, are related to quantity. For when pertains to time and where arises from place. The category of condition [*habitus*] can not be known without the category of where, as Averroës teaches in the fifth book of the *Metaphysics*. The greater part, moreover, of the category of quality contains affections and properties of quantities, because all things that are in the fourth class of quality are called qualities in quantities. And all the affections of these [quantities] which are due absolutely to them are the qualities from which the great part of geometry and arithmetic is constituted, such as right and curved and others which are due to line and triangulation and every other figuration, which are assigned to surface and body; and the prime and unfactorable in numbers, as Aristotle teaches in the fifth book of the *Metaphysics*, and other essential affections of numbers. Whatever, moreover, is worthy of consideration in the category of relation is the property of quantity, such as proportions and proportionalities, and geometrical, arithmetical, and musical means, and the kinds of greater and lesser inequality. Spiritual substances, moreover, are not known by philosophy except by means of corporeal substances and, most of all, supercelestial substances, according to what Aristotle teaches in the eleventh book of the *Metaphysics*. Inferior things are not known except through superior things, because the celestial substances are the causes of inferior substances. But the celestial substances are not known except through quantity, as is evident from astronomy. And thence all categories depend on a knowledge of quantity, concerning which mathematics treats, and therefore the whole excellence of logic depends on mathematics.

Chapter III

In which it is proved by reason that every science requires mathematics.

Moreover, what has been shown by authority concerning mathematics as a whole, can now be shown likewise by reason. And in the first place because the other sciences use mathematical examples; but examples are given to clarify the things of which the sciences treat; wherefore, if the examples are not understood, the things for the understanding of which they were adduced are not understood. Since, for example, alteration [i.e. change of quality] is not found without augmentation and diminution [i.e. change of quantity] in any natural phenomena whatsoever, and since augmentation and diminution are not found without alteration, Aristotle could not show by any natural example the difference between augmentation and alteration in their purity, because they always accompanied each other in some way; for which reason he gave the mathematical example of the quadrilateral which, when a gnomon is added, increases and is not altered. This example can not be understood before the twenty-second proposition of the sixth book of the *Elements*. For in that proposition of the sixth book, it is proved that the smaller quadrilateral is similar in every particular to the larger one. And therefore the smaller is not altered, although the larger is made of the lesser by the addition of the gnomon.

In the second place because the knowledge of mathematical things is, as it were, innate in us. For when Socrates questioned a little boy concerning geometry, as Cicero mentions in the first of the Tusculan questions, the boy replied as if he had learned geometry. And this is often found to be the case in many instances, which does not happen in other sciences, as will be more manifest in what follows. Wherefore, since this knowledge is as if innate, and as if preceding discovery and instruction, or at least requiring them less than other sciences, it will be first among the sciences and will precede the others, disposing us to them, since things which are innate or almost innate dispose to what are acquired.

In the third place because this science was found first of all the parts of philosophy. For at the beginning of the human race this was first found. Since it was known before the flood and then later by the sons of Adam and by Noah and his sons, as is evident from the prologue to the *Construction of the Astrolabe* according to Ptolemy and from Albumazar in the larger *Introduction to Astronomy*, and from the first book of *Antiquities*; and this is true as regards all the parts of mathematics, to wit, geometry, arithmetic, music, astronomy. That, however, would not have been the case except that this science is prior to the others and naturally precedes them. Wherefore, it is manifest that it should be known first that we may be advanced by it to all the later sciences.

In the fourth place because the natural way for us is from the easier to the more difficult. But this science is the easiest. This is manifest in that mathematics is not beyond the understanding of any one. In fact, the lay and the wholly illiterate know how to figure and compute and to sing, and these are mathematical operations. But one must begin first with things which are common to lay and learned; and not only is it most hurtful to the clergy, but absolutely disgraceful and abominable, that they are ignorant of what the laity knows profitably and beautifully. In the fifth place we see that the clergy, even the most unlettered, are able to understand things mathematical, even though they are not able to attain to the other sciences. Besides, a man can learn more about mathematics certainly and truly without error by listening once or twice than he can by listening ten times about other parts of philosophy, as is evident to one who tries. In the sixth place because the natural way for us is from the things which are proper to the state and ability of the child, for children begin by learning the things which are better known to us and to be acquired first. But mathematics is of this sort since children are taught first to sing, and in that same manner they can grasp the method of figuring and counting, and it would be far easier, and it would even be necessary, for them to know about numbers before singing; because in the proportions of numbers the whole rationality of number is explained in examples, as authors of music teach, as well in ecclesiastical music as in philosophical. But the rationality of numbers depends on figures, because linear numbers and superficial and corporeal and square and cubic and pentagonal and hexagonal and the others are known from lines and figures and angles. It has been found, indeed, that children learn mathematical truths better and more quickly, as is manifest in singing, and besides we know from experience that children learn and grasp mathematical truths better than the other parts of philosophy. For Aristotle says in the sixth book of the *Ethics* that youths can comprehend mathematical truths quickly, but not so with natural nor metaphysical nor moral truths. Wherefore the mind must be trained by this science before it is trained by the others.

In the seventh place when the things known to us and the things intelligible by nature are not the same, the natural way for us is from the things better known to as to those better known in nature or absolutely. And we know the things which are better known to us very easily, and we arrive with great difficulty at those which are better known in nature. And those known in nature are poorly and imperfectly known to us, because our understanding is disposed to things which are so manifest in nature as the eye of the bat to the light of the sun, as Aristotle maintains in the second book of the *Metaphysics*; among these particularly are God and the angels and the future life and heavenly things and creatures more noble than the others, because the more noble they are the less they are known to us. And these are called things known in nature and absolutely. Therefore, on the contrary when the same things are known to us and in nature, we advance a great deal in regard to things known in nature and in regard to all things which are there included, and we can attain to a perfect knowledge of them. But in mathematics only, as Averroës says in the first book of the *Physics* and in the seventh of the *Metaphysics* and in his commentary on the third book of the *Heavens and the World*, things known to us and in nature or absolutely are the same. Therefore, as we attain completely in mathematics to those things which are known to us, so we attain to those which are known in nature and absolutely. Wherefore, we can arrive absolutely at the innermost parts of that science. Since, therefore, we are not able to do this in the other sciences, it is manifest that mathematics is better known. Wherefore the beginning of our knowledge is from the acquisition of it.

Again in the eighth place because all doubt is made clear by that which is certain, and every error is wiped out by unshaken truth. But in mathematics we can come to the full truth without error and to a certitude of all points involved without doubt, since in mathematics demonstration must be made through proper and necessary cause. And demonstration makes truth to be known. And in the same way in mathematics a sensible example may be had for all things, and a sensible test in figuring and counting, so that all may be made clear to the sense; because of this there can be no doubt in mathematics. But in the other sciences, once the aid of mathematics has been excluded there are so many doubts, so many opinions, so many errors on the part of man, that the sciences can not be developed, as is manifest, since the demonstration by a proper and necessary cause does not exist in them by their own power, because there is no necessity in natural things because of generation and corruption of proper causes as also of effects. In metaphysics a demonstration can not be made except by effect [i.e. *a posteriori*], because spiritual things are discovered by corporeal effects and the creator by his creature, as is made evident in that science. In morals, demonstrations can not be from proper causes, as Aristotle teaches. And in the same way there can not be very cogent demonstrations in logical and grammatical subjects, as is plain, because of the weakness of the matter of which these sciences treat. And therefore, in mathematics alone are there most cogent demonstrations by a necessary cause. And, therefore, there alone can man come to truth by the power of that science. Similarly in the other sciences there are doubts and opinions and contrarieties on our part, so that there is hardly agreement in even one most insignificant question or in a single sophism; for the experiments of figurations and numerations are not in these sciences from their own nature, by which all must be certified. And, therefore, in mathematics alone is there certitude without doubt.

Wherefore, it is evident that if we ought to come to certitude without doubt and to truth without error in the other sciences, it is necessary that we place the foundations of knowledge in mathematics, in so far as, disposed by it, we can attain to certitude in other sciences and to truth by the exclusion of error. And this reason can be made clearer by comparison, and the principal proposition, in fact, is in the ninth book of *Euclid*. Just as, indeed, the knowledge of the conclusion is so related to the knowledge of the premises that if there be error and doubt in the premises, truth can not be had through them in the conclusion, nor certitude, for doubt is not made certain through doubt, nor is truth proved by falsity, although truth can be syllogized from false premises (the syllogism in that case inferring but not proving); so it is with all the sciences, that those in which there are violent and numerous doubts and opinions and errors (I speak at least from our part) should have doubts of this sort and falsities removed by some science certain to us

and in which we neither doubt nor err. Since indeed conclusions and principles proper to them are parts of the whole of the sciences, therefore, just as part is related to part, as conclusion is related to premises, so science is related to science, so that, obviously, the science which is full of doubts and bestrewn with opinions and obscurities, can not be made certain or clear nor be verified except by some other science known and verified and certain to us and plain, as is the case with a conclusion from premises. But only mathematics, as has been advanced before, remains certain to us and verified with the utmost certitude and verification. Wherefore it is necessary that all the other sciences be known and certified by it.

And since it has been shown already; by the property of that science, that mathematics is prior to the other sciences and is useful and necessary to them, the same thing may be shown now by reasons taken from its subject matter. And first this, that the natural way for us is from sense to understanding, because if a sense is lacking, the science which is related to that sense is lacking also, as is pointed out in the first book of the Posterior [*Analytics*], since in the degree that sense advances, human understanding advances. But quantity is in the highest degree sensible, because it pertains to the common sense and is perceived by the other senses. and nothing can be perceived without quantity, for which reason the understanding is able to advance most of all in what relates to quantity. Secondly, because the very act of understanding is not accomplished in itself without continuous quantity, since Aristotle says in the book on *Memory and Reminiscence* that all our understanding is concerned with the continuous and with time. Whence, we understand quantities and bodies by the consideration of the understanding, because their species are present, in the understanding. But the species of incorporeal things are not received thus in our understanding; or if they are produced in it, according to what Avicenna says in the third book of the *Metaphysics*, we still do not perceive that, because of the more vigorous occupation of our understanding with bodies and quantities. And, therefore, we investigate the notion of incorporeal things by way of argumentation and concern with corporeal things and quantities, as Aristotle does in the eleventh book of the *Metaphysics*. For which reason the understanding will make most progress with quantity itself, in that quantities and bodies, so far as they are such, are appropriated to the human understanding according to the common status of understanding. Each and every thing is because of some thing, and that thing is in a higher degree.

However the final reason for complete confirmation can be drawn from the experience of the wise men; for all the wise men of antiquity worked in mathematics that they might know all things, as we have seen in the case of some of our own times and as we have heard in the case of others who learned all knowledge through mathematics, which they knew well. For very famous men have been found, like Bishop Robert of Lincoln and Brother Adam of the Marsh, and many others, who knew how to explain the causes of all things through the power of mathematics and to explain sufficiently things human and divine. The certainty of this thing, moreover, is evident in the writings of these men, as on impressions, such as on the rainbow and on comets, and on the generation of heat, and the investigation of the places of the world, and on celestial things and others, of which theology as well as philosophy make use. Wherefore, it is manifest that mathematics is absolutely necessary and useful to the other sciences.

These reasons are universal, but it can be shown in particular, by going through all parts of philosophy, how all things are known by the application of mathematics. And this is nothing other than to show that the other sciences should not be known by means of the dialectical and Sophistical arguments which are introduced commonly, but by mathematical demonstrations descending to the truths and the works of the other sciences and regulating them, without which they can not be understood, nor manifested, nor taught, nor learned. If any one, moreover, should descend to the particular by applying the power of mathematics to the separate sciences, he would see that nothing magnificent in the sciences can be known without mathematics. This, however, would be nothing other than to establish sure methods of all the sciences and to verify all things which are necessary to the other sciences by the ways of mathematics. But that does not fall within the present speculation.

Second Distinction

In which it is shown that the things of this world require mathematics; in three chapters.

Chapter I

In the first chapter is taught in general that heavenly things and things below require mathematics.

What has just been shown in regard to the sciences can be made clear in regard to things. For the things of this world can not be known unless mathematics is known. Of heavenly objects, to be sure, that is certain to all, seeing that two great mathematical sciences treat of them, namely, speculative astrology and practical astrology. The first considers the quantities of all things that are included among the celestial and all things which are reduced to quantity, as well discrete as continuous quantity. For it certifies the number of the heavens and of the stars, whose quantity can be measured by instruments, and the shapes of all and the magnitudes and altitudes from the earth and the thicknesses and the number and magnitude and smallness, the rising and setting of the constellations, and the motion as well of the heavens as of the stars, and the quantities and varieties of eclipses. Again, it takes up the quantity and shape of the habitable world and of all the great divisions of it which are called climates, and it shows the diversity of the horizons and of the days and nights in every climate. These things, then, are determined in speculative astrology and many others connected with them. Practical astrology on the other hand treats of this, that we know at every hour the positions of the planets and the stars and their combinations and all things which occur in celestial things; and it treats of those things which happen in the air, such as comets and rainbows and other things that occur there, that we may know their positions and altitudes and magnitudes and shapes and many things which must be considered in them. And all these things are done by instruments suitable to them and by tables and canons, that is, rules invented to certify these things so that a way may be prepared for the judgments [i.e. horoscopes] that can be formed within the power of philosophy, not only in natural things, but in those which take their tendency from nature and follow freely the heavenly disposition; and not only for judgments [horoscopes] of things present, past, and future, but for wondrous works that all the fortunate circumstances of this world may be advanced and the adverse be held in check, usefully and magnificently. Nor are these matters doubtful. For the patriarchs and prophets from the beginning of the world have certified these as they have other matters. And Aristotle renewed the certification of the ancients and brought it out into the light. And all who are wise in great things agree in this, and experience teaches it. But exposition will be made of these matters in the proper place.

It is plain, therefore, that heavenly things are known by means of mathematics and that the way is prepared by it to things below. That, moreover, those things below can not be learned without mathematics is evident first by this, that we know things only through causes, if science be taken properly, as Aristotle says. But heavenly things are the causes of the things below. Therefore, these inferior things will not be known unless the heavenly things are known, and they can not be known without mathematics. Therefore, the knowledge of these inferior things depends on the same science. In the second place, we can see from their properties that no one of these lower or higher things can be known without the power of mathematics. For every natural thing is produced in being by an efficient cause and by the matter in which it operates, for these two concur first. The agent, indeed, by its force moves and transmutes the matter that the thing may be made. But the force of the efficient cause and of the matter can not be known without the great power of mathematics, as is the case with the force of the effect produced. There are therefore these three, the efficient cause, the matter, and the effect. And in celestial things there is set up a mutual influence of forces as of light and of other agents, and there is alteration in them, but not toward corruption. And so, too, it can be shown that nothing can be known in things without the power of geometry. We hold by this argument that the other parts of mathematics are necessary in the same way: for what applies to geometry applies likewise to them, except that it applies much more because they are nobler. If, therefore,

what was proposed is shown in geometrical things, it is not necessary to speak in this demonstration of the others.

In the first place, I show, therefore, what was proposed concerning geometry from the point of the efficient cause. For every efficient cause acts by its own force which it produces in the subject matter, as the light of the sun produces its own force in the air, which force is illumination [lumen] diffused through all the world by the solar light [lux]. And this force is called a likeness and image and species, and by many names; and it is produced by substance as well as accident and by spiritual as well as corporeal substance. And by substance more than by accident, and by spiritual more than by corporeal. And this species produces every operation in this world, for it operates on sense, on understanding, and on all the matter of the world for the generation of things, because one and the same thing is done by a natural agent on whatsoever it operates, seeing that it does not have freedom of choice; and, therefore, it produces the same thing, whatever may occur to it. But if it acts on the sense and the understanding, a species is formed, as all know. Therefore, it acts in the same way on that which is contrary to these, and a species is made in matter. And in beings that have reason and understanding, although they do many things by deliberation and freedom of the will, still this operation which is the generation of species, is natural in them as in other things. Whence, the substance of the soul multiplies its own force in the body and outside the body, and every body produces its own force outside itself, and angels move the world by forces of this sort. But God produces forces out of nothing, which he multiplies in things; created agents do not act so, but in another manner, of which there need be no concern at the present time. Forces of agents of this sort, therefore, produce every operation in this world. But now two things need be considered concerning them: one is the multiplication itself of species and of force in the place of their generation; and the other is the varied operation in this world due to the generation and corruption of things. The second can not be known without the first. And therefore, it is necessary that the multiplication itself be described first. . . .

The Fifth Part of This Demonstration[1]

ON THE SCIENCE OF PERSPECTIVE; HAVING THREE PARTS:

First Distinction

This distinction is concerned with the properties of this science and with the parts of the mind and the brain and with the organs of seeing; having five chapters.

Chapter I

On the properties of this science.

Having propounded the roots of wisdom, as well divine as human, which are found in the languages from which the sciences of the latins have been translated and likewise the roots of wisdom which are in the power of mathematics, I wish now to discuss some roots which arise from the power of perspective. And, if the consideration which has already been stated is noble and delectable, the present one is by far more noble and more delectable, since our peculiar delight is in vision; and light and color have a special beauty beyond any which are brought to our senses; and not only beauty shines forth, but utility and a greater necessity arise. For Aristotle says in the first book of the *Metaphysics* that vision alone shows us the differences of things: by it, in fact, we seek out the sure experiences of all things which are in the heavens and on earth. For those things which are in the heavens are considered by visual instruments, as Ptolemy and other astronomers teach. And similarly, too, those which are generated in the air, as comets, and rainbows, and others of this sort. For their altitude above the horizon, and their magnitude, and shape and number, and all qualities which are in them, are made certain by methods of seeing with instruments. Moreover, the things which are here on the earth we find by vision, in that the blind man is able to discover nothing of this world that is worthwhile. Hearing makes us believe because we believe what we have learned, but we can not discover what we learn except by sight. If, moreover, we should adduce taste and touch and smell, then we assume a bestial wisdom. For the brutes are conversant with gustibles and tangibles, and they exercise their sense of smell for taste and touch, but the things which these senses certify are of trifling value and few in number and common to us and to brutes and, therefore, they do not rise to the dignity of human wisdom. But sciences are constituted in view of necessity and utility and difficulty, because art is of the difficult and the good, as Aristotle says in the second book of the *Ethics*. For if what is sought is easy, there is no need that a science be constituted. In the same way, even though something is difficult and still not useful no science is made of it, because the labor would be stupid and inane. Furthermore, if it were not exceedingly useful and had not many and outstanding truths, it should not have a separate science set up, but it suffices that it be marked out in some part of a book or chapter together with other subjects in the common science. But of vision alone is a separate science formed among philosophers, namely perspective, and not of any other sense. Wherefore, through vision there must be a special utility to wisdom, which is not found in the other senses. And what I have already touched on in general. I wish to show in particular by going over the roots of this most beautiful science. To be sure some other science may be more useful, but no other science has such delightfulness and beauty of utility. And, therefore, it is the flower of all philosophy and that by which the other sciences can be learned and without which they can not he acquired. It should be known, moreover, that Aristotle first found this science, of which he speaks in the second book of the *Physics*, because the matter is a subtopic of that book, and in the book on *Sense and the Sensed*, and he confuted Democritus because he did not mention the reflections and the refractions of vision of the optic nerves and the concave visual nerves; this has been translated into latin. After him Alhazen expounds the subject fully in a book which is also to be had. Likewise Alkindi composed some things more fully and also authors of books on vision and mirrors.

Chapter II

On the internal faculties of the sensitive soul, which are imagination and the common sense.

---

[1]O. c., vol. II, pp. 1–12, and vol. III, p. 136.

Since the optic nerves, that is, the concave nerves causing sight, have their origin in the brain and since writers on perspective ascribe the formation of judgments on twenty species of visible things to a distinguishing faculty with vision mediating, which twenty will be touched on later, and since it is not known whether that distinguishing faculty is among the faculties of the soul, the organs of which are distinct in the brain, and since many other things, which will be treated below, underlie the determination of the faculties of the sensitive soul, therefore, it is necessary to begin with the parts of the brain and the faculties of the soul that we may discover those things which are necessary to sight. And writers on perspective furnish us the way to this, showing how the visual nerves descend from the membranes of the brain and from the lining of the cranium; but no one explains all the details that are necessary to this part. I say, therefore, that, as all natural and medical and perspective philosophers agree, the brain is wrapped in a double membrane of which one is called the *pia mater*, which is the one containing the brain immediately; and the other is called the *dura mater*, which adheres to the concavity of the bone of the head, which is called the cranium. For the latter is harder that it may resist the bone, and the former is softer and smoother because of the pliability of the brain, the substance of which is medullar and unctuous, and phlegm is the chief constituent, and it has three distinctions which are called chambers, and cellules, and parts, and divisions. In the first cell there are two faculties: and one is the common sense located in the anterior part, as Avicenna says in the first book on the *Soul*, which is like a fountain with respect to the particular senses and like a center with respect to the lines extending from the same point to the circumference, according to Aristotle in the second book on the *Soul*,[1] the common sense judges of individual sensible particulars. For judgment concerning the visible is not completed before the species comes to the common sense; and it is so too with the audible and the others, as is evident from the end of the work on *Sense and the Sensed* and from the second book on the *Soul*, and the common sense judges of the diversity of sensibles, as that in milk the whiteness is other than the sweetness, which sight could not do, nor taste, in that they do not distinguish extremes, as Aristotle holds in the second book on the *Soul*. And it judges of the operations of the particular senses, for sight does not perceive itself see, nor does hearing perceive itself hear, but another faculty which is the common sense does, as Aristotle holds in the second book on *Sleep and Waking*. The final operation of the common sense, however, is to receive the species coming from the particular senses and to complete judgment on them. But it does not retain them, owing to the excessive slipperiness of its organ, according to what Avicenna holds in the first book on the *Soul*. And, therefore, it is necessary that there be another faculty of the soul in the back part of the first cellule, the function of which is to retain the species coming from the particular senses because of its temperate moistness and dryness, which is called the imagination and is the treasury and repository of the common sense, according to Avicenna who uses the example of a seal, the image of which water receives well but does not retain because of its superfluous moistness: but wax retains the image well because of its moistness tempered with dryness. Whence he says that it is one thing to receive and another to retain, as appears in these examples. So it is in the case of the organ of the common sense and of the imagination. Nevertheless, the whole faculty compounded of these faculties, that is, that which occupies the whole first cellule, is called phantasy or the phantastical faculty. For it is evident from the second book on the *Soul* and from the book on *Sleep and Waking* and from the book on *Sense and the Sensed* that phantasy and common sense are the same in respect to subject and different in respect to being, as Aristotle says, and that phantasy and imagination are the same in respect to subject and different in respect to being. Wherefore, phantasy comprehends both faculties and does not differ from them except as the whole from the part. And, therefore, when the common sense receives the species and the imagination retains it, there follows a complete judgment of the thing, which judgment phantasy forms.

---

[1]The reference should be to the third book.

Chapter III

Concerning sensibles which are perceived by the senses proper and by the common sense and by imagination.

It must be noted that imagination and common sense and the particular sense judge by themselves only of twenty-nine sensibles; as sight of light and color; touch of heat and cold, moist and dry; hearing of sound; smell of odor; taste of savor. These are the nine proper sensibles which are appropriated, as I have named them, to their senses; of which no other particular sense can form a judgment. There are, however, twenty other sensibles, namely, distance, situation, corporeity, figure, magnitude, continuity, discreteness or separation, number, motion, rest, roughness, smoothness, transparency, thickness, shadow, obscurity, beauty, ugliness, and also likeness and difference in all these sensibles and in all things compounded from them. And besides these there are others which are placed under some one or more of them, as ordination under situation, and writing and painting under ordination and figure; and as straightness and curvedness, and concavity and convexity, which are placed under figure; and multitude and paucity, which are placed under number; and as equality and augmentation and diminution which are placed under likeness and diversity; and as liveliness and laughter and sadness, which are comprehended from the figure and form of the face; and as weeping which is comprehended from the figure of the face with the motion of tears; and as moistness and dryness which are placed under motion and rest, since moistness is not comprehended by the sense of sight except from the liquidity of the moist body and from the motion of one part of it before another, and since dryness is comprehended from the retention of the part of the dry thing and from the privation of liquidity. This, however, must be considered, which Aristotle maintains in the second book on *Generation*, that moist and dry are, in one manner, primary qualities inherent naturally in the elements, and because of them moistness and dryness in the things compounded of the elements[1] are reduced to the first and are caused by them. Concerning the primary qualities, therefore, it has been said that they are proper sensibles and perceptible by touch alone. Of the others the following statement is made. The primary moistness is, in fact, that which passes easily into all figures which are terminable of themselves with difficulty and readily terminable by the limit of something else, as in the case of air in the highest degree and then in the case of water. Dryness is the contrary and dryness is most of all in earth and secondarily in fire. Moreover, moistness is here used in the sense of liquid and slippery, and dry in the sense of arid and coagulated. And it is thus too with many others which are reduced to the species and principal modes of the visible objects enumerated above. And all these things are apparent from the first book of Ptolemy on *Optics* and from the second book of Alhazen on *Appearances* and from other authors on perspective. There are also the common sensibles, some of which Aristotle exemplifies in the second book on the *Soul* and in the beginning of his work on *Sense and the Sensed*, as of magnitude and figure, motion, rest, and number; but not only these are common sensibles but all those mentioned above, although the run of natural philosophers do not take that up because they are not expert in the science of perspective. For the common sensibles are not so called because they are perceived by the common sense, but because they are determined in common by all the particular senses or by several, and most of all by sight and touch, since Ptolemy says in the second book on *Perspective* that touch and sight share in all the above twenty. And these twenty-nine, together with those which are reduced to them, are perceived by the particular senses and by common sense and imagination; and these faculties of the soul can not judge by themselves of other sensibles except by accident.

Chapter IV

On the investigation of the estimative faculty and the memorative and the cogitative faculties.

There are however other sensibles per se, for brute animals use only sense because they do not have understanding. The sheep, even if he has never seen a wolf, flees from it at once, and every animal is terrified at the roar of a lion, even though it may never have heard or seen a lion before, and the same is true in the case of many things which are hurtful

---

[1]The text reads *inelementales*; it is interpreted here as *in elementatis*.

and contrary to the constitution of animals. And in the same way in the case of the useful and agreeable. For even if a lamb has never seen another lamb, it runs to one and stays willingly with it and so with other animals. Brutes, therefore, perceive something in advantageous and in hurtful things. Therefore, there is something there sensibly besides the twenty-nine sensibles enumerated above and besides those which are reduced to them. For there must be something more active and alterative of the sentient body than light and color, because it leads not only to comprehension but to the affection of fear or love or flight or tarrying. And this thing is the quality of the constitution of each thing in which the natural kinship of different individuals of the same species or genus is grounded and in consequence of which they are drawn together and strengthened and fortified by each other, or by which they differ and are opposed and made hurtful to each other. Whence, not only do light and color make their species and powers, but even more the qualities of the constitutions make them, and indeed the substantial natures themselves of things, agreeing with each other or contrary, make strong species which modify the sensitive soul strongly, that it is moved by the affections of fear and of horror and of flight or the contraries. And these species or virtues coming from the things, although they modify and alter the particular senses and the common sense and the imagination, just as they do the air through which they pass, nevertheless, none of these faculties of the soul judge of them, but it is necessary that there be a faculty of the sensitive soul far nobler and more powerful, and this is called estimation or the estimative faculty, as Avicenna says in the first book on the *Soul*, which he says perceives the unperceived forms connected with sensible matter. That is called sensible matter here which is known by the particular senses and the common sense, such as the twenty-nine enumerated above. And that is called the unperceived form which is not perceived by those senses of themselves, since they are commonly called senses, although other faculties of the sensitive soul could be called senses equally well, should we wish to call them so, since they are parts of the sensitive soul. For each part of the sensitive soul can be called a sense because it is in truth a sense and a sensitive faculty. When it is said, there-

fore, that the constitutional qualities are not perceived by the sense, it must be understood that they are not perceived by the particular sense and the common sense and the imagination; but they can very well be perceived by estimation, which although it is not called a sense, is nevertheless a part of the sensitive soul.

But estimation does not retain a species although it receives it, as does the common sense, and therefore there is needed another faculty in the last part of the posterior cellule to retain the species of the estimative faculty and to be the treasury and repository of it, as imagination is the treasury of the common sense, and this is the memorative faculty, and Avicenna says this in the first book on the *Soul*. But judgment, or the cogitative faculty, is in the middle cellule; it is the mistress of the sensitive faculty and takes the place of reason in brutes, and therefore it is called logistic, that is, rational, not because it uses reason, but because it is the ultimate perfection of brutes, as reason is of man, and because the rational soul in men is united directly to it. By virtue of it the spider weaves its geometrical web and the bee its hexagonal house, choosing one from the figures which fill space, and the swallow its nest and so with all the works of brutes which are similar to human art. Man sees wonders in dreams by that faculty, and all the faculties of the sensitive soul serve and obey it, as well the posterior as the anterior, since all of them are because of it. For the species which are in the imagination multiply themselves in cogitation, although in the imagination they are according to their first being because of phantasy which makes use of those species; but the cogitative faculty contains these species in a more noble way, and the species of the estimative and the memorative faculties acquire in the cogitative faculty a being which is nobler than the one it has in them, and therefore the cogitative faculty uses all the other faculties as its instruments. In man the rational soul comes above these from without and by creation, and it is united first and immediately to the cogitative faculty, and it uses that principally as its special instrument, and species are formed in the rational soul by it. Whence, when this faculty is injured, the judgment of reason is perverted to the highest degree, and when it is sound, then the understanding operates well and rationally.

Chapter V

On the exposition of opposed authorities concerning the aforesaid faculties.

But the Latin text of Aristotle does not disclose to us this division, for no mention is made expressly except of the common sense and imagination and memory. However, since the text of Aristotle can not be understood in these places, as elsewhere, because of perversity of the translation, and since Avicenna was almost everywhere the perfect imitator and expositor of Aristotle and the leader and prince of philosophy after him, as the Commentator says in the commentary on the chapter on the rainbow, for this reason the opinion of Avicenna which is clear and perfect, must be followed. And, although the translators of the books of Avicenna, as in that book on the *Soul* and in the book on *Animals* and in the books on medicine, have translated them differently and have changed words, so that the intention of Avicenna is not everywhere translated in the same way, since in the book on *Animals* of Avicenna it is found that the estimation is in the place of reason in brutes, and so sometimes there is found elsewhere a contrariety in respect of the things said above, still it is not important that different interpreters make differences in words and sometimes have even some difference on the part of the thing; but his opinion in the book on the *Soul* must be held to because he there discusses the faculties of the soul as his principal intention, whereas, elsewhere he rather makes mention of them incidentally. Furthermore, that book is better translated by far than the others; which is evident in that it has few or no words of other languages, while his other books have an infinite number of them. If, moreover, any one should consider what has been said above, he must assume three altogether diverse faculties distributed in three cellules. For a diversity of objects shows us a diversity of faculties. There are, in fact, two kinds of sensibles, to wit one exterior, such as the twenty-nine stated above, another internal unknown to the exterior sense, as the quality of a hurtful or useful constitution, or rather the useful or the hurtful substantial nature itself. Therefore, it fol-

lows necessarily that there be, as a consequence of this cause, two kinds of senses: namely, one which contains the particular senses and the common sense and the imagination, which are moved by the first kind of sensibles; and the other which contains estimation and memory, which are referred to the second class of sensibles. But because of the nobility of the operations which the cogitative faculty has, compared with the other faculties, the cogitative faculty is distinguished from the others. In the generally accepted translation of Aristotle, therefore, every faculty is called memory which has the power of retaining species and, therefore, as well the storehouse of common sense as the storehouse of estimation, is called memory. And, therefore, what is here called imagination is comprehended under memory in the translation of Aristotle which is in common use. But it is necessary without doubt, then, that memory is double and of very different parts, so that one will be the storehouse of common sense and the other of estimation; and they will differ according to species and according to subject and organ and operation. Moreover, although these faculties have now been located in the brain, it must be understood that the medullar substance of the brain does not perceive as Avicenna teaches in the tenth book on *Animals*; and in this he corrects Aristotle with pious and reverent interpretation.[1]

For the marrow in other places of the body does not have sense, and therefore it does not here. But it is a receptacle and treasury of sensitive faculties containing subtle nerves in which sense and sensible species are located. But that all doubt may be removed, it must be considered that the sensitive soul has a twofold instrument or subject: one is basic and original like a wellspring, and this is the heart according to Aristotle and Avicenna in their books on animals; the other is that which is first modified by the species of the sensibles and in which the operations of the senses are made more manifest and are distinguished, and this is the brain. For if the head be injured we clearly see that a lesion of the sensitive faculties follows, and head lesions are more easily dis-

---

[1]Bridges points out that a passage in *Do Animalibus*, III, c. 19, makes it clear that Aristotle was aware that the substance of the brain was not sensitive; the reference is doubtless to the discussion of marrow in the *Historia Animalium* III, 20, 521^b 4–17.

cerned by us and they occur more frequently than heart lesions, and therefore, because of [these more frequent and] more obvious manifestations [of connections as revealed by lesions] we locate the sensitive faculties in the head; and this is the opinion of physicians who do not think that the wellspring and origin of faculties is in the heart. But Avicenna says in the first book of the *Art of Medicine*, that although the opinion of the physicians is the more manifest to the sense, nevertheless, the opinion of the Philosopher is the truer, since all the nerves and veins and all the faculties of the soul arise from the heart first and principally, as Aristotle demonstrates in the twelfth book on *Animals*, and Avicenna in the third book on *Animals*. . . .

The Sixth Part
of This Demonstration[1]

AND THE SIXTH PART OF THE OPUS MAJUS IS ON EXPERIMENTAL SCIENCE

Chapter I

Having laid down the roots of the wisdom of the latins so far as they are found in languages and mathematics and perspective, I wish now to take up the roots of experimental science, because without experience nothing can be known sufficiently. There are, in fact, two ways of knowing, namely, by argumentation and experience. Argumentation concludes and makes us grant the conclusion, but does not make certain nor remove doubt that the mind may be quiet in the contemplation of truth, unless it finds truth by the way of experience; many, because they have arguments for the knowable but do not have experience, neglect the arguments and neither avoid the hurtful nor follow the good. For if a man who has never seen fire should prove by sufficient argument that fire burns and that it injures things and destroys them, the mind of one hearing it would never be satisfied by that nor would a hearer avoid fire until he had put a hand or a combustible object into the fire that he might prove by experience what argument had taught. But once he

has had experience of combustion, his mind is made sure and rests in the brightness of truth. Therefore, argumentation does not suffice but experience does.

This is evident too in mathematics, where demonstration is most convincing. But the mind of one who has a most convincing demonstration of the equilateral triangle will never adhere to the conclusion without experience nor will such an one trouble about it, but will neglect it until experience is offered him by the intersection of two circles, from the intersection of which are drawn two lines to the extremities of the given line; but then the man accepts the conclusion with full repose. What Aristotle says, therefore, to the effect that the demonstration is a syllogism that makes us know, is to be understood if the experience of it accompanies the demonstration, and it is not to be understood of the bare demonstration. What he says, likewise, in the first book of the *Metaphysics*, that those who have the reason and the cause are wiser than those who are experienced, is said of experienced men who know only the bare truth without the cause. But I speak here of the man of experience who knows the reason and cause by experience. These men are perfect in wisdom, as Aristotle holds in the sixth book of the *Ethics*,[2] and their simple statements must be believed as if they offered demonstration, as he states in the same place.

He, therefore, who wishes to enjoy without doubt[3] the truths of things, should know how to devote his time to experiment; this is evident in examples. For authors write of and the people maintain many doctrines by arguments which they fashion without experiment and which are wholly false. For it is commonly believed that the diamond can not be broken except by goat's blood, and philosophers and theologians misuse this opinion. But no certainty has been arrived at yet concerning fraction by blood of this sort although an attempt has been made at it; and without goat's blood the diamond can be broken easily. For I have seen it with my own eyes; and it is necessary, because gems can not be carved except with fragments of this stone. In the same way, it is held generally that the follicles [of beavers], which physicians

---

[1] O. c., vol. II, pp. 167–174, and vol. III, p. 141.

[2] *Eth. Nic.* VI, 2, 6.

[3] The text reads *sine demonstratione*; it is interpreted as an error for *sine dubitatione*.

use, are the testicles of the male animal. But that is not true because the beaver has them under its breast, and both the male and the female produce testicles of this sort. And besides these follicles the male has his proper testicles in their natural place; and therefore, what is added to this is a horrible lie, namely, that when hunters are tracking the beaver, he, knowing what they seek, tears off the follicles with his teeth. Moreover, it has come to be held generally that hot water congeals in vessels more quickly than cold, and it is argued as basis for this that contrary is excited by contrary, as enemies resist each other. But it is certain that cold water congeals more quickly, to any one who makes the experiment. People read this into Aristotle in the second book of the *Meteorologies*[1] but he certainly does not say that, but he does affirm something like it, by which they have been deceived, namely, that if cold and hot water be poured into a cold place, as upon ice, the hot water is congealed more quickly, and this is true. But if cold and hot water be placed in two vessels, the cold will be congealed more quickly. It is necessary, therefore, that all things be certified by the way of experience.

But experience is double: one is by means of the exterior senses, and such are those experiences which show things that are in the heavens through instruments made for these experiments and those things that we find below by visual ascertainments. We know things which are not present in the places in which we are, through other wise men who have experienced them. Just as Aristotle sent, by the authority of Alexander, two thousand men to various places of the world to learn of all things which are on the surface of the earth, as Pliny testifies in the *Natural History*. This experience is human and philosophical, as much as man can do in accordance with the grace given him; but this experience does not suffice man, in that it does not certify fully concerning corporeal things because of its difficulty, and it touches on nothing at all of spiritual things. Therefore, it is necessary that the understanding of man be aided otherwise, and therefore the holy patriarchs and prophets, who first gave the sciences to the world, received interior illuminations and were not

dependent only on sense. In the same way in the case of many of the faithful since the time of Christ. For the grace of faith illumines greatly and divine inspirations likewise, not only in spiritual but in corporeal things and in the sciences of philosophy, according to what Ptolemy says in the *Centilogium*, that the way to come to a knowledge of things is twofold, one by the experience of philosophy, the other by divine inspiration, which is far the better as he says.

There are seven grades of this interior knowledge. The first by purely scientific illuminations. The second grade consists in the virtues. For the evil man is ignorant, as Aristotle says in the second book of the *Ethics*. And al Ghazali says in his *Logic* that the soul which is cast down by sins is like a rusty mirror, in which the species of things can not be seen well; but the soul adorned with virtues is like a well-polished mirror, in which the forms of things are clearly seen. For this reason true philosophers have labored the more in morals for the integrity of virtue, concluding among themselves that they can not see the causes of things unless they have souls free from sins. Saint Augustine recounts this of Socrates in the eighth book of the *City of God* in the third chapter. For this reason the Scripture says, "wisdom will not enter into an ill-disposed soul."[2] For it is impossible that the soul repose in the light of truth while it is stained with sins, but it will recite like a parrot or a magpie the words of another which it learned by long practice. And the test of this is that beauty of a cognized truth attracts men by its refulgence to love it, but the proof of love is the exhibition of work. And, therefore, he who acts contrary to the truth, must necessarily be ignorant of it, although he may know how to put together very elegant phrases and to quote the opinions of others, like a brute animal that imitates human voices or like a monkey who attempts to perform the actions of men although it does not understand the reason of them. Virtue, therefore, clarifies the mind that man may understand more easily not only moral things, but scientific things. And I have bested this carefully in many fine youths, who because of innocence of soul advanced to greater knowledge than can be stated when they have had sound counsel on their study. Of this number is the

---

[1]Reference probably to *Meteor.* I, 13, 18.

[2]*Book of Wisdom 1:4.*

bearer of the present writings, whose foundations very few of the latins acquire. Since, indeed, he is very young, that is, about twenty years of age, and extremely poor, he could not have masters, nor has he devoted the time of one year to learning the great things which he knows, nor is he of great genius or of great memory, so that there can be no other cause than the grace of God which gave him, because of the purity of his soul, that which it has refused to give to almost all students. For he has gone from me an uncorrupted virgin nor have I been able to find in him any kind of mortal sin although I have searched out carefully, and therefore he has a soul so clear and perspicuous that he learned with little instruction more than can be judged. And I have done what I could to bring about that these two youths should be useful vessels in the Church of God to the end that they may rectify by the grace of God all the studies of the Latins.

The third step consists in the seven gifts of the Holy Spirit which Isaiah enumerates. The fourth consists in the beatitudes, which the Lord defines in the Gospels.[1] The fifth consists in the spiritual senses. The sixth is in fruits among which is the peace of the Lord which exceeds all understanding. The seventh consists in raptures [raptus] and the modes of them, according to which different men are seized differently to see many things of which it is not given to man to speak. And he who is carefully disciplined in these experiences or in several of them, can assure himself and others not only as regards spiritual things but as regards all human sciences. Therefore, since all parts of speculative philosophy proceed by arguments which are based either on grounds of authority or on other grounds of argumentation, except this part which I am now investigating, that science is necessary to us which is called experimental. And I want to explain it, as it is useful not only to philosophy but to the wisdom of God and to the guidance of the whole world, as I have shown in the case of languages and sciences above in relation to their end, which is divine wisdom by which all things are disposed.

Chapter II
And because this experimental science is wholly ignored by the general run of students, for that reason

I can not convince people of its utility unless I show at the same time its excellence and its property. This science alone, then, knows how to test perfectly by experience what can be done by nature, what by the industry of art, what by imposture; what the incantations conjurations, invocations, deprecations, sacrifices (which are magical devices) seek and dream of; and what is done in them, so that all falsity may be removed and that only the truth of art and nature be retained. This science alone teaches one to consider all the insanities of magicians, not that they may be confirmed but that they may be avoided, just as logic considers Sophistical argument.

This experimental science has three great prerogatives with respect to the other sciences. The first is that it investigates by experiment the noble conclusions of all of the sciences. For the other sciences know how to discover their principles by experiments, but their conclusions are reached by arguments based on the discovered principles. But if they must have particular and complete experience of their conclusions, then it is necessary that they have it by the aid of this noble science. It is true, indeed, that mathematics has universal experiences concerning its conclusions in figuring and numbering, which are applied likewise to all the sciences and to this experimental science, because no science can be known without mathematics. But if we turn our attention to the experiences which are particular and complete and certified wholly in their own discipline, it is necessary to go by way of the considerations of this science which is called experimental autonymically. I use the example of the rainbow and of the phenomena connected with it, of which sort are the circle around the sun and the stars, likewise the rod [virga] lying at the side of the sun or of a star which appears to the eye in a straight line and is called by Aristotle, in the third book of the Meteorologies, the perpendicular but is called the rod by Seneca, and the circle is called the corona, which often has the colors of the rainbow. The natural philosopher, to be sure, holds discussions concerning these things and the perspectivist has many things to add which pertain to the mode of seeing, which is very necessary in this case. But neither Aristotle nor Avicenna, in their Natural Histories, has given us

[1]See Matthew 5:3–11; Luke 6:20–22.

knowledge of things of this sort, nor has Seneca, who composed a special book on them. But experimental science makes certain of them.

The experimenter, then, should first examine visible things to discover colors ordered as in the above mentioned things and in the same figure. Let him, indeed, take the hexagonal stones of Ireland or India, which are called iris stones in Solinus on the *Wonders of the World*, and let him hold them in the solar ray falling through a window so that he may find in the shadow near the ray all the colors of the rainbow and ordered as in it. And further let the same experimenter betake himself to any shady place, and let him place the stone to his eye, almost closed, and he will see the colors of the rainbow clearly ordered as in the rainbow. And since many who use these stones think that it is because of a special virtue of the stones and because of their hexagonal figure, for that reason let the same experimenter proceed further and he will find this property in crystalline stones which are properly shaped and in other clear stones. Moreover not only in white stones like the irish, but in black stones, as is evident in the dark crystal and in all stones of similar transparency. He will find it, too, in another figure than the hexagonal, provided the surfaces are corrugated like the irish stone and neither altogether polished nor more rough than they are, and provided they are such property of surface as nature produces in the irish. For the diversity of wrinkles produces a diversity of colors. And after that, [the experimenter] considers rowers and he finds the same colors in the falling drops dripping from the raised oars when the solar rays penetrate drops of this sort. It is the same with waters falling from the wheels of a mill; and when a man sees the drops of dew in summer of a morning lying on the grass in the meadow or the field, he will see the colors. And in the same way when it rains, if he stands in a shady place and if the rays beyond it pass through dripping moisture, then the colors will appear in the shadow nearby; and very frequently of a night colors appear around the wax-candle. Moreover, if a man in summer when he rises from sleep and while his eyes are yet only partly opened, looks suddenly toward an aperture through which a ray of the sun enters, he

will see colors. And if, while seated beyond the sun, he extend his hat before his eyes, he will see colors; and in the same way if he closes his eye, the same thing happens under the shade of the eyebrow; and again, the same phenomenon occurs through a glass vessel filled with water, placed in the rays of the sun. Or similarly if anyone holding water in his mouth sprinkles it vigorously into the rays and stands to the side of the rays; and if rays in the proper position pass through an oil lamp hanging in the air, so that the light falls on the surface of the oil, colors will be produced. And so in an infinite number of ways, as well natural as artificial, colors of this sort appear, as the careful experimenter is able to discover. . . .

The Seventh Part of This Demonstration[1]

MORAL PHILOSOPHY

First Part

I have shown in the preceding parts that the knowledge of languages, and mathematics, and perspective as well as experimental science are extremely useful and particularly necessary in the pursuit of wisdom. Without them no one can advance as he should in wisdom, taken not only absolutely but relatively to the Church of God and to the other three sciences described above. Now I wish likewise to go over the roots of the fourth science which is better and more noble than all those previously mentioned; and it is the practical one among them all, that is, the operative one, and it consists of our actions in this life and in the other life. In fact, all other sciences are called speculative. For although certain of them are active and operative, nevertheless, they are concerned with artificial and natural actions, not with moral actions, and they consider the truths of things and of scientific activities which have reference to the speculative intellect, and they are not related to things pertaining to the practical intellect; and it is called practical because it directs *praxis*, that is, the operation of good and evil. Whence, the term practical is taken here in a restricted sense as applying to the activities of morality in accordance with which we

---

[1]O. c., vol. II, pp. 223–232, and vol. III, p. 144.

are good or evil; although if practical is taken in a broad sense for all operative science, many other things are practical; but this is called practical autonymically because of the chief operations of man which are related to virtues and vices, and to the felicity and misery of the other life.

This practical science, then, is called moral and civil science, which places man in his proper order to God and to his neighbor and to himself, and tests these orders and invites and moves us to them efficaciously. For this science is concerned with the salvation of man in fulfillment of virtue and felicity; and this science aspires to that salvation so far as philosophy can. From these things, it appears in general that this science is more noble than all the other parts of philosophy. For since it is the inward end of human wisdom and since the end is the most noble aspect in anything, this science must of necessity be the most noble. In the same way, this science alone or in the highest degree treats of the same questions as theology, because theology considers nothing except the five subjects mentioned above, although in another manner, namely, in the faith of Christ. This science contains many outstanding testimonies for the same faith; and it scents from afar the principal articles for the great aid of the Christian faith, as what follows will declare. But theology is the most noble of the sciences; therefore, this which agrees in the highest degree with it, is more noble than the others. But that the very great utility of this science may be apparent, its parts must be investigated to the end that what we wish may be drawn from the parts and from the whole.

Moreover, since moral philosophy is the end of all the parts of philosophy, the conclusions of the other sciences must be the principles in it in accordance with the relation of preceding sciences to those that follow, because the conclusions of the preceding are naturally assumed in those that follow. And, therefore, it is fitting that they be carefully proved and certified in the preceding sciences, that they may be worthy of acceptance in the sciences which follow, as is evident from metaphysics. Therefore, the principles of moral philosophy are certified in the preceding sciences; and for that reason these principles should be drawn from other sciences, not because they belong to those sciences, but because these sciences

have prepared them for their mistress. Whence, wheresoever they may be found they must be ascribed to moral philosophy, since in substance they are moral. And, although they may be repeated in other sciences, it is by the grace of moral philosophy. Wherefore, all things of this sort must be reckoned as moral philosophy and ascribed to it. Therefore, if we wish to use them according to their natural right, they must be brought together in moral science from all the other sciences. Nor is it strange if philosophers have spread moral philosophy through all speculative philosophy: because they knew that it is of the salvation of man; and therefore, they have mixed beautiful doctrines in all the sciences that men might always be directed to the good of salvation, and that all might know that the other sciences are to be sought after only for this one science which is the mistress of human wisdom. Therefore, if I adduce authorities from other places than those which are contained in the books on morals, it must be considered that they should properly be placed in this science; nor can we say that they have not been written in the books of this science, since we do not have except in part in Latin the philosophy of Aristotle, Avicenna, and Averroës, who are the principal authors in moral science. For just as theology understands that salvation-bringing truths belong to it, wheresoever they be found, as was stated in the beginning and touched on later, so too moral philosophy vindicates as its own whatever it finds written elsewhere on things of this sort. Moreover, this moral science is called by Aristotle and by others civil science, because it shows the rights of citizens and of states. And since it was ordinary that states dominate regions as Rome ruled the world, for that reason this science is called civil from the state [civitas], although it is formed to construct the laws of the kingdom and the empire.

This science, moreover, teaches in the first place to draw up the laws and the rights of living; secondly, it teaches that these rights are to be believed and approved and that men are to be urged to act and live according to these laws. The first part is divided into three sections; for first comes naturally the relation of man to God and in respect to the angelic substance; secondly, his relation to his neighbor; thirdly, to himself, as the Scripture states. For in the first place in the books of Moses are the commands and laws concerning God and divine worship. In the second place concerning the relation of man to his neighbor in the same books and those that follow. In the third place there are instructions concerning customs, as in the books of Solomon. In the same way in the New Testament, these three alone are contained. For man can not assume other relations.

Not only because of the first but because of all those which follow, it is necessary that the principles of this science, by which the others are verified, be set forth in the beginning. Of these principles, however, there are some which are purely principles and are capable of being stated only metaphysically. Others, although they are principles with respect to the sciences which follow, are nevertheless either first conclusions of this science [i.e. morals], or else, although they enjoy some of the privilege of a principle, still because of their extreme difficulty, and that they may meet with less contradiction, and because of their excellent utility in respect to the sciences which follow, they should be demonstrated sufficiently: as Aristotle in the beginning of his natural philosophy proves the first principle of that science, namely, that there is motion, against those who suppose only the one immovable being.[1] It should be noted, however, that metaphysics and moral philosophy agree with each other to the highest degree; for both have to do with God and angels and eternal life and with many subjects of this sort although in different ways. For metaphysics investigates metaphysically by means of the common properties of all the sciences: and it investigates spiritual things by way of the corporeal: and through created things it finds the Creator: and through the present life it treats of the future: and it sets forth many preambles to moral philosophy. Metaphysics investigates these subjects because of civil science, so that it is right to join this science with metaphysics, lest (since principles are assumed in this science, which have to be proved in metaphysics) I should confuse different sciences with each other, by trying to prove in this science principles which are proper to metaphysics.

I state, therefore, that God must be, just as he must be shown to be in metaphysics: second, that all men know naturally that God is: and third, that God is of infinite power and of infinite goodness, and together with that, that he is of infinite substance and essence, so that it follows thus that he is best, wisest, and most powerful. In the fourth place, that God is one in essence and not many. Fifth, that not only is he one in essence but three in another manner, which has to be explained in general by metaphysicians, but here it must be explained in the discipline itself. Sixth, that he has created all things and governs them in the being of Nature. Seventh, that besides corporeal things he has formed spiritual substances which we call Intelligences and Angels; for intelligence is the name of a nature, and angel is the name of a function; and how many they are and what their activities are, as it pertains to metaphysics, as far as it is possible for them to be known by human reason. Eighth, that besides angels he made other spiritual substances which are the rational souls in men. Ninth, that he made them immortal. Tenth, that the felicity of the other life is the highest good. Eleventh, that man is capable of this felicity. Twelfth, that God governs the human race in the way of morals just as he governs other things in the being of nature. Thirteenth, that God promises future felicity to those who live rightly in accordance with the governance of God, as Avicenna teaches in the tenth book of the *Metaphysics*, and that a horrible future infelicity is due those who live evilly. Fourteenth, that worship is due God with all reverence and devotion. Fifteenth, that as man is ordered naturally to God through the reverence due him, so he is ordered to his neighbor by justice and peace, and to himself by honorableness of life. Sixteenth, that man can not know by his own effort how to please God with the worship due him, nor how he should stand in relation to his neighbor nor to himself, but he needs the revelation of truth in these things. Seventeenth, that the revelation must be made to one only; that he must be the mediator of God and men and the vicar of God on earth, to whom is subjected the whole human race, and in whom one must believe without contradiction when it has been proved with certitude that he is such as I have just described him; and he is the lawgiver and

---

[1] The reference is to the *Physics* I, 2, 184[b] 27 ff.

the high priest who has the plentitude of power as if. God on earth in temporal and in spiritual things, as Avicenna says in the tenth book of the *Metaphysics*, whom it is proper to adore after God.

By these principles metaphysics is continuous with moral philosophy and approaches it as its end; thus. Avicenna joins them beautifully at the end of his *Metaphysics*. The other principles, however, are peculiar to this science and are not to be explained in metaphysics, although Avicenna adds a number of them. But in the beginning of his volume he gives the reason for this, that he had not constructed a moral philosophy and he did not know whether he would complete one; and therefore he mixed with these metaphysical principles many which are nevertheless proper to moral philosophy, as is evident to the inquirer. And once these have been considered, the legislator should then at the beginning take up the properties of God in particular, and of angels, and the felicity and the misery of the other life, and the immortality of bodies after the resurrection, and things of this sort to which the metaphysician could not aspire. For the metaphysician treats in all these principally of the question of whether the thing is; because it is proper for him to take up that question in regard to all things, in that he considers that which is and being in their common properties. But the other sciences take up other questions involved in things: namely, what each one is, and of what kind, and how much, and other questions of this sort, in accordance with the ten categories. The moral philosopher, however, does not have to explain all the secrets of God and of the angels and of others; but he must explain those which are necessary to the multitude, in which all men should agree, lest they fall into questions and heresies, as Avicenna teaches in the *Principles of Moral Philosophy*.

I say, therefore, that moral philosophy explains first the trinity in relation to God, which truth the legislator has by revelation rather than by reason. The reason, indeed, why philosophers have said a great deal concerning divine things in particular which exceed human reason and fall under revela-

tion, was touched on before in mathematics. For there it was shown how they could have many noble truths concerning God which were had through revelation made to them, as the Apostle says, for God revealed these things. But rather to the patriarchs and the prophets who, it is known, had revelation and from whom the philosophers learned all things, as was proved clearly above. For the patriarchs and the prophets not only treated divine things theologically or prophetically but also philosophically, because they devised all philosophy as was proved in the second part of this work. The metaphysician, however, was able to teach sufficiently that God is, and that he is known naturally, and that he is of infinite power, and that he is one, and that he is three. But how the Trinity is, he could not there explain to the full; and, therefore, that must be shown here.

There is, then, the blessed Trinity, the Father and the Son and the Holy Ghost. For Claudius, one of the expositors of the sacred Scripture, in the book in which he combats the following heresy, that God feels nothing with a sense of passion but with an affect of compassion, brings forward this argument, "Plato with praiseworthy daring, admirable skill, unchangeable purpose, sought, found, and proclaimed three persons in the Divinity: God the Father, also the paternal mind, art, or counsel, and the love of the two for each other." He taught thus not only that we must believe in one supreme equitrinal undivided Divinity, but he demonstrated that he must be thus. These things are clear from his book on *Divine Things*. Porphyry, as Augustine says in the tenth book of the *City of God*, chapter twenty-nine, spoke of the Father and his Son whom he called the paternal intellect and mind, and the medium of them whom, as Augustine says, we think he called the Holy Spirit; and following his manner he calls them three Gods, where although he uses words loosely, he sees nevertheless what should be maintained. Augustine, in the same book in the thirty-second chapter,[1] recounts that a certain platonic philosopher, whose name he does not give, stated the beginning of the Gospel according to John as far as the incarnation of Christ, in which the distinction of

_____

[1]*De Civit. Dei*, X, 29.

[2]*De Civit. Dei*, X, 32.

the divine persons is stated clearly. Augustine, also in the tenth book of the *City of God* in the thirty-sixth and the thirty-seventh[2] chapters, insists that Porphyry says in the first book on the *Return of the Soul* that sins can not be purged except by the Son of God. And Aristotle says in the beginning of the *Heavens and the World* that in divine worship we exercise ourselves to magnify the one God by the number three, which is prominent in the properties of the things which are created. And therefore, since every creature, as is evident from the *Metaphysics*, is a trace and imprint of the Trinity, there must be the Trinity in the Creator. And since Aristotle completed the philosophy of his predecessors to the limit of the possibility of his times, he had to feel far more certainly concerning the blessed Trinity of persons that he might confess the Father and the Son and the Holy Spirit. For this reason there were three sacrifices in the law of Aristotle and three prayers, as Averroës says in his commentary on the beginning of the *Heavens and the World*: and this is manifest from the politics of Aristotle, which is the *Book of Laws*. Avicenna, moreover, the most outstanding expositor of Aristotle, assumes the Holy Spirit in the principles of moral philosophy.

But he [i.e. Aristotle] could perceive the truth of the Father and the Son far better, because it is more difficult to understand the procession of the Holy Spirit from two distinct persons than the generation of one of them from the other. For this reason philosophers failed more in the comprehension of the Holy Spirit than in the knowledge of the Father and the Son. And therefore they who were able to have a knowledge of the Holy Spirit, had far more knowledge of the other persons. The philosopher Ethicus in his book on divine and human and natural things, which he wrote in the Hebrew, the Greek, and the Latin languages, because of the greatness of the secrets, places in God, the Father, and the Word of the Father, and the Holy Spirit, and maintains that there are three persons, namely, the Father and the Son and the Holy Spirit. This must also be held by reason. This reasoning, nevertheless, could not have been given before the things which have to he expressed of God in particular nor before the authorities of the great philosophers, which are introduced to this same end in this science as in the place appropriate to them.

I say, therefore, that God is of infinite power; and infinite power is powerful of infinite operation; therefore, something infinite can be made by God, but not something infinite in essence, because then there could be several Gods; the contrary of which has been shown in the section on mathematics. Therefore, that which is begotten of God must be God since it has the essence of its progenitor; but it is different in person. And since this which is begotten has infinite power, and since it is infinite good, it can bring forth something infinite: therefore it is able to bring forth another person. Either, then, the Father brings forth the same person, and then the Holy Spirit will proceed from both of them; or he will be brought forth from the Son only, and in that case he will not pertain to the Father and the relationship will not be full and there will not be complete agreement in the divine persons, which is contrary to reason. Further, there can not be parity of love according to this view, because the Father would love the Son more than the Holy Spirit, because he begets the Son and does not bring forth the Holy Spirit. But since the Holy Spirit is God, because he has the divine essence, an infinite love must be due him; and therefore, the Father will love him with an infinite love as he does the Son. And likewise because the love of the Father can not be other than infinite, because his love is in accordance with his power, it remains, therefore, that the love of the Father for the Holy Spirit will be as great as the love of the Son for the Holy Spirit. Wherefore, the Holy Spirit as well as the Son must be brought forth from the Father. That however, there are not and can not be more persons, can not and should not be explained here, but must be assumed until it is proved in the fourth part of this science [of morals], to which the full measure of the demonstration will be assigned. But it was necessary that the trinity of persons, namely, of the Father and the Son and the Holy Spirit be proved and expounded here because it is the radical foundation of this science for establishing divine worship and for many other things. Nor should it be alleged in opposition that no science has to prove its principles. For how that is to be understood has been shown above. But other things which can be inquired concerning God and in which there should be probable doubt, are conclusions of the fourth part and, therefore, will be determined there. . . .

The Second Part of Moral Philosophy[1]

Chapter I

On observance of the laws of matrimony and of the commonwealth.

The second part treats of the laws and statutes of the relations of men to each other. In the first place, the welfare of the human species is considered in the line of propagation, to bind people by laws in their increase. Therefore, laws of marriage are given and how marriages must be made is determined and how impediments are to be removed; and most of all, that fornicators and sodomites be excluded from states, who are inimical to the construction of the state, since they draw men away from that which is better in states, namely, from marriage, as Avicenna and others maintain.

Next, laws are given in accordance with which subjects are ordered in respect to prelates and princes, and contrariwise, and servants to masters according to every type of servitude and mastership; and laws are given in accordance with which the fathers of families must live in guiding their offspring and family, and the master is ordered in respect to his disciples. Next, the doctors and the skilled in each of the sciences and arts are appointed; and those best suited to engage in studies and duties of this sort are chosen according to the advice of the wise men from the youths who are to be instructed; and the rest are deputed to the military service to execute justice and to check malefactors. And it is necessary, as Avicenna says, that this be the first intention in instituting the law, namely, to order the state in three parts, that is, into disposers, ministers, and those learned in the law, and that in each of them some one in charge be appointed. After him, other officials inferior to him should be appointed, and after these still others, until few remain; to the end that no one be useless in the state and not have some praiseworthy function, and that some utility to the state may be derived from each one. Whence, in

Plato, that state is held to be most justly ordered in which each one knows his own condition. Therefore, as Avicenna says, the prince of the state should prohibit idleness and disoccupation. Those, moreover, who can not be curbed should be expelled from the state, unless the cause is infirmity or old age; and then a place should be set apart in which people of that sort should remain and have a procurator allotted to them. It is necessary, moreover, that there be in the state a certain place for the moneys of the commonwealth, which should be derived partly from the law governing contracts, partly from fines which are inflicted for punishment, partly from the estates and spoil of rebels, partly from other sources; and to the end that this public fund be available partly for those who can not acquire money for themselves because of infirmity and old age and partly for teachers of law and medicine, and partly for public uses.

And then, the legislator instructs men to make patrimonies and inheritances and testaments, because Avicenna says that the substance necessary for life is partly the branch and is partly the root. But the root is the patrimony and anything bequeathed and given by testament, of which three roots the most secure is patrimony. The branch of substance, however, comes from gains derived from kinds of business. Then laws should be published concerning contracts in all sorts of business, in buying, selling, leasing, hiring, borrowing, lending, paying, saving and the like, that whatever can do harm in contracts may be removed, as Avicenna says.

Then, laws must be framed in accordance with which it may be shown in all lawsuits and in all cases what rights and wrongs are, and according to which legal processes may be terminated that peace and justice may be fostered among the citizens. Later, as Avicenna says, activities by which inheritances and fortunes are lost and by which the peace and concord of citizens are disturbed, must be prohibited; and those who set up and practise these pursuits are people who wish to win for the sake of some gain, such as the wrestler, the dice player, and others of this sort. In the same way, activities should be prohibited which lead to things contrary to the utilities, such as he

[1]O. c., vol. II, pp. 250–255, and vol. III, p. 145.

exemplified in his teaching concerning stealing and plundering and other acts of this sort.

And further ordinances should be made, as Avicenna says, that men aid and defend each other, and that they be unanimous against the enemies of the law even to subduing them by violence. If, however, there be another commonwealth and another regimen of good constitutions and laws, this is not opposed to the first unless the time should come when there must be no other law than this one, the establishment of which, since it is the best, must then be extended throughout the whole world. And in this statement the Christian law is signified, as will be explained below. If, however, there should be some among those who are at variance with the law, they should first be corrected that they may return to their senses; but if they do not wish to do that, they should be put to death.

Chapter II

The last point that is required here is that the legislator set up a successor to himself. This is done, according to Avicenna, in the following manner. For he should do it with the consensus of the nobles and of the people; and he should choose such an one as can rule well and be prudent and be of good morals, brave, kind, skilled in governing and learned in the law, than whom none is more learned, and this should be manifest to all. But if thereafter they should so disagree that they wish to choose another, they have in that denied God, and therefore the legislator should interpose in his law enactments to the effect that the entire state should fall unanimously upon any one who should wish to intrude himself by power or money and should kill him. But if they shall be able to do this and shall not have done it, they have in that contradicted God, and he is not guilty of blood who has killed one of this sort provided, however, it is previously known to the people. If, on the other hand, he who should be made successor is not worthy and has been so proved, another should be appointed.

And so in a summary way the intention and aims of the fundamental parts [the roots] of this second section [of moral philosophy] and of those matters that proceed from such fundamentals have been brought to a close. In this part is comprehended the civil law, which is now in use among the latins, as is

manifest from the roots of this part. Moreover, it is certain that the Latins have derived their rights and laws from the Greeks; that is, from the books of Aristotle and Theophrastus, his successor, as well as the laws of the twelve tables which were taken first from the laws of Solon the Athenian.

The Third Part of Moral Philosophy

Chapter I

On the guidance of man relative to himself.

The third part of moral and civil science is concerned with the practices of each person relative to himself, that everyone may have honorableness of life and may pass over the foulness of vices because of future felicity and the horror of eternal punishment. That this should be the third part appears evidently, since it is plain that that part which contains the worship of God is first, as has been declared. The common good, moreover, is set before the private good, as Aristotle says in the first book of the *Metaphysics*. But the preceding part has to do with the common good; whereas this part advances the private good. For charity is the greatest virtue, and it is ordered with reference to the common good, and peace and justice attend it, which virtues go beyond the morals of individual persons. For man is a social animal and it is one of his properties, as Avicenna says in the fifth book on the *Soul*, that he should not live alone like the brute animal which in its life suffices to itself alone. Therefore the laws which order men to their neighbor are the more important.

According to Aristotle and Averroës, in the tenth book of the *Metaphysics*, the hermit man who is not part of the state, but is concerned with himself alone, is not good nor is he evil. And Cicero, in the book on *Duties*, quoting the words of Plato says that Plato wrote very truly that we are not born for ourselves alone. Our native land claims part of our origin; our friends part; and as the stoics are pleased to believe that all things are created for the use of men, men are generated for the sake of men, that they may be able to aid one another. As Cicero himself, in the fifth book of the *Academics*, says, "Nothing is so noble as the communication of benefits." It is, in fact, innate in man that he have something of the civil and the popular, which something the Greeks call *politicon*. Whence, in the book on the *Happy Life*, Seneca says, "This word is required of man that he aid all, if he is able to, or many; if he is less able, a few; if still less, his neighbors; if less, himself." Wherefore, the second principal part of moral philosophy must be concerned with public laws, as has been stated; and the third will be on the life and the honor which each one should pursue. This, moreover, is true according to the order of the dignity of nature and absolutely speaking, although Aristotle does not adopt this manner in his books, for he proceeds according to the way of investigation and therefore goes from the things which are better known to us and not from those better known to nature. But since we have already made certain through him and others what the power of this science requires, therefore, we can arrange its parts according to the order which the dignity of nature demands.

And here the philosophers have said wondrous things concerning virtues and vices; so that every christian may be confounded when we conceive that unbelieving men had such sublimities of virtues and we seem to fall ignominiously from the glory of virtues. For the rest, we should be greatly encouraged to aspire to the apex of virtue, and stirred by noble examples we should give forth more noble fruits of the virtues, since we have greater aid in life than those philosophers, and since we are assured we shall receive greater aids beyond comparison by the grace of God. I shall first quote certain phrases relating to virtues and vices in general: secondly, I shall pass on to particulars. . . .

The Fourth Part
of Moral Philosophy[1]

Chapter I

I have dwelt on this third part of *Moral Philosophy* at length because of the beauty and utility of moral sentiments and because the books from which I have gathered these roots, flowers, and fruits of morals, are rarely found. Now, however, I wish to go on to the fourth part of this science [of morals] which, although it is not so copious and so pregnant as the third, is nevertheless more wonderful and more worthy, not only than that part, but than all the parts of the science,

since it consists in the elucidation of the belief, and the love, and the proof by works, of the religion of the faithful which the human race should accept. Nor is there anything of philosophy more necessary for man or of so great utility or dignity. For it is especially on account of this part [of morals] that all the sciences are subordinate to moral philosophy. In fact, all wisdom is ordered with a view to knowing the salvation of the human race; and this salvation consists in the perception of the things which lead man to the felicity of the other life. Avicenna says of this felicity that it is such as eye has not seen nor ear heard, as has been touched on above. And since this fourth part of philosophy purposes to investigate this salvation and to attract men to it, therefore, all the sciences, arts, and functions, and whatever falls under the consideration of man, are bound to this most noble part of civil science; and this is the goal of human consideration.

For this reason it is most useful to consider the intention of this part; and it is fitting that every christian do so for the confirmation of his profession and that he may have wherewith to correct those who have wandered astray. Assuredly, God can never deny to the human race a knowledge of the way of salvation, since he wishes all men to be saved according to the Apostle. And his goodness is infinite, wherefore he has always left men means by which they may he enlightened to know the ways of truth. Aristotle indeed in his *Politics* takes up the different kinds of religions, and says that he wishes to consider the religions and the laws of four or five simple commonwealths and to see what laws corrupt commonwealths and kingdoms, and what laws do not. He says, moreover, that there are four or five simple corrupt religions, intending that the religion or law be called simple because of a simple end and composite because of a composite end, since every religion varies according to the condition of the end, as Al Farabi teaches in the book on the *Sciences*, expounding the view of Aristotle concerning religions. And these simple ends, according to Al Farabi, but more clearly according to Boethius in the third book of the *Consolation of Philosophy*, are: pleasure, riches, honor, power, fame or glory of name.

And now I shall tell of the principal nations among which are varied throughout the world, the

---

[1]O. c., vol. II, pp. 866–68, and vol. III, pp. 149–150.

religions which still continue, and they are, saracens, tartars, pagans, idolaters, Jews, Christians. For there are no more principal religions, nor can there be until the religion of the Antichrist. But religions are compounded from all these, or from some four, or three, or two, according to various combinations.

But besides the ends enumerated, there is another, namely, the felicity of the other life, which different religions seek and strain toward in different ways, because some place it in the delights of the body, some in the delights of the soul, some in the delights of both. In addition there are religions compounded of this felicity and all the other ends, or from several, and this in diverse manners. For although they seek after a future felicity, nevertheless many men give themselves up to pleasures, and others strive eagerly after riches, and some aspire after honors, and some after the power of dominion, and some after the glory of fame. I shall touch, however, on the three divisions of the religions first, that the end to which they tend may be clear. Then I shall deal with the choice of the religion of the faithful, which alone should be spread throughout the world. . . .

Chapter I (continued)[1]

Having set forth these principal religions in respect to the use of peoples as well as in respect to the ways of astronomy and in respect to the diversities of their ends, the consideration proceeds to the means of persuading men of the truth of religion. It was said above in the section on mathematics, in relation to the conversion of unbelievers, that the persuasion of the religious truth which is contained in the Christian religion alone, is brought about in a twofold manner, since it is either by miracles which are beyond us and beyond unbelievers, and concerning this way no man can presume; or else it is by a way, common to unbelievers and to us, which is in our power and which they can not deny, because it proceeds along the ways of human reason and by the ways of philosophy. Philosophy belongs especially to unbelievers, since we have derived the whole of philosophy from them, and not without the greatest reason, that we may have confirmation of our faith for ourselves, and that we

may pray efficaciously for the salvation of unbelievers. Nor should the statement of Gregory be urged in objection, that faith has no place where human reason lends proof. For this statement must be understood of the Christian man who would lean only or principally on human reason. But this should not be done: on the contrary, he must believe in the Church and the Scripture and the Saints and the Catholic doctors, and that he should do principally.

But for the solace of human frailty, that it may avoid the attacks of error, it is useful for the Christian to have effective reasons for the things which he believes, and he should have a reason for his faith for any occasion that requires it, as the blessed Peter teaches in his first Epistle, saying,[2] "but sanctify in your hearts Christ as Lord; being ready always to give answer to every man that asketh you a reason concerning the faith and hope that is in you." But we can not argue this by quoting our law, nor the authorities of the saints, because unbelievers deny the Lord Christ and his law and saints. Wherefore it is necessary to seek reasons in another way, and this way is common to us and to unbelievers, namely, philosophy. But the power of philosophy in this part accords in the highest degree with the wisdom of God; indeed, it is the trace and imprint of the divine wisdom given by God to man, that by this trace man may be moved to divine truths. Nor are these things proper to philosophy, but are common to theology and philosophy, to believers and unbelievers, given by God and revealed to philosophers, to the end that the human race might be prepared for special divine truths. And the reasons of which I speak are not unrelated to faith nor outside the principles of faith, but are dug from its roots, as will be manifest from only stating them.

I could, of course, set forth the simple and crude methods suited to the mass of unbelievers, but that is not worth while. For the crowd is too imperfect, and therefore the conviction of faith which the crowd must have is crude and confused and unworthy of wise men. I wish, therefore, to go higher and give a demonstration of which wise men must judge. For in every nation there are some men who are assiduous and apt to wisdom, who are open to rational convic-

---

[1] O. c., vol. II, pp. 872–79, and vol. III, p. 150.

[2] *First Epistle of Peter* 3:15.

tion; so that once they have been informed, persuasion through them of the crowd is made easier.

I assume in the beginning, of course, that there are three kinds of knowledge; one is in the effort of personal discovery through experience. Another is by the learning of others. The third precedes these, and is the way to them, called natural knowledge; and it is so named because it is common to all. That, in fact, is natural which is common to all members of the same species, as burning is natural to fire, according to the example of Aristotle in the fifth book of the *Ethics*; and Cicero says this same thing in the first of the *Tusculan Questions*, and we see it in an infinite number of examples. For we say the cries of brutes have a natural significance, because they are common to the individuals of their species; and things are known naturally by us of the sort in which we all agree, as that every whole is greater than its part, and others of this sort, as well simple as complex. We know likewise that the rational soul is formed to learn the truth and to love it, and the proof of this love is the exhibition of action, according to Gregory and all the saints and philosophers. There are some, however, who think that there are two distinct parts in the soul, or two faculties, so that there is one by which the soul knows the truth, another by which it wishes to seize on[1] the truth when learned. On the other hand some believe that there is one substance of the soul which performs both functions, because its acts are coordinated to each other, in that the knowledge of truth exists on account of the love for it; for it is one and the same faculty. According to them the soul first apprehends the truth and then loves it when known and completes it in action. Whence Aristotle holds in the third book on the *Soul*,[2] that the speculative intellect is made practical by the extension of knowledge of truth to the love of it. Nor does he ever make a specific difference between the speculative intellect and the practical as he does between the intellect and the sense and the vegetative soul. For he argues, in the second book on the *Soul* that these three

are diverse in species, because their operations are diverse in species, that is, understanding, perceiving and vegetating; nor are they ordered in relation to each other. But the knowledge of truth is ordered toward the love of it, and it is formed because of it; and therefore there is one faculty, or nature, or substance of the rational soul which knows truth and loves it. Whence in the third book on the *Soul*,[3] Aristotle begins thus: "however, concerning the part of the soul with which it knows and judges, I must now speak"; meaning that it is the same part which has both functions; just as it is in the sensitive part; because it is the same faculty which perceives and desires, as is evident in every sense. For the sense of touch knows the hot and desires it; and the sense of taste knows flavors and desires them, and so with others.

But it is not of great moment how we may speak of these matters. For we know that the rational soul is formed to know and to love the truth. But the truth of religion is perceived only so far as the knowledge of God overflows in one, for every religion is referred to God; and therefore he who wishes to come to a certain knowledge of religion must begin with God. But the knowledge of God, so far as concerns the question of whether he is, is known to all naturally, as Cicero teaches in his book on the *Immortality of the Soul*. And he proves it saying, "no nation is so savage and monstrous that its mind has not been imbued with an opinion of God nor is there a people that does not show some form of divine worship."[4] But if Avicenna says in the first book of the *Metaphysics*[5] that this science seeks to prove the being of God, it must be said that this is true as regards full certitude. For the natural knowledge which every one has of God is weak, and it is weakened by the sins which are numerous in everyone. For sin obscures the soul and most of all in what concerns the divine.

Therefore, it is necessary that this knowledge be aided by argument and faith. But the knowledge of the unity of God, and of what God is, and how, and of

---

[1] *Audire* in the text has been interpreted as erroneous, probably, for *adpetere*.

[2] *De An.* III, 7, 431ᵃ 10–20.

[3] *De An.* III, 4, 429ᵃ 10.

[4] Probably from *De Nat. Deorum* I, 16 and 23.

[5] *Met.* I, 1.

what sort, is not known naturally. For in these matters men are always in disaccord, some maintaining several gods, others considering that the stars are gods, others, things here below, as, for example, the pure pagans and the idolaters. And so they must err in religion. All others who say that there is one God do not understand other points which are true of God. And therefore one who advances a religion must know in the beginning how to present the attributes which are required in general of God. However, it is not necessary that he go into all the particular truths in the beginning; but he should proceed little by little and he should begin with the easier questions in this way. For as the geometer sets down his definitions that the things he deals with may be known in respect to what they are and what they are called, so one must proceed here: because unless one knows what it is that is meant by a name, there will be no demonstration.

God, therefore, is the first cause antecedent to which there is no other, and which did not emerge into being, nor will it be possible for it not to be, of infinite power, wisdom, and goodness, Creator of everything and director of everything, according to the susceptibility of the nature of individual things. And in this definition tartars, Saracens, Jews, and Christians agree. The wise men also of the idolaters and the pagans, when they have been given the reason for this, can not contradict it; nor consequently can the multitude over whom the wise men stand as directors and leaders. For two ways of arguing to this end will be presented for them: one by the consensus of all other nations and religions and of all the rest of the human race. But the lesser should conform itself to the greater part; and that part is disgraceful which does not accord with its whole. It is well known that there are wiser men in the other religions; and the pagans and the idolaters are not ignorant of this. For when a meeting is arranged with them they are convinced easily, and they perceive their own ignorance clearly; as appeared in the case of the emperor of the tartars who summoned before him Christians, Saracens, and idolaters to confer on the truth of religion; and forthwith the idolaters were confounded and convinced. This fact appears in the book on the *Practices of the Tartars* addressed to our lord the present King of France. And when Christians confer with pagans, like the Prusceni

and the other adjoining nations, they yield easily and see that they are held by errors. The proof of this is that they wished most willingly to be made Christians if the Church were willing to permit them to retain their freedom and to enjoy their goods in peace. But the Christian princes who labor for their conversion, and most of all the brothers of the Teutonic house, wish to reduce them to servitude, as is known to the dominicans and franciscans and other good men throughout Germany and Poland. And, therefore, they offer opposition; whence, they stand against oppression, not against the arguments of a better religion.

Further, one who advocates the religion of the faithful has from the part of *Metaphysics* and of this moral science another manner by which he may proceed in arguing. This I wish only to indicate until such a time as the treatise which Your Highness demands will be completed. And, indeed, it can be set down as a postulate for the man who is assiduous and amenable to the efficacy of reason, that causes do not go back *in infinitum*, since an infinite number of causes can not be nor be understood. For all things which are and which are understood are comprehended in some number, as Aristotle says in the third book of the *Physics*. There is not therefore cause preceding cause *in infinitum*. Therefore we must stop at some first cause which does not have a cause before it, and all the multitude is reduced to unity. And in every genus there is one first to which the others are reduced. But if this be the first cause, with no other cause antecedent to it, it is manifest that it did not come forth into being through a cause; not is anything else the cause of its being; nor does it make itself to be after not being, because then it would have to be when it was not, that it might make itself be. For everything which causes something else to be after not being, has being while it does this: therefore, nothing is cause of its own being. Wherefore, this first cause never had non-being: therefore, it always was. But if that is the case, then it will always be, since there are many things which will always be, and nevertheless have not always been, as angels and souls and the heavens and the earth and others of this sort. And, therefore, that which never had non-being will conserve its being far more easily in eternity. Furthermore, that which never had non-being is removed infinitely from non-being; and therefore it is impossible that it fall into non-being. Some things, in fact, which have come forth into being are able not to be, because they are not infinitely removed from non-being, for at one time they were not: therefore, since non-being is removed *in infinitum* from that which always was, there is no proportion between it and this other. And, therefore, such a thing will not be able not to be: and this is more acceptable than any of the doctrines which have been spoken of here, and therefore it is rather conceivable than in need of proof.

It is evident, however, that the thing which always was and will be is of infinite power. Because if it is of finite power, then its power is imperfect, since something can be added to all finite things, and every imperfect thing is naturally subject to change; but it is not possible to assume any change unless the first be assumed. For the first is naturally prior to the posterior. And therefore since the first change is in respect to being and non-being, it must be possible in that which has finite power. But this change does not occur in that which always was and always will be: wherefore, neither does finitude in power pertain to it.

Further, Philosophy argues in the third book of the *Consolation*[1] in this fashion. In every genus in which the imperfect is found, it is natural that the perfect be found. And, therefore, in the genus of power a perfect power must be found after we find an imperfect one. But the perfect is that from which nothing is lacking, nor can anything be added, according to Aristotle in the third book of the *Physics* and the fifth of the *Metaphysics*. And that to which nothing can be added is infinite; because an addition can be made to every finite thing in so far as it is such, and something else can be understood beyond it. It is necessary, therefore, that the perfect power be infinite. But there is no perfect and infinite power in things other than this cause which we seek: therefore, in this cause there will be such power. But if its power is infinite, then its essence is infinite; because power does not exceed essence. For essence is either equal to power or greater. And demonstrations have already

been given for this in the observations which were made concerning matter. It is manifest, therefore, that the essence of the first cause is infinite.

And certainly if its essence and power are infinite, its goodness must be infinite, since a thing whose essence is finite has finite goodness. Therefore the infinite will have infinite goodness; and otherwise there is no proportion of goodness to essence in this cause; which can not be in so great majesty. And if its goodness were finite, it would be imperfect, and something could be added to it and taken from it, and thus it could be subjected to transmutation; and therefore it would be natural for it to have non-being, as was argued previously of power. Nor is it possible that that which has infinite majesty in essence and power and goodness, should lack knowledge, because a thing which is of this sort [i.e. deficient] has a lowliness[2] and can not be related to the infinity of majesty, as is the case with elements and stones and vegetables.

Moreover, we see that things lacking infinite power, as animals and men and angels, have knowledge because of the nobility of their nature: therefore, since the nature of the cause which is now sought is infinitely more noble than anything of this sort, it will have the power of knowing. But since all other things which are in it are found to be infinite, this cause has infinite wisdom. Again, if it were finite, it would be imperfect and subject naturally to transmutation into greater and lesser, as is clear in the case of other things that know, as in every imperfect thing. And therefore the first mutation which is in respect to being and non-being could be discovered here, as was shown above. It is necessary, therefore, that there be infinite wisdom in this cause; but if its power is infinite it is able to produce this world, and its infinite wisdom knows how to order it best, and its goodness requires that that be done, because it is the property of the best to do the best and to communicate its goodness to others, so far as goodness is adaptable to them. Therefore, this cause has necessarily produced the world. . . .

---

[1]*Consol. Phil.* III, prosa 10.

[2]The text reads *utilitatem*; this has been interpreted as an error for *vilitatem*; an Interpretation which is reinforced by the contrast below to *nobilitas*, i.e. *nobilis=non vilis*.

STUDY QUESTIONS: BACON, *OPUS MAJUS*

1. What are the two components of wisdom? How are they related?
2. What are the main causes of error in our thinking?
3. What is Bacon's view of the Scriptures? Are they to be accepted on faith? Why?
4. Is experience more or less certain than the truths taught by religious authority? Why?
5. What is the right relationship between philosophy and theology?
6. What is the importance of Augustine and why does Bacon bring him up?
7. Why is language important? How do we study and learn languages?
8. What is the "utility" of mathematics?
9. What is the significance of the "science of perspective," and what function does it serve?
10. What is experimental science? How does it work? How is it related to philosophy? To theology?
11. What is Bacon's view of morality? Is moral philosophy a separate branch from other philosophical disciplines? How is morality acquired?
12. What is Bacon's view of Avicenna's political philosophy?
13. What is the four parts of moral philosophy? How are they related?
14. What is Bacon's view of Al Farabi's moral teachings?

Philosophical Bridges: Roger Bacon

Bacon's integration of experimental methods into philosophy independently of theological considerations both signaled and inspired a return to the sort of empiricism to which Aristotle aspired but never fully achieved: practitioners of the "dark arts," crafting methods of experimentation, the "magic" of what would eventually come to be known not as alchemy or astrology or witchcraft but science. It is perhaps ironic that the sort of collective epistemology developed by the Scholastics, in which inquiry was done as a group enterprise, would turn out to be an environment more conducive to science than to theology. The notion that controlling experience, and thereby nature, by testing hypotheses and correcting and improving the mind's innate ideas, was in part the legacy that Roger Bacon bequeathed to the next generation of thinkers and helped herald the modern era.

JOHN DUNS SCOTUS (1266–1308)

Biographical History

Born in the village of Duns, Berwickshire, John Duns Scotus joined a Franciscan seminary in Scotland at the age of 14. In 1291, he was ordained and then continued studying theology and philosophy at the Universities of Oxford and Paris. About his short life (he died at the age of 42), very little is known. He got in trouble for siding with the Pope against King Philip IV regarding some dispute, for which he was forgiven. For the Church, he defended the notion of the Immaculate Conception, which the councils of Basel (1439) and Trent (1546) officially adopted as one of the central tenets of Roman Catholic Dogma; Pope Pius IX even issued the bull *Ineffabilis Deus*, which declared what came to be called the "Scotist opinion" was a divine revelation and believed without question.

Scotus wrote numerous works that are extremely technical and hard to follow because of their complex terminology. For this reason he was dubbed, "the Subtle Doctor." After receiving his doctorate in 1305 from Paris, he was appointed professor at Cologne, where he remained until his death.

Philosophical Overview

The Islamic philosophers, most notably Avicenna and Averroës, also influenced Scotus. He is generally regarded as the most important British medieval thinker. His students have compiled most of his extant writings from their various lectures, drafts and notes. These rely on many obscure Latin terms in addition to which Scotus coined many of his own terms that later became standard medieval parlance.

One key idea in his thinking is the notion that the world is *univocal* rather than *equivocal*, meaning that there is but one best interpretation of the true meaning of things, not many. In other words, the world according to Dun Scotus is not just One, as Parmenides and so many other philosophers have claimed, it has an unambiguous, single *meaning*. We can discover the true meaning of reality using our own reason and experience as guides. He thus sides with Aquinas, against both Averroës and Maimonides, in thinking that the human mind can fully understand the world without resort to divine revelation or some sort of mystical illumination. All that we need is a deeper, more precise, and subtle language. Like mathematicians, philosophers are free to invent new distinctions and terms as needed to capture the true meaning of the world. It is as if we are increasing the resolution power of our minds using language as a technology.

Scotus turns away from Platonic dualism, arguing that knowledge is not based on innate ideas but must begin, instead, with individual experience. The primary objects of our thought are not mere representations of some universal idea, as Plato and Aristotle each in his own way thought, nor some divine essence, as Augustine thought. Rather, Scotus evokes the doctrine of what he calls *hylomorphism*, the view that all existent things are a combination of Aristotelian forms and primordial matter. The various individual things that are the objects of our thoughts he calls *haecceity*, which means, literally, "thisness." Things have "thisness." It is the same logical type as a universal. So although he rejects universal hylomorphism, Scotus argues that material things exist as a conjunction of matter and form, each of which is a different principle. Each thing has *esse*, being as such, which can be predicated univocally of all things and without which nothing is comprehensible. The mind according to Scotus has a primary intellectual intuition of each individual thing it itself. His argument is that it would be impossible to abstract the universal idea from the individual thing unless this were so. A previous intellectual intuition of the individual thing is what makes perception possible.

For example, consider that Garrett is human and Dan is human. As distinct individuals, Garrett and Dan are different humans. Yet there must be some amorphous aspect of their being that allows of distinct individuations. "Humanness" would be that amorphous aspect, their "thisness (haecceity)" would be what allows their existence as distinct entities. Scotus thus argues that we can distinguish "Garretness" and "Danness" from general concepts such as "humanness." Now, but on what could the distinction be based? In no way is Dan's individual essence, his "Danness," separable in actuality from his "humanness," his existence as a human being. Remove the human being from existence and you remove the individual Dan. This deep and subtle distinction, what he called a "formal objective distinction," is something that according to Scotus not even God could destroy.

Duns Scotus' subtle notion of being involves not a genus but the concept of opposition to non-being, or nothingness. There are various types of oppositions to nothings, from God at the highest level to human and inanimate objects at the lowest. The opposition is manifested in part in the will, both divine and human. Moreover, neither God nor individual human beings are bound by necessity to act according to the dictates of deterministic providence, not even to the dictates of logically guided reason (as both the Arabic neo-Platonic and Aristotelian intellectualist philosophers believed). Both exist as autonomous individual agents in the universe. The world is apprehended through the primacy of being itself. This is because being as such is known directly and immediately by all sentient beings who are aware of themselves and the world.

THE OXFORD COMMENTARY
ON THE FOUR BOOKS
OF THE MASTER OF THE SENTENCES
John Duns Scotus

In the following selection, John Duns Scotus starts out by applying Aristotelian concepts and arguments to a basically Augustinian metaphysics, an improved modification of earlier positions against which Thomas Aquinas had argued. In Aquinas' view, various individuals belonging to a particular species were all of the same kind yet numerically different, a consequence of his fundamental position that the principle of individuation is matter itself. In Scotus' view, it is not matter but form that provides the principle of individuation, a consequence of his doctrine of *hecceity* (discussed earlier). Knowledge a priori is limited to concepts and although it guides our interpretation of experience it cannot every fully explain experience, the items of which must be accounted for *a posteriori*. The mind must rely on yet abstract from experience in order to make knowledge of all sciences possible. And although the particular truths of science are variable, the epistemic principles themselves are invariable and infallible. The truths of these principles however depend on the understanding, not on data derived from the senses.

A special, third, category of certain knowledge is that of our own existence and actions. Like Augustine before him and Descartes after him, he argues that I can know with absolute certainty that I think, that I exist, that I am being appeared to some way rather than another. Thus, regardless of how I may be deceived by my senses, the certainty of the existence of the being thus deceived is logically guaranteed, regardless. From such certainties, derived as it were from variations in experience or even illusions, we can ascertain logical principles that guarantee the possibility of certain knowledge at all levels.

John Duns Scotus, from *The Oxford Commentary on the Four Books of the Master of the Sentences*, translated by Richard McKeon in Richard McKeon, ed., *Selections from Medieval Philosophers*, Vol. 2, Charles Scribners Sons, 1929, pp. 313–350.

BOOK I. DISTINCTION III, QUESTION IV[1]

The Question is proposed. Finally, with reference to this matter of knowability, I ask:

Whether any sure and pure truth can be known naturally by the understanding of the wayfarer without the special illumination of the uncreated light?

Principal Arguments. And I argue that it can not. Augustine says *On the Trinity*, book IX, Chapter 6: "But we perceive the inviolable truth, from which we may determine perfectly, so far as we are able, not how the mind of each man is, but how it must be in the sempiternal reasons." And again in Chapter 6 of the same work: "When we approve or disprove something rightly, we are inwardly convinced in approving and disproving, all other criteria remaining unchangeably above our mind." And again in the same work, Chapter 6: "Grasping the ineffably beautiful art of such figures above the perception of the mind by simple intelligence." And in Chapter 7 of the same work: "Therefore in that eternal truth, from which all temporal things are made, we perceive by the vision of the mind the form according to which we are and according to which we perform anything with true or right reason, whether in ourselves or in bodies, and thence we have the true knowledge of things conceived as if a word within us." Again in book XII, Chapter 2 of the same work: "But it is of more sublime reason to judge concerning these corporeal things according to incorporeal and eternal reasons." Again in the same book Chapter 14: "However, not only do the intelligible and incorporeal reasons of sensible things located in places persist without local spaces, but also the reasons of motions extended in time exist simultaneously without temporal duration as intelligible and not sensible reasons."

And that Augustine is speaking there of *eternal reasons* truly in God and not of *first principles*, is seen by the fact that he has said in the same place, that it is the privilege of few to attain to them; but if he were speaking of first principles, it would not be the privilege of few to attain to them but of many, because they are known to all. Again, in book XIV Chapter 15, speaking of the unjust man who rightly praises and vituperates many things in the customs of men, he says: "By what rules do they judge these things except by those in which they see in some fashion how everyone should live?" And at the end he adds: "Where then are they written unless in that book of that light which is called truth.'" That book of light is the divine understanding. Therefore, he means that in that light the unjust man sees what actions are to be done justly. And this is to be seen by means of something which is stamped or impressed by it [the light], for he says in the same place: "Whence, all just law is marked off, and it is transferred to the heart of man who does justice, not by migrating, but as if by being impressed, as the image passes from a ring to way and yet does not leave the ring." Therefore, we see in that light by which justice is imprinted in the heart of man; but that is the uncreated light. Again, in the XIIth book of the *Confessions*, Chapter 25: "If both of us see the true, you do not see it in me, nor I in you, but both of us in that which is above the mind in immutable truth." There are moreover in many places many other authorities of Augustine to prove this conclusion.

To the contrary: the Epistle to the Romans 1:20: "The invisible things of God, understood by means of those things that have been made, are clearly comprehended from the creation of the world";[2] but these reasons are the invisible things of God: therefore, they are known from creatures: therefore, before the vision of them sure knowledge of creatures is had.

The opinion is expounded which holds that no sure and pure truth can be known by us naturally without special illumination of the uncreated light. In this question there is one opinion[3] that there is a natural order per se among *general intentions*. We speak of the two intentions which are relevant to the question propounded, namely, of the intention of *that which is* [ens] and of *the true*.

---

[1] B. Ioannis Duns Scoti, from *Commentaria Oxoniensia ad IV. Libros Magistri Sententiarum*, ed. P. Marianus Fernandez Garcia. Ad Aquas Claras (Quaracchi): Ex Typographia Collegii S. Bonaventurae, 1912, vol. I, pp. 357–383.

[2] *A creatura mundi* is usually interpreted in english translations, *since the creation of the world*.

[3] Attributed to Henry of Ghent.

a) The first intention is of *that which is*. This is proved by the statement of the book *On Causes* in the fourth proposition: *the first of created things is being,* and in the commentary on the first proposition: *being is of more vehement adherence.*

b) This is proved likewise by reason: because *entity is absolute:* whereas truth indicates a reference to an exemplar. From this it follows that that which is can be known under the relation of *entity,* but not under the relation of *truth.*

c) This conclusion furthermore is proved from the part of the *intellect:* because *that which is* can be conceived by simple understanding, and hence, *that which is true* is conceived; but the relation of *truth* is conceived only by the understanding *compounding* and *dividing;* simple understanding however precedes composition and division.

If, therefore, it is inquired, in the question proposed, concerning knowledge of *that which is,* or concerning *that which is true* of that which is, the reply is that the intellect can know *the true* thus by pure natural causes. This is proved: because it is contradictory that a nature be untrained in its own operation, according to Damascenus, and that is more contradictory in a more perfect and superior nature according to the Philosopher in the second book *On the Heavens and the World,* where he speaks of stars, because it would be extremely contradictory for the stars to have a progressive power and not have the natural instruments for progression: therefore, since the proper operation of the intellect is to understand the true, it seems improper that nature should not concede to the intellect that which suffices for that operation.

d) But if we speak of the knowledge of *truth,* it is replied that as there is a *double exemplar,* created and uncreated, according to Plato in the first part of the *Timaeus,* that is, a made and an unmade or a created and an uncreated exemplar: the *created* exemplar is the *universal species* caused by the thing: the *uncreated* is the idea in the *divine mind;* thus there is a *double conformity* to the exemplar and a *double truth:* one is the conformity to the *created* exemplar, and in this fashion Aristotle stated that the truths of things are known by their conformity to the intelligible species; and Augustine seems to say this in the IXth book *On the Trinity,* chapter 7, where he holds that we have a special and a general knowledge of things, each of which is collected from sensibles, according to which we judge the truth of anything that turns up, that the thing itself is such or such.

But that we should have an absolutely *certain* and *infallible knowledge of the truth* of a thing through the *acquired exemplar* in us, this is said to be utterly impossible. And it is proved by a threefold reason, according to those holding this doctrine: the first reason is taken from the part of the *thing* from which the exemplar is drawn: the second from the part of the *subject* in which it is: the third from the part of the *exemplar* in itself.

e) The *first* reason is this: that object from which the exemplar is abstracted is *mutable:* therefore, it can not be the cause of anything *immutable;* but sure knowledge of any truth concerning anything is had of it under an immutable relation: therefore, it is not had by such an exemplar.

This is said to be the reason of Augustine in the *LXXXIII Questions,* question 9, where he holds that *pure truth is not to be sought from sensible things,* because sensible things change without intermission.

f) The *second* reason is this: the soul in itself is mutable and passive to error: therefore, it can be rectified by nothing more mutable than itself that it err not; but such an exemplar in it is more mutable than the soul itself: therefore, that exemplar does not regulate the soul perfectly that it err not.

This is said to be the reason of Augustine in the book *On True Religion:* "Since the law of all arts is absolutely immutable, and since the human mind, to which it has been conceded to see such a law, can suffer the mutability of error, it is sufficiently apparent that there is above our mind a law which is called truth."

g) The *third* reason is: no one has certain and infallible knowledge of truth, unless he has that by which he can distinguish truth from verisimilitude; for if he can not distinguish truth from *falsity* or *verisimilitude,* he can doubt whether he is deceived: but truth can not be distinguished by means of the aforesaid created exemplar from verisimilitude, therefore etc. *Proof of the minor premis:* such a species can represent itself *as itself,* or in another fashion it can represent itself *as object,* as is the case in dreams. If it represents itself as object, it is falsity: if as itself, it is truth: therefore, through such a species it is not known sufficiently distinctively when it represents itself as itself, and when it represents itself as object; and thus it is not sufficiently distinctive of truth from falsity.

h) From these considerations it is concluded that if it happen that man knows a sure knowledge and infallible truth, that does not happen to him by looking at an exemplar derived from the thing by sensation, howsoever much it be purified and made universal, but it is necessary that he look upon the *uncreated exemplar*.

And, therefore, this mode is stated: God, not as that which is known, has the significance of an *exemplar* looking to which pure truth is: for the known is in *general attribute*, but he is the reason of knowing as naked exemplar, and the proper reason of the created essence. The fashion, however, in which he may be the *reason of knowing* and not the *known* is shown in an *example*: for just as the ray of the sun is sometimes projected from its source in an *oblique* line, sometimes in a *direct* line: and although the sun is the reason of seeing of that which is seen in the ray projected in the first manner, nevertheless it is not seen as it is in itself; but the sun is the reason of knowing of that which is seen in the ray in the second manner, in such wise that it too is known; thus, therefore, the uncreated light illumines the angelic intellect as in direct view, and then as seen, it is the reason of seeing other things in itself; but it illumines our understanding, while we are on the way, as in an oblique view; and therefore it is the reason of seeing to our intellect and not the seen.

i) It is held, moreover, that the uncreated exemplar has a triple relation in respect to the act of seeing, namely, that of the *kindling light*, and that of the *changing species* and that of the *configuring character or exemplar*.

And from this it is concluded finally that a special influence is required, because just as that essence is not seen by us naturally in itself, so likewise, as that essence is the exemplar in respect to any creature, it is not seen naturally, according to Augustine when he writes on seeing God: *for it is in his power to be seen: if he wishes, he is seen, if he does not wish, he is not seen.*

j) Finally it is added that there is a perfect knowledge of truth when two exemplar species concur in the mind, one *inhering*, that is, caused, the other *having penetrated from without*, that is, not caused, in illuminating the mind. The mind conceives the *word*

of truth perfectly when out of these two species of the thing it has compounded one reason or criterion for understanding the thing of which it is the criterion.

Division of the Question. Against this opinion I show *first*, that these reasons are not the fundamental reasons of any true opinion, nor are they according to the intention of Augustine, but lead to the opinion of the academics. In the *second* place, I show how that opinion of the academics, which seems to follow from these reasons, is false. In the *third* place, I reply to those reasons, in so far as they do not hold. In the *fourth* place I argue against the conclusion of this opinion. In the *fifth* place, I resolve the question. In the *sixth* place, I show how these reasons (in so far as they are Augustine's) lead to that intention of Augustine, but not that intention to which they were drawn here.

Article 1

It is shown that the proposed reasons are not the fundamental reasons of any true opinion, nor are they according to the intention of Augustine, but lead to the opinion of the academics.

It is demonstrated that the above mentioned reasons lead to all incertitude. *In the first place, these reasons seem to lead to the impossibility of sure natural knowledge.*

a) In the first place this is so,[1] because if an object is changed continually, no certitude of it can be had under an immutable reason, nor indeed could certitude be had in any light, because there is no certitude when the object is known in another way than it is itself: therefore, there is no certitude in knowing a mutable thing as immutable. It is evident likewise that the antecedent of this reason, namely, *that sensible things are changed continually*, is false; this is, indeed, the opinion attributed to Heraclitus in the IVth book of the *Metaphysics*.

b) In the same way, if there could not be certitude because of the mutability of the exemplar which is in our soul,[2] since whatsoever is placed in the soul subjectively is mutable, so too the very act of understanding will be mutable, and therefore it follows that the soul is rectified by nothing in the soul that it err not. It would follow likewise that the very act of understanding, since it is more mutable than the soul

---

[1] See above. e) p. 317.

[2] See above, f) pp. 317–318.

in which it is, will never be true, nor will it contain truth; which is false.

c) In the same way, according to this opinion, the caused *inhering* species concurs with that *penetrating* species; but when something which is incompatible with certitude concurs, no certitude can be had: for just as from a necessary and a contingent proposition only a contingent conclusion may be drawn, so from certainty and uncertainty concurring for some point of knowledge, no certain conclusion follows.

d) The same conclusion is likewise evident from the third reason,[1] because if that species abstracted from the thing concurs for all knowledge, and if it can not judge distinctly, because sometimes it represents itself as itself and sometimes it represents itself as object: therefore, whatever else concurs, no certitude can be had by which truth may be distinguished from verisimilitude.

e) Therefore, these reasons are seen to lead to all incertitude and thus to the opinion of the academics.

It is proved that the aforestated conclusion is not according to the mind of Augustine. I prove however that this conclusion is not according to the mind of Augustine:

a) Augustine in the second book of the *Soliloquies*: "Everyone concedes without hesitation that the proofs of the sciences are very true." And Boethius *De hebdomadibus:*[2] "A common conception of the mind is that which when heard anyone proves." And the Philosopher in the second book of the *Metaphysics*: "First principles are known to all, like the door in a house," because the door is concealed to no one, although things within the house may be concealed. From these three authorities it is argued as follows: that which is proper to *all* members of any species follows from the *specific nature*: therefore, since everyone has infallible certitude of *first principles*, and further since the *form of the perfect syllogism* is naturally evident to every one, according to the first book of the *Prior Analytics*, but knowledge of the conclusion depends only on the evidence of the principles and on the evidence of the syllogistic inference; therefore any demonstrable conclusion can be known naturally to every one from premises known through themselves.

b) In the second place, it is clear likewise that Augustine concedes the certitude of those things which are known through the *experience of the senses*; wherefore he says in the XVth book *on the Trinity*, chapter 12: "May we be spared from doubting that those things which we learn through the senses of the body are true, for through them we learn the heaven, the earth, and the things which are known to us in these, so far as he who made us and them wished us to know." If therefore we do not doubt their truth and we are not deceived, as is clear, then we are certain of things known by way of sense, for *certitude* is had when doubt and deception are excluded.

c) In the third place it is evident that Augustine concedes in the same work book XV, the same chapter, certitude concerning our actions: "He lives whether he be asleep or awake, for it is part of living also to sleep and see in dreams."

d) But if you say: to live is not a second act but a first act; he continues in the same place: "If anyone should say, I know that I know, he can not be mistaken," even by reflecting as many times as you wish on the first known. And in the same work: "If anyone should say, I wish to be happy, how would the reply be made not impudently, perhaps you are mistaken? And if he says I know that I wish this, and I know that I know this, then he can add a third to these two that he knows these two, and a fourth that he knows that he knows these two, and so he can proceed to an infinite number." And in the same work: "If anyone should say, I do not wish to err, will it not be true, whether he errs or does not err, that he nevertheless does not wish to err? And other arguments," he says, "are found which hold against the academics who contend that nothing can be known by man." And there follows in the same work, "There are then our three books[3] written in the first period of our conversion; the many arguments which have been found by the academics against the perception of truth will not in the least prevail on him who had been able to and has wished to read them and having read them has understood them." Again in the same book XV, chapter 15: "Those things too which are known in such wise that they can not slip from the mind, since they are present

---

[1] See above, g) p. 318.

[2] See above, p. 160, note 3.

[3] *The Three Books Against the Academics.*

and pertain to the nature of the mind itself, of which sort is the following, that we know we live; for this remains as long as the mind remains, and because the mind always remains, this also remains always."

And thus the first article is evident, that the reasons of that opinion are not conclusive, and that this first opinion is false and against Augustine.

Article II

It is shown in what that opinion of the academics is false.

Division of the Article. With respect to the second article, that the error of the academics has no place in any knowable things, it must be seen how infallible certitude can be had naturally of the three kinds of knowables mentioned above, namely, of *principles known through themselves* and of *conclusions*, secondly of *things known by experience*, thirdly, of *our actions*.

The certitude of first principles is shown. With reference to certitude of *principles* I say this: that the terms of principles known through themselves have such an *identity*, that one term known *evidently* includes the other necessarily; and therefore the understanding compounding those terms, from the fact that it apprehends them, has in itself the *necessary* cause of the *conformity* of that act of compounding to the terms themselves of which the composition is and likewise the *evident* cause of that conformity; and therefore, that conformity is evident to it necessarily. The necessary and evident cause of that conformity it apprehends in the terms: therefore, the *apprehension* of terms and their *composition* can not be in the understanding, unless the *conformity* of that composition to the terms stands, just as whiteness and whiteness can not stand unless *likeness* stands. But this conformity of composition to terms is the *truth of composition*: therefore, the composition of such terms can not stand unless there is truth, and thus the perception of that composition and the perception of terms can not stand, unless the perception of conformity of composition to terms stands and thus the perception of truth, for the first percepts obviously include the perception of that truth.

The Philosopher confirms this reasoning by likeness in book IV of the *Metaphysics*, where he insists that the opposite of a first principle, such as, "it is impossible that the same thing be and not be," can

not come into the understanding of any one, because then there would be contrary opinions in the mind at the same time. This is undoubtedly true of contrary opinions, that is of opinions formally contradictory, for the opinion attributing being to something and the opinion attributing non-being to the same thing are formally contradictory. Thus I may state in the question proposed that there is some contradiction to the intellections in the mind, although not a formal contradiction; for if there exists in the understanding a knowledge of the whole and the part and a composition of them, since they include as a necessary cause the conformity of the composition to the terms, and if there exists in the understanding this opinion, that this composition is false, contradictory ideas will be present: not formally, but the one notion will stand with the other, and nevertheless one will be the necessary cause of an idea opposed to the other; which is impossible. For just as it is impossible for white and black to be at the same time, because they are contrary formally, so it is impossible that white and that which is the precise cause of blackness stand, so it is necessary that it can not be without the other without contradiction.

The certitude of conclusions is shown. When the evidence or the certitude of first principles has been had, it is evident how certitude may be had of conclusions inferred from them, because of the evidence of the perfect form of the syllogism, since the certitude of the conclusion depends only on the certitude of the principles and on the evidence of the inference.

The understanding does not err, although the senses err. But will not the understanding err in this knowledge of principles and conclusions, if the senses are deceived concerning all the terms? I reply, that with respect to this knowledge the understanding does not have the senses for cause, but only for occasion, for the understanding does not have knowledge of simples unless it has received that knowledge from the senses; still, having received it, it can compound simples with each other by its own power; and if from the relation of such simples there is a combination which is evidently true, the understanding will assent to that combination by its own power and by the power of the terms, not by power of the sense by which it receives the terms from without. For example, if the reason of whole and the reason of greater are received from sense, and the understanding compounds the following: *every whole is greater than its part*, the understanding by its own power and that of these terms assents indubitably to this combination, and not only because it sees the terms conjoined in the thing, as it assents to the following. *Socrates is white*, because it saw that the terms are united in the thing. Moreover, I say that if all the senses were false, from which such terms are received, or, what would lead even more to deception, if some senses were false, and some true, the understanding would not be mistaken concerning such principles, because it would always have in itself terms which were the cause of truth: just as, if the species of whiteness and blackness had been impressed miraculously in dreams on one blind from birth, and if they remained subsequently in waking, the understanding abstracting from them would compound the following proposition, *white is not black*; and the understanding would not be deceived concerning this, even though the terms be received from erring sense; for the formal relation of the terms, to which it has reached, is the necessary cause of this negative truth.

The certitude concerning things known by experience is shown. Concerning the second type of knowables, namely concerning things known through experience, I say that although experience is not had of all singulars, but of a large number, and that although it is not always had, but in a great many cases, still one who knows by experience knows infallibly that it is thus, and that it is always thus, and that it is thus in all, and he knows this by the following proposition reposing in the soul, *whatever occurs as in a great many things from some cause which is not free, is the natural effect of that cause*, which proposition is known to the understanding, even though it had accepted the terms of it from erring senses; for *a cause which is not free* can not produce *as in a great many things* an effect to the opposite of which it is ordered, or to which it is not ordered by its form: but a casual cause is ordered to the producing of the opposite of the casual effect or to not producing it; therefore, nothing is the casual cause in respect to an effect produced frequently by it, and if it is not free, it is a natural cause.

That, however, this effect occurs by such a cause producing *as in a great many cases*, this must be learned through experience; for to discover such a nature at one time with such an accident, at another with such another accident, it must be discovered

that, howsoever great might be the diversity of such accidents, such an effect always followed that nature; therefore, such an effect follows not through some accident accidentally of that nature, but through the very nature in itself.

But it must be noted further that sometimes experience is had of a conclusion, as for example, *that the moon is frequently eclipsed*; and then having supposed the conclusion because it is so, the cause of such a conclusion is inquired by the method of division, and sometimes one proceeds from the conclusion experienced to principles known from the terms, and then from such a principle known from the terms, the conclusion, previously known only by experience, can be known more certainly, namely, by the first kind of knowledge, for it can be known as deduced from a principle known in itself: just as the following is known through itself, that, namely, *an opaque object interposed between a luminous and a transparent object impedes the multiplication of light to such a transparent object*; and if it were found by division that the earth is such a body interposed between the sun and the moon, it will be known most certainly by demonstration based on the essence [*propter quid*] and through causes, and not only through experience as that conclusion was known before the discovery of the principle.

Sometimes, however, there is experience of the principle in such a manner that it is not possible to discover further by division the principle known through the terms, but one must stop at some truth which holds as in many cases, of which the extremes are frequently experienced united, as for example, that *a herb of such a species is hot*, nor is any other middle term discovered prior by means of which the passion is demonstrated of the subject because of its nature [i.e. a priori], but one must stop at this as at the first thing known by experience. Then although incertitude and fallibility may be removed by the following proposition, *the effect as in a great many cases of any cause which is not free is the natural effect of it*, nevertheless, this is the last grade of scientific knowledge; and perhaps necessary knowledge is not had there of the actual union of extremes, but only of an aptitudinal union; for if the passion is another thing separated from the subject, it could without contradiction be separated from the subject, and the person who knows by experience would not have knowledge that it is so, but that it is formed apt to be so.

Certitude concerning our actions is shown. Concerning the third type of knowable things, namely, concerning our actions, I say there is certitude concerning many of them just as of principles known through themselves, as is obvious from book IV of the *Metaphysics*, where the Philosopher says of the reasons of those who say that all appearances are true, that these reasons inquire whether we are now dreaming or awake: "All these doubts, however, amount to the same, for they all think that there is a reason for all things. And he adds, "they seek the reason for things of which there is no reason, for there is no demonstration of a principle of demonstration." Therefore, according to the same Philosopher in the same place, that we are awake is known through itself as is a principle of demonstration.

Nor does it matter that it is contingent, for as has been said elsewhere, there is an order in contingent things, because something is first and immediate; otherwise there would either be a regress *in infinitum* in contingent things, or else something contingent would follow from a necessary cause: both of which are impossible.

And as there is certitude concerning waking as concerning something known through itself, so likewise of many other actions which are in our power, as that I understand, that I hear, and thus of others which are perfect acts; for although there is no certitude that I see white which is located without, either in such a subject or at such a distance, because an illusion can be caused in the medium or in the organ and in many other ways, nevertheless there is certitude that I see, even though an illusion be caused in the organ, which illusion in the organ seems to be the greatest of illusions, as for example, when an act is caused in the organ itself, not by a present object, but such as is made naturally by a present object. And thus the faculty would have its act, if such an illusion or passion were supposed, and that would truly be what is called vision there, whether it be action, or passion, or both. But if the illusion were not caused in the organ itself, but in something proximate to it, which seems to be the organ, as, if the illusion were not caused in the concourse of nerves, but if the impression of the species such as is naturally made by the object were caused in the eye itself, still sight would see; because such a species, or what is naturally seen in it, would be seen, for it would have sufficient distance with respect

to the organ of sight, which is in the concourse of those nerves, as is evident from Augustine in book VI *On the Trinity*, chapter 2, because the remains of things seen, remaining in the eye when the eyes are closed, are seen; and according to the Philosopher *On Sense and the Sensed*, because the fire which is generated by the violent elevation of the eye and which is multiplied as far as the closed eyelid, is seen; these are true visions, although they are not the most perfect visions, because there are here sufficient distances of the species to the principal organ of sight.

On the certitude of those things which are under the actions of the senses. But how is certitude had of those things which are under the actions of the senses, as for example, that something outside is white or hot as it appears to be? I reply: either opposites appear to the diverse senses concerning something known thus, or else not, but all the senses knowing it, have the same judgment concerning it. If in the second manner, then certitude is had of the truth of such a thing known by the senses, and by that proposition which precedes, namely, *what occurs as in a great many cases from something, is the natural effect of it, if it is not a free cause;* therefore, since the same alteration [or immutation] of sense occurs in a great many cases when this thing is present, it follows that this sensitive alteration or the generated species [i.e. impression] is the natural effect of such a cause, and thus such a thing outside will be white or hot or such as is naturally represented by the species generated by it as in a great many cases. If, however, the diverse senses have diverse judgments concerning something seen outside, as, for example, sight says that the staff is broken of which part is in water and part in air, and touch can discover the contrary: as sight likewise always says that the sun is of a quantity less than it is, and everything seen from a distance is less than it is; in such judgments there is certitude of what is true and of what sense errs, by a proposition reposing in the soul more certain than any judgment of sense and by the concurrent actions of many senses, so that some proposition always rectifies the understanding of actions of sense, as to which is true and which is false, in which proposition the understanding does not depend on the sense as on a *cause*, but as on an *occasion*. For example, the understanding has this proposition reposing in it, *nothing which is harder is broken on the contact of something soft receding from it;* this is so known through itself from its terms, that even if it were received from erring senses, the understanding could not doubt that proposition, for the opposite involves a contradiction: but that the staff is harder than water, and that the water withdraws from it, both senses testify this, as well sight as touch. It follows therefore that the staff is not broken as the sense of sight judges it broken; and thus the understanding judges, by something more certain than any act of sense, which sense errs and which does not with respect to the fracture of the staff.

In the same way from another part, that *the same quantity added to a quantity is absolutely equal to itself,* this is known to the understanding, howsoever much the knowledge of terms may be received from erring senses; but that the same quantity can be added to an object of sight nearby or distant, this the sense of sight as well as touch testifies: therefore, a quantity seen, whether nearby or at a distance, is equal: therefore, when sight testifies that it is less, it errs. This conclusion is concluded from principles known through themselves and from the actions of two senses knowing it is thus in a great many cases; and thus wherever reason judges that the sense errs, it does this not by some knowledge acquired positively from the senses as from a cause, but through some knowledge occasioned from sense, in which it is not deceived even if all the senses are deceived and through some other knowledge acquired from sense or from the senses as in a great many cases, which are known to be true by the often quoted proposition, namely, *that which occurs in a great many cases,* etc.

Article III

A reply is given to the reasons in so far as they do not hold.

The first reason of the contrary opinion is solved and it is demonstrated that the mutability of the object in itself does not stand in the way of certitude of knowledge. With respect to the third article, replies to the three reasons stated above must be derived from these points. To the first,[1] that is, to the objection concerning the change of the object, the *antecedent* is false; for sensible things are not in continual motion, but they remain the same in another duration. Nor is it the opinion of Augustine, but that of Heraclitus and of his disciple, Trachilus, who did not wish to speak but to move his finger, as is related in the IVth book of the *Metaphysics.*[2] And likewise the consequence does not hold, even if it were granted that the antecedent was true, because then according to Aristotle, certain knowledge could still be had of this truth, *that all things are moved continually.* Again, it does not follow: if the object is mutable: therefore, what is produced from it is not representative of anything under the aspect [*ratio*] of immutability; because *mutability* in the object is not the reason for producing; but the *nature* of the object itself, which is mutable, is that reason; that which is produced by it, therefore, represents the nature essentially, because the nature is essentially the reason for producing it; therefore, if there is a nature, from which a nature has some immutable relation to something else, that something else and that nature, each through its own exemplar, are represented as immutably united. And thus, knowledge of the immutable union of them can be had through two exemplars produced from two mutable things, not in so far as they are mutable, but in so far as they are natures.

It is evident also that something can be represented under the aspect of the immutable by a representative which is mutable in itself; for the essence of God is represented to the understanding under the aspect of the immutable by something entirely mutable, whether it be a species or an act. This is evident by a like case, for something under the aspect of the infinite can be represented by a finite.

The second reason is solved. To the second[3] I say that two kinds of mutability can be understood in the soul: one from *affirmation* to *negation,* and conversely: as for example, from ignorance to knowledge, or from not understanding to understanding. Another is as from *contrary* to *contrary:* as for example, from rectitude to deception, and conversely. The soul, however, is mutable by the first mutability with reference to any object, and such mutability is removed from it by

---

[1]See above, e) p. 317.

[2]The reference is to Cratylus; see Aristotle, *Met.* IV, 5, 1010–13.

[3]See above, f) pp. 317–318.

nothing existing formally in it; but it is not mutable according to the second mutability, except concerning those complexes which are not evident from their terms; concerning those however which are evident from their terms, it can not be changed according to the second mutability, because the apprehended terms themselves are the necessary cause of the conformity of the composition to those terms. Therefore, if the soul is mutable from rectitude to error absolutely, it does not follow that it can be rectified by nothing other than itself, for it can at least be rectified by those objects concerning which the understanding can not err, once it has apprehended the terms.

The third reason is solved. To the third[1] I say: if it had some cogency, it would hold rather against that opinion which denies the intelligible species, for that species which can represent itself as object in dreams is a phantasm, not an intelligible species: therefore, if the understanding uses only a phantasm, through which the object is present to it, and not any other intelligible species, it does not seem that it can discern, through something in which the object lights up itself, truth from verisimilitude. But the reason does not hold when the intelligible species is posited in the understanding, for the understanding can not use that as the object in itself, for it is not possible to use the intelligible species in dreaming.

Objections and doubts are solved.[2]

a) If you object that the phantasm can represent itself or the object; that therefore the understanding can err because of that error of the faculty of phantasy or it can be bound so that it can not operate, as is evident in dreams and in frenzies, it can be said that if it be bound when there is such error in the faculty of phantasy, the understanding nevertheless does not err, because it does not then have any act.

b) But how will the understanding know or how will it be certain when the faculty of phantasy does not err, which however must not err in order that understanding may not err? I reply: the following truth reposes in the understanding, that *a power* [i.e. a faculty] *does not err concerning the object proper and proportioned to it unless it is indisposed*; and it is known to the understanding that the faculty of phantasy is not

indisposed in waking by such an indisposition which makes the phantasm represent itself as object, for it is known self-evidently [i.e. through itself] to the understanding, that when it understands it is awake, and thus it is that the faculty of phantasy is not bound in waking as it is in dreams.

c) But a further argument against the stated certitude concerning actions is the following: it seems to me that I see or I hear when I nevertheless do not see or hear: therefore, there is no certitude concerning this. I reply, that it is one thing to show, against some one denying a given proposition, *that it is true*, and it is another to show, to some one admitting it, *how it is true*. For example, in book IV of the *Metaphysics*, when the Philosopher does not bring forward against those denying the first principle the following inconsistency, that *contrary opinions would be in the soul at the same time*, [since] they would concede this as a premiss; but he shows them other inconsistencies manifest to them, although not manifest in themselves. But to *those who accept the first principle* he shows *how* the first principle is known, for it is known thus, that the opposite of it can not occur in the mind; he proves this, because otherwise contrary opinions could be present at the same time: such a conclusion is more inconsistent with itself than the hypothesis.

Thus at this point, if you contend against me that no proposition is *known through itself*, I do not wish to dispute with you: for it is shown that you are shameless, because you are not persuaded, as is evident in your actions, as the Philosopher argues in book IV of the *Metaphysics*: for dreaming of obtaining something as if hard by and later awaking, one does not pursue it, as one would to attain it in waking if it were thus close by. But if you admit that *some* proposition is *known through itself*, it is necessary that it can be known; and concerning anything an indisposed power [i.e. faculty] can err, as is evident in dreams: therefore, from the fact that some things are known to be *known through themselves*, it can necessarily be known when a power is indisposed and when not; and consequently knowledge can be had of our actions, because a power is disposed so that those

---

[1] See above, g) p. 318.

[2] See above, g) *Proof of the minor premiss*, p. 318.

things are known through themselves which appear to it to be known through themselves.

d) I say then to the form of that bit of sophistry, that just as it appears to one dreaming that he sees, so the opposite of any speculative principle known through itself may possibly appear to one; and still it does not follow that that principle is known through itself. Thus it does not follow that that which one hears is known through itself to one who hears it, for the indisposed power can err concerning either, but not the disposed power. And when it is disposed and when not, is *known through itself*; otherwise it could not be known that anything else is known through itself for it could not be known what was known through itself to the understanding, [that is,] whether it was that to which the understanding thus or thus disposed would assent.

Article IV

It is argued against the conclusion of the aforestated opinion.

The aforestated conclusion is impugned by five reasons. With respect to the fourth article against the conclusion of the opinion, I argue thus:

a) I ask, what is understood by *sure* and *pure truth?*[1] Either the *infallible* truth, that is, truth without doubt or deception; and it has been proved above and it has been declared in the second and third articles that such truth can be had from pure natural things. Or else the question is understood of the truth which is *a passion of that which is*; and then since that which is can be understood naturally, therefore also the true, since it is a passion of it. And if the true, then also *truth* by abstraction, because whatever form can be understood as in the subject, can also be understood as in the abstract in itself and in the abstract from the subject. Or in the third place, by truth is understood a *conformity to an exemplar;* and if it is to the created exemplar, the proposition is proved; but if to the uncreated exemplar, the conformity to that can not be understood except if that exemplar is known; for the relation is not knowable unless the extreme is known: therefore, what is assumed in the opinion is false, namely, that *the eternal exemplar is the reason of knowing, not the known.*

b) Moreover, in the second place thus: the simple understanding can know definitively that which it understands confusedly, by seeking by the method of division the definition of that which is known. This definitive knowledge seems the most perfect knowledge pertaining to the simple understanding. From such preliminary knowledge of terms the understanding can know the principle most perfectly, and from the principle, the conclusion: and in this, intellectual knowledge seems to be completed, so that necessary knowledge of truth does not seem to be had beyond the aforesaid truths.

c) Again in the third place: either the eternal light causes something prior naturally in actuality or not. If it does, it does it either in the object or in the understanding. Not in the object; for the object in so far as it has being in the understanding, does not have real being, but intentional being: therefore, it is not capable of any real accident. If in the understanding, then the uncreated light does not change for the understanding of the pure truth, except through the mediation of its effect: and thus the common opinion seems to posit knowledge in the uncreated light as perfectly as this opinion for it posits that it is seen in the active intellect, which is the effect of the uncreated light, and more perfect than would be the accidental, caused light.

If, however, it causes nothing actual prior, either therefore the light alone causes the actuality, or the light together with the understanding and the object. If the light alone, then the active intellect has no operation in the knowledge of the pure truth: which seems inconsistent because this operation is the most noble operation of our understanding: therefore, the active intellect which is the most noble faculty in the soul, concurs in some way in that action.

d) In the same way likewise according to the Philosopher, in book III *On the Soul*, the active intellect corresponds to the active reason, the possible intellect to the passive reason: therefore, the active intellect is related in some manner actively to whatever the possible intellect receives.

e) The following contradiction likewise which is brought forward at that point is derived from the aforesaid opinion by another method, for according

---

[1]See above, h) p. 318–319.

to those holding this opinion, the agent using the instrument cannot have an action exceeding the action of the instrument: therefore, since the power of the active intellect has no application in the knowledge of the pure truth, the eternal light using the active intellect will have no application in the knowledge or in the action of this knowledge of pure truth, so that the active intellect has there the relation of instrument.

f) If you say that the uncreated light together with the understanding and the object causes this pure truth, this is the common opinion, which considers that the eternal light, as the remote cause, causes all certain knowledge and truth. Either therefore this opinion [which is being examined] will be contradictory, or it is not at variance with common opinion.

Article V

The question is solved.

The fourfold way in which necessary truths can be seen in eternal rules. Therefore, I say in answer to the question, that it is necessary, because of the statement of Augustine, to concede that "infallible truths are seen," or understood or known, "in eternal rules." Note here in the first place that the *in* can be taken objectively, and this can be done in four ways: as in a *proximate object*, or as in *that which contains the proximate object*, or as in that *by virtue of which the proximate object moves*, or as in *the remote object*.

The first way of seeing necessary truths in eternal rules is expounded. For the understanding of the first way I say that all actual intelligibles of the divine understanding have intelligible being, and in them all truths concerning them shine forth, so that the intellect, understanding them, and by virtue of them understanding the necessary truths concerning them, sees in them, as in objects, those necessary truths. The latter, however, in so far as they are secondary objects of the divine understanding, are truths (because they are in conformity with their exemplar namely, with the divine understanding) and quiddities; they are light, because they are manifestive, and they are immutable there and necessary; but they are eternal in some one respect [*secundum quid*], because eternity is a condition of an existing thing, and they do not have existence except in some one respect

only. Thus, therefore, we can in the first place be said to see in the *eternal light*, that is, in the *secondary* object of the divine understanding, which is *truth* or the *eternal light* in the manner set forth.

The second way is expounded. The second way is clear similarly, for the divine understanding contains these truths like a book, as that authority of Augustine states *On the Trinity*, book XIV, chapter 15,[1] that these rules are written in the book of eternal light, that is, in the divine understanding, in so far as it contains these truths. And although that book is not seen, still those quiddities or truths which are written in that book are seen. And to that extent our understanding can be said to see truths in the eternal light, that is, in that book, as in *that which contains the object*, and this is done according to the second way; or even in those truths which are *the eternal light in some one respect only*, just as we see in objects, and that is done according to the first way. And either of these ways seems to be dependent on the understanding, for Augustine in book XII *On the Trinity*, chapter 14, says that, "the relation or reason of the square body remains incorruptible and immutable," etc.: but it does not remain thus except as it is the secondary object of the divine understanding.

A doubt concerning the first way is solved and the third is expounded.

a) There is, however, a doubt directed against the first way: for if we do not see these truths as they are in the divine understanding, because we do not see the divine understanding, how are we said to see in the uncreated light from the fact that we see in such light eternal in some one respect only, which has being in the uncreated light, as in the understanding which knows?

b) To this the third way affords answer, that those things, as they are a secondary object of the divine understanding, do not have being, except in some one respect only; however, a truly real operation does not belong absolutely to any being in some one respect by virtue of itself; but if it belongs to it in some manner, it must be by virtue of something to which *being absolutely* [*esse simpliciter*] belongs. Therefore, it is not the property of these secondary objects to move the understanding absolutely except by virtue of the divine understanding, which is being absolutely, and

---

[1] See above, *Principal Arguments*, p. 314.

through which these objects have being in some one respect. Thus, therefore, we see in the light which is eternal in some one respect as in a proximate object; but we see in the uncreated light according to a third manner, namely, as in a proximate cause, *by virtue of which the proximate object moves.*

c) In relation to this, likewise, it can be said that as regards the third way, we see in the uncreated light as in the proximate cause of the object in itself; for the divine understanding produces objects by its own actuality in intelligible being, and by its own actuality it gives to this object such being, and to that object such, and consequently it gives them such a reason of object, by which reason they first move the understanding to such certain knowledge.

And that it can properly be said that our understanding sees in an uncreated light, because the eternal light is the cause of the object, appears from a comparison, for we are said properly to understand in the light of the active intellect, although none the less that light is only the active cause, namely, either making the object in actuality, or by virtue of which the object moves, or both.

d) This double causality of the divine understanding, therefore, which is the true uncreated light, namely, that it produces secondary objects in intelligible being, and that it is that by virtue of which secondary objects already produced move the understanding actually, can, as it were, integrate a third member as the cause by which we are said truly to see in an eternal light.

The objection is solved. And if you object against these two modes integrating a third member as cause, because then it seems that we should be said to see in God willing, or in God as he is will, rather than in God as he is light, for the divine will is the immediate principle of any action directed outward; I reply: the divine understanding, in so far as it is prior in any manner in the act of the divine will, produces these objects in *intelligible* being; and thus in respect of them it seems to be a purely *natural* cause, for God is not a *free* cause in respect of anything except what presupposes before itself in some manner a willing according to the act of will; and just as the understanding as prior to the act of the will produces objects in intelligible being, so as prior cause it seems to cooperate with those intelligibles toward their natural effect, namely, that apprehended and com-

pounded they may cause a *conformity of apprehension to themselves.* It seems, therefore, to involve a contradiction, that any understanding form such a composition, and the composition not be in conformity with the terms, although it is possible that it may not conceive those terms; for although God voluntarily constrains to the end that the understanding compound the terms or not, nevertheless, when it has compounded them, that that composition he in conformity with the terms seems to follow necessarily from the relation of the terms, which relation they have from the understanding of God causing those terms naturally in intelligible being.

Corollary. It is apparent from this why special illumination is not necessary for seeing in eternal rules; for Augustine does not hold that anything is seen in them except truths which are necessary by the strength of the terms, and there is the greatest necessity in such things as well of remote cause as of proximate cause in respect to the effect: for example, as well of the divine understanding with reference to moving objects as of those objects with reference to the truth of combination of them. And although likewise there is not so great a necessity to the perception of that truth, that the opposite involves a contradiction, nevertheless the necessity is from the part of the proximate cause, with the remote cause coassisting it, for the terms apprehended and compounded are formed naturally to cause the evidence of conformity of the composition to the terms, even though it is held that God constrains terms to this effect by a general influence, but not by a natural necessity.

But whether there is a general influence, or what is more, a natural necessity of influencing the terms to this effect, it is clear that no special illumination is needed.

The doctrine of Saint Augustine is expounded. That which has been assumed concerning the intention of Augustine is evident from his own statement in book IV *On the Trinity,* chapter 15, in which he speaks of infidel philosophers: "Some of them were able to raise the sight of their mind beyond any creature and to attain to the light of immutable truth in howsoever small a degree, for not yet having attained which they deride many Christians who live meanwhile from faith alone." Therefore, he holds that Christians do not see the things they believe in the eternal rules; but philosophers see many necessary truths in them. In the same place, in book IX *On the Trinity*, chapter 6: "Not as the mind of every man is, but as it must be in sempiternal reasons," as if to say, contingent things are not seen there, but necessary things. And in the same work, book IV, chapter 16, he argues against those philosophers,

> Because they dispute most truly and because they persuade by most certain proof; that all temporal things are made by eternal reasons, have they therefore been able to perceive in those reasons themselves, or to gather from them, how many the genera of animals are, what the seeds of each are in the beginnings, what the mode is in increments, what the numbers are by conceptions, by births, by ages, by deaths, what motions in desiring those things which are according to nature and of avoiding the contraries? Have they not sought all these things, not by that immutable wisdom, but by the history of places and times, and have they not credited the things discovered and written by others?

Therefore, he understands that those contingent things which are known only by the senses or are believed by stories, are not known by eternal rules; and yet special illumination is needed more in believing contingent things than in things known necessarily; indeed, special illumination is removed most especially in necessary truths and general illumination alone suffices.

The objection against the aforestated exposition is solved. To the contrary: why then does Augustine say in book XII *On the Trinity*, chapter 14, that, "it is in the power of only few to attain by keenness of mind to the intelligible reasons," and in the LXXXIII Questions, question 46, that only the pure of soul attain to them? I reply: that purity must not be understood as a purity from vices, for in book XV *On the Trinity*, chapter 15, he holds that the unjust see in the eternal rules what is to be perceived in them,[1] and in book IV, in the chapter quoted above, he holds that the philosophers saw the truth in the eternal rules without faith; and in the same question he holds that no one can be wise without knowledge of ideas, in the manner in which Plato, for example, would be conceded to be wise. But this *purity* must be under-

stood by elevating the understanding to considering truths as they shine forth in themselves, not only as they are revealed in the phantasm.

It must be considered here that the sensible thing outside causes a confused phantasm and single accidentally in the faculty of phantasy, that is, representing the thing according to quantity, figure, color, and other sensible accidents; and as the phantasm represents only confusedly and accidentally, so, many men perceive only that which is by accident. Truths, however, are purely and absolutely such from the *very nature of terms*, in so far as those terms are abstracted from all thing; conjoined by accident to them: for this proposition, *every whole is greater than its part*, is true in the first place, not as the whole is in a stone or in wood, but as the whole is abstracted from all things with which it is conjoined by accident; and therefore the understanding which never understands totality except in the accidental concept, as for example in the totality of the stone or the wood, never understands the pure truth of this principle, for it never understands the absolute reason of the term, by which truth is.

Therefore, it is in the power of few to attain to the eternal reasons, because it is in the power of few to have essential intellections, and of many to have such accidental concepts—But these few are not said to be distinguished from others by a special illumination, but by better natural powers, for they have an understanding which is more abstractive and more perspicacious, or else because of a greater searching out, through which one person succeeds in knowing those quiddities which another, equally ingenious, but not inquiring, does not know.

And in this manner is to be understood that saying of Augustine concerning one looking out on a mountain and having below the cloudy air and above pure light, in book IX *On the Trinity*, chapter 6; for he who always understands only the accidental concept, in the manner in which phantasms represent such objects as accidental entities, is like one placed in a valley surrounded with cloudy air; but he who separates quiddities by understanding them absolutely by an essential concept, which quiddities notwithstanding are apparent in phantasm with many other accidents joined to them, has the lower phantasm, like

---

[1]See above, *Principal Arguments*, p. 314.

cloudy air, and he is in the mountain, in so far as he knows that truth, and he sees the true above, as that superior truth in the power of the uncreated understanding, which is the eternal light.

The fourth way of seeing necessary truths in eternal rules is expounded. And in this last manner it can be conceded that pure truths are known in the eternal light as in a *remote known object*, for the uncreated light is the first principle of speculative things and the final end of practical things; and therefore speculative as well as practical things are derived from principles themselves. And, therefore, the knowledge of all, of speculative as well as practicable, by principles derived from the eternal light as known, is more perfect and purer than knowledge derived by principles in the class itself, as has been said in the question on the subject of theology, and it is more eminent than any other kind whatsoever. And in this manner the knowledge of all things pertains to the theologian, for to know that a triangle has three sides, as it is a certain participation of God, and having such an order in the universe that it expresses as it were the perfection of God, this is to know that the triangle has three sides in a more noble way than by the reason of triangle: and thus to know that one must live temperately because the final beatitude is to follow, which consists in attaining to the essence of God in himself, is to know this practical knowable more perfectly than by any principle in the class of morals, as for example by this, that *one should live honorably*.

And in this manner Augustine speaks of the uncreated light as known, in book XV *On the Trinity*, chapter 27, where addressing himself, he says, "certainly, therefore, you have seen many true things and you have drawn them from that light in which you saw them shining forth to you; turn your eyes up to the light itself and fasten them on it if you can; for thus you will see what distinguishes the nativity of the Word of God from the procession of the Gift of God." And a little later, "This light has shown these and other things similarly certain, to your interior eyes. What cause is there therefore why you can not see with fixed glance that light itself, save only weakness?"

The principal arguments are solved. From the things that have been said it is clear concerning all the authorities of Augustine to the contrary[1] and the authorities of Augustine which occur concerning this matter, can be expounded according to some of the mentioned modes of seeing.

Article VI

It is shown how the reasons of the contrary opinion prove the intention of Augustine, but not the intention for which they are brought forth here.

With respect to the sixth article it must be seen how those three reasons stated for the first opinion prove something of truth in so far as they are taken from Augustine, although they do not prove that false conclusion for which they were adduced.

Another Solution of the Reasons of Henry.

a) It must be known here that from sensible things as from a primary and essential cause, pure truth must not be expected, for the knowledge of the sense is truly something by accident, as has been said,[2] although some acts of the senses are certain and true; but by virtue of the active intellect, which is a participation of the uncreated light, illumining the phantasms, the quiddity of the thing is known, and from this, true purity [of truth] is had. And by this the first argument of Henry[3] is solved; and it no longer holds according to the intention of Augustine.

b) To the second reason of Henry[4] I say that the soul is mutable from one disparate act to another, according to the diversity of objects, because of its own unlimitedness and immateriality, for it is in respect to any thing that is; in the same way from actuality to non-actuality, for it is not always in actuality; but in respect of first principles, the truth of which is known from the terms and in respect of conclusions deduced evidently from the terms, it is not mutable from contrary to contrary, from true to false. For the rules rectify the thing understood in the light of the active intellect; and although the intelligible species itself of the

---

[1]See above, pp. 313–315.

[2]See above, p. 346.

[3]See above, e) p. 317.

[4]See above, f) pp. 317–318.

terms is mutable in being, still in representing in the light of the active intellect, the intelligible species represents immutably, and the terms of the first principle are known by two intelligible species, and thus that union is true and certain evidently.

To the third[1] it must be said that the conclusion is against him, for he posits only sensible species or phantasms [i.e. sensible impressions or images][2] there is no conclusion concerning intelligible species representing the quiddity.

It must be said, however, that if the sensitive powers are not impeded, the sensible species represents the thing truly; but in sleep the powers of the exterior senses are bound: therefore, the imaginative faculty, conserving the sensible species, in accordance with the diversity of flux of the humors of the head, apprehends them as the things of which they are the likenesses, for they have the force of things, according to the Philosopher, *On the Motions of Animals.* The third reason proves no more than this.

STUDY QUESTIONS: SCOTUS, *OXFORD COMMENTARY ON THE FOUR BOOKS OF THE MASTER OF THE SENTENCES*

1. What is the eternal truth "from which all temporal things are made?"
2. How do we perceive the form of a thing?
3. What does Scotus mean by "double exemplar?" Why is this important?
4. What is an "uncreated exemplar?" What is the significance?
5. What is Scotus' main disagreement with the academics?
6. Can the senses err? Can the understanding? Why?
7. What does Scotus mean by claiming that every whole is greater than its part?
8. How can we be certain of our own actions? Why is this different from being certain of the actions of others?
9. Are there any propositions that are known through themselves?
10. What is the fourfold way in which necessary truths can be seen?

ORDINATIO

In the following selection, John Duns Scotus starts from Avicenna's point of view regarding the nature of essences. "Horseness is just horseness," wrote Avicenna, "it is not of itself either one or many, either universal or particular." He also distinguishes first from second intentions; particulars are first intentions, universals are second intentions. Scotus then develops a brilliant and original theory as to how some particular essence can be both a universal and a particular individual. He integrates aspects of both Plato and Aristotle in developing his overall view of nature and the place and function of mind within it. He explains how some particular nature that individual members of a species all have in common *contracts*, or is compactified, into one individual that is thereby a member of a class with a distinct existence yet common to all; moreover, this common nature, or essence, is equally real, equally "there" in all the various individuals whose particular existences are contractions (compactifications) thereof. This is the fundamental notion that will be attacked by Ockham (see the Ockham section).

---

[1] See above, g) p. 318.

[2] See above, pp. 334–335.

John Duns Scotus, from *Ordinatio*, translated by M. M. Tweedale, in *Basic Issues in Medieval Philosophy*, Orchard Park, NY: Broadview Press 1999, pp.404–418.

NATURES ARE NOT OF THEMSELVES INDIVIDUATED (*ORDINATIO* II, DIST.III, PT.1, QU.1)

As regards the third distinction we must inquire into the personal distinction in the angels. But in order to get a view of that distinction in them we first have to inquire into the individual distinction in material substances. Different people have said different things about this and as a consequence they have differed on the matter of a plurality of individuals in the same species of angel. So that we may see distinctly what each of the different opinions thinks the question is regarding the distinction or indistinction of material substance, I am going to pose separate questions for each of the different ways of approaching the matter; and first:

Is it on account of itself, that is on account of its own nature, that a material substance is individual or singular?

[1] In favor of an affirmative answer: In *Metaphysics* VII[1] the Philosopher shows—against Plato—that "the substance of any thing whatsoever is peculiar to that of which it is the substance and does not belong to anything else." Therefore, a material substance in virtue of its own nature, everything else left aside, is peculiar to that in which it exists, and this in such a way that in virtue of its own nature it cannot belong to anything else. Therefore, in virtue of its own nature it is individual.

[2] Against this: [2.1] whatever belongs to something in virtue of its own essential character belongs to it in any instance; therefore, if the nature of stone were of itself *this*, no matter what item the nature of stone is in, that nature would be *this* stone. The consequent here is absurd when we speak of determinate singularity, as we are in this question.

[2.2] Moreover, what of itself possesses one of a pair of opposites will of itself reject the other opposite. Therefore, if a nature were of itself one in number,[2] it would reject numerical multiplicity.

[3] Here it is said that just as a nature of itself is formally a nature so also it is of itself singular, and this

in such a way that there is no need to seek cause of its singularity other than the cause of the nature, as if the nature were a nature before (temporally or naturally)[3] it was a singular and then were contracted to make a singular by something arriving in it.

[3.1] This is shown by an analogy: just as a nature of itself has true being outside the soul but has being in the soul only in virtue of something else, that is, in virtue of the soul itself (the reason for this is that true being belongs to it unqualifiedly, but being in the soul is its being qualifiedly),[4] so universality belongs to a thing only in virtue of its qualified being, namely being in the soul. Singularity, on the other hand, belongs to a thing in virtue of its true being and thus belongs to it of itself and unqualifiedly. Therefore, we should seek a cause for why a nature is universal and we have to propose the intellect as this cause. But we need not seek some cause for why a nature is singular, that is a cause, other than the nature of the thing, that acts as an intermediary between it and its singularity. Rather the same causes which cause the unity of the thing also cause its singularity.

[4] Against this proposal it is argued as follows:

[4.1] The object insofar as it is the object is naturally prior to the act itself, and, according to you, as prior the object is of itself singular, because this is always the case with a nature when it is not considered as qualified or in respect of the being which it has in the soul. Therefore, an intellect that ideates that object under the character of a universal ideates it under a character opposed to its own character, because as it precedes that act it is determined of itself to the opposite of that character, that is of that character of a universal.

[4.2] Moreover, what has a real unity, peculiar to it and sufficient for it, but less than a numerical unity, is not of itself one by a numerical unity (i.e. is not of itself *this*). But the nature existing in this stone has a real and sufficient unity peculiar to it, and one less than numerical unity.

The major is self-evident because nothing is of itself one by a unity greater than the unity sufficient

---

[1] Ch.13, 1038b 10–11. See selection VI.2.5.

[2] See selections V.1.1–3, for the notion of something 'one in number.'

[3] See glossary entry for 'order of nature.'

[4] See glossary entry for 'qualified/unqualified.'

for it. For if its own peculiar unity, which is due to something of itself, were less than numerical unity, numerical unity would not belong to it from its own nature and in virtue of itself. Otherwise just from its own nature alone it would have both a greater and lesser unity. But these when taken as about the same item and in respect of the same item are opposed, because a multiplicity opposed to the greater unity can co-exist without contradiction with the lesser unity, but this multiplicity cannot co-exist with the greater unity because it rejects it; therefore etc.

Proof of the minor: if there is no real unity of the nature less than singularity and every unity other than the unity of singularity, and which belongs to a specific nature, is less than a real unity, then there will be no real unity less than numerical unity. The consequent is false as I will prove in five or six ways.

[4.2.1] The first way runs as follows: According to the Philosopher in *Metaphysics* X,[1] "in every genus there is one primary item which is the standard and measure for everything which belongs to that genus." This unity of the primary measure is real, because the Philosopher shows[2] that the primary character of a measure belongs to one item, and explains through ranking how in every genus that to which the character of measuring belongs is one. But this unity belongs to something insofar as that item is primary in its genus; therefore, it is real, because the items that are measured are real and they are really measured, but a real being cannot be really measured by a being of thought.[3] Therefore, this unity is real.

Further, the unity is not numerical because there is no singular in a genus which is the measure of all the items in that genus. For, according to the Philosopher in *Metaphysics* III,[4] "in individuals of the same species it is not the case that this one is prior and that one posterior."

Although the Commentator explains[5] the notion of something prior that constitutes something poste-rior, this makes no difference to the minor premiss, because The Philosopher there intends to give as the reason why Plato posited a separated character for a species but not in the case of a genus, that there is in species an essential ranking on account of which the posterior can be reduced to the prior, and therefore, according to him it is not necessary to posit the idea of a genus through participation in which the species are what they are, but rather only the idea of a species to which all the other species are reduced. On the other hand, according to Plato and according to The Philosopher who relates this, in individuals there is no such ranking whether or not one constitutes another. Therefore etc. Thus it is the Philosopher's intention here to agree with Plato that among individuals of the same species there is no essential ranking. Therefore no individual is through itself a measure of the items in its own species; consequently no numerical or individual unity [is such a measure].

[4.2.2] Further I show in a second way that that same consequent is false, because, according to the Philosopher in *Physics* VII,[6] comparison takes place within an indivisible species because in that case there is a single nature, but not in a genus because a genus does not have that sort of unity.

This difference of unities is not due to thought, because the concept of the genus is one in number in the same way as the concept of the species is; otherwise, no concept would be said *in quid*[7] of several species (and thus no concept would be a genus), but rather just as many concepts would be said of species as there are concepts of species, and so in each predication the same item would be predicated of itself. Likewise the unity of the concept or of the non-concept is irrelevant there to the intention of the Philosopher, that is to the question of whether there is comparison or not. Consequently, the Philosopher means there that the specific nature is one by the unity of the specific nature, but he does not mean

---

[1]Ch.1, 1052b18.

[2]*Ibid.* 19–24.

[3]See glossary entry for 'being of thought.'

[4]Ch.3, 999a12–13.

[5]Averroës, Comment 11 on *Meta*.III.

[6]Ch.4, 249a3–8.

[7]See glossary entry for *'in quid.'*

that it is one by a numerical unity, because comparison does not occur in the case of numerical unity.

[4.2.3] Further, in a third way, according to The Philosopher in *Metaphysics* V, (the chapter about relation),[1] same, similar and equal are based on one in such a way that, although similarity has for its basis[2] a thing in some qualitative genus, the relation is real only if it has a real basis and a real proximate character of being based. Therefore, the unity which is required of the basis of the relation of similarity is real; but it is not a numerical unity, because nothing one and the same is similar or equal to itself.

[4.2.4] Further, in a fourth way, for a single real opposition there are two real primary terms; but contrariety is a real opposition. This is clear because one really corrupts or destroys the other even when every operation of the intellect has been excluded; this occurs only because they are contraries. Therefore each primary term of this opposition is real and one by some real unity; but not by a numerical unity, because then exclusively *this* white would be the primary contrary to *this* black, or exclusively *that* white to *that* black, which is absurd because then there would be just as many primary contrarieties as there are contrary individuals.

[4.2.5] Further, in a fifth way, for a single action of a sense there is an object that is one in virtue of some real unity; but not a numerical unity. Therefore, there is some other real unity than numerical unity.

Proof of the minor premis: A power that apprehends an object in this way, that is, insofar as it is one by this unity, apprehends it insofar as it is distinct from anything which is not one by this unity. But a sense does not apprehend an object insofar as it is distinct from anything which is not one by that numerical unity. This is clear because no sense discerns that this ray of sunlight numerically differs from some other ray, and yet they are diverse on account of the sun's motion. If all common sensibles, for example diversity of location or situation, were eliminated, and if through divine power two quantities were put in existence at the same time and these were completely similar and equal in whiteness, sight would not discern that there were two whites there. Yet if it apprehended one or the other of them insofar as that item were one by a numerical unity, it would apprehend that item insofar as it is one item *distinct* by a numerical unity.

On this point it can also be argued that the primary object of a sense is one in itself by some real unity, because just as an object of this power, insofar as it is an object, precedes the intellect, so also in respect of its real unity it precedes every action of the intellect.

But this argument is not as conclusive as the prefor one can propose that some primary object, as it is adequate to a faculty, is something common, abstracted from all particular objects, and thus it has only the unity of commonness to those several particular objects. At any rate, this proposal does not seem to deny that the single object of a single act of sensing necessarily has a real unity that is less than numerical unity.

[4.2.6] Further, in a sixth way, if every real unity is numerical, then every real diversity is numerical. But the consequent is false, because every numerical diversity, insofar as it is numerical, is equal, and thus all things would be equally distinct. Then it follows that the intellect would no more be able to abstract something common from Socrates and Plato than from Socrates and a line, and every universal would be a pure fabrication of the intellect.

The first consequence [that if every real unity is numerical, then every real diversity is numerical] is shown in two ways: first, one and several, same and diverse, are opposites (see *Metaphysics* X, ch.5).[3] But one of a pair of opposites is said just as often as the other one is said (see *Topics* I).[4] Therefore, to any unity corresponds its own peculiar diversity.

Secondly, each of the terms of any diversity is in itself one, and it is diverse from the other term in the very same way by which it is one in itself, so that the unity of one term seems to be through itself the reason for the diversity of the other term.

---

[1] Ch.15, 1021a9–12.
[2] See glossary entry for 'basis of a relation.'
[3] Actually ch.3, 1054b22–23.
[4] Perhaps *Topics* II, 7, 113a34.

This conclusion is defended in another way. If in this thing there is only a real numerical unity, then any entity there is in that thing is of itself one in number. Therefore, this and that are primarily diverse in virtue of every entity in them, because they are diverse items that in no way agree in some one item.

It is also defended in this way: numerical diversity is for this singular not to be that singular, given the entity of both terms. But such unity necessarily belongs to either term.

[4.2.7] Further: Even if no intellect existed, fire would generate fire and destroy water, and there would be some real unity between the generator and the generated in virtue of a form on account of which there would be univocal generation. For the intellect that considers it does not make the generation be univocal; rather it apprehends it to be univocal.

[5] To the question, then, I concede the conclusions of those arguments, and I say that a material substance is not on account of its own nature *this* of itself, because, as the first argument proves [4.1], if it were, the intellect would not be able to ideate it under an aspect opposed [to *this*] without ideating its object under an aspect of ideation that conflicts with the character of such an object.

Also, as the second argument [4.2] with all its proofs deduces, there is some real unity in things, apart from all operations of the intellect, which is less than numerical unity or the unity proper to a singular, and this unity belongs to the nature in virtue of itself. In virtue of this unity that is peculiar to the nature as it is a nature, the nature is indifferent to the unity of singularity; therefore, it is not of itself one by that unity, that is by the unity of singularity.

How to understand this can in some way be seen from the remark of Avicenna in *Metaphysics* V, chapter 1 where he maintains that "horseness is just horseness; it is not of itself either one or many, either universal or particular." I read this as meaning: It is not of itself one by a numerical unity nor many by a plurality opposed to that unity; neither is it actually universal, that is in the way that something is universal when it is an object of the intellect, nor is it of itself particular. For although it is never really apart from some of these, of itself, nevertheless, it is not any of them, but rather is naturally prior to them all.

In virtue of its natural priority it is what something is and by itself an object of the intellect, and by

itself as such it is studied by the metaphysician and is expressed through a definition. Propositions that are true in the first mode are true by reason of a quiddity taken in this way, because nothing is said per se in the first mode of a quiddity unless it is essentially included in it, insofar as it is abstracted from all those items which are naturally posterior to it.

But not only is the nature itself of itself indifferent to being in the intellect and in the particular, and consequently to being universal and particular or singular, but also when it has being in the intellect it does not have universality primarily in virtue of itself. For although it is ideated under universality as under a mode of ideating it, still universality is not part of its primary concept, because it is not a metaphysician's concept but a logician's, for, according to him [Avicenna], the logician studies second intentions that are applied to first intentions. Therefore, the primary ideation is of the nature as not ideated along with some mode, neither a mode which belongs to it in the intellect nor one which belongs to it outside the intellect, even though universality is the mode of ideating that ideated item, but it is not a mode that is itself ideated.

And just as the nature is not of itself universal in virtue of that being, but rather universality happens to that nature in virtue of the first character of it in virtue of which it is an object, so also in things outside where the nature exists with singularity the nature is not of itself determined to that singularity; rather it is naturally prior to the character that contracts it to that singularity, and insofar as it is naturally prior to that contracting factor it is not repellent to it to be without that contracting factor. And just as the object in the intellect in virtue of *that* entity of it and universality has true intelligible being, so also in reality the nature has in virtue of *that* entity true real being outside the soul—also in virtue of *that* entity it has a unity proportional to itself which is indifferent to singularity in such a way that it does not of itself conflict with that unity which is given with any unity of singularity.

This is what I mean by saying that the nature has a real unity that is less than numerical unity. And although it does not of itself have it in such a way that it is within the definition of the nature (since "horseness is just horseness," according to Avicenna in *Metaphysics* V), still that unity is an attribute peculiar to the nature in virtue of its primary entity, and consequently it is not of itself *this* either intrinsically or in virtue of the entity peculiar to it that is necessarily included in the nature itself in virtue of its primary entity.

[6] But against this there seem to be two objections:

[6.1] One arises because this view seems to propose that a universal is something real in things, which runs counter to what the Commentator [Averroës] says in *De Anima* I, comment 8: "the intellect produces universality in things in such a way that it exists only through the intellect." Thus it is just a being of thought. For that nature, as it exists in this stone and yet is naturally prior to the singularity of the stone, is, according to what was said, indifferent to this singular and to that one.

[6.2] Further, Damascene[1] says in chapter 8 [of *De Fide Orthodoxa*], "we have to realize that it is one thing to consider something as it is in reality, another to consider it as it is in reason and thought. Therefore, and more specifically, in all creatures the separation of substrates is considered to be in reality (for Peter and Paul are considered to be separate in reality), but commonness and linkage [of predicate to subject] are considered by reason and thought as in the intellect alone (for we apprehend by the intellect that Peter and Paul are of a single nature and have one common nature)"; "for these substrates are not in each other; rather each is set apart on its own, i.e. is separated as a thing." Later he says, "but the reverse is the case in the holy and super-substantial Trinity, for there, a single common item is considered to be in reality," "while later the division is considered to be in thought."

[7. Replies]

[7.1] To the first objection [6.1] I say that the actual universal is what has an indifferent unity in virtue of which it is the same in its proximate potential for being said of any *suppositum* whatsoever, since, according to the Philosopher in *Posterior Analytics* I,[2] "the universal is what is one in many and of many." For nothing, no matter what unity it has, is such in reality that in virtue of that precise unity it has a proximate potential in respect of every *suppositum* for a predication that says *this* is *this*. This is because,

although there is something that exists in reality which does not reject being in a singularity other than the one in which it is, still it cannot be truly said of any item beneath it that it is it. This is possible only for an object which is the same in number and actually before the intellect. Certainly this, as an object of the intellect, has even a numerical unity of an object, and in virtue of this it is the same item predicable of every singular by saying that *this* is *this*.

From this it is clear how to refute the remark that the agent intellect produces universality in things by the fact that of every item which is what something is and exists in the imagination it can be said that it does not reject being in something else, and by the fact that the intellect strips bare this item existing in the imagination. For no matter where it exists before it has objective being in the intellect, whether in reality or in the imagination, whether it has certain existence or existence inferred by argument (and so such a nature is not by means of some light, but rather always of itself, something which does not reject being in something else), still it is not such that being said of anything belongs to it by a proximate potential, rather it is such by a proximate potential only when it exists in the possible intellect.

Therefore, there is in reality a common item which is not of itself this, and consequently it of itself does not reject being *not-this*. But such a common item is not actually universal, because it lacks that indifference in virtue of which the complete universal is universal, that is in virtue of which as the same item by some identity it is predicable of any individual in such a way that any one of them is it.

[7.2] To the second objection from Damascene [6.2] I say that there is not in creatures a common item that is really one in the way in God there is a common item that is really one. For in God the common item is singular and individual, since the divine nature itself of itself is *this*, and it is obvious that no universal in creatures is really one in that way. To propose otherwise would be to propose that some individual created nature was predicated of many individuals by a predication that says *this* is *this*, just as we say that the Father is God and the Son is the same God.

---

[1]St. John Damascene, who in the eighth century led the Christian community in Damascus when it was already under Muslim rule.

[2]Ch.4, 73b26–33.

Nevertheless, there is in creatures something common that is one by a real unity but a unity less than numerical unity. Certainly this common item is not so common that it is predicable of many, although it is so common that it does not reject being in something other than that in which it is.

Thus it is clear in two ways how the authority [i.e. Damascene] is not against me. First, because he talks of the unity of singularity in God, and in this sense not only the created universal is not one but neither in creatures is the common item one.

Secondly, because he speaks of a common predicable, not just of the common item that is in fact determined [to an individual] even though it does not reject being in something else. Such a common item can be posited as real only in creatures.

[8] From what has been said it is clear how to reply to the principal argument [1]: the Philosopher refutes the fiction he credits to Plato, namely that this human being who exists per se and who is posited as an Idea is through itself universal to every human being, because "every substance that exists *per se* is peculiar to that of which it is [the substance]," that is either it is of itself peculiar or it is made peculiar by something that contracts it, and once the contracting factor is given it cannot belong to something else, although it does not of itself reject belonging to something else.

This gloss is also true when we use 'substance' in the sense in which it means a nature. Then it follows that an Idea will not be the substance of Socrates because it is not the nature of Socrates, because it is neither of itself peculiar to Socrates nor made peculiar to Socrates so that it is only in him—rather according to him [Plato] it is also in something else.

But if 'substance' is taken for primary substance, then it is true that any substance is of itself peculiar to that of which it is [the substance], and then it follows much more that the Idea, which he claims is a substance that exists per se, cannot in that sense be the substance of Socrates of Plato. But the first alternative suffices for what we have said.

[9] In response to the defense of the opinion [3]: It is clear that commonness and singularity do not relate to a nature in the way being in the intellect and true being outside the soul do, because commonness belongs to the nature as outside the intellect, as

does singularity. Commonness belongs to the nature of itself, while singularity belongs to the nature through something in reality that contracts it. But universality does not belong to the thing of itself.

Therefore, I allow that we do need to seek a cause of universality, but we do not need to seek a cause of commonness other than the nature itself. And given there is commonness in the nature itself in virtue of its own entity and unity, we necessarily need to seek a cause of the singularity, which adds something further to the nature to which it belongs.

VI.8.2. WHAT MAKES A SUBSTANCE INDIVIDUAL (FROM *ORDINATIO* II, DIST.3, QU.6)

[1] Therefore, in answer to the question I say that yes [a material substance is individual on account of some positive entity that of itself determines a nature to singularity].

[1.1] For this I add the following argument: just as unity in general is itself a consequence of entity in general, so any sort of unity is of itself a consequence of some entity. Therefore, unqualified unity, such as is the unity of the individual which we have often described above as that which rejects division into several subjective parts[1] and which rejects not being *this*, that is a signed item, if it exists in beings (which everyone supposes), is of itself a consequence of some per se entity. But it is not a consequence of the per se entity of the nature, because that has its own per se real unity, just as was proven in the resolution of the first question. Therefore, it is a consequence of some other entity that determines that [nature], and this [other entity] with the entity of the nature produces something that is one per se, for the whole possessing this unity is complete of itself.

[1.2] Again, every difference of differences ultimately leads back to something primarily different (otherwise there would be no point at which we stop finding differences). But individuals are different in the strict sense because they are different beings with something the same. Therefore, their differences lead back to some items which are primarily different. Moreover, these primarily diverse items are not the nature in this and the nature in that, because that by which items agree formally is not the same as that by

---

[1]That is, "parts" which it could be predicated of in the way 'animal' is predicated of 'rabbit,' 'goose,' 'cow,' etc.

which they differ really, although what is really distinct can be the same as what really agrees. For being distinct is quite different from being that by which something is primarily differentiated, and consequently likewise for unity. Therefore besides the nature in this and in that there are some items that are primarily different by which this and that differ (one of them in this and another in that). These cannot be negations—see the second question; nor can they be accidents—see the fourth question. Therefore they will be some positive entities that of themselves determine the nature.

[2] Against the first argument [1.1] it is objected that if there is some real unity less than numerical unity, it belongs to something that is either in numerically the same item or is in something else. Not to something in numerically the same item, because whatever is in numerically the same item is one in number; not to something in two items because in them there is nothing that is really one, since that feature is exclusive to the case of the divine *supposita* (as we explained in discussing above what John Damascene said).

[3] I answer: Just as was said on this subject in the resolution of the first question, the nature is naturally prior to *this* nature and its own distinctive unity, consequent on the nature as a nature, is naturally prior to its unity as *this* nature, and it is under this character that there is metaphysical consideration of the nature, a definition is assigned to it and we have per se in the first way propositions. Therefore in the same item that is one in number there is some entity on which is consequent a unity that is less than numerical unity, and it is real. That to which such a unity belongs is not formally of itself one item by a numerical unity. I allow, then, that a real unity does not belong to something that exists in two individuals but rather [to something that exists] in one.

[4] And when you object: "whatever is in numerically the same individual is numerically the same,"

[4.1] I answer first by citing an analogous and clearer case: this argument is invalid: Whatever is in a single species is one in species. Therefore, color in whiteness is one in species. Therefore, color does not have a unity less than the unity of a species. For, just

as we said elsewhere (namely in book I, the question about attributes,[1] before the resolution of the principle argument about attributes, by way of resolving the first point of doubt) that something can be called alive denominatively, as a body is, or per se in the first way, as a human being is (also in this way a surface is called white denominatively while a white surface is called white per se in the first way, because the subject includes the predicate), so I say that a potential which is restricted by an actual item, is informed by that actual item, and through that is informed by the unity consequent on that actuality or that act is one by that actual item's own unity, but it is one this way denominatively. It is not, however, this way one of itself, not in the first way, nor through an essential part. Therefore, color in whiteness is one in species, but it is not one of itself, not per se, nor primarily, but rather only denominatively. The specific difference, however, is primarily one because it primarily rejects being divided into items that are many in species. Whiteness is one in species per se, but not primarily, because it is one in species by something intrinsic to itself, that is by the difference. Thus I allow that whatever is in this stone is one in number either primarily, or per se, or denominatively. Primarily [one in number], perhaps, is that by which such a unity belongs to this composite. *Per se* [one in number] is this stone, of which that is a part which is primarily one by this unity. Only denominatively [one in number] is that potential which is perfected by this actual item and which sort of denominatively relates to its actuality and unity.

[4.2] Further by explaining this resolution: What this entity is in virtue of which the perfect unity exists can be explained by analogy with the entity from which we get the specific difference. Certainly the specific difference, or the entity from which we get the specific difference can be related to that which is beneath it, or to that which is above it, or to that which is on its own level.

[4.2.1] In the first way [i.e. as related to what is beneath it], the specific difference and the specific entity reject being divided into items essentially many in species or nature, and in virtue of it the whole of which that entity is a per se part rejects such

---

[1]*Ord.*I, d.8, n.214 (Balic IV, p.271).

division. Likewise in the case we propose, this individual entity primarily rejects being divided into any subjective parts whatsoever, and in virtue of it the whole of which that entity is a part rejects such division. The only difference between these cases lies in this, that the unity of the specific nature is less than that unity [of the individual], and for that reason the former unity does not exclude every division into subjective parts but only that division which is of essential parts. The latter unity, however, excludes all division. This sufficiently confirms what we proposed, for, given that any unity less than that unity [of the individual] has its own entity on which it is of itself consequent, it seems unlikely that this most perfect unity would not have its own entity on which it is consequent.

[4.2.2] When we relate the specific nature to what is above it, I say that the reality from which we get the specific difference is actual in relation to the reality from which we get the genus or generic character. This is the case in such a way that the one reality is not formally the other; otherwise, in the definition there would be redundancy because the genus alone (or the difference alone) would suffice for the definition, since it would indicate the whole entity of the defined.

Nevertheless, sometimes the restricting item is different from the form from which we get the generic character, namely, when the species adds some thing over and above the nature of the genus. Sometimes, however, it is not another thing but only another formality or another formal concept of the same thing. On account of this some specific differences have concepts that are not unqualifiedly simple, for example those we get from the final abstraction of the form. (In dist. 3 of book I we spoke of this distinction among specific differences, how some specific differences include being and some do not.)

The reality of the individual is similar to the specific reality in this respect: it is a sort of act that determines the reality of the species, which is a sort of possible and potential item. But it is dissimilar in this respect: we never get it from an added form; rather we get it exclusively from the final reality of the form. Also it is dissimilar in this respect: the specific reality establishes the composite of which it is a part in quidditative being, because it is a quidditative entity; this reality of the individual, however, is primarily diverse from all quidditative entity.

This is shown by the fact that when we apprehend any quidditative entity (speaking now of limited quidditative entity), we find it is common to many and it does not reject being said of many items each of which is it. Therefore, this entity, which of itself is an entity different from a quiddity or a quidditative entity, cannot establish the whole of which it is a part in quidditative being, but rather in some other sort of being.

Also since in the works of the Philosopher quiddity is frequently called 'form' (this is clear in *Metaphysics* V, the chapter on 'cause,'[1] as well as in many other places; also in *Metaphysics* VII, the chapter on parts of a definition,[2] he says, "in any items where there is no matter the what-it-is is the same as that of which it is [the what-it-is]. As we will explain, he speaks here of matter and form.) and in his works 'material' means whatever has a restricted quiddity (also Boethius in his little book *On the Trinity*[3] claims that no form can be the subject of an accident, because a form is said *in quid* of anything else. Also if humanity is a subject, this belongs to it not insofar as it is a form. Certainly humanity is not the form of one or the other part of the composite, that is of the form or of the matter; rather it is the form of the whole composite that has a restricted quiddity or in which there is a restricted quiddity.) Given this, every specific reality establishes [the whole of which it is a part] in formal being since in quidditative being, and the reality of the individual establishes [the whole of which it is a part] exclusively in material being, i.e. in restricted being. From this follows the logical distinction that the one is essentially formal, the other material, because the latter establishes [the whole of which it is a part] in the character of a subject while the former establishes [the whole of which it is a part] exclusively in the

---

[1] Ch.2, 1013a26–28.

[2] Ch.11, 1037a32–b5.

[3] Ch.2, (PL64,1250).

character of a predicable, and a formal predicate has the character of a form while a subject has the character of matter.

[4.2.3] Thirdly, when we relate the specific difference to what is on the same level as it, that is to another specific difference, we find that although sometimes it can be non-primarily diverse from another, as is the entity which we get from the form, still the ultimate specific difference is primarily diverse from another, that is the one which has an unqualifiedly simple concept [is primarily diverse]. In this regard I say that the individual difference resembles the specific difference of the ultimate sort, because every individual entity is primarily diverse from any other.

From this it is clear how to answer the following objection: this [individual] entity and that [individual] entity are either of the same sort or not. If they are, then some entity can be abstracted from them, and this will be specific. Then of this entity we will have to ask what restricts it to this entity and that entity. If we say it is restricted of itself, then with equal reason we could have stopped with the nature of a stone; if we say it is restricted by something else, then we have an infinite regress. If they are of different sorts, then also the item they are a constituent of will be of different sorts and thus will not be individuals of the same species.

I answer: ultimate specific differences are primarily diverse, and therefore from them nothing that is per se one item can be abstracted. But from this it does not follow that the items they are a constituent of are primarily diverse and not of some one type. For that some items are equally differentiated can be understood in two ways: either that they are equally incompatible, that is that they cannot belong to the same thing, or that they equally lack agreement in anything. In the first sense it is true that differentiated items are just as diverse as the very items that differentiate them, for the differentiating items cannot be incompatible without the differentiated items being incompatible. In the second sense it is universally impossible [for the differentiated items to be just as diverse as the items that differentiate them]

because the differentiated items not only include the differentiating items but something else as well which is a sort of potential in respect of the distinguishing items, and yet the distinguishing items in it have nothing in common.

As regards individual entities I answer, just as for the primarily diverse differences, that they are primarily diverse, that is they have nothing the same in common, and yet it is not necessary for the differentiated items to be unqualifiedly differentiated. Still, just as those [individual] entities are incompatible, so also are the individuals having those entities.

[5] And if you ask me what is this individual entity from which we get the individual—is it matter or form or a composite?

I answer: Every partial or total quidditative entity, belonging to a genus is of itself indifferent as a quidditative entity to this entity and to that, in such a way that as a quidditative entity it is naturally prior to that entity as it is *this*. And since it is naturally prior, just as being *this* does not belong to it so it does not in virtue of its own character reject its opposite. Also, just as a composite does not insofar as it is a nature include its own entity by which it is formally *this*, so neither does the matter insofar as it is a nature include its own entity by which it is *this* matter, nor does the form insofar as it is a nature include its own. Therefore, this entity is neither matter nor form nor the composite insofar as any of these is a nature. Rather it is the ultimate reality of the being which is the matter or which is the form or which is the composite. In just the way that any common but determinable item, however much it is a single thing, can still be distinguished into several formally distinct[1] realities of which one is not formally the other, so here the one is formally the entity of the singular and the other is formally the entity of the nature. Neither can these two realities be a thing and a thing, as can the reality from which we take the genus and the reality from which we take the difference and from both of which is taken the specific reality. Rather, in the same item (whether in a part of it or the whole of it) there are always formally distinct realities belonging to the same thing.

---

[1]Formal distinction is explained by Scotus in selection V.4.1.

VI.8.3. IS A UNIVERSAL SOMETHING IN THINGS? (FROM *QUAESTIONES SUBTILLISIMAE SUPER LIBROS METAPHYSICORUM ARISTOTELIS, LIB. VII, QU.18*)

Is a Universal Something in Things?

[1] This question can be treated first by arguing against the position of Plato, who, according to Aristotle,[1] posited Ideas on account of the formal entity of things . . . , and on account of scientific knowledge, since it is only about necessary items while singulars are corruptible; and also on account of generation, since more is needed than the particular generator.

If this view proposes that an idea is some substance apart from motion and from accidental accidents, which has nothing in itself except the separated specific nature complete to the extent that it can be complete, and which perhaps has in itself attributes of the species (otherwise nothing would be known about it), this view cannot be validly disproved, because such a singular having such a nature does not seem to be rejected by the notion of unqualified entity.

And neither does Aristotle unqualifiedly disprove it. Rather in so far as it is viewed as incorruptible he argues against it at the end of book X.[2] But here in book VII he argues not its impossibility but its lack of necessity. For here he argues against Ideas as follows: nothing which is not obvious is to be posited by philosophers without necessity. There is no necessity in the reasons for positing Ideas; therefore, they should simply not be posited. That it is not necessary on account of entity or knowledge he argues in [Ch 6 of] *Metaphysics* VII, which begins: "moreover is that which is a what. . . ."

But if someone further proposes that this idea is formally universal in such a way that it is predicated as identical with this corruptible item by a predication which says this is this, immediately a contradiction arises, because numerically the same item is the quiddity of many different items and yet is outside them (for otherwise it would not be incorruptible).

[2] Setting aside this approach we can treat the question by following the view Aristotle takes in speaking of the universal. We find here two opposed opinions:

[2.1] The first is that the universal is in things. There are three arguments for this:

[2.1.1] The first of these is that the universal is that which is naturally suited to be said of many. But a thing naturally suited to be said of many. But a thing naturally suited to be said of many is so *of itself*. If it were not, that suitability would be contrary to it and could not be conferred on it, at least not by the intellect, for then the intellect could give Socrates such a suitability.

[2.1.2] Moreover, the universal, about which we are speaking, is predicated of a thing, for example of a singular, by a predication that says this is this, for example, 'Socrates is a human.' But it is impossible for something to be predicated of a thing and not be in things.

[2.1.3] Also, a "what" taken completely absolutely is a true thing, because it is a principle and a cause, as we see in *Metaphysics* VII, the last chapter [ch.17]. But when taken absolutely it is a universal. Proof: what is taken absolutely is expressed by a definition; but definitions are only of universals.

[2.2] The way this is posited is as follows: as was said in the question on individuation, in a thing with the grade of limitation by which it is *this* singular, there is also a nature limited by that grade. This nature is not only intelligible without that grade but is also prior in the thing; and as such it does not reject being in something else, because as prior in this way it is not as a result limited to *this*. Therefore, as prior in this way it is universal.

[2.3] Against this view there are three ways of arguing.

[2.3.1] First, as follows: the universal is a numerically single object of the intellect and is understood by numerically one act of understanding. This occurs in such a way that the intellect in attributing it to different singulars attributes numerically the same object conceived many times as a predicate of different

---

[1]*Meta.* 1,6 987b1–11, 9 991b3–9; XIII,4 1078b12–17.
[2]Cf.1059a10–14.

subjects by saying this is this. But it seems to be impossible that something which is in things is numerically the same intelligible item and is attributed as such to different items.

This reasoning is bolstered because even *this* nature as prior to its limiting grade, if it were understood, would be correctly attributed to only one item. For *this* concept is not correctly attributed to another singular, but rather there is another concept of another nature which is in the other [singular].

[2.3.2] Secondly, an attribute of a subject belongs to whatever its subject belongs to under the character by which it is the subject [of that attribute]. Therefore, if human belongs to Socrates under that thought by which human is truly universal, Socrates is truly universal. This reasoning does not involve the fallacy of accident since the middle term stays the same.

[2.3.3] Thirdly, it would follow that the senses would have as their *per se* objects universals. For, as was said in the question on the intellectual apprehension of the singular, although nature does not cause motion unless it is *this* nature, it does not cause motion in as much as it is *this* nature. Also it follows that if every universal is of itself actually in things, it is completely superfluous to propose an agent intellect.

[2.4] Against the way of positing this view: It follows that there would be as many universals as singulars, because any nature in any individual has this assigned character of a universal; and there is no nature other than those of individuals, as the first argument above showed. Thus any nature is a universal and there is none [other than those of individuals].

Also in the predication of a universal of a singular the same item would be predicated of itself.

[2.5] The other opinion is that the universal is only in the intellect. In support of this: the authority of the Commentator in *De Anima* I[1] the intellect makes the universality in things, otherwise the agent intellect would not seem to be necessary. This point is bolstered by the fact that the agent intellect is not a productive power, and therefore does not cause anything outside the intellect. Also Boethius, speaking about unity and 'one': "everything which is one in

number." In support of this there is the argument that "the universal is one in many and of many" (*Posterior Analytics* I).[2] It includes essentially, then, a relationship with *supposita*, as a predicable is related to a subjectible. But such a relationship is not in the things, but only in an intellect relating them.

For this view and the mode of proposing it we have the authority of Avicenna in *Metaphysics* V, chapter 2, where he intends that the intelligible form is singular in relation to the soul and forms in different intellects are different. But the same form is universal in respect of individuals outside the mind.

[2.6] Against this opinion:

[2.6.1] The object naturally precedes the act. Therefore, the universal naturally precedes the ideation when it is ideated. But it is actually in the intellect only by an ideation. This is bolstered by the fact that if the object, as object and as prior to the ideation, were not universal, it could not be related by the intellect to the many items outside the mind.[3]

To these points it can be said that although the object is prior by nature to the act, still this need not be in the object necessarily, especially when it is a matter not of the mode of the known but of a mode under which it is known, and especially if the object exists only at the same time as the act, as Avicenna claims of the universal.

But, contrary to this, it would follow that if no one were thinking there would not be an actual universal, and thus habitual scientific knowledge would not be of an actually universal object.

Furthermore, in so far as the object is prior to the act it is not ideated under this mode; therefore, it is ideated either under no mode or under the opposite mode, for since it is an object it determines some mode for itself.

[2.6.2] Moreover, the subject of scientific knowledge, insofar as it is a subject, precedes the ideation. But as such it is universal, because as a subject it is primarily such in its relationship to its own distinctive attribute; and if it is this primarily, then [that attribute is said] of everything [that falls under that subject], and thus there can be scientific knowledge of it.

---

[1]Averroes, comm.18, AOAC Supp.II, 161F.

[2]Ch.171a7.

[3]The following 2 paragraphs are out of place in the Wadding/Vives edition.

This is bolstered as follows: Just as a first principle, which is a universal proposition, can be conceived as prior to the complex act, so its term outside the mind under that character by which it is its term, can be conceived as prior to the incomplex act of ideation. But the term within the first principle is universal, because it can be taken universally.

[2.6.3] Thirdly, universality would be a condition of what is a being in the intellect, just as *true* is. Thus, the former would weaken the sense of 'being' just as the latter does. Thus, some scientific knowledge would no more be of the universal than of the true.

[2.6.4] Against the mode of proposing this view: This intelligible form is subjectively[1] in the soul and really in it; if the universal is in the intellect, it will seem to be there as an object known is in the knower. These modes of being are different. And thus, the arguments already given disprove this opinion.

[3] Concerning the solution of this question:

[3.1] First we must distinguish the senses of 'universal,' for it is taken or can be taken in three ways: It can be taken for a second intention which is a certain relation of thought in the predicable directed to that of which it is predicable. The noun 'universal' signifies this relation concretely just as 'universality' does abstractly.

In another sense 'universal' is taken for that which is denoted by that intention, which is a thing of first intention, for second intentions are applied to first intentions. In this sense it can be taken in two ways: In one way for that which is denoted by this intention as a sort of remote subject. In another way, for the near subject. In the first way a nature taken absolutely is called universal, because it is not of itself a *this*. and thus it is not contrary to it of itself to be said of many. In the second way only that is universal which is actually indeterminate in such a way that numerically one intelligible is sayable of every *suppositum*. This is the complete universal.

The second opinion [2.5] can be interpreted as about the first sense, because that relationship which is a second intention, belongs to the object only as it is in an intellect that is relating [it to something]. The first opinion [2.1] can be interpreted as about the second sense, for the nature is not of itself a *this*. But the first opinion does not posit a complete universal because it is not sufficiently indeterminate, since it is not contrary to determination, but sort of deprived of it or contradictory to it.

The second opinion does not speak of the complete sort of universal either, since the question is difficult. Rather it speaks of a certain intention naturally posterior to the complete sort [or universal]. For the indetermination which is sort of contrary [to determination] and by which human being is indeterminate in such a way that when quidditatively conceived it belongs to every human being, naturally precedes that second intention which is logical universality or a relationship to many.

[4] Therefore, it remains to see whether the universal taken in the third sense is primarily in the intellect.

[4.1] Just as we can speak of two ways of being in, so we can speak in two ways of being in the intellect objectively. In one sense we speak of it as habitual, in another as actual whether in the primary act or in the secondary act. In the first sense it is there when it is there as immediately motivating to an ideation. In the second sense, when it is actually ideated. According to Avicenna's position, these are simultaneous, although the first is prior in nature. For although he does not propose that an intelligible species by which an object is present in the first sense remains in the intellect even while the intellect is not actually ideating, still the present object as a motivator is prior in nature to the actual ideation. For the first precedes the ideation as its cause; the second follows or accompanies it.

To someone else who denies the intelligible species it is not clear how these two beings can be distinct, since according to him an object in the intellect has no being except by way of an act of ideation. Thus, it does not have the first sort of being at all, and in no way does it move the intellect. Nevertheless, [Avicenna] holds the contrary of this.

There is a third approach that is common and which says that the first being precedes temporally and naturally the second and stays on without it in the way those propose who maintain that the intelligible species remains without the act. For it seems absurd to deny to the intellect (in as much as it is a created intellect) the retention after the act of its

---

[1]That is, in it as in a subject, as opposed to being in it objectively, that is, as the object of some psychological act or state.

peculiar object, when this capacity is found in the senses. And although the intellect is joined to phantasms, I ask what is the intrinsic perfection of the intellect? For in so far as it is an intellect it accidentally happens to it that it is joined to phantasms; and although it would be less perfect if not joined to phantasms, still it would not, to be sure, be a different type of power. Therefore, just as a separated intellect is intrinsically retentive, so also ours, although less so.

[4.2] To the question as posed in this section I say that the universal spoken of in the third sense is not necessarily in the intellect in the second way, that is it is not as though such a being belonged to it necessarily. The arguments [2.6] against the second opinion prove this. But necessarily it is in the intellect in the first way, that is universality would not belong to it if this did not accompany the object. This is proved by the first argument [2.3.1] against the first position. But what is the cause of this indeterminacy by which the object when it has this first being in the intellect is completely universal?

I answer that not just the thing [is the cause], for in it there is not that much indeterminacy, as the first argument proves. And not the possible intellect either, for it does not more indeterminately receive than the object is productive.

In every nature (as Aristotle argues in *De Anima* III[1] text commentary 17 & 18),[2] given something which is made into everything, there is something which makes everything. That is generally in all of nature to any passive power there corresponds an active power; and if it is not extrinsic, then it is intrinsic in the same nature. Therefore, since we experience that there is some intellect in us which is made universal (i.e. to which belongs something through which the object is present as a universal), there must be something active. And this is not outside the mind (as has been argued); therefore, it is within.

Therefore, the agent intellect in conjunction with a nature which is in some way indeterminate of itself is the whole effective cause of the object in the possible intellect in respect of its first being. And this

is the case as regards the complete indetermination of the universal. And just as there is no reason why what is warm makes things warm other than the existence of an appropriate power, likewise there is no other cause why the agent intellect in conjunction with the nature makes the object exist in this way. Therefore, a nature has a remote potency toward the determination of singularity and toward the indetermination of a universal. And just as it is joined to singularity by its producer, so it is joined to universality by the thing as an agent in conjunction with an agent intellect. It is in this way that Avicenna is correctly interpreted when he says (*Metaphysics* V, ch.1)[3] that a nature of itself is neither universal nor particular, but only a nature. It is this second form of indeterminacy which the third argument [2.1.3] along with its supporting arguments proves, not the indeterminacy of a universal, because this lesser indeterminacy saves similarity, contrariety, etc. And in this way we speak of a 'what.' This indeterminacy is privative; the other greater one is a contrary universality.

[4.3] As for the second part of the question: Is it in things? I answer that being in the intellect in the first way or the second is only to have a relation of thought to the intellect. But that which is in things does in fact have this relation; therefore, that which is universal is in things.

This is bolstered as follows: otherwise in knowing something about universals we would not know anything about things but only about our concepts. Neither would our opinion change from true to false on account of a change in the existence of a thing. Thus, a universal can be in things in such a way that it is the same nature which is determinate by being in existence through a grade of singularity and which is indeterminate by being in the intellect, that is by having a relation to the intellect of known to knower. And just as these two beings occur together accidentally in the same nature and each can be without the other, so also the determinacy and indeterminacy we spoke of. And from this we see that it is not necessary that what is universal be in things, although it can, but it is necessary that it be in the intellect.

---

[1]Ch.5 430a 10–14.

[2]That is, Averroës's commentary.

[3]*Philosophia Prima (sive Metaphysica)* 11, 228.

STUDY QUESTIONS: SCOTUS, *ORDINATIO*

1. Are natures in and of themselves individuated? Why?
2. Is every real unity numerical? Why? What about every real diversity?
3. What does Scotus mean by saying that "the nature has a real unity that is less than numerical unity?" How is this related to Avicenna's view? To Aristotle's?
4. Aristotle says that "the universal is what is one in many and of many." How does Scotus use this notion?
5. According to Scotus, what is the "fiction" that Aristotle credits to Plato, and how does Aristotle refute it?
6. What makes a substance an individual?
7. What does Scotus mean by "difference of differences?"
8. Do universals exist in individual things?
9. What are attributes? How are they related to a subject?
10. What are the three different senses of a universal?
11. What is the role of the agent intellect in relation to individuals and universals?

Philosophical Bridges: The Influence of John Duns Scotus

The first and foremost influence of Scotus was on Ockham (see the following section). In particular, Scotus' shift from the logical derivation of propositions (truths) to their evidential basis signaled a significant turn in subsequent philosophy towards a more scientific outlook on experience, the world, and our place in nature. Overall, Duns Scotus' most important contribution, the legacy for which he was nicknamed the "Subtle Doctor," was the refinement of the distinctions and concepts that influenced philosophers throughout the ages, among them Gottfried Leibniz, Martin Heidegger, and Charles Peirce. In recent decades there has been a great resurgence of interest in John Duns Scotus. His technical distinctions, both logical and what we would now refer to as phenomenological, are deeply relevant to questions having to do with the nature of perception, especially in object formation and the relationship between subject (perceiver) and object (perceived). Both in contemporary analytic philosophy and in phenomenology the subtleties of Duns Scotus' terminology have shed new light on perennial and what some would call intractable philosophical problems.

WILLIAM OF OCKHAM (1280–1349)
Biographical History

William, named after the village of Ockham in Surrey, near London, England, where he was born, studied theology and the arts at Oxford University. His primary focus while working on his doctorate was Peter Lombard's (1100–1160) *Books of Sentences*, the official theology textbook, and all students were required to write detailed commentaries and disputations consisting of questions with replies and rebuttals. Ockham's comments got him in trouble with the chancellor, a devout Thomist, who promptly had him arrested for heresy. Instead of defending himself before the Holy See at Avignon, the young Ockham took every opportunity to further criticize the currently accepted interpretations, such as whether Jesus and his disciples possessed any (e.g. real estate) property, raising questions about the relationship between papal and secular authority. The Holy See reprimanded him for his views but stopped just short of outright condemnation. Ockham was not intimidated. He went on to publish his controversial ideas. His *Dialogus de Potestate Papae et Imperatoris* (*Dialogue on the Power of the Emperor and the Pope* (1339–1342), a charged critique of the temporal supremacy of the pope in favor of the idea of a secular state, lay the foundations for modern theories of government.

Throughout his life Ockham criticized Pope John XXII. He joined forces in 1328 with the Franciscan General Michael of Cesena. In Pisa they formed a new Franciscan order called the Spirituals. But eventually they too found him too critical and expelled him from the order that he helped form. King Ludwig of Bavaria offered him protection in Munich.

Philosophical Overview

Ockham's famous principle of ontological economy—Ockham's razor—is that "multiplicity ought not to be posited without necessity." Any word or concept that does not have to be regarded as being real should be dismissed as a fiction having intensional meaning only, without reference or extension. Positing the existence of universals as mind-independently real entities, for instance, as realists like Duns Scotus do, is thus dismissed as an unnecessary fiction in Ockham's view, called *nominalism*. Other nominalists, also known as "terminists," rallied around this innovative purging of unnecessary metaphysical entities from language, calling it the *via moderna*, "the modern way," in contrast to the *via antiqua*, "the ancient way."

Ockham's nominalist, or terminist logic, is the precursor of modern analytical, critical, and empirical approaches to the analysis of language and the functions of individual terms within propositions. It brought into play the distinction, influential to this day, between a term's meaning and that which it stands for, which he called *suppositio*, which means, "standing for." In the first book of the *Prior Analytics*, Aristotle defined terms as follows:

> I call a term that into which a proposition is resolved (namely, the predicate, or that of which something is predicated) when it is affirmed or denied that something *is* or *is not* something.

Ockham asks, what type of existence do such terms have, when they seem to involve universal rather than particular entities? A term can refer to something in three different ways. Consider the sentence, "this person, Robert DeNiro, is an actor." The term "this person" refers to a particular individual named Robert DeNiro. On the other hand, consider, "Robert DeNiro is a strange person." In this case, the term "person" stands for a class. Or, consider " 'person' is a noun." In this case, the term "person" stands for the word. Now, a printed word in a book exists as marks on paper. When you read and say the word, that word exists as a sound. The third, most important aspect of a word, is *the concept*. But what is a concept? A concept is to the written and spoken word that expresses it as a number is to a numeral. Numerals are not numbers, they are symbols, representations of numbers. A concept is not a symbol. Thus, according to Ockham, a symbol expresses a concept that is itself the mental concept or impression, and that is what has meaning. Contrary to Plato, a term does not stand for some mind-independent universal entity, or some abstract thing that all the individual instances have in common.

SUMMA LOGICAE
William of Ockham

Ockham argues that conceptual terms and propositions are "mental words" that belong to no language. They are but signs subordinated to mental concepts that exist as such in the mind only; they cannot even be uttered. Only the meanings of terms themselves—names as such—are universals, not any actual things-in-themselves to which they refer. Only individuals exist. Names do *seem* to stand for universals, but in reality they are signs for classes of individuals.

This does not mean that spoken words are signs of mental concepts. Rather, spoken words signify the same things as mental concepts. Whereas a concept signifies "primarily and naturally," the word signifies "secondarily." This, according to Ockham, is what Aristotle himself meant when he wrote that "Words are signs of the impressions in the soul." By thus arguing that all knowledge must ultimately come from the senses and cannot be had without them, Ockahm lay the foundation for the revival of Aristotelian empiricism. According to Plato, a thing external to the mind must correspond exactly and perfectly to its mental representation, otherwise knowledge is impossible. According to Aristotle, universals exist in the mind and are related to external reality, but without having to correspond exactly. For Ockham, only particular individuals exist, each having its own nature. There is no identity, only similarity. The distinction between essence and existence is in Ockham's view itself fictitious: "existence and essence signify one and the same thing."

PART I

Chapter 14: On the Universal

It is not enough for the logician to have a merely general knowledge of terms; he needs a deep understanding of the concept of a term. Therefore, after discussing some general divisions among terms we should examine in detail the various headings under these divisions.

First, we should deal with terms of second intention and afterwards with terms of first intention. I have said that "universal," "genus," and "species" are examples of terms of second intention. We must discuss those terms of second intention which are called the five universals, but first we should consider the common term "universal." It is predicated of every universal and is opposed to the notion of a particular.

First, it should be noted that the term "particular" has two senses. In the first sense, a particular is that which is one and not many. Those who hold that a universal is a certain quality residing in the mind which is predicable of many (not suppositing for itself, of course, but for the many of which it is predicated) must grant that, in this sense of the word, every universal is a particular. Just as a word, even if convention makes it common, is a particular, the intention of the soul signifying many is numerically one thing a particular; for although it signifies many things it is nonetheless one thing and not many.

In another sense of the word we use "particular" to mean that which is one and not many and which cannot function as a sign of many. Taking "particular" in this sense no universal is a particular, since every universal is capable of signifying many and of being predicated of many. Thus, if we take the term "universal" to mean that which is not one in number, as many do, then, I want to say that nothing is a universal. One could, of course, abuse the expression and say that a population constitutes a single universal because it is not one but many. But that would be puerile.

Therefore, it ought to be said that every universal is one particular thing and that it is not a universal except in its signification, in its signifying many things. This is what Avicenna means to say in his commentary on the fifth book of the *Metaphysics*. He says, "one form in the intellect is related to many things, and in this respect it is a universal; for it is an intention of the intellect which has an invariant relationship to anything you choose." He then continues, "although this form is a universal in its relationship to individuals, it is a particular in its relationship to the particular soul in which it resides; for it is just one form among many in the intellect." He means to say that a universal is an intention of a particular soul. Insofar as it can be predicated of many things not for itself but for these many, it is said to be a universal; but insofar as it is a particular form actually existing in the intellect, it is said to be a particular. Thus, "particular" is predicated of a universal in the first sense but not in the second. In the same way we say that the sun is a universal cause and, nevertheless, that it is really and truly a particular or individual cause. For the sun is said to be a universal cause because it is the cause of many things (i.e., every object that is generable and corruptible), but it is said to be a particular cause because it is one cause and not many. In the same way the intention of the soul is said to be a universal because it is a sign predicable of many things, but it is said to be a particular because it is one thing and not many.

But it should be noted that there are two kinds of universals. Some things are universal by nature; that is, by nature they are signs predicable of many in the same way that the smoke is by nature a sign of fire; weeping, a sign of grief; and laughter, a sign of internal joy. The intention of the soul, of course, is a universal by nature. Thus, no substance outside the soul, nor any accident outside the soul is a universal of this sort. It is of this kind of universal that I shall speak in the following chapters.

Other things are universals by convention. Thus, a spoken word, which is numerically one quality, is a universal; it is a sign conventionally appointed for the signification of many things. Thus, since the word is said to be common, it can be called a universal. But notice it is not by nature, but only by convention, that this label applies.

Chapter 15: That the Universal Is Not a Thing Outside the Mind

But it is not enough just to state one's position; one must defend it by philosophical arguments. Therefore, I shall set forth some arguments for my view, and then corroborate it by an appeal to the authorities.

That no universal is a substance existing outside the mind can be proved in a number of ways:

No universal is a particular substance, numerically one; for if this were the case, then it would follow that Socrates is a universal; for there is no good reason why one substance should be a universal rather than another. Therefore no particular substance is a universal; every substance is numerically one and a particular. For every substance is either one thing and not many or it is many things. Now, if a substance is one thing and not many, then it is numerically one; for that is what we mean by "numerically one." But if, on the other hand, some substance is several things, it is either several particular things or several universal things. If the first alternative is chosen, then it follows that some substance would be several particular substances; and consequently that some substance would be several men. But although the universal would be distinguished from a single particular, it would not be distinguished from several particulars. If, however, some substance were to be several universal entities, I take one of those universal entities and ask, "Is it many things or is it one and not many?" If the second is the case then it follows that the thing is particular. If the first is the case then I ask, "is it several particular things or several universal things?" Thus, either an infinite regress will follow or it will be granted that no substance is a universal in a way that would be incompatible with its also being a particular. From this it follows that no substance is a universal.

Again, if some universal were to be one substance existing in particular substances, yet distinct from them, it would follow that it could exist without them; for everything that is naturally prior to something else can, by God's power, exist without that thing; but the consequence is absurd.

Again, if the view in question were true, no individual would be able to be created. Something of the individual would pre-exist it, for the whole individual would not take its existence from nothing if the universal which is in it were already in something else. For the same reason it would follow that God could not annihilate an individual substance without destroying the other individuals of the same kind. If He were to annihilate some individual, he would destroy the whole which is essentially that individual and, consequently, He would destroy the universal which is in that thing and in others of the same essence. Consequently, other things of the same essence would not remain, for they could not continue to exist without the universal which constitutes a part of them.

Again, such a universal could not be construed as something completely extrinsic to the essence of an individual; therefore, it would belong to the essence of the individual; and, consequently, an individual would be composed of universals, so that the individual would not be any more a particular than a universal.

Again, it follows that something of the essence of Christ would be miserable and damned, since that common nature really existing in Christ would be damned in the damned individual; for surely that essence is also in Judas. But this is absurd.

Many other arguments could be brought forth, but in the interests of brevity, I shall dispense with them. Instead, I shall corroborate my account by an appeal to authorities.

First, in the seventh book of the *Metaphysics*, Aristotle is treating the question of whether a universal is a substance. He shows that no universal is a substance. Thus, he says, "it is impossible that substance be something that can be predicated universally."

Again, in the tenth book of the *Metaphysics*, he says, "thus, if, as we argued in the discussions on substance and being, no universal can be a substance, it

is not possible that a universal be a substance in the sense of a one over and against the many."

From these remarks it is clear that, in Aristotle's view, although universals can supposit for substances, no universal is a substance.

Again, the Commentator in his forty-fourth comment on the seventh book of the *Metaphysics* says, "In the individual, the only substance is the particular form and matter out of which the individual is composed."

Again, in the forty-fifth comment, he says, "let us say, therefore, that it is impossible that one of those things we call universals be the substance of anything, although they do express the substances of things."

And, again, in the forty-seventh comment, "it is impossible that they (universals) be parts of substances existing of and by themselves."

Again, in the second comment on the eighth book of the *Metaphysics*, he says, "no universal is either a substance or a genus."

Again, in the sixth comment on the tenth book, he says, "since universals are not substances, it is clear that the common notion of being is not a substance existing outside the mind."

Using these and many other authorities, the general point emerges: no universal is a substance regardless of the viewpoint from which we consider the matter. Thus, the viewpoint from which we consider the matter is irrelevant to the question of whether something is a substance. Nevertheless, the meaning of a term is relevant to the question of whether the expression "substance" can be predicated of the term. Thus, if the term "dog" in the proposition "The dog is an animal" is used to stand for the barking animal, the proposition is true; but if it is used for the celestial body which goes by that name, the proposition is false. But it is impossible that one and the same thing should be a substance from one viewpoint and not a substance from another.

Therefore, it ought to be granted that no universal is a substance regardless of how it is considered. On the contrary, every universal is an intention of the mind which, on the most probable account, is identical with the act of understanding. Thus, it is said that the act of understanding by which I grasp men is a natural sign of men in the same way that weeping is a natural sign of grief. It is a natural sign

380 SECTION SIX / THIRTEENTH CENTURY AND LATE MEDIEVAL PHILOSOPHERS

such that it can stand for men in mental propositions in the same way that a spoken word can stand for things in spoken propositions.

That the universal is an intention of the soul is clearly expressed by Avicenna in the fifth book of the *Metaphysics*, in which he comments, "I say, therefore, that there are three senses of 'universal.' For we say that something is a universal if (like 'man') it is actually predicated of many things; and we also call an intention a universal if it could be predicated of many." Then follows the remark, "an intention is also called a universal if there is nothing inconceivable in its being predicated of many."

From these remarks it is clear that the universal is an intention of the soul capable of being predicated of many. The claim can be corroborated by argument. For every one agrees that a universal is something predicable of many, but only an intention of the soul or a conventional sign is predicated. No substance is ever predicated of anything. Therefore, only an intention of the soul or a conventional sign is a universal; but I am not here using the term "universal" for conventional signs, but only for signs that are universals by nature. That substance is not capable of functioning as predicate is clear; for if it were, it would follow that a proposition would be composed of particular substances; and, consequently, the subject would be in Rome and the predicate in England which is absurd.

Furthermore, propositions occur only in the mind, in speech, or in writing; therefore, their parts can exist only in the mind, in speech, and in writing. Particular substances, however, cannot themselves exist in the mind, in speech, or in writing. Thus, no proposition can be composed of particular substances. Propositions are, however, composed of universals; therefore, universals cannot conceivably be substances.

Chapter 16: Against Scotus' Account of the Universal

It may be clear to many that a universal is not a substance outside the mind which exists in, but is distinct from, particulars. Nevertheless, some want to claim that the universal is, in some way, outside the soul and in particulars; and while they do not want to say that a universal is really distinct from particulars, they say that it is formally distinct from particulars.

Thus, they say that in Socrates there is human nature which is contracted to Socrates by an individual difference which is not really, but only formally, distinct from that nature. Thus, while there are not two things, one is not formally the other.

I do not find this view tenable:

First, in creatures there can never be any distinction outside the mind unless there are distinct things; if, therefore, there is any distinction between the nature and the difference, it is necessary that they really be distinct things. I prove my premise by the following syllogism: the nature is not formally distinct from itself. This individual difference is formally distinct from this nature; therefore, this individual difference is not this nature.

Again, the same entity is not both common and proper, but in their view the individual difference is proper and the universal is common; therefore, no universal is identical with an individual difference.

Again, opposites cannot be attributed to one and the same created thing, but *common* and *proper* are opposites; therefore, the same thing is not both common and proper. Nevertheless, that conclusion would follow if an individual difference and a common nature were the same thing.

Again, if a common nature were the same thing as an individual difference, there would be as many common natures as there are individual differences; and, consequently, none of those natures would be common, but each would be peculiar to the difference with which it is identical.

Again, whenever one thing is distinct from another it is distinguished from that thing either of and by itself or by something intrinsic to itself. Now, the humanity of Socrates is something different from the humanity of Plato; therefore, they are distinguished of and by themselves and not by differences that are added to them.

Again, according to Aristotle things differing in species also differ in number, but the nature of a man and the nature of a donkey differ in species of and by themselves; therefore, they are numerically distinguished of and by themselves; therefore, each of them is numerically one of and by itself.

Again, that which cannot belong to many cannot be predicated of many; but such a nature, if it really is the same thing as the individual difference, cannot belong to many since it cannot belong to any other particular. Thus, it cannot be predicable of many; but, then, it cannot be a universal.

Again, take an individual difference and the nature which it contracts. Either the difference between these two things is greater or less than the difference between two particulars. It is not greater because they do not differ really; particulars, however, do differ really. But neither is it less because then they would admit of one and the same definition, since two particulars, can admit of the same definition. Consequently, if one of them is, by itself, one in number, the other will also be.

Again, either the nature is the individual difference or it is not. If it is the difference I argue as follows: this individual difference is proper and not common; this individual difference is this nature; therefore this nature is proper and not common, but that is what I set out to prove. Likewise, I argue as follows: the individual difference is not formally distinct from the individual difference; the individual difference is the nature; therefore, the nature is not formally distinct from the individual difference. But if it be said that the individual difference is not the nature, my point has been proved; for it follows that if the individual difference is not the nature, the individual difference is not really the nature; for from the opposite of the consequent follows the opposite of the antecedent. Thus, if it is true that the individual difference really is the nature, then the individual difference is the nature. The inference is valid, for from a determinable taken with its determination (where the determination does not detract from or diminish the determinable) one can infer the determinable taken by itself; but "really" does not express a determination that detracts or diminishes. Therefore, it follows that if the individual difference is really the nature, the individual difference is the nature.

Therefore, one should grant that in created things there is no such things as a formal distinction. All things which are distinct in creatures are really distinct and, therefore, different things. In regard to creatures modes of argument like the following ought never be denied: this is A; this is B; therefore, B is A; and this is not A; this is B; therefore, B is not A. Likewise, one ought never deny that, as regards creatures, there are distinct things where contradictory notions hold. The only exception would be the case where contradictory notions hold true because of some syncategorematic element or similar determination, but in the same present case this is not so.

Therefore, we ought to say with the philosophers that in a particular substance there is nothing substantial except the particular form, the particular matter, or the composite of the two. And, therefore, no one ought to think that in Socrates there is a humanity or a human nature which is distinct from Socrates and to which there is added an individual difference which contracts that nature. The only thing in Socrates which can be construed as substantial is this particular matter, this particular form, or the composite of the two. And, therefore, every essence and quiddity and whatever belongs to substance, if it is really outside the soul, is just matter, form, or the composite of these or, following the doctrine of the Peripatetics, a separated and immaterial substance.

STUDY QUESTIONS: OCKHAM, *SUMMA LOGICAE*

1. What does Ockham mean by the "general knowledge of terms" versus the "concept of a term?"
2. What does the word "particular" mean, as Ockham uses it, and what is its significance?
3. What does the word "universal" mean, as Ockham uses it, and what is its significance?
4. What is the nature of the relationship between particulars and universals?
5. Do universals exist outside the mind? Why?
6. What are the two kinds of universals? How are they distinguished?
7. Does Ockham agree with Aristotle's view, in his *Metaphysics*, that a universal is a substance? Why?
8. How does Ockham's view of universals differ from that of Duns Scotus?
9. What is the nature of the relationship between propositions and the mind?

10. Why is the particular form the only substantial part of a particular substance? What is the importance of this thesis, and how does Ockham defend it?

THE SEVEN QUODLIBETA

Here Ockham uses Aristotelian logic to develop his nominalism, the view that universals (abstract or general terms) do not represent any objectively real entities, but are mere words, verbal expressions that stand for names. Universals are *flatus vocis*, empty vocal utterances without real referents. Reality, on the other hand, consists of actual substance, such that universals exist *post res*, not *ante res*, as realists suppose. The first version of the position, originally put forth by Boethius in the sixth century, was occasionally considered but never fully caught on until Ockham's development which began with the distinction between real and grammatical meanings of terms.

According to Ockham, outside the mind there are no universals, only individuals, particular entities. Knowledge would, therefore (it would seem), have to begin with particulars. But the objects of the understanding—those parts of the mind that perceive, know, interpret experience, and think—are universals. How then to get from one to the other? Ockham's leading argument throughout the following reading is that the object of sense and the object of understanding are one and the same.

QUODLIBET I.

QUESTION XIII.

Whether that which is known by the understanding first according to a primacy of generation is the individual.

Principal Argument: And it seems in the first place that it is not. For the universal is the first and proper object of the understanding. Therefore, in point of primacy of generation it is known first.

To the contrary, the object of sense and the object of understanding are absolutely the same. But the individual is the first object of sense by such a primacy.

Conclusion: The meaning of the question must be stated first here. In the second place the question is to be answered.

1. With respect to the first part it must be known that individual is taken here not as everything which is one in number, for taken thus, each and every thing is individual. But it is taken to mean that thing which is one in number and is not a sign, whether natural or voluntary (or at good pleasure), common to many things, for the written word, the concept, and the spoken word, which are significative of many things, are not individuals, but only the thing which is not a common sign is individual.

In the second place [with respect to this first part] it must be known that this question is not understood to be about any knowledge whatsoever of the individual, for any universal knowledge taken thus is knowledge of the individual. For nothing is understood by such universal knowledge except an individual and individuals. However, such knowledge is common; but the question is understood to be about knowledge which is properly speaking simple and individual.

2. With respect to the second part, having supposed that the question is understood to be about knowledge properly individual, then I say first that, taking individual in the said manner to mean knowledge which is properly individual and simple, the individual is known first.

This is proved by the following reason, that the thing outside the soul which is not a sign is under-

Quodlibeta septem una cum tractatu de sacramento altaris Venerabilis inceptoris fratris Guilhelmi de Ockam anglici, sacre theologie magistri, de ordine fratrum minorum, Strasbourg, 1491.

The Seven Quodlibeta, translated by Richard McKeon in Richard McKeon, ed., *Selections from Medieval Philosophers*, Vol. 2. Charles Scribners Sons, 1929, pp. 360–421.

stood by such knowledge first. But every thing outside the soul is individual.

Moreover, the object precedes its own act and is first in the primacy of generation. But nothing precedes such an act except the individual.

In the second place [with respect to the second part] I say that knowledge which is simple and peculiarly individual and first by such a primacy is intuitive knowledge. That this knowledge, however, is first, is evident because of the fact that abstractive individual knowledge presupposes intuitive knowledge in respect to the same object, and not conversely. Moreover, that it is properly and peculiarly individual is evident from the fact that it is caused immediately by the individual thing, or it is its nature to be caused by it, nor is it its nature to be caused by any other individual thing, even of the same species.

3. In the third place, I say that the abstractive knowledge which is first by the primacy of generation and simple (1) is not knowledge peculiarly individual, but (2) on the contrary is sometimes, nay always, common knowledge.

(1) The first is evident because one does not have properly simple knowledge of any individual at the moment when specific knowledge of the individual can not be had; but now and then there is such knowledge [i.e. abstract knowledge which is not properly individual], as is clear in the case of something coming from a distance which causes a sensation by virtue of which I am able only to judge that that which is seen is a being. It is manifest that in that case the abstractive knowledge which I have first according to the primacy of generation is knowledge of being and of nothing lower. And consequently, it is not a concept having to do with the species nor is it a proper concept of the individual.

(2) The second is clear because no abstract simple knowledge is more the likeness of one thing than another in respect of like things, nor is it caused by a thing, nor is it its nature to be caused by it: therefore, no such knowledge is properly an individual knowledge; but all such knowledge is universal.

Doubts: But perhaps there are some doubts at this point. First because it seems that intuitive knowledge is not proper knowledge, because whatever is given by intuitive knowledge is assimilated equally to one individual and to another which is like it, and it represent one individual equally with the rest. There-

fore, it does not seem to be knowledge of one thing more than another.

The second doubt is that if first abstract knowledge is occasionally a knowledge or concept of being, such as was given in the case of something coming from a distance, then in the same way first intuitive knowledge in the same situation will be knowledge of all being, because it is impossible that there be many simple proper concepts of the same thing. But I can have one perception of one thing coming from distant places, by which I only judge it to be being, another by which I judge it to be animal, a third by which I judge it to be man, a fourth by which I judge it to be Socrates. But these perceptions are not of different kinds [ratio]: therefore, all of them can not be proper notions of the same individual thing.

The third doubt is that it seems that first abstract knowledge is most of all proper, since the object is approximated in the manner in which it should be, because we are able by the first abstract knowledge to recall the same thing previously seen, which could not be done if abstract proper knowledge were not had concerning the same thing previously seen.

The fourth doubt is that it seems from what has been said already, as if the concept of the genus could be abstracted from one individual, for example the concept of animal, as is evident in the case of one coming from distant places, since I have a perception such that I can judge by it that that is an animal.

Resolution of Doubts: I say, therefore, to the first of these doubts that intuitive knowledge is proper individual knowledge, not because of the greater assimilation to one thing than to another, but because it is caused naturally by the one and not by the other, nor can it be caused by the other. If you say that it can be caused by God alone, that is true, but it is the nature of such a perception to be caused by one created object and not by another. And if it is caused, it is always caused by one object and not by another. Whence it is no more called intuitive proper singular knowledge because of likeness, than it is called first abstract knowledge, but only because of causality; nor can any other cause be assigned.

To the second doubt I say that sometimes those perceptions are of the same species and differ only as more and less perfect in the same species, as, if a concept were perceived from parts of the same reason or kind [ratio], in which there were no more accidents sensible to sight, then by the approximation of that visible, as for example white, perception is intensified and is made clearer. And in this way one and another individual can be caused, for such a perceived thing is being or body or color or whiteness. But you say that those things differ in species which can not cause an effect of the same species; but clear and obscure vision are of this sort: I say that whenever causes which are augmented and intensified can not cause an effect of the same species, they differ in species then and not otherwise. Now, however, this perception, when it is augmented and intensified, can accomplish every effect that a clear sight can; and consequently they are of the same reason or of the same species. Yet clear perception and obscure perception are sometimes of different species, as for example when different objects are seen, as, if something were seen colored in different colors, according to a lesser and a greater approximation. But these perceptions are not of the same object but of different objects.

To the third doubt I say that by seeing something I have some proper abstract knowledge; but this is not simple but composed from simples. And this composite notion is the beginning of recollection, for by it I recall Socrates, because I saw him formed thus or figured thus, colored thus, of such a length, breadth, and in such a place; and by that composition I recall that I have seen Socrates. But if you circumscribe all simple concepts except one, I no more recall Socrates because of it, than I recall another man extremely like him. Whence I can recall that I have had sight of a man; but I do not know whether it is Plato or Socrates; and, therefore, a simple abstractive notion is not proper absolutely; but a composite notion can well be proper.

To the fourth doubt I say that the concept of genus is never abstracted from one individual. To the other argument [of this doubt] concerning something coming from distant places, I say that I judge it to be animal because I have previously the concept of animal, which concept is the genus; and, therefore, by the concept I am led to recollective knowledge. Whence, if I did not previously have the concept of the genus of animal, I would judge only that this thing seen is something.

And if you ask what abstractive conception is first formed by the medium of intuitive knowledge, I

say sometimes only the concept of that which is or being, sometimes the concept of genus, sometimes the concept of the most special species according to whether the object is less or more removed. The concept of that which is or being, however, is always impressed, because when the object is approximated in the required manner, the specific concept and the concept of being are caused at the same time by the individual thing without.

To the principal argument, I say that the universal is the first object by the primacy of adequation, not by the primacy of generation.

QUODLIBET I.

QUESTION XV.

Whether our understanding by its nature [pro isto statu] knows sensible things intuitively.

Principal argument: And it seems in the first place that it does not, because sensitive sight suffices together with abstractive knowledge for the knowledge of sensible things: therefore, intuitive sight is superfluous.

To the contrary, whatsoever perception sense can accomplish, understanding also can accomplish: but this is proper to the perception of sense.

Conclusion: To this question I say that our understanding does know sensible things intuitively, because our understanding knows evidently the first contingent proposition concerning sensibles: therefore, it has an incomplex conception sufficient to cause this complex conception evidently; but abstract knowledge of sensibles does not suffice: therefore etc.

To the arguments to the contrary,[1] I say that in holding the sensitive soul to be the same form as the intellective soul it is not necessary to say that the sensitive sight is received in the intellective soul; but it is received in the body or in the soul which is distinct from the intellective soul in the body. For if it were received in the intellective soul, then a separated soul, at least by the power of God, could have in itself all such sensation and it could perceive; which does not seem to be true: because if it were thus, the angel would lack some natural perfection, for it seems that the angel also could have such forms naturally; for corporeal things would be only the efficient causes of

---

[1]The statement of the *arguments to the contrary*, to which the following are replies, seems to be lacking.

these forms. But if they are diverse forms, as I believe that they are, then I say that the sensitive seeing does not suffice to cause assent to a contingent proposition however much it may suffice to cause an act in the sensitive appetite; for they are not similar in that the same form would then be subject of the sensation and of the act of desiring. If you say that the intellective and the sensitive are not distant from each other in location, that does not hold, for what sees and what assents must be the same in number [i.e. the same individual]. The question concerning the understanding of the head and of the foot has been answered above.

To another [argument to the contrary], I say that there is a difference between sensitive seeing and intellectual seeing, which is noticed by us partly through reason, partly through experience. By experience because the child sees by sensitive sight and not intellectual; for he does not understand by reason that the separated soul can have intellective sight, not sensitive.

To another [argument to the contrary], I say that the separated soul can have such sight, otherwise the separated soul could not have knowledge of sensibles. Similarly, the angel can have such knowledge: therefore, the separated soul likewise. To the proof of this I say that the separated soul can naturally see the complex and incomplex secrets of hearts in the mind of the angel.

To the Scripture I say that the statement is of a fact and natural power suspended from actuality.

To another [argument to the contrary], I say that it requires speech and illumination for two reasons. The first is that perhaps it is not permitted to understand naturally what it could understand [super]naturally. The second, that many things are revealed to one angel which are not revealed to another nor to the separated soul, as was said in the question on the speech of angels.

To another [argument to the contrary], I say that one can not acquire the sight of God and beatitude naturally, because it can not be caused except by God alone. And further it does not follow: he can see the less visible, therefore, the more visible, just as it does not follow that my understanding can see whiteness which is less visible, therefore, it can see the angel which is more visible; and this is so because the sight

of the angel can not be caused in me naturally, and thus it is in this question.

To another [argument to the contrary], I say that sensitive sight is the partial cause of intellectual sight, but it is not the partial cause of the act of assenting without the intellectual seeing, for complex knowledge presupposes incomplex knowledge in the same subject; just as the will can not proceed to action, unless knowledge precedes in the understanding, howeversomuch intuitive knowledge there be in sense.

To another [argument to the contrary], I concede that sensitive sight is subjectively in the sensitive appetite, for sense and appetite are the same: therefore, whatever is subjectively in one is also subjectively in the other.

To the principal argument, I say that sensitive seeing does not suffice, but requires intellectual seeing.

QUODLIBET V.

QUESTION V.

Whether intuitive and abstractive knowledge differ.

Principal argument: And it seems that they do not, because a plurality must not be asserted without necessity, but the same notion, according to substance, can be called intuitive when the thing is present, and abstractive when the thing is absent, in that intuitive knowledge connotes the thing present, and abstractive, the thing absent.

To the contrary, a contingent proposition can be known evidently by the understanding, as for example that this whiteness is, and not by abstract knowledge, for that knowledge abstracts from existence; therefore by intuitive knowledge; therefore, they differ really.

The conclusion of this question is certain and can be proved by the separateness of the acts of the two kinds of knowledge; but how they differ is doubtful. And I say for the present that they differ in two ways. In one way in that by intuitive knowledge assent is given to a contingent proposition,[1] and by abstract knowledge it is not. In another way through the fact that by intuitive knowledge I not only judge that a thing is when it is, but also that it is not when it is not; by abstract knowledge I judge in neither of these manners. The second is manifest. I prove the first because

---

[1]The 1491 edition has *primo* instead of *propositioni*.

although it is contradictory that the same idea be the total cause of one judgment and of the contrary of the judgment in respect of the same experience of it, yet it is not contradictory that it be the partial cause of one judgment when the thing exists and that it be the partial cause of the contrary judgment when the thing does not exist, and thus it is in the question proposed. Furthermore, God sees by the same idea that the thing is when it is and that it is not when it is not; therefore, it can be thus without contradiction in the case proposed.

1. But to the contrary, if this is granted, it follows that God could not cause in us a single act of knowing by which it appears to us that a thing is present when it is absent; which is false, since this does not involve a contradiction. The assumption is proved, because that knowledge is not intuitive because of the thing, since by intuitive knowledge the thing appears to be when it is and not to be when it is not; nor abstract knowledge, since by abstract knowledge the thing does not appear to be present.

2. Moreover, that which agrees with an act according to the substance of the act, if the substance of it remains the same, whatsoever else is posited it can still agree with it. But the substance of seeing remains the same by the divine power when no thing exists: therefore, it is not contradictory for it to cause at least partially such an assent as previously, now that the thing does not exist; and consequently, that can be proper to it.

3. Moreover, if this is granted it follows that seeing could be, and yet by it the thing would appear neither to be nor not to be. The consequence is contrary to fact. The assumption is proved by the following common principle: where anyone at all of certain given things is in accord with a given thing contingently, if there is no contradiction God can make that thing without all those certain things at once. For thus it is proved most cogently that matter can be without any form. But by virtue of seeing, someone can sometimes know that a thing is and sometimes know that it is not: therefore, there is no contradiction that neither being or non-being accords with it.

4. Moreover, if this is granted, God could not cause evident assent in respect of the following contingent proposition, *this whiteness is*, when whiteness is not existent, for the sight of whiteness causes the

evident assent in respect of the proposition, *this whiteness is not*; and the understanding does not seem to assent to the opposite.

1. To the first of these I say that God can not cause in us knowledge such that by it a thing appears evidently to be present when it is absent, for that involves a contradiction, because such evident knowledge conveys that it is thus in fact as is denoted by the proposition to which assent is given. And consequently since evident knowledge of this proposition, *the thing is present*, conveys that the thing is present, it is necessary that it be present; otherwise it would not be evident knowledge. And you posit that it is absent. And thus from that hypothesis there follows a manifest contradiction with evident knowledge, namely, that the thing is present and that it is not present. And, therefore, God can not cause such evident knowledge. Nevertheless, God can cause a creditive act by which I believe that a thing which is absent is present. And I say that that creditive idea will be abstract, not intuitive. By such an act of faith a thing can appear to be present when it is absent; yet not by an evident act.

2. To the other I answer by conceding that if the sight of the thing remain by the power of God when the thing is non-existent, it is not inconsistent for vision to cause partial assent, if all other causes requisite concur, but it is inconsistent that it cause such assent totally and partially without other causes; and thus since the existence of the thing is the partial cause of that evident assent, it is impossible that it be caused naturally without the existence of the thing.

3. To the other, I concede the principle and the confusion and the whole deduction, for it is not a contradiction that seeing be and still by that seeing I neither judge the thing to be nor not to be, because God can make sight without any such assent; but this can not be done by nature.

4. To the last, I say that God can not make evident assent of the following contingent proposition, *this whiteness is*, when the whiteness is not, because of the contradictions which follow, because evident assent conveys that it is thus in fact as is conveyed by the proposition to which assent is given; but by this proposition, *this whiteness is*, is conveyed that this whiteness is, and consequently if the assent is evident, this whiteness is, and it has been asserted that this whiteness is

not; and thus that hypothesis involves manifestly a contradiction with evident knowledge, namely, that whiteness is and that it is not. And yet I concede that God can make assent which is of the same species with that evident assent in respect of that contingent proposition, *this whiteness is*, when it is not; but that assent is not evident, because it is not in fact as is conveyed by the proposition to which assent is given.

And if you say that God can bring about evident assent of this contingent by way of the existence of this thing as a mediating secondary cause: therefore, he can do it by himself alone; I reply that this is the fallacy of a figure of speech; as the following argument, God can bring about a meritorious act with a created will mediating: therefore, he can do it by himself alone. And this is because of the different connotation herein.

To the principal argument I say that there is a necessity of asserting a difference between these kinds of knowledge.

QUODLIBET VI.

QUESTION VI.

Whether there can be intuitive knowledge of a non-existent object.

Principal argument: And it is argued that there can not be, because it is a contradiction that sight be and nothing be seen: therefore, it is a contradiction for sight to be and for the object seen not to be.

To the contrary, sight is a quality absolutely distinct from the object: therefore, it can be without contradiction without the object.

Conclusion: 1. In this question I assert two conclusions. The first is that there can be by the power of God intuitive knowledge concerning a non-existent object; this I prove first by an article of faith: I believe in God, father almighty; which I understand thus, that everything which does not involve a manifest contradiction is to be attributed to the divine power; but for this to be done by God does not involve a contradiction: therefore etc. Moreover, in that article is based the following famous proposition of theologians: *whatsoever God produces with secondary causes mediating, he can produce and conserve immediately without them.* From this proposition I argue thus: every effect which God causes with a secondary cause mediating

he can produce immediately through himself. But he has power in intuitive corporeal knowledge with the object mediating: therefore, he is effective in it immediately through himself. Moreover, every absolute thing distinct in place and subject from another thing can exist by the divine power if the other absolute thing has been destroyed. But the sight of the stars in the sky which I see is of this sort.

And if you say that according to this opinion it follows that God can be seen beatifically and intuitively, when his actual presence is not displayed, as [*in ratione*] an object actually present to the understanding itself: which is false and erroneous; I reply that there is a condition involved in arguing that because God can make such a vision without a created object on which it depends only as on a second cause, therefore, God can be seen intuitively and beatifically, when his actual presence is not displayed, as [*in ratione*] an actuality present to the understanding itself, on which object that vision depends as on a first cause. For although, according to the doctors, God can produce effects proper to secondary causes without those secondary causes, still he can not produce any effect without a first cause. Whence, just as it is not possible that color cause effectively the sight of color in the eye unless it is actually present, so it is not possible that God cause sight in the understanding unless he has displayed his actual presence.

2. The second conclusion is that intuitive knowledge can not be caused or conserved naturally when the object is not existent. The reason of this is that a real effect can not be produced from non-being to being nor conserved by that which is nothing, and consequently, naturally speaking, a producing cause is required for existing as much as a conserving cause. And if you say that if one sees the sun and later enters a dark place, it appears to one that one sees the sun in the same place and of the same magnitude: therefore, the sight of the sun remains when it is itself absent; and for the same reason it would remain if it were itself nonexistent; I reply that the sight of the sun does not remain, but there remains some quality, namely, the light impressed on the eye, and that quality is seen; and if the understanding forms such a proposition as this, *the light is seen in the same place* etc. and assents to it, it is deceived because of that impressed quality which is seen.

To the principal argument I say that it is a contradiction for sight to be and for that which is seen not to be in effect and for it not to be able to be: therefore, it is a contradiction that a chimera be seen intuitively. But it is not a contradiction that that which is seen be nothing in actuality outside the soul, so long as it can be in effect or was at some time in the nature of things. It is thus in the question proposed. Whence, God saw from eternity all makeable things and yet none were from eternity.

QUODLIBET V.

QUESTION II.

Whether the same conclusion in number can be known evidently by demonstration and experience.

Principal argument: 1. And it seems that it can not, because seeing the thing and later not seeing it, one forms simple absolute concepts of different kinds [ratio]: therefore, composite conclusions from them will be of different kinds [ratio], of which the nature of one is to be known by demonstration, that of another to be known by experience. The consequence is clear of itself. The antecedent is proved because otherwise the wayfarer and the blessed would form equally evident propositions concerning God, because they would be composed from concepts of the same kind; which is false.

2. Moreover, the necessary is not contingent, but the conclusion of a demonstration is necessary; and the proposition known by experience immediately is contingent: wherefore etc.

To the contrary, the following conclusion can be known by experience, *all fire is heat-giving*; and the same conclusion in number can be known by demonstration by heat as by a middle term.

Conclusion: To this question I say briefly that the same conclusion not only in species but in number can be known evidently by demonstration and by experience and by the same condition in number. This I prove because some condition verificative of the conclusion is acquired from experience and no other from knowledge. This is clear inductively, and knowledge of the same conclusion is acquired by demonstration.

Moreover, demonstration based on the nature of things [*propter quid*, i.e. a priori demonstration] and

demonstration on the grounds of some one thing only [*quia*, i.e. *a posteriori* demonstration] can cause knowledge of the same species in respect of the same conclusion: therefore, in the same manner demonstration and experience can do it.

Moreover, a principle and a conclusion differ in this, that a principle can be known only from its terms or by experience without demonstration; but the same conclusion can be known evidently by experience and by demonstration.

Moreover, causes distinct in species can have effects of the same species; this is clear above: therefore, it is thus in the question proposed.

1. But to the contrary, a single proposition is not more evident or less evident. But a proposition which is formed with sight mediating is compounded from conceptions more evident than the proposition which is formed with only demonstration mediating, because seeing a thing one assents more evidently than having a demonstration only without experience.

2. Moreover, if the condition of the conclusion caused by demonstration and [that caused by] experience are of the same species, then no way is apparent for proving a distinction of species between the acts of believing, of having an opinion, and of knowing, because the conclusion is the same in itself, and thence the premises can cause an act of the same species.

3. Moreover, knowing a conclusion by demonstration or experience, howsoever much that assent may be intended, one would never assent so evidently as when one has demonstration and experience. For otherwise assent could be increased by frequent repetition of that demonstration to equal evidence with that which experience caused; which is false: therefore, these kinds of knowledge differ in species by the following principle, *those things which have no power in effects of the same kind* [ratio] *are not of the same kind*.

4. Moreover, if thus the same conclusion is in the syllogism from true premises and from false premises, the false premises would cause assent of the same species with the true premises, and consequently the sophistical, the falsigraphic, and the demonstrative syllogisms will cause knowledge of the same species.

5. Moreover, the same conclusion in number can be proved from the thing philosophically from specu-

lative premises and can be demonstrated by practical premises, such as the following, *the act is generative of the habit or condition.* Therefore, if this assent will be the same, then the same knowledge will be practical and speculative; which seems absurd.

Resolution of objections: 1. To the first of these I say that the same proposition can not be more evident and less evident at one and the same time to one and the same person; nevertheless the same proposition can at one and the same time be more evident to one and less evident to another. In the same way the same proposition can be less evident to one person at one time and more evident to the same person at another time.

For proof of this, I say that if some one knows a conclusion at one time by demonstration only and at another time knows the same conclusion by demonstration and experience, then to such an one that conclusion is first less evident and later more evident.

2. To the other I deny the consequence, because the act of having an opinion of and the act of knowing the same conclusion are formally contradictory, because one is evident and the other is unevident and entertained with fear. Two such, however, can not at the same time be in the same understanding, and consequently they are distinct in species; just as it is proved that the acts of loving and of hating the same man differ in species because they are contradictory formally.

For proof of this, I say that not all premises can cause knowledge of a conclusion of the same species, but some can and some can not, because it is certain that the premises of a Sophistical syllogism and of a falsigraphic syllogism do not cause knowledge of the same species in respect of the same conclusion. In the same way premises of creditive, opinionative, and demonstrative syllogisms in respect of the same conclusion do not cause assent of the same species, but rather opposed assents, as faith, opinion, and knowledge are opposed. And, therefore, I say that some causes of different kinds [*ratio*] can sometimes cause effects of the same species, but not all causes of different kinds can do this. Nor is any other cause to be sought than that that is the nature of the thing.

But there remains a doubt with reference to this: how is a determination of species proved between these acts? The reply is proved by reason of the contra-

diction between the acts of knowing, having an opinion, and believing in respect of the same conclusion.

3. To the other I say that if that argument were conclusive, it would prove that heat which is caused by the sun and by fire, and heat which is caused by two fires are not of the same species, because howsoever much the power of the sun were increased it can not by itself cause such perfect heat as it can together with fire. And likewise, howsoever much the power of one fire be augmented, it can not by itself cause so perfect heat as with another fire. And consequently these heats would be of different species by this argument; which is false. Therefore, I say that just as the power of the sun can be increased so much that it can cause as perfect heat as fire can cause by itself without the sun, and yet with the sun it can cause a still more perfect heat than this, so by demonstration assent can so be increased to a very great degree, if possible *in infinitum*, that it is equally evident and equally perfect as that assent which experience would cause by itself without demonstration. Nevertheless, it can never be increased by demonstration so much that it causes assent equally perfect and equally evident by itself without experience, as it can cause together with experience. And the principle quoted is to be understood in this sense: *those things which have no power in any effect of the same species are of different kinds* [ratio] *or species, and otherwise they are not.*

4 and 5. To the last I say that the same conclusion can be in the syllogism from true premises and from false, but besides that, the consequence does not hold: that, therefore, these premises can cause knowledge of the same species, because I have not said universally that all premises cause assent of the same species, but I have said particularly that some premises etc. And, therefore, I say that false premises are not formed naturally to cause assent of the same species with true premises. For false premises cause opinion; true evident premises cause evident assent. However, if they are believed, they cause faith.

1. To the principal argument, I say that, seeing a thing and later not seeing it, one can form two propositions composed from abstract conceptions, as Paul after the rapture. And one is composed from conceptions causing evident assent and the other not, but [the latter] will be [un] evident, as that proposition which he had of God before the rapture which was

only believed by faith; and he had another after, which was evident to him by demonstration before the rapture, and the same demonstration in species or in number was more evident after the rapture, with the vision of God mediating.

2. To the other, I say that the necessary is not known through the contingent syllogistically as through premises, but evident contingent knowledge can be the efficient cause partial to causing evident knowledge in respect of the necessary; and thus it is in the question proposed.

QUODLIBET V.

QUESTION VI.

Whether the act of apprehending and the act of judging[1] differ really.

Principal argument: And it seems that they do not, because it is a contradiction that there be a demonstration in the soul if the soul does not know the conclusion; but demonstration can be in the soul with only the composition of the propositions of the demonstration: therefore, knowledge is something of demonstration. Not the principle nor any term: therefore, the conclusion.

To the contrary, they can be separated: therefore, they differ. The antecedent is clear, because some propositions are neutral, to which our understanding does not assent nor dissent at first, and later it assents because of some middle term.

Conclusion: I reply that I shall first assert two distinctions. Secondly, I shall answer the question.

Concerning the first I say that *assent* is of two sorts. One by which the understanding assents that something is or that something is not, or that something is good or white; another by which the understanding assents to some complex.

The second distinction is that *apprehension* is of two sorts. One is composition or division, or the formation of a proposition; there is another, which is a knowledge of the complex itself already formed, as knowledge of whiteness is called apprehension.

In the third place, I state two conclusions

1. The first is that the act of assenting taken in either mode is different from the [first] apprehension which is the formation of the proposition. This I prove first as follows. The same conclusion is proved a priori and *a posteriori* and by authority as has been shown before. If therefore the conclusion or the formation of the conclusion were knowledge, which is an act of assenting, it follows that then the same knowledge would be a priori and *a posteriori*. In the same way faith and opinion; and the same conclusion would at one and the same time be evident and not evident to the same person, because it is by hypothesis knowledge and faith. For the same conclusion in number can first be believed and later be known.

Moreover, the act of doubting is not contradictory to the conclusion of the demonstration, because it is not contradictory to the subject nor the predicate, nor the copula; but the act of doubting is incompossible with knowledge. Therefore, knowledge is not the conclusion nor the formation of the conclusion.

Moreover, the act of believing and the act of knowing are simple and brought forth of necessity immediately. The conclusion itself however is composite, because the composition of the conclusion is the conclusion and not part of it.

2. The second conclusion is that assent, taken in either mode, differs from the second apprehension which is knowledge of the complex already formed. I prove this first as follows: believer and unbeliever contradict each other concerning this article of faith. *God is three and one.* Either, therefore, this article formed in the mind is apprehended and known by both, or not. If it is and the act of believing is not in both, then the act of believing differs not only from this article formed in the mind, but also from the apprehension of it. If not, it is apprehended in both.

To the contrary, it may be argued by asserting all things in these two to be equal, except the act of believing, and then it is manifest that one can apprehend that article. In the same way no one assents or dissents except concerning something known; but the unbeliever dissents from this article immediately and denies it: therefore, be knows this article.

Moreover, the apprehensive act causes the judicative act: therefore, they differ. The consequence is manifest. The antecedent is proved by experience, for however frequently one apprehends a complex and

---

[1]The 1487 edition has (erroneously) *act of seeing.*

does not at first assent, if later because of some middle term one should assent to it only once, one is inclined later promptly to assent to it, and not from the habit of assenting, because as yet it is not had so perfectly that it could incline to that assent: therefore, that promptitude is effectively from the apprehensive habit. But no habit inclines to another act except with its own act mediating: therefore, the apprehensive act immediately causes the judicative act.

Moreover, some apprehend a neutral proposition to which they neither assent nor dissent: therefore, apprehension, assent, and dissent differ.

Moreover, some first deny a proposition, and later concede it, and apprehend it always: therefore, this apprehension differs from the assent and dissent, for it is related successively to both when one denies and when one concedes.

To the principal argument it is said that it is no contradiction for a demonstration to be in the soul without the act of knowing, because the act of doubting is not contradictory formally to the conclusion nor to the demonstration: although perhaps it is contradictory to it virtually; and consequently by the power of God the act of doubting could be caused in the soul at the same time with the demonstration.

QUODLIBET IV

QUESTION XVII.[1]

Whether every act of assenting presupposes an act of apprehending with respect of the same object.

Principal argument: And it seems that it does, because the understanding assents only to what it considers true, nor does it dissent except to what it considers false. But the understanding considers nothing true or false except what is known and apprehended: therefore, all assent necessarily presupposes apprehension.

To the contrary, having formed the following immediate proposition, *every whole is greater than its part*, without any apprehension of the proposition, the understanding straightway assents necessarily: therefore, that assent does not presuppose apprehension.

Conclusion: Here I shall first make a distinction. Secondly I shall answer the question.

Concerning the first I say, as has been said elsewhere, in quodlibet III, question VI, that the act of assenting is of two sorts: one by which I assent that something is or is not, as I assent that *God is three and one*, and that *God is not the devil*; and yet I do not assent to God or to the devil, but I assent that God is not the devil. Whence by the power of word I assent by the latter act to no thing, yet by the same act I apprehend God and the devil, because every act of assenting is an act of apprehending and not conversely. Another kind is the act of assenting by which I assent to something so that the act of assenting is referred to something by assenting or dissenting to a complex, as by assenting to this proposition, *man is an animal*, because I consider that it is true, and I assent not only to this proposition, *this proposition man is an animal is a true proposition*, in which this proposition, *man is an animal*, is subject, but I assent to this proposition, *man is an animal*, in itself and absolutely; and this is so because I know that as it is in fact, so it is conveyed by this proposition.

Concerning the second I say in general that the first assent never presupposes necessarily the apprehension of a complex, because this assent is not in respect of a complex as object, but it presupposes the apprehension of individual things, although the understanding may not assert to the individual things. But the second assent, naturally speaking, presupposes necessarily the apprehension of a complex, and this indifferently,[2] whether that complex is compounded of conceptions of [individual] things or not. And the reason is that this assent has a complex for object. Now, however, none of us naturally assent or dissent except concerning that which is known and apprehended: therefore, it is impossible that I assent to some complex naturally unless I apprehend it.

1. But to the contrary, if the understanding form this proposition, *the whole is greater than its part*, having circumscribed all other apprehension of the complex except this composition, this evident assent' is caused instantly. Otherwise it would not be a proposition known through itself. In the same way if this understanding form the proposition, *God is three and one*, without any other apprehension, it can, together

[1]This question is numbered XVI in the 1487 edition.

[2]The 1491 edition has *et in hoc differunt* instead of *et hoc indifferenter*.

with a command of the will, cause an act of belief of that article: therefore, such assent does not presuppose apprehension.

2. Moreover, apprehension of a complex is not a proposition, because the understanding can form a proposition although it does not know it or apprehend it, just as I can know a stone although I do not know that knowledge. Nor is the apprehension part of the proposition, because every part of the proposition can be knowledge of an external thing and no other knowledge is necessary to the act of assenting.

3. Moreover, assent with respect to a thing is one thing and assent with respect to a complex is another, just as apprehension of a thing is one thing and apprehension of a complex another. Therefore, assent at least in respect of a thing does not presuppose apprehension of a complex.

1. To the first of these [arguments to the contrary], I say that the argument, as well with respect to the act of assenting in common as with respect to the act of believing the article, proceeds from the first assent and not from the second.

2. To the second, I say that the apprehension of a complex is neither a part of the proposition compounded from notions of external things, nor is it the proposition itself, although it could be part of another proposition; but it is another kind of knowledge distinct as well from proposition as from assent; and assent which has a complex for object presupposes this knowledge; and this is true not only when one assents to a complex which is compounded from conceptions of things, as in the following, *man is an animal, man is not an ass*, but also when one assents to some proposition whose subject, and predicate are propositions; propositions concerning the sense of a composition are commonly of this sort, such as the following, *this proposition, man is an animal, is true, or necessary, or contingent*; or *this proposition, man is an ass, is impossible*, because in order that I may assent to such complexes it is necessary that I first apprehend and know them.

3. To the third, I say that there is no assent in respect of the thing because nothing is said when I assent to a stone or an ox.

To the principal argument, the answer is clear from what has been said.

QUODLIBET IV.

QUESTION XIX.[1]

Whether first and second intentions are really distinct.

Principal argument: And it seems that they are not, for an essence of the reason is not distinct really; but intentions, as well first as second, are only entities of the reason: therefore etc.

To the contrary, first and second intentions are things, and are not the same things but distinct things: therefore, they are distinguished really.

Conclusion: In the first place, what first and second intentions are must be considered here. In the second place, the question must be answered.

Concerning the first I say that both first and second intention can be taken in two ways, broadly and strictly. Broadly the first intention is said to be the intelligible sign existent in the soul which does not signify an intention or a concept in the soul or any other signs precisely, and I say this, whether sign be taken for that which can stand [for a thing] in a proposition and be part of a proposition, of which sort are categorematic terms, or whether sign be taken for that which can not stand [for a thing] nor be the extreme terms of a proposition when it is taken significatively, of which sort are syncategorematic terms. And in this manner not only mental categorematic terms which signify things which are not themselves significative, but also mental syncategorecatic terms and verbs and conjunctions and others of this sort are called first intentions.

Example: For in this manner not only the concept of *man* which signifies all men and can stand for them and be part of a proposition, and the concept of *whiteness*, and the concept of *heat*, and such concepts are properly called [first] intentions; but such syncategorematic concepts as the following, *if, nevertheless, not, while, is, and, runs, reads*, are called first intentions, and this is because although they do not stand, taken in themselves, for things, yet conjoined with others they make the others stand [for things in diverse manners, as *every* makes *man* stand for][2] and be

---

[1]This question is numbered XXXV in the 1487 edition.

[2]Omitted in the 1491 edition.

distributed over all men, as in this proposition, *every man runs;* and yet this sign *every* signifies nothing through itself, because it signifies neither an external thing nor an intention of the soul.

But strictly the first intention should be a mental name formed precisely to be the extreme term of a proposition and to stand for a thing which is not a sign; as the concept of *man,* of *animal,* of *substance,* of *body.* And briefly all mental names which naturally signify individual things which are not signs.

In the same way, taken broadly, that concept of the soul is called a second intention, which signifies not only the intentions of the soul which are natural signs of things (of which sort are the first intentions taken strictly) but also as it were mental signs signifying at will syncategorematic mental signs. And we have perhaps in this way only a word corresponding to the second intention.

However, taken strictly, that concept is called a second intention which signifies precisely intentions naturally significative, of which sort are *genus, species, difference,* and others of this sort, for as the concept of man is predicated of all men, as in saying, *this man is a man, that man is a man,* and thus of the others, so too one common concept, which is the second intention, is predicated of first intentions which stand for things, as in saying, *man is a species, ass is a species, whiteness is a species, animal is a genus, body is a genus, quantity is a genus;* in the manner in which *name* is predicated of different names, as in saying, *whiteness is a name, man is a name;* and this second intention thus signifies first intentions naturally and can stand for them in a proposition, just as the first intention signifies external things naturally and can stand for them.

Concerning the second, some say that first and second intentions are certain fictive entities which are only objectively in the mind and nowhere subjectively.

On the contrary, when a proposition is verified by things, if two things suffice for the truth of it, it is superfluous to assert another thing; but according to all such propositions as, *man is understood: man is subject: man is predicate: man is a species: animal is a genus,* and similar propositions in which such fictive being is asserted, the propositions are verified by things, and two things suffice for verifying all such propositions. The assumption is proved because having posited

knowledge of man in the understanding, it is impossible that this proposition be false, *man is understood.* In the same way, having posited the intention of man in common and the intention of subject in common, and having formed this mental proposition, *man is subject,* in which one intention is predicated of the other, it is necessary that this proposition be true, *man is subject,* without anything fictive.

Moreover, such a fictive thing hinders the knowledge of the thing: therefore, it is not to be asserted because of knowledge. The assumption is proved because that fictive thing is neither the idea, nor is it the external whiteness known, nor is it both together; but a certain third thing, medium between knowledge and the thing: therefore, if that fictive thing is understood, then the thing outside is not understood, and then when I form the following mental proposition, *God is three and one,* I do not understand God in himself but that fictive thing; which seems absurd.

Moreover, for the same reason, in understanding other things God would understand such fictions; and to from eternity there was coordinated as many fictive beings as there could be different intelligible beings which were so necessarily that God could not destroy them; which seems false.

Moreover, such a fictive being does not have to be posited in order that a subject and predicate may be had in a universal proposition, because the act of understanding suffices for this: for that fictive being is as individual in being and in representing as the act. This is evident from the following, that one fiction can be destroyed while another remains as actual, for either that fiction depends essentially on [some] act [of reason] or not. If it does, then, when one act ceases, that fiction is destroyed, and yet the fiction remains in another act, and consequently there are two individual fictions as there are two acts. If it does not depend on this individual act, it does not consequently depend essentially on any act of the same reason, and thus that fiction will remain in objective being without any other act; which is impossible.

Moreover, it is no contradiction that God form such real knowledge without such a fiction [for knowledge does not depend on such a fiction] essentially; but the contradiction is that the intention be posited in the understanding lest something be understood:

therefore, the intention must not be posited because of a common intention.

Therefore, I say that as well the first intention as the second intention is truly an act of understanding, for by the act can be saved whatever is saved by the fiction. For in that the act is the likeness of the subject, it can signify and stand for external things; it can be the subject and the predicate in a proposition; it can be genus, species etc. just as the fiction can. Wherefore, it is clear that the first and second intention are really distinct, for the first intention is the act of understanding signifying things which are not signs. The second intention is the act signifying first intentions. Therefore, they are distinguished.

As regards the principal argument, it is clear that both first and second intentions are truly real entities, and they are truly qualities subjectively existent in the soul.

QUODLIBET V.

QUESTION XXV.[1]

Whether the absolute, connotative, and relative concepts are really distinct.

Principal argument: And it seems that they are not, because plurality must not be asserted without necessity; but this is not necessary: therefore etc.

To the contrary, words are distinct: therefore, concepts; the consequence holds because they are ordered signs.

Conclusion: I reply that the conclusion is certain according to the philosophers. For the concept of man is absolute; the concept of white is connotative; and the concept of father is relative; and they do not coincide except as inferior and superior, for every relative concept is connotative, and not conversely.

But it is doubtful how they differ. And therefore I say that they differ in this, that the absolute concept signifies all the things it signifies equally in the first and single mode of signifying, namely, in the direct mode, as is clear from this name *man* and similar words, for it signifies all men equally, and not first one and secondarily another. Nor does it signify one

directly and another obliquely. And such a name is truly predicated of something without the addition of any term in an oblique case, as *Socrates is a man*, although he is not a man of anything. And such a name, properly speaking, does not have a definition expressing the essence of the name [*quid nominis*].

The connotative name, however, properly signifies one thing first and another secondarily, and one thing directly and another obliquely. And such a name properly has a definition expressing the essence of the name, nor can it be predicated truly of anything unless an oblique case can be added to it. An example of this is in the concept *white* and in similar concepts. First, it signifies *white* and second, *whiteness*; it signifies the subject directly, and whiteness obliquely. Nor can Socrates be white unless this is true; Socrates is white by whiteness; Socrates is so much by quantity; long by length.

The concrete relative concept, however, has in the highest degree the aforesaid conditions which this connotative concept has. But they differ in that whenever the connotative concept is predicated truly of anything, its abstract can properly be added to it only in an oblique case, for nothing is white unless it is white by whiteness, nor warm unless it is warm by warmth. But when the relative concept is predicated truly of anything, an oblique case which is not the abstract of it can always properly be added to it. An example is in the case of *master, father*, and others, for Socrates is not master unless he is master of some servant. Nor can he be a father unless he is father of some son. Nor can he be like except to some one having a like quality. Nor equal except to some one having quantity; and thus it is with all relative nouns.

To the principal argument the conclusion is clear from what has been said.

QUODLIBET II.

QUESTION XII.

Whether the direct and reflex act are the same act.

Principal argument: And it seems in the first place that they are, because otherwise there would be a process *in infinitum* in reflex acts: therefore etc.

---

[1]This question does not appear in the 1487 edition.

To the contrary, in us the understanding and its object are not the same; but the direct act is the object of the reflex act.

Conclusion: In the first place I shall expound here the meaning of the question. In the second place I shall reply to the question.

Concerning the first I say that the direct and reflex acts are not taken here in their proper sense, for that is called reflex properly, which begins from a given thing and terminates in the same thing. And therefore no act is properly called reflex. But direct and reflex are taken improperly, for that act is called direct by which the understanding understands an object outside the soul, and that act reflex by which this direct act is understood.

Concerning the second I say that the direct act and the reflex act are not the same act. I prove this first as follows. Whatever is known by a power through some act of a kind [ratio] other than the object, can be known through a consimilar act by another power of the same kind. But one angel knows the act of another angel by an act distinct from the act known: therefore, the angel whose act is known by the other can know its own act by a knowledge consimilar to this knowledge which another angel knows. But that knowledge is distinct in species from the object: therefore, it is other. For this reason seems more cogent than all the others which are relative to this part.

Again, intuitive knowledge and abstractive knowledge are distinct; that is certain; but abstract knowledge can be known intuitively as is clear in the first quodlibet: therefore etc.

Again, the direct and the reflex acts of will are not the same: therefore, the understandings of them are not the same. The antecedent is clear because the act of love and of hate are not the same; but some one sometimes loves hate.

1. To the contrary, if this is so, then infinite acts could be at the same time, because there is a process *in infinitum* in them; and the posterior always requires that the prior exist, just as intuitive knowledge requires naturally the existence of the object.

2. Moreover, there would then be some act which could not be apprehended intuitively by the understanding.

1. I reply, therefore, to the first of these by conceding a process *in infinitum* in abstractive but not in intuitive ideas. The first is clear because any intuitive and abstract knowledge can be known abstractly when it is not itself existent. For this perception can cease and then it can be known abstractly; and that knowledge can cease and then be known in another abstract idea; and thus *in infinitum*. But from this there does not follow any actual infinity nor any great magnitude, as for example that a thousand perceptions exist at the same time, which we do not experience: therefore, in this process there is given an ultimate perception which can not be seen. For of it we have experience through its status itself [i.e. through the fact that perception comes to rest in it]. But what the cause is I do not know.

And by this the conclusion to the other argument and to the principal argument is clear; obviously no multitude follows from this necessarily.

2. The second is clear likewise, because in intuitive ideas the posterior always requires that the prior exist; and therefore if there were a process *in infinitum*, one greatest multitude could be made; which is not true.

QUODLIBET I.

QUESTION XIV.

Whether our understanding by its nature [pro isto statu] knows its own acts intuitively.

Principal argument: And it seems in the first place that it does not, for nothing is known by the understanding except that which previously fell under sense; but acts of understanding were never under sense.

To the contrary, abstract knowledge presupposes intuitive. But intellectual conceptions are known abstractively: therefore, intuitively.

Conclusion: Replying to this question I say that our understanding does know its own acts intuitively. And the reason is that a contingent proposition is formed concerning the knowledge of the understanding and concerning the will, which is known evidently by our understanding, namely, such a proposition as the following, *there is an understanding, there is a will*: therefore, either by means of intuitive or abstract knowledge of the act of understanding. If in the first manner, the proposition is granted. The second can not be held because abstract knowledge is abstracted from an actual existence.

Again, experimental knowledge is not without intuitive knowledge; but one who lacks all intuitive sensitive knowledge, experiences intellectual knowledge.

Resolution of Objections: To the first argument to the contrary, I say that that does not follow because there would then be infinite perceptions in actuality. For proof of this I say, that if it is held that direct and reflex acts are not distinct, it can be said that the seeing of a stone is seen by itself when the stone is seen. And then it can be said that that proposition which is composed from the seeing of the stone and the concept of the stone can not remain when the seeing of the stone is not, although another proposition which is composed out of these conceptions can remain without the sight of the stone. But if it be held that the reflex act is distinct from the direct act, I say that the seeing of the stone will be by another seeing, but in the end one will come to a seeing which is not seen by a seeing naturally distinct from it, although it could be seen if there were no impediment, and I concede a regress *in infinitum* by the divine power; but speaking naturally there will be seeing which can not be seen; and for the following reason, that our understanding is a limited power: therefore, it has power only for a certain number of sight and not for more. But in what seeing one must stop I do not know. Perhaps one should stop in the second seeing, because it perhaps can not be seen naturally.

To another [objection] I say that one can not experience the first and the second seeing equally and an *in infinitum*, because one is stopped at some sight which can not be seen because of the limitation of the understanding, which has power for so many sights and no more. I concede, none the less, that one can naturalists have several perceptions at once, at least two or three of the same object.

To another [objection] I concede that I assent evidently to the following proposition, *I see*. And I say that the assent is caused by the seeing of that seeing; but from this it does not follow that there will be infinite perceptions at the same time; nor can there be a process *in infinitum* naturally; but a stop must be made at some seeing which is not naturally visible. Nor can one assent evidently to a complex formed as the following, *I see that sight at which the seeing has come to a stop.*

To another [objection] I concede that if there were in the soul a second sight, it could be seen if there were no impediment, and yet if it were in my soul I would not be able to see it, because the first act impedes the second so that it can not be seen with the first seeing. And I say it is not impossible, by the fact that it is in the understanding, that it could not be seen because if it were in the understanding it could be seen through itself; but because it is in the understanding at the same time as another act, it comes about that it can not be seen. And I say that I experience the vision of a stone, but I do not experience the vision of that vision. And by that reason the example of Augustine in book VI *On the Trinity*, chapter 8 near the end, is explained, in which he says that he often read and did not know what he read; clearly this happened because of destruction through the act of the other power, and still there is no contradiction between those acts, just as likewise a man intent on seeing does not perceive himself hear, when nevertheless he hears, and yet between sight and hearing there is no contradiction. So it is in the question proposed that although there is no contradiction between the last perceiving to which one comes naturally and the perceiving of that or of any of the preceding perceivings, yet one act can impede the other by the fact that it is.

To another I say that I am certain that I understand a stone in virtue of the sight of the stone, and in virtue of the perception of the first sight, and sometimes perhaps in virtue of these perceptions and in virtue of some proposition habitually known. For example, I am certain that I understand by experience because I see the seeing of the stone. But I am certain that I understand the stone by discourse from effect to cause as I know fire by smoke, when I see smoke alone, and this is so because I have on another occasion seen smoke caused by the presence of fire. And in the same manner because on another occasion I have perceived intellectually such a seeing caused in me by the presence of a stone.

Again I argue, such effects are of the same species, as has been expounded above in reference to the speech of angels. The proposition habitually known is this, *all such effects of the same species have causes of the same species*. I do not say in general all effects of the same species have a cause of the same species.

To the principal argument, I say that Aristotle says that nothing of those things which are external is understood unless first it falls under sense, and they are sensibles only according to sense, and that authority is true concerning them, but concerning spirits it is not.

QUODLIBET II.

QUESTION X.

Whether the sensitive soul and the intellective soul are really distinct in man.

Principal argument: And it seems in the first place that they are not, for there is only a single being of a single composite thing: therefore, only a single form, for the form gives being.

To the contrary, any animal is prior in nature to man: therefore, man is by one form and animal by another.

Conclusion: I reply to this question that they are distinct; but it is difficult to prove this, because it can not be proved from propositions known through themselves. I prove, nevertheless, that they are distinct really.

1. In the first place thus. It is impossible that there be contraries at the same time in the same subject; but the act of desiring something and avoiding or rejecting the same thing are contrary in the same subject: therefore, if they are at the same time in the nature of things, they are in different subjects; but it is clear that they are at the same time in man, for this same thing which man desires by the appetite he rejects by the understanding.

And in the same way by Aristotle in book III *On the Soul*, where he says that there are in the same person contrary appetites, that is, they would be contrary if it was their nature to be received in the same subject. If you say that these appetites are called contrary because they are inclinative to contrary effects, and they are thus virtually contrary, because the one inclines to pursuing, the other to flight, which is incompossible with the first, and such contraries can well be in the same subject; but they are not formally contrary; on the other hand by that reason you would say just as easily that willing and denying are not contraries formally, but only virtually, for it is their nature to incline to contrary

effects, and thus the way disappears for proving anything to be contrary.

Moreover, the same substantial form can not at one and the same time have two acts of desiring in respect to the same object. But in man there are frequently acts at the same time of willing some good and of desiring it by the sensitive appetite: therefore, these acts are not in the same subject.

Moreover, the same form does not bring forth at one and the same time an act of desiring something naturally and something else freely; but man wishes something freely, and the sensitive appetite desires it naturally.

2. In the second place, I argue thus principally. Sensations are subjectively in the sensitive soul immediately and immediately; and they are not subjectively in the intellective soul: therefore, they are distinct. The major premise is clear because nothing else can be assigned as the subject of sensations except the sensitive soul or power. And if the power is an accident of the soul, it will be subjectively in the sensitive soul; this is proved because otherwise every apprehension of the sensitive soul would be an act of understanding, for it would be subjectively in the intellective soul. Similarly, then, the separated soul could perceive, for sensation is therefore subjectively in the intellective soul, and God can conserve every accident in its subject or in any other; and consequently he could conserve the sensitive soul in the separated soul; which is absurd. If you say that the composite whole is the immediate subject of sensation or of the sensitive power, and no form; on the contrary, accident is not more simple than its first subject, as will be shown clearly at another time: therefore, sensation, since it is a simple accident, can not be subjectively and immediately in the composite and first [subject]. In the same way having granted this, those powers would not be powers of the soul more than of the body: wherefore, they are not subjectively more in one than in another.

3. In the third place I argue thus. The same form in number is not extended and unextended, material and immaterial; but the sensitive soul in man is extended and material, and the intellective soul is not, for it is all in all.

Objections: But against these [arguments] there are arguments of many sorts.

1. In the first place thus, that Augustine in his book on Ecclesiastical Dogmas attacks two souls in man and says that it is the error of some.

2. In the second place, that either that sensitive soul remained three days with the body or with the soul; and whichever be granted it follows that Christ was not dead univocally with other men, or else he was corrupted and then Christ put off one soul which he had taken on; which is contrary to the holy doctors.

3. In the third place, that the Parisian article says the doctrine that, when the rational soul recedes from the body, the animal remains still alive, is an error. But if they are distinct the sensitive soul remains after the separation of the intellective, for nature proceeds in the same order in generating and in corrupting. But in generating, the sensitive is introduced prior to the intellective if they are distinct; and the Philosopher says this in his book on Animals.

4. Again, if the sensitive soul remains without the intellective, that composite would be neither man nor rational animal; and thus it would not be rational nor irrational.

Resolution of Objections: 1. I reply and I say to the first of these, that Augustine attacked two intellective souls in man of which one is from God and the other from the devil; and this is the mind of Augustine if any one examines his book in that place.

2. To the second, I say that the sensitive soul of Christ in those three days remained where God pleased, but thus that it was always united to deity. But whether it remained with the body or with the intellective soul, only God knows; yet both can well be said. And I deny that he was not then dead univocally with other men, because for the same reason it could be said that he was not univocally dead, for the body of Christ is not corruptible as the bodies of other men are corruptible: therefore, it does not follow that he was not univocally dead because of the separation of the intellective soul.

3. To the third, I say that after the separation of the intellective soul the sensitive soul does not remain, nor was the sensitive soul introduced in the generation of man prior in time to the intellective. To the Philosopher I say that the sensitive soul is prior in nature in the body, but not prior in time, for they are introduced and expelled at the same time.

4. To the last, I say that if by the power of God the sensitive soul remained in the body, that composite would be alive, and still it would be neither rational animal nor irrational, nor would it be animal truly contained under animal, which is the genus. And the reason of this is that it would not be a being complete through itself in the genus, but it would be its nature to be an essential part of something existing through itself in the genus; and no such thing would be through itself in the genus of substance, or in any other genera essentially. Nor would any genus be predicated of it essentially in the first manner. Yet if all that which has this sensitive soul be called animal, then this is truly animal; but then animal would be spoken of equally of that and of other animals.

To the principal argument, I say that there is only one total being of man, but many partial beings.

QUODLIBET II.

QUESTION XIII.

Whether the act of a more perfect object is more perfect.

Principal argument: And it seems in the first place that it is not, because if it were, then the act of an infinite object would be infinite and consequently every act in respect to God would be infinite.

To the contrary, if it is not, then there would be no way of proving that any act is more perfect than any other.

Conclusion: I shall first set down one distinction here. In the second place I shall reply to the question.

Concerning the first I say that for anything to be more perfect than another thing can be taken in two ways. In one way according to things distinct in species. In a second way in those things which are of the same species. In the first way the angel is more perfect than man and man is more perfect than the ass. In the second way one whiteness is more perfect than another, and any form in which there are more parts of the same quantity of mass or power than in another form of the same species, as one whiteness is more perfect than another, because it has more parts of whiteness of the same quantity, and in the same way one love is more perfect than another.

Concerning the second article, I assert two conclusions.

1. The first is that it is not necessary that the act of the more perfect object always be more perfect; and this so whether the object be complex or incomplex. And I prove this first as follows. A principle is a more perfect object than the conclusion, and in respect of the same principle there can be acts of erring and of doubting, both of which are more imperfect according to species than the act of knowing: therefore, an act related to a more perfect object can be more imperfect than the act of a more imperfect object.

Moreover, let us take two incomplex objects, such as an angel and a man. Then I argue thus: the act of hating is more imperfect in respect of either than the act of loving; but I can hate the angel and love the man.

Moreover, a remiss act is more imperfect than an intense act, at least speaking of perfection of the second sort, although it may not be necessary that it be thus always in the first sort, but [it is] when some one loves a better and more perfect object less intensely; and this holds as well of objects of the same species as of objects of different species, as a man sometimes loves the greater love with less intensity than the lesser love, and loves the angel less than the man, which is clear because sometimes he thinks less intensely of the more perfect object than of the more imperfect object.

2. The second conclusion is this: the act of the more perfect object can always be more perfect than the act of the more imperfect, so that some act in respect of the more perfect object is more perfect than any act in respect of the more imperfect object, as well complex as incomplex.

Wherefore, it must be known that in respect of the same object, as well complex as incomplex, there can be different acts, just as in respect of the same conclusion there can be different acts, such as erring and doubting. And similarly in respect of the same thing there can be the act of loving and of hating. And although the act of erring could be more perfect than some act in respect of the more perfect object, yet the most perfect act among these is the act more perfect in respect to the more perfect object than

any act in respect to a more imperfect object. Just as the most perfect act in respect of one more perfect conclusion is more perfect than any other act in respect of a more imperfect conclusion. And in the same way I conclude of incomplex objects distinct in species. However, the most perfect act in respect of the more perfect object is more perfect than any other act in respect of a more imperfect object. Just as the most perfect act which is brought forth concerning an angel is more perfect than any other act which is brought forth concerning a man. I prove this as follows: because those two are of different species, and the most perfect act in respect of the more imperfect object is not more perfect than the most perfect act in respect of the more perfect object, it appears manifestly: therefore, since one act is necessarily more perfect than another, by the fact that they differ in species, it follows that the most perfect act in respect of the more perfect object is more perfect than the most perfect act in respect of the more imperfect object. But that these acts are distinct in species, is proved because contrary acts in respect of the same object differ in species, such as the act of erring and knowing therefore, much the more the most perfect acts of objects distinct in species. If you say that the acts of complex objects are of different species, but not the acts of incomplex objects, there is not, on the contrary, greater reason for the latter than for the former. Moreover, then the act of hating would be of the same species as the act of loving, for both are in respect of incomplex objects. In the same way the vision of a creature according to this could be beatific, because if it is of the same species as the vision of God to whomsoever it should be intended, it would arrive at an equal grade with the beatific vision.

To the first principal argument, I say that such a mode of arguing does not hold, unless it happens to fill in proper order the process *in infinitum*, that is, when the act in respect of the infinite presupposes of necessity infinite acts of infinite objects having an order according to greater and less perfection. But it is not, thus, in the question proposed, as is manifestly clear, because God can be understood and loved after or before any created object, and the act by which he is loved is necessarily finite.

1. To the contrary, if the act in respect of the infinite is finite, and the act of anyone in respect to that which is a created subject is similarly finite, since the act in respect of the infinite exceeds the other act in respect of the other subject in a double proportion, as I suppose, God can, therefore, make some object doubly more perfect than A, and let that be B. Then the most perfect act in respect to B, according to what has been said, exceeds the most perfect act in respect to A doubly. And again let God make an object excelling B doubly, and let that be C. Then because the most perfect act in respect of C excels the most perfect act in respect of B doubly, and because consequently by chance the most perfect act in respect of B is made equal to an act which is in respect of the infinite, it follows necessarily that the most perfect act in respect of C exceeds the act in respect of the infinite doubly, and thus an act in respect of the infinite would exceed in perfection an act is respect of the infinite.

To this answer can be made in a number of ways. In one way by positing a status among species distinct in respect to perfection [i.e. a species than which there could not be one more perfect], because then the chance is not possible, and, therefore, if the act in respect of the infinite exceeds in a double perfection the act in respect to that which is an individual of the highest species, God could not make another species in double perfection of that, and thus according to this way the argument is made void.

1. But against that there is that difficulty of the process *in infinitum* of acts of understanding by reflex acts, of which each posterior is more perfect than the prior. Because of the more perfect object I say that the more perfect act having whiteness for object is more perfect than whiteness: therefore, the first reflex act is more perfect than the direct act because of a more perfect object. For the same reason the second reflex act is more perfect than the first, and thus with all: therefore, there can be a process *in infinitum* in objects distinct in species according to greater and less perfection.

I say that it can be said in answer to this that in such things there is a process *in infinitum,* and one would never arrive none the less at any act of perfection equal to A. And thus it can be said in the question proposed, notwithstanding such a process *in infinitum,* one never arrives none the less at any

equally perfect act, such as an act in respect of the infinite. And this is so because they are of different kinds [*ratio*], nor is it the nature of the one to be equalled to the other in perfection. If you say that the act in respect of the infinite excels the direct act in a certain proportion of quantity, let us say, twenty times, and the first reflex act excels the first direct act in as much perfection, and the second excels the first as much or in as much, and the third excels the second as much; but every finite amount is transcended by the addition of the same quantity: therefore, one must come to some reflex act which will be more perfect than the act in respect of the infinite.

I say here that properly speaking it is not to be conceded with respect to proportion that the act in respect of the infinite exceeds the direct act in equal proportion, because this is true only when one happens to suppose equal or unequal parts by the composition of which something more perfect is made, as is the case with two parts of water and fire; and thus with similar things. But in the question proposed there is an excess of one act over another act according to itself whole and totally, so that every part of one exceeds the whole of the other, not only in species but also in perfection, just as every part of whiteness is more perfect than any blackness.

So I say that that proposition which has been accepted, *every finite,* has truth in those things which are of the same kind [*ratio*], in which one is added truly to the other, just as a part of water is added to a part of water, and a part of whiteness is added to the preceding whiteness. It has truth, likewise, when it happens to assert an equal part and another part exceeding. But it does not have truth in those things in which one can proceed *in infinitum* according to perfection by the addition of some things not of the same quantity, but of some things of the same proportion, which according to themselves as wholes are unequal, and yet one never comes to any great perfection of quantity, for one does not come in the least to the perfection of substance, and thus, it is in the question proposed concerning reflex actions.

1. But still the position advanced is proved because when something is added to something else according to your gloss, that if someone grieves concerning something sad, he will grieve so much more concerning something greater, as a man grieves more

because he is punished for two days than for one day, and so forth for the rest. And consequently through an infinite time he will grieve infinitely, and here a part of grief is added to part.

2. Moreover, a remiss habit sets up a difficulty for the will, and the more intense the habit the greater the difficulty: therefore also, some habit sets up an impossibility for conquering the sensitive appetite.

1. Replying to the first of these I say that it is possible that one man be saddened as much and not more concerning an infinite intensive pain than another man may be, or the same man at another time, concerning a finite pain. And if you argue in the same manner as above concerning that man who according to right reason sorrows so much, that he sorrows more concerning a greater thing, I say that it is possible that he sorrow according to right reason, as much by fear of a finite pain as another man, or the same man at another time, concerning an infinite pain. The reason of this is that every creature is limited, and, therefore, has power for so great an effect and not a greater. And, therefore, when he comes to the ultimate to which he is able to go, then he can do no more.

To the contrary, right reason declares repeatedly to you that you grieve more concerning an infinite pain than concerning a finite pain. I say that that is not so, but it would be necessary that one grieve more, if one could. And in the same way it can be said that such a man who is in the ultimate act can desire the vision of God as intensively through one time as through infinite time, because of the defect of his power.

If you say: I assert that God may cause grief concerning infinite pain and desire of beatific vision to endure *in infinitum*; since he is not himself limited, he can communicate infinite grief concerning infinite pain; this can be said in two ways. First from any such quality caused by God, God can make a more intense quality *in infinitum*; but one will never arrive at the infinite. It can likewise be said in another way, that there is a state [i.e. a point is reached] in the augmentation of form that must give some act so intense in respect of an infinite object.

2. Now, therefore, I say to the second instance that habit can not make a difficulty for the will, because if it were thus, it would be because of some

productive or destructive action neither of which can be asserted in the question proposed; nevertheless the will, as is commonly the case, follows the passion freely without any compulsion, and the saints call this a difficulty of the will in genus.

If you say that then it would be no more culpable for the will to follow a small passion than a great one, I reply and I say that it can well be said that it is not more culpable because of the difficulty which is brought to the will, but it is more laudable because it wills to undergo more evil or sorrowful passions for God, and it is more culpable because it does not will patiently to bear fewer adversities or it is more laudable because it flees more and greater delights, and more vituperable because it does not flee fewer and small delights, but acquiesces in them.

It can, likewise, be said in another way, namely, that habit brings difficulty to the will. And I concede that habit can be so intense that it inclines the will sufficiently to action in conformity with the sensitive appetite, so that it can in no manner act in the contrary, unless perchance there be a state [i.e. a point beyond which it can not go] in the increase of passion, and then will can conquer the supreme passion, and consequently any more remiss passion. And perhaps the sensitive appetite is not capable of such habit or passion beyond a certain grade which the will can conquer. And according to the first way, if the habit can increase so much that it necessitates the will, one must say that the will in such an act could not sin. Whence, it would then have no hope of liberty; yet not absolutely, because in respect of other objects it could sin, and likewise in respect of that object it could sin if the habit or the passion be relaxed.

To the other preceding argument answer can be made in another way, that some act in respect of a finite thing can be more perfect than some act which is in respect of an infinite.

QUODLIBET IV.

QUESTION XVIII.[1]

Whether the wayfarer has any simple and proper concept of God before [discursive knowledge by] composition and division or after.

---

[1]This question is numbered XVII in the 1487 edition.

Principal argument: And it seems that he has, because the concept is simple of which are sought such composite concepts as the following: *whether God is an infinite being: whether he is the first actuality.* But such questions are raised concerning the concept of God. The major premise is clear because such questions are not raised concerning the proper composite concept of God. because then the same thing could be asked concerning itself; which is false.

To the contrary, no creature contains a proper and simple concept of God essentially nor virtually: therefore, no creature can cause it.

Conclusion: 1. To this question I say that the wayfarer can not have from pure natural things any knowledge of God which is absolute not connotative, affirmative not negative, simple not composite, proper not common, before composition and division. The reason of this is that otherwise no one would be able to deny that God is, because if it is supposed that no proper knowledge of any impossible thing is caused by sensation of the thing before composition and division; then since sensation has no relation to the impossible that it may cause proper knowledge of it; then since for the same reason sensation would cause proper notions of infinite impossible things, because it has the same relation to all impossibles; then I argue thus, that you concede that proper knowledge of God is caused before composition and division, and not from faith because we agree in faith, and yet do not affirm this: therefore, it is known evidently that proper knowledge of God is caused by sensation, and consequently it is evident to every unbeliever that God is by the fact that he sees that whiteness is. For he could argue evidently that the concept caused by sensation mediating is not of anything impossible, but possible; wherefore, by the sensation of whiteness mediating for the thing, there is proper knowledge of God before composition; and this knowledge is not of anything impossible; it is possible therefore that any unbeliever be able to know God evidently. And since in perpetual things being does not differ from being able, any unbeliever can know evidently that God is: which is false. Therefore, I say that before composition and division, the wayfarer has no such concept not can he have it.

Moreover, it is not of the nature of complex knowledge of one thing to cause first incomplex, simple, and proper knowledge of another thing, because it is not intuitive, for such knowledge is caused immediately by the thing, speaking naturally. Nor again is it abstractive, because if such knowledge were simple proper knowledge, it necessarily presupposes intuitive knowledge. Since, therefore, the wayfarer can not see God intuitively in this state he can have no such knowledge of God.

2. To the second, I say that the wayfarer can not have such a simple and proper concept after composition and definition. The reason of this is that discourse is properly among complexes: therefore, by discourse alone only complex knowledge can be acquired, and not incomplex knowledge which is presupposed in composition and division.

But to the contrary: 1. Because if this were granted we would then understand God by understanding nothing else; this is proved because these common concepts, *being, first, three and one,* follow each other in the same order of time in mind as in word. But when the first concept is in mind, God is no more understood than creature, nor when the second is in mind, nor when the third: therefore, God is never understood by a proper concept, unless these concepts formed successively contain the simple and proper concept.

2. Moreover, to understand God otherwise it is necessary to begin with being and descend by composition and definition; and thus, it will be a long time before and could again understand God.

3. Moreover, the definition of a created substance can cause a simple concept proper to the thing defined: therefore, the description of God can cause a simple concept of God. The consequence holds, because otherwise a definition and a simple concept of the thing defined would not be distinguished in the predicamental use, nor would there be three terms in demonstration because there would not be in demonstration a simple concept of the thing defined.

4. Moreover, otherwise there would not be a relative concept in us, because neither extreme can cause a concept of the other, nor is the extreme concept caused before composition and division, because experience teaches that understanding does not have

a relative concept before it compares one thing to another by composition and division, as when the understanding forms the following complex: *this whiteness is such as that is.*

5. The concept of the likeness of a chimera is caused. Moreover, then, we would not be able to have an act of understanding in one instant, for the parts of the composite concept follow each other in mind as in word, as has already been said.

6. Moreover, when the understanding forms the following complex, *God is distinguished from anything else which is not he,* either the subject of that proposition in the mind is a simple concept of God, and the proposition is had; or else it is not, and then I shall make the proposition by demonstrating the thing which God is thus: this thing which is signified by this complex is distinguished from every other which is not it; and then I demonstrate God by one actuality, and the proposition is had. Or else by composition from many acts, and there will be a process *in infinitum.*

1. To the first of these, I concede that the wayfarer can not naturally understand God, understanding nothing else, because although by the total concept alone I understand only the being which is God, nevertheless by any partial concept of that composite I understand something other than God, because any such concept is common to God and others. But further, I say that the proof is incomplete because although it is possible in some case that common concepts follow each other in the same order in mind as in word, yet it is necessary that one can form some proposition in which many common concepts are predicated or subjected at the same time, and consequently in such a composite concept God can be understood.

2. To the second, I say that it is not necessary to begin from being, because one can begin from the first being or from the ass. Nor is such a descent or discourse by composition and division required for understanding God again, nor is a great amount of time required, because when God is understood first by any composite concept, he can be understood again in an instant by an interior habit inclining to a consimilar notion, just as in an instant a whole proposition can be formed.

3. As regards the third, I deny the assumption, that the concept of the thing defined is presupposed

by a common law in the definition. For knowledge of the thing defined by definition properly so called is caused because of the mediating of intuitive knowledge of one individual, because the concept of the species can be abstracted from one individual. Division, however, can not be caused with respect to every part of it except by knowledge of many individuals. For proof of this I say that neither of these impossibles follows, for the concept of the thing defined is not distinguished from definition because of the fact that it is caused by it, because it is in no manner caused by it. But they are distinguished from each other and causally from their causes because they are diverse.

4. To the fourth, I say that the argument is to the contrary because the relative concept is compounded and distinguished positively at the same time from both extremes. I prove this because the subject and predicate of a proposition precede the composition at least in order of nature. Now the understanding however in the very formation of the following complex, *this whiteness is similar or equal to another,* asserts the relative concepts from the part of the predicate: therefore, these concepts precede the proposition. There is this one order, therefore, because when two whitenesses have been seen, a specious concept [i.e. a concept of the species] of whiteness is caused in the mind, and I say this immediately from the whitenesses themselves or from the ideas of them, and the proposition is formed later, at least according to the order of nature. To the proof of this I say that experience teaches that one does not judge by an act of assenting that those whitenesses are similar before the understanding compares one to the other by composition and division; and this is so because such assent presupposes composition and division, as has been said above. But experience does not teach that one does not have a relative concept before composition and division.

5. To the fifth, I say that we can understand a chimera in one instant by a composite concept involving a contradiction, but in no wise by a simple proper conception. And further I say that the proof makes a false assumption, namely, that the parts of a composite concept follow each other in the mind as in the word, because the concepts exist together in the indivisible subject, but in the word they do not.

6. To the last I say that the subject of this proposition: *God is distinguished* is not a simple concept but a composite one. In the same way I say that in forming the following proposition: *this thing signified by this composite concept is distinguished*, the subject of this second proposition is composite of the concept of God and the demonstrative pronoun. And further, in forming the proposition which states the following: *this thing signified by this second composite concept is distinguished*, the subject is still a composite concept. And therefore I concede a process *in infinitum* in forming such propositions distinct at least in number, and the subject in each proposition is always a composite and not a simple concept.

To the principal argument, I say that such composite concepts as *infinite being, pure act*, are sought and demonstrated of the concept of being taken particularly, as when it is asked whether there is in the universe *any infinite being* and pure act. The subject of this proposition, however, is a concept compounded from the concept of *being in common* and of this syncategorematic, *any*, and thus it is not improper that one composite concept be sought and proved of another composite concept.

QUODLIBET V.

QUESTION VII.

Whether several proper concepts can be had of God.

Principal argument: And it is argued that they can not, because either absolutely the same thing corresponds to these concepts or not. If it does, then the concepts are synonymous. If not then there is some real distinction in the divine beings besides the distinction of persons.

To the contrary, the supreme good, infinite being, pure act, which are several concepts proper to God, are predicated of God.

Conclusion: To this question I say that concerning God there can not be had several concepts proper and convertible with him, all of which are absolute not connotative, affirmative not negative, simple not composite. By the first are excluded such concepts as first cause, creative, governing, glorifying. By the second are excluded such concepts as incorporeal, immortal, and infinite. By the third are excluded such concepts as infinite being, being intensively, supreme good, pure act. But when these conditions are circumscribed no one can have two proper quidditative concepts of God, nor one quidditative and another denotative. And I speak of the concept which is abstract knowledge.

1. The first is proved because if it is thus, then for the same reason an infinite number of quidditative concepts can be had of God, because no cause can be given wherefore they may be reduced to a certain number if two can be had, since argument is impossible from the simplicity of an object, for notwithstanding the simplicity you posit two proper quidditative concepts, and thus another for the same reason would posit an infinite number.

Moreover, a thing is not otherwise perceptible by abstractive concepts than by intuitive concepts; but only intuitively is the thing which is visible by a single vision, distinct and clear by a single conception which is the proper idea: therefore, only one such proper concept is possible of God.

Moreover, if the understanding is the same and the object the same, and there is no diversity, then the concept which is the effect will be the same and only one: otherwise every way of proving the unity of the effect would disappear.

2. The second is proved because such distinct concepts of different[1] kinds [*ratio*] can not be had of the same thing of which one concept is quidditative and another connotative without any distinction in the thing, and without any extrinsic connotation, and without any grammatical and logical mode. Wherefore, if all these are set aside, whatever is signified by the one is signified by the rest and in the same mode of signifying, and thus both will be quidditative or neither.

3. Moreover, of the same simple there are not two proper abstractive likenesses of which neither is like the other. But the concept is like that of which it is [the concept]: therefore, there could not be two such concepts, one quidditative, another denominative.

---

[1]The 1491 edition has *the same kind*.

4. Moreover, by each concept the whole quiddity is expressed and nothing else: therefore, each is quidditative, because it is this for a concept to be quidditative.

[1. No reply to the first argument is given in either edition, doubtless because the argument is in accordance with the conclusion.]

2. To the second, I say that one such proper concept of God can not be had naturally, neither before composition nor after, together with all the aforesaid conditions, as has been shown in another quodlibet.

3. To the third, I say that the blessed, seeing God for the first time, has only one such proper concept if God after such a vision, because he has one abstractive notion which is the proper concept of God, absolute, affirmative, and simple, which can not correspond to any other.

4. To the fourth, I say that our understanding can have no such simple, proper concept of any creature without sight of the creature, nor can it with any sight whatever, and this is because any such notion or concept is equally a likeness and represents all very similar individuals, and thus it is no longer the concept of one more properly than of the other.

1. But to the contrary, the negative concept is not predicated affirmatively of the thing of which it is [the concept]. This is proved because the affirmative and the negative concepts of the same thing are contradictory concepts, such as white and not-white, and clearly they signify the same thing, otherwise they would not be contradictory, and consequently these two concepts are not predicated affirmatively of the same thing; but infinite is predicated affirmatively of the divine wisdom, wherefore the following is true: *the divine wisdom is infinite.*

2. Moreover, although infinite, which is part of the complex concept, is negative, yet the whole complex concept is affirmative, because it is equivalent to an affirmative proposition such as the following: *the divine wisdom is infinite.*

1. To the first of these I say that the negative concept signifies something negatively, something

affirmatively. For example, not-white signifies whitenesses negatively, of which it is not verified, nor does it stand for them. Affirmatively, however, it signifies all things other than whiteness, and concerning these it is predicated affirmatively, and it stands for them because, whatsoever else may have been demonstrated from whiteness, this is true, *this is not-whiteness.*

2. And by this [distinction] I say to the argument, that the negative concept is not predicated affirmatively of the thing which it signifies negatively, yet it is truly predicated affirmatively of the thing which it signifies affirmatively; and therefore infinite is predicated affirmatively of no finite thing, because infinite signifies all finite things negatively; but it signifies all infinite things affirmatively; and, therefore, I say that it is predicated truly of all these, and it stands for them truly.

To the proof, I say that although affirmative and negative concepts are contradictory, yet obviously they do not signify the same thing, except this contradiction, *being and non-being,* because whatever being signifies affirmatively, non-being signifies negatively; and it signifies nothing else affirmatively.[1] In other contradictories the negative concept signifies many things affirmatively, which the affirmative concept does not signify, as not-white signifies many things affirmatively which white does not signify. But such concepts are said to be contradictory, because that which one signifies affirmatively, the other signifies negatively.

To the question proposed, I say that finite and infinite are opposed: therefore, infinite is predicated affirmatively of nothing of which finite is predicated affirmatively, and this is because infinite signifies all finite things negatively. but of those things which are not finite, of which sort God is, infinite is predicated affirmatively. By this the answer to the second is clear.

To the principal argument, I say that several composite concepts can be had of God formally and equivalently, but not simple in the stated way.

---

[1]The edition of 1491 has *negatively.*

STUDY QUESTIONS, OCKHAM, *THE SEVEN QUODLIBETA*

1. Are intuitive and abstract knowledge the same, or do they differ? Why? What is the significance?
2. Can you have intuitive knowledge of an object that does not exist? Why?
3. Can some particular thing be known two different ways—for example, by logical demonstration and by experience? What does this show?
4. Is the act of judging different from the act of apprehending? Why?
5. What is the significance of the example of the proposition, "God is three and one?"
6. What are first and second intentions? Are they different or the same? Why is this important?
7. How are absolute, connotative, and relative concepts related?
8. Do we understand our own acts intuitively? Or by some other means?
9. Are the sensitive soul and the intellective soul distinct?

Philosophical Bridges: Ockham's Influence

Modern British Empiricist John Locke used Ockham's distinction between a concept that signifies "primarily and naturally," and the word that signifies "secondarily" to explain the relationship between mind and world. All subsequent nominalists, influenced by Ockham, regard words as signifying, or being the signs of, mental impressions: words are signs that signify secondarily what the impressions of the mind import primarily.

A spoken or written term can be changed at will, whereas the meaning of a conceptual term cannot be changed. Ockham not only continued the medieval tradition of advancing Aristotelian logic, he envisioned it a science of language with the power to reveal what the mind thinks and how it represents the world and itself to itself. Ockham made it a central task of virtually all philosophy thereafter to precisely formulate what words signify, or refer to, and to explain their mode of signification.

According to Ockham's theory of perception, the objects presently before you are what he calls *intellectual intuitions*. They are not things as they exist in themselves independently from the mind. Rather, perceptions exist as such only in your mind. This notion, which he calls "intuitive vision," provided a logical and ontological grounding in language for the transcendental idealist philosophical innovations of Immanuel Kant, whose own notion of perceptions as intellectual intuitions Ockham influenced. Ockham also furthered the method already begun by Augustine for what would ultimately culminate in the method of Cartesian doubt: the finding of absolute certainty. This is done using propositions that are themselves immune to doubt, such as the affirmation of one's own existence as thinker in the act of thinking, based on the having of mental events regardless of whether they are *of* anything actual or not. The fact that I am thinking is evidence for my existence as *something*.

Ockham distinguishes, as modern and post-modern philosophers also would, between intention in the sense of "the sign of something not itself a sign," or a "mental name meant to stand for its signified object"—and intention in the sense of "something in the mind which is applicable to things and is predictable of the names of things when they do not stand in personal supposition but in a simple one." Universals are intentions not in the first but in the second sense. Intentions, as such, have being only in the logical sense; intentions exist, as such, in the logical realm. The logical realm, according to Ockham, subsists in the soul but does not consist of psychological elements (sensations, images, figments of the imagination, and so on). Rather, intentions exist in the logical realm just as external objects exist in the ontological realm, and can thus be called *real*, without our thereby having to posit them as existing independently of our minds. By providing the first clear intentional theory of mind, Ockham laid the conceptual foundation for the work of nineteenth-century philosophers such as Brentano, Husserl, and other pioneers in the method of phenomenology. His version of nominalism, which accords real status to universals that exist in the mind and thus affords simultaneously a subjective and objective aspect, influenced many logical positivists of the early part of the twentieth century.

Nicholas of Cusa (1401–1464)

Biographical History

Born Nicholas Krebs in the German village of Cusa on the Moselle River, Nicholas of Cusa honored his birthplace by taking the name Nicholas of Cusa. As a young man he was "discovered" by the Brothers of the Common Life at Deventer in the Lowlands, a mystical group in search of "unity with God," and devoted to following the methods laid out in one of the most widely read books of the time, written by one of their fellows, called *The Imitation of Christ*. Cusa joined the group but quickly outgrew it, and over the next 12 years he went on to study philosophy, mathematics, science, law, the arts, and theology at the universities of Rome, Cologne, Padua, and Heidelberg, earning his Ph.D. in 1433. He practiced law but was later ordained as a priest. He became cardinal in 1448, and in 1450, was appointed to the position of bishop of Brixen. Throughout his career Cusa tried to resolve political, social, and philosophical differences among differing, and sometimes warring, religious factions. One of the biggest debates of the time was whether the highest authority was the Church itself, or the church council, or the pope; Cusa tried to get all the sides to reach consensus. When he rode on horseback throughout Byzantium, trying to end the schism between the Latin and Greek churches, he earned the title "mystic on horseback." In his first published work, *On Catholic Concordance (De Concordantia Catholica,* 1433), Cusa lays out a global plan for peace and harmony organized along the lines of the church conceived as the highest level of human civilization.

Philosophical Overview

Nicholas of Cusa is the key transitional figure between the Middle Ages and the Renaissance. His opposition to Scholastic Aristotelianism led him to develop a unique blend of neo-Platonic philosophy with thirteenth-century mysticism, a synthesis of mathematical and experimental methods with mysticism. Moreover, unlike any of his contemporaries, Cusa cared little for making his philosophy fit any particular school.

Throughout his theological and political career, Cusa worked continuously on philosophical problems with the same idea of achieving unity through synthesis of opposing viewpoints. This is not merely an overriding theme throughout his work, it is a precise method worked out in great detail. The main idea is his notion of the identity of opposites (*coincidentia oppositorun*). According to this principle, all distinctions and contradictions among views expressed by finite minds can be resolved into unity at the infinite, absolute level of understanding. This may sound like the sort of mystical doctrine expressed by the

Brothers of the Common Life or some esoteric discipline. However, Cusa works this out in precise mathematical detail. For instance, draw a series of concentric circles, all of which touch line *l* on point *p*, thus:

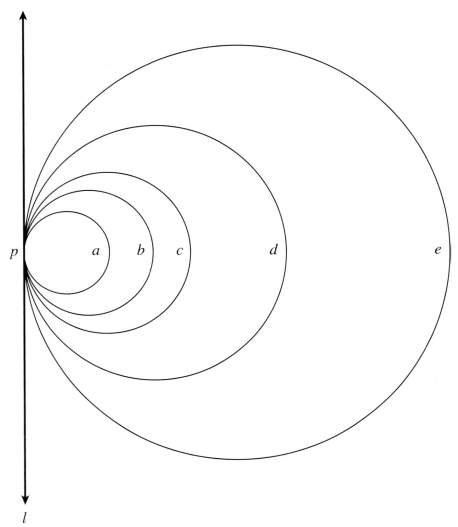

Notice that as you go from circle *a* to circle *b* to circle *c* to circle *d* to circle *e*, and so on ad infinitum (the circles get bigger and bigger, forever), the curve of each circle appears to "flatten out" relative to line *l*. For instance, to represent a circle whose radius is the size, say, of the distance between the earth and the sun, you would not be able, on this page, to tell the difference between the straight line *l* and the arc of the side of the circle whose radius is 93 million miles. But now imagine representing on this page a circle whose radius was the entire universe. The curvature across these ten inches would be imperceptible. Yet Cusa goes even further: imagine an *infinite* sphere, whose radius is infinite. Now the difference between the "curved" line of the circle and the "straight" line would disappear. This is how Cusa argues, with precision, that *at infinity* all distinctions between opposites vanish and the opposites become one. As he puts it: "an infinite line . . . would be at once a straight line, a triangle, a circle, a sphere; similarly, if there were an infinite sphere, it would at once be a circle, a triangle, and a line; and it would be likewise with the infinite triangle and infinite circle." In this way he leads up to his mind-boggling conclusion, which would be echoed by various philosophers throughout the subsequent ages, namely, "everything is everything."

OF LEARNED IGNORANCE
Nicholas of Cusa

Nicholas of Cusa's major philosophical work, *Of Learned Ignorance (De Docta Ignorantia,* 1440), relies heavily on the medieval method of *via negativa,* literally the "negative way." This is a process of transcending the built-in limitations of the human mind that prevent it from fully understanding anything that is greater than what can be comprehended by the limited logical categories (e.g., "either/or") available to the conscious ego. To fully grasp what something is, one must begin not with trying to state its essence in some positive terms (since to fully and directly know the essence of an infinite thing by a finite mind is impossible) but, rather, by finding out what is left over after one has exhausted all positive statements about its essence. That is how an individual human mind can ascend to knowledge of what is beyond either the direct reach of the senses or the intellect. Even God can be in this way known. But unlike, for example, Maimonides, who relies solely on this method, Cusa combines this principle with his method of "learned ignorance." This method owes much to Socrates, who defined wisdom as knowing how little you know. By thus struggling with insoluble puzzles, paradoxes, and dilemmas about God, the world, and ourselves, we transcend the limits of our own understanding; because what the mind is trying to understand are infinities, and even though the mind itself is an infinity, the concepts available to consciousness are conscripted to finite terms by *language.*

Moreover, the problem, as Nicholas lays it out, is that reason *(ratio)* is itself *discursive,* meaning that any truths attained by our propositions are the result of inference, not direct insight. The intellect transcends such limitations only through intuitive cognitions, "mystical" insights that cannot ever adequately be expressed by our language, nor etched into our ordinary experience. Thus, for instance, the ultimate unity of all opposites cannot be directly seen nor stated in ordinary language. However, once we see that this is impossible, we become enlightened: the mind at that moment transcends its limitations and mystical insight is attained because the mind suddenly sees its own limits of expression and thought, thereby witnessing the infinite within the finite, and vice versa.

Such a state of "learned ignorance" is not the same as being dumb or stupid or naïve. On the contrary, as mentioned above, it is exactly the sort of wisdom sought by Socrates and the great ancient sages. Moreover, it can be reconciled with the claims of Pythagoras, whom he also credits for inspiring his method.

From Jasper Hopkins. *Nicholas of Cusa on Learned Ignorance: A Translation and an Appraisal of De Docta Ignorantia,* Chapters 1–4 (Minneapolis. MN: Banning Press, 2nd edition. 2nd printing. 1990). Reprinted by permission.

CHAPTER 1: HOW IT IS THAT KNOWING IS NOT KNOWING.

We see that by the gift of God there is present in all things a natural desire to exist in the best manner in which the condition of each thing's nature permits this. And [we see that all things] act toward this end and have instruments adapted thereto. They have an innate sense of judgment which serves the purpose of knowing. [They have this] in order that their desire not be in vain but be able to attain rest in that [respective] object which is desired by the propensity of each thing's own nature. But if perchance affairs turn out otherwise, this [outcome] must happen by accident—as when sickness misleads taste or an opinion misleads reason. Wherefore, we say that a sound, free intellect knows to be true that which is apprehended by its affectionate embrace. (The intellect insatiably desires to attain unto the true through scrutinizing all things by means of its innate faculty of inference.) Now, that from which no sound mind can withhold assent is, we have no doubt, most true. However, all those who make an investigation judge the uncertain proportionally, by means of a comparison with what is taken to be certain. Therefore, every inquiry is comparative and uses the means of comparative relation. Now, when the things investigated are able to be compared by means of a close proportional tracing back to what is taken to be [certain], our judgment apprehends easily; but when we need many intermediate steps, difficulty arises and hard work is required. These points are recognized in mathematics, where the earlier propositions are quite easily traced back to the first and most evident principles, but where later propositions [are traced back] with more difficulty because [they are traced back] only through the mediation of the earlier ones.

Therefore, every inquiry proceeds by means of a comparative relation, whether an easy or a difficult one. Hence, the infinite, qua infinite, is unknown, for it escapes all comparative relation. But since comparative relation indicates an agreement in some one respect and, at the same time, indicates an otherness, it cannot be understood independently of number. Accordingly, number encompasses all things related comparatively. Therefore, number, which is a necessary condition of comparative relation, is present not only in quantity but also in all things which in any

manner whatsoever can agree or differ either substantially or accidentally. Perhaps for this reason Pythagoras deemed all things to be constituted and understood through the power of numbers.

Both the precise combinations in corporeal things and the congruent relating of known to unknown surpass human reason—to such an extent that Socrates seemed to himself to know nothing except that he did not know. And the very wise Solomon maintained that all things are difficult and unexplainable in words. And a certain other man of divine spirit says that wisdom and the seat of understanding are hidden from the eyes of all the living. Even the very profound Aristotle, in his *First Philosophy*, asserts that in things most obvious by nature such difficulty occurs for us as for a night owl which is trying to look at the sun. Therefore, if the foregoing points are true, then since the desire in us is not in vain, assuredly we desire to know that we do not know. If we can fully attain unto this [knowledge of our ignorance], we will attain unto learned ignorance. For a man even one very well versed in learning—will attain unto nothing more perfect than to be found to be most learned in the ignorance which is distinctively his. The more he knows that he is unknowing, the more learned he will be. Unto this end I have undertaken the task of writing a few things about learned ignorance.

CHAPTER 2: PRELIMINARY CLARIFICATION OF WHAT WILL FOLLOW.

Since I am going to discuss the maximum learning of ignorance. I must deal with the nature of Maximality. Now, I give the name "Maximum" to that than which there cannot be anything greater. But fullness befits what is one. Thus, oneness—which is also being—coincides with Maximality. But if such oneness is altogether free from all relation and contraction, obviously nothing is opposed to it, since it is Absolute Maximality. Thus, the Maximum is the Absolute One which is all things. And all things are in the Maximum (for it is the Maximum) and since nothing is opposed to it, the Minimum likewise coincides with it, and, hence, the Maximum is also in all things. And because it is absolute, it is, actually, every possible being; it contracts nothing from things, all of which [derive] from it. In the first book I shall strive to investigate—

incomprehensibly above human reason—this Maximum, which the faith of all nations indubitably believes to be God. [I shall investigate] with the guidance of Him "who alone dwells in inaccessible light."

Secondly, just as Absolute Maximality is Absolute Being, through which all things are that which they are, so from Absolute Being there exists a universal oneness of being which is spoken of as "a maximum deriving from the Absolute [Maximum]"—existing from it contractedly and as a universe. This maximum's oneness is contracted in plurality, and it cannot exist without plurality. Indeed, in its universal oneness this maximum encompasses all things, so that all the things which derive from the Absolute [Maximum] are in this maximum and this maximum is in all [these] things. Nevertheless, it does not exist independently of the plurality in which it is present, for it does not exist without contraction, from which it cannot be freed. In the second book I will add a few points about this maximum, namely, the universe.

Thirdly, a maximum of a third sort will thereafter be exhibited. For since the universe exists in plurality only contractedly, we shall seek among the many things the one maximum in which the universe actually exists most greatly and most perfectly as in its goal. Now, such [a maximum] is united with the Absolute [Maximum], which is the universal end; [it is united] because it is a most perfect goal, which surpasses our every capability. Hence, I shall add some points about this maximum, which is both contracted and absolute and which we name *Jesus*, blessed forever. [I shall add these points] according as Jesus Himself will provide inspiration.

However, someone who desires to grasp the meaning must elevate his intellect above the import of the words rather than insisting upon the proper significations of words which cannot be properly adapted to such great intellectual mysteries. Moreover, it is necessary to use guiding illustrations in a transcendent way and to leave behind perceptible things, so that the reader may readily ascend unto simple intellectuality. I have endeavored, for the purpose of investigating this pathway, to explain [matters] to those of ordinary intelligence as clearly as I could. Avoiding all roughness of style, I show at the outset that learned ignorance has its basis in the fact that the precise truth is inapprehensible.

CHAPTER 3: THE PRECISE TRUTH IS INCOMPREHENSIBLE.

It is self-evident that there is no comparative relation of the infinite to the finite. Therefore, it is most clear that where we find comparative degrees of greatness, we do not arrive at the unqualifiedly Maximum: for things which are comparatively greater and lesser are finite: but, necessarily, such a Maximum is infinite. Therefore, if anything is posited which is not the unqualifiedly Maximum, it is evident that something greater can be posited. And since we find degrees of equality (so that one thing is more equal to a second thing than to a third, in accordance with generic, specific, spatial, causal, and temporal agreement and difference among similar things), obviously we cannot find two or more things which are so similar and equal that they could not be progressively more similar *ad infinitum*. Hence, the measure and the measured—however equal they are—will always remain different.

Therefore, it is not the case that by means of likenesses a finite intellect can precisely attain the truth about things. For truth is not something more or something less but is something indivisible. Whatever is not truth cannot measure truth precisely. (By comparison, a noncircle [cannot measure] a circle, whose being is something indivisible.) Hence, the intellect, which is not truth, never comprehends truth so precisely that truth cannot be comprehended infinitely more precisely. For the intellect is to truth as [an inscribed] polygon is to [the inscribing] circle. The more angles the inscribed polygon has the more similar it is to the circle. However, even if the number of its angles is increased ad infinitum, the polygon never becomes equal [to the circle] unless it is resolved into an identity with the circle. Hence, regarding truth, it is evident that we do not know anything other than the following: that is to say, that we know truth not to be precisely comprehensible as it is. For truth may be likened unto the most absolute necessity (which cannot be either something more or something less than it is), and our intellect may be likened unto possibility. Therefore, the quiddity of things, which is the truth of beings, is unattainable in its purity; though it is sought by all philosophers, it is found by no one as it is. And the more deeply we are instructed in this ignorance, the closer we approach to truth.

CHAPTER 4: THE ABSOLUTE MAXIMUM, WITH WHICH THE MINIMUM COINCIDES, IS UNDERSTOOD INCOMPREHENSIBLY.

Since the unqualifiedly and absolutely Maximum (than which there cannot be a greater) is greater than we can comprehend (because it is Infinite Truth), we attain unto it in no other way than incomprehensibly. For since it is not of the nature of those things which can be comparatively greater and lesser, it is beyond all that we can conceive. For whatsoever things are apprehended by the senses, by reason, or by intellect differ both within themselves and in relation to one another—[differ] in such way that there is no precise equality among them. Therefore, Maximum Equality, which is neither other than nor different from anything, surpasses all understanding. Hence, since the absolutely Maximum is all that which can be, it is altogether actual. And just as there cannot be a greater, so for the same reason there cannot be a lesser, since it is all that which can be. But the Minimum is that than which there cannot be a lesser. And since the Maximum is also such, it is evident that the Minimum coincides with the Maximum. The foregoing [point] will become clearer to you if you contract maximum and minimum to quantity. For maximum quantity is maximally large: and minimum quantity is maximally small. Therefore, if you free *maximum* and *minimum* from *quantity*—by mentally removing *large* and *small*—you will see clearly that maximum and minimum coincide. For *maximum* is a superlative just as *minimum* is a superlative. Therefore, it is not the case that absolute quantity is maximum quantity rather than minimum quantity; for in it the minimum is the maximum coincidingly.

Therefore, opposing features belong only to those things which can be comparatively greater and lesser: they befit these things in different ways: [but they do] not at all [befit] the absolutely Maximum, since it is beyond all opposition. Therefore, because the absolutely Maximum is absolutely and actually all things which can be (and is so free of all opposition that the Minimum coincides with it), it is beyond both all affirmation and all negation. And it is not, as well as is not, all that which is conceived not to be. But it is a given thing in such way that it is all things; and it is all things in such way that it is no thing: and it is maximally a given thing in such way that it is it minimally. For example, to say "God, who is Absolute Maximally, is light," is [to say] no other than, "God is maximally light in such way that He is minimally light." For Absolute Maximally could not be actually all possible things unless it were infinite and were the boundary of all things and were unable to be bounded by any of these things—as by the graciousness of God. I will explain in subsequent sections. However, the [absolutely Maximum] transcends all our understanding. For our intellect cannot, by means of reasoning, combine contradictories in their Beginning, since we proceed by means of what nature makes evident to us. Our reason falls far short of this infinite power and is unable to connect contradictories, which are infinitely distant. Therefore, we see incomprehensibly, beyond all rational inference, that Absolute Maximality (to which nothing is opposed and with which the Minimum coincides) is infinite. But "maximum" and "minimum," as used in this [first] book, are transcendent terms of absolute signification, so that in their absolute simplicity they encompass—beyond all contraction to quantity of mass or quantity of power—all things.

STUDY QUESTIONS: NICHOLAS OF CUSA, *OF LEARNED IGNORANCE*

1. What does Nicholas mean by saying that knowing is not knowing? Does this make sense?
2. What is the end to which all things tend?
3. What is the role of the "innate" faculty of inference?
4. How does every inquiry proceed?
5. How is the infinite known?
6. Does evoking the Pythagorean claim that number is not just a quantity but "in all things" help with understanding what everything is? Why?
7. How does Nicholas reconcile the apparently different methods and positions of Pythagoras, Socrates, and Aristotle?

8. What does Nicholas mean by "maximum?"
9. What is the "absolute one?"
10. Who "alone dwells in inaccessible light?"
11. What are the "intellectual mysteries?"
12. Is there any comparative relation of the infinite to the finite? Why?

Philosophical Bridges: Nicholas of Cusa's Influence

Nicholas of Cusa inspired many subsequent philosophers and philosophical systems, such as for instance the great German idealists of the nineteenth century, particularly Schelling's "philosophy of identity." His synthesis, on the one hand, of mathematics and empirical methods and, on the other, mystical and transcendental methods of inquiry, paved the way for philosophers such as Kant who claimed that the categories of reason, consisting essentially of opposites and contradictions, give us only a limited representation of truth and reality. Nicholas' theologically inspired cosmological philosophy, according to which experience of ourselves and the world—nature itself—is the direct experience of God, inspired not only philosophers but scientists such as Galileo. Galileo's notion that in studying the world we are studying God, implies that what we need is not divinely inspired scripture or church authority but our own wits and methods to inquiry into the nature of God and reality; in fact, this is precisely what got Galileo (and others) in trouble with the Church. Other philosophers, such as Berkeley, would similarly argue that during each and every moment of our existence we are immediately and directly experiencing God's mind in action (otherwise everything would instantly disappear). The world according to Cusa is a *theophany*, or an "appearance of God." Spinoza would thus likewise conceive of reality as an endless series of unfoldings of God. Because according to Cusa, the present existence of the world is itself the result of a divine "contraction," the unity of God "unfolds" into multiplicity, such that the world itself is infinite. This leads Cusa to reject the notion of fixed points in space and time, thereby anticipating Albert Einstein's relativity of space and time. The idea that no entity in the universe, not even the Earth or the sun, has a priviledged position, first stated by Cusa, means that all judgments of location are relative; he even questioned the geocentric view of the solar system as laid out in the Bible.

Inspired by the forbidden views of Averroës, Cusa's arguments that each individual entity is a direct manifestation of God, form part of an elaborate mosaic in which harmony is achieved between part and whole; his evocation of Anaxagoras' fundamental proposition that "everything is everything," became a foundation for many subsequent philosophies in which everything in one way or another mirrors the entire universe. As Nicholas puts it, "all is in all, and each in each . . . each creature receives all, so that in any creature all creatures are found in a relative way." This anticipates and later influences the thought of Spinoza and Leibniz, who echoed Cusa's claim that "all things are what they are, because they could not be otherwise nor better."

Cusa's view that the mind must transcend the limitations of sensory knowledge to attain by its own limited means an intellectual intuition beyond reason, logic, and language, is an idea that continues to this day to inspire philosophers and scientists trying to understand the universe and themselves. Cusa's vision of enlightenment is as profound as it is enduring: the knower is a living bridge between the finite, relative domain and the infinite, absolute domain, a comprehensive expression of the ultimate oneness of being.

Bibliography

BACON

Primary

The Opus Majus of Roger Bacon, translated by R. B. Burke, University of Pennsylvania Press, 1928

Roger Bacon Essays, A. G. Little, ed., Clarendon Press, 1914

Secondary

Bridges, J. H., *The Life and Work of Roger Bacon: An Introduction to the Opus Majus,* William & Norgate, 1914

Westacott, E., *Roger Bacon in Life and Legend,* Philosophical Library, 1953

JOHN DUNS SCOTUS

Primary

The Oxford Commentary on the Four Books of the Master of the Sentences, translated by R. McKeon in R. McKeon, ed., *Selections from Medieval Philosophers,* vol. 2, Charles Scribners Sons, 1929

A Treatise on God as First Principle, translated by A. B. Wolter, Franciscan Herald Press, 1969

Duns Scotus Philosophical Writings, translated by A. B. Wolter, Macmillan/Library of Liberal Arts, 1962

Secondary

Bettoni, E., *Duns Scotus: The Basic Principles of His Philosophy,* translated by B. Bonansea, Catholic University of America Press, 1961

Harris, C. R. S., *Duns Scotus,* Humanities Press, 1959

Wolter, A. B., *The Philosophical Theology of John Duns Scotus,* Cornell University Press, 1990

OCKHAM

Primary

Ockham's Theory of Terms: Part I of the Summa Logicae by William of Ockham, translated by M. J. Loux, University of Notre Dame Press, 1974

Ockham's Philosophical Writings, ed. P. Boehner, Nelson Philosophical Texts, 1957

Secondary

Bohner, P., ed., *Collected Articles on Ockham,* Franciscan Institute, 1958

Carré, M. H., *Realists and Nominalists,* Oxford University Press, 1946

Leff, G., *William of Ockham: The Metamorphosis of Scholastic Discourse,* Manchester University Press, 1975

McGrade, A., *The Political Thought of William of Ockham,* Cambridge University Press, 1974

Moody, E. A., *The Logic of William of Ockham,* Russell and Russell, 1965

Shapiro, H., *Motion, Time and Place According to William Ockham,* Franciscan Institute, 1957

Wood, R., *Ockham on the Virtues,* Purdue University Press, 1997

NICHOLAS OF CUSA

Primary

Nicholas of Cusa on Learned Ignorance: A Translation and an Appraisal of De Docta Ignorantia, Banning Press, second edition, 1990

Secondary

Bett, H., *Nicholas of Cusa,* Methuen, 1932

Hopkins, J., *A Concise Introduction to the Philosophy of Nicholas of Cusa,* second ed., University of Minnesota Press, 1980

Christianson, G. and I., Thomas, M., eds., *Nicholas of Cusa, in Search of God and Wisdom,* E. J. Brill, 1991

Watts, P. M., *Nicolaus Cusanus, a Fifteenth-Century Vision of Man,* E. J. Brill, 1982

Philosophical Bridges: The Medieval Influence

Without medieval philosophy, modern philosophy would have been impossible. The transmission and translation of ancient philosophy into the codified system of thought sustained during the thousand-year reign of Christendom not only preserved but advanced many of the key elements of inquiry essential for the pursuit of wisdom in the western Socratic tradition. With the influence of Plato, especially in the early and later medieval times, the role of metaphysics, epistemology, and ethics as an integrated system based on reason was secured. The influence of Aristotle throughout the middle period made argument, logic, and empiricism central pursuits of all aspects of the knowledge-seeking enterprise.

Second, the slow but sure forging of the concept of the individual soul, whether as a separately existing entity or as part of a cosmic world soul, provided the foundation for subsequent theories of mind that would have a lasting influence on our concept of ourselves, etching in our minds the very notion of what it means to be human, to live justly, to be free, and to ask the right questions about ourselves and the world. Moreover, the medieval lack of constraint with regard to the most outlandish or even bizarre metaphysical positions created a vast ontological framework within which to conceive the universe and the place of the mind within it.

Third, the role and notion of God, whether conceived in a traditional religious perspective, be it Christian, Jewish, or Islamic, or even in the Asian traditions of Hinduism and Buddhism, so central to medieval conceptions of everything, becomes, under the medieval banner, a way of conceiving and relating with a wholly alternate realm of being. To be able to conceive, contemplate, and formulate arguments for and against such matters requires logical and metalogical techniques that would forever become the technological staple of philosophical inquiry, religious or secular. At the same time, attempts to ground human political institutions in more than purely human terms, regardless of whether such urges are regarded as divinely inspired or simply misguided, fostered an ambition to achieve a just and lasting system of government, education, and economics, tempered by ethical ideals.

Fourth, there can be no overstating the importance of the advances made by medieval philosophers in what have now become tools of the trade—namely, the understanding of concepts through a rigorous analysis of logic, language, meaning, and the nature of thought in relation to matters of being and what is. The categories of thought forged by the medievals from the raw materials provided to them by their ancient predecessors became the staple of modern thought, and their principles still exert influence on philosophy today.

◆ SOURCES ◆

SECTION I: PLOTINUS

Page 1: Plotinus, *Enneads*, translated by Stephen MacKenna: Medici Society, 1917. *First Ennead*: Sixth Tractate—Beauty; *Fourth Ennead*: Ninth Tractate—Are All Souls One?

SECTION II: AUGUSTINE

Page 13: Augustine,
1. *Confessions*, translated by Edward Pusey, Collier and Sons, 1909: Book X, Book XI.
2. *Against the Manichaeans and Against the Donatists*, from a Select Library of the Nicene and post-Nicene Fathers, First Series, edited by Philip Schaff, vol. IV, The Christian Literature Publishing Co., 1886–1890.
3. *Enchiridion*, translated by J. F. Shaw, in *The Works of Aurelius Augustine*, edited by M. Dods, T. & T. Clark, 1892, chaps 12–17, 32.
4. "Self Knowledge and the Three-Fold Nature of Mind," from i) *The City of God* translated by Marcus Dods, Modern Library, 1950: Book XI, Ch 26, and ii) *On the Trinity* in *History of the Christian Church, Nicene and Post-Nicene Fathers*, vol. III, Philip Schaff, ed., Charles Scribner's Sons, 1884.
5. *On Free Will*, Book II, 1–46, translated by Richard McKeon in Richard McKeon, ed., *Selections from Medieval Philosophers*, vol. 1, Charles Scribners Sons, 1929, pp. 11–64.

SECTION III: THE EARLY MEDIEVALS

Page 54: Boethius,
1. *The Second Edition of the Commentaries on the Isagoge of Porphyry*, translated by Richard McKeon in Richard McKeon, ed., *Selections from Medieval Philosophers*, vol. I, Charles Scribners Sons, 1929, pp. 70–99.
2. *Consolation of Philosophy*, Book V, translated by W. V. Cooper, J. M. Dent, 1902, pp. 101–120.

Page 67: John Scotus Eriugena, *On the Division of Nature*, Book IV, Chs 7-9, translated by Richard McKeon in Richard McKeon, ed., *Selections from Medieval Philosophers*, vol. 1, Charles Scribners Sons, 1929, pp. 106–141.

Page 82: Anselm,
1. *Proslogion*, translated by Sidney Norton Deane, Open Court, 1926. Preface, Chs. 1–8.

2. "In Behalf of the Fool," An Answer to the Argument of Anselm by Guanilo, a Monk of Marmoutier, with Anselm's response, translated by Sidney Norton Deane, Open Court, 1926.

Page 90: Abelard,
1. *Ethics, or the Book Called "Know Thyself,"* edited and translated by Eugene R. Fairweather, *The Library of Christian Classics, vol. X, A Scholastic Miscellany: Anselm to Ockham*, Philadelphia: The Westminster Press, 1956, pp. 288–297.
2. *The Glosses of Peter Abailard on Porphyry*, edited and translated by Richard McKeon, New York: Charles Scribners Sons, 1929, pp. 208–258.

Page 108: Hildegard of Bingen, *Scivias* Book I, Vision IV, chs. 16–26, translated by Mother Columba Hart and Jane Bishop, New York: Paulist Press, 1990 (Copyright Abbey of Regina Laudis: Benedictine Congregation Regina Laudis of the Strict Observance, Inc.).

Page 113: John of Salisbury,
1. *Metalogicon*, from *The Metalogicon of John Salisbury: A Twelfth-Century Defense of the Verbal and Logical Arts of the Trivium*, Book II, Ch. 17, translated by Daniel D. McGarry, Berkeley: University of California Press, 1955.
2. *The Policraticus (An Excerpt from the Fourth Book)*, edited and translated by Eugene R. Fairweather, *The Library of Christian Classics, vol. X, A Scholastic Miscellany: Anselm to Ockham*, Philadelphia: The Westminster Press, 1956, pp. 247–260.

SECTION IV: ISLAMIC AND JEWISH PHILOSOPHY

Page 127: Avicenna (Ibn Sina)
1. Avicenna, "Essay on the Secret of Destiny," translated by George F. Hourani, in John F. Wippel and Allan B. Wolter, eds., *Medieval Philosophy*, New York: The Free Press, 1969, pp. 229–232, originally published in the *Bulletin of the School of Oriental and African Studies*, University of London, vol. 29, Pt. 1, 1966, pp. 31–33.
2. Avicenna, "Concerning the Soul," from *Concerning the Soul from Avicenna's Psychology*, translated by Fazlur Rahman, London: Geoffrey Cumberlege, Oxford University Press, 1952.
3. "The Nature of Universals," translated by Martin Tweedale, in *Basic Issues in Medieval Philosophy*, ed. Richard N. Bosley

and Martin Tweedale, Orchard Park, NY: Broadview Press 1999, pp. 401–403.

4. *Metaphysics*, from *The Metaphysica of Avicenna (Ibn Sina)*, translated by Parviz Morewedge, Persian Heritage Series No. 13, New York: Columbia University Press, 1973, pp. 47–60.

Page 142: al-Ghazali,

1. *The Incoherence of the Philosophers (Tahāfut al-Falāsifah)*, translated by Sabih Ahmad Kamali, Lahore, Pakistan: Pakistan Philosophical Congress, 1963, pp. 1–5.

2. *The Book of Fear and Hope*, translated by W. McKane, Leiden: E. J. Brill 1965, pp. 1–25.

Page 156: Averroës (Ibn-Rushd)

1. *The Incoherence of the Incoherence (Tahāfut al-Tahāfut)*, translated by Simon Van Den Bergh, Unesco Collection of Great Works Arabic Series, London: Luzac & Co. Ltd, 1969, pp. 1–36 and 235–241.

2. *Long Commentary on De Anima*, translated by Arthur Hyman, in A. Hyman and J. Walsh, eds., *Philosophy in the Middle Ages*, New York: Harper & Row, 1967.

Page 202: Maimonides (Moses Ben Maimon)

Maimonides, *Guide for the Perplexed*, translated by M. Friedlander, Part I: chs 50–52, 60–62, Part II: Propositions 1–26, London: Routledge & Kegan Paul, 1904.

SECTION V: AQUINAS

Page 217: Aquinas

1. *Summa Contra Gentiles*, selections, translated by Joseph Rickaby, 1905, Burns and Oates, London.

2. *Summa Theologica*, translated by Laurence Shapcote, London: O. P. Benziger Brothers, 1911.

SECTION VI: THE THIRTEENTH CENTURY AND LATE MEDIEVAL PHILOSOPHERS

Page 259: Roger Bacon, *The Opus Majus*, translated by Richard McKeon in Richard McKeon, ed., *Selections from Medieval Philosophers*, vol. 2, Charles Scribners Sons, 1929, pp. 7–110.

Page XX: John Duns Scotus,

1. *The Oxford Commentary on the Four Books of the Master of the Sentences*, translated by Richard McKeon in Richard McKeon, ed., *Selections from Medieval Philosophers*, vol. 2, Charles Scribners Sons, 1929, pp. 313–350.

2. *Ordinatio*, translated by M. M. Tweedale, in *Basic Issues in Medieval Philosophy*, Orchard Park, NY: Broadview Press 1999, pp. 404–418.

Page XX: William of Ockham

1. *Summa Logicae*, from *Ockham's Theory of Terms: Part I of the Summa Logicae* by William of Ockham, translated by Michael J. Loux, University of Notre Dame Press, 1974.

2. *The Seven Quodlibeta*, translated by Richard McKeon in Richard McKeon, ed., *Selections from Medieval Philosophers*, vol. 2, Charles Scribners Sons, 1929, pp. 360–421.

Page XX: Nicholas of Cusa, *Of Learned Ignorance*, from Nicholas of Cusa *On Learned Ignorance: A Translation and an Appraisal of De Docta Ignoranita*, Jasper Hopkins, Ch. 1–4, Minneapolis: Banning Press, second edition, 1990.

◆ CREDITS ◆